# Approaches
# to Child Study.

## John Touliatos
Texas Christian University
Fort Worth, Texas

## Norma H. Compton
Purdue University
West Lafayette, Indiana

 **Burgess Publishing Company**
Minneapolis, Minnesota

Editor: Kay Kushino
Copy Editor: Judy O'Donnell
Production: Priscilla Heimann, Judy Vicars
Compositor: Loni Hansen

**Library of Congress Cataloging in Publication Data**
Touliatos, John.
    Approaches to child study.

    Includes bibliographical references and index.
    1. Child psychology—Methodology.    2. Child
psychology—Research.    3. Psychological tests for
children.    I. Compton, Norma H.    II. Title.
BF722.T68    1983            155.4            82-19741
ISBN 0-8087-3636-1

Burgess Publishing Company
7108 Ohms Lane
Minneapolis, Minnesota 55435

BF
722
T68
1983

J  I  H  G  F  E  D  C  B  A

**CREDITS**

*Figure 2.2.* Reprinted from "Criteria for Use in Describing Facial Expressions of Children" by N. G. Blurton
Jones in *Human Biology*, Volume 43, Number 3 (1971) by permission of the Wayne State University Press. Copy-
right 1971 by Wayne State University. *Table 2.3.* Adapted from N. G. B. Jones, "Criteria for Use in Describing
Facial Expressions of Children," *Human Biology* 43 (1971): 365-413. By permission of the Wayne State University
Press. *Table 3.1.* Reprinted from *Ecological Psychology* by Roger G. Barker, with the permission of the publishers,
Stanford University Press. Copyright 1968 by the Board of Trustees of the Leland Stanford Junior University.
*Tables 3.4 and 3.5* From *Environmental Psychology: Man and His Physical Setting* edited by Harold M. Proshansky,
William H. Ittelson, and Leanne G. Rivilin. Copyright 1970 by Holt, Rinehart and Winston, Inc. Reprinted by
permission of Holt, Rinehart and Winston. *Table 7.2.* Table 7.1 (p. 208) in *Essentials of Psychological Testing,* 3rd
edition by Lee J. Cronbach. Copyright 1960, 1970 by Lee J. Cronbach. Reprinted by permission of Harper & Row,
Publishers, Inc. *Pages 167-168:* Excerpt from *Principles of Educational and Psychological Testing* by Frederick G.
Brown. Copyright 1970 by the Dryden Press, Inc. Reprinted by permission of Holt, Rinehart and Winston. *Page
209:* Excerpt reprinted from *The Fourth Mental Measurements Yearbook* by Oscar Krisen Buros by permission of
University of Nebraska Press. Copyright 1953 by Oscar Krisen Buros. *Page 210:* Excerpt reprinted from *The Sixth
Mental Measurements Yearbook,* Oscar Krisen Buros, editor, by permission of University of Nebraska Press. Copy-
right 1965 by Oscar Krisen Buros. *Pages 232-234:* Excerpted from *Patterns of Child Rearing,* by Robert R. Sears,
Eleanor E. Maccoby, and Harry Levin, with the permission of the publishers, Stanford University Press. Copyright
1957 by the Board of Trustees of the Leland Stanford Junior University.

To my wife Paula and daughter Kara for their inspiration and support in the development of this book.

John Touliatos

and

To my children Bill and Anne and my grandchildren Amy and Daniel through whom I have gained my direct experiences in child study.

Norma Compton

# Contents

# Preface

In this book we define *child study* as the process of collecting, organizing, synthesizing, and interpreting pertinent information of many kinds about individual children.* Scientific study, regardless of subject matter, consists of formulating and verifying general principles through the joint application of logic and objective controlled observation. Our subject matter is children, and the study of children is complex. This book is designed for those who want to learn more about children through their own scientific observations or who want to be better "consumers" of scientific studies of children conducted by researchers, teachers, and others concerned with child development. There are many sources of information available. Knowledge of how to tap these sources is important. There are also many available diagnostic tools. Similarly, knowing how to use these tools and how to interpret them is important.

*Approaches to Child Study* should be appropriate for use at whatever level and in whatever course scientific child study is introduced at a college or university. The book is published as part of the Burgess Home Economics Series because home economics (or human ecology, consumer and family sciences, etc.) will most likely be its primary market. However, since programs such as early childhood education and child guidance and counseling are often offered in departments or schools of education, this market should be an important one too. The book could also be used in undergraduate courses devoted entirely to child study. Moreover, this text would be appropriate for beginning graduate-level courses with observation assignments and/or more specialized offerings with course titles such as Psychological Assessment of Children, Child and Family Study, Systems and Methods of Observing Children's Behavior, and Ecological Observation for Intervention. The book would also be appropriate as a supplementary text in general home economics core courses that require laboratory observation and other child study experiences, in traditional child development courses with observations arranged in the department's nursery school, as well as in courses concerning the guidance of children.

*Approaches to Child Study* is organized into twelve chapters. Chapter 1 provides the overall framework for the scientific study of children, including a brief review of the historical development of the field and the primary theoretical and methodological approaches applied in studying children. Chapter 2 emphasizes the appropriateness of direct observation for the study of behavior either in natural settings or in the laboratory. Language behavior, paralinguistic behavior, gestures, posture, facial expressions, eye behavior, spatial behavior, touching behavior, personal appearance, and environments are discussed as types of data that can be obtained through observation. In Chapter 3 six observational techniques employed in the study of child behavior and development are discussed: anecdotal records, specimen records, running records, time sampling, event sampling, and environmental analysis. Chapter 4, "Methodological Issues in Observational Study," emphasizes the resurgence of interest in observational study in natural settings and the importance of choosing methods that meet the goals of the investigator and the nature of his or her subjects. This chapter focuses on the advantages and problems in systematic observation, including observer errors and interference, reliability, validity, and norms. Aids are available that are designed to make the task of observation easier and more precise. Chapters 5 and 6 describe the use of various observational aids. Both paper-and-pencil aids, such as rating scales and checklists, and mechanical aids, such as sound recorders and videotape techniques, are discussed in these chapters.

Scientific approaches to child study require the quantification of the variables under study through testing and measurement techniques and statistical tools appropriate to them. These topics are discussed in Chapter 7, "Structured Tests and Scales." An array of objective tests and scales, as

*The authors have adopted the definition by Gibson and Higgins, from *Techniques of Guidance: An Approach to Pupil Analysis.*

well as interview, questionnaire, and projective techniques are covered in detail in numerous other books. However, at the introductory level in child study, it is important to begin to think in terms of the development of the whole child and to become familiar with a wide sampling of instruments and techniques that are available to professionals studying children. Therefore, these instruments and techniques are introduced and other references are suggested as sources for greater detail. Chapter 7 also deals with test selection and includes brief descriptions of several intelligence and aptitude tests, achievement tests, personality scales, and attitude, value, and interest scales. Sociometric techniques along with other self-report methods that often accompany direct observation of children are examined in Chapter 8, "Self-Report Methods: Interviews and Questionnaires." Chapter 9 provides examples from four types of projective techniques used with children: association techniques (e.g., Rorschach), construction techniques (e.g., TAT, figure drawing), completion techniques (e.g., structured doll play), and choice or ordering techniques.

Because the family exerts the single greatest influence on the behavior and development of a child, Chapter 10 is devoted to the topic of "Studying the Child's Family." This chapter is organized within the following taxonomy which classifies aspects of family life that are closely related to child behavior and development: (a) parental background and current family status, (b) personal characteristics of parents, (c) parental perceptions of their roles and relationships in the home, (d) child-oriented parental attitudes, (e) parental behavior patterns, and (f) child's perceptions of parents and family relationships. Since family dimensions are studied in many of the same ways as individual children, the family assessment techniques described in this chapter are similar to those described in previous chapters as being applied to children, such as direct observation, structured tests and scales, interviews and questionnaires, and projective techniques.

The case study is a process that brings together data collected by a variety of child study techniques in such a manner as to permit systematic review and analysis. Therefore, we chose to cover the case study in Chapter 11, as our last "approach" to child study. Finally, we are concerned about the serious consequences of a nonscientific approach to observing and recording, interpreting and distributing data collected about children. Chapter 12, "Ethical Guidelines for Child Study," reflects this concern. The chapter enumerates many guidelines for protecting the rights and well-being of children and other humans participating in various types of studies. It also points to the need to consider risks versus benefits, for the development of all children may be improved through scientific studies.

We hope that students, by understanding and using the techniques described in *Approaches to Child Study*, will become better teachers, parents, and/or researchers of children.

We are grateful to our colleagues, former professors, and students for many of the ideas expressed in this book. We extend special thanks to these reviewers who offered helpful suggestions on the first draft of the manuscipt:

Richard M. Brandt, Dean, Curry Memorial School of Education, University of Virginia

John L. Carter, Director, Diagnostic Education Center, and Psychologist, University of Houston at Clear Lake City

Damaris Pease, Distinguished Professor, Child Development, College of Home Economics, Iowa State University

At Purdue University we owe special thanks to Dianne Cherry for her assistance with innumerable telephone communications and manuscript typing. We also gratefully acknowledge Paula Touliatos's assistance with the indexing. Finally, appreciation is expressed to Kay Kushino of Burgess Publishing Company for her continuous support during several years of writing and revision.

J. T. and N. C.

# 1

# Introduction to Child Study

Children represent experiences common to all humanity. The vast literature concerning children runs the gamut from folklore based upon superstition to imaginative fiction to philosophical speculation to popularized magazine articles and finally to professional articles that describe scientific observations and research studies of children. The latter scientific studies of children form the focus of this book, for, in fact, *child study* is the process of collecting, organizing, synthesizing, and interpreting pertinent information of many kinds about individual children.

The study of children has interested adults for several reasons, including these:

1. *Guiding children in their development.* Individuals involved with the development and rearing of children in many settings (the home, the school, the church, the community) need to understand children and the theories of child development in order to guide their behavior and the learning process.

2. *Intellectual curiosity and "science for science's sake."* Some individuals have a curiosity about the world around them that prompts them to seek a personal understanding of a variety of natural phenomena and to contribute to scientific knowledge. People are a very important part of that world.

3. *Understanding ourselves.* "The child is father of the man." Therefore, we must understand ourselves. Freud's psychoanalysis added support to this long-held belief that in order to understand ourselves we must understand the role played by our childhood experiences in shaping our behavior. Transactional analysis (TA) is also based on the idea that there are three figures within each of us: an adult (rational, objective, and decision making); a parent (incorporated largely from the behavior of our own parents and other authority figures toward us); and a child (carefree, joyful, dependent, and demanding).[1]

## DEVELOPMENT OF THE FIELD OF CHILD STUDY

The history of child study is different from traditional scientific disciplines. As Sears has indicated, other life sciences developed within the academic structure and were stimulated by a scientist's desire to know more about the phenomena of his or her discipline. "Histories of biology, psychology, biochemistry and anthropology are largely intellectual histories, the records of developing theories, accumulating facts, of more and more precise instrumentation, and of biographies of scientists who performed these feats."[2] In contrast, child development evolved as a result of social pressures arising from many different sources. These external pressures were based on desires to improve the health, education, rearing, and the legal and occupational treatment of children.

Long before attempts were made to study children scientifically, parents and teachers followed traditional beliefs as guides in rearing children and in teaching them to become useful, moral citizens. Many of these traditional beliefs are still held as firmly today as they were in the past because of insufficient evidence to prove that they are not true. It was not until recently that scientists began to subject these beliefs to carefully controlled and established research procedures.[3]

## PIONEERING EFFORTS

One of the first to study the child as an individual with an essential child nature instead of as a miniature adult was John Comenius, the famous Slavic educational reformer of the seventeenth century. Comenius's purpose was to understand the capacities of children and to learn how to deal with them.

Following Comenius's pioneer work, two trends appeared in the study of children: (1) philosophical treatises on education in which children were studied only indirectly were written, and (2) daily notes of direct observations of children were compiled. Although valuable education philosophies about children were contributed, the direct observations that focused attention on the child proved to contain far more fruitful information. The first scientific record of the development of a young child was published in 1774 by Pestalozzi of Switzerland. This record was based upon observational notes that Pestalozzi made regarding his 3½-year-old son. Several years later in Germany, Tiedemann recorded the developmental behavior of his children. The best known and most thorough of the early American studies was Millicent Shinn's *The Biography of a Baby* which was published in 1900.[4] This biography was based upon Shinn's observations of her niece from birth through the first year of life and was modeled along the lines of the German baby biographies.[5]

Until the end of the nineteenth century most child care advice was moral, focusing on the building of self-control and proper character as defined by the Protestant ethic. Then, as Sears points out, with the sudden blooming of scientific medicine in the 1870s and 1880s, a new element was introduced.[6] The child's physical welfare became an important focus. In 1874, Holt's *The Care and Feeding of Children* provided a landmark for public adoption of scientific procedures that dealt with children's health and well-being.[7] Pediatric clinics, state-supported institutions for neglected children, and social welfare programs soon followed.

The late nineteenth century witnessed the replacement of belief and opinion with scientifically determined facts. During that period three professions became committed to work on behalf of children—medicine, education, and social work. Scientific methods grew most rapidly in medicine, but new technical tools also were developed in education in response to pressures for improvement. The new profession of social work was formed in response to problems of social advising.[8]

By the beginning of the twentieth century, political leaders in the United States were becoming concerned about children. The first White House Conference was called in 1909 by Theodore Roosevelt, and its focus of discussion was what the government should do about children. The United States Children's Bureau was organized as a result of this conference.

## G. STANLEY HALL AND THE CHILD STUDY MOVEMENT

The scientific study of children received great impetus from the work of G. Stanley Hall, a psychologist and president of Clark University. Hall's study of children's concepts, which was reported in 1891 in his *Contents of Children's Minds on Entering School,* emphasized that children should not be considered miniature adults. Because of the interest that Hall stimulated, he has come to be regarded as the "father of the child study movement." This movement was the preeminent influence in educational reform circles in the 1890s.[9] Hall also was considered "without qualification the founder of child psychology in the United States."[10]

> . . . He was incontestably the most prominent psychologist of the late nineteenth century; . . . he was the first to legitimate and institutionalize within the universities the study of children and . . . he more than anyone popularized the idea that the study of children would revolutionize the pedagogy of home and school.[11]

Hall approached his studies genetically and emphasized the idea that education should focus on the natural stages of children's growth. He was widely acclaimed by teachers, parents, and religious educators. In fact, Hall was considered the "intellectual patron saint of the PTA," a group that was a staunch partisan of his ideas during the progressive period of education.[12]

Hall also was widely acclaimed by physicians and public health workers because of his emphasis on children's health. However, Hall's fellow psychologists condemned his use of questionnaires filled out by teachers, parents, and other amateur child observers and considered his research methods unscientific.[13]

## THE CHILD DEVELOPMENT MOVEMENT AND LAWRENCE FRANK

The groundwork for the scientific study of children had been laid by the 1920s, but it was this decade that provided the climate for the systematic and organized study that would characterize the child development movement. Faith in science was rising. Business was generating funds for research. Rapid strides were being made in the disciplines to be applied to child development—biology, chemistry, psychology, nutrition, and medicine. Concern and support were forthcoming from the progressive movement in education and from the National Child Labor Committee. Another impetus for the child development movement was provided by World War I. Physical and psychological examinations of military recruits revealed that the development of the young adult American male left much to be desired. The American people rallied to remedy this situation by establishing well-baby clinics, school health programs, child guidance clinics, mental hygiene programs, and public health clinics.

At the same time, numerous university-based institutes were founded to conduct research in child development. Many of these institutes were established and supported through funds provided by the Laura Spelman Rockefeller Memorial. Lawrence Frank was the organizing force for these institutes. To meet one of the primary purposes of the memorial, Frank promoted research in child development and parent education throughout the United States. Additional institutes were formed with other sources of funds. Nursery schools were established in many institutes to provide settings for observational study of children. Within a few years the various institutes had turned out vast literature on all facets of child development.

These are the primary child study institutes or the programs that were established by universities during this period:

**1917**   Iowa Child Welfare Research Station

**1920**   Merrill Palmer School, Detroit, Michigan (later the Merrill Palmer Institute)

**1924**   Teachers College, Columbia University

**1925**   University of Minnesota
Toronto University
Cornell program in child development and family life

**1926**   Yale Psychological Clinic (Prior to World War I, a Clinic of Child Development had been set up at Yale by Arnold Gesell primarily for the study of infants.)

**1927**   Brush Foundation at Western University
University of California at Berkeley
Child Research Council at Denver

**1929**   Fels Institute at Antioch College

**1930**   University of Michigan Center

Other ongoing programs during this period were the Harvard Growth Study, which was initiated by Dearborn in the early twenties, and studies on ability and achievement tests for children that were conducted by Thorndike.

To provide for information exchange and coordination of efforts concerning child development, the National Research Council activated its Committee on Child Psychology in 1925. The committee's name was subsequently changed to Committee on Child Development in order to recognize a broader approach to the study of children. The Society for Research in Child Development, which was officially organized in 1933, was an outgrowth of this committee. It undertook publication of *Child Development Abstracts, Child Development* (which originally was published at Johns Hopkins University), and a monograph series. Robert Woodworth, a professor of psychology at Columbia University and one of the original members of the Committee on Child Development, was instrumental in these developments.

Several other organizations and movements also reinforced the work of the institutes in the 1920s. These included the preschool movement, the National Committee on Nursery Schools, and the National Association for Nursery Education. The latter association, under the direction of Lois Meek Stolz who served as its first president, became one of the bonds that pulled the institutes together. As Senn[14] points out, Stolz and Frank held different opinions about how nursery schools should be developed. Frank believed that the schools should be part of the home economics field because they were a supplement to the family. In contrast, Stolz viewed nursery schools as educational and therefore advocated that they be tied in with the whole school system. That these differences still exist today is evidenced by the existence of preschool and early childhood education programs in schools of home economics at some universities and in schools of education at others. Some of the larger universities even offer programs in both schools, with each program being slanted to the philosophy and mission of the school in which it is administered.

Frank supported his conviction by funneling foundation funds to college and university home economics schools or departments for the establishment of child development programs and nursery schools. These home economics nursery school laboratories were set up at Cornell University, Georgia State University, Iowa State University, Spelman College, Atlanta University, and several other smaller institutions.

## OTHER LEADERS IN CHILD DEVELOPMENT

Pauline Park Wilson Knapp was a pioneer in broadening the study of home economics to include child development. Her first job was as nursery school teacher in the Department of Child Development at Cornell. She then became head of a similar department at the University of Georgia when it was established in 1928. Knapp also introduced child development programs at the University of Kentucky and the University of Alabama before becoming director of the Merrill-Palmer Institute in Detroit, a position she held from 1952 until her retirement in 1967.

Other leaders in the field of child psychology in the early 1900s included John Watson and Arnold Gesell. Watson reflected the need for psychology to be a respectable science. His behavioristic approach and contributions to scientific research continue to be recognized today, however his approach to child rearing has fallen into disrepute. Dr. Gardner Murphy, who was at Columbia when Watson's research was becoming important to psychology, has stated this opinion of Watson's contribution to the field of child psychology: "I think Watson was the most important single influence in child psychology from the period of the First World War until the thirties. It was part of a general expression of protest against the introspective psychology."[15]

Arnold Gesell received a Ph.D. in psychology at Clark University and an M.D. at Yale where he was associated with the Yale Clinic for Child Development. Gesell shared G. Stanley Hall's view of heredity as the prime molder of the developing child. However, unlike Hall, Gesell conducted carefully controlled observational research and accurately recorded his data. Gardner Murphy reports that

Gesell was considered a pioneer in longitudinal methods of investigation rather than a proponent of any specific theoretical position.[16] Two of Gesell's innovative research observation techniques have become well known around the world: the one-way vision screen and the cinematograph.

An account of the beginnings of child study would not be complete without mention of the contributions of Lewis M. Terman. He was a pioneer in mental testing in the United States, and is especially known for his longitudinal studies of gifted children. The Stanford Revision of the Binet Scale, the first significant and most widely used intelligence test in the United States, was developed by Terman.

## SIGMUND FREUD AND PSYCHOANALYSIS

The child guidance clinics established in the 1920s grew out of the mental hygiene movement and were aimed at preventing juvenile delinquency. These clinics adopted a clinical psychiatric approach that emphasized the psychoanalytic principles of Sigmund Freud, principles which were not generally accepted in academic circles in the twenties.

David Levy, a psychoanalyst who worked with Herman Adler in Chicago, became chief of staff of the Institute for Child Guidance in New York in 1927. Two years previously, Levy had introduced the Rorschach test in America. Work by Levy and fellow psychoanalysts Anna Freud, Melanie Klein, and Susan Isaacs broadened research studies with children. Lois Stolz was among those who recognized the contributions of these psychoanalysts to the child development movement: "I don't think there's any question that Freudian psychology . . . pushed us to ask the question *Why* instead of *What*. The early child development movement was trying to answer the question: *What* are children like? and I think Freudians began to say *Why* are they like this?"[17]

## KURT LEWIN

Kurt Lewin, the last of the Gestalt psychologists, came to the United States in 1932. With his field theory life-space approach, he promoted the study of the whole personality in its setting. Lewin's experiments in the late thirties at the Iowa Child Welfare Research Station provided new insights into relationships between the child and his or her environment. These experiments also gave credibility to the study of behavior in natural settings as a scientific method parallel to laboratory experiments. Additional reference is made to Lewin's work later in this chapter under the section entitled "Ecological Approaches."

## JEAN PIAGET

Jean Piaget's influence was not widespread in the early days of child study. While other investigators emphasized measurement and experimental method dealing with simple forms of behavior, Piaget employed the clinical method and focused on complex behavior and higher thought processes. However, since the early 1950s, Piaget has been recognized by child psychologists, educators, and others in diverse areas as the foremost contributor to the study of intellectual development. From 1920 to the present time, Piaget and his collaboraters have produced more worthwhile research and theory in child psychology than any other investigators.[18]

## SUMMARY OF THE EARLY DEVELOPMENT OF CHILD STUDY

In the beginning of the twentieth century, two essentially different approaches to child study evolved as a result of the prevailing social pressures and the available resources. One was the clinical approach. This approach arose from medical and psychological developments in the last part of the nineteenth century, and employed case studies from the clinics. The other approach was more formally structured; it was oriented to laboratory experimentation and measurement and carefully controlled field studies. What is today labeled child development is patterned after this second approach.[19]

## CHILD PSYCHOLOGY VERSUS CHILD DEVELOPMENT

Hurlock makes several distinctions between the fields of child psychology and child development. Essentially, child development is a broader field than child psychology. More specifically, child development differs from child psychology in four ways:

1. Child psychology focuses primarily on the content or products of development, while child development focuses more on the process itself. In the area of speech, for example, child psychology emphasizes children's vocabularies and what they say. Child development emphasizes how children learn to speak, characteristic speech patterns, and the conditions that cause variations in these patterns.

2. Child development puts more emphasis on the role played by environment and experience than child psychology does.

3. Child psychology has one major objective: to study the different areas of child behavior. Child development has six objectives: (a) to determine the characteristic age changes from one developmental period to another in appearance, behavior, interests, and goals; (b) to determine when these changes occur; (c) to determine under what conditions these changes occur; (d) to determine how these changes influence the child's behavior; (e) to determine the predictability of these changes; and (f) to determine whether these changes are individual or characteristic of all children.

4. Early studies by child psychologists concentrated on preschool and school-age children. Developmental psychology has extended the area of study in both directions.[20]

## THEORETICAL APPROACHES TO CHILD STUDY

Early studies of children were based upon traditional beliefs and attempted merely to catalog physical and behavioral changes at each age and to set up norms. Such observations and descriptions of behavior are important, since scientific investigators must first have an accurate picture of the behavior they are studying. But they cannot stop with a mere description of the behavior; they need to understand *why* the behavior occurs if they are to devise effective methods of predicting and guiding future behavior. In an attempt to provide such explanations for behavior, scientific investigators have constructed *theories*. Observations can be understood by relating them to theories. In fact, the maturity of a science is generally gauged by the extent to which it has developed a solid and valid foundation for the construction of theories.

Former President Conant of Harvard University defined science as "an interconnected series of concepts and conceptual schemes."[21] It is from such a body of relationships among variables that theories are built. Kerlinger defined theory as "a set of interrelated constructs (concepts), definitions, and propositions that present a systematic view of phenomena by specifying relations among variables, with the purpose of explaining and predicting the phenomena."[22]

Theory and practice are not antagonists in science. A good theory is very practical. It can be applied in many situations and reduces the complexity of understanding. Not only are theory and practice compatible but each is at its best when they are used together. As Leonardo da Vinci said many years ago: "Those who are enamoured of practice without science are like a pilot who goes into a ship without rudder or compass and never has any certainty where he is going."

Another factor that has a significant effect on the construction of theories is common sense. Common sense can positively or negatively influence the development of scientific theories to explain behavior. In every science theories are preceded by a naive, commonsense knowledge of nature. If these ideas are refined and formalized, scientific problems and hypotheses may emerge to be tested for their accuracy. On the other hand, some commonsense ideas may result in misleading hypotheses that can hamper the development of a field of study.

The theories of child development are varied, and therefore contribute numerous explanations for the behavior of children. This variety of theories is essential because an in-depth understanding of children requires the application of many theories and many levels of analysis. Some of the most widely used theories in child study are summarized in the sections which follow. Since this is not a textbook on theories, the reader should seek additional references for more detailed coverage.[23] The theories are briefly described here in order to emphasize their diversity and complexity and to stress the importance of approaching the study of children within a theoretical framework. The seven basic theoretical approaches to child study that will be discussed are psychoanalytic, cognitive, behavioristic, social-learning, organismic, ethological, and ecological.

## PSYCHOANALYTIC APPROACH

The psychoanalytic frame of reference was originally developed by Sigmund Freud in an attempt to discover a treatment for neuroses. Therefore, it stems historically from the medical clinic rather than from the university laboratory, from attempts to help patients rather than from attempts to test theories on normal subjects. Freud considered an individual's primary motives to be sexual, aggressive, and survival drives, and placed emphasis upon wishes, dreams, feelings, and other emotional states rather than upon behavior. Based upon his use of the free association technique with patients (recall of ideas and experiences as they come to awareness following verbal stimuli), Freud became convinced that an individual's early childhood experiences are responsible for most of his or her behavior. Freud's most significant contributions to the field of child study are his concepts regarding developmental stages and data regarding the importance of the first five or six years of life for personality development.

Three interlocking elements constitute the structure of personality in psychoanalytic thought: the id, the ego, and the superego. The id is the primitive source of a person's instincts, is entirely unconscious, and presses for gratification of instincts which are the primary motivators of behavior. These instincts or innate needs are in conflict with the cultural norms of society. The ego represents reality and the self, including all of a person's mental functions. The superego, which evolves from the child's early experiences with the parents, represents a person's conscience or "internalized parent," or the moral aspect of personality. A stable balance among the id, the ego, and the superego constitutes character structure.

Freud's psychosexual developmental stages through which personality unfolds are divided into three principal periods: (1) *the infantile period* from birth to age five or six, which consists of the oral stage whereby satisfaction is attained through the mouth, the anal stage with satisfaction centered on eliminative functions and organs, and the phallic stage in which pleasure is associated with the genital organs; (2) *the latent period* from age five or six to the beginning of adolescence; and (3) *the adolescent period* or beginning of the genital stage from puberty to about age twenty.

With respect to child study, the psychoanalytic frame of reference is often applied to parent-child relationships and to sibling relationships. It has made an impact on various aspects of family study, including anthropological studies dealing with the family. However, as Bayer points out:

> . . . psychoanalytic theory has become a thorn in the side of orthodox empirical validation in sociology because its conceptual basis is the unconscious, its complementary concepts allow contradictory interpretations, and its nature is relatively impervious to operational definition[24]

Sears also recognized this problem and came to this conclusion after a review of numerous psychoanalytic studies:

> Psychoanalysis relies upon techniques that do not admit of the repetition of observation, that have no self-evident or denotative validity, and that are tinctured to an unknown degree with the observer's own suggestions. These difficulties may not seriously interfere with therapy, but when the method is used for uncovering psychological facts that are required to have objective validity, it simply fails.[25]

Although Freud's model has frequently been criticized on scientific grounds, it has provided ideas that have been the focus of investigation by some reputable researchers. Also, his system has served as a foundation for a number of other theories. The most notable variation on the Freudian theme has been presented by Erik Erikson.[26] Erikson, who accepted much of Freud's theory, is best known for the extension of Freudian psychosexual stages to include his own concept of psychosocial crises that an individual must work through at various stages of development in order to achieve a healthy personality.

## COGNITIVE APPROACH

Cognitive theorists are involved with the development of thought processes at each developmental stage from infancy through adolescence. They have contributed three important concepts to the science of child psychology:

1. A child's strategies of organizing and interpreting events in the environment are qualitatively different from an adult's.

2. There is a definite link between the structural properties of the sense receptors, the brain and the nervous system, and the capacity to know the world.

3. The acquisition of knowledge is an active, ongoing process: the needs to find meaning in experience and to reduce uncertainties serve as internal motives for cognitive change.[27]

Since the early 1950s, it has become increasingly clear to child psychologists, educators, and others in diverse areas that Jean Piaget is the foremost contributor to the field of intellectual development.[28] Piaget's work at the University of Geneva aroused interest in the United States around 1930, but that interest died shortly thereafter and was not actively revived until about 1955. His approach to the problems of psychology reflects his training in biological science.[29] He adapts two features of biological evolution to his theories of human development. First, old structures are continuously fitted into new functions, and new structures are developed to fit old functions under changed circumstances. Therefore, development is solidly rooted in what already exists and has a continuity with the past. Second, these adaptations do not develop in isolation. Piaget studies development at each age level and shows how each learning process interacts with environmental demands.

**Scheme.** After his early work in biology, Piaget turned to the psychological development of the child, seeking a link between the biological study of life and the philosophical study of knowledge. For Piaget, the scheme in behavioral science is like structure in biology. In its simplest form, a *scheme* is a response to a stimulus but it becomes complicated since it soon includes a variety of acts in many different circumstances, not just a simple response to a specific stimulus. It is an organized pattern of behavior. The concept of scheme can refer to innate reflexes such as sucking, however the vast majority of schemes are not innate but are based upon experience. A scheme involves activity on the part of the child. The concept describes things the child does that are generalized by repetition. For example, the scheme of sucking begins in infancy as a reflex or a response to stimulation on the inside of the mouth. However, the response also involves turning the head, opening the mouth, swallowing milk, and so on. The scheme soon expands to include nonnutritive thumb sucking and chewing many objects in the environment. The older child performs classifying *operations,* such as putting things together and forming hierarchies of classes. These intellectual activities constitute another psychological structure.

**Adaptation.** The second aspect of general functioning in Piaget's theory is adaptation, which is further subdivided into accommodation and assimilation. *Accommodation* refers to an organism's tendency to modify its structures according to environmental pressures, while *assimilation* involves the use of current structures to deal with the environment. Eventually the organism tends toward equilibrium, aiming toward a balance between its structures and the requirements of its world.[30]

**Stages of Development.** These are the different stages of a child's development as delineated by Piaget:

1. *Sensorimotor intelligence* exists from birth until approximately eighteen months.

2. *Preoperational thought* begins when the child uses symbols (words or drawings) to represent actions and ends at about age five or six.

3. *Concrete operational thought* begins at about age five to six and ends at about age eleven or twelve. This stage involves the manipulation of categories and classification systems and problem solving with a clear tie to physical reality. At this stage children are less skilled in dealing with purely philosophical or abstract concepts.

4. *Formal operational thought* begins in adolescence and continues through adulthood. This level of thought leads to conceptualization about many variables interacting simultaneously. Laws or rules to be used for problem solving—the kind of thought on which science and philosophy are built—are developed at this level.[31]

Ginsberg and Opper suggest several implications of Piaget's views in regard to educational practices:

1. Children's language and thought are different from adults'. Therefore, a teacher must observe children very closely to determine their unique perspectives.

2. Children need to manipulate things in order to learn. They must physically act on their environment. Therefore, formal verbal instruction is generally ineffective.

3. Children are most interested and learn best when experience is moderately novel. Since children's cognitive structures differ at a given age level, all children will not find the same new event interesting. Therefore, group instruction is generally ineffective. Children should work individually at tasks of their own choosing.

4. Children's thought processes progress through a series of stages. Therefore, children should not be forced to learn material for which they are not ready. A teacher must be sensitive to an individual child's strengths and weaknesses.

5. Social interaction, especially when it is centered around relevant physical experience, promotes intellectual growth. Therefore, children should talk, argue, and debate in school.[32]

This statement by Piaget summarizes his educational goals:

The principal goal of education is to create men who are capable of doing new things, not simply of repeating what other generations have done—men who are creative, inventive, and discoverers. The second goal of education is to form minds which can be critical, can verify, and not accept everything they are offered. The great danger today is of slogans, collective opinions, ready-made trends of thoughts. We have to be able to resist individually, to criticize, to distinguish between what is proven and what is not. So we need pupils who are active, who learn early how to find out by themselves, partly by their own spontaneous activity and partly through material we set up for them; who learn early to tell what is verifiable and what is simply the first idea to come to them.[33]

## BEHAVIORISTIC APPROACH

The behavioristic movement in psychology began about 1910 with the work of John B. Watson. Watson believed that all behavior is learned by associative processes and that only overt, observable behavioral concepts belong in psychology. He considered concepts such as thoughts, goals, and feelings to be nonbehavioristic and therefore discarded them. Behavioristic psychologists are often referred to as stimulus-response (S-R) theorists. Although behavioristic S-R psychologists do not reject all thought processes as rigidly as Watson did, their approach to child study is very different from the two approaches previously described.

The behavioristic theorists approach the study of human behavior experimentally in the laboratory where conditions can be controlled. Their procedure is sometimes called the "black-box approach" because they view behavior from the outside, ignoring the fact that the experimenter is also a person. The advantage of the black-box strategy is that the subject can be considered as an objective "thing" with various appendages that act and respond to stimuli, and this objective view allows the experimenter to develop a theory about the mechanism inside the box to explain its reactions.[34] Many of the behaviorists' theories of learning have been worked out through animal experiments with the results applied to human behavior. Most significant are the contributions of B. F. Skinner.

The behaviorists apply their theories sparingly. Instead of seeking global explanations for behavior, they deal with their concepts in simple, uncomplicated experimental situations. With respect to learning, some of their basic principles are that behavior is learned, that such behavior is the result of many independent learning processes, and that it is learned through *external reinforcement* (such as the individual being rewarded by someone for the learned behavior). The unit of behavior studied is a specific act and each act is independently learned. This view is in contrast to Piaget's groupings of organized behavioral acts. Behavior need not be reinforced each time for learning to occur. Reinforcement may be presented on different schedules (fixed interval, variable ratio, etc.).

*Conditioning* is an important process in behavioristic theory. Of course, classical conditioning is associated with Pavlov and his conditioning of the salivary response in a dog. The dog, who salivated when a food powder was put into its mouth, was conditioned to salivate in response to a bell. This learning response was accomplished by ringing a bell at approximately the same time the food stimulus was presented (S-R application). After repeating the bell and food stimuli contiguously, the ringing bell stimulus was presented alone and evoked the salivary response without any food. Therefore, the bell became the conditioning stimulus, and the salivation to the bell the conditioned response.

Newman and Newman apply the principles of conditioning relative to children acquiring a fear of the dark.[35] If a child is startled from partial sleep on a dark night by a loud noise, the child may become anxious and upset. The next night the dark room alone may generate anxiety in the child. Over a period of time, if the darkness is no longer linked to the startling noise, the fear response should subside. This is called *extinction*. However, sometimes the child continues to fear the dark long after the initial startling experience. *Operant conditioning* offers one explanation for this continuing fear response. If an experience—the stimulus—is followed by a positive consequence—the *reinforcement*—a response can be strengthened. In this example, if the child's cries and fear bring parental attention in the form of extra affection or even a snack, the strength of the habit will increase. The basic behavioristic explanatory concept for relating S to R is *habit*.

The behavioristic concept of operant conditioning has been incorporated into an applied system of interventions called *behavior modification*.[36] This is a process in which reinforcements are made to encourage some responses in order to shape behavior in the desired direction and reduce undesired responses. The effectiveness of behavior modification is described in detail by Risley and Baer.[37]

## SOCIAL-LEARNING APPROACH

Although social-learning theory continues to be modified, essentially it emphasizes imitation and observational learning: children learn and therefore change their behavior by watching and imitating others. The basic elements of social-learning theory are the role of dependency in infancy and dependency anxiety.

> Dependency is seen as the root of nearly all socialization, the gradual taming of
> aggression into a socially acceptable form, the appearance of various adult behavior
> patterns enforced through fear of punishment, and the appearance of identification
> and conscience.[38]

Sometimes social-learning theory is said to be a translation of Freudian theory into S-R terminology. Psychoanalytic writers disagree with this observation, however.[39] Yet, while social-learning theory does ignore the psychoanalytic formulation of psychosexual development (the unconscious and basic instinctual drives), it does incorporate certain Freudian hypotheses related to the child's personality and social relations that have been tested within the S-R experimental framework. Such research has led to revisions of the theory and differences among social-learning theorists regarding empirical child development data.

One of the leaders of S-R theory was Clark L. Hull of Yale University. Hull's research, which dealt with experiments using rats as subjects, contributed to general theory on behavior. Some of his students and colleagues combined S-R and psychoanalytic theory into the social-learning approach to the study of children. The leaders of this approach include O.H. Mowrer, Robert R. Sears, Neal Miller, John Dollard, Albert Bandura, and Richard Walters.

The field of anthropology has also contributed to the development of social-learning theory, especially in regard to environmental factors that cause children to learn the same things at approximately the same age. The constant realities of the physical environment and customary patterns of child rearing are two factors that produce similar learning environments. Cross-cultural studies of child-rearing practices have greatly increased understanding of the consequences of the *socialization process,* or the process by which a society teaches its children to behave like adults.

## ORGANISMIC APPROACH

The organismic approach is a holistic one which focuses on the entire organism as an organized system: not only is all behavior essentially interrelated but it has physiological genetic underpinnings. This approach is in contrast to that espoused by theorists who focus upon separate traits or habits. Although numerous organismic theories exist, there are several common features among them:

1. Organization is the natural state of the organism. Inherent genetic factors operate in this organization on the basis of biological processes which put some constraints upon a child's development and learning.

2. The individual is motivated by one sovereign drive: self-actualization or self-realization. This means that he or she strives continuously to reach potential growth and capabilities by making use of all available resources.

3. The influence of the external environment is minimized. The organism will select the features of the environment to which it will react. If an individual cannot control the environment, he or she will try to adapt to it. If an individual's potentialities are allowed to unfold in an orderly way in an appropriate environment, a healthy, integrated personality will develop. Similarly, an inadequate environment can destroy or cripple an individual.

4. A comprehensive study of one person is done rather than an extensive investigation of isolated psychological functions abstracted from many individuals. Therefore, organismic theories tend to be more popular with clinical psychologists who are concerned with the whole person than with experimental psychologists who are interested in studying separate functions such as perception and learning.[40]

Although individual theories will not be discussed here, the interested reader is referred to the writings of several leading exponents of organismic and related theories: Kurt Goldstein, Heinz Werner, Gardner Murphy, Prescott Lecky, and Abraham Maslow.[41] Goldstein, a neuropsychiatrist, is considered to be the leading exponent of organismic theory. This set of directions, which is based on a survey of Goldstein's research activities, is suggested to the investigator who wishes to conduct studies using the organismic approach:

1. Study the whole person.

2. Make intensive studies of individuals using tests, interviews, and observations under natural conditions.

3. Study behavior in terms of such principles as "self-actualization" and "coming to terms with the environment."

4. Use both qualitative and quantitative methods in collecting and analyzing data.

5. Do not use experimental controls and conditions which make the behavior artificial.

6. Remember that the organism is complex and that behavior is the result of a vast network of determiners.[42]

## ETHOLOGICAL APPROACH

Ethology is the study of the biological basis of behavior, and the movement has focused primarily on animal behavior. Ethologists believe that animals inherit response patterns to environmental stimuli through biological evolution.

The ethological approach to child study has emerged from the work of several European zoologists, most notably Konrad Lorenz and Niko Tinbergen.[43] Lorenz and Tinbergen shared the Nobel prize in physiology in 1973 with Karl von Frisch for their work dealing with early attachment in ducks, mating behavior of fish, and instinctual aggression in a variety of species. Such innate tendencies are observed more easily in lower animals because they are not modified by the complex learning that takes place in humans.[44]

In studying children, ethologists observe them in their natural environment and employ experimental techniques to supplement and confirm their observations. Exhaustive descriptions of all behaviors occurring in specific environmental settings are called *ethograms.*[45] While ethologists emphasize the importance of innate behavioral responses, they also recognize learning and the interaction between innate and learned factors. In this respect, Ginsburg and Pollman studied the aggressive behaviors of children during school recess periods. They observed that fighting among boys was momentarily halted when one of the fighters stopped or knelt down. Typically, such a child would try to tie his shoelace or fix his shoe even if tying or fixing did not appear necessary. The researchers concluded that the ritual of halting the fight when one child is in an indefensible position is likely innate—like instances observed in the animal kingdom—but that the shoe tying activity is a learned response to the ritual.[46]

Numerous psychologists are now adopting the ethological approach to help them understand how a child's biological heritage influences growth. Jones and McGrew have focused more on this approach to child development than earlier ethologists who were more animal-oriented.[47] McGrew lists six classes of behavior that should be explored in human ethology: facial patterns, head patterns, gestures, postures and leg patterns, gross body pattern, and locomotion. Each of these patterns is presumed to be determined by genetically transmitted forces.[48]

## ECOLOGICAL APPROACH

> The child . . . is a *psychobiological system* that exists within the context of social and physical systems. The development of the child can only be fully understood through an analysis of the psychobiological system and its relationship to the social and physical systems within which it exists.[49]

An ecological approach focuses on the study of children in *interaction* with their environment. "Human ecology focuses on the individual and his reciprocal relationships with other men and technology in the settings most critical for human development: the family, home, and community."[50] The community includes many settings, such as the school, the church, and the neighborhood playground. "A setting is defined as a place with particular physical features in which the participants engage in particular activities in particular roles (e.g., daughter, parent, teacher, employee) for particular periods of time. The factors of place, time, physical features, activity, participant, and role constitute the elements of a setting."[51] See Chapter 3 for a discussion of behavior settings and their measurement.

**Microsystem and Macrosystem.** The relationships between the developing person and the environment in an immediate setting containing that person such as the home or school is called a *microsystem.* Another term used in ecological study in the *macrosystem.* This system differs from a microsystem in that it refers not to specific contexts affecting the life of the individual but to general patterns existing within the culture. Bronfenbrenner defines a macrosystem in this manner:

> A macrosystem refers to the overarching institutional patterns of the culture or subculture, such as the economic, social, educational, legal, and political systems . . . What place or priority children and those responsible for their care have in such macrosystems is of special importance in determining how a child and his or her caretakers are treated and interact with each other in different types of settings.[52]

**Kurt Lewin.** Ecological theory employs many of the topological "life-space" ideas conceived by Kurt Lewin.[53] Lewin's structure includes the inner person and the psychological environment (life space) and the foreign hull or objective physical world surrounding the life space. The inner person affects the psychological environment, and likewise the life space affects the person through the process of interaction. Unfortunately, heredity and maturation are ignored in Lewin's life space. These two factors exist outside the life space except in adolescence where the body influences the psychic structure. Therefore, according to Lewin, a person's needs are determined largely by social factors.

Roger Barker, a postdoctoral student with Lewin in the 1930s, established the Midwest Psychological Field Station at Lawrence, Kansas with some associates in the early 1950s. The methods of the ecological psychologists were first developed there.[54] Barker's *Ecological Psychology*[55] is considered a sequel to Lewin's earlier work with children.[56]

## APPLICATION OF OTHER THEORIES TO ECOLOGY

The ecological approach, due to its broad interdisciplinary nature, draws upon a wide array of theories and methods. In fact, each of the theories summarized in this chapter offers an application to the ecological approach to child study. Psychoanalytic theory credits a child's early experiences for most of the child's later behavior. Piaget, the foremost contributor to cognitive theory, has shown how the learning process at each developmental stage interacts with environmental demands. Adaptation is an important concept of Piaget's. According to this concept and the related subconcepts of accommodation and assimilation, an organism modifies its structures according to environmental pressures (accommodation) and uses current structures to deal with the environment (assimilation). Eventually, the organism tends toward an equilibrium and maintains a balance between its needs and the requirements of its environment.

Behavioristic (stimulus-response) theorists, with their emphasis on an organism's responses to environmental stimuli and their concepts of external reinforcement and behavior imitation in learning, have contributed to the ecological approach. Social-learning theorists have contributed to knowledge of the socialization process, especially with cross-cultural studies of physical environments and patterns of child-rearing as they produce learning environments.

The organismic theorists minimize the influence of the external environment but emphasize the study of the whole person and the observation of children under natural conditions. They also focus on the genetic factors influencing the child's potential development, factors which have been given little attention by most other theorists.

The ethological perspective is similar to the ecological perspective of studying individuals as they interact in the natural environment. However, Hutt and Hutt identify several important differences between the two approaches, including these:

1. Ethologists focus on smaller units of behavior than ecologists.

2. Ethologists focus on motor patterns of the subjects being observed, while ecologists think of behavior episodes in relation to the achievement of a goal.

3. Ethologists regard the ecologists' use of the "psychological habitat," or the person's attitudes and motives, as being unscientific.[57]

The ecological approach adopts the "best" of all these theories. To refer to Newman's and Newman's definition on page 13, adequate child study must include the physical, psychological, and social systems in interaction. The methodological approaches for ecological study of children also should be varied.

> There is a great need for studies in which the techniques and advantages of laboratory control and naturalistic observation are combined, and in which the traditional experimenter-subject dyad is replaced by or supplemented with a more meaningful, natural social structure.[58]

## AUTHORS' PERSPECTIVE

This formula best summarizes the authors' conception of the interaction of numerous factors in the development of the child:

$$OH \ (CH + SG) \ UE = TS$$

**organic heritage (cultural heritage + social groups) unique experiences = tentative self**

The child's psychological and social development—the formation of his or her "tentative self"—is the summary of the interaction of the child's organic heritage, the cultural beliefs in which the child was raised, the social groups in which the child has been a part, and unique personal experience.[59]

**Organic Heritage.** At the outset of life, behavior is biological and a number of well-defined response patterns are set up in the organism. Very important to the operation and equilibrium of these bodily processes is the autonomic nervous system, which is fully developed at the time of birth. The central nervous system is immature at birth and represents a blank tablet upon which environmental factors make impressions as they are experienced. However, the impressions made are in turn dependent upon further and continuous maturing of the nervous system. Thus, the nervous system serves as the integrating point of the organism and sets the limits or capacities of the individual for learning. Physical maturity and the amount of prior learning set the rate.

**Cultural Heritage.** The child is born into a society with well-established material and nonmaterial components, through which the "progress" or complexity of the society may be determined. The material components of culture—the "near environment"—consist of housing, clothing, food, tools, and concrete presentations of ideas such as books and paintings. Nonmaterial components include the ideas and techniques behind the material components as well as ways of thinking and behaving, values, language, science, law, and religion.

With respect to the nonmaterial cultural heritage, a child is conditioned, through the socialization process, to conform to society's well-established patterns of thinking and behaving. Whether the child accepts these patterns with ease or whether they must be forced upon the child depends upon other factors (organic heritage, social groups, and personal experiences). The child's reaction to these cultural environmental pressures plays an important part in his or her future psychological adjustment.

Probably the greatest contribution of the cultural heritage to the development and adjustment of the self in its environment lies in that heritage's provision of supplies or resources for reaching potentialities. Early environmental stimulation, such as visual and tactile stimuli and communication with other humans, is considered essential to cognitive and emotional development.

**Social Groups.** The social groups in a society are organized and held together by a common cultural heritage. The family is an important social group and the most significant molder of personality. Family members exert a primary influence on an individual's concept of self and of the environment and on the individual's development and adjustment to the environment. Gradual independence from the family becomes important as the individual performs the various developmental tasks toward adulthood. A step toward independence begins with peer group interaction. The peer group provides the beginning for genuine relations with others in the broader environment outside the child's family. The child is required to play rather specific roles in the peer group. Moreover, the child measures self according to the reactions of others concerning the number of roles which the child plays and his or her skill in playing these roles.

**Unique Experiences.** Organic heritage, cultural heritage, and social groups have important meanings for the individual. These meanings are derived from the individual's interpretations of his or her unique experiences, based upon what these experiences imply for need-satisfaction. Ecologists may sometimes reduce culture to patterns of instinctual or conditioned responses to environmental conditions. Such a reduction ignores the interpretative or subjective aspects of meaning. The fact that societal as well as individual responses to similar environments vary indicates that these environments alone do not determine responses. Giving meaning to the environment implies having emotions and making evaluations about it. Thus, the environment may be interpreted as being comfortable or uncomfortable, friendly or hostile, beautiful or ugly, and so on. Individuals tend to interpret the environment in terms of its relevance to the self—in terms of the extent to which the environment satisfies their needs and aspirations.

**The Tentative Self**. The tentative self is the end product of the interaction of a person's organic and cultural heritages, social groups, and personal experiences. It takes such forms as attitudes, values, goals, drives, levels of aspiration, self-concepts, and codes of conduct—all of which are fairly consistent with one another.

The word *tentative* indicates that no life pattern is static. The self, once organized, exerts itself in *self-control*. Although a human being is never completely free of the influence of social and physical factors, he or she is not a passive component in an adaptive system. The individual does not simply react to the environment. He or she responds to it. Moreover, these responses are not always aimed at blindly adapting to the environment. Instead, they often reflect a need for exploration, activity, and manipulation. These three drives have much in common and are therefore classified under the single concept of *competence*. This opens the way for considering those aspects of behavior in which stimulation and contact with the environment seem to be sought, in which raised tension, mild excitement, novelty, and variety are enjoyed for themselves.

Through the process of *perception* the individual tends to protect his or her already achieved self-organization. Moreover, through selective perception the individual selects stimuli supportive of his or her present self-development.

The individual must master or "come to terms with" the environment not only because it affords the means by which self-actualization can be achieved but also because it contains obstructions in the form of threats and pressures that hinder self-actualization. Dealing with the environment is the most fundamental element of motivation.

By applying an S-R framework to the ecological approach, Compton has developed a model for an ecological approach to research in human ecology and related fields of study.[60] This model is shown in Figure 1.1.

## METHODOLOGICAL APPROACHES TO CHILD STUDY

Knowledge of how to conduct an objective and comprehensive appraisal of individual children is vital to those who educate children or provide other services for them. Such an appraisal requires the collection of many kinds of information about the child and his or her family. Methods or techniques of data collection may be classified into four general types: observational; structured tests and scales; self-report methods; and projective and other indirect methods.

### OBSERVATIONAL TECHNIQUES

People are constantly observing events and behavior in progress around them. However, accounts of witnesses to crimes and other events reveal that two observers may interpret an incident quite differently and often inaccurately. Such everyday observations are far from scientific. The observation of people and events becomes scientific only to the extent that it involves a "deliberate and systematic search, carried out with planning and forethought."[61]

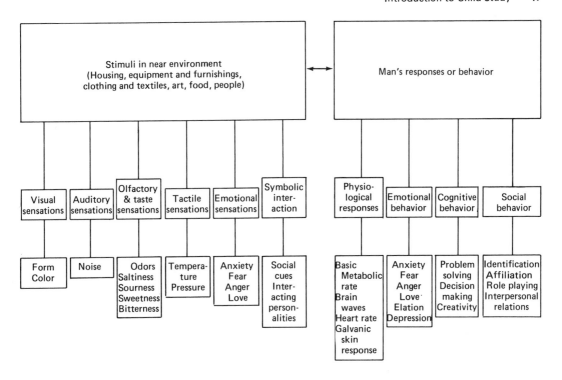

**Figure 1.1.** Interaction Between Man and His Near Environment

The observational method makes it possible to observe behavior as it occurs, either in a laboratory or real-life situation. Detailed discussion of data for observation and observational techniques is included in Chapters 2 through 6.

## STRUCTURED TESTS AND SCALES

As measuring instruments, tests and scales are similarly defined. A person participating in a test is presented with a set of constructive stimuli to which he or she responds, and these responses enable the tester to assign a numeral or numerals to indicate the person's possession of the attributes that the test is supposed to measure. Likewise, a scale indicates the individual's possession of whatever attributes the scale is supposed to measure.

Structured tests and scales can be divided into several classes such as intelligence and aptitude tests, achievement tests, personality scales, interest scales, attitude scales, and value scales. They are used in a variety of ways that may range from the rating of an object to the evaluating of personal traits. Some can be scored quickly and without much thought, while others are complex with the rater being forced to make fine discriminations between degrees of behavior or preference.

Many tests and scales are available in published form. The question that must be asked is, Does a good measure for a particular variable exist? The answer will require much searching and studying. First, the kind of variable that is to be measured must be determined. Once the variable has been identified as an aptitude, personality trait, attitude, or some other kind of variable, the next step is to consult books that discuss measurement instruments. Periodical research journals also should be searched, since many worthwhile instruments have never been published commercially. The availability and adequacy of measures can be checked through *Psychological Abstracts, Review of Educational Research, Encyclopedia of Educational Research,* and the *Mental Measurements Yearbooks.* The latter books present reviews of various instruments.

## SELF-REPORT METHODS

The observational method makes it possible to record behavior as it occurs and eliminates the disadvantage of depending upon someone else's memory and interpretation of an event. However, the observational method is useless when the concern is to secure information about past behavior and about perceptions, feelings, attitudes, and goals. In such instances, a self-report method must be used.

Questionnaire and interview techniques have been devised to collect data directly from subjects in the form of verbal or written self-reports. The validity of these reports is open to question, especially with young children. People may not only be reluctant to express their personal feelings and attitudes, but they also may not have sufficient understanding of themselves to give accurate appraisals. In spite of these limitations, the self-report method provides information that may not be available through other techniques or that may be expensive and time-consuming to obtain by other means. In instances where the information needed is straightforward and not threatening to a subject, valid information may be obtained if a questionnaire is constructed properly and if an interview is conducted by a well-trained interviewer.

## PROJECTIVE AND OTHER INDIRECT METHODS

Projective tests probe into the unconscious depths of feelings, emotions, and determinants of behavior in order to provide a more complete picture of personality than is usually possible with most other instruments. They do this by using relatively unstructured stimuli for which there are no obvious or socially acceptable responses.

When an individual is presented with objective items to test knowledge of a subject, the likelihood of self-projection occurring is minimal. There are few choices and little opportunity for interpretation. On the other hand, relatively ambiguous, unstructured stimuli have no meaning in themselves and therefore force an individual to "project" something into his or her responses. The stimuli used in projective tests have many forms, such as describing inkblots, using finger paints, describing pictures, playing with dolls, and reacting to colors and sounds. A wide variety of responses can be made to such stimuli. An individual must choose an interpretation or reaction from within and thereby express perception of self and of his or her individual world.

Projective techniques were developed originally for use in clinical psychology, but today applications are being made in many research fields. The techniques are largely independent of a subject's self-insight and willingness to reveal self. In fact, the subject is generally unaware of what is being measured. In a projective test, an individual's responses are not taken at face value with the meanings that he or she would expect them to have, but are interpreted in terms of preestablished conceptualizations with respect to what his or her responses to the test stimuli mean. Such conceptualizations provide the framework for interpreting the responses. Usually a total record of numerous replies must be studied before a response tendency for an individual is derived.

Use of a projective technique is not advisable if a more objective instrument that adequately measures the same variable is available. Many projective techniques require highly specialized training and a great deal of questionable interpretation.

## PRINCIPLES OF ANALYSIS

As was indicated in the introduction of this chapter, *child study* is the process of collecting, organizing, synthesizing, and interpreting pertinent information of many kinds about individual children. Various techniques for collecting data on children will be described in this book. These data must be analyzed and interpreted by teachers, guidance personnel, and others who work with children. Gibson and Higgins offer ten principles of analysis to serve as guidelines in this appraisal process. These principles are reprinted in Figure 1.2.

---

1.  Every individual is unique.

2.  Variation exists within the individual as well as between individuals.

3.  Analytical techniques provide only samplings.

4.  Analytical techniques do not always reveal a trait directly.

5.  Supposedly similar analytical tools may vary considerably.

6.  Analytical tools cannot provide information of pinpoint accuracy.

7.  All aspects of the use of analytical tools require specific training.

8.  Norms are not standards.

9.  Analytical measures may be weakened by failure to include the subject's views.

10.  The use of any analytical technique must be governed by rigid adherence to ethical standards.

---

**Figure 1.2.** Ten Principles of Analysis

## CHAPTER NOTES

1.  G. R. Medinnus, *Child Study and Observation Guide* (New York: Wiley, 1976).
2.  R. R. Sears, "Your Ancients Revisited: A History of Child Development," *Review of Child Development Research*, vol. 5, ed. E. M. Hetherington (Chicago: University of Chicago Press, 1975), pp. 1-73.
3.  E. B. Hurlock, *Child Development*, 6th ed. (New York: McGraw-Hill, 1978).
4.  M. W. Shinn, *The Biography of a Baby* (New York: Macmillan, 1900).
5.  Hurlock, *Child Development.*
6.  Sears, "Your Ancients Revisited."
7.  L. E. Holt, *The Care and Feeding of Children* (New York: Appleton, 1894).
8.  Sears, "Your Ancients Revisited."
9.  M. Senn, *Insights on the Child Development Movement in the United States*, Society for Research in Child Development Monographs, 40, 1975.
10.  W. Kessen, *The Child* (New York: Wiley, 1965), pp. 147-148.
11.  S. L. Schlossman, "Before Home Start: Notes Toward a History of Parent Education in America, 1897-1929," *Harvard Educational Review* 46 (1976): 441.
12.  Ibid.
13.  Senn, *Insights.*
14.  Ibid.
15.  G. S. Murphy and J. K. Kovach, *Historical Introduction to Modern Psychology*, rev. ed. (New York: Harcourt Brace Jovanovich, 1972).
16.  Murphy and Kovach, *Historical Introduction.*
17.  H. R. Stolz and L. M. Stolz, *Somatic Development of Adolescent Boys* (New York: Macmillan, 1951).
18.  H. Ginsburg and S. Opper, *Piaget's Theory of Intellectual Development* (Englewood Cliffs, N.J.: Prentice-Hall, 1969), p. ix.
19.  Sears, "Your Ancients Revisited."
20.  Hurlock, *Child Development*, p. 3.
21.  J. Conant, *Science and Common Sense* (New Haven: Yale University Press, 1951), p. 25.
22.  F. N. Kerlinger, *Foundations of Behavioral Research* (New York: Holt, Rinehart and Winston, 1964).
23.  A. L. Baldwin, *Theories of Child Development* (New York: Wiley, 1967).
      W. C. Crain, *Theories of Development* (Englewood Cliffs, N.J.: Prentice-Hall, 1980).
      J. Langer, *Theories of Development* (New York: Holt, 1969).
      H. W. Maier, *Three Theories of Child Development* (New York: Harper, 1978).
      R. E. Muuss, *Theories of Adolescence* (New York: Random House, 1975).
      R. M. Thomas, *Comparing Theories of Child Development* (Belmont, Calif.: Wadsworth, 1979).
24.  A. E. Bayer, "The Psychoanalytic Frame of Reference in Family Study," in *Emerging Conceptual Frameworks in Family Analysis*, eds. E. Nye and F. Berardo (New York: Macmillan, 1966), p. 169.
25.  R. R. Sears, "Survey of Objectives Studies of Psychoanalytic Concepts," *Social Science Research Bulletin*, 1 (1943): 133.
26.  E. Erikson, *Childhood and Society* (New York: Norton, 1963).
27.  B. Newman and P. Newman, *Infancy and Childhood* (New York: Wiley, 1978).
28.  H. Ginsburg and S. Opper, *Piaget's Theory.*
29.  A. L. Baldwin, *Theories of Child Development* (New York: John Wiley, 1967).
30.  Ginsburg and Opper, *Piaget's Theory*, pp. 230-31.
31.  Newman and Newman, *Infancy and Childhood.*
32.  Ginsburg and Opper, *Piaget's Theory*, pp. 230-31.
33.  J. Piaget, "Development and Learning," in *Piaget Rediscovered*, eds. R.E. Ripple and V.N. Rockcastle (Ithaca, N.Y.: Cornell University Press, 1964), p. 5.

34. Baldwin, *Theories.*
35. Newman and Newman, *Infancy and Childhood.*
36. Ibid.
37. T. R. Risley and D. M. Baer, "Operant Behavior Modification: The Deliberate Development of Behavior," in *Review of Child Development Research,* vol. 3, eds. B. M. Caldwell and H. N. Riccuiti (Chicago: University of Chicago Press, 1973).
38. Baldwin, *Theories,* p. 473.
39. Baldwin, *Theories.*
40. C. S. Hall and G. Lindzey, *Theories of Personality* (New York: Wiley, 1970).
41. K. Goldstein, *The Organism* (New York: American Book Co., 1939).
    H. Werner, *Comparative Psychology of Mental Development,* rev. ed. (Chicago: Follet, 1948).
    G. Murphy, *Personality: A Biosocial Approach to Origins and Structure* (New York: Harper, 1947).
    P. Lecky, *Self-Consistency* (1945; reprint ed., Garden City, N.Y.: Doubleday, 1968).
    A. H. Maslow, *Motivation and Personality* (New York: Harper, 1954).
42. Hall and Lindzey, *Personality.*
43. K. Lorenz, *On Aggression* (New York: Harcourt, 1966).
    N. Tinbergen, *The Study of Instinct* (New York: Oxford University Press, 1969).
44. S. R. Yussen and J. W. Santrock, *Child Development* (Dubuque, Iowa: Wm. Brown, 1978).
45. Ibid.
46. H. J. Ginsburg and V. A. Pollman, "An Ethological Analysis of Nonverbal Inhibiters of Aggressive Behavior in Elementary School Children" (Paper presented at the annual meeting of the Society for Research in Child Development, Denver, April, 1975).
47. N. Blurton Jones, ed., *Ethological Studies of Child Behavior* (New York: Cambridge University Press, 1972).
    W. C. McGrew, *An Ethological Study of Children's Behavior* (New York: Academic Press, 1972).
48. McGrew, *Ethological Study.*
49. Newman and Newman, *Infancy and Childhood,* p. 36.
50. D. Knapp, *The New York State College of Human Ecology at Cornell University* (Ithaca, N.Y.: Cornell University, 1970), p. 3.
51. U. Bronfenbrenner, "Toward an Experimental Ecology of Human Development," *American Psychologist,* July 1977, p. 514.
52. Ibid., p. 515.
53. K. Lewin, *A Dynamic Theory of Personality* (New York: McGraw-Hill, 1935).
54. O. M. Irwin and M. M. Bushnell, *Observational Strategies for Child Study* (New York: Holt, 1980).
55. R. Barker, *Ecological Psychology* (Stanford, Calif.: Stanford University Press, 1968).
56. Sears, "Your Ancients Revisited," p. 54.
57. S. J. Hutt and C. Hutt, *Direct Observation and Measurement of Behavior* (Springfield, Ill.: Thomas, 1970).
58. Social Research Group, *Toward Interagency Coordination—An Overview of Federal Research and Development Activities Relating to Early Childhood,* Third Annual Report (Washington, D.C.: George Washington University, December 1973).
59. N. Compton and O. Hall, *Foundations of Home Economics Research—A Human Ecology Approach* (Minneapolis: Burgess, 1972).
60. Ibid.
61. B. Kleinmuntz, *Personality Measurement* (Homewood, Ill.: Dorsey, 1967), p. 83.

# 2

# Systematic Observation: Introduction

On the surface, observation seems to be a very simple process in which we all engage. It is the way we obtain information about the world around us. In a characteristically casual manner, we observe the weather, our surroundings, what our friends are wearing, and the mannerisms of our instructors. More systematic observation such as that used in child study is essentially an application in the scientific area of a general skill which most of us have to some degree. However, since the purpose of observational child study is the pursuit of knowledge about children, it necessarily entails "planned, methodical watching that involves constraints to improve accuracy."[1]

Observation becomes scientific to the extent that it serves a formulated purpose, is planned methodically, is recorded systematically and related to certain questions or propositions, and is subjected to checks and controls with respect to reliability and validity.[2] Systematic observation, although different in some ways from informal observation, is not without fallibility. Yet, the trained observer is cognizant of his or her limitations: he or she approaches the tasks methodically, and is also armed with specialized techniques and equipment that increase the scientific quality of the observations. Systematic observation may involve such diverse facilities as category systems, rating scales, checklists, interval timers, event recorders, and cameras as well as pencil and notebook.

The observational study of children, which has a history encompassing more than 100 years,[3] has been employed for a variety of purposes in the behavioral sciences and education:

> It may be used in an exploratory fashion, to gain insights that will later be tested by other techniques; its purpose may be to gather supplementary data that may qualify or help interpret findings obtained by other techniques; or it may be used as the primary method of data collection in studies designed to provide accurate descriptions of situations or to test causal hypotheses.[4]

Direct observation is appropriate for the study of behavior either in natural settings or in the laboratory. The investigation of behavior at school, at home, on the playground, or at the grocery store is called naturalistic observation. In these everyday settings, the behavior in question is observed under natural conditions. If the subjects are in a laboratory, their behavior is observed under more controlled conditions. Such studies may or may not utilize the experimental method in which the effects of the independent variables (i.e., those manipulated by the researcher) on the dependent variables (i.e., subject's behavior) are investigated and the responses are recorded through observational techniques.

## DEFINITION OF SYSTEMATIC OBSERVATION

*Webster's Third New International Dictionary* defines *observation* as " . . . an act of recognizing and noting a fact or occurrence often involving measurement of some magnitude with suitable instruments . . . a record so obtained."[5] *Systematic* is defined as "marked by . . . method or orderly procedure."[6] A number of authors have proposed formal definitions of systematic observation that combine these elements. Jones, Reid, and Patterson have described observational study as "the practice of noting and recording facts and events in accordance with, or in imitation of, the essential character of a thing."[7]

Weick has provided perhaps the most comprehensive definition of systematic observation, although his pertains primarily to naturalistic observation. According to this researcher, systematic observation is:

> . . . the selection, provocation, recording, and encoding of that set of behaviors and settings concerning organisms in situ which is consistent with empirical aims.[8]

Weick uses the term *selection* to point out that some editing takes place in all observation whether it is intentional or not. This and other perceptual errors that plague the observer are discussed in Chapter 4. *Provocation* refers to modifications of the natural setting made by the observer to increase clarity and to improve the quality of observational study. In Weick's estimation, these changes do not necessarily destroy the richness of the natural event. The word *recording* underscores the aspect of observational study that is noted in some way and subjected to analysis at a later time. Anecdotal and specimen records as well as films are examples of records. Methods of recording data are treated in some detail in Chapter 3. By *encoding,* Weick means the simplification and objectification of observation data through the use of aids such as ratings, categories, and frequency counts (see Chapter 5). The phrase *that set* implies the use of more than one behavioral measure. Employment of multiple measures overcomes the limitations of individual techniques and provides a more comprehensive picture of the child and the event. In this regard, Weick's point of view is consistent with one theme of this book: that different approaches to behavioral assessment should be interlinked systematically in order to understand the total child. *Organisms* is used synonymously with *persons*. The phrase *in situ* suggests that an observer concentrate on natural settings where a particular behavioral phenomenon might occur. Finally, Weick chooses the phrase *empirical aims* to emphasize the potential that observational studies have for description and for the formulation and testing of hypotheses. He is aware of the popular notion that observation, in contrast to experiment, is often thought to refer to hypothesis-free inquiry, unselective recording, and avoidance of manipulations in the independent variable. Weick argues that this traditional and limited view of observation has served to constrain the different ways in which the method may be used and suggests that the observational technique can be made into a more valuable and potent child study method.

Systematic observation, then, is a planned process of looking at and recording behavior and/or describing aspects of the environment for the purpose of understanding a child better. It may be done in a natural setting or in a laboratory situation that has been arranged for the isolation and study of certain variables. Observational study may be undertaken with the assistance of devices like rating scales, checklists, and category systems as well as special equipment that is designed to help make the observations more complete and scientific. Increasingly, systematic observation has become a widely accepted method of investigating human behavior, and for many, it is the preferred approach in behavioral science and educational research.

## DATA OBTAINED THROUGH OBSERVATION

The way a child looks and acts and the context of the child's behavior are rich sources of data for observational study. All provide valuable information about a youngster. As observers, we may choose to examine one or more of these child-related variables, but with any of the categories alone, we cannot always expect to draw sound inferences. It is therefore preferable to employ in our observations multiple indicators of personality and development to help us reach valid conclusions. In order to illustrate this point, Mehrabian and Ferris derived a formula that demonstrates the differential contributions of verbal and nonverbal behaviors in communication: total impact = .07 (verbal) + .38 (vocal) + .55 (facial).[9] *Verbal* represents attitude communicated in the verbal component alone; *vocal,* attitude communicated in the vocal component alone; and *facial,* attitude communicated in the facial component alone. This equation indicates that the combined effect of simultaneous verbal, vocal, and facial attitude communications is a weighted sum of their independent effects. Although the formula is limited by the design of Mehrabian's and Ferris's study, it does point up the contributions made by verbal, vocal, and facial cues, and it suggests that both verbal and non-verbal channels carry different classes of information that are important for the observer. Several investigations have demonstrated that there are indeed multiple channels for communicating attitudes, feelings, and emotions.[10] That there is information or message value in *all* observed behavior is emphasized by Brooks when he says that "one cannot not communicate."[11]

In the sections which follow, language behavior, paralinguistic behavior, kinesic behavior—gestures, posture, facial expressions, eye behavior, spatial behavior, and touching behavior—personal appearance, and environmental descriptions will be discussed as types of data that can be obtained through observation.

## LANGUAGE BEHAVIOR

Since human social behavior consists, to a large degree, of the exchange of verbal utterances, language behavior understandably provides an observer with a wealth of information about a subject. *Webster's Third New International Dictionary* lists approximately one-half million vocabulary entries, so there is a seemingly infinite number of words at our disposal. Language is the basis for cultural activities; through language, we question, convey information, and establish and sustain interpersonal relationships.

Traditionally, language has been viewed from two major perspectives: content and structure. However, it has not been uncommon for researchers to examine simultaneously both features of language. The most widely used method to study language content is content analysis: "a research technique for the objective, systematic, and quantitative description of the manifest content of communication."[12] Although this method has been employed to examine data that are already available in documents such as newspapers, books, letters, and speeches,[13] it also has been used effectively to analyze oral language produced by subjects in experimental, therapeutic, and naturalistic settings.[14]

A widely known general purpose content analysis system is the Bales Interaction Process Analysis.[15] Using twelve categories, it classifies what is said in the course of group interaction into six areas: communication, evaluation, control, decision, tension reduction, and reintegration. A limited number of nonverbal components are also included. The Bales method is discussed further in Chapter 5. Other content analysis systems are available which are topic-free and can be applied to a variety of social interaction situations.[16]

Despite the overlap between content and linguistic analysis, there are some essential differences between the two approaches to language study:

> The area of "who says what to whom under what circumstances for what purpose and with what effect," which presumably defines the variables in communication analysis, would in general serve as an adequate definition of precisely what linguists are *not* concerned with. Linguistic analysis deals with the code per se; the statements which describe the code enable one to generate an infinite number of utterances, a very high percentage of which will be acceptable to native speakers of the language.[17]

Accordingly, linguistic analysis focuses on the properties of language as a code, on identification of the minimal units of the code (i.e., phonemes and morphemes), and on statement of permissible sequences of these units.[18] Linguists are less occupied with meanings and are more interested in the structure of language habits and the relation of the linguistic symbols themselves. They consider speech apart from its interpersonal setting and concentrate their efforts on three levels of linguistic behavior: phonology, morphology, and syntax. Several good sources are available which discuss the structural considerations of language and linguistic analysis.[19]

At this time, there are no fully standardized procedures specifically designed for the observation of language behavior and development in children, although some authors[20] have provided preliminary guidelines. Typically, an observer uses toys or books to help elicit speech from a child. This may be done in the child's home or in a laboratory setting. The youngster's utterances are tape-recorded, with the observer taking notes to indicate contextual information or to decode unintelligible utterances. The very difficult job of transcription follows. Dale describes the complexity of this task:

> On the one hand, the untrained ear is likely to hear sentence elements that are required in adult English but not produced by young children (such as articles and inflections), and a skeptical attitude is necessary. On the other hand, young children have deviant phonological systems which may obscure elements that are present. Reliability of transcription is seldom assessed, and in fact it is not clear how best to do so.[21]

After the transcript is prepared, the child's discourse is segmented into distinct utterances which are usually calculated for mean length of utterance (MLU) and subjected to grammatical analyses. Once the observer has listed the utterances, he or she then determines underlying patterns. A number of primary sources that describe research methods and report findings regarding children's language behavior are available.[22]

## PARALINGUISTIC BEHAVIOR

There is a close relationship between language behavior and paralanguage.

> A number of noncontent vocal cues usually accompany speech behavior. When a person says something, the words or linguistic content actually constitute a relatively small portion of the verbal behavior which the alert observer can record. These noncontent behaviors are significant indices of psychological processes; consequently, the observer should consider them carefully when choosing the behaviors to record.[23]

With the exception of only a few investigations,[24] paralinguistic research has dealt mainly with adults and not children. Moreover, it has concentrated largely on monologue material, with data being derived mostly from clinical settings. Yet, despite the paucity of paralinguistic studies involving children and the limited samples obtained in everyday situations, paralinguistic behavior has been demonstrated as an important scientific datum. Since paralanguage conveys information that is essential to behaviorial assessment, it is certainly worthy of consideration when observing children.

Traeger describes several studies which represent a cooperative endeavor by anthropologists, linguists, and psychiatrists to investigate vocal behaviors that are collectively termed "paralanguage."[25] According to Traeger, paralanguage is comprised of two components: vocalizations and voice qualities. Vocalizations are "variegated . . . noises, not having the structure of language."[26] The three types of vocalizations are vocal characterizers (e.g., laughing, crying, giggling, snickering, whimpering, sobbing, yelling, whispering, moaning, groaning, whining, breaking, belching, yawning), vocal qualifiers (e.g., intensity, pitch height, extent), and vocal segregates (e.g., "uh-uh" for negation, "uh-uh" for affirmation, "uh" for hesitation, coughs, snorts, sniffs). Voice qualities are recognizable speech events that are "modifications of all the language and other noises."[27] These include pitch range, vocal lip control, glottis control, pitch control, articulation control, rhythm control, and tempo. Other related systems for the study of paralanguage have been developed in addition to Traeger's initial outline of the subject.[28]

Paralinguistic variables that have been subjected to examination by Traeger and other scholars include: (a) length of verbal production; (b) latency or interval between presentation of stimulus and

**Table 2.1** Characteristics of Vocal Expressions Contained in the Test of Emotional Sensitivity

| Feeling | Loudness | Pitch | Timbre | Rate | Inflection | Rhythm | Enunciation |
|---------|----------|-------|--------|------|------------|--------|-------------|
| Affection | Soft | Low | Resonant | Slow | Steady and slight upward | Regular | Slurred |
| Anger | Loud | High | Blaring | Fast | Irregular up and down | Irregular | Clipped |
| Boredom | Moderate to low | Moderate to low | Moderately resonant | Moderately slow | Monotone or gradually falling | ... | Somewhat slurred |
| Cheerfulness | Moderately high | Moderately high | Moderately blaring | Moderately fast | Up and down; overall upward | Regular | |
| Impatience | Normal | Normal to moderately high | Moderately blaring | Moderately fast | Slight upward | ... | Somewhat clipped |
| Joy | Loud | High | Moderately blaring | Fast | Upward | Regular | |
| Sadness | Soft | Low | Resonant | Slow | Downward | Irregular pauses | Slurred |
| Satisfaction | Normal | Normal | Somewhat resonant | Normal | Slight upward | Regular | Somewhat slurred |

initiation of response; (c) speech and interaction rate; (d) hesitation phenomena including unfilled pauses (silent) and filled pauses (*er, um, ah,* etc.); (e) intrusions, both verbal (*you know, but, I don't know, I mean,* etc.) and nonverbal (brief laughs, coughs, belches, sniffs, throat-clearing, yawns, sighs, etc.); (f) nonfluencies (interchanges of words and syllables, anticipations, omissions, tongue slips, stutters, repetitions, etc.); and (g) voice quality, including pitch, loudness, and timbre. A good deal of research has examined these variables, including their relationships to emotions and attitudes.[29] Rather than survey the voluminous literature here, a summary is given in Table 2.1. This table indicates how Davitz has represented the correlation between vocal cues and emotional expressions. According to Davitz, it is possible to communicate emotional meanings by vocal expression.

One of the paralinguistic studies involving younger subjects, which was conducted by Levin and Silverman, examined hesitations in children's speech.[30] The paralinguistic variables treated in the study included two broad groups of measures: fluency and hesitation in speech. Here are descriptions of these two noncontent properties of children's language behavior:

1. **Fluency variables**

    a.  Seconds speaking (length of presentation in seconds)

    b.  Number of words (word count excluding hesitation phenomena)

    c.  Rate of speaking (ratio of words spoken to number of seconds speaking)

2. **Hesitation variables**

    a.  Vocal segregates (noises like *uh, er,* and *um*)

    b.  Sentence correction (grammatical correction, word order correction, lexical correction, accentual correction, or phonological change)

    c.  Sentence incompletion following a phrase, a single word, or in the middle of a word or phoneme

    d.  Repetitions of a phrase, word, or phoneme

e.   Slips of the tongue

f.   Omissions of words or parts of words

g.   Parenthetic remarks (*oh, well, see, for example, I mean, you know, for some reason,* etc.)

h.   Zero segregates (unfilled pauses)

i.   Drawls (lengthening of a phoneme)

The research subjects included thirty-four male and twenty-four female upper-middle-class fifth graders with a mean IQ of 124 on the Lorge-Thorndike Test. They were instructed to tell stories and to respond to story stems in each of two situations: (1) to an audience of four adults and (2) to a microphone with no one present. After the stories were taped, verbatim transcriptions were coded for type of hesitation phenomena, their frequency, and their duration. On the average, the children emitted 500 words per session, uttered in a period of 238 seconds of speaking. The average frequencies per session of fluency and hesitation variables can be seen in Figure 2.1. Since certain of the variables occurred infrequently, several of them were combined or omitted from further consideration. The categories that were retained for subsequent statistical analyses consisted of words, seconds, rate, zero segregates, long pauses, vocal segregates, corrections, and repetitions. Although our interest

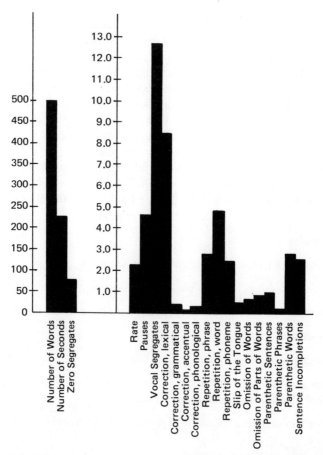

**Figure 2.1.** Average Frequencies Per Session of Fluency and Hesitation Variables

rests primarily with the normative data illustrated in Figure 2.1, we will summarize some of the other findings of the study: (a) boys speak faster than girls; (b) highly exhibitionist subjects pause for longer periods than more self-conscious subjects; and (c) more brief pauses and vocal segregates occur during the public speaking situations than during the private situations.

Finally, it should be mentioned that in recent years many researchers have successfully employed instrumentation to study paralinguistic phenomena. Perhaps the most notable of the devices used is the voice spectrometer developed by Hargreaves and Starkweather.[31] This voice filter eliminates the higher frequencies of speech so that words become unintelligible but vocal qualities remain.

## KINESICS

Kinesics consists of bodily movements and motor expressions that originate in various parts of the body. According to Knapp, kinesic behavior includes "gestures, movements of the body, limbs, hands, head, feet, and legs, facial expressions (smiles), eye behavior (blinking, direction and length of gaze, and pupil dilation), and posture."[32] The importance of kinesics or nonverbal body motion would be undeniable if sheer quantity were the only measure: nonverbal behavior comprises approximately 65 percent of all communication, and verbal, only 35 percent.[33] Though nonverbal behaviors are less well codified and more ambiguous with respect to meaning or intent than verbal behavior, they do have significant communicative value. Invariably, we observe and respond not only to the content of what a child is saying but also to the nonverbal signals that the child emits. We can learn a great deal about a youngster by observing his or her body movements, including gestures, postures, facial expressions, eye behavior, touching behavior, and proxemic behavior. These kinesic behaviors may serve as highly informative indices of the child's feelings, attitudes, and psychological processes.

Some bodily movements are made for the purpose of performance, and others, for expression.[34] Expressive behavior is that which is spontaneously emitted by the child such as walking, talking, posturing, and gesturing. It is uncontrolled and largely unconscious. On the other hand, coping behavior, such as throwing a baseball or riding a bicycle, is purposive, controlled, and consciously performed. It is influenced by awareness of environmental stimuli. As the coping or adjustive component in behavior increases, the expressive component diminishes. Therefore, an observer studying a youngster in a task-oriented situation will probably not view many expressive acts and those which are viewed will probably assume a limited number of forms. Expressive behaviors can be observed with greater frequency in less structured situations.

Birdwhistle, one of the foremost taxonomists and lexicographers of body behavior, has built on the linguistic tradition in anthropology and has sought to extend the linguistic model to body motion.[35] He describes the specific units of body movement in terms that parallel language structure, and he argues that elemental units of body movement, like language, can be isolated and combined into larger wholes. Since this system of body movement is learned and practiced by members of a culture, the linguistic methods that are appropriate for language study are equally applicable to it. Knapp has summarized the more specific characteristics of the linguistic-kinesic analogy that underlie Birdwhistle's methodology:

> Just as there are subdivisions of linguistic study (descriptive and historical), there are also subdivisions of kinesic study (microkinesics, prekinesics, and social kinesics). While there is no kinesic analog to historical linguistics, such work will be plausible in future kinesic study—using the vast number of reels of films and video tapes currently capturing man's body motions in a variety of contexts and in a variety of cultures. Microkinesics and prekinesics seem to parallel descriptive linguistics. Prekinesics deals with the physiological study of the limits of movement and the physiological determinants of movement; microkinesics deals with the derivation of units of movement. Social kinesics concerns the study of units and

patterns of movement in context in order to determine their function in communication.[36]

In addition, Knapp points out that bodily movements have dialects and regionalisms just as a spoken language.[37] Moreover, we use only a fraction of the total sounds and motions that are at our disposal. That is, our reading vocabulary is far more extensive than our speaking vocabulary; likewise, our awareness of visible bodily movement and gestures exceeds our actual use of them. As the voice has certain qualities such as pitch range, intensity, and timbre, there are also parakinesic phenomena that parallel these paralinguistic or extralinguistic behaviors. For example, the amount of muscular tension involved in forming a certain movement may be considered "intensity," and the extent of the movement, its "range." Finally, the units of analysis in linguistic and kinesic behavior are related. In vocal behavior, allophones are the smallest unit of movement, and in kinesic behavior, allokines are the simplest unit. Larger categories that include allophones and allokines are phones and kines, respectively. Whereas sequences of phonemes constitute words, and the minimum sequence of phonemes is called a morpheme, kinemes also combine to form kinemorphemes. Kinemorphs represent a range of movement that is meaningful in the context of larger patterns.

> These kinemes combine to form *kinemorphs,* which are further analyzed into *kinemorphemic classes* which behave like linguistic morphemes. These analyzed, abstracted and combined in the full body of the behavioral stream, prove to form *complex kinemorphs* which may be analogically related to words. Finally, these are combined by syntactic arrangements, still only partially understood, into extended linked behavioral organizations, the *complex kinemorphic constructions,* which have many of the properties of the spoken syntactic sentence.[38]

Although the linguistic-kinesic analogy is an interesting one, it is not without its critics.[39] However, the foregoing description of the two systems and the brief consideration of their units of analysis, though limited by Birdwhistle's hypotheses and coding scheme, illustrate the complexity of body motion. They also suggest the wealth of information available to the observer within the purview of body movements.

**Gestures.** Gestures may be considered language substitutes, language supplements, punctuation marks for verbal conversation, interaction markers, and indicators of mood or emotional intensity.

> Gestures are hard to classify and it is difficult to make a conscious separation between that in gesture which is of merely individual origin and that which is referable to the habits of the group as a whole . . . we respond to gestures with an extreme alertness and, one might say, in accordance with an elaborate and secret code that is written nowhere, known by none, and understood by all.[40]

Freud, in *The Psychopathology of Everyday Life,*[41] and others wrote many years ago that gestures and related mannerisms are symbolic of unconscious processes that provide clues to a person's emotional life. In an early study of gesticulations, Krout examined autistic manual gestures and found that they did indeed represent certain psychological states.[42] He discovered that hand-to-nose gestures represented fear; fist gestures, aggression; fingers at the lips, shame; and hands dangling between legs, frustration. In all, Krout identified over 5,000 distinct manual gestures. Numerous other investigations have studied the symbolism of this nonverbal modality in adults,[43] but surprisingly few have focused on children. We will highlight some of the limited research dealing with children.

A study by Michael and Willis examined the development of gestural behavior as a function of social class, education, and sex.[44] Initially, the researchers identified the gestures that were most frequently employed by four- to seven-year-old children at play and in the classroom. These gestures included those used to indicate these communications: go away, come here, yes, no, be quiet, how many, how big, shape, I don't know, goodbye, hi, and give me your attention. Next, the researchers determined if each child could communicate each of the gestures and if the child could decode gestures transmitted by the interviewer. Results indicated that middle-class children were more accurate in transmitting and interpreting gestures than their lower class counterparts; youngsters with a year of school experience were better than children with no prior school; and boys were more proficient than girls in the interpretation of gestural behavior.

Kumin and Lazar asked three- and four-year-old children to view a videotape containing thirty nonverbal acts including these emblem gestures: no, quiet, hello, I won't do it, yes, come here, naughty, good-bye, stop, who me, and get up.[45] They found that age was related to accuracy in encoding and decoding gestures. This ability increased from ages three to three-and-one-half and from four to four-and-one-half, with males interpreting a greater number of gestures in the younger group and girls decoding more in the older group. Although three subjects in the younger group could not interpret any emblem gestures at all, older children generally did not appear to encode or employ more than the younger group. But during free play, girls at both age levels interpreted the meaning of more gestures than boys.

Another related investigation examined "listener responses" of children.[46] The exploratory phase of this study by Dittmann revealed that head-nods, smiles and eyebrow raises, and comments such as "yeah" and "I see" were almost completely absent in a seven-year-old-boy. The listener responses that the child did make seemed to be inaccurately placed in his speech rhythm, occurring somewhat late and giving the appearance of overtalking or interruption. Dittmann then expanded his sample to include first-, third-, and fifth-grade youngsters. He observed his subjects and wrote notes to help him remember the interaction situation, how strongly the situation "pulled" listener responses, and the number of such responses that occurred. Dittmann found that listener responses took place only under strong social pull by the interactant; there were minimal differences in response rates in grades one, three, and five; the rates were low (twenty-five listener responses in 246 minutes of observation); and there was wide individual variation within grades. Generally speaking, younger children produced fewer listening responses in comparison to older children and adults.

Evans and Rubin studied hand gestures as a communicative mode in boys and girls in kindergarten and grades two and four.[47] A board game was used as the subject matter to be communicated. The youngsters were taught how to play the game by an experimenter and were later asked to explain it to a same-sex experimenter. In order to limit the effect of the experimenter's game description on the child's subsequent explanation in his or her own words, no hand gestures or irrelevant verbal information were included in the description. Results showed that children in all three age groups expressed most of the rules of the game with accompanying gestures, although kindergartners relied more on hand movements than the older children. A hand gesture appeared for about every seven words, and approximately half of the gesticulations provided information that was supplementary to the verbal communication.

In an investigation of communicative hand and arm movements in four- to eighteen-year-old children, Jancovic and others departed from tradition and predicted either no change or an increase in the overall number of gestures emitted with increasing age.[48] The long-standing view holds that communicative use of the gestural channel is expected to decrease as the child achieves greater verbal fluency. Additionally, the researchers hypothesized a shift in the kinds of gestures used from less complex for younger children to more complex for older children. Their findings revealed that the use of hand and arm movements increases over age and that more complex gestures (e.g., semantic modifiers and relationals) increase as age increases. They pointed out that they would have found that less complex gestures do decrease with age if they had focused only on those gestures appearing in the very young (e.g., deictics and pantomimics) and omitted consideration of more complex gestures. But the inclusion of hand and arm movements of greater complexity generated results that supported the hypotheses. Jancovic and her associates suggested that the notion that nonverbal communicative behaviors are simply precursors to more complex verbal communicative behaviors may be unfounded.

Rekers and his associates studied the occurrences of nine body gestures in male and female adolescents, eleven to eighteen years of age, who were playing a tic-tac-toe game with a bean bag.[49] There was a significant sex difference in regard to "palming" (touching the palms to the back, front, or sides of the head above ear level), with girls exhibiting more of these gestures than boys. There was also a developmental increase in the frequency of "limp wrist" (flexing the wrist toward the palmar surface of the forearm and/or upper arm while the elbow is either fixed or extended). The same increase was found for both males and females.

A well-known ethologist, W. C. McGrew, has carefully outlined and described the elements of behavior observed in three- and four-year-old children in social situations at nursery school. McGrew's book *An Ethological Study of Children's Behavior* contains a fairly inclusive repertoire of children's behavior patterns, or an ethogram for young homo sapiens as ethologists would prefer to call it.[50] Behaviors specifically categorized as gestures (those that involve hand and arm movements) are listed in the middle column under III in Table 2.2. All of the behaviors are defined precisely with simple and nonmotivational terms which refer specifically to the body part involved (e.g., forearm raise) or to everyday English usage (e.g., wrestle). Since a complete glossary of McGrew's behavioral elements are provided elsewhere,[51] only three behaviors will be presented here to illustrate the detailed nature of the descriptions used in ethological studies.

> **Hand Cover.** The open, partially flexed hand moves to the head, where the bunched fingers and palms are held close to or in contact with the eyes, ears, nose, and/or mouth.
>
> **Pinch.** The thumb and index finger are forcibly opposed with an object or part of another's body in between.
>
> **Repel.** The arms are spasmodically extended away from and in front of the body, not necessarily horizontally, hands open and palm-first. The movements are usually rapidly repeated and accompanied by negative expletives. The movements somewhat resemble pushing intention movements or lowered incomplete open beating.[52]

**Posture.** Body posture and orientation may reflect personality characteristics and feelings and consequently merit consideration by an observer. Traditionally, psychoanalysts have suggested a relationship between posture and affect, but their evidence has been primarily anecdotal in nature. More systematic studies have been undertaken, however. In an early investigation by James, four broad postural categories were identified from 347 different postures: approach, withdrawal, expansion, and contraction.[53] *Approach* refers to a posture that is adopted by an individual who is examining an external object with attention, interest, curiosity, or scrutiny. It involves forward lean of the body. In contrast to this attentive posture, *withdrawal* means that the individual is drawing back or turning away, indicating negation, refusal, and repulsion. The term *expansion* signifies an expanded chest, an erect or backward-leaning trunk, erect head, and raised shoulders. It suggests such states as pride, conceit, arrogance, disdain, mastery, and self-esteem. *Contraction* is characterized behaviorally by a forward-leaning trunk, bowed head, dropping shoulders, and sunken chest. It is expressive of a depressed, abased, and downcast mental state. According to James, head and trunk positions are the most important indicators for each of the four generic categories, although hand and arm position should also be considered.

Mehrabian has proposed a two-dimensional scheme to describe posture and position cues and their role in the communication of liking and status relations.[54] His first dimension of *immediacy* refers to touching, closer position, forward lean, eye contact, and more direct body orientation. We assume

**Table 2.2** Repertoire of Preschool Children's Behavior Patterns, Arranged by Body Parts Involved

| I. Facial | III. Gestures | V. Gross |
|---|---|---|
| 1. Bared Teeth | 1. Automanipulate | 1. Arms Akimbo* |
| 2. Blink* |    Finger | 2. Body Oppose |
| 3. Eyebrow Flash* |    Fumble | 3. Fall |
| 4. Eyes Closed* | 2. Beat | 4. Flinch |
| 5. Grin Face |    Incomplete | 5. Hug |
| 6. Low Frown |    Object | 6. Jump |
| 7. Mouth Open |    Open | 7. Lean Back |
| 8. Narrow Eyes* |    Up | 8. Lean Forward |
| 9. Normal Face | 3. Beckon* | 9. Physical Contact |
| 10. Nose Wrinkle* | 4. Clap Hands* | 10. Quick Hop |
| 11. Play Face | 5. Digit Suck | 11. Rock |
| 12. Pout* | 6. Drop* | 12. Shoulder Hug |
| 13. Pucker Face | 7. Fist* | 13. Shrug |
| 14. Red Face | 8. Forearm Raise | 14. Stretch* |
| 15. Smile | 9. Forearm Sweep | 15. Turn |
| 16. Wide Eyes | 10. Hand Cover* | 16. Wrestle |
|  | 11. Hand on Back* |  |
| II. Head | 12. Hold Hands | VI. Posture |
|  | 13. Hold Out* |  |
| 1. Bite | 14. Knock* | 1. Climb* |
| 2. Blow* | 15. Pat | 2. Crouch |
| 3. Chew Lips* | 16. Pinch | 3. Immobile |
| 4. Chin In* | 17. Point | 4. Kneel* |
| 5. Face Thrust | 18. Pull | 5. Lie* |
| 6. Gaze Fixate | 19. Punch | 6. Play Crouch* |
| 7. Glance* |    Incomplete | 7. Sit* |
| 8. Grind Teeth* |    Object | 8. Slope* |
| 9. Head Nod* |    Open | 9. Stand* |
| 10. Head Shake |    Side |  |
| 11. Head Tilt* | 20. Push | VII. Locomotion |
| 12. Kiss* | 21. Reach |  |
| 13. Laugh | 22. Repel* | 1. Back |
| 14. Lick* | 23. Scratch | 2. Back Step |
| 15. Look | 24. Shake* | 3. Chase |
| 16. Mouth* | 25. Snatch* | 4. Crawl* |
| 17. Spit | 26. Throw | 5. Flee |
| 18. Swallow* | 27. Tickle* | 6. Gallop* |
| 19. Tongue Out* | 28. Underarm Throw | 7. March* |
| 20. Verbalize | 29. Wave* | 8. Miscellaneous |
| 21. Vocalize |  |    Locomotion |
| 22. Weep | IV. Leg | 9. Run |
| 23. Yawn |  | 10. Sidle |
|  | 1. Kick | 11. Sidle Step |
|  |    Incomplete | 12. Skip* |
|  |    Up | 13. Step |
| * Not recorded in | 2. Shuffle* | 14. Walk |
| original Slade study | 3. Stamp* |  |

more immediate positions with people we like, while body orientation is least direct toward low status females and most direct toward high status males who are disliked. The second dimension of *relaxation* is characterized by cues that indicate an asymmetrical rather than symmetrical position of posture and limbs. We tend to be moderately relaxed with people we like and to be posturally very relaxed or very unrelaxed with people we dislike. We become tense around threatening people and extremely relaxed with nonthreatening, disliked people. Males become tense when addressing other males whom they dislike, whereas females talking to men or women they dislike and men talking to women they dislike appear extremely relaxed. In regard to status, people seem to relax their posture when they are around lower-status addressees and relax least with those of higher status. Several studies have associated numerous other variables with body posture and orientation.[55]

McGrew has isolated nine different postural categories which should be kept in mind while observing children: climb, crouch, immobile, kneel, lie, play crouch, sit, slope, and stand.[56] *Climbing* seems to be related to the newborn's grasping reflex and involves the extension and flexure of the limbs. In *crouching,* the knees are flexed and the child's head and trunk are lowered from an upright or standing posture, or the back may be flexed from a sitting position. Extreme crouching refers to a position in which the upper legs and chest are brought together. *Immobility* indicates the cessation of gross trunk, limb, and head movements for a minimum of three seconds. This usually occurs while the child is standing or sitting. The *kneeling* posture is signified by a lowered trunk and by a forward lean by hip and knee flexion that allows the trunk to rest on the knees and feet. After this posture is assumed, the child may straighten his or her trunk and position the head vertically and forward. The *lying* posture requires that the legs be flexed at the knees, the arms extended toward the ground, and the trunk tilted so that the main body axis is lowered from a higher position to one that is horizontal to the ground. Following this, the legs are flexed, the trunk is moved forward until it attains a kneeling position, and the trunk and arms are moved forward into a prone reclining posture. A version of the crouching posture previously described is called the *play crouch.* In this position, the child's head and trunk are posturally erect, and the legs are flexed slightly. The feet are spaced wider apart than the shoulders, and the arms are likewise flexed and extended from the trunk. *Sit* refers to the position in which the child's body is supported by the buttocks after the trunk has been lowered from a higher posture by hip and knee flexion. *Slope* is a posture characterized by backward lean from the hips while the child is looking directly at another person. The chin is tucked in, and the hands are clasped in front of the body at waist level or behind the back. Youngsters frequently assume this position when they have ambivalent feelings about fleeing a situation or complying with a dominant person's wishes. *Standing* involves movement of the body by extension of the knees, hips, and back into an upright position with the feet at about shoulder's width supporting the body's weight. The head is usually held in an erect position, and arms hang freely.

**Facial Expressions.** With the possible exception of speech, the face is the richest source of information about a person's emotional state. The face has been appropriately called the primary site of our affect.[57] Although we usually limit our vocabulary describing facial behavior to general words such as smile, frown, squint, and grin, there is evidence that the facial musculature permits the creation of more than 1,000 different expressions,[58] many of which are micromomentary in nature.[59] Some facial expressions last more than one second, but others extend only between $\frac{1}{25}$ to $\frac{1}{5}$ of a second. Further complicating matters, the face can communicate multiple feelings rather than just single emotions.[60] Expressions showing more than one emotion are called blends. To say the least, facial affect is most complex and difficult to describe accurately.

Some major categories of facial affect have been demonstrated consistently in research over the past thirty to forty years: happiness, surprise, fear, sadness, disgust/contempt, and interest.[61] Other studies have indicated that information from facial cues can be described in terms of dimensions such as pleasant-to-unpleasant, active-to-passive, and intense-to-controlled.[62] Research also has shown that it is possible to measure facial behavior in a systematic manner,[63] the most elaborate of measures of adult facial behavior being the Facial Affect Scoring Technique (FAST) developed by Ekman, Friesen, and Tomkins.[64] FAST distinguishes among six emotions and allows the scoring of observable facial movements in each of three areas of the face: brows-forehead area; eyes-lids; and lower face, including cheeks, nose, mouth, and chin. Here is how Ekman describes the application of FAST:

> FAST is applied by having independent coders view each of the three areas of the face separately, with the rest of the face blocked from view. It should be emphasized that the FAST measurement procedure does *not* entail having the coder judge the emotion shown in the face he is coding. Rather, each movement within a facial area is distinguished, its exact duration determined with the aid of slowed motion, and the type of movement classified by comparing the movement observed with the atlas of FAST criterion photographs.[65]

FAST atlas photographs are available for each of the three facial areas. This very ambitious effort to measure facial expressions represents a significant breakthrough in the area of nonverbal behavior.

Facial expressions in infants and children also have been subjected to considerable investigation. Over a century ago, Darwin initiated his studies of expression in human beings and devoted a good deal of his work to the observation of children. In his classic *Mind* paper, Darwin described seven emotional states in infants that are accompanied by distinctive facial expressions: anger, fear, affection, amusement, discomfort, jealousy, and shyness.[66] In another publication, Darwin identified three additional emotions that older children are capable of expressing through facial behavior: shame, embarrassment, and grief.[67] More recent research has extended the work of Darwin and has examined expressive behaviors such as crying, smiling, and laughing and more global expressions of emotions like anger, fear, delight, surprise, and shyness.[68] Not only can children encode some facial expressions reasonably well but they also can decode these nonverbal behaviors, with their accuracy increasing as they grow older.[69]

One technique for the analysis of facial components has been designed specifically for use with children. It is an ethologically based approach devised by Blurton Jones.[70] Realizing that the study of facial behavior by direct observation required precise descriptions of the various forms of expression, this researcher developed criteria for representing the morphology of facial expressions in children. He divided a child's face into a number of possible states called components, described each component, delineated the range of possible facial shape changes, and produced categories of facial behavior patterns which observers could use reliably. According to Blurton Jones, there are fifty-two different states or components that comprise the nine segments of a child's face. The segments and their components are presented in Table 2.3. Blurton Jones points out that the segments have no particular significance except as useful groupings of the components or as guides for an observer studying children's facial behavior. An excerpt from Blurton Jones's description of children's facial components is provided, along with an illustration of the cues used for determining the child's brow positions (Figure 2.2).

### Raised Brows

A very conspicuous movement of raising the eyebrows which can be rather difficult to judge on photographs because of the individual variation in the resting position of the brows. One or more of the following criteria could apply:

a.   The height of the brow above the eye corner appears to be equal or more than the width of the open eye.

b.   Horizontal lines visible across the forehead above the brows.

c.   There is an enlarged area between the brow and the eyelids which is often highlighted (very pale) in photographs.

d.   There is a less sharp fall from the brow into the eye socket (orbit) because the brow is raised beyond the edge of the orbit which it normally covers. Therefore there is less shadow between brow and eye than usual.

e.   The shape of the eyebrows change, becoming more curved when they are raised (but they are not curved when the brows are slanted or oblique as well as raised).[71]

This technique has not been experimentally validated, but it does represent significant progress in the field that will improve the quality of observational study of nonverbal behavior in children.

**Eye Behavior.** Although visual behavior is a very important aspect of social interaction, we usually give very little conscious thought to our eye behavior patterns or to those of others. However, research has shown that the eyes are the center of focus in the visual examination of human faces.[72]

**Table 2.3.** The Nine Segments of a Child's Face and Their Components

| Segment A: | Brow position | Segment E: | Tongue position |
|---|---|---|---|
| | 1.  Raised brows | | 1.  Tongue invisible |
| | 2.  General frown | | 2.  Tongue visible |
| | 3.  Oblique brows | | 3.  Tongue pushed forward |
| | 4.  Weak frown | | 4.  Tongue out of mouth |
| | 5.  Strong frown | Segment F: | Eye direction |
| | 6.  Contraction around the eye | | 1.  Upwards |
| Segment B: | Mouth shape | | 2.  Downwards |
| | 1.  Squared upper lip | | 3.  Sideways |
| | 2.  Squared lower lip | Segment G: | Lip separation |
| | 3.  Lips retracted | | 1.  Lips touching |
| | 4.  Corners raised | | 2.  Lips slightly apart |
| | 5.  Corners lowered | | 3.  Lips clearly apart |
| Segment C: | Lip position | | 4.  Lips wide apart |
| | 1.  Lower lip pout | Segment H: | Teeth |
| | 2.  Two lip pout | | 1.  No teeth showing |
| | 3.  Lips pressed together | | 2.  Upper teeth visible |
| | 4.  Lower lip bitten | | 3.  Lower teeth visible |
| | 5.  Upper lip bitten | | 4.  Both show equally |
| | 6.  Lips rolled in | | 5.  Upper show more |
| | 7.  Lengthening upper lip | | 6.  Lower show more |
| | 8.  Contraction of m. orbicularis oris | Segment I: | Others—Miscellaneous |
| Segment D: | Eye openness | | 1.  Wrinkling the nose |
| | 1.  Wide | | 2.  Bilateral asymmetry |
| | 2.  Bit wide | | 3.  Indented cheeks |
| | 3.  Normal | | 4.  Puffed cheeks |
| | 4.  Bit narrow | | 5.  Clenched incisors |
| | 5.  Very narrow | | 6.  Lower jaw sideways |
| | 6.  Upper lid down | | 7.  Clenched molars and toothgrinding |
| | | | 8.  Face direction |
| | | | 9.  Head on side |
| | | | 10.  Head shake |

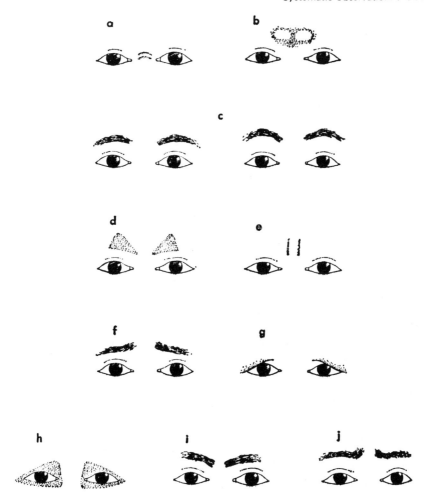

**Figure 2.2.** Cues in Determining Brow Positions. (a) Horizontal lines across nose; (b) bulges on brows; (c) curvature of brow, resting brows slightly curved, raised brow more curved; (d) triangular shadows on forehead; (e) vertical lines on forehead; (f) hairy part of brow sloping obliquely up to center; (g) upper eyelid folded down over eye at outer end; (h) shadow in orbit shows oblique upper edge; (i) hairy part of brow straightened and inner end lowered; (j) inner end turned up.

There seems to be a pattern to visual behavior. According to Argyle, two people engaged in a conversation on an emotionally neutral topic and spaced about six feet apart would probably exhibit this eye behavior:

| | |
|---|---|
| Individual gaze | 60 percent |
| while listening | 75 percent |
| while talking | 40 percent |
| length of glance | 3 seconds |
| Eye-contact (mutual gaze) | 30 percent |
| length of mutual glance | 1½ seconds[73] |

Should a third person join the conversation, each individual would divide his or her gaze between the other two. If there is a physical task at hand, the individuals would look less at each other and attend more closely to the problem. Apart from the *amount* of gaze, there are several other factors that are related to the *quality* of gaze:

1. Pupil dilation (from 2-8 mm in diameter)

2. Blink rate (typically every 3-10 seconds)

3. Direction of breaking gaze, to the left or right

4. Opening of eyes, wide-open to lowered lids

5. Facial expression in the area of eyes, described as "looking daggers," "making eyes," etc.[74]

Some of the more important terms used in the research literature to describe visual behavior are defined in Table 2.4.

Kendon has identified four functions of visual behavior: cognitive, monitoring, regulatory, and expressive.[75] The *cognitive* function is shown by a person's tendency to look away during difficult encoding situations such as when confronted with difficult material or when listening to nonfluent passages. Apparently, there is a need to avoid the distraction of additional inputs of information, and this is accomplished by aversion of gaze. *Monitoring* involves looking at another person in order to see his or her reactions or level of attentiveness as well as to indicate the conclusion of thought units. The *regulatory* function is illustrated by eye behavior that either demands or suppresses the responses of others. When we seek eye contact, we are indicating that our communication channel is open and that we wish to interact. Contrariwise, visual avoidance is likely to minimize interaction. The fourth or *expressive* function refers to the extent that eye behavior signals a person's involvement or arousal. These major functions of visual behavior do not necessarily operate independently. For example, by looking at another person, your eye behavior not only transmits information but also collects it. Or by looking at your interactant, you may be indicating that you have finished speaking and that it is now his or her turn to talk. This eye behavior also provides an opportunity for you to monitor feedback regarding your previous utterance.

Eye behavior provides information regarding one's feelings toward others. For instance, we tend to have more visual contact with people we like and less with disliked persons and those who make unfavorable comments about us.[76] Another aspect of eye behavior, pupillary response, is associated with emotional arousal, interest, and attitudes. An excellent review of the literature on pupillary behavior is presented in Janisse's book *Pupillometry*.[77] Eyeblink may also reflect a person's internal state, such as tension or anxiety.[78] Children frequently blink when startled by a sudden movement

**Table 2.4.** Definitions of Eye Behavior

| Term | Definition |
| --- | --- |
| Gaze | Looking behavior that may or may not be directed at the other person. |
| Mutual gaze | Two people looking at each other, usually in the face region. |
| Gaze avoidance | Avoidance of another person's gaze. |
| Eye contact | Two people looking into each other's eyes. |
| Pupillary response | Dilation and constriction of the pupils of the eyes. |
| Blinking | Rapid and successive lowering and raising of the eyelids. |

near the head or by a loud sound and they may also blink in nonstartling situations such as when a threatening child is nearby.[79]

Several studies have demonstrated that eye behavior in adults is associated with sex,[80] ethnicity,[81] and status.[82] Investigations of children's visual behavior are far more limited, but some tentative generalizations are possible based upon available research. Eye contact between the infant and mother has been demonstrated as early as the first month of life.[83] Also, by the first month, pupil dilation may be seen in the infant's responses to faces, with increased dilation exhibited specifically toward the mother's face at four months of age.[84] There appears to be more eye contact between child and mother in higher socioeconomic families than in lower socioeconomic ones.[85]

When children in preschool, kindergarten, and grades two, five, and eight were compared in one study, eye contact reached a peak at kindergarten and second grade and a low point at fifth grade, with girls looking more than boys while speaking but not while listening.[86] The sex difference was consistent with findings in adult studies.

Another investigation revealed that there is an increase in gazing from ages four, five, and six to ages seven, eight, and nine; a slight decrease at ages ten, eleven, and twelve; and an increase for adults, with more gazing occurring during listening than speaking.[87] There are no significant age changes in this behavior during the performance of a task, but, overall, less gazing is found during structured task situations than during conversations. Females seem to gaze more than males while conversing. In contrast to adults who are inclined to gaze at the beginning and end of an utterance, children tend not to gaze at either point.

Finally, research has shown that children use eye contacts as cues to the appropriate interaction distances with both their age mates and adults[88] and that early elementary-aged, but not preschool children, indicate a preference to affiliate with people who exhibit eye contact.[89] The area of children's eye behavior awaits further systematic investigation.

**Spatial Behavior.** Hall coined the term *proxemics* to mean the "interrelated observations and theories of man's use of space as a specialized elaboration of culture."[90] Elsewhere, he described this field as "the study of how man unconsciously structures microspace—the distance between man in the conduct of daily transactions, the organization of space in his houses and buildings and ultimately the layout of his towns."[91] This anthropologist has developed a model for classification of proxemic behavior which is comprised of three levels.[92] The first, the *infracultural,* deals with the spatial behavior that has its base in our biological past. This includes territoriality and crowding. There is an abundance of anecdotal evidence regarding the existence of territoriality in humans, including dad's easy chair, mother's desk, sister's bathroom, a neighborhood gang's territory, and a traveling sales representative's district or region. Comparative studies of animal territorial behavior[93] have provided a basis for the understanding of environmental influences on human space requirements and have stimulated a number of investigations of territoriality in humans.[94] The second of Hall's levels, the *precultural,* is physiological and is concerned with our capacity to perceive space through our senses. Our sensory apparatus are classified as distance receptors (e.g., eyes, ears, nose) and immediate receptors (e.g., skin, membranes, muscles). Thus, we have visual, auditory, and olfactory space as well as thermal and tactile space. Hall's third level of proxemic behavior, the *microcultural,* involves the structuring of space as it is affected by culture. This is the level at which most proxemic observations are made, according to Hall. Therefore, it will be discussed in somewhat more detail.

There are three aspects of the microcultural level in Hall's model: fixed-feature, semifixed-feature, and informal. *Fixed-feature space* includes those features that are materially "fixed" such as buildings and the very layouts of towns and cities. In addition, architecture and the arrangement of interior spaces are subsumed under fixed-feature space. The second aspect of the microcultural level, *semifixed-feature space,* involves the placement of movable objects such as furniture, screens, and movable partitions. Spaces that tend to bring people together are called sociopetal, and those which keep people apart and discourage interaction are termed sociofugal.[95] Sociopetal arrangements focus people toward the center of a room and bring them together, whereas sociofugal arrangements drive people toward the periphery of a room. The sidewalk cafe and the tavern are good examples of sociopetal arrangements that encourage sociability; libraries and waiting rooms, which are designed to keep people out of each other's way, are examples of sociofugal arrangements. The third type of spatial organization on the microcultural level is called *informal space*. Hall uses this term to refer to distances that are maintained in interactions with others. These zones or interpersonal distances are called informal because they are unstated and not because they lack form. Largely outside our level of awareness, these spatial patterns have distinct bounds and such a deep, though unvoiced, significance that they are an essential part of our everyday lives. This particular aspect of proxemic behavior overlaps with what is commonly referred to as ecological psychology.

According to Hall, there are four divisions of informal space, each of which has a close and far phase. Here is his statement of the hypothesis that underlies this proxemic classification scheme:

> . . . It is the nature of animals, including man, to exhibit behavior which we call territoriality. In doing so, they use the senses to distinguish between one space or distance and another. The specific distance chosen depends on the transaction; the relationships of the interacting individuals, how they feel, and what they are doing. The four-part classification system used here is based on observations of both animals and men. Birds and apes exhibit intimate, personal, and social distances just as man does.[96]

Hall has provided a description of his four-part classification of distances for middle-class American adults. This is a summary of these classifications:

**Intimate Distance**

Close phase: 0 to 6 inches. Presence of the other person is conspicuous and may even be overwhelming because of increased sensory inputs. Physical contact and involvement is possible, including love-making, comforting, and protecting. Vocalization is not necessary. All senses can be brought to bear, but sharp vision is impossible.

Far phase: 6 to 18 inches. Certain parts of the body, with the possible exception of the hands, are not easily brought into contact. This area of interaction is common in interfamilial interactions and is appropriate for the discussion of confidential matters. Voice is usually held to a whisper or at a low level. There is some visual distortion. Use of this distance in public by younger people is acceptable but is considered improper for adults.

**Personal Distance**

Close phase: 1½ to 2½ feet. This is the distance that typically separates us from others. It is a comfortable distance for discussing personal topics. One can still hold or grasp the other person. There is less sensory involvement than in intimate distance. Vision of the other person is clearer.

Far phase: 2½ to 4 feet. This is the limit of physical domination, extending to arm's length. It is used for discussing subjects of personal interest and involvement. Voice level is usually moderate, vision is better, and odor cannot be detected except among persons who use strong smelling colognes or do not bathe regularly.

### Social Distance

Close phase: 4 to 7 feet. Used for impersonal business by people who work together, this distance does not violate another person's personal space. It is the common distance for people at social gatherings and at work. Clear perception of the other person is possible, and the eye can view a greater portion of the person than at closer distances.

Far phase:    7 to 12 feet. More formal business is transacted at this phase. Voice level is usually louder than for the close phase and can be heard in the next room if the door is open. It is impossible to distinguish the finest details of the person's face, but everything else is visible.

### Public Distance

Close phase: 12 to 25 feet. This distance is generally used in addressing an informal group or small audience. Voice is not full-volume but is loud. Some physical attributes of the other person are no longer clearly visible.

Far phase:    25 feet or more. The far phase is used by public figures who do not wish to become involved with persons nearby. It is the outside area of involvement with others. Voices and gestures are necessarily exaggerated so that both verbal and nonverbal behaviors can be detected by listeners.

There are, then, distance sets that are associated with different types of interpersonal interaction. Informal space expands and contracts under varying conditions. As we move closer to or farther from someone, the potential for body contact, visual and verbal communication, and the amount of heat and olfactory cues are affected. In proxemic perception, there is an interplay of all of our senses.

The physical distances at which interactions take place generally suggest to the observer the kind of interpersonal exchange that is occurring. A measure of the interpersonal distance between two people may also provide clues concerning the nature and quality of their relationship. This is not to say that distance sets do not sometimes reveal incongruities such as when formal conversation is carried on at an intimate distance.[97]

Research has shown that the use of space is consistently related to sex;[98] ethnicity;[99] status and social class;[100] physical characteristics, including handicaps and other stigmatizing features;[101] personality and behavior pathology;[102] value congruence and attitude similarity;[103] characteristics of the interpersonal relationship;[104] topic under discussion;[105] and setting.[106] Studies also have demonstrated that variations in interpersonal distance may affect the amount and type of interaction,[107] relating, perhaps, to Freedman's "density/intensity" model which suggests that close proximity magnifies the impact of the stimulus properties of a person.[108] Depending on other cues associated with the person, close distance to another individual produces either intense positive or negative effects.

Several investigations of proxemic behavior have been conducted with child subjects. These have approached the measurement of personal space through the use of simulation, paper-and-pencil, and direct observation techniques. An observational study by Aiello and Aiello revealed that there is a gradual expansion in interpersonal distances between grades one and five, more dramatic increases between grades five and seven, and a slight decline or leveling off thereafter.[109] Their findings were not completely consistent with previous research. While some investigations have shown that very young children prefer to interact at the closest range and that their interpersonal distances increase with age,[110] other studies have demonstrated that personal distance shrinks with age.[111] By the age of twelve, children generally stand at distances of 1½ to 2½ feet, which is essentially Hall's Personal Distance Zone (close phase). Apparently, they have internalized adult personal space norms by this time. The Aiello and Aiello study also revealed that boys maintain greatest distances at all grade levels. Although the trend in studies of gender effects has been for boys to prefer greater distances in most situations,[112] numerous other investigations have shown no sex differences.[113] In some cases, sex differences have been found to be age and partner specific.[114]

Research with children has revealed ethnic differences in the use of space, with blacks usually preferring lower mean distances than whites[115] and with Mexican-Americans spacing themselves significantly closer than white children.[116] Youngsters with social and emotional disturbances require greater interpersonal distance from others than do normal children.[117] And as with adults, positive relationships and degree of acquaintance are associated with smaller personal space zones or closer distances in children.[118] One simulation study showed that parent-child figures were placed closer together when the parent was described as praising rather than as criticizing the child.[119]

There is reason to suspect the quality of some of the data amassed over the past decade. As Evans and Howard have written, personal space data are "often inconsistent and ambiguous. Those that are not have generally been collected by poor techniques, which make positive conclusions possible only in cases where the data overwhelmingly supports the conclusion."[120] Striking an equally pessimistic note, Hayduk has concluded that "if one accepts findings based only on the strongest measurement techniques, considerable reevaluation of research on personal space appears necessary."[121]

One very interesting study has been carried out in an attempt to resolve inconsistencies in the research literature. Severy, Forsyth, and Wagner employed multiple assessment techniques to determine the influence of age, sex, and ethnicity on 144 children matched for socioeconomic status.[122] These investigators used behavioral, paper-and-pencil, and simulation techniques and found that the most pronounced effects obtained across the three assessment procedures concerned developmental changes. They discovered that personal space shrinks steadily from ages seven through fifteen, although the decrease is less dramatic in black youngsters than in white. Younger blacks tended to require less space than younger whites. Regarding sex of children, mixed-sex dyads maintained greater distances than same-sex pairings. For the most part, the effects of sex and race were not as robust as those for age and were more measurement method specific.

It is clear that the personal space phenomenon operates in children as well as in adults. However, because of diverse methodological approaches, it is difficult to compare results and to state generalizations. This field of interest is still in its infancy.

In concluding this section, something should be said about research dealing with the impact of spatial density on children's behavior. With a few exceptions,[123] most studies have shown that children are more aggressive in high density environments.[124] Research also has demonstrated that high density is associated with less gross motor activity,[125] less social interaction,[126] and more tension and discomfort.[127]

**Touching Behavior.** Although personal space has become a very popular area of inquiry, comparatively less work has been done on another type of proxemic behavior—touching. This is surprising inasmuch as interpersonal touching may be considered as the extreme end of the personal space continuum.[128] The significance of tactile behavior did not escape Hall, the father of proxemics. He wrote that many researchers "have failed to grasp the deep significance of touch, particularly active touch. They have not understood how important it is to keep the person related to the world in which he lives."[129] Touch conveys love, affection, tenderness, support, encouragement, dominance, and hate, among other things. Some researchers have indicated that physical contact is necessary for normal development and continues to be important throughout life.[130] The importance of touch is understandable when we consider that "the skin is the outer boundary, the envelope which contains the human organism and provides its earliest and most elemental mode of communication."[131] Sometimes referred to as the "mother sense,"[132] the skin is the largest organ of the body and is made up of thousands of receptors for pressure, pain, hot, and cold, all of which provide the individual with distinct signals.

Touching behavior has been classified in different ways. Heslin has proposed a system which specifies five levels of touching based upon the context of the interpersonal relationship: functional/ professional level (e.g., physician examining a patient), social/polite level (e.g., handshake), friend-ship/warmth (e.g., touching between friends), love/intimacy level (e.g., embrace), and sexual arousal (e.g., touch between individuals considered sex objects).[133] This taxonomy represents a continuum from impersonal to personal touching.

Gibson has approached the classification of tactile communication differently.[134] In his model, there are two broad categories of touch. The first is *active* touch which is what is ordinarily consid-ered touching or tactile scanning. The second is *passive* touch or being touched. In active touch, the impression on the skin is brought about by the perceiver, whereas in passive touch, by an outside agency. Both kinds will be considered in this chapter.

One of the first researchers to systematically examine tactile behavior was Jourard. In his now classic study, he investigated what parts of the body are touched most often.[135] He administered a "body-accessibility questionnaire" to unmarried male and female college students. The purpose of the questionnaire was to determine the extent to which the students allowed their parents and friends of both sexes to see and touch their bodies and the extent to which they had seen and touched the bodies of these target persons in the past twelve months. Among other things, Jourard found that most tactual exchanges occurred between the subjects and their closest opposite-sex friends. Also, females were more accessible to touch than males. A decade later, Rosenfeld, Kartus, and Ray replicated the study and found minimal overall changes in touching behavior except that males and females had become more accessible to opposite-sex friends, particularly in the chest, stomach, hip, and thigh regions.[136]

In regard to the social patterns of touch, research has shown that sex,[137] age,[138] and status,[139] are all related to touch exchange. Females touch and are touched more often than males; older persons initiate physical contact more often than younger persons; and individuals of higher status touch their inferiors more. There are also cultural and subcultural variations in touching behavior.[140] The amount of touching behavior in persons from "contact" cultures (e.g., Arabs, Latin Americans, Southern Europeans) as opposed to those from "noncontact" cultures (e.g., Americans, Indians, Pakistanis, Northern Europeans) is sometimes dramatic as any world traveler can attest. Similarly, different sub-cultures within the United States exhibit certain patterns of tactile contact. Johnson has written an interesting paper on black kinesics in which he describes touching behavior and other types of body movements that communicate meaning specific to the black subculture.[141] Finally, touching behavior may have special affective and evaluative effects, both favorable and unfavorable.[142]

In the past few years, several studies that focus on children's tactual behavior have been conducted. Goldberg and Lewis found that mothers touch their six-month-old daughters more than sons of the same age and that thirteen-month-old girls touch their mothers more than do boys.[143] Lewis observed that boys receive more proximal stimulation than girls until six months of age, but from that time until two years of age, the direction of this difference is reversed with girls receiving more touch.[144] Lewis, Weintraub, and Ban discovered that both boys and girls decrease proximity seeking over the first two years of life.[145] Clay demonstrated that mothers tended to touch their daughters more than their sons before the age of four but that there was more bodily contact between boys and mothers after that time.[146] Two studies have revealed social class differences in parent-child touching, with the lower class mother-child dyads engaging in more contact than their middle- and upper-class counterparts.[147] Age and sex variables are relevant: the amount of touching declines from five to twelve years but still exceeds adult rates in adolescence, and touch is more likely to occur between girls and same-sex children.[148] Interpersonal touch is also more frequent between black children and between Mexican-American children than between whites.[149]

A recent study by Williams and Willis examined interpersonal touch among 274 black and white preschool children at play.[150] Each of the eight cooperating nursery schools were either predominately black or white. Observers recorded the identity of the child whom the subject touched or who touched the subject and the body area used to touch or that was touched. Body areas included head, face, shoulder, arm, elbow, hand, fist, chest, back, trunk, butt, leg, knee, and foot. Tactual behavior was recorded whether it was intentional or not, and no notation was made regarding the duration of touch. The mean frequency of touches was .74 per minute, with rates of touch being higher for same gender pairs both indoors and outdoors. The incidence of bodily contact for different-sex dyads was the same in inside and outside play areas. Highest rate of touch was seen between black females. Hands were used more by girls than by boys and more by middle-class youngsters than by lower-class youngsters.

Another recent investigation of children's tactile behavior focused on patterns of touching between preschool pupils and male and female teachers.[151] Four types of touch were observed: friendly (touches expressing nurturance or approval), helpful (touches occurring while the teacher was helping the child or vice versa), attentional (touches focusing or controlling behavior), and incidental (accidental touching). The sample consisted of thirty-one boys, twenty-five girls, and eight undergraduate student teachers (four males and four females). Observations were made from a booth equipped with a one-way mirror. Results indicated that teachers directed more touches to youngsters of their own sex. When male teachers touched little girls, it was more likely to be of a "helpful" nature than when they touched little boys. Boys tended to use all of the four categories of touch more frequently with male teachers rather than with female teachers, while girls directed their touches to male and female teachers at approximately the same rate. The findings were interpreted in terms of sex-role development.

## OTHER DATA FOR OBSERVATION

Two other types of data merit consideration in observational study. They are personal appearance and the environmental settings in which child development and behavior occur. These will be considered here because of their importance in understanding children.

**Personal Appearance.** Forming judgments based upon only superficial assessment of outward appearance, though often imperfect, may also be quite sensitive. The way in which we are physically perceived frequently determines how people react to us; likewise, our perceptions of people, based upon physical appearance, influence our attitudes and behavior toward them.[152]

> Physical appearance conveys a variety of information about a person. With briefest visual perception, a complex mental process is aroused, resulting within a very short time, 30 seconds perhaps, in judgment of the sex, age, size, nationality, profession and social caste of the stranger, together with some estimate of his temperament, his ascendence, friendliness, neatness, and even his trustworthiness and integrity. With no further acquaintance many impressions may be erroneous, but they show the swift totalizing nature of our judgments.[153]

Descriptions of physique have been used for some time as indices of personality traits. For example, considerable stereotyping has been encouraged by Sheldon's formulation of three somatotypes: endomorph, ectomorph, and mesomorph.[154] Wells and Siegel[155] have found that the endomorphic type, who is characterized by roundness of shape and fat, is usually considered good natured, agreeable, dependent, and trusting. On the other hand, the ectomorph, who is angular and possesses sharp features, is rated as tense, stubborn, ambitious, pessimistic, and suspicious. The mesomorphic type, who is big-boned, muscular, and athletic, creates the impression of masculinity, maturity, and self-reliance. Other studies have investigated the attribution of behavioral and character traits to Sheldon's three body types.[156] The shape and configuration of the human body obviously has message value to most people.

In addition to our tendency to link body type to temperament, we frequently make generalizations based on observations of other related exterior cues. One study[157] reported the tendency of people to ascribe friendliness, humor, and easygoingness to persons with wrinkles at the eye corners. And whereas blonds and fair-skinned people were judged to have favorable qualities, dark-skinned people were perceived as unfriendly, hostile, and having a lack of humor. In another study,[158] it was demonstrated that personality impressions of social acceptability are related to good grooming, and sexual attractiveness, to narrowed eyes and full, relaxed lips. Bowed lips contributed to impressions of conceit and immorality. People also seem to respond to beardedness and length of hair in men.[159] Men with beards are usually judged more positively than clean-shaven males (e.g., more masculine, sophisticated, mature, and of higher status), while those with long as opposed to short hair create a negative impression. Numerous other investigations have also shown that other aspects of a person's physical appearance are frequently judged to be associated with certain qualities.[160]

Clothing provides clues to a person's personality, attitudes, interests, values, social status, and identification with specific groups.[161] The clothing one is wearing makes a difference particularly when strangers are formulating judgments about you; clothing is less important when you are being judged by acquaintances.[162] It also has been found that people dressed in high-status clothes are frequently more influential than those who wear low-status clothes.[163] Artifacts (perfume, lipstick, eyeglasses, wigs, false eyelashes, etc.), though subjected to very little research, have been shown to possess some communicative value. McKeachie examined the influence of lipstick on observations of personality in girls who behaved similarly in an interview situation.[164] He found that girls wearing lipstick were judged to be frivolous, anxious, and silent as well as markedly interested in the opposite sex. The same girls without lipstick were considered conscientious, serious, talkative, placid, and not interested in men. Men and women who wear eyeglasses, in contrast to those who do not, are rated higher in intelligence and industriousness.[165] These artifactual objects probably interact with other clothing, verbal, and body features to tell us something about a particular person. Although the accuracy of judgments that are based upon outward appearance varies considerably, the more concrete items such as age, sex, nationality, and social status may be signaled with greater exactitude than more abstract qualities such as attitudes, values, and personality.

Bijou has pointed out that a youngster's physical appearance can be reinforcing, calling attention to him or her and insuring adequate opportunities for positive experiences, or it can be nonreinforcing or aversive to others, leading to avoidance of the child and deprivation of growth-promoting experiences.[166] The majority of studies investigating the relationship of appearance to children's behavior or the impact of children's physical appearance on others have examined either body build or physical attractiveness. As with adults, somatotype has certain connotations with children.[167] By the age of five, youngsters hold a favorable view of the mesomorph relative to the ectomorph or endomorph. The chubby physique is least preferred and endowed by the perceiver with negative descriptors; moreover, significantly greater interpersonal distances are maintained between endomorphs than between either of the other two body types. The favorable stereotype of the mesomorph may be related to the American society's emphasis on health and athletics. At any rate, an increasing fund of research is demonstrating that morphological characteristics play an important role in children's peer relationships and may influence self-concept.

Another major line of inquiry regarding children's appearance has demonstrated that youngsters' judgments of the physical attractiveness of their peers are associated with evaluations that include high self-concepts, independence, self-assuredness, social influence, popularity, and behavioral adjustment.[168] Adults, including teachers, sometimes have been shown to moderate their evaluations of a child in relation to his or her physical attractiveness, judging more attractive children as having greater intellectual potential, as enjoying better social relationships, and as having parents who are more interested in their child's education.[169] Undoubtedly, children of different body builds and degrees of attractiveness receive different socializations. Observers must guard against the tendency to stereotype children on the bases of physique and other aspects of appearance and must report data as objectively as possible.

**Environments.** Insel and Moos suggest that environments are as amenable to assessment as personality and behavior:

> Like people, environments have unique personalities. Just as it is possible to characterize a person's "personality," environments can be similarly portrayed with a great deal of accuracy and detail.[170]

We will explore Insel and Moos's assumption further in this section. You will note that the plural of *environment* was used in order to indicate that environment is not a single entity but is composed of a number of subunits.[171] Each of us has many environments or subenvironments. For example, a child has a home environment, neighborhood environment, church environment, school environment, and so on. The school setting may have its own subenvironments such as classroom, cafeteria, library, and playground.

A child also has a physical and psychological environment. The *physical environment* is "objective"; it is defined in terms of discrete and quantifiable stimuli without regard for individual differences in the way these stimuli are perceived. We can see, hear, feel, and smell a child's physical environment. This interpretation of physical environment is founded on experimental psychophysics and behaviorism. In contrast, *psychological environment* represents a phenomenological orientation. This view defines environment as it is experienced and not by its physical aspects alone. Such a subjective frame of reference implies that behavior is related to how one perceives his or her environs. As was mentioned in Chapter 1, Lewin explained the phenomenal environment in terms of his field theory of life-space.[172] According to Lewin, behavior is not a function of the objective properties of one's surroundings, but of an environment transformed into an "inner" world by a cognizant organism. Following this line of thinking, an observer who is assessing someone else's environments must go beyond the observable data. In child study, it may be necessary to interview the child to find out the real meaning of his or her environments. What is considered by the observer to be an unsightly and even unhealthful trash pile behind a youngster's house may turn out to be the child's favorite place of play. Therefore, an objective description of the physical aspects of a child's environments may be quite inconsistent with the child's own perception of them. Consequently, the observer must exercise caution in his or her interpretations. More will be said about environmental descriptions in the next chapter.

Other classification schemes for human environments that go beyond the theoretical dualism of physical/objective and phenomenological/subjective and conceptualize the environment in several different ways have been developed.[173] In fact, the interrelationship between environment and behavior has long been emphasized in the developmental literature. Barker stressed the importance of settings for behavior when he reported that three children who were each observed for an entire day interacted with 571, 671, and 749 different objects.[174] The numbers of interactions with these objects were 1,882, 2,282, and 2,590, respectively, and each of these interactions had many different attributes. It is not surprising, then, that a substantial portion of variance in behavior has been attributed to environmental variables.[175] Of particular interest are studies which have demonstrated that children's behavior is markedly and differentially affected by changes in milieu.[176] Since environments play such a prominent role in child development and behavior, they should be given their proper share of attention in child study. Like human beings, environments are complex, multidimensional entities,[177] and in spite of their complexity, both lend themselves to systematic observation and measurement. A number of recent publications provide theoretical and empirical perspectives on children's environmental domains and should be required reading for students engaging in child study.

## CHAPTER NOTES

1.  K. E. Weick, "Systematic Observational Methods," in *The Handbook of Social Psychology,* vol. 2, eds. G. Lindzey and E. Aronson (Reading, Mass.: Addison-Wesley, 1968), p. 358.
2.  C. Selltiz et al., *Research Methods in Social Relations* (New York: Holt, 1959).
3.  M. G. Cooper, "Observational Studies of Children from Diary to Ethogram: A Century of Progress," *Child: Care, Health, and Development* 3 (1977): 283-92.
4.  Selltiz et al., *Research Methods,* p. 204.
5.  P. B. Gove, ed., *Webster's Third New International Dictionary* (Springfield, Mass.: Merriam, 1971), p. 1558.
6.  Gove, *New International Dictionary,* p. 2322.
7.  R. R. Jones, J. B. Reid, and G. R. Patterson, "Naturalistic Observations in Clinical Assessment," in *Advances in Psychological Assessment,* vol. 3, ed. P. McReynolds (San Francisco: Jossey-Bass, 1975), p. 45.
8.  Weick, "Observational Methods," p. 360.
9.  A. Mehrabian and S. R. Ferris, "Inference of Attitudes from Nonverbal Communication in Two Channels," *Journal of Consulting Psychology* 31 (1967): 248-52.
10.  P. Ekman, "Differential Communication of Affect by Head and Body Cues," *Journal of Personality and Social Psychology* 2 (1965): 726-35. P. Ekman et al., "Relative Importance of Face, Body, and Speech in Judgments of Personality and Affect," *Journal of Personality and Social Psychology* 38 (1980): 270-77. R. M. Krauss et al., "Verbal, Vocal, and Visible Factors in Judgments of Another's Affect," *Journal of Personality and Social Psychology* 40 (1981): 312-20. S. F. Zaidel and A. Mehrabian, "The Ability to Communicate and Infer Positive and Negative Attitudes Facially and Vocally," *Journal of Experimental Research in Personality* 3 (1969): 233-41.
11.  W. D. Brooks, *Speech Communication* (Dubuque, Iowa: Brown, 1972), p. 176.
12.  B. Berelson, *Content Analysis in Communication Research* (Glencoe, Ill.: Free Press, 1952), p. 18.
13.  O. R. Holsti, *Content Analysis for the Social Sciences and Humanities* (Reading, Mass.: Addison-Wesley, 1969). I. Pool, ed., *Trends in Content Analysis* (Urbana, Ill.: University of Illinois Press, 1959).
14.  K. Berger, "Conversational English of University Students," *Speech Monographs* 34 (1968): 65-73. P. Cameron, "Frequency and Kinds of Words in Various Social Settings, or What the Hell is Going On?" *Pacific Sociological Review* 12 (1969): 101-04. L. C. Haggerty, "What a Two-and-one-half-year-old Child Said in One Day," *Journal of Genetic Psychology* 37 (1930): 75-101. G. Maroden, "Content-Analysis Studies of Therapeutic Interviews: 1954 to 1964," *Psychological Bulletin* 63 (1965): 298-321. R. S. Uhrbrook, "The Vocabulary of a Five-year-old," *Educational Research Bulletin* 14 (1935): 85-97. E. J. Webb et al., *Unobtrusive Measures: A Survey of Non-reactive Research in Social Science* (Chicago: Rand McNally, 1981). H. M. Wellman and J. D. Lempers, "The Naturalistic Communicative Abilities in Two-year-olds," *Child Development* 48 (1977): 1052-57.
15.  R. F. Bales, *Interaction Process Analysis: A Method for the Study of Small Groups* (Cambridge, Mass.: Addison-Wesley, 1950).
16.  E. F. Borgatta, "A Systematic Study of Interaction Process Scores, Peer and Self-assessments, Personality and Other Variables," *Genetic Psychology Monographs* 65 (1962): 219-91. R. O. Mann, *Interpersonal Styles and Group Development* (New York: Wiley, 1967). T. M. Mills, *Group Transformation: An Analysis of a Learning Group* (Englewood Cliffs, N.J.: Prentice-Hall, 1964).
17.  S. Saporta and T. A. Sebeok, "Linguistic and Content Analysis," in *Trends in Content Analysis,* ed. I. Pool (Urbana, Ill.: University of Illinois Press, 1959), pp. 131-132.
18.  Ibid.
19.  P. S. Dale, *Language Development: Structure and Function* (New York: Holt, 1976). Z. S. Harris, *Structural Linguistics* (Chicago: University of Chicago Press, 1960). A. A. Hill, *Introduction to Linguistic Structures* (New York: Harcourt, 1958). D. Ingram, *Procedures for the Phonological Analysis of Children's Language* (Baltimore: University Park Press, 1981). N. A. McQuown, "Linguistic Transcription and Specification of Psychiatric Interview Methods," *Psychiatry* 20 (1957): 79-86. R. E. Pittinger, C. F. Hockett, and J. J. Dahney, *The First Five Minutes: A Sample of Microscopic Interview Analysis* (Ithaca, N.Y.: Martineau, 1960).
20.  M. Blank and E. Franklin, "Dialogue with Preschoolers," *Applied Psycholinguistics* 1 (1980): 127-50. L. Bloom, *Language Development: Form and Function in Emerging Grammars* (Cambridge, Mass.: M.I.T. Press, 1970). J. G. de Villiers and P. A. de Villiers, "Language Development," in *Strategies and Techniques of Child Study,* ed. R. Vasta (New York: Academic Press, 1982). P. Dale, "What Does Observing Language Mean?" in *Observing Behavior,* vol. 1, ed. G. P. Sackett (Baltimore: University Park Press, 1978). M. Hughes et al., "Recording Children's Conversations at Home and at Nursery School: A Technique and Some Methodological Considerations," *Journal of Child Psychology and Psychiatry* 20 (1979): 225-32. J. F. Miller, *Assessing Language Production in Children: Experimental Procedures* (Baltimore: University Park Press, 1978). D. Tyack and R. Gottsleben, *Language Sampling, Analysis, and Training* (Palo Alto, Calif.: Consulting Psychologists Press, 1974).
21.  Dale, "Observing Language," p. 221.
22.  Bloom, *Language Development.* Bowerman, *Early Syntactic Development.* T. L. Layton and B. L. Stick, "Use of Mean Morphological Units to Assess Language Development," *Journal of Communication Disorders* 12 (1979): 35-44. L. Lee, *Developmental Sentence Analysis* (Evanston, Ill.: Northwestern University Press, 1974). W. D. Loban, *The Language of Elementary School Children* (Champaign, Ill.: National Council of Teachers of English, 1963). D. A. McCarthy, *The Language Development of the Preschool Child* (Minneapolis: University of Minnesota Press, 1930). M. E. Smith, "A Study of Some Factors Influencing the Development of the Sentence in Preschool Children," *Journal of Genetic Psychology* 46 (1935): 152-212. M. C. Templin, *Certain Language Skills in Children: Their Development and Interrelationships* (Minneapolis: University of Minnesota Press, 1957).
23.  Weick, "Observational Methods," p. 391.
24.  L. Dimitrovsky, "The Ability to Identify the Emotional Meaning of Vocal Expressions at Successive Age Levels," in *The Communication of Emotional Meaning,* ed. J. R. Davitz (New York: McGraw-Hill, 1964). H. Levin and I. Silverman, "Hesitation Phenomena in Children's Speech," *Language and Speech* 8 (1965): 67-85. H. Levin, I. Silverman, and B. Ford, "Hesitations in Children's Speech During Explanation and Description," *Journal of Verbal Learning and Verbal Behavior* 6 (1967): 560-64.

W. C. Olson and V. S. Koetzle, "Amount and Rate of Talking of Young Children," *Journal of Experimental Education* 5 (1936): 175-79.

W. C. Sheppard and H. L. Lane, "Development of the Prosodic Features of Infant Vocalizing," *Journal of Speech and Hearing Research* 11 (1968): 94-108.

B. Wood, *Children and Communication* (Englewood Cliffs, N.J.: Prentice-Hall, 1976).

25.  G. L. Traeger, "Paralanguage: A First Approximation," *Studies in Linguistics* 13 (1958): 1-12.

26.  Ibid., p. 4.

27.  Ibid.

28.  W. M. Austin, "Some Social Aspects of Paralanguage," *Canadian Journal of Linguistics* 11 (1965): 31-39.

D. Crystal and R. Quirk, *Systems of Prosodic and Paralinguistic Features in English* (London: Mouton, 1964).

Pittinger, Hockett, and Dahney, *The First Five Minutes.*

29.  M. Argyle, *Bodily Communication* (London: Methuen, 1975).

S. Duncan, Jr., "Nonverbal Communication," *Psychological Bulletin* 72 (1969): 118-37.

R. G. Harper, A. N. Wiens, and J. D. Matarazzo, *Nonverbal Communication: The State of the Art* (New York: Wiley, 1978).

R. P. Harrison, *Beyond Words: An Introduction to Nonverbal Communication* (Englewood Cliffs, N.J.: Prentice-Hall, 1974).

G. F. Mahl and G. Schulze, "Psychological Research in the Extralinguistic Area," in *Approaches to Semiotics* (London: Mouton, 1964).

W. von Raffler-Engel, *Aspects of Nonverbal Communication* (Lisse: Swets and Zeitlinger, 1980).

30.  Levin and Silverman, *Hesitation Phenomena.*

31.  W. A. Hargreaves and J. A. Starkweather, "Recognition of Speaker Identity," *Language and Speech* 6 (1963): 63-67.

J. A. Starkweather, "The Communication Value of Content-free Speech," *American Journal of Psychology* 69 (1956): 121-23.

32.  M. L. Knapp, *Nonverbal Communication in Human Interaction* (New York: Holt, 1978), p. 12.

33.  Ibid.

34.  G. W. Allport, *Pattern and Growth in Personality* (New York: Holt, 1961).

35.  R. Birdwhistle, *Introduction to Kinesics* (Louisville: University of Kentucky Press, 1952).

R. Birdwhistle, *Kinesics and Context* (Philadelphia: University of Pennsylvania Press, 1970).

36.  Knapp, *Nonverbal Communication*, p. 198.

37.  Knapp, *Nonverbal Communication.*

38.  R. Birdwhistle, "Communication Without Words," in *L'adventure Humaine*, ed. P. Alexandre (Paris: Société d'Etudes Litteraires et Artistiques, 1965), p. 36.

39.  A. T. Dittmann, "Review of Kinesics in Context," *Psychiatry* 34 (1971): 334-342.

40.  E. A. Sapir, "The Unconscious Patterning of Behavior in Society," in *Selected Writings of Edward Sapir in Language, Culture, and Personality*, ed. D. G. Mandelbaum (Berkeley: University of California Press, 1949), p. 556.

41.  S. Freud, "The Psychopathology of Everyday Life," in *The Standard Edition of the Complete Psychological Works of Sigmund Freud*, vol. 6, ed. J. Strachey (1901); reprint ed. (London: Hogarth, 1960).

42.  M. H. Krout, "Autistic Gestures: An Experimental Study in Symbolic Movement," *Psychological Monographs* 46 (1935).

M. H. Krout, "An Experimental Attempt to Determine the Significance of Unconscious Manual Symbolic Movements," *Journal of General Psychology* 51 (1954): 121-52.

43.  P. Ekman, "Differential Communication of Affect by Head and Body Cues," *Journal of Personality and Social Psychology* 2 (1965): 726-35.

N. Freedman and S. Hoffman, "Kinetic Behavior in Altered Clinical States: Approach to Objective Analysis of Motor Behavior During Clinical Interviews," *Perceptual and Motor Skills* 24 (1967): 527-39.

W. V. Friesen, P. Ekman, and H. Wallbott, "Measuring Hand Movements," *Journal of Nonverbal Behavior* 4 (1979): 97-112.

F. Hayes, "Gestures: A Working Bibliography," *Southern Folklore Quarterly* 21 (1957): 213-317.

44.  G. Michael and N. Willis, Jr., "The Development of Gestures as a Function of Social Class, Education, and Sex," *Psychological Record* 18 (1968): 515-19.

45.  L. Kumin and M. Lazar, "Gestural Communication in Preschool Children," *Perceptual and Motor Skills* 38 (1974): 708-10.

46.  A. T. Dittmann, "Development Factors in Conversational Behavior," *Journal of Communication* 22 (1972): 404-23.

47.  M. A. Evans and K. H. Rubin, "Hand Gestures as a Communicative Mode in School-aged Children," *Journal of Genetic Psychology* 135 (1979): 135, 189-96.

48.  M. A. Jancovic, S. Devoe, and M. Wiener, "Age-related Changes in Hand and Arm Movements as Nonverbal Communication: Some Conceptualizations and an Empirical Exploration," *Child Development* 46 (1975): 922-28.

49.  G. A. Rekers, J. A. Sanders, and C. C. Strauss, "Developmental Differentiation of Adolescent Body Gestures," *Journal of Genetic Psychology* 138 (1981): 123-31.

50.  W. C. McGrew, *An Ethological Study of Children's Behavior* (New York: Academic Press, 1972).

51.  S. J. Hutt and C. Hutt, *Direct Observation and Measurement of Behavior* (Springfield, Ill.: Thomas, 1970).

52.  McGrew, *Ethological Study*, pp. 76, 79, 83.

53.  W. James, "A Study of the Expression of Bodily Posture," *Journal of General Psychology* 7 (1932): 405-36.

54.  A. Mehrabian, *Nonverbal Communication* (New York: Aldine Atherton, 1972).

55.  P. Ekman, "Body Position, Facial Expression and Verbal Behavior During Interviews," *Journal of Abnormal and Social Psychology* 68 (1964): 295-301.

G. T. Hewes, "The Anthropology of Posture," *Scientific American* 196 (1957): 123-32.

K. R. Johnson, "Black Kinesics—Some Non-verbal Communication Patterns in the Black Culture," in *Messages: A Reader in Human Communication*, ed. J. M. Civikly (New York: Random House, 1974).

A. Mehrabian, "Significance of Posture and Position in the Communication of Attitude and Status Relationships," *Psychological Bulletin* 71 (1969): 359-71.

56.  McGrew, *Ethological Study.*

57.  S. S. Tomkins, *Affect, Imagery, and Consciousness: The Positive Affects*, vol. 1 (New York: Springer, 1962).

58.  P. W. Ekman, V. Friesen, and P. Ellsworth, *Emotion in the Human Face: Guidelines for Research and an Integration of the Findings* (New York: Pergamon, 1972).

59.  E. A. Haggard and K. S. Isaacs, "Micromomentary Facial Expressions as Indicators of Ego Mechanisms in Psychotherapy," in *Methods of Research in Psychotherapy*, eds. L. A. Gottschalk and A. H. Auerbach (New York: Appleton, 1966).

60.  P. Ekman, W. V. Friesen, and S. S. Tomkins, "Facial Affect Scoring Technique (FAST): A First Validity Study," *Semiotica* 3 (1971): 37-58.

S. S. Tomkins and R. McCarter, "What and Where Are the Primary Affects? Some Evidence for a Theory," *Perceptual and Motor Skills* 18 (1964): 119-58.

61.  N. H. Frijda, "Recognition of Emotion," in *Advances in Experimental Social Psychology*, vol. 4 ed. L. Berkowitz (New York: Academic Press, 1968).

62.  N. H. Frijda and E. Philipszoon, "Dimensions of Recognition of Emotion," *Journal of Abnormal and Social Psychology* 66 (1963): 45-51.

H. Schlosberg, "Three Dimensions of Emotions," *Psychological Review* 61 (1954): 81-88.

63.  E. Grant, "Human Facial Expression," *Man* 4 (1969): 525-36.

Haggard and Isaacs, "Micromomentary Facial Expressions."

J. O. Jecker, N. Maccoby, and H. S. Breitrose, "Improving Accuracy in Interpreting Non-verbal Cues of Comprehension," *Psychology in the Schools* 2 (1965): 239-44.

N. G. B. Jones, "Criteria for Use in Describing Facial Expressions of Children," *Human Biology* 43 (1971): 365-413.

64.  P. Ekman, W. V. Friesen, and S. S. Tomkins, "Facial Affect Scoring Technique (FAST): A First Validity Study," *Semiotica* 3 (1971): 37-58.

65.  Ekman, Friesen, and Ellsworth, *Emotion in the Human Face*, p. 114.

66.  C. Darwin, "A Biographical Sketch of an Infant," *Mind* 2 (1877): 285-94.

67.  C. Darwin, *The Expression of Emotions in Man and Animals* (London: Murray, 1972).

68.    J. A. Ambrose, "The Development of the Smiling Response: A Contribution to the Ontogenesis of Social Relations," *Genetic Psychology Monographs* 34 (1946): 57-125.
       W. E. Blatz and D. A. Millichamp, "The Development of Emotion in the Infant," *University of Toronto Studies, Child Development Series*, no. 4 (1935).
       K. M. B. Bridges, *The Social and Emotional Development of the Pre-school Child* (London: Kegan Paul, 1931).
       L. A. Camras, "Facial Expressions Used by Children in a Conflict Situation," *Child Development* 48 (1977): 1431-35.
       W. R. Charlesworth, "Instigation and Maintenance of Curiosity Behavior as a Function of Surprise Versus Novel and Familiar Stimuli," *Child Development* 35 (1964): 1169-86.
       N. G. B. Jones, "An Ethological Study of Some Aspects of Social Behavior in Nursery School," in *Primate Ethology*, ed. D. Morris (Chicago: Aldine, 1967).
       A. F. Ricketts, "A Study of the Behavior of Young Children in Anger," *University of Iowa Studies in Child Welfare* 9 (1934): 163-171.
69.    M. Zuckerman and S. I Przewuzman, "Decoding and Encoding Facial Expressions in Preschool-age Children," *Environmental Psychology and Nonverbal Behavior* 3 (1979): 147-63.
       N. L. Morency and R. Krauss, "Children's Nonverbal Encoding and Decoding of Affect," in *Development of Nonverbal Behavior in Children*, ed. R. S. Feldman (Seacaucus, N.J.: Springer-Verlag, 1982).
70.    Jones, "Describing Facial Expressions of Children."
71.    Jones, "Describing Facial Expressions of Children," p. 375.
72.    S. W. Janik et al., "Eyes As the Center of Focus in the Visual Examination of Human Faces," *Perceptual and Motor Skills* 47 (1978): 857-58.
73.    Argyle, *Bodily Communication*, p. 229.
74.    Argyle, *Bodily Communication*, p. 220.
75.    A. Kendon, "Some Functions of Gaze-Direction in Social Interaction," *Acta Psychologica* 26 (1967): 22-63.
76.    J. Efran and A. Broughton, "Effect of Expectancies for Social Approval on Visual Behavior," *Journal of Personality and Social Psychology* 4 (1966): 103-07.
       R. Exline, D. Gray, and D. Schuette, "Visual Behavior in a Dyad As Affected by Interview Content and Sex of Respondent," *Journal of Personality and Social Psychology* 1 (1965): 201-09.
       R. V. Exline and L. C. Winters, "Affective Relations and Mutual Glances in Dyads," in *Affect, Cognition, and Personality*, eds. S. Tomkins and C. Izard (New York: Springer, 1965).
77.    M. P. Janisse, *Pupillometry* (New York: Wiley, 1977).
78.    C. S. Harris, R. I. Thackery, and R. W. Shoenberger, "Blink Rate As a Function of Induced Muscular Tension and Manifest Anxiety," *Perceptual and Motor Skills* 22 (1966): 155-60.
       F. G. Kanfer, "Verbal Rate, Eyeblink, and Content in Structured Psychiatric Interviews," *Journal of Abnormal and Social Psychology* 61 (1960): 341-47.
       E. Ponder and W. P. Kennedy, "On the Act of Blinking," *Quarterly Journal of Experimental Physiology* 18 (1927): 89-110.
79.    McGrew, *Ethological Study*.
80.    D. R. Buchanon, M. Goldman, and R. Juhnke, "Eye Contact, Sex, and the Violation of Personal Space," *Journal of Social Psychology* 103 (1977): 19-25.
       Exline and Winters, "Affective Relations."
       Exline, Gray, and Schuette, "Visual Behavior."
       A. Mehrabian, "Nonverbal Betrayal of Feelings," *Journal of Experimental Research in Personality* 5 (1971): 64-73.
81.    E. Goffman, *Relations in Public: Microstudies of the Public Order* (New York: Basic Books, 1971).
       Johnson, "Black Kinesics."
       M. LaFrance and C. Mays, "Racial Differences in Gaze Behavior During Conversations: Two Systematic Observational Studies," *Journal of Personality and Social Psychology* 33 (1976): 547-52.
       A. Scheflen, *Body Language and the Social Order* (Englewood Cliffs, N.J.: Prentice-Hall, 1972).
82.    J. S. Efran, "Looking for Approval: Effects on Visual Behavior of Approbation from Persons Differing in Importance," *Journal of Personality and Social Psychology* 10 (1968): 21-25.
       R. V. Exline, "Visual Interaction: The Glances of Power and Preference," in *Nebraska Symposium on Motivation*, ed. J. K. Cole (Lincoln: University of Nebraska Press, 1971).
83.    P. H. Wolff, "Observations on the Early Development of Smiling," in *Determinants of Behaviour*, vol. 2, ed. B. M. Foss (London: Methuen, 1963).
84.    H. E. Fitzgerald, "Autonomic Pupillary Reflex Activity During Early Infancy and Its Relation to Social and Non-social Stimuli," *Journal of Experimental Child Psychology* 6 (1968): 470-82.
85.    W. H. O. Schmitt and T. Hore, "Some Nonverbal Aspects of Communication Between Mother and Preschool Child," *Child Development* 41 (1970): 889-96.
86.    V. Ashear and J. R. Snortum, "Eye Contact in Children As a Function of Age, Sex, Social, and Intellective Variables," *Developmental Psychology* 4 (1971): 479.
87.    M. H. Levine and B. Sutton-Smith, "Effects of Age, Sex, and Task on Visual Behavior During Dyadic Interaction," *Developmental Psychology* 9 (1973): 400-05.
88.    E. H. Eberts and M. R. Lepper, "Individual Consistency in the Proxemic Behavior of Preschool Children," *Journal of Personality and Social Psychology* 32 (1975): 841-49.
89.    R. Abramovitch and E. M. Daly, "Children's Use of Head Orientation and Eye Contact in Making Attributions of Affiliation," *Child Development* 49 (1978): 519-22.
90.    E. T. Hall, *The Hidden Dimension* (Garden City, N.Y.: Doubleday, 1966), p. 1.
91.    E. T. Hall, "A System for the Notation of Proxemic Behavior," *American Anthropologist* 65 (1963): 1003.
92.    Hall, *Hidden Dimension*.
93.    J. B. Calhoun, "Population Density and Social Pathology," *Scientific American* 206 (1952): 139-46.
       C. R. Carpenter, "Territoriality: A Review of Concepts and Problems," in *Behavior and Evolution*, eds. A. Roe and G. G. Simpson (New Haven: Yale University Press, 1958).
94.    I. Altman and W. W. Haythorn, "The Ecology of Isolated Groups," *Behavioral Science* 12 (1967): 169-82.
       A. H. Esser et al., "Territoriality of Patients on a Research Ward," in *Recent Advances in Biological Psychology*, vol. 7, ed. J. Wortis (New York: Plenum, 1965).
       H. Garfinkel, "Studies of the Routine Grounds for Everyday Activities," *Social Problems* 11 (1964): 225-50.
       C. Hutt and M. J. Vaizey, "Differential Effects of Group Density on Social Behavior," *Nature* 209 (1966): 1371-72.
       R. Sommer, *Personal Space: The Behavioral Basis of Design* (Englewood Cliffs, N.J.: Prentice-Hall, 1969).
95.    H. Osmond, "The History and Social Development of Mental Hospitals," in *Psychiatric Architecture*, ed. G. Goshen (Washington, D.C.: American Psychiatric Association, 1959).
96.    Hall, *Hidden Dimension*, pp. 120-121.
97.    Weick, "Observational Methods."
98.    J. C. Baxter, "Interpersonal Spacing in a Natural Setting," *Sociometry* 33 (1970): 444-56.
       G. W. Evans and R. B. Howard, "Personal Space," *Psychological Bulletin* 80 (1973): 334-44.
       Garfinkel, "Routine Grounds."
       J. J. Harnett, F. Bailey, and W. Gibson, "Personal Space As Influenced by Sex and Type of Movement," *Journal of Psychology* 76 (1970): 139-44.
       J. L. Kuethe and G. Stricker, "Man and Woman: Social Schemata of Males and Females," *Psychological Reports* 13 (1963): 655-61.
       M. Leibman, "The Effects of Sex and Race Norms on Personal Space," *Environment and Behavior* 2 (1970): 208-46.
99.    Baxter, "Interpersonal Spacing."
       S. E. Bauer, "Personal Space: A Study of Blacks and Whites," *Sociometry* 36 (1973): 402-08.
       A. S. Frankel and J. Barrett, "Variations in Personal Space As a Function of Authoritarianism, Self-esteem, and Racial Characteristics of a Stimulus Situation," *Journal of Consulting and Clinical Psychology* 37 (1971): 95-98.
       Johnson, "Black Kinesics."

S. E. Jones, "A Comparative Proxemic Analysis of Dyadic Analysis of Dyadic Interaction in Selected Subcultures of New York City," *Journal of Social Psychology* 84 (1971): 35-44.

K. B. Little, "Cultural Variations in Social Schemata," *Journal of Personality and Social Psychology* 10 (1968): 1-7.

100.  Goffman, *Relations in Public.*
       A. Mehrabian, "Significance of Posture and Position in the Communication of Attitude and Status Relationships," *Psychological Bulletin* 71 (1969): 359-72.

101.  R. J. Comer and J. A. Piliavin, "The Effects of Physical Deviance upon Face-to-face Interaction: The Other Side," *Journal of Personality and Social Psychology* 23 (1972): 33-39.
       R. E. Kleck et al., "Effect of Stigmatizing Conditions on the Use of Personal Space," *Psychological Reports* 23 (1968): 111-18.

102.  M. Cook, "Experiments on Orientation and Proxemics," *Human Relations* 23 (1970): 61-76.
       Frankel and Barett, "Variations in Personal Space."
       M. J. Horowitz, "Spatial Behavior and Psychopathology," *Journal of Nervous and Mental Disease* 146 (1968): 24-35.
       M. J. Horowitz, D. F. Duff, and L. O. Stratton, "Body-buffer zone," *Archives of General Psychiatry* 11 (1964): 631-56.
       J. Luft, "On Nonverbal Interaction," *Journal of Psychology* 63 (1960): 261-68.
       R. Sommer, "Studies in Personal Space," *Sociometry* 22 (1959): 246-60.
       J. L. Williams, "Personal Space and Its Relation to Extroversion-Introversion," *Canadian Journal of Behavioral Science* 3 (1971): 156-60.

103.  J. Conroy and E. Sundstrom, "Territorial Dominance in a Dyadic Conversation As a Function of Similarity of Opinion," *Journal of Personality and Social Psychology* 35 (1977): 570-76.
       Little, "Cultural Variations."

104.  J. Gullahorn, "Distance and Friendship As Factors in the Gross Interaction Matrix," *Sociometry* 15 (1952): 123-34.
       Little, "Cultural Variations."
       F. N. Willis, "Initial Speaking Distance As a Function of the Speaker's Relationship," *Psychonomic Science* 5 (1966): 221-22.

105.  S. Albert and J. N. Dabbs, Jr., "Physical Distance and Persuasion," *Journal of Personality and Social Psychology* 15 (1970): 265-70.
       K. B. Little, "Personal Space," *Journal of Experimental Social Psychology* 1 (1965): 237-47.

106.  N. Bass and M. Weinstein, "Early Development of Interpersonal Distance in Children," *Canadian Journal of Behavioral Science* 3 (1971): 368-72.
       D. T. Campbell, W. H. Kruskal, and W. P. Wallace, "Seating Aggregation As an Index of Attitude," *Sociometry* 29 (1966): 1-15.
       P. A. Hare and R. F. Bales, "Seating Position and Small Group Interaction," *Sociometry* 26 (1963): 480-86.
       D. V. Lott and R. Sommer, "Seating Arrangements and Status," *Journal of Personality and Social Psychology* 7 (1967): 90-94.
       N. J. Russo, "Connotation of Seating Arrangement," *Cornell Journal of Social Relations* 2 (1967): 37-44.

107.  Sommer, "Studies in Personal Space."
108.  J. L. Freedman, *Crowding and Behavior* (San Francisco: Freeman, 1975).
109.  J. R. Aiello and T. D. C. Aiello, "The Development of Personal Space: Proxemic Behavior of Children 6 Through 16," *Human Ecology* 2 (1974): 177-89.
110.  Ibid.
       Bass and Weinstein, "Interpersonal Distance."
       Baxter, "Interpersonal Spacing,"
       J. Lomranz et al., "Children's Personal Space As a Function of Age and Sex," *Developmental Psychology* 11 (1975): 197-205.
       G. F. Melson, "Sex Differences in Proxemic Behavior and Personal Space Schemata in Young Children," *Sex Roles* 3 (1977): 81-89.
       G. H. Tennis and J. M. Dabbs, Jr., "Sex, Setting, and Personal Space: First Grade Through College," *Sociometry* 38 (1975): 385-94.

111.  S. E. Jones and J. R. Aiello, "Proxemic Behavior of Black and White First-, Third-, and Fifth-grade Children," *Journal of Personality and Social Psychology* 25 (1973): 21-27.
       M. Meisels and C. J. Guardo, "Development of Personal Space Schemata," *Child Development* 40 (1969): 1167-78.
       L. J. Severy, D. R. Forsyth, and P. J. Wagner, "A Multimethod Assessment of Personal Space Development in Female and Male, Black and White Children," *Journal of Nonverbal Behavior* 4 (1979): 68-86.

112.  Aiello and Aiello, "Development of Personal Space."
       R. Gifford and J. Price, "Personal Space in Nursery School Children," *Canadian Journal of Behavioral Sciences* 11 (1979): 318-26.
       L. Harper and K. M. Sanders, "Preschool Children's Use of Space: Sex Differences in Outdoor Play," *Developmental Psychology* 11 (1975): 119.
       Lomranz et al., "Children's Personal Space."

113.  Bass and Weinstein, "Interpersonal Distance."
       R. M. Lerner, S. A. Karabenick, and M. Meisels, "Children's Personal Space As a Function of Age and Sex," *Developmental Psychology* 11 (1975): 541-45.
       Meisels and Guardo, "Personal Space Schemata."
       J. Smetana, D. L. Bridgeman, and B. Bridgeman, "A Field Study of Interpersonal Distance in Early Childhood," *Personality and Social Psychology Bulletin* 4 (1978): 309-13.
       Tennis and Dabbs, "Sex, Setting, and Personal Space."

114.  Meisels and Guardo, "Personal Space Schemata."
115.  J. R. Aiello and S. E. Jones, "Field Study of the Proxemic Behavior of Young School Children in Three Subcultural Groups," *Journal of Personality and Social Psychology* 19 (1971): 351-56.
116.  Baxter, "Interpersonal Spacing."
       J. G. Ford and J. R. Graves, "Differences Between Mexican-American and White Children in Interpersonal Distance and Social Touching," *Perceptual and Motor Skills* 45 (1977): 779-85.

117.  T. R. DuHame and H. Jarmon, "Social Schemata of Emotionally Disturbed Boys and Their Male Siblings," *Journal of Consulting and Clinical Psychology* 36 (1971): 281-85.
       R. C. Newman and D. Pollack, "Proxemics in Deviant Adolescents," *Journal of Consulting and Clinical Psychology* 40 (1973): 6-8.
       A. Tolar, "Psychological Distance in Disturbed and Normal Children," *Psychological Reports* 23 (1968): 695-701.
       L. Weinstein, "Social Schemata of Emotionally Disturbed Boys," *Journal of Abnormal Psychology* 70 (1965): 457-61.

118.  Bass and Weinstein, "Interpersonal Distance."
       R. O. Blood and W. P. Livant, "The Use of Space Within the Cabin Group," *Journal of Social Issues* 13 (1957): 47-53.
       R. Castell, "Effect of Familiar and Unfamiliar Environments on Proximity Behavior of Young Children," *Journal of Experimental Child Psychology* 9 (1970): 342-47.
       B. W. Estes and D. Rush, "Social Schemas: A Developmental Study," *Journal of Psychology* 78 (1971): 119-23.
       Gifford and Price, "Nursery School Children."
       M. G. King, "Interpersonal Relations in Preschool Children and Average Approach Distance," *Journal of Genetic Psychology* 109 (1966): 109-16.
       E. K. Morris and G. L. Smith, "A Functional Analysis of Adult Affection and Children's Interpersonal Distance," *Psychological Record* 30 (1980): 115-63.

119.  C. J. Guardo and M. Meisels, "Child-Parent Spatial Patterns Under Praise and Reproof," *Developmental Psychology* 5 (1971): 365.
120.  G. W. Evans and R. B. Howard, "Personal Space," *Psychological Bulletin* 80 (1973): 334.
121.  L. A. Hayduk, "Personal Space: An Evaluative and Orienting Overview," *Psychological Bulletin* 85 (1978): 117-34.
122.  Severy et al., "Multimethod Assessment."
123.  C. Loo, "The Effects of Spatial Density on the Social Behavior of Children," *Journal of Applied Social Psychology* 2 (1972): 372-81.
124.  C. Hutt and J. Vaizey, "Differential Effects of Group Density on Social Behavior," *Nature* 209 (1966): 1371-72.
       A. T. Jersild and F. V. Markey, *Conflicts Between Preschool Children* (New York: Columbia University Press, 1935).
       McGrew, *Ethological Study.*

125.  Loo, "Effects of Spatial Density."
       McGrew, *Ethological Study.*

P. Smith and K. Connelly, "Patterns of Play and Social Interaction in Preschool Children," in *Ethological Studies of Child Behavior*, ed. N. Blurton Jones (Cambridge, England: Cambridge University Press, 1972).

126. Hutt and Vaizey, "Differential Effects."
Loo, "Effects of Spatial Density."
McGrew, *Ethological Study*.

127. J. R. Aiello, G. Nicosia, and D. E. Thompson, "Physiological, Social, and Behavioral Consequences of Crowding on Children and Adolescents," *Child Development* 50 (1979): 195-202.

128. S. J. Williams and F. N. Willis, Jr., "Interpersonal Touch Among Preschool Children at Play," *Psychological Record* 28 (1978): 501-08.

129. Hall, *Hidden Dimension*, p. 57.

130. S. Escalona, "Emotional Development in the First Year of Life," in *Problems of Infancy and Childhood*, ed. M. J. E. Sean (New York: Macy Foundation, 1953).
H. F. Harlow, "The Nature of Love," *American Psychologist* 13 (1958): 673-85.
A. Montagu, *Touching: The Human Significance of the Skin* (New York: Columbia University Press, 1971).

131. L. K. Frank, "Tactile Communication," *Genetic Psychology Monographs* 56 (1957): 211.

132. F. B. Dresslar, "Studies in the Psychology of Touch," *American Journal of Psychology* 6 (1884): 313-68.

133. R. Heslin, "Steps Toward a Taxonomy of Touching" (Paper presented at the annual meeting of the Midwestern Psychological Association Chicago, 1974).

134. J. J. Gibson, "Observations on Active Touch," *Psychological Review* 69 (1962): 477-91.

135. S. M. Jourard, "An Exploratory Study of Body-Accessibility," *British Journal of Social and Clinical Psychology* 5 (1966): 221-31.

136. L. B. Rosenfeld, S. Kartus, and C. Ray, "Body Accessibility Revisited," *Journal of Communication* 26 (1976): 27-30.

137. N. M. Henley, "Status and Sex: Some Touching Observations," *Bulletin of the Psychonomic Society* 2 (1973): 91-93.
N. M. Henley, *Body Politics: Power, Sex, and Nonverbal Communication* (Englewood Cliffs, N.J.: Prentice-Hall, 1977).
Jourard, "Exploratory Study."
J. Nguyen, R. Heslin, and M. L. Nguyen, "The Meaning of Touch: Sex Differences," *Journal of Communication* 25 (1975): 92-103.

138. Henley, "Status and Sex."
Henley, *Body Politics*.
F. N. Willis, C. M. Rinck, and L. M. Dean, "Interpersonal Touch Among Adults in Cafeteria Lines," *Perceptual and Motor Skills* 47 (1978): 1147-52.

139. Frank, "Tactile Communication."
E. Goffman, "The Nature of Deference and Demeanor," in *Interaction Ritual* (Garden City, N.Y.: Doubleday, 1967).
Henley, *Body Politics*.
D. L. Summerhayes and R. W. Suchner, "Power Implications of Touch in Male-Female Relationships," *Sex Roles* 4 (1978): 161-65.

140. D. Efron, *Gesture, Race, and Culture* (The Hague: Mouton, 1946).
Johnson, "Black Kinesics."
Jourard, "Exploratory Study."
O. M. Watson, *Proxemic Behavior: A Cross-cultural Study* (The Hague: Mouton, 1972).
Willis et al., "Interpersonal Touch."

141. Johnson, "Black Kinesics."

142. Argyle, *Bodily Communication*.
J. D. Fisher, M. Rytting, and R. Heslin, "Hands Touching Hands: Affective and Evaluative Effects of an Interpersonal Touch," *Sociometry* 29 (1976): 416-21.
Henley, *Body Politics*.
C. L. Kleinke, "Compliance to Requests Made by Gazing and Touching Experimenters in Field Settings," *Journal of Experimental Social Psychology* 13 (1977): 218-23.
Nguyen et al., "Meaning of Touch."
S. J. Whitcher and J. D. Fisher, "Multidimensional Reaction to Therapeutic Touch in a Hospital Setting," *Journal of Personality and Social Psychology* 34 (1979): 87-96.

143. S. Goldberg and M. Lewis, "Play behavior in the Year-old Infant: Early Sex Differences," *Child Development* 40 (1969): 21-31.

144. M. Lewis, "Parents and Children: Sex-role Development," *School Review* 80 (1972): 229-40.

145. M. Lewis, M. Weintraub, and P. Ban, *Mothers and Fathers, Girls and Boys: Attachment Behavior During the First Two Years of Life* (Princeton, N.J.: Educational Testing Service, 1972).

146. V. S. Clay, "The Effects of Culture on Mother-Child Tactile Communication" (Ph.D. diss., Columbia University 1966).

147. Ibid.
Schmidt and Hore, "Nonverbal Aspects."
Ford and Graves, "Mexican-American and White Children."
Williams and Willis, "Interpersonal Touch."
F. N. Willis and G. E. Hoffman, "Development of Tactile Patterns in Relation to Age, Sex, and Race," *Developmental Psychology* 11 (1974): 866.

148. Ford and Graves, "Mexican-American and White Children."

149. Ford and Graves, "Mexican-American and White Children."
Williams and Willis, "Interpersonal Touch."
F. N. Willis and D. L. Reeves, "Touch Interactions in Junior High Students in Relation to Sex and Race," *Developmental Psychology* 12 (1976): 91-92.

150. Williams and Willis, "Interpersonal Touch."

151. V. P. Perdue and J. M. Connor, "Patterns of Touching Between Preschool Children and Male and Female Teachers," *Child Development* 49 (1978): 1258-62.

152. E. Berscheid and E. Walster, "Physical Attractiveness," in *Advances in Experimental Social Psychology*, vol. 7, ed. L. Berkowitz (New York: Academic Press, 1974).

153. G. W. Allport, *Personality: A Psychological Interpretation* (New York: Holt, 1937), p. 500.

154. W. H. Sheldon, *Atlas of Men: A Guide for Somatotyping the Adult Male at All Ages* (New York: Harper, 1954).

155. W. Wells and B. Siegel, "Stereotyped Somatypes," *Psychological Reports* 8 (1961): 77-78.

156. S. A. Gacsaly and C. A. Borges, "The Male Physique and Behavioral Expectancies," *Journal of Psychology* 101 (1979): 97-102.

157. P. F. Secord, "Facial Features and Inference Processes in Interpersonal Perception," in *Person Perception and Interpersonal Behavior*, eds. R. Taguiri and L. Petrullo (Stanford, Calif.: Stanford University Press, 1958).

158. P. F. Secord and J. E. Muthard, "Personality in Faces: IV. A Descriptive Analysis of the Perception of Women's Faces and the Identification of Some Physiognomic Determinants," *Journal of Psychology* 39 (1955): 269-78.

159. D. G. Freedman, "The Survival Value of the Beard," *Psychology Today* 3 (1969): 36-39.
S. M. Pancer and J. R. Meindl, "Length of Hair and Beardedness As Determinants of Personality Impressions," *Perceptual and Motor Skills* 46 (1978): 1328-30.
R. Pellegrini, "The Virtue of Hairiness," *Psychology Today* 6 (1973): 14.

160. Berscheid and Walster, "Physical Attractiveness."

161. L. Aiken, "Relationships of Dress to Selected Measures of Personality in Undergraduate Women," *Journal of Social Psychology* 59 (1963): 119-28.
H. M. Buckley and M. E. Roach, "Clothing As a Nonverbal Communicator of Social and Political Attitudes," *Home Economics Research Journal* 3 (1974): 94-102.
N. H. Compton, "Personal Attributes of Color and Design Preferences in Clothing Fabrics," *Journal of Psychology* 54 (1962): 191-95.
P. N. Hamid, "Style of Dress As a Perceptual Cue in Impression Formation," *Perceptual and Motor Skills* 26 (1968): 904-06.

162. Knapp, *Nonverbal Communication*.

163. M. Lefkowitz, R. R. Blake, and J. R. Mouton, "Status Factors in Pedestrian Violation of Traffic Signals," *Journal of Abnormal and Social Psychology* 51 (1955): 704-06.

164. W. McKeachie, "Lipstick As a Determinant of First Impressions of Personality: An Experiment for the General Psychology Course," *Journal of Social Psychology* 36 (1952): 241-44.

165. G. Thornton, "The Effect of Wearing Glasses upon Judgments of Personality Traits of Persons Seen Briefly," *Journal of Applied Psychology* 28 (1944): 203-07.

166. S. W. A. Bijou, "A Functional Analysis of Retarded Development," in *International Review of Research in Mental Retardation,* vol. 1, ed. N. Ellis (New York: Academic Press, 1966).

167. E. Gellert, J. S. Girgus, and J. Cohen, "Children's Awareness of Their Bodily Appearance: A Developmental Study of Factors Associated with the Body Percept," *Genetic Psychology Monographs* 84 (1971): 107-74.
    R. M. Lerner and E. Gellert, "Body Build Identification, Preference and Aversion in Children," *Developmental Psychology* 1 (1969): 456-62.
    R. M. Lerner and C. Schroeder, "Physique Identification, Preference and Aversion in Kindergarten Children," *Developmental Psychology* 5 (1971): 538.
    R. M. Lerner, J. Venning, and J. R. Snapp, "Age and Sex Effects on Personal Space Schemata Toward Body Build in Late Childhood," *Developmental Psychology* 11 (1975): 855-56.
    J. R. Staffieri, "Body Build and Behavioral Expectancies in Young Females," *Developmental Psychology* 6 (1972): 125-27.
    R. N. Walker, "Body Build and Behavior in Young Children: I. Body Build and Nursery School Teachers' Ratings," *Monographs of the Society for Research in Child Development* 27 (1962).

168. Berscheid and Walster, "Physical Attractiveness."
    K. K. Dion and E. Berscheid, "Physical Attractiveness and Peer Perception Among Children" *Sociometry* 37 (1974): 1-12.
    J. H. Langlois and A. C. Downs, "Peer Relations As a Function of Physical Attractiveness: The Eye of the Beholder or Behavioral Reality," *Child Development* 50 (1979): 409-18.
    J. Salvia, J. B. Sheare, and B. Algazzine, "Facial Attractiveness and Personal-Social Development," *Journal of Abnormal Child Psychology* 3 (1975): 171-78.

169. G. R. Adams and A. S. Cohen, "An Examination of Cumulative Folder Information Used by Teachers in Making Differential Judgments of Children's Abilities," *Alberta Journal of Educational Research* 22 (1976): 216-25.
    G. R. Adams and P. Crane, "An Assessment of Parents' and Teachers' Expectations of Preschool Children's Social Preference for Attractive or Unattractive Children and Adults," *Child Development* 51 (1980): 224-231.
    M. M. Clifford and E. Walster, "The Effect of Physical Attractiveness on Teacher Expectations," *Sociology of Education* 46 (1973): 248-58.
    K. L. Marwit, S. J. Marwit, and E. Walker, "Effects of Student Race and Physical Attractiveness on Teachers' Judgments of Transgressions," *Journal of Educational Psychology* 70 (1978): 911-15.

170. P. M. Insel and R. H. Moos, "Psychological Environments: Expanding the Scope of Human Ecology," *American Psychologist* 29 (1974): 179.

171. R. Wolf, "The Measurement of Environments," in *Testing in Perspective,* ed. A. Anastasi (Washington, D.C.: American Council on Education, 1966).

172. K. Lewin, *Principles of Topological and Vector Psychology* (New York: McGraw-Hill, 1936).

173. R. Moos, "Conceptualizations of Human Environments," *American Psychologist* 28 (1973): 652-65.

174. R. G. Barker, "The Ecological Environment," in *Big School, Small School,* eds. R. G. Barker and P. V. Gump (Stanford, Calif.: Stanford University Press, 1964).

175. J. W. B. Douglas, *The Home and the School* (London: MacGibbon & Kee, 1964).
    N. Endler and J. McV. Hunt, "S-R Inventories of Hostility and Comparisons of the Proportion of Variance from Persons, Responses, and Situations for Hostility and Anxiousness," *Journal of Personality and Social Psychology* 9 (1968): 309-15.
    R. Moos, "Sources of Variance in Responses to Questionnaires and Behavior," *Journal of Abnormal Psychology* 74 (1969): 405-12.

176. R. G. Barker, and P. V. Gump, *Big School, Small School* (Stanford, Calif.: Stanford University Press, 1964).
    P. Gump, P. Schoggen, and F. Redl, "The Behavior of the Same Child in Different Milieus," in *The Stream of Behavior,* ed. R. G. Barker (New York: Appleton, 1963).

177. K. H. Craik, "The Assessment of Places," in *Advances in Psychological Assessment,* vol. 2, ed. P. McReynolds (Palo Alto, Calif.: Science and Behavior, 1971).

# 3

# Studying the Child
# Through Systematic Observation

Various observational techniques have been employed in the study of child behavior and development. Of these, anecdotal records, specimen records, running records, time sampling, and event sampling will be treated in some detail in this chapter. Another observational approach, called environmental assessment, combines features of these five techniques, and it also will be discussed in this chapter.

## ANECDOTAL RECORDS

The anecdote is the most frequently used means of describing what has been observed. It is simply a brief written account of an incident. Rather than trust to memory, physicians, social workers, psychologists, and teachers note and preserve descriptions of behavior and events through anecdotal records. Early diary descriptions were the forerunners of the anecdotal method as a technique for studying child development. These diaries were of two types. The first comprehensive diaries, or baby biographies as they are sometimes called, were used to record the behavior and development of young children in a sequential, narrative form.[1] They resembled the lay diary and were usually kept by parents or guardians who were in continuous, close contact with the child. The second type, topical diaries, focused only on certain aspects of behavior such as language, social-emotional behavior, and sensorimotor behavior.[2] The topical approach was more selective than the comprehensive method. Although anecdotal records and the early diary methods are similar in some ways, anecdotal records cover a wider sampling of behavior. According to Prescott, any incident that seems important should be recorded. However, an attempt should be made to build a balanced picture of the child without undue emphasis on either good or bad behaviors.

> In general, the description should give a cross section of the pupil's life at school and show how he acts in a variety of situations. Some children behave so differently in different classes and with different teachers that one would hardly recognize them as the same individuals; a proper distribution of anecdotal material should demonstrate this. It is as important to see what bores a child as to see what excites his interests, and a good case record would reveal how he acts under both circumstances. It would show him in action when things are going well and when they are not going well; interacting with his teacher, the principal, other adults, his peers, and younger and older children; studying, loafing, creating, sulking, or pursuing an interest alone; interacting with his parents, siblings, and near-neighbor children; informal situations such as eating lunch or playing. In short, samplings from the whole range of his life experience in and around the school are needed.[3]

Use of the term *anecdote* originated many years ago,[4] but Randall was one of the first authors to describe the anecdotal method in great detail. He defined it as:

> . . . a record of some significant item of conduct; a record of an episode in the life of a student; a word picture of the student in action; the teacher's best effort at taking a word snapshot at the moment of the incidents; any narrative of events in

which the student takes such a part as to reveal something which may be significant about his personality.[5]

Other authors have defined anecdotal records as:

> . . . a specialized form of incidental observation. It is a description of the child's conduct and personality in terms of frequent, brief concrete observations of pupils made and recorded by the teacher.[6]

> . . . a description made by each instructor of any behavior which he observed which he thought significant . . . collected from a number of instructors over a period of time, it was found possible by reading these cumulative descriptions of behavior to reach an interpretation which did not fluctuate widely from one competent reader to another.[7]

All of these definitions have certain elements in common. They suggest that anecdotal records are descriptive; that they are objective and factual accounts of behavior; that they are brief and report one incident of behavior at a time; that they are continuous and cumulative; and that they reveal information which is considered significant in understanding a child's growth and development.

There are many reasons why anecdotal records should be kept.

1. Anecdotal records provide a variety of descriptions concerning the unconstrained behavior of pupils in diverse situations and thus contribute to an understanding of the core or basic personality pattern of each individual and of the changes in pattern.

2. They substitute specific and exact descriptions of personality for vague generalizations.

3. They direct the attention of teachers away from subject matter and class groups and toward individual pupils.

4. They stimulate teachers to use records and to contribute to them.

5. They relieve individual teachers of the responsibility of making trait ratings and provide a basis for composite ratings. Moreover, they provide a continuous record, while trait ratings are usually made only at certain points in a pupil's school experience.

6. They encourage teacher interest in and understanding of the larger school problems that are indicated by an accumulation of anecdotes.

7. They provide the information which the counselor needs to control the conferences with individual pupils. An appropriate starting point for each conference can be found in the data, and the discussion can be kept close to the pupil's needs.

8. They provide data for pupils to use in self-appraisal. While in some cases the anecdote should not be shown to the pupils, each pupil can profitably study the indications in many of the anecdotes about him in order to decide what he needs to do to improve.

9. Personal relationships between the pupil and the counselor are improved by anecdotal records, for these records show the pupil that the counselor is acquainted with his problems.

10. Anecdotal records aid in the formulation of individual help programs and encourage active pupil participation in remedial work.

11. They show needs for the formation of better work and study habits.

12. Curriculum construction, modification, and emphasis may be improved through reference to the whole volume of anecdotal record material collected by a school. The anecdotes indicate where there should be general presentation of material in character development to satisfy the needs of the whole school community.

13. An appropriate summary of anecdotes is valuable for forwarding with a pupil when he is promoted to another school.

14. Anecdotal records may be used by new members of the staff in acquainting themselves with the student body.

15. The qualitative statements contained in anecdotal records supplement and assist in the interpretation of quantitative data.

16. Collections of anecdotal records may provide the necessary validating of evidence for various evaluating instruments.

17. Anecdotal records aid in clinical service. When pupils are referred to clinical workers for special study of their problems, there is great advantage in having anecdotal records available.[8]

These reasons and additional positive features of anecdotal record keeping have been discussed by several authors.[9]

There are essentially three types of anecdotes:

1. *Anecdote with no comment.* Ben borrowed a ruler from Mary this morning. When the bell rang at the end of the period at lunchtime, he called across the room to Mary: "Hey! Your ruler!" Mary: "Well, hurry up." Ben: "Wait until I draw two lines." Mary: "Bring it to fifth period class with you." Ben: "No—wait! I don't want to carry it to the lunch room."

   Elizabeth asked if she might stay in my room during lunch hour. I asked her if she wasn't going to lunch. She said she couldn't go as she had no money but that it was all right, as she wanted to reduce anyway.

2. *Anecdote with interpretation.* George did part of a motor experiment today in which the instructions specifically stated that the instructor must be present. George sought the aid of a student instead. He pulled the switch promptly and avoided trouble.

   *Interpretation:* It should be noted that he had the presence of mind to save the situation. He goes ahead by himself too much, without regard to instructions.

3. *Anecdote accompanied by a recommendation.* Henry stopped after class today and gave me an opportunity to lead him to say that he felt he was not doing himself justice because he did not know how to take part in discussions effectively. He said this had been a difficulty with him all through high school.

*Treatment recommendation:* I told him that I had been aware from his attitude that he was in the habit of following the trend of thought in the discussion. I advised him, when he was studying, to pick out one or two points each day which he definitely planned to bring up and discuss in class.[10]

With the exception of Randall[11] and a very few others,[12] most authors recommend that interpretation should *not* be a part of the anecdotal record. Their point is well justified. It would seem logical to postpone interpretation until several anecdotes have been obtained. Evaluations based upon single incidents are likely to be invalid, since an isolated incident may represent atypical behavior. For example, if only one observation of destructive behavior has been recorded in a child's file, it should be considered inconsequential. But if there are several anecdotes describing destructiveness, the behavior pattern takes on greater significance; it reveals a trend and has greater interpretive value. It is preferable to avoid premature appraisals and to offer interpretations only after the observer has had an opportunity to collect a number of anecdotes. A larger and more representative sample of behavior helps guard against misinterpretation.

Although no prescribed procedure for writing anecdotal reports exists, there are a number of guidelines which, if adhered to, increase the quality and usefulness of this technique. The anecdote should cover a *single* incident and should be written as soon after the behavior episode as possible. When this is impossible, a few phrases or key words should be noted for elaboration at a later time. The period of time between the observation and the completed write-up may affect the accuracy of the record. Such a concern led the Council for Exceptional Children to recommend that anecdotal records be written within twenty-four hours of the behavioral incident or action.[13] Included in the record should be the date, time, setting, and situation which provided the background for the incident. All persons involved in the episode should be clearly identified. Responses, reactions, and especially direct quotations should be recorded. "Mood cues,"[14] such as postures, gestures, facial expressions, and voice qualities also should be noted. (These very important aspects of behavior were discussed in Chapter 2.) It is imperative that the anecdote maintain the original sequence of action: (1) a beginning that includes details regarding the setting; (2) a description of the action in the sequence observed; and (3) an ending that describes how the episode was concluded. The length of time covered by the observation also should be indicated in some way. If the behavior recorded in the anecdote was previously observed, this should be specified along with a notation of the past frequency of the behavior.

Forms for reporting observations are available, and two are shown in Figures 3.1 and 3.2. Anecdotal record forms usually provide space for identifying information, description of the behavioral episode, and the observer's comments or interpretations. As suggested by the formats of the record forms in Figures 3.1 and 3.2, interpretation of an incident, if included, is separated from factual material. Interpretation composed of personal comments or hypotheses is noted in a special section or is written on the reverse side. If opinions and comments are not put into a separate section, there is likely to be a distortion of facts as Kiley[15] illustrates in the two anecdotes related in Figures 3.3 and 3.4. Both anecdotes describe the same incident. The anecdote reported in Figure 3.3 represents a fairly objective presentation of the observed incident, although the phrase *each time it seemed to make more noise* could possibly be questioned on the grounds that it is judgmental. But that phrase does help the reader understand what prompted the teacher to tell Tricia not to keep stacking the books over and over again. Ideally, the teacher should have included exactly what he or she said to the student and the manner in which it was said. The student could very well have been reacting to the manner (e.g., tone of voice) in which the teacher corrected her. The record is concluded with a somewhat questioning and even sympathetic attitude on the part of the teacher. The version of the anecdote presented in Figure 3.4 shows how evaluative statements mixed with factual information can affect the description of an event. The phrases *as usual, deliberately, another*

## Anecdotal Record Form

Child's name _____    Date _____

Observer _____    Place _____

| Incident observed | Comments |
|---|---|
|  |  |

Figure 3.1. Anecdotal Record: Form A

Anecdotal Record Form

Child Development Laboratory

Child _____          Observer _____

Where observed _____          Time and date _____

Anecdote:

Interpretation:

Recommendations:

**Figure 3.2.** Anecdotal Record: Form B

Anecdotal Record

Student's name:  Tricia "X"                                    Date:  10/12/7-
Age:  13                                                       Length of observation:  15 minutes
Name of observer:

Description of Incident

   Tricia came into the English class about five minutes after the bell had rung and dropped her
books on her desk; two of them slipped to the floor. It took her a few minutes to get them back into
order. Some of the class laughed when the books hit the floor. After picking them up, she stacked
them in rows, over and over again at her desk. Each time it seemed to make more noise. When I told
her to stop doing this, she said, "Yeah, O.K., you don't have to holler." A few minutes later, she put
her head down on the desk. When I asked her to sit up, she said, "Ah, let me sleep. Your class is so
boring, it would put anyone to sleep." Again there was some laughing. I told Tricia that she couldn't
sleep in class, but I would give her a pass to go to the nurse's office for the rest of the period and that
I would see her after class. She took her books and went to the nurse's office.

Interpretation

   Tricia was making a bid for attention today, and she got it. I did not report her to the principal,
but later in the nurse's office, I tried to talk to her. She would not discuss her behavior. I warned her
that I would not allow any further activities of this kind. I don't know what caused her to act like
this. She has never been any problem in class before; she may have been seeking attention or releasing
some frustration which was already built up before she got to my class.

**Figure 3.3.** Sample of an Anecdotal Record Without Judgmental Statements Included in the Description

Anecdotal Record

Student's name:  Tricia "X"                                    Date:  10/12/7-
Age:  13                                                       Length of observation:  15 minutes

Description of Incident

   Tricia came into the English class late as usual and deliberately dropped her books on her desk,
another of her attention-getting tactics. They scattered and fell to the floor, disrupting the class.
Students went off into gales of laughter. She wasted as much time as she could picking them up and
getting into her seat. During class, she shuffled her books repeatedly and was very fidgety. I told her
to stop and she made one of her smart remarks. Later she put her head down on the desk, which she
knows is against the school rules, and I told her to sit up straight or to go to the nurse's office if she
felt ill, though I knew she was faking. Again, she answered rudely and loudly. Naturally, I could not
tolerate this kind of insolence, but after a few minutes, I gave her a note to go to the nurse's office.

Interpretation

   Tricia needs discipline. If you don't stop her, she'll disrupt the class all period long.

**Figure 3.4.** Sample of an Anecdotal Record with Judgmental Statements in the Description

*one of her attention-getting tactics,* and *I could not tolerate this kind of insolence* suggest that the teacher was quite angry and not completely objective. The contents of Tricia's "smart remarks" are not reported as in the first anecdote nor are the specifics of her rude and loud remarks given. Finally, in the interpretation, no allowance is made for possible mitigating circumstances, and there is no mention of questions that remain to be answered. This comparison of the two anecdotal records emphasizes how important it is for the observer to confine subjective thoughts and feelings to an interpretive comments section.

This anecdote illustrates an adequate descriptive write-up:

> *May 28, 1975, 1:40 P.M.* During free play, Lance and three other children were playing in the sandbox. They had been playing for about five minutes. [Setting is established.] I noticed that the other children would not give a shovel and sand pail to Lance. I walked over and asked why they would not share their sand toys. Lance said, "They don't like me. They won't let me play." Mary, one of the playmates, said, "Lance uses bad words." Lance lowered his head. "Is it true?" I asked. Lance replied in a soft voice, "Sometimes." [Objective description includes actions of the child and others involved, with direct quotations and "mood cues."] I urged the children to try hard to play together nicely and to get along. Lance was given a shovel and the group played together until we asked all the children to come inside at 2:00 P.M. [Episode is complete and reveals the outcome.]

Although a single ancedote, such as the foregoing, usually provides only limited insight into development and behavior, the accumulation of anecdotal information over a period of time contributes toward a total picture of an individual child. Anecdotal information, which is often unavailable by other means, is especially valuable in generating hypotheses to explain a child's behavior. Hypotheses based on anecdotal data as well as on the observer's knowledge of child behavior and development may be tested against facts accumulated through additional observations. If these observations do not validate all of the hypotheses, more information about the child may be secured through such means as additional anecdotes, standardized test results, and interviews. In light of these new data, the hypotheses may be reevaluated, and if confirmed, considered validated conclusions.

Anecdotes reporting a child's behavior in or out of the classroom may describe either routine behavior or what seems to the observer to be significant behavior episodes. Conversations with the child also may reveal noteworthy information that should be recorded. Of particular importance are reports stimulated by parent conferences and home visits. In view of a teacher's busy schedule, several weeks or even months may be required before a meaningful amount of anecdotal data can be accumulated regarding an individual child. Yet, a few anecdotes on a child each month should give a good idea of what the child is like. Work conducted at the University of Maryland Institute for Child Study has revealed that the average amount of time needed to write an anecdotal description is approximately eight minutes.[16] This implies that some anecdotes may take less time and that other more complex ones may require longer than the average amount of time.

The anecdote has been used sparingly in child development research. Navarra investigated the development of scientific concepts in a young child using the anecdotal method.[17] These three anecdotal reports illustrate a child's use of self-references in conceptual development.

> **6PE1055—January 29, 1952**
> L. B. recalled a story which had been read to him two days ago. He made reference to the fact that the tiger had killed some people and asked, "What do tigers do when they are happy?" Mother replied, "They don't seem to be happy very often, do they?" L. B. persisted, "Aren't they happy when they're with children?" Mother said, "Well, tigers usually stay by themselves; and mothers and fathers wouldn't allow them near children."

**7PE1188—February 20, 1952**

L. B. saw a picture of a crocodile swimming after a person and attempting to eat him. When this scene was over, L. B. asked, "Why are crocodiles hard?" His mother explained that the skin was quite rough and hard. L. B. pinched his own flesh and said, "My skin isn't hard." He poked at his mother and remarked, "Yours isn't hard either." Then he added, "Mommy, if I was a crocodile, I would be a good crocodile."

**8PE1910—May 15, 1952**

L. B. had just awakened. He was sitting on the edge of the bed when he inquired, "Mommy, why do they keep gorillas locked in cages?" His mother explained that it would be dangerous to have a gorilla free among people since it might attack someone. L. B. listened attentively and then asked, "Are monkeys bad animals?" Mother asked, "Do you think they're bad animals?" L. B. quickly replied, "No, but sometimes they're locked in cages. Mommy, are the gorillas nice to other gorillas?"[18]

The purpose of Navarra's study was to provide for the full and immediate recording of child behavior unrestrained by preconceived hypotheses. All pertinent information was noted as the observations were made. Each episode included the date, time of day, and sometimes the duration of activity. No interpretations were offered at the time of recording; only what the child said and did was included in the record. Since some of the child's activity was not accompanied by verbalization, Navarra supplemented the anecdotal descriptions with photographs as a means of recording nonverbal behavior. The method of analysis involved the making of inferences or of tentative hypotheses based on aspects of behavior. Navarra used these hypotheses as a foundaton for theoretical segments of the data. Organization of the more than 4,500 anecdotes according to conceptual topics was completed later.

Other research has utilized the anecdotal technique as a method of data collection. Wann and his co-workers studied the intellectual development of three- to six-year-old children.[19] Through anecdotal reports, they discovered what the children understood about their world of people and things. Children's concern with weather phenomena is illustrated by these anecdotes:

Four-year-old Warren thought ice was made of air but Bobby corrected this impression, "No, Warren, water makes ice."

"Yes," replied Warren, "and snow is a pillow on the ice. It's different than water."

Five-year-old Alyson presses the teacher for information about snow.

Alyson:  Teacher, what causes snow?

Teacher:  When the air on the earth where we live is warmer than the air up in the sky, the warm and cold air mix and cause water. If it is cold enough, the water freezes and causes snow.

Alyson:  Well, why is it white?

Teacher:  When drops of water freeze they become white. You know, sometimes when it is cold outside water gets on the warm window.

Alyson:  Yes, it's white, and I wipe it off with my hand so I can see outside.

Teacher:  Yes, that is the same thing that happens in the sky.[20]

The researchers also found that young children are aware of certain social amenities as reflected in these anecdotes:

"You didn't have to throw my girl friend on the floor. You don't dance like that. You better watch out because I'm going to marry Cheryl when I grow up and just don't treat her like that. Right, teacher? Boys don't throw girls down on the floor when dancing. You are suppose to act nice to the girls."

Anita is talking to the teacher as she undresses after outdoor play. "Would you unbutton my top button, please? I always say please because it's nice to say please."

On the way in from outdoor play, five-year-old Larry had tried to choke Luke.

Dana:      I'll sure be glad when Larry learns his lesson.

Teacher:  What lesson does he need to learn?

Luke:      Not to touch things.

Lisa:      He needs a good lesson.

Teacher:  What kind of lesson?

Lisa:      A good lesson. How to do good things.[21]

Wann found that children actively strive to understand the world beyond the here and now. Such an attempt is illustrated by this anecdote which is based upon a group interaction of five-year-old children:

Many of the children had seen dinosaurs on television, and at their request, the teacher read them *The Book of Prehistoric Animals.* One morning Teddy brought some plastic dinosaurs from home. He put them in a circle around a small piece of white paper and pretended they were dancing around a pudding.

Fred joined him and said, "I have some dinosaurs too."

Mat, who was nearby, exclaimed, "Let's make a family of them!"

Chris, John, and Brandon joined the group, who by this time had moved to the block area.

Mat informed the newcomers, "We're building a home for the dinosaurs."

"Don't you need some people for the animals to eat?" asked Brandon.

"The people will eat the dinosaurs," responded Chris.

"Dinosaurs didn't eat people. They weren't around at the same time as dinosaurs," said Fred.

John, who was at work with the blocks, exclaimed, "I'm building a dinosaur track. Dinosaurs at fifty miles per hour."

"This is a dinosaur fort," exclaimed Brandon.

"Do you think there were railroad tracks as that time?" asked the teacher.

"Yes," replied John.

"No!" exclaimed Chris.

"Railroad tracks came very, very much later than dinosaurs," the teacher added.[22]

With the use of anecdotal records, Wann and his co-workers believed that they had overcome many of the limitations inherent in obtaining young children's responses in structured interviews and laboratory settings. Also, they seemed to have accomplished most of the objectives of their investigation by employing the anecdotal method.

As with all direct observation methods, the anecdotal record is not without its limitations. Traxler has listed some of them.

1. It is apparent, of course, that an anecdotal record can be valuable only if the original observation is accurate and is correctly recorded; otherwise, it may be worse than useless.

2. Many persons find it extremely difficult to write with complete objectivity, but practice will do a great deal to overcome the tendency to intersperse the report of behavior with statements of opinion.

3. A pernicious but fortunately rare use of anecdotal records is the employment of them for defense purposes.

4. It is evident that there is danger in lifting a behavior incident out of the social setting in which it occurred and reporting it in isolation.

5. At best, only a small proportion of the total number of significant behavior incidents for any pupil will find their way into anecdotal records.

6. Some persons fear that anecdotes, through preserving a record of unfortunate behavior incidents on the part of certain pupils, may prejudice their success long afterward, when the behavior is no longer typical of them.

7. It cannot be too strongly emphasized that the adoption of a system of anecdotal records is no small commitment and that it will inevitably add to the load of the entire staff, particularly the counselors and the clerical staff.

8. There is some danger that anecdotal records will throw the need for better adjustment of certain pupils into such high relief that too marked an effort will be made to short-cut the adjustment process.

9. Undesirable behavior, because of its nuisance aspect, is likely to make a stronger impression on teachers than desirable behavior.

10. Occasionally teachers will observe incidents that are not at all typical of the behavior of the pupil concerned.[23]

In addition to these limitations cited by Traxler, anecdotal records also present some practical problems. Anecdotal records are time-consuming to write.[24] Collected over a year or even a semester, they can create a storage problem.[25] Although qualitatively a very rich source of data, anecdotal descriptions do not lend themselves to quantitative analysis. Still, in the final analysis, the advantages of anecdotal records can be weighed successfully against their limitations. Anecdotes that describe child behavior in a number of settings and under a variety of circumstances provide information which is not readily available to all professionals who deal with children. When the anecdotal record is considered as one part of the total evaluation of an individual child and is integrated with all other available information, it can illuminate important characteristics of the child and help us see patterns of behavior that lead to a better understanding of the youngster. Greater understanding of individual children is the first step toward providing for the next steps in their development, guidance, and education.

A final word should be said about the maintenance and use of anecdotal reports. The Council for Exceptional Children has issued a policy statement that is appropriate for consideration as we conclude this section.

> All recorded descriptions shall be placed in the child's "education records" (cumulative, permanent) within five school days after completion.
>
> All anecdotal records in the Child's education records shall be evaluated in relation to the child's present individual education plan each time that the plan is reviewed which must occur no less than annually.
>
> If, after a determination has been made that an individual anecdotal record has no relation to the child's individual education plan and program, it shall be removed from the record and destroyed.
>
> Anecdotal records shall remain within the child's official records for as long as they remain directly related to the child's education plan and program.
>
> In all instances the collection, maintenance, and use of anecdotal records shall conform to all other requirements relating to the collection, maintenance, and use of school records.[26]

These ethical guidelines guard against the potentially damaging effects of an outdated single anecdote or an isolated interpretation that may remain in a child's file for many years. One possible solution to this, other than the preceding recommendations, is to maintain ancedotal material in a confidential file separate from the permanent record or cumulative folder. Teachers and counselors would therefore continue to have the benefit of these materials but would be reminded periodically to destroy reports that have outlived their usefulness, without disturbing more permanent materials. Also, other personnel who have access to a child's cumulative folder would not necessarily be allowed entry into the anecdotal file.[27] In summary, Kiley has written that "used in a positive manner and fully cognizant of the variety of errors which can occur . . . anecdotal records can evidence sincere interest by the teacher and counselor to understand their students and counselees."[28]

## SPECIMEN RECORDS

A specimen record is "a detailed, sequential, narrative account of behavior and its immediate context as seen by skilled observers. The account describes in concrete particulars the stream of an individual's behavior and habitat."[29] This narrative technique has been used to describe the behavior of children in school, in the home, at camp, and in other settings within the community.[30] Recorded sequences have spanned periods ranging from a few minutes to a full day.[31] The time and place are selected by the observer, but the behavior and events are not observed in any selective manner; specimen records are atheoretical. The observer "aims to make a faithful record of 'everything' as it comes in the behavior and situation of the child."[32]

This is a sample of one of Barker and Wright's specimen descriptions:

> Raymond continued climbing the tree, cautiously grasping one branch and then another, and fixing his feet firmly. He called out to Stewart in a playfully boastful manner. "Stewart, this tree is harder to climb than the other one."
>
> Stewart called back very firmly and definitely, "No, it isn't."
>
> When Raymond was as high as it seemed safe to climb, he settled in a crotch of the tree with his hands gripped tightly around the branches.

Exuberantly, he sang out, "Owww, owww, whee. Do you see me?" Since the evening was very still and there were few distracting noises, his voice carried far.

Raymond cocked his head as if listening for an echo, but there was none. It seemed that he listened with pleasure to the effect his singsong had upon the quiet evening air.[33]

As can be seen from this protocol, the specimen record provides a description of the child's behavior and its context. It may also include interpretations about the situation and behavior. These *immediate inferences* are usually differentiated from objective material by italics, although this is not shown above. Words and phrases such as *cautiously, very firmly and definitely,* and *exuberantly* provide inferences about the child's perceptions, feelings, and motives and are typically noted in the specimen description. According to Wright, such spur-of-the-moment judgments enrich the record without measurably reducing its validity.[34] *Minor interpretations* based upon observations over a period of time are also permitted. These interpretative statements offer information that might otherwise be overlooked. They are set apart in an indented paragraph and are sometimes italicized.

7:03  It seemed that Raymond tried to figure out a good retort, for he sat motionless.

Suddenly he yelled with playful intensity, "No, in bed!"

> *Raymond was evidently getting a good deal of pleasure from this conversation.*

Stewart's immediate answer was, "Yeah. In the hospital. In bed in the hospital." He spoke somewhat derisively.

Raymond seemed at a loss for an answer.

After a brief silence he climbed up a little farther.

> *He seemed satisfied with his achievement in reaching the new position.*[35]

Finally, there may be generalizations in the protocol based upon theories of child behavior and development. Called *professional or technical interpretations,* they are allowed only after the specimen description has been completed and are separated in some way from the narrative record.

> *The evidence suggests that in "accidentally" breaking the new briar pipe, after listening in on the argument between his parents, Tom was manifesting repressed aggression against his father.*[36]

It should be emphasized again that theorizing is done only *after* the specimen record has been made.

Analysis of observational data obtained through specimen recording may be approached in several ways.[37] The raw material of a specimen record can be examined for instances of certain behaviors by using scale values such as *very often* (3), *sometimes* (2), *infrequently* (1), and *never* (0), which allow the summation of scores for broad categories of behavior such as language, perceptual-motor, and social. Another possible analytical scheme is to calculate scores by adding the time spans of different recurring behaviors or by summing the number of time intervals that encompass selected behavioral phenomena. Existing observer systems also can be applied to the mass of data available in the specimen record. The record can be coded, after the fact, using the categories of a system, and the frequency of the various types of behavior can be figured. The most widely known method of analyzing specimen records has been developed by Wright, but it is also the most complex of the procedures used to divide the stream of behavior.[38] This is an excerpt from a specimen record which has been broken down into parts for purposes of analysis:

1

The mother went into the bedroom and said, "Margaret, Margaret, it's time to get up; you have to go to Bible School," coaxingly calling Margaret out of her sleep.

Margaret muttered very, very sleepily, "I hope they don't start," as if she didn't want Bible School to be.

> I took this to mean that if Bible School didn't start she wouldn't have to get up.

The mother said very pleasantly, "Yes, dear, it does start."

Margaret rolled over.

Mrs. Reid walked out of the room.

Margaret was again seemingly sound asleep.

2

8:11. Returning, the mother said more firmly, "Margaret, get up so you can get to Bible School on time."

Then she turned to me and said, "She's sleeping so soundly I hate to wake her."

Turning to Margaret, she said coaxingly and in a loving tone of voice, "Come on, honey, get up; you have to get ready for Bible School."

3

Margaret groaned and stretched way out.

The mother pulled down the covers.

Margaret put her arms clear above her head and raised herself by using her heels and her head as supports, wiggling as she did so.

The mother then asked, "Well, how do you feel?" in a very pleasant tone of voice, as she sat on the edge of Margaret's bed.

Margaret said very, very sleepily, "O.K.," and the mother absently murmured, "Huh?"

Margaret said, "O.K., I don't have a cold."

This was said a little less sleepily in the tone of one who is telling something of great interest.

The mother asked, "You don't have a cold?"

Margaret muttered, "Huh," still rather sleepily, lapsing back to her former sleepy state.

The mother asked pleasantly, "Do you want to go to Bible School?"

Margaret murmured, so sleepily as hardly to say a word at all, "Yes."

*(Left margin labels: Coming Awake — bracketing section 1; Stretching — bracketing section 3; Exchanging Remarks with Mother — bracketing sections 2 and 3)*

4

8:12. The mother urged, "Well, let's get dressed."

As Margaret started to slide off the bed, her mother said quickly, "Wait." Then she explained, "Get your shoes and socks so you won't have to get your feet dirty."

Margaret sat on the edge of the bed where she was before her mother's voice arrested her slide to the floor.

5

As the mother reached for her foot, Margaret said sleepily, "I want to lie down."

The mother laughed and said, "So you want to lie down and go to sleep again."

She let Margaret lie down.

Margaret lay with her head at the foot of the bed this time.

6

Margaret then stretched as far as she could with her arms back, raising up and wiggling.

It was almost as if she were shedding her sleep like a snake sheds its skin.

Her mother laughed at her pleasantly.

7

Margaret said cautiously, "A hairpin came out."

> Her hair was done up in bobby pins for curling purposes.

Then she asked with a great deal more interest, much more animated than she had been, "Do you see a curl?"

Margaret wiggled some more.

The mother didn't say anything.

"I took a hairpin out," said Margaret with firmness, almost with a note of defiance.

The mother said, "So you took a hairpin out," as if "so what."

> I gathered that Margaret was pestering her mother. After saying the hairpin came out had brought no reprimand, she seemed to be trying to get one by saying she took it out.

Margaret took out several more hairpins, reaching rather lazily up to remove them.

She looked cautiously at her mother.

Getting no response, she didn't bother to look at her mother any more.

Margaret watched her mother's hand as if to make sure she was keeping the hairpins safely.

*(margin labels:* Getting Dressed; Lying Down; Stretching; Taking Bobby Pins Out*)*

Getting Dressed ⎰ Taking Bobby Pins Out ⎰ Discussing ⎰ Curls with Mother

8

8:13. She took several more hairpins from her hair and said, "Do you see a curl?" rather eagerly.

The mother said, "I see a lot of them that are going to be curls."

Margaret took a few more bobby pins out and said again, "Do you see a curl now?" a bit more eagerly.

The mother answered, "Yes, I see a curl," as if she knew she had to say so before she would have any peace.

The mother finished putting on the shoes and socks for Margaret and told her to take off her pajamas and put on her panties.

Without saying anything, Margaret put her feet off the bed rather lazily.

She slid slowly to her feet.[39]

According to Wright's method of analyzing specimen records, a record must first be read in its entirety. Then, the behavioral stream must be divided into segments that indicate the beginning and ending of episodes. Behavior episodes are units of action and the coexisting situation. Each episode is identified by a title and number, with numbering being consecutive. Usually, a participial phrase is chosen that reflects as clearly and precisely as possible what the child did during an episode. Action may be singular and undivided as shown in "Stretching," or it may be broken down into subordinate parts as in "Getting Dressed." It also can be seen that Margaret did more than one thing at a time at some points; during parts of the behavioral sequence, two or even three episodes took place concurrently. For instance, "Lying Down" overlapped with the initial part of "Getting Dressed," and the early phase of "Discussing Curls with Mother" overlapped with the concluding segment of "Taking Out Bobby Pins." Overlapping is indicated by the parallel placement of brackets. Readers who are interested in learning more about Wright's complicated process of dismantling and analyzing specimen records are referred to his excellent book *Recording and Analyzing Child Behavior*.[40]

There are some guidelines that have proved to be beneficial to observers in the development of specimen records.[41] First, the length of the observation needs to be limited, preferably to no longer than thirty minutes at a time. Should extensive records be necessary, more than one observer is required. For example, in a now classic study, Barker and Wright used eight observers to record the behavior of a seven-year-old boy for an entire day.[42] Another guideline recommends that the observer make notations at the scene of the observed behavior in order to insure detailed and accurate reporting of events and circumstances in their true order. Observations also should be timed in some way so as to allow the observer to later determine the approximate duration of an episode. Indications of time can be made at intervals of one minute or more. If possible, the behavioral accounts should be recorded by dictation immediately after they are observed. When this is done, an interrogator who has listened to the original dictation should be called upon to question points that are unclear and to request further elaboration where needed. Ideally, the edited report should then be subjected again to interrogation and revised in a final form. Instead of writing a record, an observer may use a tape recorder in order to dictate his or her commentary coincidentally with the occurrence of a child's behavior.

To enhance the quality of specimen records, Wright has offered what he calls rules of reporting. The rules, which have proven to be of value in the writing of good records, are provided here.

1. Focus upon the behavior and the situation of the subject.

2. Observe and report as fully as possible the situation of the subject.

3. Never make interpretations carry the burden of description . . . . In the written version, all interpretative comments should be bracketed.

4. Give the "how" of everything the subject does.

5. Give the "how" of everything done by any person who interacts with the subject.

6. Report in order, in the final writing, all of the main steps through the course of every action by the subject.

7. Wherever possible, state descriptions of behavior positively.

8. Describe in some detail the scene as it is when each behavior setting is entered.

9. Put no more than one unit of molar behavior in one sentence . . . . In our record typescripts, every paragraph about a single molar behavior unit is blocked and single spaced, and a double space precedes and follows every such paragraph. This format is strongly urged for analysis purposes.

10. Put in one sentence [a description of] no more than one thing done by a person in the situation of the child.

11. Do not report observations in terms of time intervals . . . . The observer should let the behavior set its own limits.[43]

The specimen record and the anecdotal record have often been compared as observational child study techniques. The former method is assumed to be more "scientific" than the latter. However, anecdotal records can approach specimen records in scientific quality if some system is adopted whereby recording is done at preselected times or when certain situational or contextual conditions prevail.[44] Both techniques record the sequence of behavior in its original order, but differ in regard to reporting behavioral events and duration of observation. In specimen recording, the observer's responsibility is to describe continuously over a specified period of time (usually a relatively brief period) the behavior of the child being observed and the habitat or situation in which the behavior takes place. On the other hand, in anecdotal recording, the accounts of certain behavioral events that may or may not appear to be especially significant to the observer are chosen from episodes occurring over a relatively long period of time. Moreover, it is not uncommon for the writer of an anecdote to recount a situation after the total event has occurred. This is especially true for teachers who are responsible for large groups of children. In the specimen record, the observer divides the stream of behavior into segments after the description is completed, while the person developing the anecdotal description is concerned primarily about including a definitive beginning and end. Both techniques describe behavior in context. Specimen records covering only a few minutes are quite lengthy, whereas anecdotal records are characteristically brief. Inferences are usually discouraged in anecdotal descriptions, but they are encouraged in specimen descriptions. Finally, the observation and recording for specimen descriptions are intentionally unselective. Although the observer selects a child, time, and place for observation, he or she is entirely unselective with respect to his or her observation and recording. The observer records everything that is seen and heard. In contrast, the writer of the anecdote employs a method that is more selective and not as comprehensive.

There are a number of advantages to the use of specimen records. One obvious advantage is that no special observer skills are required by the procedure.[45] Other positive characteristics of the method include face validity;[46] permanence and comprehensiveness; recording of the behavior in context; narration in lay language; continuity; absence of theoretical bias; and freedom from the restriction of precoded categories, rating scales, and checklists.[47] Limitations of the specimen record include a lack of built-in provisions for quantification; dependence upon observation usually without instrumental aids; sheer bulk;[48] the difficulty in recording rapid, complex interacton;[49] and predisposition to measurement of individuals and not groups.[50] Despite its limitations, specimen recording is an indispensable part of child study. The richness of data obtained by this method cannot be surpassed by other observational strategies.

## RUNNING RECORDS

A recording technique that has been called a "close relative" to specimen descriptions is the running record.[51] Evolving from early diary descriptions and anecdotal records, the running record may be classified somewhere in between anecdotal and specimen records. Running records are more complete than anecdotes but less precise, less comprehensive, and more informal than specimen records. Unlike specimen recording which requires that the observer be a nonparticipant in the action so that he or she can record *everything* without interruption, the running record demands less rigorous detail. Consequently, it is used frequently by classroom teachers who are directly involved on a day-to-day basis with students and who have little time to themselves to record material. Usually the teacher jots down notes at the actual moment and develops a fuller record later in the day as time allows. These on-the-spot narrative records provide a chronological and unclassified account of a child's behavior in various situations (e.g., at arrival and dismissal, snack time, toileting, story time, and free play). When accumulated over a period of time, running records reveal patterns of responses and changes in behavior. They provide data regarding intellectual development, physical style and growth, and adjustment to school—information that is of great value to the teacher, next year's teacher, the guidance counselor, and parents. The running record is the basis for most case studies of children.

Although many of the same guidelines for the preparation of specimen records and anecdotal records also apply to running records, a few suggested practices are listed here:

1. Take records as often as possible and at many different periods of the day.

2. Record behavior in a variety of situations and over an extended period of time.

3. Indicate the setting, the stimulus for the activity, the child's reactions, and the child's behavior after the episode. Pay special attention to the child's interaction with the environment.

4. Be sensitive to the child's verbal and nonverbal behavior.

5. Use precise words that describe not only what the child does but also *how* he or she does it.

6. Interpret the behavior by relying primarily on objective data.

7. Prepare a final summary that includes trends of behavior, problems, evaluations of growth and development, prediction of future behavior and development, and recommendations.

The reader is referred to Cohen and Stern's *Observing and Recording the Behavior of Young Children*[52] for additional guidelines and for examples of descriptive records. An on-the-spot record of a two-year-old's experience with play materials is provided here for illustrative purposes:

Two-year-old Penny at the sandbox:

Penny runs to sandbox carrying tablespoon, empty orange juice can, and toy plastic teacup. She climbs down into sandbox, sits down in corner, and silently and intently begins to fill can with sand, using spoon. She is oblivious to several other children around her. She stands up, dumps sand from can onto asphalt outside sandbox. She bangs can down on sand several times, then gently pats sand with open palm, saying "Cake." Rene, aged four, comes up. She starts to take can from Penny, saying, "Can I have that?" Penny pulls the can away and stands still, staring at Rene. Teacher gives Rene a small spoon and plastic cup. She stands beside Penny and they both begin to spoon sand, occasionally smiling at each other. Penny climbs out of the sand to bench where teacher is sitting. She dumps the sand onto the bench and then spoons it back into can. She dumps it onto the bench again, and pats it gently. "I'm making cake." She takes a spoonful of sand and puts it on teacher's hand. She looks up and sees Patty on the swing. She runs over to her, carrying spoon with her . . . [53]

The running record has been used in systematic studies of children. During the 1930s, Susan Isaacs, a teacher in Cambridge, England, used the running record as her method of data collection and published *Intellectual Growth in Young Children*[54] and *Social Development in Young Children*.[55] Another teacher, Louise Woodcock, collected detailed running records of two-year-old children in a nursery school setting and published her findings a few years later in *Life and Ways of the Two-Year-Old: A Teacher's Study*.[56] This monograph is still considered one of the best descriptions of two-year-olds in child development literature.

## TIME SAMPLING

Time sampling is a very popular method of recording observation data. In contrast to the anecdotal record, specimen description, and running record which impose little or no structure on the behaviors to be recorded, the time sampling technique employs constraints on the behavioral units that can be recorded by specifying what, when, and how recording is to take place. The origin and development of this child study technique has been described by Arrington[57] and by Olson and Cunningham.[58] According to Arrington, the primary assumption underlying time sampling is that

> . . . reliable quantitative measures of the frequency with which an individual nor-
> mally displays a given behavior in a given situation can be obtained from records of
> the occurrence of the behavior in a series of randomly distributed short-time inter-
> vals of uniform length, and that similar measures descriptive of the normal inci-
> dence of a given behavior in a group of individuals can be derived by combining
> such records for the individual members of the group.[59]

In a later publication, Arrington formally defined time sampling as a "method of observing behavior of individuals or groups under the ordinary conditions of everyday life in which observations are made in a series of short-time periods so distributed as to afford a representative sampling of behavior under observation.[60] Goodenough described time sampling in a similar manner:

> . . . the observation of everyday behavior of an individual or a group of individuals
> for definite short periods of time and the recording of the occurrence or non-
> occurrence of certain specified and objectively defined forms of behavior during
> each of these periods.[61]

With time sampling techniques, the observer first defines the behavioral event as precisely as possible. For example, *talking* might be defined as "anything said by the child to a classmate or teacher." The behavior must be described clearly so that an observer can discriminate between it and other similar responses. Next, the observer divides the observation period into intervals and notes these preselected times on an observation form. The data sheet usually consists of rows and columns with each row designated for a category of behavior and each column assigned to an observation interval. If an observation period is sixty minutes, the child can be observed for evidence of the target behavior(s) for successive intervals of one minute or any other interval (e.g., fifteen seconds, thirty seconds, etc.) that would seem appropriate for study of the behavior in question. A timing device may be used to remind the observer to prepare to record. At the appropriate recording time, the behavior of the child is coded as *present* or *absent.* Using "talking" as an example, if the child is actively talking at the prescribed time, the observer marks a *1* on the recording sheet, but if the child is not talking, the observer puts a *0* in the square corresponding to that interval. For this reason, time sampling has sometimes been called zero-one sampling.[62] Other symbols may be used to denote occurrence or nonoccurrence.

Time sampling does not result in frequency measures; occurrence or nonoccurrence rather than frequency is scored. Therefore, scores reflect the number of intervals or the percentage of intervals that included at least one incidence of the behavior(s) being studied. The scores may be combined or averaged over many time sampling sessions or calculated for several children. When time samples are gathered during the same observation period each day, such as between 9:00 A.M. and 10:00 A.M., they are called *fixed* samples. Often there is some temporal delimitation of the behavior being studied, and a specific time for observation is indicated. Time samples also may be obtained at randomly selected periods of time. These are called *randomized* samples. The random method probably provides a more representative sample of behavior, assuming that behaviors at school or at home from 9:00 A.M. to 10:00 A.M. may be different from those at other times during the day. It should be noted that several behaviors can be recorded simultaneously and that more than one child can be studied at a time.

## POINT VERSUS INTERVAL SAMPLING

There are two basic types of time sampling: time *point* and time *interval.* In time point sampling, coding occurs precisely at the end of an interval. Notation of occurrence or nonoccurrence is made at that instantaneous point, without regard for any activity not at that point. If the record is divided into thirty-second intervals, the observer determines whether the target behavior is occurring at the end of each half minute by looking for the behavior in question for one or two seconds following the interval. In time *interval* sampling, the observation session is divided into a number of equal, continuous intervals, and each behavior under study is scored once and only once if it occurs during the interval, rather than at the exact instant the interval is over. The behavior is scored as an occurrence if it spanned the entire interval, took place several times for brief durations during the interval, happened during the last seconds of the interval, or extended from the previous interval to the present one. In the latter case, the behavior would be scored in both intervals. Again, the only criterion for occurrence is if the behavior was observed at least once during an interval. Hence, a behavior that was initiated in one interval, continued through a second, and ended sometime during the third would receive three scores—one for each of these intervals. A behavior that occurred three times during one interval would result in only one score.

**Time Point Sampling.** Of the many studies using time point sampling, only one will be cited as an example of child development research. Employing a multi-baseline design, Ayllon et al. explored the feasibility of a behavioral education alternative to drug control of hyperaction children.[63] They used a time point sampling procedure to record the hyperactive behavior of children in math and reading classes of a self-contained learning disability section in an elementary school. Arrangements were made to observe six children who had been identified as being hyperactive and who were taking medication for the condition. The response definition for hyperactivity included gross motor behaviors, disruptive noise with objects, disturbing others, orienting responses, blurting out, talking, and other miscellaneous behaviors. Math and reading performances were defined as responses to workbook problems. The children were observed for the forty-five-minute math and reading class periods. Each child was observed in successive order, using a time sample of twenty-five seconds. At the end of the twenty-five-second interval, the child's behavior was recorded as showing hyperactivity or not. The observer marked a slash (/) in the appropriate interval, if one or more hyperactive behaviors took place. If no hyperactive behaviors occurred at that interval, a zero (0) was recorded. The percentage of intervals in which the child displayed hyperactivity was calculated by dividing the number of intervals with such behavior by the total number of intervals the child was observed. During baseline, three of the most hyperactive children were identified for inclusion in the treatment program: an eight-year-old girl and nine- and ten-year-old boys. For the remainder of the experiment, these chronically hyperactive children were sampled every eighteen seconds for fifty times during each of the two class periods. A second baseline was obtained while the children were not on medication. Discontinuation of medication resulted in an increase in hyperactivity and a slight increase in math and reading performances. The behavior program for academic performance, which used token reinforcement, was then introduced to the children while they were off their medication. The contingency management techniques controlled the children's hyperactivity at a level comparable to that when they were using drugs. During the behavioral program, math and reading performances also improved substantially in the absence of medication.

**Time Interval Sampling.** Time interval sampling has been used a great deal in child development research. One interesting study by Allen and her associates examined the effects of social reinforcement on isolate behavior of a four-year-old girl who was enrolled in a university laboratory pre-school.[64] The child's teachers had become concerned because the youngster tended to isolate herself from other children but frequently sought the attention of adults. By closely examining the situation, the teachers discovered that the adult attention which was given to the little girl seemed to be contingent upon behaviors that were incompatible with behavioral interaction with peers. The staff subsequently developed a procedure to effect change in the child's isolate behavior.

> A plan was instituted to give Ann maximum adult attention contingent on play with another child, and minimum attention upon isolate behavior or upon interactions with an adult when alone. Approximately the same total amount of adult attention was available to Ann each day provided she met the criteria for obtaining such behavior from teachers.[65]

An attempt was made to control all variables except adult social interaction.

> No changes were to be made in the regular nursery school program or in supervisional assignments of the three teachers. Teachers were to continue to be physically present, as usual. The only change instituted was in the condition under which they were to give Ann attention, and this was governed by the schedule of reinforcement in effect at a given phase of the study.[66]

To evaluate changes in the girl's behavior, it was necessary to observe her proximity with adults and children and her interaction with them. A line from the observational record that shows five minutes of recorded behavior broken down into ten-second intervals is presented in Figure 3.5. The upper row of the record reveals that there were four intervals of proximity (i.e., physical closeness within three feet) and seven intervals of interaction (i.e., conversing, smiling, looking toward, touching, and/or helping) with adults during the five-minute period. The bottom row indicates that there was an increase in intervals showing interaction with other pupils toward the end of the five-minute period. During the first two minutes and twenty seconds there were six intervals of proximity to children and only one interval of interaction with children in contrast to two intervals of proximity and six intervals of interaction in the last one minute and thirty seconds. Additional

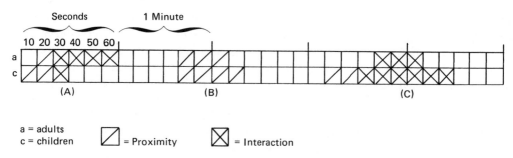

a = adults
c = children      ◩ = Proximity      ⊠ = Interaction

**Figure 3.5.** Sample Line from a Data Sheet Illustrating the Use of Time Interval Sampling in Child Development Research.

procedures were utilized that will not be discussed here, but the study demonstrated that application of reinforcement principles by teachers in a classroom setting increased the child's interaction with peers.

Since interval sampling, like point sampling, allows the study of many behaviors and more than one child at a time, elaborate symbol systems may be necessary for multiple event and/or multiple subject recording. Mattos describes a sample interval recording form that makes possible the simultaneous notation of sixteen different behavior categories.[67] The record in Figure 3.6 indicates that the three-minute observation period was divided into eighteen intervals of ten seconds each. For most of the first minute, the child was alone and nontask oriented. During this time, she emitted at least two eye grimaces and two rapid head jerks. Her fingers were in her mouth at some time during the first five intervals. She then emitted eye-mouth grimaces during the seventh and eighth intervals and jerked her head also in the eighth interval. During this period, she momentarily engaged in some task-oriented behavior. In the last seventy seconds of the observation period, the subject interacted in close proximity to another child, during which time she put her fingers in the mouth and emitted at least one eye-mouth grimace and one head jerk.

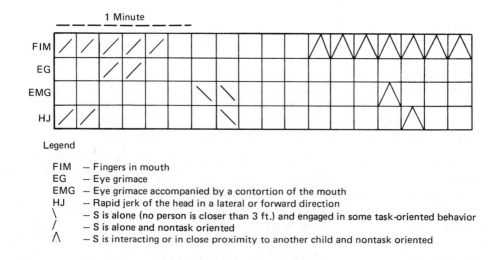

Legend

FIM — Fingers in mouth
EG — Eye grimace
EMG — Eye grimace accompanied by a contortion of the mouth
HJ — Rapid jerk of the head in a lateral or forward direction
\ — S is alone (no person is closer than 3 ft.) and engaged in some task-oriented behavior
/ — S is alone and nontask oriented
∧ — S is interacting or in close proximity to another child and nontask oriented

**Figure 3.6.** Illustration of Coded Recording of Multiple Behavior Categories

Mattos also addresses the problems of behavior sample selection, observation period duration, number of behavioral categories, and interval duration. The reader should consult that source as well as others[68] for further guidelines on issues relating to time sampling recording procedures.

Variations of time sampling have been used to study a number of child variables.[69] The popularity of this technique is attributable, in part, to its many advantageous qualities, some of which have been summarized by Wright:

> It limits with exactitude observed contents as well as temporal lengths of the behavior stream. It permits systematic control by selection of phenomena to be observed and studied. It insures representativeness and reliability by recording large numbers of commensurable observations. It is economical of research time and efforts. Its coding schemes minimize equivocal judgments and prescribe definite ways to quantify whatever is observed. It goes far to achieve standardization of observer and analyst as measuring instruments.[70]

But as with all child study techniques, time sampling has some delimitations. Its most outstanding shortcoming is that it divorces behavior from its coexisting situation. The method just yields relative frequencies of actions or situations and typically does not describe the components of an episode. Since time sampling lends itself to problems of incidence, it is appropriate only for behaviors or situations that occur with some degree of regularity. If the objective of the observation is that of estimation of the incidence of certain behaviors, time sampling is a highly regarded technique of child study.

## EVENT SAMPLING

Event sampling, another direct observation technique, focuses on unitary behavioral events as they naturally occur. Its main purpose is to examine the conditions under which certain kinds of events are triggered or to describe operationally recurring patterns of behavior. After deciding on events of a given class to be studied, the observer carefully defines the behavior, identifies the setting in which the event is likely to occur, waits for the event, and then records the episodes. Pilot observations may be helpful in defining the event and in determining where the observer should be stationed. For example, after the properties of a certain type of behavior like aggression had been specified in order to distinguish it from other forms of behavior, the observer probably would choose to pursue the aggressive events in a play-yard where there would be a greater probability of such behavior occurring than in a classroom. Each aggressive incident in the naturally occurring behavior stream of children would represent a sample of its class, regardless of its duration. The specific class of behavior or behavioral event labeled as "aggressive" might be defined as cursing, shoving, tripping, striking others, and throwing things at classmates. Whenever the observer saw an aggressive event occur on the playground, he or she would check the appropriate categories on a form or would record the event with a cassette tape recorder. Notations would be made regarding the children involved in the incident, the cause of the aggression, the outcome, and so on.

Although event sampling can describe in detail the behavioral sequence in context like the example just given, some observers prefer to note only the number of occurrences of a given event, since simply counting the number of times a discrete behavior occurs is also a legitimate form of event sampling. Examples of event sampling without narrative include counting the number of times a child goes to the restroom without assistance, the number of cooperative episodes, or the number of quarrels. This type of frequency recording obviously does not describe the behavior in relation to its contemporaneous conditions. Lack of information regarding precipitating states of affair, participants in the event, and the setting, as well as the absence of direct quotes and mood cues, may render the simple notation of occurrence less meaningful to the practitioner than records that also include narration. To facilitate the recording of events, an increasing number of observers are making use of carefully designed checklists and complex category systems. Still others are abandoning paper-and-pencil event sampling in favor of electronic event recorders (see Chapter 6).

In an early study, Helen Dawe used event sampling to investigate children's quarrels as they arose spontaneously in a nursery school setting.[71] Her subjects were forty children, about equally divided with regard to sex. They ranged in age from twenty-five to sixty months. From a convenient, central vantage point, Dawe watched for the development of quarrels among the children during morning free play. When a quarrel took place, she moved quickly and as unobtrusively as possible to the scene of action and used mimeographed forms to describe the episodes and the participants.

> Mimeographed blanks prepared in advance provided space for recording and check-ing the name, age, and sex of the children, the duration of the quarrel, what the children were doing and what difficulty arose, the types of behavior under proper categories (to be described), the motor and vocal activity, the outcome of the quarrel, and the aftereffects.[72]

The difficulties over which the quarrels started were categorized and defined. They included posses-sions, physical violence, interference with activity, and social adjustment. The type of behavior exhibited by a child during the quarrel was specified and coded according to seven categories: nonparticipator, precipitator, aggressive behavior, retaliative behavior, objecting behavior, undirected energy, or passive behavior. Under type of activity were included the motor and verbal accompani-ments of the quarrel. When possible, the children's conversation also was recorded. Outcome was categorized as yielding, compromise, or unsettled, and aftereffects were classified as cheerful or resentment. Event sampling of the children's difficulties revealed, among other things, that more quarrels occurred indoors than outdoors; quarrels outside lasted longer than those inside; the average duration of a quarrel was 23.62 seconds, with very few lasting more than one minute; quarrels of the older children lasted longer than those of the younger ones; boys quarreled more than girls; motor activity characterized almost all of the quarrels; silence, crying, or forbidding comments were common verbal accompaniments of the encounters; yielding to force was the most typical outcome; and quick recovery and little resentment characterized the majority of aftermaths.

Event sampling lends itself to the study of many different kinds of child behavior,[73] since any behavioral event that engages the observer's interest can be studied with this method. Kerlinger has identified a number of virtues of event sampling.[74] First, the events possess inherent validity because, unlike time sampling, they are natural lifelike situations. As such, they enable the observer to investi-gate relationships between behavior and its contemporaneous situation. The integral event also possesses a continuity of behavior not found in the more piecemeal behavioral units of time samples. Still another advantage of event sampling is related to its feasibility in studying episodes that are infrequent. Event sampling lends itself to the study of behavior with low incident rates, although it can be used equally well with frequently occurring behaviors. Conversely, other techniques, such as time sampling, may miss sporadic events altogether. It is not uncommon for observers to ask parents and other lay adults who are around the child for long periods of time to assist in the collection of certain event samples whose incidence is low and/or whose occurrence is typical in only certain settings. In spite of these advantages, event sampling may be viewed as violating the even larger continuity of behavior found in specimen descriptions. The solution to this problem is the use of event sampling with specimen narration in order to preserve at least the smaller continuities of behavior.[75]

## ENVIRONMENTAL ASSESSMENT

Children's behavior always occurs someplace, within the limits of a particular setting. Consequent-ly, ecologists urge us to examine not only behavioral units but also behavioral-environment units.

Description and evaluation of a child's environment provides valuable information regarding the external forces that shape the youngster's behavior. The study of a child is therefore incomplete without some assessment of his or her environments.

After the observer has identified the unit of environment to be studied, he or she must determine how to obtain a picture of that environment in a manner that will capture its full and complex character within a reasonable time span. A variety of techniques are available for this purpose: direct observation, still photography, motion pictures, videotapes, sketches, and drawings. There are also several different response formats for recording the observer's responses. Craik, a noted environmental psychologist, has described two formats that are especially applicable for our purposes.[76] In the first, called *free description,* the observer describes what is seen in his or her own words. The second is called *standardized description.* Here, the observer indicates his or her reactions by means of ratings, checklists, or other structured measures including observer systems. A number of scales are available to aid in the assessment of environments, and a few will be discussed later in this chapter.

## FREE DESCRIPTION

**Ecological Descriptions of the Home and Neighborhood.** This is an example of an ecological description of a child's home:

> The farm consists of several acres of farming land, and there is also some woodland. The house is a remodeled old house which gives the appearance of a new home. The outside is green asbestos siding. The porches are cement. The house is underpinned with cement blocks.
>
> The front yard is bare. There is no grass except tall Bermuda grass in the backyard that needs to be mowed down. The boys' wagons, tricycles, and other playthings were under one of the big trees in the front yard. The well is about ten feet from the back porch. Its curb is made of brick. Clapboards are laid across the top of the brick. The top hasn't been fixed yet. The backyard is comparatively small. The pasture fence comes to the edge of the yard. Inside the pasture are the truck garage, barn, and pigpens. The outdoor toilet is at the edge of the yard and fence, under some trees.
>
> The house has six rooms: two bedrooms, a living room, a kitchen, a dining room, and a place for a bath.
>
> Apparently Mrs. Beach is a good housekeeper. She has the shades, curtains, rugs, and furniture arranged neatly. The rugs were clean and the floor waxed. There was no bed in the living room. The living room furniture had some type of cover over it, probably old bedspreads. The covers were clean. In one corner was a tall cabinet radio. A heater (Warm Morning) was in the living room. In the kitchen Mrs. B has two stoves—one wood and one gas. There were built-in wooden cabinets along one wall. A dinette set was in the kitchen.[77]

The significance of the home aspect of a youngster's life space is emphasized by Gump: "The behavior opportunities available to a child are determined to a large extent by how much space is available within and around the home and how that space is structured and furnished."[78] Although the observer is limited in the conclusions that can be drawn from such general, free, descriptive information, the data do provide the basis for certain hypotheses regarding social class, values, and family life. They also are the source of many answers to questions posed by a child's behavior.

An excellent ecological write-up is presented by Brandt in *Studying Behavior in Natural Settings.*[79] The case is especially instructive because it illustrates the range of interpretations stimulated by descriptions of the microecology of the home environment.

**Data**

1. *Neighborhood.* Located on the fringe of a small New England town, a block away from storehouses, a rail line, supply depots, and rolling pastureland. The neighborhood houses are uniformly brick with white-painted wood trim; concrete walks connect these homes to a blacktop street. The lots are a quarter-acre in size with a larger backyard than front. The houses cover a rectangular ground space of 20 X 30 feet and are all single story. The probable room number would include a living room, kitchen, bath, two bedrooms, a hallway, and basement.

   The yards contain evergreen shrubs for landscaping, crabgrass, and small trees.

   Mrs. D's yard is unique in that it has two overturned metal lawn chairs in the front yard under a small beech tree. The backyard contains a black, small Scotch terrier chained to a small doghouse, a circular aluminum rope clothesline, and a small (possibly homemade) grill and pit. The yard generally appears as not so tidy or so well kept as adjacent yards. Weeds show here and there on the lawn, several papers are strewn about, and two large cans are under the beech tree.

2. *House Interior.* The front door, at middle front of the house, has cracking veneer at the base and three diagonally placed square windows in the top. It opens into the living room, a 10 X 20 foot room and directly opposite the opening into the hall. The floor is the most obvious part of the living room—creating an effect that is intensified by the soiled, pictureless, dark brown walls and ceiling. The wall is especially soiled at the corner of hall entrance and living room. The floor is rugless and very worn, covered with a moderate amount of dust. The lack of decoration and simplicity of furnishings further contribute to the plain effect of the room. The rest of the room is neat and free of clutter.

   A cloudy picture window at the front of the house is graced by a pink, new-looking Singer sewing machine on a worn wooden table. A faded slip-covered sofa is opposite the window, angled against the wall (slightly away from the wall at one end)—allowing for placement of TV dinner trays behind it. One end of the room, bounded by the front and hall entrances, is centered by a large-screen TV set upon which rests a contrastingly expensive looking man's black felt hat. The opposite side of the room is lined by two worn chairs—one forward of the other. End tables bound the sofa arms, and are topped by multicolored, crocheted, ruffled doilies, and by lamps. These doilies underlie and decorate cut-glass dishes of lemon drops and the lamps on each table.[80]

From the description, the observer singled out important details and formulated hypotheses followed by an interpretation of available data.

| Details | Suggesting the Following Hypotheses |
|---|---|
| 1. Yard not so well kept as neighboring yards; overturned lawn chairs; papers, cans, weeds | Inability or lack of interest in aspiring to middle-class ideal of neatness of yard, gardening, etc. (The neighborhood is obviously middle class, as seen by uniformity and size of homes, near-suburb location and landscaping.) |

| Details | Suggesting the Following Hypotheses |
|---|---|
| 2. Lack of rug; worn floors | No interest in caring for a rug or floors; difficulty in caring for or using a rug; insufficient funds for a rug purchase. |
| 3. Dirty walls, especially near hall entrance | Dirt concentrated at entrance to hallway suggests that corner might be used as a pivot point for young children or others. |
| 4. Lack of pictures, mirrors, faded slip cover, dust on floor, cloudy picture window; room arrangement lines walls without any esthetic flourish | Inability (physical, perceptual) or disinterest in cleaning or decorating. |

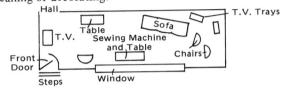

| Details | Suggesting the Following Hypotheses |
|---|---|
| 5. Large-screen TV; arrangement of a chair and sofa (see diagram) toward TV; TV dinner trays in living room | Meals accompany TV viewing; TV viewing is a popular form of recreation for a usual maximum of four seated people (3, sofa; 1, chair). |
| 6. Multicolored doilies and lemon drops placed together | Only form of decoration in room is placed with food, suggesting interest in food. |
| 7. One chair placed before the other, out of usual conversational grouping | Possibly easier seating for head of the house, perhaps a disabled or poorly sighted person. |
| 8. Expensive hat in cheaply furnished home | Male visitor's hat; husband's hat—who might have to dress expensively for a job with well-dressed people. |
| 9. Sewing machine in room; uncluttered room | Woman of house sews frequently; feminine member of house values neatness. |

## Interpretation

Neatness that would require hard labor is nonexistent in this house; for example, floors unwaxed, walls dirty, lawn chairs overturned, crabgrass lawn that is uncut. Certain aspects of esthetics usually observed were ignored: soiled walls, lack of decoration, dirty picture window, nonesthetic arrangement of furniture. The only esthetic part of the room were the doilies. Details from the above subconclusions further suggest:

1. This family ignores the esthetic for the pragmatic.

2. This family aspires somewhat to middle-class values in neatness (uncluttered room) and dressing well for the job (provided the hat is the husband's).

3. The lack of esthetics along with an emphasis on the pragmatic suggests that probably the feminine member or wife might have some physical disability or perceptual difficulty.

4. The family, as seen by the size of the house and amount of money spent on furnishings, appears to belong to the lower-middle-class socioeconomic bracket.[81]

To seek support for these interpretations, the observer interviewed residents of the house and obtained this information:

1. Mr. A. is unable to push a lawnmower or work in a garden easily. He also works at night, sleeps by day, and cannot devote much time to the yard.

2. Mr. A. is paralyzed from the waist down, walks on crutches, using a swing-through gait and leg-length braces. Therefore, he cannot use rugs on the floor and maintain maximum stability and mobility.

3. Mrs. A. is blind and walks into the wall when seeking the entrance to the hallway—hence the concentration of soil on that corner of the wall.

4. Mrs. A. has been blind since birth and therefore fails to show the same amount of attention as sighted wives to the front yard, pictures, sweeping up of floor dust, or window washing.

5. The family often eats and watches **TV** at dinner time.

6. Mrs. A. enjoys candy and is slightly overweight. It is interesting to note that the candy dish, which she frequents, is decorated by lacy doilies—items that by touch are esthetic to her.

7. The furniture is arranged for convenience. Mr. A. sits in the forward chair because it is easier for him to approach with crutches and he can better view the TV. (Last year he had his cataracts taken out and can see best at that distance.)

8. Mr. A. works a night shift as a receptionist at an exclusive country club; hence, he dresses well for his job.

9. Mrs. A. sews her own clothes, provided someone cuts the pattern for her.

10. Mrs. A. feels most comfortable when every item is in its customary place; thus the room is tidy and her memory does not fail her often.[82]

Descriptions of a youngster's environment by an outside observer should always be supplemented by discussions with the child in order to obtain his or her perceptions of the surroundings, because the "observed" environment is not always the "real" environment. Procedures such as interviews, life space surveys, or neighborhood mapping provide additional information about the child's range of environmental experiences to supplement the objective observations.[83]

**Ecological Descriptions of the School.** Assessment of the school environment is vital to the understanding of child behavior. Gump explains why:

Schools are where people live. The here-and-now quality of life for millions of children (and their teachers) is shaped by the conditions of the school environment. Each child between six and sixteen spends about 1,200 hours a year in a setting

cluster of society's choosing. The quality of these clusters and of children's experiences within them—apart from their capacity to train for the future—is surely
an important issue.[84]

Cartwright and Cartwright have identified four components of the instructional environment that
should be observed: people in the setting, the space and objects in it, the time arrangements, and the
management and teaching procedures used.[85] People in the school environment include teachers,
teacher aides, counselors, nurses, principals, coaches, custodians, cafeteria workers, and of course,
other children. Individuals within the setting interact to provide an overall climate which, in turn,
affects the student in different ways. Therefore, the number of children in the class, the ratio of boys
to girls, and the number of adults present should be considered when observing. The behavior of these
individuals also should receive attention. Because of their crucial implications for learning, teacher
behaviors are perhaps of greatest interest. Amount of space available, what is included in that space,
and how the objects within it are arranged represent dimensions of instructional environments that
are likewise important for observation. The size and arrangement of the classroom as well as available
materials and equipment are worthy of notation. Playgrounds also should be observed. It is helpful if
the observer makes a sketch of the classroom layout, indicating the location of learning centers, art
area, library corner, bookshelves, desks, storage closets, doors, windows, and so on. Notation of other
physical characteristics of the classroom also should be made, such as temperature, lighting, acoustics,
and room color. The outdoor play space should be diagrammed to show not only constructed
permanent structures (climbers, sandboxes, etc.) but also aspects of the natural environment (trees,
shrubbery, etc.). Movable equipment (tricycles, digging tools, exercise mats, etc.) should be included
in the pictorial diagram. Also deserving of the observer's attention are time variables in the classroom
environment. These include the manner in which routines are established, the schedules that are used,
and the length and variety of activities in which the children engage. Teaching methods and management procedures comprise another significant part of the classroom environment that should be
subjected to direct observation. All of the instructional environment components identified by
Cartwright and Cartwright influence the behavior of students.

Data on the educational environment can be described narratively and supplemented by diagrams
as recommended by the Cartwrights, or the information can be organized using the guidelines for
ecological write-ups recommended by Brandt.[86] Yet another possibility for describing the child's
educational setting has been suggested by Boehm and Weinberg.[87] They advocate the use of a chart
or worksheet to summarize the key components of the school setting. An example of their approach
is shown in Figure 3.7.

**Guidelines for Write-ups.** Brandt has written some helpful guidelines for the preparation of ecological descriptions. They apply equally to ecological write-ups regarding a child's home and neighborhood and to those concerning the child's school.

1.  Think ahead about items you will want to look for when you arrive on the
    scene.

2.  Develop a system for observing the environment such as noting the furnishings
    in each room, condition of the walls, ceiling, etc., as well as other materials in
    the room.

3.  Restrict the write-up to an objective and comprehensive itemization of what
    the environment comprises.

4.  Adequate time should be allowed for the write-up, after visiting the scene.[88]

**Key Components of a Setting**

Setting:  Middle-school library
Time:    Library period for eighth-grade pupils

| Physical Features | Objects | People | Activities |
|---|---|---|---|
| Rectangular room<br>Entrance and exit turnstile<br>Yellow colored walls<br>One large glass window<br>One small glass window<br>Two pillars<br>One adjoining room with a<br>  window door<br>One big door leading into library<br><br>Check out counter<br>Overhead fluorescent light turned<br>  on | Three rows of steel bookshelves<br>  outside<br>One wooden bookshelf against the<br>  'wall<br>Two yellow and one green chair<br>  with a small table in one corner<br>Six round tables, "natural wood,"<br>  each with five chairs<br>Index card boxes<br>Books on the counter<br>Books in the shelves<br>Duplicating machine<br>Painting of a man<br>Three plants<br>Paper slips, pins, stamps on the<br>  counter<br>Bulletin board | One adolescent girl in blue dress<br><br>One middle-aged woman in green<br>  dress<br><br><br>Two adolescent boys in the rows of<br>  bookshelves<br><br>Three adolescent girls sitting at one<br>  of the round tables | Putting cards back in the books<br>  repeatedly<br><br>Often coming out from the<br>  adjoining room with a paper<br>  in hand<br>Checks the paper with the girl<br>Goes back to her room<br><br>Searching for books<br><br>Two girls writing in notebooks; one<br>  girl looking at book in front of<br>  her |

**Summarizing Characteristics**

—Presence of only six students in the library suggests that only small groups of eighth-grade pupils use the library at a time, not the entire class, because, at the time of the observation, only the six students were there, although there was ample room for a class.
—Turnstile present for counting or control.
—All individuals present seem occupied.

**Figure 3.7.** Worksheet for Analysis of the Key Components of a Setting

**Behavior Setting Survey**. The behavior setting survey is another observational method for environmental assessment. Behavior setting is a concept that was first introduced by Barker and Wright in *Midwest and Its Children*[89] and which was subsequently elaborated and refined in two later volumes, *Ecological Psychology*[90] and *Qualities of Community Life.*[91] Behavior settings are "stable extra-individual units with great explanatory power with respect to the behavior occurring with them."[92] As defined using ecological terminology, behavior settings are "a standing pattern of behavior and part of the milieu which are synomorphic and in which the milieu is circumjacent to the behavior."[93] Bechtel translates these highly technical definitions into simpler language for us:

1. A behavior setting is a standing pattern of behavior that occurs over and over again in a given place and at a given time. You can go to the *place* where it occurs at the *time* it occurs and see the behavior repeated each time the setting happens.

2. Yet behavior settings, even though they are defined as separate entities, are part of the flow of behavior in a community. People move in and out of settings but the settings do not disappear when different people arrive; they have a life of their own. Yet when the community changes, settings change also.[94]

In the Kurt Lewin Memorial address in 1963, Barker provided a concrete example of a behavior setting.

It is not often that a lecturer can present to his audience an example of his phe-nomena, whole and functioning in situ—not merely with a demonstration, a descrip-tion, a preserved specimen, a picture, or a diagram of it. I am in the fortunate position of being able to give you, so to speak, a real behavior setting.

If you will change your attention from me to the next most inclusive, bounded unit, to the assembly of people, behavior episodes, and objects before you, you will see a behavior setting. It has the following structural attributes which you can observe directly:

1. It has a space-time locus: 3:00-3:50 P.M., September 2, 1963, Clover Room, Bellevue-Stratford Hotel, Philadelphia, Pennsylvania.

2. It is composed of a variety of interior entities and events: of people, objects (chairs, walls, a microphone, paper), behavior (lecturing, listening, sitting), and other processes (air circulation, sound amplification).

3. Its widely different components form a bounded pattern that is easily dis-criminated from the pattern on the outside of the boundary.

4. Its component parts are obviously not a random arrangement of independent classes of entities; if they were, how surprising, that all the chairs are in the same position with respect to the podium, that all members of the audience happen to come to rest upon chairs, and that the lights are not helter-skelter from floor to ceiling, for example.

5. The entity before you is a part of a nesting structure; its components (e.g., the chairs and people) have parts; and the setting, itself, is contained within a more comprehensive unit, the Bellevue-Stratford Hotel.

6. This unit is objective in the sense that it exists independently of anyone's perception of it, qua unit.[95]

Thus, a behavior setting is an environmental unit that is highly visible and is independent of a person's perception. It is a naturally occurring unit, having temporal, physical, and behavioral attributes. There are several other dimensions of behavior settings. An important one is that they have one or more *standing patterns* of behavior. Called "program" by Gump,[96] these are comprised of a regime, a set of procedures, or a way of doing things. Such behavioral patterns are not those of individual people, but of a group of people, as the overall patterns of behavior that you would see at a ball game, at church, or in the park. One other characteristic of standing patterns of behavior is that they are not completely dependent on the particular people within the setting at a certain point in time. The people are interchangeable and replaceable. The same entity continues with new people. Another dimension of behavior settings is *milieu*. Milieu refers to the fact that behavior settings have physical features that exist even when the standing pattern of behavior is not occurring. The physical or nonpsychological aspects of the setting—including mountains, streets, buildings, desks, and chairs—exist independently of the standing pattern of behavior and independently of anyone's perception of it. A football field with stands, turf, and goal posts is a milieu and becomes a setting only when certain behavior patterns—a football game—are enacted on it. This temporal-spatial milieu encloses the behaviors that exist in the setting. When Barker and Wright speak of the "circumjacent" milieu, they are referring to walls, ceilings, and other properties of the physical environment that surround, enclose, or encompass behavior.[97] An additional aspect of behavior settings is that the standing patterns of behavior within the setting are *synomorphic* or are similar in structure to the milieu. That

**Table 3.1.** Sample List of Potential Behavior Settings

| Category | Setting |
|---|---|
| Business | 1. *Drugstore |
| | 2. Fountain of Drugstore |
| | 3. Pharmacy of Drugstore |
| | 4. Variety Department of Drugstore |
| | 5. *J. Wiley, Attorneys Office |
| | 6. *Barber Shop |
| | 7. *J. Wiley, Music Lessons |
| Church | 8. Methodist Church |
| | 9. *Joash Worship Service at Methodist Church |
| | 10. *Adult Choir Practice at Methodist Church |
| | 11. Presbyterian Church |
| | 12. *Worship Service at Presbyterian Church |
| | 13. Anthem by Presbyterian Church Choir |
| Government | 14. *County Treasurers Office |
| | 15. *Payment of Taxes at County Treasurers Office* |
| | 16. *Courthouse Square |
| | 17. *Sitting on Benches of Courthouse Square* |
| Voluntary Association | 18. *Boy Scout Troop 72 Meeting |
| | 19. Tenderfoot Test at Scout Meeting |
| | 20. Beaver Patrol Activities at Scout Meeting |
| | 21. *4-H Club* |
| | 22. *Skating Party of 4-H Club |
| | 23. *Regular Meeting of 4-H Club |
| | 24. Election of 4-H Club Officers |
| | 25. *Achievement Banquet of 4-H Club |
| | 26. *Hopscotch Games* |
| | 27. March 3 Meeting of Couples Bridge Club |
| | 28. April 1 Meeting of Couples Bridge Club |
| | 29. May 2 Meeting of Couples Bridge Club |
| School | 30. High School |
| | 31. *High School Senior Class* |
| | 32. *Box Social by Senior Class |
| | 33. Bingo Game |
| | 34. Walk for a Cake |
| | 35. *High School Gym* |
| | 36. *Girls Locker Room |
| | 37. *Brick-paved Area in Front of High School* |
| Miscellaneous | 38. *Trafficways |
| | 39. *State Highway* |

is, there is an interdependence or synomorphic relationship between the pattern of behavior and the pattern of the nonbehavioral or physical components of the setting. In Barker's memorial address, he indicates that the chairs face the speaker for listening, illustrating that the milieu is synomorphic to the behavior. Finally, a person who is in a behavior setting is influenced by the standing patterns of behavior and its milieu. Commenting on the influence of behavior settings, Gump explains that one's "behavioral opportunities and constraints come from the setting; that which he can experience is markedly influenced by the setting he inhabits."[98]

The systematic method of collecting information about behavior settings is the behavior setting survey. This entails an inventory and description of the behavior settings in a community or institution. Three basic operations are involved: (1) identification and listing of all possible behavior settings; (2) editing the list so that potential settings that do not meet predetermined limiting conditions are eliminated; and (3) description of the behavior settings. Newspapers, telephone books, handbills, church bulletins, school programs, as well as other public media provide sources of many potential behavior settings. Informants from the community also can offer ideas concerning behavior settings. These are listed and grouped by setting and subsetting on an initial inventory such as the one compiled by Barker that is shown in Table 3.1. The next step in the survey is to discard nonsettings that do not possess the defining attributes of a behavior setting. Potential settings that do not meet these criteria are eliminated from the preliminary list: (a) recurrent bounded patterns of behavior of people en masse, (b) anchored to a particular physical structure or milieu complex, (c) occurrence at a specific time and space, (d) synomorphy or congruent relation between behavior and physical structure, and (e) circumjacency of milieu to behavior. Three tests are applied to the potential behavior settings. The *structure* test asks if the community part is a behavior-milieu synomorph (characteristics *a-c*). In Barker's summary table, the items not in italics were classified as synomorphs. The behavior-milieu synomorphs are then subjected to the *internal dynamics* test (characteristic *d*) which requires synomorphs that are structurally adjoined to other synomorphs to be examined for interdependence. Of the thirty-one behavior-milieu synomorphs in Barker's study, only six potential behavior settings (1, 12, 18, 23, 32, and 38) were judged to have interjacent synomorphs with the degree of internal unity required. Three items (8, 11, and 30) were not classified as behavior settings because their synomorphs were too independent. The remaining potential settings are subjected to the test of *external dynamics;* they are examined for their degree of interdependence with regard to structurally external synomorphs. All of Barker's remaining items except three (27, 28, and 29) met this criterion. The potential settings with asterisks in Table 3.1 passed all three tests and could be labeled behavior settings or K-21 behavior settings to be exact.

The general basis and importance of interdependence of behavior-milieu synomorphs have already been discussed. The assumptions underlying the basis for determining the interdependence index $K$ of pairs of synomorphs are

> (1) that interdependence between synomorphs occurs (a) via behavior, which has effects across synomorphs, (b) via inhabitants, who migrate between synomorphs, and (c) via leaders, who are common to synomorphs; and (2) that the amount of interdependence that occurs via these channels is a direct function of (a) the amount of behavior, the number of inhabitants, and the number of leaders that span the synomorphs, (b) the closeness of the synomorphs in space and time, and (c) the similarity of the synomorphs with respect to behavior objects and behavior mechanisms.[99]

The $K$ value for two synomorphs is based upon ratings that reflect the extent to which

1. behavior or its consequences span the synomorphs;

2. the same inhabitants enter the synomorphs;

3. the same leaders are active in the synomorphs;

4. the synomorphs use the same physical space or spaces that are near together;

5. the synomorphs occur at the same time or at times that are near together;

6. the synomorphs use the same or similar behavior objects;

7. the same kinds of behavior mechanisms occur in the synomorphs.[100]

The degree of interdependence of two behavior settings is estimated by rating each of these seven criteria on a seven-point scale, with 1 indicating the greatest and a rating of 7 indicating the least similarity or commonality between the settings. The total interdependence scale may range from 7 (maximal interdependence or minimal independence) to 49 (minimal interdependence or maximal independence). A $K$ value of 21 is used as the cutting point for distinguishing between behavior settings. Pairs of settings with a $K$ value of less than 21 are considered as single behavior settings, and those with a value of 21 or more are evaluated as separate or discrete settings. A two-day study of a nine-year-old boy at home and at camp revealed that the child entered over seventy behavior settings each day.[101] Since this is of interest to us, the classes of behavior settings which the boy entered are listed in Table 3.2.

The final step in the behavior setting survey involves a description of the behavior setting. Through observation, through the use of informants, or by examination of existing data such as minutes, work logs, and other documents, the observer is able to record who the participants in the settings are and their characteristics, as well as what they do and how long they do it. Barker has delineated categories for the description of behavior settings. In addition, he has provided suggestions concerning ratings for these categories. These are Barker's eleven categories:

1. *Occurrence.* Number of days a year the behavior setting occurs for any amount of time.

2. *Duration.* Total number of hours spent in the setting.

3. *Population.* Number of different persons who inhabit the behavior setting for any period of time.

4. *Occupancy Time.* Total number of person hours spent in a setting for a period of time.

5. *Penetration of Behavior Settings.* Degree of involvement or responsibility of the occupants.

6. *Action Patterns.* Distinguishable features of standing patterns of behavior settings (e.g., aesthetics, business, education, government, nutrition, personal appearance, physical health, professionalism, recreation, religion, and social contact).

7. *Behavior Mechanisms.* Extent to which certain mechanisms occurred in the standing patterns of behavior settings (e.g., affective behavior, gross motor activity, manipulation, talking, and thinking).

8. *Richness of Behavior Settings.* Variety of behavior possibilities within it.

9. *Pressure.* Degree to which outside forces act upon an individual to enter or leave a behavior setting.

10. *Welfare.* Extent to which the behavior setting serves the welfare of its inhabitants.

11. *Local Autonomy.* Degree to which decisions regarding the operation of the behavior setting are made by persons or agencies within differing levels of proximity (e.g., within the town, outside the town but within the school district, etc.).[102]

This abbreviated and simplified treatment of behavior setting theory and techniques does not do justice to the highly technical problems involved in the subject. The reader is referred to the numerous references cited in this section. Also, Wicker has written an interesting article which

**Table 3.2.** Varieties of Behavior Settings Entered by Wally at Camp and at Home

| Camp | Home |
|---|---|
| Cabin M Indoors | Home, Meals |
| Paths in Camp | Home, Indoors |
| Camp (Boys') Toilet | Home, Outdoors |
| Washing Machine & Clothes Line Area | Home, Bathroom |
| Flag Ceremony | City Streets and Sidewalks |
| Main Lodge, Meals | Booster Park |
| Clean-Up of Crafts Shop | Total no. entered—6 |
| Woods | |
| Luke's Dispensary, Outside | |
| Luke's Dispensary, Clinic | |
| Swimming | |
| Cook-Out in Woods | |
| Athletic Field | |
| Crafts in Craft Shop | |
| Main Lodge, Free Play | |
| Main Lodge, Outside | |
| Indian Council Fire | |
| Total no. entered—17 | |

discusses recent and prospective developments in ecological psychology.[103] He points out the relevance of behavior setting theory and research to other areas within the behavioral and social sciences, and indicates that the field of ecological psychology has shown an increasing concern with direct and practical applications of its research. Moreover, he attempts to eliminate the notion that the field is an isolated and even esoteric area by demonstrating how ecological psychology, and behavior setting technology in particular, can help us to understand our environment and how that understanding can lead to improved conditions for all.

**Environmental Force Units.** In the previous section, the behavior setting survey was discussed as a valuable way to describe the places and occasions (i.e., context) of a child's behavior. Another method of environmental study that was developed by a psychological ecologist is called the environmental force unit (EFU). Analogous to the behavior episode methodology which is used to analyze the behavior streams of children by identifying goal-directed molar actions as recorded in specimen descriptions, the EFU focuses more on environmental inputs to the behavioral stream. It unitizes environmental action. As defined by Schoggen, the EFU is "an action by an environmental agent which (1) occurs vis-a-vis the child, and (2) is directed by the agent toward a recognizable end-state with respect to the child, and (3) is recognized as such by the child."[104] While behavior episodes correspond to a youngster's behavioral goals, EFUs refer to the agent's goals as they relate to the child. The EFU is an observable molar action by another person (or pet) who responds to, directs, controls, assists, supports, or interacts in any way with the child in his or her immediate presence. It can involve either verbal or nonverbal behavior.

After the observer has compiled a specimen record on a child and has had the manuscript typed, he or she draws brackets in the margins to indicate initiation and termination points of the EFU. The units are given brief descriptive titles that identify both the agent and the action, and they are numbered consecutively (e.g., EFU 1—Teacher: Planning Next Activity With Class; EFU 2—Teacher: Giving Chalk to Pupils). Examination of the EFU titles in a record gives the observer a good idea of the various ways in which a child's social environment impacted on the youngster during the observation period.

Through a study of the environmental forces in the everyday home lives of children, Schoggen and Schoggen[105] revealed a number of interesting material-content features of the active social environments of three-year-olds. Among other things, they found subcultural differences as well as inter-group variations for social classes and ethnic groups.

1. Environmental agents were most frequently female and the mother, not surprisingly, was the most active agent in the environment for the majority of these three-year-old children.

2. Agents were responsive to, attentive to, and interfering with the children in one group as often as in another.

3. Children in middle-income homes, compared with children in low-income homes, had higher percentages of EFUs in which they were given or asked for information, engaged in more extended interaction, were given an obligation to perform some specific action, were in harmony with the goal of the agent, and received and gave messages through a verbal medium.

4. No differences could be detected on any of the variables when the sample of urban black families was compared with the urban white families.

5. Although children in low-income homes received as much total input from the environment as children in middle-income homes, the children in low-income homes did receive less verbal input, more inhibiting behavior, and less input directed toward specific behavior of the subject.

6. Comparison of these data with those from a related study suggested that disturbances (environmental interferences with the child's pursuits) occur much more frequently at home than in nursery school and outdoor settings.[106]

The work of the Schoggens illustrates the kind of analyses possible after the EFUs are initially defined in terms of their structural and dynamic properties.

## STANDARDIZED DESCRIPTION

**HOME Inventory.** A relatively recent approach to environmental assessment that was developed by Caldwell and Bradley employs a combination of direct observation and interview procedures in which the social (parent-child relationships) and physical features of the home environment are examined.[107] Designed primarily as a measure of social stimulation in the child's home, the Home Observation for Measurement of the Environment (HOME) Inventory lends itself well to child study. The form, which is designed for families of infants and toddlers, is composed of forty-five items that are organized into six subscales: (1) emotional and verbal responsivity of mother; (2) avoidance of restriction and punishment; (3) organization of physical and temporal environment; (4) provision of appropriate play materials; (5) maternal involvement with children; and (6) opportunities for variety in daily stimulation. The observer checks under *yes* or *no* to indicate the presence or absence of a behavior or object in the home. An interview probe may be necessary unless the mother offers the information spontaneously or unless behavior or items in question can be readily seen by the observer (see Table 3.3). Subscores are obtained for each of the subtests by adding the positive responses; total scores are calculated by summing the subtest scores. Raw scores for both the subscales and the total scale are then converted into percentile bands. A second form of the HOME Inventory is available for families of preschool-aged children. This fifty-five item version includes eight subscales: (1) stimulation through toys, games, and reading materials; (2) language stimulation;

**Table 3.3.** Sample Items from the HOME Inventory (Birth to Three)

| Subscale | Item |
|---|---|
| Emotional and verbal responsivity of the mother . . . . . . . . . . . . | Mother responds to child's vocalization with a vocal or verbal response. |
| | Mother caresses or kisses child at least once during visit. |
| Avoidance of restriction and punishment . . . . . . . . . . . . . . . | Mother does not scold or derogate child during visit. |
| | Mother does not interfere with child's actions or restrict child's movements more than three times during visit. |
| Organization of physical and temporal environment . . . . . . . . . . | When mother is away, care is provided by one of three regular substitutes. |
| | Child's play environment appears safe and free of hazards. |
| Provision of appropriate play materials. . . . . . . . . . . . . . . . | Child has some muscle activity toys or pieces of equipment. |
| | Provides toys for literature and music. |
| Maternal involvement with the child . . . . . . . . . . . . . . . . . | Mother talks to child while doing her work. |
| | Mother structures child's play periods. |
| Opportunities for variety in daily stimulation . . . . . . . . . . . . . | Father provides some caregiving every day. |
| | Mother reads stories at least three times weekly. |

(3) physical environment: safe, clean, and conducive to development; (4) pride, affection, and warmth; (5) stimulation of academic behavior; (6) modeling and encouragement of social maturity; (7) variety of stimulation; and (8) physical punishment. Like the HOME Inventory for families of infants and toddlers, items on the preschool version receive binary scores—yes or no—and the raw scores are then transformed into percentile bands reflecting the lower 10 percent, lower 25 percent, middle 50 percent, upper 25 percent, and upper 10 percent. Studies using the HOME Inventory have been summarized elsewhere.[108]

**Other Environmental Checklists and Rating Scales.** Other inventory approaches are available in which the observer evaluates aspects of the physical features of the home or school environment. Four such instruments will be described.

Rheingold and Cook canvassed the furnishings and toys in the rooms of ninety-six boys and girls under six years of age in a study of room contents as an index of parents' behavior.[109] They proposed that the manner in which mothers and fathers furnish their children's rooms, including the toys they purchase, reflect either directly or indirectly parental behavior toward their sons and daughters. Although children may express certain preferences between the ages of one and six, it is the parents who ultimately determine what toys, curtains, pictures, and furniture are bought.

The observer recorded all toys and furniture in the youngster's bedroom on a checklist called The Child's Room (see sample items in Figure 3.8). To supplement the checklist data, color photographs were taken. Observations revealed thirteen major classes of items:

C.  Pattern  Edges

Walls       — ——

          — ——

Floors ( )

Wood __    — ——

Vinyl __    — ——

Carpet__    — ——

Rugs __    — —— ——

(N.) __    — —— ——

          — —— ——

Curtains    — —— ——

          — —— ——

Bed (D/S/C)    — ——

Bedspread    — —— ——

Blanket    — —— ——

Pillows    — —— ——

(N.) __    — —— ——

Desk    — —— ——

Table    — —— ——

Chest of Drawers __ —— ——

Dresser    — —— ——

Light Switch    — —— ——

Books:

Adventure _____ Paperback _____

Nature _____ Hardback _____

Religious _____ 0 _____

Comic _____ _____

Fairy tales _____

Sports Equipment

Balls _____ Basketball _____

Baseball _____ Roller skates _____

Football _____ Jump rope _____

0 _____

Educational Toys:

Globe _____ Blackboard _____

Tool kit _____ Typewriter _____

Telephone _____ Bldg. blocks _____

Tinker toy _____ Dr/nurse kit _____

Clay _____ Crayons/paint _____

0 _____

Games (list) _____

Flora & Fauna (list) _____

**Figure 3.8.** Items from The Child's Room Checklist

1. *Animal furnishings* (e.g., bedspreads and curtains bearing the figures of animals)

2. *Books* (e.g., children's books)

3. *Dolls* (e.g., small-scale figures of human beings)

4. *Educational-art materials* (e.g., charts of numbers or letters, typewriters, and drawing/coloring materials)

5. *Floral furnishings* (e.g., furnishings bearing flower and plant figures)

6. *Furniture* (e.g., beds and dressers)

7. *Musical items* (e.g., radios, record players, and instruments)

8. *Ruffles* (e.g., items like curtains and bedspreads bearing ruffles, lace, or fringe)

9. *Spatial-temporal objects* (e.g., outer-space toys, clocks, and shape-sorting toys)

10. *Sports equipment* (e.g., balls, skates, and kites)

11. *Stuffed animals* (e.g., any material stuffed and shaped like an animal)

12. *Toy animals* (e.g., toy animals and their houses)

13. *Vehicles* (e.g., cars, trains, and planes)

Results demonstrated that boys had more vehicles, animal furnishings, educational-art materials, spatial-temporal toys, sports equipment, and toy animals. Girls' rooms contained more dolls, floral furnishings, and "ruffles." The findings suggested that parents provide different types of environments for male and female children. Moreover, the investigators showed how observations, structured by the use of a checklist, can yield a wealth of data about children's home environments.

Laumann and House conducted home interviews to study the ecological arrangement of objects and designed components in homes located in a major metropolitan area.[110] They used an instrument called the Living Room Checklist to indicate the presence or absence of fifty-three attributes in the subjects' living rooms (Figure 3.9). This checklist inventory can be conveniently used to assess the contents and characteristics of the child's home as can other similar observational recording procedures such as Chapin's Living Room Scale and Social Status Scale.[111]

Stallings and her associates at the Stanford Research Institute have developed a Physical Environment Information Checklist to evaluate the physical features of a classroom.[112] Aspects of the classroom environment that are evaluated include its size, shape, lighting, ventilation, noise level, and seating patterns as well as the equipment and materials available for instructional purposes (Figure 3.10).

Frost has developed a detailed Playground Rating System to assess the child's play environment.[113] Unlike the Stallings et al. checklist which only allows judgments regarding the presence or absence of certain features, materials, and equipment in the classroom, the Frost measure allows finer discriminations and asks the observer to indicate the degree to which a quality or feature is present in an outdoor play area. The forty items that comprise the instrument are shown in Figure 3.11. Each item is rated on a five-point scale, indicating nonexistence (0) to excellent (5). Checklists and rating scales are treated in greater detail in Chapter 5.

**Behavioral Mapping.** Yet another potential observation technique for the study of a child's environment is behavioral mapping. Originally developed by Ittelson, Rivlin, and Proshansky, behavioral maps are "descriptions of behavior and of participants and statements relating the behavior to its physical locus."[114] Such maps are qualitative since they describe settings, and yet at the same time, they are quantitative because they indicate how much activity occurs in a given setting. The initial phase in the development of behavioral maps is the identification of observational categories. This can be achieved by looking at and recording in narrative style the behaviors that take place in the areas to be mapped. The observation record is later analyzed for the key behavioral examples that are relevant to the problem being studied. The behaviors that are finally selected should be overt and require a minimum of observer inference. Observational forms are then prepared which contain summary behavioral and analytic categories based upon the initial exploratory pilot observations. Afterwards, specific activity arenas to be mapped (street, neighborhood, recreation center, school, playground, etc.) are identified. Mapping is subsequently done, usually on a time sampling basis. Narrative records also can be made if smaller areas are studied. The behavior of one child or a group of children can be examined as it relates to the physical surrounding.

Since behavioral mapping is a relatively new technique, only a few investigations have been reported which have used this method with children.[115] Pioneering work on mapping was conducted by Ittelson and his associates,[116] and their model has been adapted for use in other studies including those involving younger subjects. Therefore, their frequently cited work with adults will be described briefly before we consider research with child subjects. Although their study focused on the mapping of psychiatric wards, the procedures used can be generalized to a variety of other settings. First, the investigators observed and recorded, for each of the predetermined locations on the ward, the major examples of patients' behavior. Next, they examined their inventory of behaviors and eliminated

**Floor**
—— highly polished wood
—— unpolished wood
—— covered
—— other

**Carpet**
—— wall-to-wall carpeting
—— standard size rug
—— scatter rugs
—— other

**Main carpet design**
—— no carpet
—— solid color/tweed
—— floral
—— braided
—— oriental
—— other

**Curtains and drapes**
Translucent
—— lacy, ruffled
—— straight-hanging
—— other

Opaque
—— floral pattern
—— geometric design
—— light, neutral, solid color
—— dark, solid color
—— other

—— number of complete window
    casements

**Furniture**
—— modern functional
—— bulky old-fashioned, stuffed
—— traditional American
—— mixture, no consistent style
—— other

**Walls**
—— neutral or pastel paper or paint
—— bright color paper or paint
—— ornate paper
—— other

**Books**
—— many in shelves
—— a few around
—— none

**General space factor (density, not size)**
—— rather bare
—— below average
—— average
—— above average
—— densely furnished

**General condition of living room and furniture**
—— excellent
—— above average
—— average
—— below average
—— poor

**General neatness**
—— exceptionally orderly, nothing
    out of place
—— average neatness and order
—— things in disarray

**Miscellaneous items**
—— fireplace
—— piano
—— television
—— hi-fi set
—— candle holder of any type
—— religious objects
—— Bible
—— vases
—— enlarged photographs
—— knickknacks
—— artificial flowers
—— large potted plants on floor
—— antimacassars (doilies covering
    furniture)
—— encyclopedia set
—— clock (type:          )
—— picture window over four feet wide
—— wall mirror(s)
—— outdoor nature scene painting
—— painting: people as subject
—— abstract painting
—— religious painting
—— still life painting
—— cut flowers
—— small potted plants on tables or sills
—— trophies, plaques, or similar objects

**Figure 3.9.** Living Room Checklist

PHYSICAL ENVIRONMENT INFORMATION — Mark all that apply.

### Playground Facilities/Use/Activities
- O Playground equipment in new condition.
- O Playground equipment in old condition.
- O Playground equipment seems to be used a lot.
- Playground activity directed by adults:
  - O Always
  - O Sometimes
  - O Never

### Condition of Building
Yes  No
O    O  Is the school building in good condition?

### Noise Level
Yes  No
O    O  Adults seem to have difficulty making themselves heard (have to repeat questions, ask the children to be quiet, etc.)
O    O  Children are noticeably disturbed in their work by the noise level.

### Lighting
Yes  No
O    O Physical lighting seems adequate.
O    O Some areas of the room are noticeably lighter/darker than the rest.

### Heating and Ventilating
Yes  No
O    O Some areas of the classroom are noticeably warmer/cooler than the rest. (Direct sunlight, proximity to heating system, etc.)
O    O Classroom is comfortably heated.

### Displays in Classroom
Yes  No
O    O Children's own art on display.
O    O Photographs of the children on display.
O    O Pictures of various ethnic groups on display.
O    O Community events posted.
O    O Other (Specify) ⟶

NOTE: Do not write outside this box ⟶

### Description of Classroom Space
Yes  No
O    O Single contained classroom within a building.
O    O Open classrooms.
O    O Portable classrooms.

### Space per Child
Yes  No
O    O Does there seem to be adequate space per child?

For each of the items below, mark all that apply:

① Present
② Used today

### GAMES, TOYS, PLAY EQUIPMENT
- ①② small toys (trucks, cars, dolls and accessories)
- ①② puzzles, games
- ①② wheel toys
- ①② small play equipment (jumpropes, balls)
- ①② large play equipment (swings, jungle gym)
- ①② children's storybooks
- ①② animals, other nature objects
- ①② sandbox, water table
- ①② carpentry materials, large blocks
- ①② cooking and sewing supplies

### INSTRUCTIONAL MATERIALS
- ①② Montessori, other educational toys
- ①② children's texts, workbooks
- ①② math/science equipment, concrete objects
- ①② instructional charts

### AUDIO, VISUAL EQUIPMENT
- ①② television
- ①② record or tape player
- ①② audio-visual equipment

### GENERAL EQUIPMENT, MATERIALS
- ①② children's own products on display
- ①② displays reflecting children's ethnicity
- ①② other displays especially for children
- ①② magazines
- ①② achievement charts
- ①② child-size sink
- ①② child-size table and chairs
- ①② child-size shelves
- ①② arts and crafts materials
- ①② blackboard, feltboard
- ①② child's own storage space
- ①② photographs of the children on display

### OTHER
- ①② please specify . . . . . .

### Seating Patterns:
- O Movable tables and chairs for seating purposes.
- O Stationary desks in rows.
- O Assigned seating for at least part of the day.
- O Children select their own seating locations.
- O Teacher assigns children to groups.
- O Children select their own work groups.

**Figure 3.10.** Physical Environment Information Checklist

## PLAYGROUND RATING SYSTEM*

*Instructions:* Rate each item on a scale from 0-5. High score possible on Section I is 100 points; Section II is 50 points and Section III is 50 points, for a possible grand total of 200 points. Divide the grand total score by 2 to obtain a final rating.

### Section I.   What does the playground contain?

Rate each item for degree of existence and function on a scale of 0-5 (0 = not existent; 1 = some element(s) exists but not functional; 2 = poor; 3 = average; 4 = good; 5 = all elements exist, excellent function).

_____ 1. A hard-surfaced area with space for games and a network of paths for wheeled toys.

_____ 2. Sand and sand equipment.

_____ 3. Dramatic play structures (play house(s), old car or boat with complementary equipment, such as adjacent sand and water and housekeeping equipment).

_____ 4. Climbing structure(s) (with room for more than one child at a time and with a variety of entries, exits and levels).

_____ 5. Mound(s) of earth for climbing and digging.

_____ 6. Trees and natural areas (including weed areas).

_____ 7. Zoning to provide continuous challenge; linkage of areas, functional physical boundaries, vertical and horizontal treatment.

_____ 8. Water play areas, with fountains, pools and sprinklers.

_____ 9. Construction area with junk materials such as tires, crates, planks, boards, bricks and nails. Tools should be provided and demolition allowed.

_____10. An old vehicle, train, boat, car that has been made safe, but not stripped of its play value. (This item should be changed or relocated after a period of time to renew interest.)

_____11. Equipment for active play: A *slide* with a large platform at the top (best if slide is built into side of a hill);

*swings* that can be used safely in a variety of ways (use of old tires as seats); *climbing trees* (mature dead trees that are horizontally positioned); *climbing nets.*

_____12. A large grassy area for organized games.

_____13. Small private spaces at the child's own scale: tunnels, niches, playhouses, hiding places.

_____14. Fences, gates, walls and windows that provide security for young children and are adaptable as opportunities for learning/play.

_____15. Natural areas that attract birds and bugs. A garden and flowers located so that they are protected from play, but with easy access for the child to tend them.

_____16. Provisions for the housing of pets. Pets available.

_____17. A transitional space from outdoors to indoors. This could be a covered play area immediately adjoining the playroom areas which will protect the children from the sun and rain and extend indoor activities to the outside.

_____18. Adequate protected storage for outdoor play equipment, tools for construction area, and maintenance tools. Storage can be separate, wheel toys stored next to the roadway; sand equipment near or next to the sand enclosure; tools in the workshop area. Or storage can be the lower level of the climbing structure, or separate structures attached to the building or fence. *But storage should aid in pick-up* (that is, make it easy for children to put equipment away at the end of each play period).

_____19. Easy access from outdoor play areas to coats and toilets.

_____20. Places for adults, parents and teachers, to sit within the outdoor play areas. Shade structures with benches can provide for this as well as for seating for children.

_____
*Joe L. Frost © 1977

**Figure 3.11.** Playground Rating System

**Section II.   Is the playground in good repair and relatively safe?**

Rate each item for condition and safety on a scale of 0-5 (0 = not existent; 1 = exists but extremely hazardous; 2 = poor; 3 = fair; 4 = good; 5 = excellent condition and relatively safe yet presents *challenge*).

_____ 1. A protective fence next to hazardous areas (streets, etc.).

_____ 2. Eight to ten inches of noncompacted sand (or equivalent) under all climbing and moving equipment, extending through fall zones and secured by retaining wall.

_____ 3. Size of equipment appropriate to age group served.

_____ 4. Area free of litter (e.g., broken glass, rocks).

_____ 5. Moving parts free of defects (e.g., no pinch and crush points, bearings not excessively worn).

_____ 6. Equipment free of sharp edges, protruding elements, broken parts, toxic substances.

_____ 7. Swing seats constructed of soft material (e.g., rubber, canvas).

_____ 8. All safety equipment in good repair (e.g., railings, padded areas, protective covers).

_____ 9. Fixed equipment secure in ground and concrete footings recessed in ground.

_____10. Equipment structurally sound. No bending, warping, breaking, sinking, etc.

**Section III.   What should the playground do?**

Rate each item for degree and quality on a scale of 0-5 (0 = not existent; 1 = some evidence but virtually nonexistent; 2 = poor; 3 = fair; 4 = good; 5 = excellent). Use the space provided for comments.

_____ 1. Encourages Play:
Inviting, easy access
Open, flowing and relaxed spaces
Clear movement from inside to outside
Appropriate equipment for the age group

_____ 2. Stimulates the Child's Senses:
Change and contrasts in scale, light, texture and color
Flexible equipment
Diverse experiences

_____ 3. Nurtures the Child's Curiosity:
Equipment that the child can change
Materials for experiments and construction

_____ 4. Allows Interaction Between the Child and the Resources:
Systematic storage which defines routines
Semi-enclosed spaces to read, work a puzzle, or be alone

_____ 5. Allows Interaction Between the Child and Other Children:
Variety of spaces
Adequate space to avoid conflicts
Equipment that invites socialization

_____ 6. Allows Interaction Between the Child and Adults:
Easy maintenance
Adequate and convenient storage
Organization of spaces to allow general supervision
Rest areas for adults

_____ 7. Supports the Child's Basic Social and Physical Needs:
Comfortable to the child
Scaled to the child
Free of hazards

_____ 8. Complements the Cognitive Forms of Play Engaged in by the Child:
Functional, exercise, gross-motor, active
Constructive, building, creating
Dramatic, pretending, make believe
Organized games, games with rules

_____ 9. Complements the Social Forms of Play Engaged in by the Child:
Solitary, private, meditative
Parallel, side-by-side
Cooperative interrelationships

_____10. Promotes Social and Intellectual Development:
Provides graduated challenge
Integrates indoor/outdoor activities
Involves adults in child's play
Adult-child planning
The play environment is dynamic—continuously changing

**Figure 3.11** *(Continued)*

duplicate, trivial, or especially peculiar observations. The resulting list included approximately 300 behavioral descriptions. Because of their extremely large number, these behaviors were sorted into summary observational categories. To facilitate analysis, the observational categories were further combined into analytic categories. Table 3.4 presents some of the observational and analytic categories along with sample behaviors for each. The data were then collected by observers who were familiar with the patients as well as with the functioning of the ward. The observations were recorded on data sheets and included the number of patients, staff, and visitors who were seen engaging in the predetermined categories of behavior. All areas of the ward were observed in three- to four-minute intervals every fifteen minutes. Table 3.5 presents the analytic behavior categories (columns) and the major areas of the ward (rows) in terms of the percentage of patients who were observed behaving in the manner indicated at a particular location between the hours of 9:30 A.M. to 12:30 P.M., 1:30 to 4:30 P.M., and 6:00 to 9:00 P.M. Finer discriminations of spatial locations also were made and other analyses done, but they will not be reported here.

A study by Beeken and Janzen used behavioral mapping of student activity at school in order to examine behavior in open-area and traditional classroom settings.[117] With minor changes, they adopted the Ittelson model for use in the project. The independent variable was architectural design of the educational space (open concept vs. traditional). Dependent variables included pupil behavior (writes, reads a notebook, attends to teacher, travels, etc.), location (assigned class, table; library, aisle; hall, etc.), and social settings (alone, one same-sex peer, assigned teacher, librarian, etc.). Observations were made of three male and three female pupils from each of two fifth-grade language arts sections for fifteen minutes apiece on two different occasions. Data were coded using a time sampling schedule of ten seconds. At the end of every interval, the child's behavior, his or her location, and social setting were noted on the observation form. Analysis involved the calculation of frequency counts for the categories and computation of percentages to reflect the proportion of total behavior that was subsumed in each category for the two types of schools. Frequencies in the

**Table 3.4.** Categories for Behavioral Mapping

| Behavior | Observational Categories | Analytic Category |
|---|---|---|
| Patient reclines on bench, hand over face, but not asleep Patient lies in bed awake | lie awake | |
| Patient sleeps on easy chair One patient sleeps while others are lined up for lunch | sleeping | Isolated Passive |
| Patient sits, smiling to self Patient sits, smoking and spitting | sitting alone | |
| Patient writes letter on bench Patient takes notes from a book | write | |
| Patient sets own hair Patient sits, waiting to get into shower | personal hygiene | |
| Patient reads newspaper and paces Patient reads a book | read | Isolated Active |
| Patient and nurses's aide stand next to alcove Patient stands in doorway smoking | stand | |
| Patient paces between room and corridor Patient paces from room to room saying hello to other patients | pacing | |

**Table 3.5.** Behavior on an Average Psychiatric Ward

|  | Traffic | Visiting | Social | Mixed Active | Isolated Active | Isolated Passive | Total |
|---|---|---|---|---|---|---|---|
| Bedrooms | 0.1 | 3.2 | 3.9 | 0.8 | 5.7 | 10.4 | 24.1 |
| Public rooms | 2.7 | 6.5 | 14.3 | 9.4 | 4.6 | 2.6 | 40.1 |
| Total | 2.8 | 9.7 | 18.2 | 10.2 | 10.3 | 13.0 | 64.2 |

categories for the different educational settings were compared with chi-squares and revealed that reading and writing were less frequent in open areas, while social behavior, travel, and housekeeping activities were more common in contrast to traditional classrooms. In open concept schools, more locations were used, less time was spent at desks, and there was greater interaction among peers and less with teachers.

A variation of behavioral mapping has been used by Wahler and Cormier in conjunction with their clinical ecological interview process.[118] Using as their basis the theory that behavior is situation specific, these investigators emphasize the identification of environmental settings and subsettings in which certain child behaviors occur, and suggest the use of a behavior checklist which enumerates various physical settings and behaviors that might take place in them. One of their checklists appears in Table 3.6. Although the Wahler-Cormier mapping procedure is designed for use in behavior modification programs, their approach can be adapted to child study in general, as they have indicated. It "can assist in mapping the kind of social attention (positive, negative, neutral, or none at all) the child

**Table 3.6.** Child Community Behavior Checklist

The following checklist allows you to describe your child's problems in various situations outside the house. The situations are listed in the column at left and common problem behaviors are listed in the row at the top. Examine each situation in the column and decide if one or more of the problem behaviors in the row fits your child. Check those that fit the best—if any.

|  | Always has to be told | Doesn't pay attention | Forgets | Dawdles | Refuses | Argues | Complains | Demands | Fights | Selfish | Destroys toys or property | Steals | Lies | Cries | Whines | Hangs on or stays close to adult | Acts silly | Mopes around | Stays alone | Has to Keep things in order | Sexual play |
|---|---|---|---|---|---|---|---|---|---|---|---|---|---|---|---|---|---|---|---|---|---|
| In own yard | | | | | | | | | | | | | | | | | | | | | |
| In neighbor's yard or home | | | | | | | | | | | | | | | | | | | | | |
| In stores | | | | | | | | | | | | | | | | | | | | | |
| Public park | | | | | | | | | | | | | | | | | | | | | |
| Downtown in general | | | | | | | | | | | | | | | | | | | | | |
| Church or Sunday School | | | | | | | | | | | | | | | | | | | | | |
| Community swimming pool | | | | | | | | | | | | | | | | | | | | | |
| In family car | | | | | | | | | | | | | | | | | | | | | |

is receiving in a particular subsetting as a consequence of deviant as well as desirable behavior."[119]

In addition to providing descriptions of a child's behavior within certain settings, behavioral maps can supply information about a child's use of space and can be used to compare the behaviors of different children. By tracking the movements of a child through physical settings and by observing behavior that occurs in these settings, we can make a number of generalizations regarding the child and his transactions with the environment.

## SUMMARY OF OBSERVATIONAL APPROACHES TO CHILD STUDY

In this chapter we have discussed some of the major observational approaches that have been employed in the study of child behavior and development. A summary of the important elements of each of these approaches is provided in Table 3.7.

A final word should be said about the importance of concealing the child's identity in observatonal records. Student observers should assign a code number or fictitious name to their study child. Teachers who record observations for their own purposes should likewise use some system to insure the anonymity of the student. Researchers usually assign a research number to each subject. When names must be used in anecdotes, case studies, or reports of parent conferences that are filed in a student's permanent folder, care must be taken to make certain that the files are secured. Professional ethics in child study will be discussed in Chapter 12.

**Table 3.7.** Summary of Observational Approaches to Child Study

| Method | Time Unit | Material Coverage | Recording Technique |
|---|---|---|---|
| Anecdotal Records | Irregular intervals over a relatively long period of time | Any incident that is considered to be significant. May be a unique episode or behavior in a routine situation. | Brief, sequential narrative description. Can be recorded after-the-fact. |
| Specimen Records | Continuous behavior sequences | "Everything" related to behavior and setting (unselective) | On-the-spot detailed, sequential narration |
| Running Records | Continuous behavior sequences | Unclassified recording of behavior in context | Sequential narration recorded either on-the-spot or soon after the episode |
| Time Sampling | Intermittent and uniform time segments | Selected aspects of behavior or situation or both | On-the-spot coding, usually as "present" or "absent" |
| Event Sampling | Continuous within limited time periods (such as one hour) | Preselected behavioral events of a given class | On-the-spot coding or narration or both. Entry and notation is made only if and when the event occurs. |
| *Environmental Assessment* | *Selected intervals (or intermittent short and uniform time intervals if time sampling is used)* | *Features of the environment (and their relationships to behavior)* | *Free narration or standardized description (including on-the-spot recording) or both* |

## CHAPTER NOTES

1.  C. Darwin, "A Biographical Sketch of an Infant," *Mind* 2 (1877): 285-294.
   W. Preyer, *The Mind of the Child* (New York: Appleton, 1888).
   M. W. Shinn, *The Biography of a Baby* (Boston: Houghton Mifflin, 1900).
   J. Sully, *Studies of Childhood* (New York: Appleton, 1895).
   D. Tiedemann, *Beobachtungen Über Die Entwicklung der Seelenfahrigkeiten Bei Kindern* (Altenburg: Bonde, 1787).
2.  W. G. Bateman, "The Language Status of Three Children at the Same Ages," *Pedagogical Seminary* 23 (1916): 211-39.
   G. V. N. Dearborn, *Motor-Sensory Development: Observations on the First Three Years of Childhood* (Baltimore: Warwick and York, 1910).

3.  D. A. Prescott, *The Child in the Educative Process* (New York: McGraw-Hill, 1957), p. 155.
4.  W. H. Burnham, "A Scheme of Classification for Child Study," *Pedagogical Seminary* 2 (1892): 191-98.
    W. W. Charters, "A Character Development Study," *The Personnel Journal* 12 (1933): 110-23.
    E. M. Haskell, ed., *Child Observations; First Series: Imitation and Allied Activities* (Boston: Heath, 1896).
    E. H. Russell, "The Study of Children at the State Normal School, Worcester, Mass.," *Pedagogical Seminary* 2 (1892): 343-57.
5.  J. A. Randall, "The Anecdotal Behavior Journal," *Progressive Education* 13 (1936): 22.
6.  R. Strang, *Counseling Technics in Colleges and Secondary Schools* (New York: Harper, 1937), p. 37.
7.  R. W. Tyler, "Techniques for Evaluating Behavior," *Educational Research Bulletin* 13 (1934): 10.
8.  A. E. Traxler, *The Nature and Use of Anecdotal Records* (New York: Harper, 1949), pp. 21-22.
9.  R. M. Brandt, *Studying Behavior in Natural Settings* (New York: Holt, 1972).
    M. Brown and V. Martin, "Anecdotal Records of Pupil Behavior," *California Journal of Education* 13 (1938): 205-08.
    C. Froehlich and K. Hoyt, *Guidance Testing* (Chicago: Science Research Associates, 1959).
    A. E. Hamalainen, "An Appraisal of Anecdotal Records," in *Contributions to Education*, no. 891 (New York: Bureau of Publications, Teachers College, Columbia University, 1943).
    D. B. Harris, "Use of the Behavior Journal in a Correctional School for Boys," *Journal of Juvenile Research* 22 (1938): 162-68.
    M. A. Kiley, *Personal and Interpersonal Appraisal Techniques* (Springfield, Ill.: Thomas, 1975).
    W. A. Mehrens and I. J. Lehmann, *Measurement and Evaluation in Education and Psychology* (New York: Holt, 1973).
    Prescott, *Educative Process.*
    Randall, "Behavior Journal."
    Strang, *Counseling Technics.*
10. Randall, "Behavior Journal."
11. Randall, "Behavior Journal."
12. Froehlich and Hoyt, *Guidance Testing.*
13. Council for Exceptional Children, "Policies for the Development and Use of Anecdotal Records," *Exceptional Children* 43 (1976): 113.
14. Prescott, *Educative Process.*
15. Kiley, *Appraisal Techniques*, pp. 120-121.
16. Prescott, *Educative Process.*
17. J. G. Navarra, *The Development of Scientific Concepts in a Young Child* (New York: Bureau of Publications, Teachers College, Columbia University, 1955).
18. Ibid., p. 88.
19. K. D. Wann, M. S. Dorn, and E. A. Liddle, *Fostering Intellectual Development in Young Children* (New York: Bureau of Publications, Teachers College, Columbia University, 1962).
20. Ibid., p. 59.
21. Ibid., p. 71.
22. Ibid., p. 40.
23. Traxler, *Anecdotal Records*, pp. 17-20.
24. Kiley, *Appraisal Techniques.*
    Mehrens and Lehmann, *Measurement and Evaluation.*
25. Mehrens and Lehmann, *Measurement and Evaluation.*
26. Council for Exceptional Children, "Policies."
27. Kiley, *Appraisal Techniques.*
28. Ibid., p. 128.
29. H. F. Wright, *Recording and Analyzing Child Behavior* (New York: Harper, 1967).
30. R. G. Barker, ed., *The Stream of Behavior* (New York: Appleton, 1967).
31. R. G. Barker and H. F. Wright, *One Boy's Day* (New York: Harper, 1951).
32. H. F. Wright, "Observational Child Study," in *Handbook of Research Methods in Child Development*, ed. R. H. Mussen (New York: Wiley, 1960).
33. Barker and Wright, *One Boy's Day*, pp. 392-393.
34. Wright, *Child Behavior.*
35. Barker and Wright, *One Boy's Day*, p. 394.
36. Wright, *Child Behavior*, p. 39.
37. Wright, "Child Study."
38. Wright, *Child Behavior.*
39. Ibid., pp. 57-60.
40. Wright, *Child Behavior.*
41. Ibid.
42. Barker and Wright, *One Boy's Day.*
43. Wright, *Child Behavior*, pp. 48-53.
44. Brandt, *Natural Settings.*
45. R. W. Heyns and R. Lippitt, "Systematic Observational Techniques," in *Handbook of Social Psychology*, vol. 1, ed. G. Lindzey (Reading, Mass.: Addison-Wesley, 1954).
46. R. G. Barker et al., *Specimen Records of American and English Children* (Lawrence, Kan.: University of Kansas Publications, Social Science Studies, 1961).
47. Wright, "Child Study."
48. Wright, *Child Behavior.*
49. K. E. Weick, "Systematic Observational Methods," in *Handbook of Social Psychology*, vol. 2, eds. G. Lindzey and F. Aronson (Reading, Mass.: Addison-Wesley, 1968).
50. E. J. Webb et al., *Unobtrusive Measures: Nonreactive Research in the Social Sciences* (Chicago: Rand McNally, 1981).
51. D. M. Irwin and M. M. Bushnell, *Observational Strategies for Child Study* (New York: Holt, 1980).
52. D. H. Cohen and V. Stern, *Observing and Recording the Behavior of Young Children* (New York: Teachers College Press, 1958).
53. Ibid.
54. S. Isaacs, *Intellectual Growth in Young Children* (New York: Harcourt, 1930).
55. S. Isaacs, *Social Development in Young Children* (New York: Harcourt, 1933).
56. L. P. Woodcock, *Life and Ways of the Two-Year-Old: A Teacher's Study* (New York: Dutton, 1941).
57. R. E. Arrington, "Time Sampling in Studies of Social Behavior," *Psychological Bulletin* 40 (1943): 81-124.
58. W. C. Olson and E. M. Cunningham, "Time-Sampling Techniques," *Child Development* 5 (1934): 41-58.
59. R. E. Arrington, "Time-Sampling of Child Behavior," *Psychological Monographs* 51 (1939): 28.
60. Arrington, "Time-Sampling in Studies," p. 82.
61. F. L. Goodenough, "Measuring Behavior Traits by Means of Repeated Short Samples," *Journal of Juvenile Research* 12 (1928): 23.
62. J. Altmann, "Observational Study of Behavior: Sampling Methods," *Behaviour* 40 (1974): 227-67.
63. T. Ayllon, D. Layman, and H. J. Kandel, "A Behavioral-Educational Alternative to Drug Control of Hyperactive Children," *Journal of Applied Behavior Analysis* 8 (1975): 137-46.
64. K. E. Allen et al., "Effects of Social Reinforcement on Isolate Behavior of a Nursery School Child," *Child Development* 35 (1964): 511-18.
65. Ibid., p. 512.
66. Ibid., pp. 512-513.
67. R. L. Mattos, "Some Relevant Dimensions of Interval Recording," *Academic Therapy* 6 (1971): 235-44.
68. M. R. Yarrow and C. Z. Waxler, "Observing Interaction: A Confrontation with Methodology," in *The Analysis of Social Interactions*, ed. R. B. Cairns (Hillsdale, N.J.: Erlbaum, 1979).
69. C. L. Feldbaum, T. E. Christenson, and E. O'Neal, "An Observational Study of the Assimilation of the Newcomer to the Preschool," *Child Development* 51 (1980): 497-507.

R. A. Feldman, J. S. Wodarski, and N. Flax, "Antisocial Children in a Summer Camp Environment: A Time Sampling Study," *Community Mental Health Journal* 11 (1975): 10-18.

H. Malley, "A Study of Some Techniques Underlying the Establishment of Successful Social Contacts at the Preschool Level," *Journal of Genetic Psychology* 47 (1935): 431-57.

W. C. Olson and V. S. Koetzle, "Amount and Rate of Talking of Young Children," *Journal of Experimental Education* 5 (1936): 175-79.

H. R. Quiltich, E. R. Christopherson, and T. R. Risley, "Evaluation of Children's Play Materials," *Journal of Applied Behavioral Analysis* 10 (1977): 501-02.

N. J. Reynolds and T. R. Risley, "The Role of Social and Material Reinforcers in Increasing Talking of Disadvantaged Preschool Children," *Journal of Applied Behavioral Analysis* 1 (1968): 253-62.

D. D. Richey and J. D. McKinney, "Classroom Behavioral Styles of Learning Disabled Boys," *Journal of Learning Disabilities* 11 (1978): 297-302.

R. E. Shores, P. Hester, and P. S. Strain, "The Effects of Amount and Type of Teacher-Child Interaction on Child-Child Interaction During Free Play," *Psychology in the Schools* 13 (1976): 171-75.

P. S. Strain and D. Ezzell, "The Sequence and Distribution of Behavioral Disordered Adolescents' Disruptive/Inappropriate Behaviors: An Observational Study in a Residential Setting," *Behavior Modification* 2 (1978): 403-25.

70.  Wright, "Child Study," p. 99.
71.  H. C. Dawe, "An Analysis of Two Hundred Quarrels of Preschool Children," *Child Development* 5 (1934): 139-57.
72.  Ibid., pp. 142-43.
73.  E. Clifford, "Discipline in the Home: A Controlled Study of Parental Practices," *Journal of Genetic Psychology* 95 (1959): 45-82.

G. F. Ding and A. T. Jersild, "A Study of the Laughing and Smiling of Preschool Children," *Journal of Genetic Psychology* 40 (1932): 452-72.

F. Goodenough, *Anger in Young Children* (Minneapolis: University of Minnesota Press, 1931).

R. C. Savin-Williams, "An Ethological Study of Dominance Formation and Maintenance in a Group of Human Adolescents," *Child Development* 47 (1976): 972-79.

A. M. Sluckin and R. K. Smith, "Two Approaches to the Concept of Dominance in Preschool Children," *Child Development* 48 (1977): 917-23.

M. J. Wright, "Measurement of the Social Competence of Preschool Children," *Canadian Journal of Behavioral Science* 12 (1980): 17-32.

74.  F. N. Kerlinger, *Foundations of Behavioral Research* (New York: Holt, 1973).
75.  Wright, "Child Study."
76.  K. H. Craik, "Environmental Psychology," in *New Directions in Psychology,* vol. 4, ed. K. H. Craik et al. (New York: Holt, 1970).
77.  Prescott, *Educative Process,* p. 171.
78.  P. V. Gump, "Ecological Psychology and Children," in *Review of Child Development Research,* vol. 5, ed. E. M. Hetherington (Chicago: University of Chicago Press, 1975).
79.  Brandt, *Natural Settings.*
80.  Ibid., pp. 72-73.
81.  Ibid., pp. 73-74.
82.  Ibid., pp. 74-75.
83.  R. B. Bechtel, *Enclosing Behavior* (Stroudsburg, Pa.: Dowden, 1977).

R. G. Heckelman, *The Life Space Survey* (San Rafael, Calif.: Academic Therapy Publications, 1972).

F. C. Ladd, "Black Youths View Their Environment: Neighborhood Maps," *Environment and Behavior* 2 (1970): 74-99.

F. G. Shelton, "A Note on 'the World Across the Street,'" *Harvard Graduate School of Education Association Bulletin* 12 (1967): 47-48.

84.  Gump, "Ecological Psychology," p. 108.
85.  C. A. Cartwright and G. P. Cartwright, *Developing Observational Skills* (New York: McGraw-Hill, 1974).
86.  Brandt, *Natural Settings.*
87.  A. E. Boehm and R. A. Weinberg, *The Classroom Observer: A Guide for Developing Observation Skills* (New York: Columbia University Teachers College Press, 1977).
88.  Brandt, *Natural Settings.*
89.  R. G. Barker and H. F. Wright, *Midwest and Its Children: The Psychological Ecology of an American Town* (New York: Row and Peterson, 1955).
90.  R. G. Barker, *Ecological Psychology: Concepts and Methods for Studying the Environment of Behavior* (Stanford, Calif.: Stanford University Press, 1968).
91.  R. G. Barker and P. Schoggen, *Qualities of Community Life* (San Francisco: Jossey-Bass, 1973).
92.  Barker, *Environment of Behavior,* p. 17.
93.  Barker and Wright, *Midwest and Its Children,* p. 45.
94.  Bechtel, *Enclosing Behavior,* pp. 22-23.
95.  R. G. Barker, "On the Nature of Environment," *Journal of Social Issues* 19 (1963): 17-38.
96.  Gump, "Ecological Psychology."
97.  Barker and Wright, *Midwest and Its Children.*
98.  Gump, "Ecological Psychology," p. 80.
99.  Barker, *Environment of Behavior,* p. 40.
100.  Ibid.
101.  P. V. Gump, P. Schoggen, and F. Redl, "The Behavior of the Same Child in Different Milieus," in *The Stream of Behavior,* ed. R. G. Barker (New York: Appleton, 1963), p. 173.
102.  Barker, *Environment of Behavior.*
103.  A. W. Wicker, "Ecological Psychology: Some Recent and Prospective Developments," *American Psychologist* 34 (1979): 755-65.
104.  P. Schoggen, "Environmental Forces in the Everyday Lives of Children," in *The Stream of Behavior,* ed. R. G. Barker (New York: Appleton, 1963), p. 47.
105.  M. Schoggen and P. Schoggen, "Environmental Forces in the Home Lives of Three-year-old Children in Three Population Sub-groups," JSAS *Catalog of Selected Documents in Psychology* 6 (1976): 8(ms. no. 1178).
106.  P. Schoggen, "Ecological Psychology and Mental Retardation," in *Observing Behavior,* vol. 1, ed. G. P. Sackett (Baltimore: University Park Press, 1978), p. 48.
107.  B. M. Caldwell and R. H. Bradley, "Home Observation for Measurement of the Environment" (ms., University of Arkansas at Little Rock, 1979).
108.  R. H. Bradley and B. M. Caldwell, "Screening the Environment," *American Journal of Orthopsychiatry* 48 (1978): 114-30.

Caldwell and Bradley, "Home Observation."

R. Elardo and R. H. Bradley, "The Home Observation for Measurement of the Environment (HOME) Scale: A Review of Research," *Developmental Review* 1 (1981): 113-45.

109.  H. L. Rheingold and K. V. Cook, "The Content of Boys' and Girls' Rooms As an Index of Parents' Behavior," *Child Development* 46 (1975): 459-63.
110.  E. O. Laumann and J. S. House, "Living Room Styles and Social Attributes: The Patterning of Material Artifacts in a Modern Urban Community," *Sociology and Social Research* 54 (1970): 321-42.
111.  F. S. Chapin, *Contemporary American Institutions* (New York: Harper, 1935).
112.  J. A. Stallings, *Learning to Look* (Belmont, Calif.: Wadsworth, 1977).
113.  J. Frost and B. Klein, *Children's Play and Playgrounds* (Boston: Allyn and Bacon, 1979).
114.  W. H. Ittelson, L. G. Rivlin, and H. M. Proshansky, "The Use of Behavioral Maps in Environmental Psychology," in *Environmental Psychology; Man and His Physical Setting,* eds. H. M. Proshansky, W. H. Ittelson, and L. G. Rivlin (New York: Holt, 1970), p. 658.
115.  N. Auslander, J. Juhasz, and F. Carrusco, "Chicano Children and Their Outdoor Environments" (ms., University of Colorado, 1977).

D. Beeken and H. L. Janzen, "Behavioral Mapping of Student Activity in Open-Areas and Traditional Schools," *American Educational Research Journal* 15 (1978): 507-17.

G. Coates and H. Sanoff, "Behavior Mapping: The Ecology of Child Behavior in a Planned Residential Setting," in *Environmental Design: Research and Practice,* ed. W. J. Mitchell, Proceedings of the EDRA3/AR8 Conference (Los Angeles: University of California at Los Angeles, 1972).

C. Cooper-Marcus, "Children's Play in a Low-rise, Inner-city Housing Development," in *Childhood City, Man-Environment Interactions,* vol. 12, ed. R. C. Moore (Milwaukee: EDRA, 1974).

D. G. Hayward, M. Rothenberg, and R. Beasley, *School-aged Children in Three Urban Playgrounds* (New York: Environmental Psychology Program, City University of New York, 1973).

V. Hole, *Children's Play on Housing Estates,* National Building Studies Research Paper 39 (London: Her Majesty's Stationery Office, 1966).

C. S. Weinstein, "Modifying Student Behavior in an Open Classroom Through Changes in the Physical Design," *American Educational Research Journal* 14 (1977): 249-62.

M. Wolfe and L. Rivlin, "Evolution of Space Utilization Patterns in a Children's Psychiatric Hospital," in *Environmental Design: Research and Practice,* ed. W. J. Mitchell, Proceedings of the EDRA3/AR8 Conference (Los Angeles: University of California at Los Angeles, 1972).

116.  Ittelson et al., "Use of Behavioral Maps."

117.  Beeken and Janzen, "Behavioral Mapping."

118.  R. G. Wahler and W. H. Cormier, "The Ecological Interview: A First Step in Out-patient Child Behavior Therapy," *Journal of Behavior Therapy and Experimental Psychiatry* 1 (1970): 279-89.

119.  Ibid., p. 289.

# 4
# Methodological Issues
# in Observational Study

The frequency of observational studies seemed to peak in the 1930s with a number of now classic investigations that were published at the University of Minnesota, the University of Iowa, and Columbia University. In a 1939 article on observation in the *Review of Educational Research,* Jersild and Meigs wrote that "direct observation is the oldest, and remains the commonest instrument of scientific research."[1] During the next thirty years, however, the use of systematic observation in research declined.[2] In 1960, Wright reported that of the empirical studies involving children which were conducted from 1940 to 1958, those using direct observation represented only a little more than 5 percent of all research in the area.[3] At about the same time, Medley and Mitzel noted that although "there is no more obvious approach to research on teaching than direct observation . . . it is a rare study indeed that includes any formal observation at all."[4] A decade later, Herbert remarked that the underutilization of systematic observation was puzzling "in view of the recent emphasis on individual differences, the trend from prescriptive to descriptive studies, and the enormous increase in ease and accuracy of recording made possible by the new technological devices."[5]

The disenchantment with observational techniques during the 1940s and 1950s was related to the growing acceptance of the laboratory experiment as *the* approach to child development research. In addition to the laboratory experiment's methodological rigor which insured internal validity, it also had many other positive features which led to its widespread respect: easy isolation of variables, control of extraneous situational influences that might affect dependent variables, random assignment of subjects and treatments, and precise and highly objective measurement techniques.[6] In many cases, laboratory studies with children bypassed the human observer altogether by completely mechanizing the subject's responses. The purpose of this method was to supposedly eliminate the methodological problems of observational study that had been recognized during the early child development movement. Perhaps the move to the laboratory was associated with the mistaken notion that naturalistic studies and observation were synonymous; or maybe the change in research settings was due in part to the common error of equating the laboratory with experimental design and field studies with non-experimental procedures.[7] Traditionally, naturalistic or field studies have been considered less scientific than laboratory research.[8]

Heavy reliance on standardized tests, questionnaires, and interview measures also may have been responsible for the lost impetus of direct observation between 1940 and 1960. Not surprisingly, these more economical means of data collection developed into methodological mainstays and quickly became the choice of most investigators. Commenting on this transition in child development research, Wright has indicated that

> Psychological science began with a leap from the armchair to the laboratory and has since generally preferred to do things with its subjects, to give them tasks or problems, to interrogate them, to test them, or at least to draw them into prearranged situations.[9]

However, in spite of their popularity, tests and measurements are not infallible, nor are laboratory studies without their shortcomings. There are numerous examples of elegantly designed experiments that are seriously restricted in scope, as Bronfenbrenner explains:

This limitation derives from the fact that many of these experiments involve situations that are unfamiliar, artificial, and short-lived and that call for unusual behaviors that are difficult to generalize to other settings.[10]

As a consequence of the preoccupation with laboratory experimentation, we have really learned very little about how people act outside of laboratories or clinics.[11] Bronfenbrenner has commented that much of child development is "the science of the strange behavior of children in strange situations with strange adults for the briefest periods of time."[12] In fact, there is evidence that results obtained in laboratories may be different from those secured in natural settings.[13] Therefore, greater attention should be given to the selection of a setting that is appropriate for a research problem. Some hypotheses require a laboratory setting, and others, a field setting.[14] Still other research problems call for both laboratory and naturalistic components.[15] Similarly, certain studies can be better served by tests and questionnaries, and others, by direct observation. The goals of the investigator and the nature of his or her subjects should determine which methods are employed.

A recent survey of child development research reports published in three major developmental journals during 1972 to 1974 revealed that 8 percent of the investigations were observational studies; 17 percent employed paper-and-pencil measures; and 76 percent used the experimental laboratory paradigm.[16] On the other hand, Haynes has estimated that anywhere from 30 to 95 percent of all clinical research with children has employed observation as the method of data collection for pre-intervention assessment or for evaluating the effects of intervention procedures.[17] In the past five years, there has been an obvious dramatic increase in the number of naturalistic and laboratory studies using direct observation. A perusal of the professional journals reveals a gradually increasing balance among the major research approaches, with the observational study of children re-emerging as a method of investigation. Some possible reasons for the renewed enthusiasm for systematic observation will be considered next.

## ADVANTAGES OF SYSTEMATIC OBSERVATION

There are a number of attractive features of systematic observation, most of which pertain primarily to observation in naturalistic settings. Among the most important advantages of naturalistic observation is external validity. Laboratory studies, because of their control of extraneous variables, can boast of high internal validity (i.e., related to the question of whether differences that are found are true rather than artifacts of measurement). However, the results of laboratory studies cannot always be generalized beyond the limits of the contrived experimental environment. Studies conducted in the laboratory may have great precision, but they are notoriously weak on external validity or representativeness of their findings. For instance, educators sometimes question the generalizing of results of animal learning experiments to the learning of school children. They argue that the phenomena measured in animal research are not necessarily representative of learning in the classroom. Their point is well taken. Observational studies conducted in the natural setting do not suffer from this problem of artificiality. The researcher can extrapolate or generalize easily from the data, because naturalistic studies are as close to true life as you can get. They also permit the recording of behavior contemporaneously with its natural occurrence,[18] provide data that pertain directly to typical behavior settings or situations,[19] and do not disturb the natural stream of behavior.[20]

There are other characteristics of natural or field settings which, because of their unavailability or difficulty to manipulate in the laboratory, make the naturalistic study appealing. Kerlinger has said that "the more realistic the research situation, the stronger the variables."[21] By this, he means that the study variables in the natural setting usually have stronger effects than those in experimental settings. And the independent variable may manifest a range of intensity that cannot be produced in the laboratory because of ethical or other restrictions.[22] Phenomena in the natural setting also display a wider range of variation than could be simulated in the laboratory environment.[23] Another advantage of field studies is that they typically span a longer time period than laboratory investigations and thereby avoid problems created by the ability of most people to buffer wide ranges of stimulation when exposed to them for a short time span.[24] Laboratory experiments may not provide conditions which cross the subject's response threshold;[25] therefore, an effect may be revealed in the natural setting, but not in the laboratory.

Some child developmentalists have abandoned traditional methods of research in favor of observational approaches for other reasons. Bersoff, in a somewhat controversial article that discusses the decline of psychological testing and suggestions for its redemption, has pointed out that many of the variables which were once thought to be amenable to measurement only in conventional ways can now be assessed through direct observation.[26] He has coined the term *psychosituational assessment* for data gathering techniques about behavior that are rooted to environmental events. The primary thrust of this contextual assessment "is the analysis of behavior and the delineation of the immediate antecedent and consequent conditions that evoke, reinforce, and perpetuate that behavior."[27] The procedures are considered valid because they are based on direct and continuous measurement of performance. Bersoff recommends both time and event sampling as useful direct measures in natural settings. A number of observational procedures are already available for the measurement of personality,[28] and the development of observational methods for the study of other behavior variables appears promising.

Lambert, Cox, and Hartsough attempted an evaluation of the intellectual functioning of elementary school children through the use of observational methods.[29] They found that six areas of Intellectual Functioning Events (IFEs) lent themselves to direct observation and measurement in the classroom. The six classes of IFEs, which are based on Piagetian theory, include basic language skills, concepts of time and space, logical concepts, math concepts, reasoning skills, and general signs of development. The investigators argue quite convincingly that intellectual behavior, which is measured through observational procedures in a classroom setting, may actually be more relevant than an intelligence test score in appraising current functioning, in developing teaching and intervention strategies, and in monitoring behavior change. Indeed, more and more researchers who are displeased with certain aspects of traditional methods, such as laboratory procedures or standardized tests, are turning to alternative approaches like behavioral observation. Practitioners also have expressed a preference for observation over experimental methods. Anthony, a noted child psychiatrist, has written that the advantages of direct observation are great enough to make it the preferred method whenever it is available.[30]

Other general merits of observation, whether it is conducted in naturalistic or in laboratory settings, are these: it is independent of the subject's willingness to report;[31] it is preferable when the subject is a very young child or is mentally ill and considered an inadequate direct source of information;[32] it avoids the fallibilities of retrospective data;[33] it eliminates much of the ambiguity that is associated with projectively derived data;[34] it is the least inferential approach to data collection;[35] and it is very useful in the exploratory stages of research in providing the investigator with some idea of relevant parameters.[36]

Although the resurgence of interest in observational study can be attributed to its many virtues, several other reasons for its growing acceptance may also be suggested. One reason may be attributable to the behavior therapy boom of the past decade. Because of the importance of observation in behavior therapy, some have written that a major contribution to the behavioral sciences from this new therapeutic technique has been a growing awareness of the value of systematic observation as a supplement to more traditional methods of assessment.[37] A second factor that may help explain the recent enthusiasm for observational studies in natural settings is the new emphasis on research dealing with practical problems. As Brandt indicates, "Naturalistic field studies . . . have the advantage over other research types of being heuristic, highly realistic, relevant to social problems, and oriented toward significant theoretical issues."[38] No one would deny that there is a pressing need to conduct research that will have an impact on our everyday lives. A third trend that has probably influenced the renewal of interest in behavioral observation is the increasing acceptance of ecological psychology and ethology, both of which require observation for data collection. A fourth reason for the return to direct observation may be related to the recent growth of day care and early education. Many of the traditional laboratory techniques and tests and measurements for studying older children are inappropriate for younger subjects; therefore, observation has become the logical choice. Finally, the development of observer systems (see Chapter 5) and advances in technology (see Chapter 6) have facilitated the recording and analysis of data obtained through behavioral observation and have encouraged more and more researchers and practitioners to use observational strategies in studying children.

The contrasts we made earlier between naturalistic and laboratory research should not be interpreted as endorsement of one method over the other; some problems are better studied in the field, and others, in highly controlled experiments. In fact, interesting arguments have been made for a closer articulation between the laboratory and the field.[39] At any rate, direct observation as a medium of data collection in both naturalistic and laboratory settings is here to stay. There are indications that, with more refinement, observational techniques may replace many of the more traditional research methods. Undoubtedly, systematic observation will help accelerate our efforts to find answers to many of the complex questions regarding child development and behavior.

## PROBLEMS IN SYSTEMATIC OBSERVATION

### OBSERVER ERRORS

**Perceptual Errors.** The issue of observer bias has received considerable attention in the literature on observational study. Campbell has written perhaps the most definitive paper concerning errors made by humans when they are links in the communication chain.[40] He classifies systematic errors in observation as duplicatory transmission assignments, reductive coding assignments, and a combination of these two processes. Duplicatory assignment involves relaying a message without intended change in form. Reductive assignment, on the other hand, involves a decision-making function in which complex input signals are coded into a simpler output format. In combination, the two assignments contain elements common to both. Subsumed under these three rubrics are twenty-three systematic errors that Campbell has identified.

One of the most pervasive systematic error tendencies in duplicatory transmission is *abbreviation*. This occurs when part of the stimulus that confronts the observer is omitted from his or her response, and usually happens when the stimulus situation is extremely complex. Consistently, the "output will be shorter, simpler, and less detailed than input."[41] Abbreviation is related to what Dittman calls the problems of channel capacity of the observer.[42] All of the behavior in a behavior episode, such as spoken language, vocalizations, facial expressions, body movement, and psychophysiological responses, are available to the observer at one time, and he or she can process only so much material. As a result, there is a disposition for the observer to attend more to higher information signals than to lower ones, since higher information messages are more commanding and are more likely to get through the perceptual situation. An investigation by Dittman and his associates revealed such perceptual interference.[43] In forming judgments about how other people were feeling, observers tended to concentrate on facial expressions instead of bodily expressions. Another common perceptual-cognitive bias is *middle message loss*. In this type of selective information loss, the middle part of a message—rather than the initial or final portion—is the least well retained. This can be conveniently explained in terms of primary and recency effects. *Closure* (directional distortion) and *symmetry* (regularized distortion) occur when the input is unclear, irregular, or incomplete. Consistent with Gestalt theory, the observer exercises a systematic bias away from the input in an attempt to "fill in" or to explain the message. *Enhancement of contrast* refers to the observer's tendency to divide the content "into clear cut 'entities,' reducing gradations both by exaggerating some differences and losing others."[44] The bias toward *central tendency* involves the distortion of extreme events in the direction of the mean of the series. Here, the observer avoids judgments that are either very positive or very negative.

The second broad category of transmission functions employed in communication systems, reductive coding, may be considered a special form of filtering. Information is reduced, and consequently, the output becomes less complex than the input. One type of error in reductive coding is *coding relativism* or inclination toward systematic fluctuations in standards used for coding. Coding thresholds that are used by the observer "tend to be relative to recent inputs rather than constant for physical attributes of the stimulus."[45] The assignment of an event to one category or another is a function of what is occurring while the observer is recording the behavior. *Assimilation to prior coding assignment* is another common error in which there is a likelihood that an observer may revert to prior coding assignments if the assignment is changed or possibly if it becomes too difficult or too boring. Another influence on an observer is *coding contamination from associated cues.* If the observer has noticed that two behaviors have varied together in the past, he or she may associate certain values of one with values of the other. Consequently, both of these dimensions may contribute to coding. For example, if the observer is studying children's aggressive behavior on the basis of pushing and if he or she has previously associated aggressive pushing with face thrusting, then face thrusting may contribute to the category of aggression. *Assimilation to evaluation coding* is the tendency for an observer to perceive and categorize in terms of "good" versus "bad" or "like" versus "dislike" or some other affectively biased mode of reaction.

Some systematic errors that affect the recording process are shared by both the duplicatory transmission and the reductive coding assignments. One of these, the bias that Campbell terms *assimilation to prior input,* occurs when messages are distorted "in the direction of identity with previous inputs."[46] The distortion is usually caused by similarities in present and prior inputs. Another common bias, *assimilation to expected message,* means that an observer is prone to make output like expected input. The observer sees what he or she expects to see. Naturally, this is especially significant if the observer is also the person who formulated the hypotheses for the study. Expectation bias will be considered later in this chapter. *Assimilation to own attitudes* is a tendency for output to be colored by an observer's personal attitudes, indicating that there is an emotional as well as a perceptual component to some systematic error. Dittman has explained the inclination for an individual to become emotionally involved in the situation he or she is asked to observe:

> He becomes involved because he is a human being watching his fellow human beings, and he feels their feelings empathically, just as any person feels what others are going through. The difficulty with the observer's empathizing is that what he observes is subject to distortions based upon his own emotional history. . . .[47]

*Assimilation to reward and punishment* means that messages which are not perfectly clear may be distorted in the direction of prior messages that were rewarding or punishing. *Distortion to please receiver* occurs when output deviates from input because the observer has to transmit the message to another person and wishes to please the recipient and avoid unpleasantness. *Assimilation to prior output* is the tendency to repeat prior output even though it is not the same as the input. This error frequently occurs when communication is unclear and there is no opportunity to check the accuracy of the output.

Although the foregoing do not represent all of the possible errors made by observers, they are among the most prominent. Readers who are interested in a more thorough treatment of the topic are referred to Cambell's excellent article.[48] These types of systematic errors that people make when they are links in the communication system are closely paralleled by a number of biases in rating procedures which have been identified by Guilford.[49] Guilford's rating errors will be considered in Chapter 5. Two major solutions to observer errors are training and methodological controls. These are discussed elsewhere in detail.[50]

**Other Observer Errors.** The interesting work of Rosenthal, which culminated in the book *Experimenter Effects in Behavioral Research,*[51] has increased our awareness of the possible existence of observer bias in behavioral research. He reported several studies which demonstrated that an observer's perceptions and interpretations are affected by the knowledge of expected results. In 1967, Scott, Burton, and Yarrow examined observer expectancy bias and found that an observer who was informed of the experimental hypotheses recorded data that were more supportive of the hypotheses than uninformed observers.[52] In spite of certain methodological shortcomings, this study illustrated a definite expectation effect. Subsequent investigations have, in most cases, shown the effects of expectation bias or trait labeling bias in observational recordings.[53]

A second potential source of observer bias is related to experimenter feedback concerning the observation record. O'Leary, Kent, and Kanowitz revealed that they could shape the recordings of their observers not only by providing observers with predictions of experimental results but also by commenting on the recordings as the incoming data were reviewed.[54] Evaluative or contingent feedback differentially reinforced predicted decreases in categories of certain behaviors.

A third possible source of observer bias is introduced by overt reliability checks. Reid reported that observers who obtained median reliabilities of 75 percent when they were aware that reliability was being computed dropped to 51 percent when informed that reliability was not being assessed.[55] Other studies, including those conducted in the classroom, have also consistently found that observers record behavior more reliably when they have been informed that reliability is being computed[56] and when the reliability assessor is known.[57] Wiggins has commented on these findings:

> It makes a certain amount of sense. We all work a little bit harder when the boss is around. Our opinions are perhaps a shade closer to the boss's in his presence. And we are more accurate in describing events that have been observed by others than we are in recounting exploits that cannot be verified.[58]

Kent and Foster provide some valuable suggestions regarding ways to reduce biases in reliability assessment.[59] In addition, they discuss in considerable depth the selection of appropriate measures for computing reliability and the manner in which observational reliability should be recorded.

A fourth potential observer bias may be considered a result of the three sources already mentioned. It has been named consensual observer drift.[60] When observers are placed in fixed and unchanging pairs over a period of time, they tend to modify their interpretations of the behavioral categories to produce maximum reliability within their group. They develop idiosyncratic cues for determining the occurrence of certain behaviors. Although inter-observer agreement remains high or even increases, accuracy in terms of the original criteria decreases. Lower reliability is effected with other pairs of observers using the same category system. A number of studies have confirmed the existence of observer drift.[61]

A fifth possible source of observer bias is caused by the influence of prior information and knowledge of behavioral predictability on observational recording. Following Bruner,[62] who postulated that instructional set can affect observations, Mash and his colleagues[63] studied this potential observer error. They found that observers who had been informed prior to observation that there was a pattern to the interaction which would facilitate coding made more accurate observations than those who had been told that there was no pattern. Observers with a training history of scoring predictable interactions performed more poorly when placed in a new observation situation, whereas those with a training history of coding unpredictable interactions increased their accuracy. Of the transfer decrements made by the first group, most were related to a greater number of perseverative errors.

A sixth potential source of observer bias is caused by the behavior code that is used. Evidence for the existence of a relationship between behavioral categories and bias has been found in studies that examine complexity (i.e., a measure of the number of discriminations required of the observer) and observer agreement. The results of several investigations have shown that inter-observer reliability is negatively correlated with complexity of the protocols.[64] Complicated codes may require a large number of categories or involve complex codes that are difficult to discriminate. This has led some researchers to suggest that reliability coefficients may be very misleading because of differences in complexity of the code.[65]

## OBSERVER INTERFERENCE

The possibility that the presence of an observer might affect the behavior of those being observed has been a matter of concern for many years. One group of investigators have assumed that the intrusiveness of the observer upon the observed is inevitable. Sherif and Sherif have taken this position.

> People may lose their initial awareness of a piece of equipment or even of a live observer busily recording their words and deeds. But does reduction of initial self-awareness mean that they are behaving without regard to the very significant fact that they are being studied? It does not.[66]

Research studies carried out in a variety of settings with both children and adults have demonstrated observer effects.[67] The intrusive effects are rather complex as some authors have explained.[68] Subjects might alter their behavior so it becomes either socially desirable or undesirable, depending on the demand characteristics of the setting, or their behavior may become more variable.

Several other researchers maintain that the effect of the observer is nonreactive and that the observer becomes a neutral stimulus with the passage of time. Schoggen is one proponent of this point of view that is sometimes referred to as the "habituation hypothesis."

> One cannot completely set aside on a moment's notice the attitudes and patterns of social behavior which have been developed and practiced for years in favor of other, unnatural forms of behavior fancied to be more acceptable. Particularly this is true in dealing with children who are likely to react with blank, incredulous stares to parent behavior that deviates markedly from the usual pattern.[69]

Considerable evidence also exists that reactive effects of the observer are minimal, or that there is rapid habituation to the observer's presence.[70] To further complicate the issue, age, sex, and social class may be correlated with reactivity.[71] From all of this, it is probably safe to conclude that the observation process causes changes in the subject's behavior under some conditions but not under others.

Haynes has enumerated a number of strategies for systematically measuring reactivity:

> The most powerful method is to covertly observe target subjects and then introduce a conspicuous observer and monitor behavior rates within the two conditions. Differential behavior rates as a function of the conspicuous observation process suggest that the observation process has reactive effects on the behavior of the target subjects.

Reactivity may also be inferred from a slope in the resultant data, although slope may also be a function of other determinants. A gradual increase or decrease in rate may suggest that initial levels of the behavior were a function of the reactivity of the observation process and that because of habituation, later behavior rates are a more accurate representation of the "true" rate. It is also possible that the effects of habituation summate and the earlier data points may be more representative of the "true" value. Other empirical procedures, such as intervention or criterion-related validity assessment, may be necessary to determine which rate is a more valid representation of naturalistic values.

Reactivity may also be inferred from decreases in variability of the data across observation sessions. One effect of an assessment procedure may be increased variability in behavior. Although it is difficult to know whether observed variability is greater than what would be characteristic in the unobserved situation, changes in variability across sessions could imply that behavior during early observation sessions was influenced by the assessment procedures.[72]

Johnson and Bolstad, in a critical review of intrusive effects of the observer, warn that observer reactivity is a methodological problem that cannot be dismissed since it can limit the generalizability of observational data.[73] They recommend that factors which seem to account for reactivity should be examined more carefully and that solutions be reached to neutralize the stimulus value of the observer. Sources of interference such as conspicuousness of the observer, personal attributes of the observer, and rationale for observation should all be given greater attention in the future.

Different strategies have been employed to combat problems and potential problems of observer interference. One is the use of participant observers. An example of participant observation is when the observer also plays with the children being studied. This method has been advocated as a solution to difficulties that are sometimes encountered with the use of outside observers.[74] Participant observation, a term coined by Lindeman[75] over fifty years ago, has been defined by Schwartz and Schwartz as

> . . . a process in which the observer's presence in a social situation is maintained for the purpose of scientific investigation. The observer is in a face-to-face relationship with the observed, and by participating with them in their natural life setting, he gathers data. Thus, the observer is part of the context being observed. . . .[76]

Participant observation can occur at three levels: complete participant, participant as observer, and observer as participant.[77] The *complete participant* is the researcher who secretly becomes a member of the group in order to make observations. This involves deception and may even be considered spying, so it is discouraged on ethical grounds. The *participant as observer,* on the other hand, does not wholly conceal the purpose of his or her presence in the group. But, in an attempt not to distort the naturalness of the situation, the researcher's activities as participant assume priority over his or her observational tasks. In the role of *observer as participant,* the researcher is known at the outset to all members of the group. This is a role that is typically assumed by anthropologists. Guidelines for participant observation[78] and implications of the three levels of participation[79] are considered elsewhere.

Another similar solution to the reactive effects to observation is the use of lay observers rather than outside observers. Lay observers are persons who "belong" in the observational setting (nurses, teacher aides, etc.). Several studies which have used lay observers successfully have been reported.[80]

Concealment has been used with success in nonparticipant observation in order to handle some of the problems encountered as a result of observer effects. The ethical issues surrounding concealed observations will be discussed in Chapter 12. Observation rooms equipped with one-way mirrors or specially treated wire-mesh observation screens permit the observer to view a behavioral event without being seen by the subjects. Several technical innovations also have minimized the reactive nature of the observation process. These include audio recorders, films, and radio transmitters. Equipment and devices used to aid observational study will be considered in Chapter 6.

## RELIABILITY

In observational study, reliability refers to both accuracy and stability.[81] The most frequently used indices of *accuracy* are called observer accuracy and observer agreement. The first refers to the correspondence of an observer's coding with some previously developed criterion coding of the behaviors in question. The second involves the calculation of agreement between observers. Reliability may also indicate the *stability* of data over successive observations. For example, if an observer records a relatively stable criterion behavior for a child over a three-day period, we can assume that the behavior in question will be relatively consistent over the series of observations. Stability would be reflected by high correlation, and instability, by low correlation. Instability would suggest that the observer should exercise caution in the interpretation of his or her data.

A major drawback of systematic observation is its susceptibility to unreliability. Some reasons for low reliability, many of which have already been discussed, are summarized here.

1. Inadequate sampling

2. Lack of precision in defining behavior

3. Complexity of method of recording

4. Rapid, complex interaction

5. Difference in perspective of observers

6. Individual differences in degree of decisiveness of activities of subjects observed

7. Constant errors due to observer bias

8. Requiring high order inferences in classifying behavior

9. Demanding the simultaneous observation of too many variables

10. Excessively long periods of observation without interspersed rest periods

11. Inadequate training of observers

12. Effect of individual observers upon the behavior of the subjects

13. Degree of acquaintance with the subject[82]

Reliability in systematic observation is especially important because of its relationship to validity. Low reliability restricts validity (although high reliability does not always guarantee validity). Consideration of the different types of reliability for observational recordings and their calculations can be found in other sources.[83]

## VALIDITY

Validity refers to the degree to which an instrument measures what it purports to measure. An observation is valid if recorded differences in data yielded by it represent actual differences in behavior and not just impressions made on different observers. One important type of validity is *content validity,* or the extent to which the observed behavior is a sample from a particular behavior domain. More often than not, investigators have relied only on this type of validity. If an observer system is used, content validity refers to the degree that the codes adequately sample behavior. Logically derived content validity, rather than that empirically derived, is affected not only by the individual behaviors selected for study but also by sampling durations, frequency, and schedule. Content validity determines the generalizability and comprehensiveness of the observations.[84]

Another broad category of validity that can be measured in several ways is criterion-related validity. Comparing observational data concurrently with independent measures (i.e., outside criteria) that have already been validated is called *concurrent validity*. For example, observation data collected on a child can be compared with scores on questionnaire and interview measures obtained at a similar point in time. High intercorrelations among the three measures would give us confidence that the data collected in the course of our observations actually reflect the dimensions of behavior under investigation. (Supportive criterion-related data from a variety of sources also provide evidence of construct validity.)

Examining to see if future behavior can be predicted from current observations is called *predictive validity*. If our observations of a kindergartner's social adjustment in school correlate with a teacher's rating of the youngster's adjustment in the first grade, we can infer that our observations have predictive validity. Like concurrent validity, predictive validity is usually computed with correlational techniques, with the degree of validity indicated from the coefficient derived from the statistical procedure.

Although the criterion-related validation of observational procedures has been emphasized by some investigators, very little work has been carried out in this area.[85] As Haynes has written, "Interpretation of validation studies is confounded by the fact that the validity of criterion measures is sometimes suspect, validity of an observation system may be confined to particular research programs, and some behavior codes, but not others, may demonstrate validity."[86] An especially good synthesis of the existing literature on validity and other technical issues in direct observation has been written by Foster and Cone.[87]

The various threats to validity of observational studies (perceptual errors, observer bias, reactivity, etc.) were discussed earlier in this chapter.

## NORMS

The absence of norms is a frequently cited shortcoming of systematic observation. In contrast to standardized tests which have data available on the standardization sample, observations usually have no norms with which to compare data obtained on an individual child. The availability of norms is a decided advantage of standardized measures over observational techniques. A solution to problems created by the absence of normative data for observation is simply to collect norm data beforehand so they are available for comparative purposes. Nelson and Bowles have recommended expanding observation beyond the target child to include other children who are the same age or in the same grade in school so that information is available on the typical behavior or performance of these children.[88] Normative data are especially crucial in evaluating the effects of treatment programs. The inclusion of norms in observation will allow this technique to share one of the distinct advantages of standardized tests.

## OTHER PROBLEMS

Other disadvantages of systematic observation that have been reported are of a more practical nature. These particular difficulties are associated with such issues as cost, time, and resistance to observation.[89] Observational studies are expensive, especially if sophisticated instrumentation is used. Systematic observation also can be quite time-consuming in relation to other techniques of child study. Although there are differing points of view on the topic, the high-dross rate that is inevitable in most observations is another major complaint about observational studies. High-dross rate refers to the fact that many supposedly irrelevant events take place and are recorded by the observer before the target behavior occurs. Thus, a good deal of time and money is expended for little information. Not all researchers support this argument. As Barker explains, "data that are dross for one investigator are gold for another."[90] Regarding resistance to observation, Medley and Mitzel have written that some teachers and administrators resent the invasion of their privacy by outside observers.[91] Where the reluctance to admit observers in the classrooms exists, it can be overcome with careful planning and adequate justification of procedures to school personnel.

## THE FUTURE OF SYSTEMATIC OBSERVATION

There is a growing interest in systematic observation as a means of data collection in both structured and naturalistic or field settings. Its many positive features are responsible for the recent dramatic increase in its use. The advantages of direct observation, particularly that conducted in natural settings, make it an important approach to child study, as Bouchard so aptly states:

> . . . its advantages put it in a position of being the place where the generality, applicability, and utility of psychological knowledge are put to test. The role of the field researcher is thus an important one from the standpoint of both social utility and scientific advance. His work can enhance the usefulness of scientific theory for applied work and counter erroneous extrapolation and generalization at the theoretical level. The field researcher is the mediator of a relevant social-psychological science.[92]

### CHAPTER NOTES

1. A. T. Jersild and M. F. Meigs, "Direct Observation As a Research Method," *Review of Educational Research* 40 (1939): 472.
2. E. Gellert, "Systematic Observation: A Method in Child Study," *Harvard Educational Review* 25 (1955): 179-95.
3. H. F. Wright, "Observational Child Study," in *Handbook of Research Methods in Child Development*, ed. P. H. Mussen (New York: Wiley, 1960).
4. D. M. Medley and H. E. Mitzel, "Measuring Classroom Behavior by Systematic Observation," in *Handbook of Research on Teaching*, ed. N. L. Gage (Chicago: Rand McNally, 1963).
5. J. Herbert, "Direct Observation As a Research Technique," *Psychology in the Schools* 7 (1970): 127-38.
6. F. N. Kerlinger, *Foundations of Behavioral Research* (New York: Holt, 1973).
7. R. D. Parke, "Interactional Designs," in *The Analysis of Social Interactions*, ed. R. G. Cairns (Hillsdale, N.J.: Erlbaum, 1979).
8. H. E. Brogden, "Some Observations on Two Methods in Psychology," *Psychological Bulletin* 77 (1972): 431-37.
   W. J. Tikunoff and B. A. Ward, "Conducting Naturalistic Research on Teaching: Some Procedural Considerations," *Education and Urban Society* 12 (1980): 263-90.
9. Wright, "Child Study," pp. 71-72.
10. U. Bronfenbrenner, "Toward an Experimental Ecology of Human Development," *American Psychologist* 32 (1977): 513.
11. R. G. Barker, "Wanted: An Eco-behavioral Science," in *Naturalistic Viewpoints in Psychological Research*, eds. E. P. Willems and H. L. Raush (New York: Holt, 1969).
    R. B. McCall, "Challenges to a Science of Developmental Psychology," *Child Development* 48 (1977): 344-44.
12. Bronfenbrenner, "Experimental Ecology," p. 513.
13. J. Belsky, "Mother-Infant Interaction at Home and in the Laboratory: A Comparative Study," *Journal of Genetic Psychology* 137 (1980): 37-47.
    U. Bronfenbrenner, *The Ecology of Human Development* (Cambridge, Mass.: Harvard University Press, 1979).
    M. E. Lamb, "Interactions Between Eight-month-old Children and Their Fathers and Mothers," in *The Role of the Father in Child Development*, ed. M. E. Lamb (New York: Wiley, 1976).
    G. Ross et al., "Separation Protest in Infants in Home and Laboratory," *Developmental Psychology* 11 (1975): 256-57.
    A. Schlieper, "Mother-Child Interaction Observed at Home," *American Journal of Orthopsychiatry* 45 (1975): 468-72.
    L. A. Sroufe, "A Methodological and Philosophical Critique of Intervention-oriented Research," *Developmental Psychology* 2 (1970): 140-45.
14. Bronfenbrenner, "Experimental Ecology."
    P. C. Ellsworth, "From Abstract Ideas to Concrete Instances: Some Guidelines for Choosing Natural Research Settings," *American Psychologist* 32 (1977): 604-15.
15. Ibid.
16. M. T. Larson, "Current Trends in Child Development Research," *Tomorrow's Child* 1 (1978): 22-26.
17. S. N. Haynes, *Principles of Behavioral Assessment* (New York: Gardner Press, 1978).
18. R. W. Heyns and R. Lippitt, "Systematic Observational Techniques," in *Handbook of Social Psychology*, vol. 1, ed. G. Lindzey (Reading, Mass.: Addison-Wesley, 1954).
    C. Selltiz et al., *Research Methods in Social Relations* (New York: Holt, 1964).
19. D. A. Prescott, *The Child in the Educative Process* (New York: McGraw-Hill, 1957).
    K. Purcell and K. Brady, *Assessment of Interpersonal Behavior in Natural Settings: A Research Technique and Manual* (Denver: Children's Asthma Research Institute, 1965).
    M. W. Riley, *Sociological Research: A Case Approach* (New York: Harcourt, 1963).
    Wright, "Child Study."

20. Ibid.
21. Kerlinger, *Foundations*, p. 40.
22. T. J. Bouchard, Jr., "Field Research Methods: Interviewing, Questionnaires, Participant Observation, Systematic Observation, Unobtrusive Measures," in *Handbook of Industrial and Organizational Psychology*, ed. M. D. Dunnette (Chicago: Rand McNally, 1976).
    Ellsworth, "Abstract Ideas."
23. Bouchard, "Field Research Methods."
24. Ibid.
25. Ibid.
26. D. N. Bersoff, "Silk Purses into Sow's Ears: The Decline of Psychological Testing and a Suggestion for Its Redemption," *American Psychologist* 28 (1973): 892-99.
27. Ibid., p. 896.
28. S. Santostefano, "Performance Testing of Personality," *Merrill-Palmer Quarterly* 8 (1962): 83-97.
29. N. M. Lambert, H. W. Cox, and C. S. Hartsough," The Observability of Intellectual Functioning of First Graders," *Psychology in the Schools* 7 (1970): 74-85.
30. E. J. Anthony, "On Observing Children," in *Foundations of Child Psychiatry*, ed. L. Miller (Oxford: Pergamon, 1968).
31. Selltiz et al., *Research Methods*.
32. Gellert, "Systematic Observation."
    Heyns and Lippitt, "Observational Techniques."
33. R. G. Barker, "Observation of Behavior: Ecological Approaches," *Journal of the Mount Sinai Hospital* 31 (1964): 268-84.
34. Gellert, "Systematic Observation."
35. M. R. Goldfried and R. N. Kent, "Traditional Vs. Behavioral Personality Assessment: A Comparison of Methodological and Theoretical Assumptions," *Psychological Bulletin* 77 (1972): 409-20.
36. Bronfenbrenner, "Experimental Ecology."
    J. M. Butler, L. N. Rice, and A. K. Wagstaff, *Quantitative Naturalistic Research* (Englewood Cliffs, N.J.: Prentice-Hall, 1963).
37. S. M. Johnson and O. D. Bolstad, "Methodological Issues in Naturalistic Observation: Some Problems and Solutions for Field Research," in *Behavior Change: Methodology, Concepts, and Practice*, eds. L. A. Hamerlynck, L. C. Handy, and E. J. Mash (Champaign, Ill.: Research Press, 1973).
    A. J. Levine, "Naturalistic Observation: Validity of Frequency Data," *Psychological Reports* 40 (1977): 1311-38.
38. R. M. Brandt, *Studying Behavior in Natural Settings* (New York: Holt, 1972), p. 5.
39. Bronfenbrenner, "Experimental Ecology."
    N. L. Gage, "Paradigms for Research on Teaching," in *Handbook of Research on Teaching*, ed. N. L. Gage (Chicago: Rand McNally, 1963).
    R. Vasta, "Child Study: Looking Toward the Eighties," in *Strategies and Techniques of Child Study*, ed. R. Vasta (New York: Academic Press, 1982).
40. D. T. Campbell, "Systematic Error on the Part of Human Links in Communication Systems," *Information and Control* 1 (1958): 334-59.
41. Ibid., p. 342.
42. D. E. Broadbent, *Perception and Communication* (Oxford: Pergamon, 1958).
43. A. T. Dittman, M. B. Parloff, and D. S. Boomer, "Facial and Bodily Expression: A Study of Receptivity of Emotional Cues," *Psychiatry* 28 (1965): 239-44.
44. Campbell, "Systematic Error," p. 344.
45. Ibid., p. 353.
46. Ibid., p. 347.
47. A. T. Dittmann, *Interpersonal Message of Emotion* (New York: Springer, 1972), p. 207.
48. Campbell, "Systematic Error."
49. J. P. Guilford, *Psychometric Methods* (New York: McGraw-Hill, 1954).
50. R. N. Kent and J. L. Foster, "Direct Observational Procedures: Methodological Issues in Naturalistic Settings," in *Handbook of Behavioral Assessment*, eds. A. R. Ciminero, K. S. Calhoun, and H. E. Adams (New York: Wiley, 1977).
    K. E. Weick, "Systematic Observational Methods," in *Handbook of Social Psychology*, vol. 2, eds. G. Lindzey and F. Aronson (Reading, Mass.: Addison-Wesley, 1968).
51. R. Rosenthal, *Experimenter Effects in Behavioral Research* (New York: Appleton, 1966).
52. P. M. Scott, R. V. Burton, and M. R. Yarrow, "Social Reinforcement Under Natural Conditions," *Child Development* 38 (1967): 53-63.
53. G. G. Foster, J. E. Ysseldyke, and J. H. Reese, " 'I Would't Have Seen It If I Hadn't Believed It,' " *Exceptional Children* 42 (1975): 469-73.
    R. E. Kass and K. D. O'Leary, "The Effects of Observer Bias in Field-Experimental Settings" (Paper presented at a symposium on behavior analysis in education, Lawrence, Kansas, 1970).
    R. N. Kent et al., "Expectation Biases in Observational Evaluation of Therapeutic Change," *Journal of Consulting and Clinical Psychology* 42 (1974): 774-80.
    W. Mischel, *Personality Assessment* (New York: Wiley, 1968).
    D. W. Rapp, "Detection of Observer Bias in the Written Record," in *Experimenter Effects in Behavioral Research*, ed. R. Rosenthal (New York: Appleton, 1966).
    D. Y. Shuller and J. R. McNamara, "Expectancy Factors in Behavioral Observation," *Behavior Therapy* 6 (1976): 519-27.
54. K. D. O'Leary, R. N. Kent, and J. Kanowitz, "Shaping Data Collection Congruent with Experimental Hypotheses," *Journal of Applied Behavioral Analysis* 8 (1975): 43-51.
55. J. B. Reid, "Reliability Assessment of Observation Data: A Possible Methodological Problem," *Child Development* 41 (1970): 1143-50.
56. R. M. Kent et al., "Observer Reliability as a Function of Circumstances of Assessment," *Journal of Applied Behavior Analysis* 10 (1977): 317-24.
    R. G. Romanczyk et al., "Measuring the Reliability of Observation Data: A Reactive Process," *Journal of Applied Behavior Analysis* 6 (1973): 175-84.
    P. S. Taplin and J. B. Reid, "Effects of Instructional Set and Experimenter Influence on Observer Reliability," *Child Development* 44 (1973): 547-54.
57. Kent et al., "Observer Reliability."
    Romanczyk et al., "Measuring Reliability."
58. J. S. Wiggins, "The Quality of Observational Data: Discussion" (Paper presented at a symposium on the quality of observatonal data, Western Psychological Association, San Francisco, April, 1974), pp. 5-6.
59. Kent and Foster, "Direct Observational Procedures."
60. Johnson and Bolstad, "Methodological Issues."
61. B. DeMaster, J. Reid, and C. Twentyman, "The Effects of Different Amounts of Feedback on Observer's Reliability," *Behavior Therapy* 8 (1977): 317-24.
    Kent et al., "Expectation Biases."
62. J. S. Bruner, *Beyond the Information Given: Studies in the Psychology of Knowing* (New York: Norton, 1973).
63. E. J. Mash and J. D. McElwee, "Situational Effects on Observer Accuracy: Behavioral Predictability, Prior Experience, and Complexity of Coding Categories," *Child Development* 45 (1974): 367-77.
    E. J. Mash and G. Makohoniuk, "The Effects of Prior Information and Behavioral Predictability on Observer Accuracy," *Child Development* 46 (1975): 513-19.
64. R. R. Jones, J. B. Reid, and G. R. Patterson, "Naturalistic Observation in Clinical Assessment," in *Advances in Psychological Assessment*, vol. 3, ed. P. McReynolds (San Francisco: Jossey-Bass, 1974).
    Mash and McElwee, "Situational Effects."
    J. B. Reid et al., "The Role of Complexity in the Collection and Evaluation of Observational Data" (Paper presented at the annual meeting of the American Psychological Association, Montreal, August, 1973).
    K. D. Skindrud, "An Evaluation of Observer Bias in Experimental Field Studies of Social Interaction" (Ph.D. diss., University of Oregon, 1972).
    Taplin and Reid, "Effects of Instructional Set."

65. Jones, Reid, and Patterson, "Naturalistic Observation."
66. M. Sherif and C. W. Sherif, *Reference Groups* (New York: Harper, 1964), p. 110.
67. J. M. Arsenian, "Young Children in an Insecure Situation," *Journal of Abnormal and Social Psychology* 38 (1943): 225-49.
    H. Leventhal and K. Fisher, "What Reinforces in a Social Reinforcement Situation—Words or Expressions?" *Journal of Personality and Social Psychology* 14 (1970): 83-94.
    E. J. Mash and J. Hedley, "Effect of Observer As a Function of Prior History of Social Interaction," *Perceptual and Motor Skills* 40 (1975): 659-69.
    T. D. Meddock, J. A. Parson, and K. T. Hill, "Effects of an Adult's Presence and Praise on Young Children's Performance," *Journal of Experimental Child Psychology* 12 (1971): 197-211.
    G. R. Patterson and A. Harris, "Some Methodological Considerations for Observation Procedures" (Paper presented at the annual meeting of the American Psychological Association, San Francisco, September, 1968).
    N. Polansky et al., "Problems of Interpersonal Relations in Research on Groups," *Human Relations* 2 (1949): 281-91.
    G. D. White, "Effects of Observer Presence on Family Interaction" (Paper presented at the meeting of the Western Psychological Association, Anaheim, California, 1973).
    L. E. Zegiob, S. Arnold, and R. Forehand, "An Examination of Observer Effects in Parent-Child Interactions," *Child Development* 46 (1975): 509-12.
68. Johnson and Bolstad, "Methodological Issues."
69. P. Schoggen, "Environmental Forces in the Everyday Lives of Children with Physical Disabilities" (Unpublished manuscript, 1964), p. 56.
70. R. G. Barker and H. Wright, *Midwest and Its Children* (Evanston, Ill.: Row and Peterson, 1955).
    D. R. Dubey et al., "Reactions of Children and Teachers to Classroom Observers: A Series of Controlled Investigations," *Behavior Therapy* 8 (1977): 887-97.
    A. Harris, "Observer Effects on Family Interaction" (Ph.D. diss., University of Oregon, 1969).
    L. K. Hoover and H. H. Rinehart, "The Effect of an Outside Observer on Family Interaction" (Unpublished manuscript, Oregon Research Institute, 1968).
    W. C. McGrew, *An Ethological Study of Children's Behavior* (New York: Academic Press, 1972).
    M. F. Martin, D. M. Gelfand, and D. P. Hartmann, "Effects of Adult and Peer Observers on Boys' and Girls' Responses to an Aggressive Model," *Child Development* 42 (1973): 1271-75.
    Medley and Mitzel, "Measuring Classroom Behavior."
    T. Samph, "Observer Effects on Teacher Verbal Classroom Behavior," *Journal of Educational Psychology* 68 (1976): 736-41.
    Selltiz et al., *Research Methods.*
71. Barker and Wright, *Midwest.*
    Martin, Gelfand, and Hartmann, "Effects of Adult and Peer Observers."
    Polansky et al., "Problems of Interpersonal Relations."
    T. M. Randall, "Effect of an Observer's Presence on the Behavior of Middle- and Working-Class Mothers," *Journal of Social Psychology* 113 (1981): 193-99.
72. S. N. Haynes, *Principles of Behavioral Assessment* (New York: Halsted, 1978), p. 185.
73. Johnson and Bolstad, "Methodological Issues."
74. R. K. Bain, "The Researcher's Role: A Case Study," in *Human Organization Research,* eds. R. N. Adams and J. J. Preiss (Homewood, Ill.: Dorsey Press, 1960).
    Barker and Wright, *Midwest.*
    G. A. Fine and B. Glassner, "Participant Observation with Children: Promise and Problems," *Urban Life* 8 (1979): 153-74.
    R. A. Hilbert, "Covert Participant Observation: On Its Nature and Practice," *Urban Life* 9 (1980): 51-78.
    R. H. Wax, "Reciprocity in Field Work," in *Human Organization Research,* eds. R. M. Adams and J. J. Preiss (Homewood, Ill.: Dorsey Press, 1970).
75. E. C. Lindeman, *Social Discovery* (New York: Republic, 1924).
76. M. S. Schwartz and C. G. Schwartz, "Problems in Participant Observation," *American Journal of Sociology* 60 (1955): 344.
77. Bouchard, "Field Research Methods."
78. Fine and Glassner, "Participant Observation."
    S. M. Miller, "The Participant Observer and 'Over-rapport,' " *American Sociological Review* 17 (1952): 97-99.
    Schwartz and Schwartz, "Problems."
79. A. J. Vidich, "Participant Observation and the Collection and Interpretation of Data," *American Journal of Sociology* 60 (1955): 354-60.
    W. F. Whyte, *Street Corner Society* (Chicago: University of Chicago Press, 1955).
    W. F. Whyte, "Interviewing in Field Research," in *Human Organization Research,* eds. R. N. Adams and J. J. Preiss (Homewood, Ill.: Dorsey, 1960).
80. W. E. Bunney and D. A. Hamburg, "Methods for Reliable Longitudinal Observation of Behavior," *Archives of General Psychiatry* 9 (1963): 280-94.
    W. A. Hargreaves, "Nursing Ratings of Psychiatric Patients" (Unpublished manuscript, Langley Porter Institute, 1965).
81. A. R. Hollenbeck, "Problems of Reliability in Observational Research," in *Observing Behavior,* vol. 2, ed. G. P. Sackett (Baltimore: University Park Press, 1978).
82. G. F. King, J. C. Erkman, and D. M. Johnson, "Experimental Analysis of the Reliability of Observations of Social Behavior," *Journal of Social Psychology* 35 (1952): 151-60.
83. R. A. Berk, "An Analysis of Variance Model for Assessing Reliability of Naturalistic Observations," *Perceptual and Motor Skills* 47 (1978): 271-78.
    C. L. Booth, S. K. Mitchell, and F. K. Solin, "The Generalizability Study As a Method of Assessing Intra- and Inter-observer Reliability in Observational Research," *Behavior Research Methods and Instrumentation* 11 (1979): 491-94.
    T. Frick and M. I. Semmel, "Observer Agreement and Reliabilities of Classroom Measures," *Review of Educational Research* 48 (1978): 157-84.
    D. P. Hartmann, "Considerations in the Choice of Interobserver Reliability Estimates," *Journal of Applied Behavior Analysis* 10 (1977): 103-16.
    Haynes, *Principles.*
    Hollenbeck, "Problems of Reliability."
    Kent and Foster, "Direct Observational Procedures."
    M. Meighan, *Percentage Agreement Scores As Estimations of Nonparametric Observer Reliability* (Research training paper no. 70, Bureau of Child Research, Kansas Center for Mental Retardation and Human Development, Kansas City, Missouri, March, 1975).
84. Haynes, *Principles.*
85. Johnson and Bolstad, "Methodological Issues."
    Jones, Reid, and Patterson, "Naturalistic Observation."
    Kent and Foster, "Direct Observational Procedures."
    A. W. Statts, "Behavior Analysis and Token Reinforcement in Educational Behavior Modification and Curriculum Research," in *Behavior Modification in Education,* ed. C. E. Thorenson (Chicago: University of Chicago Press, 1973).
86. Haynes, *Principles,* pp. 176-77.
87. S. L. Foster and J. D. Cone, "Current Issues in Direct Observation," *Behaviorial Assessment* 2 (1980): 313-38.

88.  R. Nelson and P. E. Bowles, "The Best of Two Worlds—Observations with Norms," *Journal of School Psychology* 13 (1975): 309.
89.  Bouchard, "Field Research Methods."
     Gellert, "Systematic Observation."
     Herbert, "Direct Observation."
     Medley and Mitzel, "Measuring Classroom Behavior."
90.  Barker, "Wanted," p. 39.
91.  Medley and Mitzel, "Direct Observation."
92.  Bouchard, "Field Research Methods," p. 368.

# 5

# Observational Aids: Rating Scales, Checklists, and Observer Systems

Observations may be undertaken with the assistance of aids that are intended to make the complex observational task easier and more precise. This chapter describes prescaled observation methods, including ratings, checklists, and observer systems, which require the observer to judge as he or she rates, checks, or records the degree to which a child behaves in a certain manner or exhibits certain qualities or characteristics. Mechanical aids and other apparatus designed to improve the quality of observation are examined in Chapter 6.

## RATING SCALES

Rating scales are observational tools that indicate the degree to which a person, process, or thing possesses a characteristic. The observer's judgment, which may be expressed quantitatively or qualitatively, is made during the process of observation, after the observation is completed, or at some later time such as when teachers or counselors are asked to complete rating forms that provide a summary description of a child. A variety of traits are amenable to rating. Technically, traits are considered susceptible to rating procedures when there is substantial rater agreement on the traits. The possibility of satisfactory agreement among judges depends on an adequate definition of the trait and its frequent occurrence or manifestation so that sufficient samples of it can be observed.[1] Depending on the type of scale and the peculiarity of its construction, rating devices can be used for assessing a child on specific characteristics, such as aptitude or achievement in a certain subject matter area, or on more global characteristics, such as social adjustment and attitudes.

Rating scales consist of a continuum that is defined as precisely as possible and which is broken down into a sequential series of waypoints. Observers are asked to indicate the point on the continuum that describes the child best. The manner in which the waypoints are designated serves as a convenient means of categorizing rating scales. A number of classifications have been suggested for them, and at least five major groupings have emerged: numerical, graphic, cumulative points, standard, and forced-choice. We will consider two of the most widely used types of rating scales—numerical and graphic.

### NUMERICAL RATING SCALES

Numerical rating scales assign a number to indicate the degree to which a certain characteristic is present. A numerical value is usually given to descriptive categories on an a priori basis, and the observer is provided a sequence of numbers. For example, a child can be rated on a trait or on performance in the following manner:

5 = outstanding

4 = above average

3 = average

2 = below average

1 = unsatisfactory

Usually, a common set of numbers is used throughout the scale, but other formats are possible. Numerical ratings on a child can be made with a bipolar arrangement such as that developed by Ryans. Figure 5.1 illustrates his numerical scale with its verbal anchors or traits.

Perhaps the most flexible and widely used type of numerical rating scale is the Likert scale. In this approach, a statement is usually followed by a five-response continuum such as *strongly agree, mildly agree, uncertain, mildly disagree,* and *strongly disagree* or a four-response arrangement such as *very true, tended to be true, tended to be untrue,* and *very untrue.* The rater designates the category that represents his or her response to the statement. Numerous examples of Likert-type measures may be found in Shaw's and Wright's *Scales for the Measurement of Attitudes.*[2] Sometimes, the numerical scale does not use descriptive phrases at all. For instance, an observer may be requested to describe a child from 0 to 7 in order to represent the frequency of a certain behavior, with *never* indicated by 0; *sometimes,* by 4; and *very often,* by 7.

The numerical rating scale is very easy to construct and apply. It is particularly useful when the characteristics in question can be classified into a limited number of categories that are easily understood. Also, it yields numbers that facilitate statistical analyses. The numerical values, however, are sometimes vaguely described, allowing for variability in the interpretation of the ratings. Moreover, the numbers assigned to the scale categories cannot be assumed to correspond to psychological reality[3] unless this has been determined by psychophysical scaling techniques.[4] Consequently, numerical

## CLASSROOM OBSERVATION RECORD

### TEACHER CHARACTERISTICS STUDY

Teacher_____ No. _____ Sex _____ Class or Subject_____ Date_____

City _____ School_____ Time _____ Observer_____

**Pupil Behavior**                                                                     Remarks:

| | | | | | | | | | |
|---|---|---|---|---|---|---|---|---|---|
| 1. | Apathetic | 1 | 2 | 3 | 4 | 5 | 6 | 7 | N | Alert |
| 2. | Obstructive | 1 | 2 | 3 | 4 | 5 | 6 | 7 | N | Responsible |
| 3. | Uncertain | 1 | 2 | 3 | 4 | 5 | 6 | 7 | N | Confident |
| 4. | Dependent | 1 | 2 | 3 | 4 | 5 | 6 | 7 | N | Initiating |

**Teacher Behavior**

| | | | | | | | | | |
|---|---|---|---|---|---|---|---|---|---|
| 5. | Partial | 1 | 2 | 3 | 4 | 5 | 6 | 7 | N | Fair |
| 6. | Autocratic | 1 | 2 | 3 | 4 | 5 | 6 | 7 | N | Democratic |
| 7. | Aloof | 1 | 2 | 3 | 4 | 5 | 6 | 7 | N | Responsive |
| 8. | Restricted | 1 | 2 | 3 | 4 | 5 | 6 | 7 | N | Understanding |
| 9. | Harsh | 1 | 2 | 3 | 4 | 5 | 6 | 7 | N | Kindly |
| 10. | Dull | 1 | 2 | 3 | 4 | 5 | 6 | 7 | N | Stimulating |
| 11. | Stereotyped | 1 | 2 | 3 | 4 | 5 | 6 | 7 | N | Original |
| 12. | Apathetic | 1 | 2 | 3 | 4 | 5 | 6 | 7 | N | Alert |
| 13. | Unimpressive | 1 | 2 | 3 | 4 | 5 | 6 | 7 | N | Attractive |
| 14. | Evading | 1 | 2 | 3 | 4 | 5 | 6 | 7 | N | Responsible |
| 15. | Erratic | 1 | 2 | 3 | 4 | 5 | 6 | 7 | N | Steady |
| 16. | Excitable | 1 | 2 | 3 | 4 | 5 | 6 | 7 | N | Poised |
| 17. | Uncertain | 1 | 2 | 3 | 4 | 5 | 6 | 7 | N | Confident |
| 18. | Disorganized | 1 | 2 | 3 | 4 | 5 | 6 | 7 | N | Systematic |
| 19. | Inflexible | 1 | 2 | 3 | 4 | 5 | 6 | 7 | N | Adaptable |
| 20. | Pessimistic | 1 | 2 | 3 | 4 | 5 | 6 | 7 | N | Optimistic |
| 21. | Immature | 1 | 2 | 3 | 4 | 5 | 6 | 7 | N | Integrated |
| 22. | Narrow | 1 | 2 | 3 | 4 | 5 | 6 | 7 | N | Broad |

**Figure 5.1.** Classroom Observation Record

scales are frequently rejected in favor of other types of rating procedures because they are believed by some to be more vulnerable to biases and errors.[5]

## GRAPHIC RATING SCALES

Graphic rating scales are perhaps the most popular and extensively used rating devices. The trait continuum is divided into spaces which represent the possible number of judgments that can be made. A horizontal line is usually employed, although some researchers[6] have preferred a vertical format. Cues, which consist either of single words or of more complete descriptions, are written along or below the line at each end and in most cases also at intermediate points to help the rater determine precisely where to designate his or her judgment. The observer places a mark on the segment of the line which most accurately describes the child. The mark does not necessarily have to be placed directly above a given cue. For purposes of analysis, judgments are later transformed into numerical ratings using an arbitrary numerical scale.

In graphic rating scales, the same set of categories may or may not be used for each characteristic. These examples illustrate a *constant-alternatives* graphic scale in which the same descriptive words are used:

1. Does the child interact with classmates?

| never | seldom | occasionally | frequently | always |
|---|---|---|---|---|

2. Does the child interact with adults?

| never | seldom | occasionally | frequently | always |
|---|---|---|---|---|

Sometimes the descriptive categories are written so that they change from item to item within the scale. Since separate descriptions are used for the various degrees of each trait, this type of rating device is referred to as a *changing-alternatives* descriptive graphic scale.

1. Does the child interact with classmates?

| Never interacts with other pupils; unsociable | Interacts as much as other pupils in class | Interacts more frequently than other pupils |
|---|---|---|

2. Does the child interact with adults?

| Avoids or withdraws from interaction | Responds but does not initiate interaction | Readily initiates interaction, even with unfamiliar adults |
|---|---|---|

This example of a graphic rating device uses phrases rather than single words to identify points on the scale.

An old but well-known commercially available graphic rating scale is the Haggerty-Olson-Wickman Behavior Rating Schedules. This rating instrument, which is designed for the identification of maladjusted children, is presented in a changing alternatives, descriptive graphic format with weights assigned to each behavior. Figure 5.2 shows sample items from the scale. Higher weights are given to problems that are most typical of disturbed children, and lower weights, to behaviors that infrequently characterize children with difficulties.

Remmers has provided a helpful list of suggestions for the construction of graphic rating scales:

1. Introduce each trait by a question phrased to describe the trait in objective and observable terms.

## SCHEDULE B FOR HAGGERTY-OLSON-WICKMAN SCHEDULES

*Score*

**25. Is he even-tempered or moody?**

| Stolid, Rare changes of mood (3) | Generally very even-tempered (1) | Is happy or depressed as conditions warrant (2) | Strong and frequent changes of mood (4) | Has periods of extreme elations or depressions (5) | _____ |

**26. Is he easily discouraged or is he persistent?**

| Melts before slight obstacles or objections (5) | Gives up before adequate trial (3) | Gives everything a fair trial (1) | Persists until convinced of mistake (2) | Never gives in, Obstinate (4) | _____ |

**27. Is he generally depressed or cheerful?**

| Dejected, Melancholic, In the dumps (3) | Generally dispirited (4) | Usually in good humor (1) | Cheerful, Animated, Chirping (2) | Hilarious (5) | _____ |

**28. Is he sympathetic?**

| Inimical, Aggravating, Cruel (5) | Unsympathetic, Disobliging, Cold (4) | Ordinarily friendly and cordial (2) | Sympathetic, Warm-hearted (1) | Very affectionate (3) | _____ |

**29. How does he react to frustrations or to unpleasant situations?**

| Very submissive, Long-suffering (3) | Tolerant, Rarely blows up (2) | Generally self-controlled (1) | Impatient (4) | Easily irritated, Hot-headed, Explosive (5) | _____ |

**30. Does he worry or is he easy-going?**

| Constantly worrying about something, Has many anxieties (4) | Apprehensive, Often worries unduly (2) | Does not worry without cause (1) | Easy-going (3) | Entirely care free, Never worries, Light-hearted (5) | _____ |

**31. How does he react to examination or to discussion of himself or his problems?**

| Refuses flatly to coöperate (5) | Volunteers nothing, Must be pumped (3) | Conservatively coöperative (2) | Quite willing to coöperate (1) | Entirely uninhibited, Tells everything, Enjoys it (4) | _____ |

**32. Is he suspicious or trustful?**

| Very suspicious, Distrustful (5) | Has to be assured (3) | Generally unsuspicious and trustful (1) | Somewhat gullible (2) | Accepts everything without question (4) | _____ |

**33. Is he emotionally calm or excitable?**

| No emotional responses, Apathetic, Stuporous (4) | Emotions are slowly aroused (2) | Responds quite normally (1) | Is easily aroused (3) | Extreme reactions, Hysterical, High-strung (5) | _____ |

**34. Is he negativistic or suggestible?**

| Negativistic, Contrary (5) | Complies slowly (4) | Is generally open-minded (1) | Rather easily persuaded (2) | Follows any suggestion (3) | _____ |

**35. Does he act impulsively or cautiously?**

| Impulsive, Bolts, Acts on the spur of the moment (5) | Frequently unreflective and imprudent (4) | Acts with reasonable care (2) | Deliberate (1) | Very cautious and calculating (3) | _____ |

*Total, Division IV* _____

**Figure 5.2.** Haggerty-Olson-Wickman Behavior Rating Schedules

2. Make a continuous line opposite the trait so that rater can check any place on the line.

3. Adapt the words to describe each level to the understanding of the persons who will do the rating.

4. Avoid phrases at the ends which express levels of the trait so extreme that raters will never check them.

5. Make the meaning of the intermediate levels closer to the average or neutral phrase than to the extreme phrases. This might induce the raters to use a wider range of the line.

6. To reduce the halo effect, vary the desirable end of the rating line at random. This will prevent a profile from being drawn, but it may require the rater to read each degree of the trait carefully to choose the one desired.[7]

There are many advantages to graphic rating scales. They are easy to understand and use;[8] they allow fine discrimination;[9] they fix a continuum in the mind of the rater;[10] their ratings do not require numbers;[11] and behavior descriptions, when used, enhance objectivity and accuracy of judgments.[12] There are no disadvantages to graphic scales that do not apply to most other rating devices except possibly the more complicated scoring procedures required by some graphic formats.[13]

## PROBLEMS IN THE CONSTRUCTION AND USE OF RATING SCALES

There are certain problems in the construction and use of rating scales that should be mentioned. The most common difficulty in constructing these scales is the tendency to use *ambiguous categories or dimensions*. Rating scales sometimes include broad, abstract traits whose meaning may not be the same to all people. Because of this lack of uniformity in meaning, the trait must be concisely defined, preferably in operational terms. Considerable editing may be necessary before clarity is achieved. *Inadequate cues* are also an inherent weakness in most rating scales and result in rating errors. Not only should the cues be carefully selected and well written, but they also must be well placed.[14] Drawing on the early work of Champney,[15] Guilford has offered a number of criteria for developing good cues that improve the overall effectiveness of rating scales:

1. *Clarity.* Use short statements, in simple, unambiguous terminology.

2. *Relevance.* The cue should be consistent with the trait name and its definition as well as with other cues. Avoid bringing into a cue any implications of other traits. Such a slip is all too easy to make without realizing it.

3. *Precision.* A good cue applies to a point or a very short range on the continuum. There should be no doubt about its rank position among other cues, and if possible, it should not overlap them in quantitative meaning. This implies our being able to localize the cue at a point on a scale.

4. *Variety.* The use of the same terms in all or many of the cues may fail to differentiate them sufficiently. Vary the language used at different scale levels.

5. *Objectivity.* Stay clear of terminology implying ethical, moral, or social evaluations, unless dealing specifically with such types of traits. Cues with implications of good or bad, worthy or unworthy, and desirable or undesirable should generally be avoided.

6. *Uniqueness.* The cues for each trait should be unique to that trait. Avoid using cues of a very general character, such as "excellent," "superior," "poor," and the like.[16]

The matter of determining the *number of rating and scoring units* to use has plagued persons developing rating scales. The ideal number is mostly a function of what is being measured, the conditions under which the rating takes place, the precision required, and the nature and training of the observer.[17] Too few scale divisions result in coarse ratings because of the limited opportunity for the rater to discriminate. On the other hand, finely graded scales often require the rater to make differentiations he or she is unable or perhaps unwilling to provide. Conklin[18] maintains that scales designed for untrained judges should contain a maximum number of five steps for unipolar scales and nine for bipolar scales. Symonds[19] proposes that seven steps are optimal in rating human traits, although Guilford[20] considers this number as somewhat too low. Cronbach[21] recommends five to seven points for rating devices, while Gronlund[22] and Mehrens and Lehmann[23] suggest three to seven rating positions. Use of more than seven points appears to increase the inter-rater reliability very little. If the observer is untrained, the exact number of scale units should be particularly limited.[24]

In addition to errors associated with the rating scale itself, there are other problems in ratings that are linked to biases in rater judgment. Human perceptual errors in observation, which were discussed in Chapter 4, are equally applicable in rating situations. Some raters tend to rate all children approximately the same whereas others may be "easy raters" or "hard raters." Personal bias errors such as the *error of central tendency* (i.e., avoidance of extreme responses and inclination to rate "average") and the *error of leniency* (i.e., avoidance of lowest possible category ratings) may be counteracted in arrangement of the scales. To alleviate the error of central tendency, Guilford recommends that intermediate descriptive phrases be spaced far apart in graphic scales and that greater differences in the meaning of adjectives be introduced between steps near the ends of the scale than between steps near the center in numerical scales.[25] Since positive leniency or generosity errors are commonplace in ratings, the inclusion of several units on the plus side of average allows more room for differentiation without having to stigmatize a youngster as "average." Another common pitfall in rating is the *"halo effect,"* which was first identified by Wells[26] and later named by Thorndike.[27] This type of error is the tendency to rate in terms of overall general impression without differentiating specific aspects and of allowing one's total reaction to the person to color one's judgment of each specific trait.[28] To illustrate, a teacher may rate a well-behaved, cooperative pupil high in academic areas in which the pupil has performed only satisfactorily. There are several reasons for this halo effect: (a) the trait or habit is not easily observed; (b) it is one that is not commonly observed or thought about; (c) it is not clearly defined; (d) it is one which involves reactions with other people rather than "self-containing" behavior; and (e) it is one with high moral importance in its usual connotation.[29] The practices of rating one trait at a time and of having one trait per page helps remedy the halo effect.[30] Still another rater idiosyncrasy is what is termed *logical error.*[31] This error results when the observer rates two characteristics similarly because, in his or her mind, the traits seem to be logically related. For example, a rater who believes that children with very high intelligence have poor social adjustment may tend to underrate them on social relations. This defect can be mitigated by the use of objectively observable actions rather than abstract traits.[32] *Contrast error* is a source of invalidity in obtaining sound ratings that is caused by a tendency to rate others in the opposite direction from oneself on a particular characteristic.[33] This phenomenon may be related to a type of reaction formation described by psychoanalytically oriented theorists. The reverse of contrast error, the human tendency to expect others to be like ourselves, is a bias to which some raters also fall victim.[34]

In spite of their shortcomings, rating scales have many positive virtues as Kerlinger has summarized: (a) they require less time than most other methods; (b) they have a wide range of application; (c) they can be used with a large number of characteristics; (d) they are generally interesting and easy for observers to use; and (e) they are a valuable adjunct to other methods.[35] Readers who are interested in a more comprehensive treatment of rating scales are directed to Guilford[36] and Remmers.[37]

## CHECKLISTS

In many cases, checklists are similar in appearance and use to rating scales. The primary difference between the two measures is the type of judgment required of the observer. Checklists provide an opportunity to record whether or not a trait, object, condition, or event is present or whether or not a certain behavior has occurred. Therefore, they lend themselves to more qualitative judgments. Conversely, rating scales are not limited to all-or-none judgments. With a rating device, an observer is able to represent the degree to which a quality is present or the frequency with which a behavior is manifested. While checklists are especially useful in evaluating behaviors that can be divided into a series of clearly defined specific actions, they should not be used where degree or frequency of occurrence are important aspects of the appraisal.[38] In these cases, a rating scale is preferable. Likewise, rating devices should be used when an observer wishes to summarize general impressions concerning a child's personality and adjustment, particularly if fine discriminations are necessary.[39]

One example of a checklist devised as a record of childhood disorders is the Walker Problem Behavior Identification Checklist. The first ten items of this instrument are presented in Figure 5.3. Responses are made by circling the number to the right of the statement if that particular child behavior was observed during the last two months. If it was not observed, no mark is made. The numbers correspond to the five subscales of the checklist: (1) acting-out, (2) withdrawal, (3) distractability, (4) disturbed peer relations, and (5) immaturity. Checklists lend themselves not only to the measurement of specific classes of behavior such as children's disorders but also to a combination of different traits in a single format. An illustration of this type of checklist is the Trait Information checklist published by the American Guidance Service, Inc. shown in Figure 5.4. Here, the observer checks comments that apply to the child in such areas as academic abilities and talents, personality, physical condition, social development, and special problems. A performance checklist, developed by Tyler, has been used for evaluating skill in the use of a microscope. As indicated on the reproduction of this checklist in Figure 5.5, the sequence of student actions is noted by the teacher along with information regarding areas that require further training, characteristics of the student's behavior, and description of the student's mount.

The use of checklists is not necessarily limited to the recording of behavior. In child study, checklists also may be utilized to obtain routine background information about the youngster being

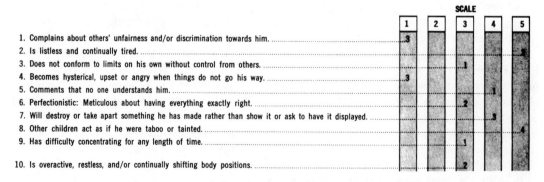

**Figure 5.3.** Walker Problem Behavior Identification Checklist

# TRAIT INFORMATION

AGCF-113

Last name_____ First name_____ Grade_____ Date_____

To aid in student's orientation, check comments that apply. Other comments are welcome.

## I — ACADEMIC, ABILITIES, & TALENTS
____Creative
____Lacks imagination
____Good judgment        ____Poor judgment
____Reliable in doing work — effort is O.K.
____Poor work habits — fails to complete work
____Fails to bring materials — pencils, book
____Learns easily        ____Learns slowly
____Reading handicap
____Needs remedial reading help
____Language skills handicap
____Math skills handicap
____Science skills handicap
____Social studies skills handicap
____Likes school
____Poor attitude toward school
____Special interests — Specify:

## II — PERSONALITY
____Daydreams
____Easily depressed
____Emotionally disturbed
____Enthusiastic
____Even-tempered
____Friendly
____Hostile
____Patient        ____Impatient
____Impulsive
____Nervous
____Easily upset by criticism
____Self-conscious
____Self-pity
____Indifferent — "don't care" attitude
____Negativistic
____Stubborn
____Sullen & surly
____Lies — About What? _____
____Steals — What? _____
____Lacks self-confidence
____Stable        ____Unstable
____Uses vulgar or obscene language often

## III — PHYSICAL CONDITION & PROBLEMS
____Diabetic
____Epileptic
____Rheumatic fever
____Allergic — To what? _____
____Asthmatic
____Frequent headaches
____Frequent pains — Specify: _____
____Frequently ill
____Poor posture
____Healthy
____Well coordinated
____Clumsy
____Energetic

____Seems usually tired
____Needs dental help
____Needs glasses or eye exam
____May have hearing problem
____Has speech problem
____Needs medical help — Specify: _____
____Handicap of____arm ____back ____leg ____foot
____Corrective surgery needed _____
____Disabling illness — Specify: _____
____Muscular control handicap
____Other handicaps — Specify _____

## IV — SOCIAL DEVELOPMENT
____Accepted by boys
____Accepted by girls
____Accepted by both boys and girls
____Rejected by classmates
____Ridiculed by classmates; "teased" often
____Prone to fight with classmates
____Interested in others
____"Lone wolf" type
____Shy or withdrawn
____Usually plays with younger children
____Usually pals with older students only
____Usually associates with adults only
____Usually associates with "troublemakers"
____Class clown or show-off
____Mature        ____Immature
____Courteous        ____Rude
____Selfish
____A leader ____Positive way ____Negative way
____Easily lead
____Seldom leads
____Cooperative        ____Uncooperative
____Popular
____Destructive
____Disobedient
____Talks excessively

## V — SPECIAL PROBLEMS & CONSIDERATIONS
____A discipline problem
____Excessive absence
____Family problems
____Need for financial help
____Lacks personal neatness or cleanliness
____Seems to have personal or emotional problems
    which appear to affect academic progress
____Need for psychological help
____Place in higher ability section
____Place in lower ability section
____Section placement O.K.

**OTHER COMMENTS:**

_____

_____

(Use reverse side of page)

**Figure 5.4.** Trait Information Checklist

| STUDENT'S ACTIONS | Sequence of Actions |
|---|---|
| a. Takes slide | 1 |
| b. Wipes slide with lens paper | 2 |
| c. Wipes slide with cloth | |
| d. Wipes slide with finger | |
| e. Moves bottle of culture along the table | |
| f. Places drop or two of culture on slide | 3 |
| g. Adds more culture | |
| h. Adds few drops of water | |
| i. Hunts for cover glasses | 4 |
| j. Wipes cover glass with lens paper | 5 |
| k. Wipes cover glass with cloth | |
| l. Wipes cover with finger | |
| m. Adjusts cover with finger | |
| n. Wipes off surplus fluid | |
| o. Places slide on stage | 6 |
| p. Looks thru eyepiece with right eye | |
| q. Looks thru eyepice with left eye | 7 |
| r. Turns to objective of lowest power | 9 |
| s. Turns to low-power objective | 21 |
| t. Turns to high-power objective | |
| u. Holds one eye closed | 8 |
| v. Looks for light | |
| w. Adjusts concave mirror | |
| x. Adjusts plane mirror | |
| y. Adjusts diaphragm | |
| z. Does not touch diaphragm | 10 |
| aa. With eye at eyepiece turns down coarse adjustment | 11 |
| ab. Breaks cover glass | 12 |
| ac. Breaks slide | |
| ad. With eye away from eyepiece turns down coarse adjustment | |
| ae. Turns up coarse adjustment a great distance | 13,22 |
| af. With eye at eyepiece turns down fine adjustment a great distance | 14,23 |
| ag. With eye away from eyepiece turns down fine adjustment a great distance | 15 |

| SKILLS IN WHICH STUDENT NEEDS FURTHER TRAINING | Sequence of Actions |
|---|---|
| a. In cleaning objective | ✓ |
| b. In cleaning eyepiece | ✓ |
| c. In focusing low power | ✓ |
| d. In focusing high power | ✓ |
| e. In adjusting mirror | ✓ |
| f. In using diaphragm | ✓ |
| g. In keeping both eyes open | ✓ |
| h. In protecting slide and objective from breaking by careless focusing | ✓ |

| STUDENT'S ACTIONS (Continued) | Sequence of Actions |
|---|---|
| ah. Turns up fine adjustment screw a great distance | |
| ai. Turns fine adjustment screw a few turns | |
| aj. Removes slide from stage | 16 |
| ak. Wipes objective with lens paper | |
| al. Wipes objective with cloth | |
| am. Wipes objective with finger | 17 |
| an. Wipes eyepiece with lens paper | |
| ao. Wipes eyepiece with cloth | |
| ap. Wipes eyepiece with finger | 18 |
| aq. Makes another mount | |
| ar. Takes another microscope | |
| as. Finds object | |
| at. Pauses for an interval | |
| au. Asks, "What do you want me to do?" | |
| av. Asks whether to use high power | |
| aw. Says, "I'm satisfied" | |
| ax. Says that the mount is all right for his eye | |
| ay. Says he cannot do it | 19,24 |
| az. Told to start a new mount | |
| aaa. Directed to find object under low power | 20 |
| aab. Directed to find object under high power | |

| NOTICEABLE CHARACTERISTICS OF STUDENT'S BEHAVIOR | |
|---|---|
| a. Awkward in movements | |
| b. Obviously dexterous in movements | |
| c. Slow and deliberate | ✓ |
| d. Very rapid | |
| e. Fingers tremble | |
| f. Obviously perturbed | |
| g. Obviously angry | |
| h. Does not take work seriously | |
| i. Unable to work without specific directions | ✓ |
| j. Obviously satisfied with his unsuccessful efforts | ✓ |

| CHARACTERIZATION OF THE STUDENT'S MOUNT | Sequence of Actions |
|---|---|
| a. Poor light | ✓ |
| b. Poor focus | |
| c. Excellent mount | |
| d. Good mount | |
| e. Fair mount | |
| f. Poor mount | |
| g. Very poor mount | |
| h. Nothing in view but a thread in his eyepiece | |
| i. Something on objective | |
| j. Smeared lens | ✓ |
| k. Unable to find object | ✓ |

**Figure 5.5.** Checklist for Evaluating Skill in the Use of the Microscope

observed. Sex, age, race, social class, family structure, and living arrangement are only a few demographic items that lend themselves to the checklist format. In addition, data regarding the behavioral setting or the child's environments can be collected and summarized effectively with checklists.[40] The values to be derived from the checklist method depend upon the skill with which it is constructed and used. These are some points that should be considered when checklists are being used: (a) checklists should be employed only when the objective is to ascertain whether a particular trait or characteristic is present or absent; (b) the traits to be observed should be clearly specified; (c) only one child should be observed at a time and a separate checklist should be used for each youngster; (d) observations should be confined specifically to the points indicated on the checklist; and (e) those behaviors for which there are insufficient data to make a valid judgment should not be recorded.[41] Used carefully, the checklist is a most valuable observational aid.

## OBSERVER SYSTEMS

According to some authors, the fundamental job of the observer is to assign behaviors to categories.[42] If there is any truth in this statement, issues pertaining to categorization are of substantial importance to observational study. There are a number of important properties of observer systems that should be considered, and six of them will be examined: exhaustiveness, amount of inference required, number of aspects of behavior scrutinized, discreteness of categories, size of units, and range of applicability.[43] Some observational systems are *exhaustive* in that all behaviors can be assigned to one of the defined categories. These exhaustive systems usually have a category labeled *neutral, other, unclassified,* or *miscellaneous* to account for undifferentiated behavior or for communication that cannot be understood by the observer. Frequent use of this residual category may create problems in interpreting behavior. Less than exhaustive systems do not permit recording of behaviors that do not fall into one of the categories; therefore, in these, it is impossible to estimate the ratio of categorized behaviors to total behaviors. Although large numbers of categories usually assure finer classificatory distinctions, they also may cause additional difficulties in the assignment of specific items. Moreover, an increased number of categories does not necessarily guarantee greater reliability and validity. At any rate, few studies have employed more than ten categories, and this number is usually considered a maximum by persons constructing standard observational schedules.[44] But, if a decision must be made, a good rule of thumb is that it is probably better to have too many categories than too few since categories can later be combined if needed.

Observational systems also differ with respect to the *amount of inference* that is expected of the observer. A two-category system that requires the observer to record verbalization and silence would involve no inference. It would necessitate only noninterpretive indications of overt behavior. If the child talked, the verbalization category would be checked; if the child was silent, the silence category would be specified. When the system calls for the notation of motives and feeling states, evaluative judgments must be made that are based upon the child's observable behavior. Inferences demand the careful examination of not only verbal behavior but also nonverbal cues.

Observer systems may vary in regard to the *number of behaviors* that are studied. Some researchers attempt to include every possible type of behavior that is related to the research problem, and others concentrate on only certain selected behaviors. Another issue concerning observer systems is the use of *discrete or continuous categories.* Most investigators employ discrete (i.e., discontinuous) categories of behavior. The observer's task is greatly complicated if he or she is expected to make judgments about greater or lesser amounts of a given behavior. Hence, aggression is more easily viewed as a category of child behavior that is distinct from hostility rather than as a lesser quality of hostility. Observer systems may differ in the *definition of the behavior unit.* Some units are defined as a single movement, and others, as entire behavioral sequences. Certain systems define their units simply as acts or natural units of behavior (a sentence, a segment of nonverbal behavior, a contact, etc.) with a tally on the observation record indicating an occurrence of the act. On the other hand, some systems define their units in terms of short periods of time. In these, each tally on the record form shows that a particular time interval includes at least one occurrence of the behavior. A few systems have combined both time and natural units.[45] Finally, observer systems may differ concerning their *range of application.* Some systems have been developed for specific situations, and others for a variety of purposes. Observer systems that are closely linked to the setting in which they were developed may be inappropriate for other settings. In other words, a system designed for use in the classroom may not be suitable for any other type of group such as an encounter group. Although a close parallel can be made between teachers in classrooms and leaders in groups, an observation system that has been developed to describe teacher behavior may not be appropriate to describe the behavior of a group leader even though both the teacher and group leader are "leaders" in their own settings. Clarity of conceptualization and level of generality of the categories determine their applicability in different situations.[46]

Two general types of observer systems are available for summarization of observations into categories: category systems and sign systems.

## CATEGORY SYSTEMS

A category system is a standard observational schedule that provides "a set of categories into one and only one of which every behavior of a certain type can be classified."[47] That is, if a behavioral act does not satisfy certain predetermined criteria, it is classified into another qualitatively different category. The record will show both the total number of behavior units and the number classified in the various categories. Typically, there is a small number (i.e., less than 10) of clearly defined categories which are used an appreciable number of times. To insure exhaustiveness, there is usually a category for undifferentiated behaviors (*other, miscellaneous,* etc.). Tallies may be based upon natural units or time units.

Hundreds of category systems have been developed for use in child development and education, many of which are summarized in a few selected sources.[48] In one anthology of observer systems, *Measures of Maturation,* Boyer and his associates describe seventy-three observation systems available for use with young children. The different observational systems are listed in Figure 5.6 along with the type of data obtained with each. One of the systems listed will be described and two others will be mentioned briefly.

APPROACH. A category system that is gaining increasing acceptance has been developed by Caldwell, Honig, and Wynn.[49] Called APPROACH (A Procedure for Patterning Responses of Adults and Children), this system helps the observer translate narrative data into a numerical code. In Chapter 3, one of the major problems of specimen recording and other narrative techniques was cited as what to do with the data once they are collected. APPROACH is one way to accomplish the sometimes overwhelming task of data reduction and conversion to numerical form for analysis and synthesis.

In the ecological tradition, Caldwell and her associates have recommended that the behavior record be obtained by having the observer stand near the subject and whisper into a small portable tape recorder all of the *behaviors* emitted by and directed toward this central figure. Also recorded are the *settings* in which the behaviors occur. Usually, twenty- or thirty-minute specimen records are made during the times of day when activities of interest to the observer are likely to occur.

All described behaviors are broken up by the observer into behavioral clauses, each of which is designated by the appearance of a verb. "Every time a verb is used by the observer, someone has done something; and that action, small or large, is coded."[50] Each behavioral clause, such as "Mary looks angrily at her homeroom teacher," is described in terms of four components and is later translated

| Systems 1 - 73 | INDIVIDUAL CATEGORY — Psychomotor: Facial Expressions | Body Activity | Level of Activity | Nervous Habits | Body Orientation | Sensory Perception | Activity: Caretaking of Self | Cognitive | Playing | Other: Expressions of Affect | Personality Traits | Background Data | SOCIAL CONTACT — Time: Number of Contacts | Duration of Contacts | Who is Contacted: Child to Child | Child to Adult | Adult to Child | Adult to Adult | Type of Contact: Leadership/Followership | Affective Communication | Reinforcement Patterns | Caretaking of/by Others | Information Processing |
|---|---|---|---|---|---|---|---|---|---|---|---|---|---|---|---|---|---|---|---|---|---|---|---|
| 1 Ainsworth | | • | • | | • | • | | | | • | | | | | | | | | • | • | • | • | |
| 2 Ainsworth-Bell-Stayton | • | • | | | • | | | | | | | | • | • | | • | • | | • | • | • | • | |
| 3 Anderson | | | | | | | | | | | | | • | | • | | | | • | | | | |
| 4 Arrington | • | • | | | | | | | | | | | • | • | • | • | • | | • | | | | |
| 5 Barker | | • | | | | | | | • | | | | • | • | • | • | • | | • | | | | |
| 6 Bee-Streissguth | | | | | | • | | | | | | | | | • | • | | | | | • | | • |
| 7 Bell-Weller-Waldrop | • | • | • | | • | • | | | | • | • | • | • | • | | | | | • | • | | • | |
| 8 Berk-Jackson-Wolfson | • | • | | | | | | | | • | | | • | | | | | | • | • | | | • |
| 9 Bing | | | | | | | | | | | | | • | | • | • | | | • | | • | | • |
| 10 Bishop | | | | | | | | • | • | • | | | • | • | • | • | | | • | • | • | | • |
| 11 Blurton Jones-Leach | • | • | | | • | | | | | • | | | • | • | | | | | • | | • | | • |
| 12 Bobbitt-Jensen | • | • | • | • | • | • | | | | | | | • | | • | • | • | | • | | | • | |
| 13 Boger-Cunningham | | • | • | | | | | • | • | | | | • | | • | • | | | • | | | | • |
| 14 Bonney | • | • | • | • | | • | | • | • | | | | • | | | | | | • | • | | | • |
| 15 Borke | | | | | | | | • | • | | | | • | | | | | | • | • | | | • |
| 16 Bott | • | • | | • | | • | | | • | | | | • | | • | • | | | • | • | | | • |
| 17 Bowman | | | | | | | | | | | | | • | | • | • | • | • | • | • | | | • |
| 18 Brody-Axelrad | | | | | • | | | | | | | | • | • | | | | | • | • | | • | |
| 19 Caldwell-Honig | | • | • | • | | • | • | • | | • | | • | • | • | • | • | • | • | • | • | • | • | • |
| 20 Coates-Anderson-Hartup | • | • | | | • | | | | | | | | • | | | | | | | | | | |
| 21 Cohen-Stern | • | • | • | • | | • | • | | | | | | • | | • | • | • | • | • | | | | • |
| 22 Coller | | • | • | | • | | | | | | • | • | • | | • | • | • | • | | | | | |
| 23 Danziger-Greenglass | | | | | | | | | | | | | • | • | | | | | • | | • | | • |
| 24 Dawe | | • | | | | | | | | • | | | • | • | • | | | | • | • | | | |
| 25 Ding | • | • | | | | | | | | • | | | • | • | • | • | • | | • | | | | |
| 26 DiNola-Kaminsky-Sternfeld (P) | | • | • | | | • | • | • | • | • | | | | | | | | | • | • | | | |
| 27 DiNola-Kaminsky-Sternfeld (Y) | | • | • | | | • | • | • | • | • | | | | | | | | | • | • | | | |
| 28 Dopyera | • | • | • | • | | • | • | | • | • | | | | | • | • | • | • | • | • | • | • | • |
| 29 Gellert | | | | | | | | | | | | | • | | • | | | | • | • | | | • |
| 30 Goodenough | • | • | • | | | | | | | | | | | | | | | | • | | | | |
| 31 Gordon-Jester | | | | | | | | | | | | | • | | • | • | • | | • | • | • | | • |
| 32 Greenberg | • | • | • | | • | • | | | | • | • | | • | • | • | • | • | | • | • | | | • |
| 33 Hartup-Charlesworth | • | | | | • | | | | | • | • | | • | | • | • | • | | • | • | • | | • |
| 34 Heathers | | | | | | | | | | • | | | • | | • | • | | | • | • | | | • |
| 35 Jack | | • | | | | | | | | | | | • | • | • | | | | • | • | | | |
| 36 Jersild-Markey | | • | | | • | | | | | • | | | • | | • | | | | • | | | | • |
| 37 Kagan | | | | | | | | | | | | | | | • | • | | | • | | • | | • |
| 38 Katz | | • | • | | | • | • | • | | • | | | • | | • | • | | | • | • | | | |
| 39 Kaufman-Rosenblum | • | • | | | • | • | • | | • | | | • | • | • | • | • | • | • | • | • | • | • | |
| 40 Kogan-Wimberger | • | • | • | | • | • | • | | | | | • | • | | • | • | | | • | • | • | | • |
| 41 Lewis | • | • | • | | • | • | • | | | | | • | • | | • | • | | | • | | | • | |
| 42 McGrew-McGrew | • | • | • | • | • | • | | | | • | | • | • | • | | | | | • | | | | |
| 43 Manwell-Mengert | • | • | | | • | | • | • | • | • | • | | | | • | • | | | • | • | | | |
| 44 Marshall-McCandless | | | | | | • | | | | • | | • | • | • | • | • | | | | | | | |
| 45 Mash-Terdal-Anderson | | | | | | | | | | • | | | • | • | • | • | | | | | • | | • |
| 46 Medley, et al. | | • | • | | • | • | • | • | | • | | • | • | • | • | • | • | • | • | • | • | • | • |
| 47 Morgan-Ricciuti | • | • | | | • | | | | | | | | • | • | • | • | | | • | | | | |
| 48 Moss-Robson | • | • | • | | • | | | | | | | | • | • | • | • | | | • | | | • | |
| 49 Murphy | • | • | • | | • | | | | | • | • | | • | | • | • | | | • | • | | | |
| 50 Ogilvie-Shapiro | | • | | | | | | | | • | • | | • | | • | • | | | | | | • | • |
| 51 Olmsted | | | | | | | | | | | | | • | • | • | • | | | | | | • | • |
| 52 Olson | • | • | • | | | | | | | | | | | | | | | | | | | | |
| 53 Parsons | | | | | | | | • | • | | | | • | • | • | • | • | • | | | • | | • |
| 54 Parten | | | | | | | | | | | | | | | | | | | • | | | | |
| 55 Ricketts | • | • | • | | | | | | | • | | | • | | • | • | | | • | • | • | | |
| 56 Rosen-D'Andrade | | | | | | | | | | • | | | • | | • | • | • | | • | • | | | • |
| 57 Schaefer-Aaronson | • | • | • | | • | | | | | • | • | | | | | | | | • | • | • | | |
| 58 Schoggen | | | | | | | | | | | | | • | • | • | • | • | • | • | • | | | |
| 59 Schroeer-Flapan | | | | | | | | | | | | • | • | | | | | | • | • | | | |
| 60 Sears-Rau-Alpert (BUO) | | • | | • | | | | | | • | | | | | | | | | • | • | | | |
| 61 Sears-Rau-Alpert (DP) | | | | | | | | • | • | • | | | | | | | | | • | • | | | |
| 62 Soar-Soar-Ragosta | • | • | | | | | • | | | • | | | • | | • | • | | | • | • | • | | • |
| 63 Spaulding | | | | | | | • | | | • | | | • | • | | | | | • | • | | | |
| 64 Stallings | | • | | | | • | • | • | • | • | | | • | | • | • | • | • | • | • | • | • | • |
| 65 Stover-Guerney-O'Connell | | | | | | • | | | | | | | | | | | | | • | • | • | | |
| 66 Tulkin-Kagan | • | • | | • | | • | • | • | | • | • | | • | • | | • | • | | • | | • | • | |
| 67 Van Alstyne | | | | | | • | | | | | | | • | • | • | | | | • | | | | |
| 68 Walters-Pearce-Dahms | • | • | | • | | | | | | | | • | • | | | | | | • | • | • | | |
| 69 Washburn | | • | • | | | | | | | | | | | | | | | | • | | | | • |
| 70 Watts, et al. | | • | | | | | • | • | • | • | | | • | • | • | • | • | | • | • | • | • | • |
| 71 White-Kaban | | • | | | | | • | • | | • | | | • | • | • | • | • | | • | | | | • |
| 72 Wright | | | | | | | | | | • | | • | • | | • | • | • | | • | | • | | • |
| 73 Yarrow, et al. | | • | • | | | • | • | • | • | • | • | | • | | • | • | • | | • | | • | | • |

**Figure 5.6.** Summary of Observation Systems

into a five-digit statement and keypunched for analysis. These are the four components that compose each behavioral clause:

1. *Subject:* who or what does something (first digit)

2. *Predicate:* what is done (second and third digits)

3. *Object:* whom or what the action is directed toward (fourth digit)

4. *Supplementary information:* usually adverbs that provide qualifying information (fifth digit)

The *subject* of a behavioral clause might include the central figure, a female adult, a male child, a setting alert (to be described later), and so forth. *Behavioral predicates* could include environmental contact, information processing, food behavior, manual activities, and the like. The *object* of the behavioral clause would include the same possibilities as the *subject* component. Finally, *supplementary information* might include such qualifiers as *with intensity, imitatively,* and *complexly.* Table 5.1 provides a summary of the major APPROACH behavior categories and the numbers assigned each in the code. Complete definitions of all behaviors are available in the APPROACH manual.[51] To give the reader some idea of the detail in which each behavior is defined, this example is presented:

> Negative Reinforcement. This area encompasses behaviors best described as disrupting the emitted behavior of another person or group.
>
> 30  Withholds sanction. Subject protests, denies, or challenges a statement made to him/her, or refuses to carry out a requested act.
>
> 31  Shows discomfort. By behavior or verbalizations, the subject gives evidence of fatigue, tension, fear, or pain.
>
> 32  Expresses displeasure. Subject emits an expression of unhappiness or some other negative affect.
>
> 33  Criticizes or derogates. Subject makes critical, derogatory, accusatory, or belligerent verbalizations.
>
> 34  Expresses hostility. Subject gives an extreme statement of dislike and antagonism.
>
> 35  Interferes or restricts. Subject physically interferes with actions of another person.
>
> 36  Resists or rejects. Subject reacts to perceived interference from another person with responses like holding back when held or led, pushing away a proffered toy, etc.
>
> 37  Threatens or frightens. Subject gesturally or verbally threatens another person with censure, loss of privileges, or punishment.
>
> 38  Assaults. Physical action which involves any assault by one person upon the body of another person, the self, or toward an item of equipment.[52]

For ecological analysis, as much attention must be given to the behavioral setting as to the emitted behaviors. Like the behavior categories, setting categories are reported in five-digit statements: setting alert (first digit), activity identification (second and third digits), geographic region (fourth digit), and social setting (fifth digit). The setting will change several times in a record. To announce this information, a *setting alert,* which always begins with the code number 9, is given. Then *activity identification* is provided (lunch or snack, pre-nap or nap, free or unstructured activity, book or story, field

**Table 5.1.** Summary of the Major APPROACH Behavior Categories and the Numbers Assigned Each in the Code

## BEHAVIORS

### I. Subject of Behavioral Clause (1st digit)

| | |
|---|---|
| 0 | Central Figure (CF) |
| 1 | The environment |
| 2 | Female adult |
| 3 | Female child |
| 4 | Item |
| 5 | Male child |
| 6 | Group, including CF |
| 7 | Group, excluding CF |
| 8 | Male adult |
| 9 | Setting alert |

### II. Behavioral Predicates (2nd and 3rd digits)

#### Environmental Contact (00-09)

| | |
|---|---|
| 00 | Ignores |
| 01 | Attends |
| 02 | Establishes or maintains contact |
| 03 | Terminates contact |
| 04 | Scans |

#### Information Processing (10-19)

| | |
|---|---|
| 10 | Confirms |
| 11 | Shows (to) or demonstrates (for) |
| 12 | Communicates or converses |
| 13 | Writes or draws (for) |
| 14 | Reads (to) |
| 15 | Corrects or disconfirms |
| 16 | Inquires |
| 17 | Informs or teaches |
| 18 | Informs about culture |
| 19 | Role plays (with) |

#### Food Behavior (20-24)

| | |
|---|---|
| 20 | Gives food (to) |
| 21 | Takes or handles food |
| 22 | Prepares food (for) |
| 23 | Transports food (to) |
| 24 | Disorganizes with food |

#### Manual Activities (25-29)

| | |
|---|---|
| 25 | Transfers item (to or toward) |
| 26 | Takes (from) or handles item |
| 27 | Manipulates item |
| 28 | Transports item (to) |
| 29 | Throws or rolls item (to) |

#### Negative Reinforcement (30-39)

| | |
|---|---|
| 30 | Withholds sanction (from) |
| 31 | Shows discomfort |
| 32 | Expresses displeasure (to) |
| 33 | Criticizes or derogates |
| 34 | Expresses hostility |
| 35 | Interferes or restricts |
| 36 | Resists or rejects |
| 37 | Threatens or frightens |
| 38 | Assaults |

#### Positive Reinforcement (40-49)

| | |
|---|---|
| 40 | Permits or sanctions |
| 41 | Expresses solicitude |
| 42 | Shows pleasure |
| 43 | Approves, encourages |
| 44 | Expresses affection |
| 45 | Facilitates |
| 46 | Excuses |

#### (Positive Reinforcement — Continued)

| | |
|---|---|
| 47 | Bargains, promises |
| 48 | Protects, defends |

#### Body Activities (50-59)

| | |
|---|---|
| 50 | Increases or accelerates |
| 51 | Decreases or retards activity |
| 52 | Perioralizes |
| 53 | Acts in situ |
| 54 | Adjusts or accommodates |
| 55 | Provides kinesthetic stimulation |
| 56 | Locomotes (toward) |
| 57 | LMAs |
| 58 | Marches, dances, or rhythmicizes |
| 59 | Voids or excretes |

#### Miscellaneous (60-69)

| | |
|---|---|
| 60 | Acts or occurs (in) |
| 61 | Caretakes |
| 62 | Consummates activity |
| 63 | Consummates activity, with failure |
| 64 | Disorganizes |
| 65 | Disintegrates emotionally |
| 66 | Makes music or sound patterns (by means of or to) |
| 69 | Garbled record |

#### Control Techniques (70-79)

| | |
|---|---|
| 70 | Suggests |
| 71 | Requests |
| 72 | Inhibits |
| 73 | Forbids |
| 74 | Offers |

### III. Object of Behavioral Clause (4th digit)

| | |
|---|---|
| 0-8 | Same as for 1st digit |
| 9 | No information or self |

### IV. Supplementary Information (5th digit)

| | |
|---|---|
| 0 | Ineptly |
| 1 | Accompanied by verbalization (or with sound if subject is 1 or 4) |
| 2 | Involving interpersonal physical contact |
| 3 | With intensity |
| 4 | In a specified manner, place, or time |
| 5 | In a manner, place, or time other than that specified |
| 6 | Imitatively |
| 7 | In continuation |
| 8 | Complexly |
| 9 | No information |

**Table 5.2.** Summary of the Major APPROACH Setting Categories and the Numbers Assigned Each in the Code

## SETTINGS

I. **Setting Alert** (1st digit)
    9    Setting code

II. **Activity Identification** (2nd and 3rd digits)
    00    Lunch or snack
    01    Pre-nap or nap
    02    Diapering or toileting or associated dressing or undressing
    03    Free or unstructured activity
    04    Structured learning time
    05    Book or story
    06    Record, singing, instrumental music, or rhythm activities
    07    Art, cutting, pasting
    08    Gym or outdoor play
    09    Transition times
    10    Medical or psychological experience
    11    Assembly or program
    12
    13    } Open
    14
    15    Perceptual-motor exercises
    16    Field trip
    17    TV time
    20    Other

III. **Geographic Region** (4th digit)
    1    School
    2    Home
    3    Laboratory or examining room
    4    Special teaching area (e.g., science corner, principal's office)
    5-9    Other

IV. **Supporting Cast** (5th digit)
    0    Central figure alone
    1    Mother (or mother figure) also present
    2    Father (or father figure) also present
    3    Mother and father (or father figure) also present
    4    One other child present
    5    More than one other child present
    6    Nonfamily adult also present
    7    Nonfamily adult or adults and child or children also present
    8    One or both parents plus other adult, with or without other children
    9    Other

trip, etc.), and this is followed by *geographic region* or the regions in which the behavior is occurring. *Social setting,* or information about people other than the central figure who are in the setting, is then noted. Table 5.2 summarizes the major setting categories and the numbers assigned to each code.

This excerpt, which relates the behavior of a young boy (two years, eight months old) during a morning's unstructured activity, shows how a narrative record can be translated into the APPROACH numerical language.

    90317               02749               35199

Richard is sitting on the floor building with shape blocks. Charean sits next to him.

30209               33301               00039

Jewell walks over to him and says, "You stupid nut." He ignores her. Charean is

35399                33307                00037        02599

standing near him. "You stupid nut," Jewell repeats. Richard ignores. Richard takes

21731-21538

a block away from his building. Mrs. Kahn says, "You forgot this is Charean and

21861

this is Ricky and you are Jewell." She says, "These are the names we use." Ricky

01076-01178                                02747

says, "One is Charean and one is Jewell and me," pointing to himself. He goes back

02741

to building with the shape blocks. Verbalizes to himself while he builds with the

02519                02649        02511

shape blocks. He's piling blocks in the cupboard now. Holds the blocks. Putting

02517

them back on the cupboard shelf, verbalizing, "One here." Verbalizes again, "One

02517                02517    02511

on top of one." He verbalizes placing the blocks one on top. Same. He takes off

02519                02740

one, says, "One on top." Takes off another. Puts another one on, but block drops
off. (He's trying to balance blocks on the pointed ends of cones and pyramids.)

01291                02511                36649

Verbalizing to himself. Puts a block on the floor, verbalizing. Looks up at Charean

00139                02591

who is hitting the xylophone. He takes a piece of paper out from underneath his

06449                06447        05399

foot and says, "Whoops." Steps on it a few times. Wipes his foot on it. Kneels

02599        02549                03191    02517

down, picks up a block. Places it alongside of his building. Coughs. Pushes another

02517                02517

block over to his building. Then back up against the toyshelf. Places the block on

02517                05449

the toyshelf. Places another block on the toyshelf. Pushes back to line it up with

02517                                02517

another block. Picks up another block and pushes it on the toyshelf. Places other

02741

blocks on the toyshelf. Puts a block on top of another block, says, "One here."

02740                                02741

He's placing blocks one on top of the other and they all fall off. He places blocks
back up, verbalizing. Tommy Horton drops all of the crayons near him. (NOTE:
Observer should have indicated whether this was inept object manipulation, as here

00159                    07151-56119

coded, or disorganized behavior.) He looks over and says, "Now you pick all of

50009        20269-24268                    04229 27051-56119

these crayons up." Mrs. Kahn smiles and walks over. Ricky smiles at her. She says,

54528                              50029              06119

"Tommy's going to help me pick them up." Tommy ignores her. Ricky throws a

02649                    02647

few crayons into their box and goes back to handling his blocks. He continues to

02517                    02517

handle his blocks. He's placing them back on the shelf again. He places one block

05249                    56119-54028

on top of another block. Puts the pointed end of the pyramid in his mouth. He

00159                    21159-27158-50149

watches Tommy put the crayons in the container. Teacher says, "Tommy, see

50149        00179        27151-52599

those blocks?" pointing. Tommy looks over. Ricky regards. Mrs. Kahn says, "You

05399

get some of those blocks and you can put them next to you." Ricky turns back to

05249                    53820

the box on the toyshelf, sucks the pointed end of the pyramid. Tommy bats at

27051-55194              50029

Mrs. Kahn, who says, "If you want to use beads, sit at the table and use them."

00179        21159-27058-52749              50027

Ricky regards. "You can give these a ride," she says to Tommy and puts a block

00177              21751        27051-55194

on his go-cart. Tommy ignores; Richard regards. "That'll sit and you can sit right

00177-05298              56449

next to it." Richard regards, finger in mouth. Tommy picks up a block, throws it

00177        20259        50323

on the floor. Richard regards. Mrs. Kahn walks over to Tommy. Tommy runs

21751-23358              00179

around the room. She says, "Tommy, you're not ready." Richard regards. Mrs.

20252              53623              00079

Kahn touches Tommy. Tommy struggles on the floor kicking. Ricky turns away

56593        00179        02511

and Tommy's screaming. Ricky regards briefly, but continues piling his blocks on
the toyshelf, verbalizing.[53]

The APPROACH system is not especially difficult to learn. Moreover, it can be readily adapted to different types of behavioral records that the observer wishes to analyze. The system is flexible inasmuch as some items may be added or substituted to adapt it more specifically to a particular research problem or behavior setting. APPROACH is a very useful tool for the systematic study of social behavior in naturalistic settings. It is especially valuable to the observer who wants to understand the sequences of behavior and the relationship between setting and behavior.

**Interaction Process Analysis.** Perhaps the best-known and most widely applicable category system is the Interaction Process Analysis (IPA). This system, which was developed by Bales,[54] can be used with both natural and laboratory groups. In the system, the observer codes every response made by an individual in a small face-to-face group into twelve categories: shows solidarity, shows tension release, agrees, gives suggestion, gives opinion, gives orientation, asks for orientation, asks for opinion, asks for suggestion, disagrees, shows tension, and shows antagonism. There are six dimensions of interaction, and the acts can be classified as either positive or negative. The dimensions include communication, evaluation, control, decision, tension reduction, and reintegration. Interrelationships among the categories are shown in Figure 5.7.

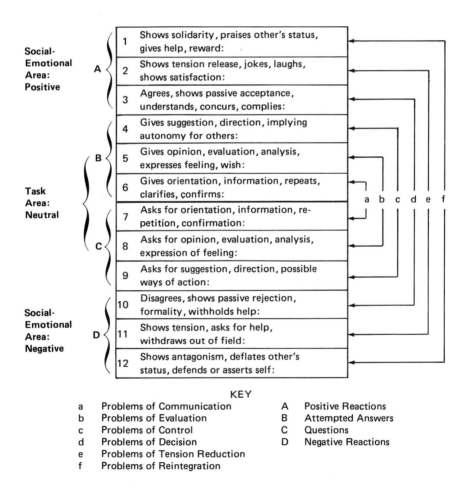

KEY

| | | | |
|---|---|---|---|
| a | Problems of Communication | A | Positive Reactions |
| b | Problems of Evaluation | B | Attempted Answers |
| c | Problems of Control | C | Questions |
| d | Problems of Decision | D | Negative Reactions |
| e | Problems of Tension Reduction | | |
| f | Problems of Reintegration | | |

**Figure 5.7.** System of Categories Used in Observation and Their Major Relations

**Teacher-Pupil Relationships.** An early category system that is used in educational studies was developed by Withall.[55] This observational system concentrates on teacher behavior and classifies verbal behaviors in terms of seven categories that range from "learner-centeredness" to "teacher-centeredness."

1. *Learner-supportive* statements that have the intent of reassuring or commending the pupil.

2. *Acceptant and clarifying* statements having an intent to convey to the pupil the feeling that he was understood and help him elucidate his ideas and feelings.

3. *Problem-structuring* statements or questions which proffer information or raise questions about the problem in an objective manner with intent to facilitate learner's problem-solving.

4. *Neutral* statements which comprise polite formalities, administrative comments, verbatim repetition of something that has already been said. No intent inferable.

5. *Directive* or hortative statements with intent to have pupil follow a recommended course of action.

6. *Reproving* or deprecating remarks intended to deter pupil from continued indulgence in present "unacceptable" behavior.

7. *Teacher self-supporting* remarks intended to sustain or justify the teacher's position or course of action.[56]

The first three categories are considered learner-centered, and the last three, teacher-centered. Thus, if the proportion of teacher statements falling into one or more of the first three categories outweighs the proportion in one or more of the last three categories, the teacher is classified as "learner-centered." If the proportion of teacher statements in the first and second categories combined exceeds those in the fifth, sixth, and seventh categories combined, the teacher may be said to be more "problem-centered" rather than "learner-" or "teacher-centered."

A more detailed treatment of observer systems and observational methods for the classroom can be found in various sources.[57]

## SIGN SYSTEMS

Used less frequently than category systems, sign systems are designed to record behaviors in incidents that take place during a specified period of time. The signs, explicitly defined discrete behaviors that have been listed beforehand, are recorded only once during an observation period no matter how many times they occur. Signs are not exhaustive, so a good many behaviors that are observed will be ignored and not recorded. Medley and Mitzel explain the differences between sign and category systems:

> A noteworthy feature of signs is that one recorder can use a relatively large number of them simultaneously. In contrast, he can normally use only one category system at a time. But, if a particular sign must be checked every few seconds, the observer is not going to be able to use many other signs with it. Important behaviors that occur frequently should, if possible, be incorporated into a category system; those that are relatively infrequent should take the form of signs.[58]

The observer using signs rather than categories must be cognizant of a larger range of possible behaviors, although fewer specific acts are usually recorded with sign systems. Normally, the behaviors that comprise a sign system occur infrequently, and therefore, long periods of time may pass during which little or nothing is recorded. One observer can use a large number of signs simultaneously in contrast to the observer who is employing categorization techniques. However, since several signs are used, it is sometimes difficult for the observer to remember them unless all of their definitions are perfectly clear in his or her mind. There is no room for ambiguity of item content. This potential problem is compounded by the fact that each sign occurs with limited frequency and may be easily forgotten.

Medley and Mitzel have suggested three characteristics that are essential to good signs.[59] A sign should be stated in the *present tense,* should refer to a *positive and not a negative occurrence,* and should be *singular in number.* An example of an item that lacks all three necessary features is "Teacher did not acknowledge the child's responses." The item, after revision to satisfy all three criteria, would read: "Teacher acknowledges the child's response."

A number of sign systems are available for the observational study of children.[60] Some systems have even been developed which combine both sign and category procedures.[61] A good example of a sign system is the Florida Taxonomy of Cognitive Behavior.[62] This procedure is made up of fifty-five behavioral items that are grouped according to seven levels of cognition: knowledge of ways and means of dealing with specifics (1.20), knowledge of universals and abstractions (1.30), translation (2.00), interpretation (3.00), application (4.00), analysis (5.00), synthesis (6.00), and evaluation (7.00). Certain student and teacher behaviors are listed under the different levels, four of which are shown in Figure 5.8. The observer marks each behavior as it occurs; the behavior is checked once in a six-minute period of time, no matter how many times it occurs. There are five separate six-minute recording intervals in each thirty-minute observation. Scoring is achieved by obtaining the median of the items recorded. All of the subtotals in the T column are summed, and the grand total is then divided by two and rounded off to the nearest whole number, which represents the midpoint number. Starting at the beginning of the record, the observer counts down the T column until the calculated midpoint number is reached. That item represents the general cognitive level at which the subject is functioning.

## EVALUATION OF OBSERVATIONAL SYSTEMS

Medley and Mitzel have commented that abstraction is the principal tool of science.[63] This observation is especially relevant to child study "not only because it is humanly impossible to record everything, but because abstraction makes the phenomena understandable."[64] Since the abstractive function of the observer is to categorize behavior and incidents as they are observed, category and sign systems help satisfy this basic scientific need. Undoubtedly, observer systems provide an efficient and reliable means of collecting data on selected events. But as with all procedures that have been utilized in observational study to any great extent, observer systems have not escaped critical assessment by their users. The primary disadvantage of structured observation systems is that, because of their selectivity, they violate the continuity and complexity of behavior[65] and distort the dynamics of behavior and interaction.[66] In some systems, however, these inadequacies can be identified and remedied.[67] Another drawback is that behaviors are frequently divorced from context.[68] The intensity and significance of certain events also may be lost.[69] If relatively long time intervals are called for, it is possible for observer variability to result.[70] Large numbers of categories cause problems in item placement, although they may allow finer discriminations.[71] In many cases, structured systems are also plagued by the problems of observer inference.[72] Additionally, recording schemes that require categorization of an event as it occurs allow fewer reliability checks, more time pressure and more errors, omission of some detail, and limited opportunity to edit the data.[73] These

FLORIDA TAXONOMY OF COGNITIVE BEHAVIOR

| TOT | | | | | | | |
|---|---|---|---|---|---|---|---|
| T | P | T/ P | T/ P | T/ P | T/ P | T/ P | **1.10  KNOWLEDGE OF SPECIFICS** |
| | | | | | | | 1. Reads |
| | | | | | | | 2. Spells |
| | | | | | | | 3. Identifies something by name |
| | | | | | | | 4. Defines meaning of term |
| | | | | | | | 5. Gives a specific fact |
| | | | | | | | 6. Tells about an event |

**1.20  KNOWLEDGE OF WAYS AND MEANS OF DEALING WITH SPECIFICS**

| | | | | | | | |
|---|---|---|---|---|---|---|---|
| | | | | | | | 7. Recognizes symbol |
| | | | | | | | 8. Cites rule |
| | | | | | | | 9. Gives chronological sequence |
| | | | | | | | 10. Gives steps of process, describes method |
| | | | | | | | 11. Cites trend |
| | | | | | | | 12. Names classification system or standard |
| | | | | | | | 13. Names what fits given system or standard |

**1.30  KNOWLEDGE OF UNIVERSALS AND ABSTRACTIONS**

| | | | | | | | |
|---|---|---|---|---|---|---|---|
| | | | | | | | 14. States generalized concept or idea |
| | | | | | | | 15. States a principle, law, theory |
| | | | | | | | 16. Tells about orgnztn or structure |
| | | | | | | | 17. Recalls name of prin, law, theory |

**2.00  TRANSLATION**

| | | | | | | | |
|---|---|---|---|---|---|---|---|
| | | | | | | | 18. Restates in own words or briefer terms |
| | | | | | | | 19. Gives cncrt exmpl of an abstract idea |
| | | | | | | | 20. Verbalizes from a graphic rprsntatn |
| | | | | | | | 21. Trans vrblztn into graphic form |
| | | | | | | | 22. Trans fig stmnts to lit stmnts, or vice v |
| | | | | | | | 23. Trans for lang to Eng, or vice versa |

**Figure 5.8.** Florida Taxonomy of Cognitive Behavior

and other shortcomings of observer systems are usually offset by more positve virtues and therefore have not discouraged the use of the systems.

Certain guidelines for developers and users of observation systems may be helpful in avoiding many potential problems.[74] Herbert and Attridge have outlined a number of such criteria under three broad headings: identifying, validity, and practicality. Identifying criteria aid in the screening and selection of observation instruments that are appropriate for a given study. Validity criteria include issues associated with degree of inference, context, and reliability, all of which are related to the accuracy with which the system represents observed behaviors and events. Practicality criteria deal with ease of implementation.

1. Identifying criteria

    1.1 Each instrument should have a title which fairly represents what it does without implying a wider purpose than is warranted.

    1.2 The instrument must be accompanied by a statement of purpose.

    1.3 The rationale or theoretical support, if any, underlying the instrument should be made clear.

    1.4 The behaviors, subjects, and substantive content on which the instrument is focused should be clearly specified.

    1.5 The applications for which the instrument is intended should be stated.

    1.6 Situations in which the instrument should not be used should be stated.

2. Validity criteria

    2.1 Item characteristics

        2.11 All terms, especially those which designate items of behaviors to be observed, must be as clearly and unambiguously defined as the behaviors under study will permit.

        2.12 Where an observation instrument and its terms are derived from theory, these terms must be defined in such a way as to be consistent with their use in the theory which they represent.

        2.13 Items comprising the instrument must be exhaustive of the dimension(s) of behavior under study.

        2.14 Items comprising the instrument must be representative of the dimension(s) of behavior under study.

        2.15 Items comprising the instrument must be mutually exclusive.

        2.16 Ground rules for the implementation of the instrument in general, and for the categorization of borderline and/or unusual behaviors, must be specified.

    2.2 Inference

        2.21 Instrument items must be as low in the degree of observer inference required as the complexity of behavior under study will permit.

        2.22 The nature and extent of observer inference and methods of reducing and/or controlling it must be explicated.

        2.23 The nature of inferences that can be made from the data obtained from the instrument subsequent to observation and coding must be carefully described and substantiated.

        2.24 Statistical and other methods of inferential treatment of data, which are recommended for use with a given instrument, should be specified.

2.3  Context

    2.31  The problem of context must be recognized and the degree and kind of context brought to bear in the instrument must be explicated.

    2.32  Methods of reducing and/or controlling use of context by observers and others must be explicated.

2.4  Observer effect

    2.41  Observer, and other effects, including those of personnel, procedures, and equipment, in and around the observation setting, should be explicated.

2.5  Reliability

    2.51  The types of reliability assessed, their meaning, and the conditions under which they were determined must be reported.

2.6  Validity procedures

    2.61  Each instrument should be accompanied by the methods employed to test its validity, the results obtained, and the purpose for which these results apply.

3. Criteria of practicality

3.1  Instrument items

    3.11  Items comprising the instrument should be relevant to its purposes.

    3.12  Codes identifying categories should be simple, easy to remember, and convenient to record.

    3.13  Categories and their codes should be capable of being learned by observers.

3.2  Observers

    3.21  Where special qualifications of observers are required, these should be made clear.

    3.22  Training procedures for observers, including number of observers, procedural steps, duration, and results must accompany the instrument. Necessary manuals, tapes, films or other training devices should be easily available.

3.3  Collection and recording of data

    3.31  The manual should recommend the number, location and functions of observers, coders, technicians and other staff needed in the observation setting and elsewhere.

    3.32  Data collection and recording procedures must accompany the instrument.

    3.33  The observation unit recommended by the system must be specified.

    3.34  The coding unit recommended by the system must be specified.

3.35 Procedures for analyzing data should be described and discussed.

3.36 Recommended data transmission and display techniques for an instrument should be described.

3.37 Costs likely to be incurred in the use of the instrument should be estimated.[75]

The number of available observational systems has grown rapidly in recent years, and methodological sophistication has also improved. A major impediment to the scientific advancement of observer systems, however, has been that the systems are usually employed only by their authors.[76] A review of child development journals reveals that there has been a tendency for investigators to develop their own systems for their specialized research. If they do happen to try the procedures of others, they frequently abandon them because sufficient reliability is not attained in their own projects. Oftentimes, this failure is due only to subtle aspects of the procedure which have not been communicated effectively.[77] Although certain methodological issues concerning observation systems still remain to be resolved, systematized approaches to observation have become indispensable in the study of children. The increased and meaningful use of observer systems in child development and education is certain to continue.

## CHAPTER NOTES

1.  J. W. Wrightstone, "Observational Techniques," in *Encyclopedia of Educational Research*, ed. C. W. Harris (New York: Macmillan, 1960).
2.  M. E. Shaw and J. W. Wright, *Scales for the Measurement of Attitudes* (New York: McGraw-Hill, 1967).
3.  H. H. Remmers, "Rating Methods in Research on Teaching," in *Handbook of Research on Teaching*, ed. N.L. Gage (Chicago: Rand McNally, 1963).
4.  W. C. Bier, "Testing Procedures and Their Value," in *Proceedings of the 1959 Sisters' Institute of Spirituality*, ed. J. E. Haley (Notre Dame, Ind.: University of Notre Dame Press, 1960).
    J. P. Guilford, *Psychometric Methods* (New York: McGraw-Hill, 1954).
5.  Guilford, *Psychometric Methods*.
6.  H. Champney, "The Measurement of Parent Behavior," *Child Development* 12 (1941): 131-66.
7.  Remmers, "Rating Methods."
8.  Guilford, *Psychometric Methods*.
    J. E. Horrocks, *Assessment of Behavior* (Columbus, Ohio: Merrill, 1964).
    F. M. Kerlinger, *Foundations of Behavioral Research* (New York: Holt, 1973).
9.  Guilford, *Psychometric Methods*.
    Horrocks, *Assessment*.
10. Kerlinger, *Foundations*.
11. Guilford, *Psychometric Methods*.
    Horrocks, *Assessment*.
12. N. E. Gronlund, *Measurement and Evaluation in Teaching* (New York: Macmillan, 1971).
13. Guilford, *Psychometric Methods*.
14. Ibid.
15. Champney, "Parent Behavior."
16. Guilford, *Psychometric Methods*, p. 293.
17. Horrocks, *Assessment*.
18. E. S. Conklin, "The Scale of Values Method for Studies in Genetic Psychology," *University of Oregon Publications* 2 (1923).
19. P. M. Symonds, "On the Loss of Reliability in Ratings Due to Coarseness of the Scale," *Journal of Experimental Psychology* 7 (1924): 456-61.
20. Guilford, *Psychometric Methods*.
21. L. J. Cronbach, *Essentials of Psychological Testing* (New York: Harper, 1960).
22. Gronlund, *Measurement*.
23. W. A. Mehrens and I. J. Lehmann, *Measurement and Evaluation in Psychology and Education* (New York: Holt, 1973).
24. H. Champney and H. Marshall, "Optimal Refinement of the Rating Scale," *Journal of Applied Psychology* 23 (1939): 323-31.
    Guilford, *Psychometric Methods*.
25. Guilford, *Psychometric Methods*.
26. F. L. Wells, "A Statistical Study of Literary Merit," *Archives of Psychology* 1 (1907).
27. E. L. Thorndike, "A Constant Error in Psychological Ratings," *Journal of Applied Psychology* 4 (1920): 25-29.
28. R. L. Thorndike and E. Hagen, *Measurement and Evaluation in Psychology and Education* (New York: Wiley, 1969).
29. P. M. Symonds, *Diagnosing Personality and Conduct* (New York: Appleton, 1931).
30. Guilford, *Psychometric Methods*.
31. T. Newcombe, "An Experiment Designed to Test the Validity of a Rating Technique," *Journal of Educational Psychology* 22 (1931): 279-89.
32. Guilford, *Psychometric Methods*.
33. H. A. Murray, *Explorations in Personality* (New York: Oxford, 1938).
34. Guilford, *Psychometric Methods*.
35. Kerlinger, *Foundations*.
36. Guilford, *Psychometric Methods*.
37. Remmers, "Rating Methods."
38. Gronlund, *Measurement*.
    Mehrens and Lehmann, *Measurement and Evaluation*.
    G. Sax, *Principles of Educational Measurement and Evaluation* (Belmont, Calif.: Wadsworth, 1974).
39. Mehrens and Lehmann, *Measurement and Evaluation*.
40. E. O. Laumann and J. S. House, "Living Room Styles and Social Attributes: The Patterning of Material Artifacts in a Modern Urban Community," *Sociological and Social Research* 54 (1970): 321-42.

H. L. Rheingold and K. V. Cook "The Contents of Boys' and Girls' Rooms As an Index of Parents' Behavior," *Child Development* 46 (1975): 459-63.

J. A. Stallings, *Learning to Look* (Belmont, Calif.: Wadsworth, 1977), pp. 27-28.

41. Mehrens and Lehmann, *Measurement and Evaluation.*
42. Kerlinger, *Foundations.*
43. R. W. Heyns and R. Lippitt, "Systematic Observational Techniques," in *Handbook of Social Psychology*, vol. 1, ed. G. Lindzey (Cambridge, Mass.: Addison-Wesley, 1954).
44. D. M. Medley and H. E. Mitzel, "Measuring Classroom Behavior by Systematic Observation," in *Handbook of Research on Teaching*, ed. N. L. Gage (Chicago: Rand McNally, 1963).
45. N. A. Flanders, *Teacher Influence, Pupil Attitudes, and Achievement* (U.S. Department of Health, Education, and Welfare, Office of Education, Cooperative Research Monograph No. 12. Washington, D.C.: U.S. Government Printing Office, 1965).
    W. W. Lewis, J. M. Mewell, and J. Withall, "An Analysis of Classroom Patterns of Communication," *Psychological Reports* 9 (1961): 211-19.
46. Heyns and Lippitt, "Techniques."
47. Medley and Mitzel, "Systematic Observation," p. 299.
48. R. D. Boyd and M. V. De Vault, "Classification of Representative Observation Systems," *Review of Educational Research* 36 (1966): 529-51.
    E. G. Boyer, A. Boyer, and G. Karafin, eds., *Measures of Maturation: An Anthology of Early Childhood Observation Instruments* (Philadelphia: Humanizing Learning Program, Research for Better Schools, Inc., 1973).
    L. Cohen, *Educational Research in Classroom and Schools: A Manual of Materials and Methods* (New York: Harper, 1976).
    M. Galton, *British Mirrors: A Collection of Classroom Observation Systems* (Leicester, England: University of Leicester, 1978).
    M. Galton, "Systematic Classroom Observation: British Research," *Educational Research* 21 (1979): 109-15.
    I. J. Gordon and R. E. Jester, "Techniques of Observing Teaching in Early Childhood and Outcomes of Particular Procedures," in *Second Handbook of Research on Teaching*, ed. R. M. W. Travers (Chicago: Rand McNally, 1973).
    Medley and Mitzel, "Systematic Observation."
    R. L. Ober, E. L. Bentley, and E. Miller, *Systematic Observation of Teaching* (Englewood Cliffs, N.J.: Prentice-Hall, 1971).
    B. Rosenshine and N. Furst, "The Use of Direct Observation to Study Teaching," in *Second Handbook of Research on Teaching*, ed. R. M. W. Travers (Chicago: Rand McNally, 1973).
    A. Simon and E. G. Boyer, eds., *Mirrors for Behavior: An Anthology of Classroom Observation Instruments*, vols. 1-6 (Philadelphia: Research for Better Schools, 1967).
    A. Simon and E. G. Boyer, eds., *Mirrors for Behavior: An Anthology of Classroom Observation Instruments*, vols. 7-14 and summary (Philadelphia: Research for Better Schools, 1970).
    A. Simon and E. G. Boyer, eds., *Mirrors for Behavior: An Anthology of Classroom Observation Instruments*, supplementary vols. A and B (Philadelphia: Research for Better Schools, 1970).
49. B. M. Caldwell, A. S. Honig, and R. Wynn, "APPROACH—A Procedure for Patterning Responses of Adults and Children" (Unpublished manuscript, 1967).
50. B. M. Caldwell, "A New Approach to Behavioral Ecology," in *Minnesota Symposia on Child Psychology*, vol. 2, ed. J. P. Hill (Minneapolis: University of Minnesota Press, 1969), p. 81.
51. B. M. Caldwell and A. S. Honig, "APPROACH, A Procedure for Patterning Responses of Adults and Children: Coding Manual" (Unpublished manuscript, University of Arkansas at Little Rock, undated).
52. Ibid.
53. Ibid.
54. R. F. Bales, *Interaction Process Analysis* (Cambridge, Mass.: Addison-Wesley, 1950).
55. J. Withall, "The Development of a Technique for the Measurement of Social-Emotional Climate in Classroom," *Journal of Experimental Education* 17 (1949): 347-61.
56. Ibid., p. 349.
57. C. W. Beegle and R. M. Brandt, *Observational Methods in the Classroom* (Washington, D.C.: Association for Supervision and Curriculum Development, 1973).
    N. A Flanders, *Analyzing Teaching Behavior* (Reading, Mass,: Addison-Wesley, 1970).
    Medley and Mitzel, 1963, "Measuring Classroom Behavior."
    Rosenshine and Furst, "Use of Direct Observation."
    G. P. Sackett, ed., *Observing Behavior* (Baltimore: University Park Press, 1977).
    R. S. Soar, R. M. Soar, and M. Ragosta, "Florida Climate and Control System (FLACCS)" (Gainesville, Fla.: Institute for Development of Human Resources, University of Florida, 1968).
    Stallings, *Learning to Look.*
    R. A. Weinberg and F. H. Wood, eds., *Observation of Pupils and Teachers in Mainstream and Special Education Settings: Alternative Strategies* (Reston, Va.: Council for Exceptional Children, 1975).
58. Medley and Mitzel, "Systematic Observation," p. 301.
59. Medley and Mitzel, "Systematic Observation."
60. W. W. Anderson, "A Study of the Effects of Self-directed Activity upon Quantity, Quality, and Variety of Responses in a Group Directed Reading-Thinking Activity" (Ph.D. diss., University of Virginia, 1971).
    B. B. Brown, R. Ober, and R. S. Soar, *Florida Taxonomy of Cognitive Behavior* (Gainesville, Fla.: Institute for Development of Human Resources, 1970).
    F. C. Cornell, C. M. Lindvall, and J. L. Saupe, *An Exploratory Measurement of Individualities of Schools and Classrooms* (Urbana, Ill.: Bureau of Educational Research, University of Illinois, 1952).
    D. C. Jayne, "A Study of the Relationship Between Teaching Procedures and Educational Outcomes," *Journal of Experimental Education* 14 (1945): 101-34.
    A. T. Jersild et al., "An Evaluation of Aspects of the Activity Program in the New York City Public Elementary Schools," *Journal of Experimental Education* 8 (1939): 166-207.
    D. G. Ryans, *Characteristics of Teachers* (Washington, D.C.: American Council on Education, 1960).
61. D. M. Medley and H. E. Mitzel, "A Techniuqe for Measuring Classroom Behavior," *Journal of Education Psychology* 49 (1958): 86-92.
    D. M. Medley et al., *The Personal Record of School Experience: A Manual for PROSE Records* (Princeton, N.J.: Educational Testing Service, 1971).
62. Brown, Ober, and Soar, *Florida Taxonomy.*
    J. N. Webb, "Taxonomy of Cognitive Behavior: A System for the Analysis of Intellectual Processes," *Journal of Research and Development in Education* 4 (1970): 23-33.
63. Medley and Mitzel, "Systematic Observation."
64. Ibid.
65. E. Gellert, "Systematic Observation: A Method in Child Study," *Harvard Educational Review* 25 (1955): 179-95.
66. R. B. Cattell and J. M. Digman, "A Theory of the Structure of Perturbations in Observer Ratings and Questionnarie Data in Personality Research," *Behavioral Science* 2 (1964): 341-58.
67. Flanders, *Teacher Influence.*
    Gellert, "Method in Child Study."
68. Gellert, "Method in Child Study."
69. E. F. Borgatta, "A Systematic Study of Interaction Process Scores, Peer- and Self-assessments, Personality, and Other Variables," *Genetic Psychology Monographs* 65 (1962): 219-91.
70. P. Ekman, "A Methodological Discussion of Nonverbal Behavior," *Journal of Psychology* 43 (1957): 141-49.

71.  K. L. Weick, "Systematic Observational Methods," in *Handbook of Social Psychology*, vol. 2, eds. G. Lindzey and E. Aronson (Reading, Mass.: Addison-Wesley, 1968), pp. 357-451.

72.  Ibid.

73.  Ibid.

74.  J. Herbert and C. Attridge, "A Guide for Developers and Users of Observation Systems and Manuals," *American Educational Research Journal* 12 (1975): 1-20.
     D. A. Jackson, G. M. Della-Piana, and H. N. Sloane, Jr., *How to Establish a Behavior Observation System* (Englewood Cliffs, N.J.: Educational Technology Publications, 1975).
     J. B. Reid, *A Social Learning Approach to Family Intervention,* vol. 2, *Observation in Home Settings* (Eugene, Ore.: Castalia, 1978).

75.  Herbert and Attridge, "Guide for Developers," pp. 4-18.

76.  Heyns and Lippitt, "Techniques."

77.  Ibid.

# 6

# Observational Aids:
# Equipment and Devices

There are several ways to instrument observational child study. Aids such as rating scales, checklists, and category or sign system recording schemes were already discussed in Chapter 5. In addition to these, there are other means to increase the feasibility and utility of direct observation and to improve the efficiency of recording. Among them are the use of sound recorders; motion picture and videotape recorders; mechanical instruments including event recorders, behavior counters, and audible timers; and one-way observation devices. The increasing demands on the observer to examine the integration among variables rather than to isolate and quantify only a few of them has required more extensive observation and complex analysis.[1] This broadened scope of observational study has frequently resulted in some dissatisfaction with exclusively paper-and-pencil recording techniques and has created a greater dependence on media. The development and use of instrumental aids may have been a response to the need to record, analyze, and understand multiple aspects of behaviors, although as some authors[2] have pointed out, the technology itself may have stimulated increased use of direct observation and greater attention to complexity.

## SOUND RECORDERS

In observational studies, sound recorders have been employed in various ways. They have been used to record an observer's spoken commentary as the behavior or events occur[3] or shortly after they have been observed.[4] Once transcription of the tape has been accomplished, the data are transferred to an analysis sheet. Sound recorders also have been used for cuing time-sampled observations.[5] The observer attaches an earplug extension to a tape recorder and turns the recorder on. At regular time intervals during the observation period, the tape recording signals the beginning and/or end of the interval and may even provide instructions to the observer. A recording sheet that coordinates with the taped time markers and directions is marked by the observer, or an electronic system is used for recording. The tape-cuing technique helps eliminate the distraction caused by visual signals such as flashing lights or watches. A third way audio recorders have been used is to make reproductions of an individual subject's speech, of vocal interaction in dyads, and of verbal interchange within groups. Subsequently, a typescript is made of the recording, and the data are then subjected to analysis (content analysis, phonemic analysis, etc.). Without a doubt, the magnetic tape recorder is probably the most commonly used mechanical auxiliary in observational study.

Using a sound recorder, Dreger conducted an investigation of children's verbal interaction to determine if their spontaneous conversation differed in style and content from that which has been recorded in children's literature and scientific writings.[6] He placed a concealed microphone in a doorway approximately forty-five feet from a tree where the children were seated or standing, and recorded a thirty-minute conversation in a naturalistic setting not directly observed by adults. Although the recordings were not ideal and did not approximate the quality of tapes produced in more controlled settings, the investigator was sufficiently convinced that the youngsters were unrestrained in their conversation and did not suspect that an adult was listening. Therefore, their verbal behavior was considered "natural." This excerpt from a transcription of a conversation about sex between two girls and a boy gives us an idea about how eight- and nine-year-old children approach this topic when there are supposedly no adults around.

John:    You tell me, too.

Katy:    Tell 'im. (scraping sounds like rasping of sandpaper on wood)

Mary:    You tell 'im.

Katy:    Why don' chu? You told me. Why don't chu fr—are you afraid to tell him?

Mary:    Well, yes—(short indistinguishable interruption). I'm sort of shy . . .

Katy:    Seems women have—women have big titties, an'—an' men don't.

Mary:    So what'll happen?

Katy:    What happen? . . .

Mary:    (interrupting) Yeah. The women have to. 'Cause you know what happens when they have a baby. The baby likes to suck on 'em. Hmm?

Katy:    Yeah, but what happened to your grand—

John:    (interrupting) He got . . .

Mary:    Yep, just like a man's.

Katy:    A man's titties get little, then . . .

John:    Don't ask me—ee? (Pause) My grandmother had her titties cut off.[7]

Satisfactory interobserver agreement was obtained. The transcription revealed far more elisions, slurrings, and unconnected statements than conversations reported in children's books and the scientific literature.

In a longitudinal study, Loban employed another type of sound recording device, the Audograph, to investigate language spoken by children in kindergarten and elementary school.[8] The 338 subjects were interviewed individually, and their spoken responses were recorded annually with the Audograph for seven consecutive years. This instrument, which reproduces sound on a plastic disk, does not provide reproductions that are of the quality of good tape recordings. But it did produce satisfactory and reliable records of the children's voices in this study. Other supplementary data were also collected, such as use of written language, proficiency in reading and listening, teachers' judgments of the children's language skill, and background information on health and family. In addition to providing developmental language data, the research demonstrated useful methods, including sound recordings, for the study of semantic and structural aspects of language.

Mahl, Dollard, and Redlich have described a number of procedures that insure optimal sound recording of verbal behavior.

1. The background noise must be reduced to permit a very wide dynamic range reproduction and still have the reproduced sound louder than the background noise of the entire recording system. (This includes all noise introduced in the acoustical, mechanical, and electrical portions of the recording and playback systems.)

2. A uniform reproduction (through the entire system) of all tones from the lowest base to the highest pitch of the overtones of the recorded sounds is required. These overtones carry much of the meaning and intelligence in the . . . emotional nuances.

3. There also should be a minimum distortion of the wave-shape of the recorded sound waves. An excessive amount of wave-shape distortion disturbs the relative intensity relationships of the fundamental tones and their associated overtones, thereby reducing the ability to interpret emotional nuances correctly.[9]

The location in which the sound recordings are to be made should also be reasonably quiet; the site should be distant from machinery that might affect the noise level (elevators, ventilation fans, etc.). Moreover, the conscientious observer should inspect the blueprints of the building to determine if the walls contain pipes for heating, plumbing, and ventilation, all of which are potential transmitters of noise. If high quality recordings are desired, other precautions should be taken to reduce potential sources of noise and sound distortion. Double-wall and ceiling construction, special floors, sound absorbent tile covers on the ceiling, weather-stripped or sound-proof doors, thermopaned windows, quiet air conditioning, good recording equipment, optimal microphone placement, and even room dimensions that insure the resonating properties are distributed throughout the sound spectrum are all variables which affect sound recordings. As many of these factors as possible should be considered when electric recording of speech is undertaken. In nonlaboratory settings, achieving ideal conditions is obviously difficult, but an attempt should be made to eliminate sources of noise and distortion. The selection of quality equipment is naturally requisite to effective observational study.[10]

A number of promising innovative techniques involving audio recordings have been used to study individuals. Jones has described an unusual use of the tape recorder in observational research.[11] The observer wears a face mask device in which a microphone and battery-operated recorder are concealed. He or she can inaudibly narrate the stream of behavior onto tape, along with contemporaneous comments. The recordings are later analyzed at the observer's leisure.

## RADIO TELEMETRY

Radio telemetry is another means of instrumenting child study through audio recordings. RTel, as the procedure is sometimes called, allows the verbal behaviors of subjects to be carried by a miniature radio transmitter to a sound recorder. (Some computer compatible systems allow the verbal behavior to be recorded directly onto computer paper tape or cards.) This mechanical innovation is viewed by many as fulfilling the need for a genuinely unobtrusive naturalistic observation methodology.[12] Considerable pilot work is necessary to determine the feasibility of using radio telemetry for study purposes, as Miklich and his associates explain:

> Pilot data may be gathered from audio recorders placed where the behavior of interest occurs. It is desirable to have the S wear or carry a microphone, since merely placing a microphone in a room often does not provide a usable record. Small, portable cassette tape recorders can be carried by an S, and they are excellent for pilot work. In fact, if the monitoring periods are short, these recorders may substitute for RTel, an especially desirable alternative in an environment in which RTel functions poorly. Initial data may be used to resolve the following issues: (1) Can different persons' voices be distinguished? (2) In particular, can S's be identified? (3) Does ambient noise prevent recovery of the data? It is also well to use pilot recordings to develop a scoring system. If sufficient scoring reliability cannot be achieved, one need not develop an RTel system. Independent behavioral observations of S's, made during pilot recording sessions, can help to determine the validity of the scoring system, as well as the extent to which nonverbal behaviors being inferred from the verbal record are missed.[13]

Before monitoring may be used, consent authorizations are required from adult subjects or from parents or legal guardians of children. Monitoring unconsenting persons is prohibited by Section 605 of the Communications Act of 1934, as amended.

Practicability of the transmitter observational technique has been demonstrated in several studies. Soskin and John used this method in an investigation of spontaneous talk.[14] The objective of their study was to examine person-environment interaction as revealed in the analysis of talk. The researchers spent a year perfecting the transmitting and recording device which they felt overcame many of the shortcomings inherent in written records:

> Chief among them is that the continuous presence of an observer unintentionally can become a stimulus to incite or inhibit certain behaviors or to modify others. Equally important, as subsequent experience has shown, it is physically impossible to write verbatim records of many interactions between adults as they occur. The rate of interaction is too rapid, especially in a small-group situation, and there is a tendency for observer-recorders to condense some utterances, completely miss others, overlook inconsistencies, neglect to record grammatical errors, etc. Moreover, it is physically impossible for an observer to record a conversation while the participants are on the move, e.g., from one location to another, just as it would be physically impossible for a single individual to sustain the set of an observer-recorder continuously over a sixteen-hour day without relaxation and at the same time attend to his own needs. Even less could one maintain such a rigorous observing schedule over a long period of days.[15]

During Soskin's and John's investigation, radio transmitters were worn continuously for fourteen to sixteen hours a day by two young married couples who were induced to participate in the experiment in return for an expense-paid vacation. A 1½-by-2½-by-5-inch miniature radio transmitter was mounted on each subject by means of a shoulder strap attached to a leather camera case so that it hung behind a subject's shoulder blade. A one-inch-square microphone was placed high on the front part of the shoulder strap. Soskin and John noted that it was difficult to determine the extent to which the behavior of the subjects was influenced by consciousness of the transmitter. However, the couples reported later that they were aware of the presence of the apparatus at some times and not at others and that self-consciousness lessened with the passage of time. This transcribed fragment from the protocols reveals the spontaneous nature of the verbal interaction:

231. *Jock* (*laughs*) Christ. That was pretty good.

232. *Roz* Which way am I supposed to be going?

233. *Jock* The other way.

234. *Roz* Oh. Maybe not.

235. *Jock* You sure are. (*reassuringly*) That's all right, by the end of this . . . our stay here, you'll be able to paddle pretty well.

236. *Roz* (*laughs*) I can paddle pretty well now.

237. *Jock* You sure can.

238. *Roz* You haven't fallen in yet, have you?

239. *Jock* No, but you almost swamped us.[16]

The investigators indicated that the tapes contained "recordings of a violent argument, of tender expressions of love, of petty behavior, of sober soul searching, and sheer, exuberant pleasure,"[17] leading one to believe that the research participants eventually became habituated to this study technique. Typed transcripts of the macrosamples of spontaneous talk were subjected to ecological, structural, functional, and dynamic analyses.

In another investigation using voice radio telemetry, Purcell and Brady studied children housed in a residential asthma rehabilitation center in order to assess the effects of monitoring children's behavior with a miniature radio transmitter.[18] Following an orientation session, the researchers enlisted the cooperation of twenty-six subjects aged twelve to sixteen. Half of them wore "live" transmitters, and the other half wore "dummies." The device used for transmitting the vocal behavior was a small unit that was attached to a waist belt. An FM receiver was installed in the attic of the children's cottage, and it relayed the conversations through telephone wires to a recorder located in another building. The investigators concluded that within a relatively short period of time, usually no more than two to four days, the youngsters adapted to the equipment. The subjects behaved naturally as judged by direct measures of attention to the apparatus, self-reports, observations by the houseparents, and the tape-recorded verbal behavior itself. In regard to the language used by the children and the nature of the interaction, Purcell and Brady noted that "their qualities of spontaneity and freedom are striking."[19] Unfortunately, no pretransmitter conversations were available for comparison.

Radio-voice telemetry has many advantages, some of which are shared by all types of audio recordings. RTel generates a far more complete record than is possible with a human observer; it picks up whispers, changes in inflections, and quiet remarks; it eliminates the problems associated with accustoming subjects to rotating observers; and it prevents observer fatigue.[20] Moreover, the permanent record provided by the recordings allows playback and re-analysis, if necessary. Other positive attributes of transmitter methods relative to the use of human observers were presented earlier in the lengthy quotation from Soskin and John.[21]

Remote instrumentation in child study also has some disadvantages. Since the verbal data can be accumulated more rapidly and more cheaply than they can be analyzed, a problem of data reduction exists. This difficulty can be overcome, however.[22] Data management may be facilitated by using a coding system and eliminating transcripts completely or by selecting only parts of the data for analysis. Another potential shortcoming of RTel relates to sex of the subject. Experience with telemetry has revealed that boys' voices are easier to distinguish than girls'.[23] Certain aspects of the physical setting may likewise limit the practicality of telemetry. Problems are created if there is a large area to be monitored, if there is an irregular and cluttered topography, and if the buildings that intervene between the subject and the receiving antenna are constructed of concrete and metal.[24] Professional engineering may be necessary to overcome serious problems of physical setting. With RTel, there is a loss of vital information about the child, such as his or her gestures, postures, facial expressions, and other types of body language.[25] The cost of establishing and maintaining a remote instrumentation system is very substantial and is increasing.[26] Finally, there are restrictions on transmitter power output which have been set by the Federal Communications Commission. Although a license is sometimes necessary, none is usually required for low-power transmitting devices that are used only in a particular building.[27] A number of sources are available which discuss the highly technical aspects of radio telemetry.[28]

## MOTION PICTURE AND VIDEOTAPE TECHNIQUES

Michaelis has written that the motion picture film is of great value to many different fields of human endeavor but that perhaps its noblest use has been as a scientific instrument.[29] There are at least five general types of investigations for which motion pictures and/or videotapes are especially appropriate:

1. Where the action proceeds so swiftly that it is not possible to record all of the required elements by any other method

2. Where the action is so complex that attention is focused on certain components rather than others

3. Where changes in the behavior are so subtle that satisfactory morphological delineation between one act and another is difficult

4. Where sequential changes in fairly complex behavior are being considered

5. Where it is required to measure precisely, specific, parameters of certain brief or complex behavioral events[30]

The choice of film or videotape is an important consideration in child study because both have their own virtues and shortcomings. Motion picture recording has two distinct advantages over videotape: (a) higher resolution, and (b) convenience, ease, and generality of use.[31] Regarding the first advantage, motion picture film permits the definition of fine details and therefore allows microanalysis. The feasibility of microanalysis with videotape is less because of the distances necessary for framing more than one person. And unlike videotape, motion pictures are available in color. Regarding the second advantage, completed motion picture films can be used more easily and in more ways than videotapes. Film projectors can be obtained almost anywhere and are easy to operate, making screening more practicable. If the material is to be subjected to intensive analysis, film is clearly the choice over videotape because of the availability of film analysis equipment, the potential for expansion (i.e., running the film slowly or shooting the film at high speed on an editor or taking the shots at spaced intervals), and its flexibility for temporal measurements and the location of events within time which is made possible with a frame counter.

On the other hand, videotape may be preferred over motion pictures for certain reasons: (a) lower cost, (b) easy operation, (c) minimal illumination requirement, (d) instant playback, and (e) closed circuit features.[32] Although the initial costs for cinematographic and video equipment are about the same, the operation costs for video are considerably less. Videotapes can be erased and reused, while movie film cannot. Video recording also does not require a special photographer or other technicians since operation of video equipment is relatively uncomplicated. In some cases, no special lighting is necessary for video. Another advantage of video recordings is that they can be replayed immediately and for an indefinite number of times. Many video units are equipped with dual audio channels which permit recording of the subject's speech in one channel and simultaneous comments of the observer in the other. And with a few adaptions, a video set-up can be developed into a closed circuit system. A number of technical references are available which treat videotape production in detail.[33] In comparing the film and videotape approaches, Scheflen concludes that "while the motion picture film is easier to use *once it has been made,* the video recording is cheaper and easier to make."[34] However, as already indicated, there are uses which dictate the choice of one or the other.

In response to the growing interest in film techniques, Dittmann, Stein, and Shakow have outlined some guidelines for persons who want to use this method of recording to instrument observational study.[35] These recommendations pertain primarily to motion picture production, although they may be equally applicable to video recording and merit consideration if ideal records are desired. First, Dittmann and his co-workers emphasize the importance of consulting with technical people before undertaking a major project that requires filming.

> Consultants from a number of fields will be needed to collaborate in the design— from architecture, heating and air-conditioning, lighting, acoustics, electronics, and photography. Since no one person has enough training and experience in all these

fields to do the complete job, the final design will be the result of the work of varied specialists.[36]

Second, a good deal of thought should be given to the design of the room that will be used for the filming. Soundproofing is important for the reduction of transmitted noise and reverberation, and high lighting levels are needed. Unless extremely high levels of diffused overhead fluorescent lighting are used, illumination can be a problem because of heat and obtrusiveness. Commenting on the physical features of the recording site, Dittmann writes:

> The design of the recording room will be a compromise of interrelationships among heat, light, and sound level. Photography requires lights; lights produce heat; removing heat is noisy; but sound recording requires low background noise levels. The design from any one of these standpoints is easy: A great deal of light can be provided unobtrusively, for example, if the scene to be filmed is so short that heat build-up is not a consideration. But combining the requirements of light, heat and sound leads to inevitable compromises. Many engineers are challenged and intrigued by such design problems.[37]

Third, the type of film selected for use in observational studies is dictated by the objectives of the investigation. The usefulness of a film is determined by resolution (i.e., detail) of the picture. The relative meaning of this term is explained by Dittmann:

> If an investigator wishes to study facial expressions of several members of a group, the requirements are very stringent. He must have the very best lens and use the finest grain film available, but the image size of each face will be so small that only the grossest expressions can be studied. If he can take a close-up of an individual face, on the other hand, a great deal of grain can be tolerated, and light levels can be reduced.[38]

Thus, there is a functional relationship between film speed, film grain, and lighting level. Higher speed films have large grains, and slower speed films have finer silver granules in the emulsion. The size of the field to be filmed influences the image size of each subject, and image size determines the grain size per subject. A fourth guideline enumerated by Dittmann and his associates concerns microphone placement; careful microphone placement is essential for clear audio signals. A fifth and final consideration has to do with playback. Not all projectors can be stopped and started again and again without damaging the film. This is not a problem with video recorders, however. Remote-control projectors that operate at different speeds can be used, but they are usually not designed for sound films. Rooms utilized for playback should have less reverberation than the recording room if the soundtrack is to be clear and easily understood.

A number of positive attributes inherent in scientific cinematography make it an attractive and reliable means of collecting records. Several of these virtues are also shared by video recordings.

1. The film has permanency.

2. There are no limits to the range and complexity of events that can be recorded.

3. The range of time and velocity of the camera is superior to the human eye.

4. Film records allow time sampling.

5. Frame analysis facilitates the transformation of visible and invisible events into quantitative data.

6. The camera can be concealed easily and can be operated automatically.

7. The camera is relatively unaffected by variations in atmospheric and climatic conditions.

8. The data can be analyzed at the observer's leisure.[39]

Peery has reported how frame-by-frame analysis of social action enhances the observer's ability to make inferences regarding the affective component of the interaction.[40] Using a super-8-mm camera, Peery filmed leave-taking behavior between parents and nursery school children and found that repeated slow-motion viewing permitted him to draw out of the interaction certain subtle emotional behavioral components not seen at normal speed. Although Peery used frame analysis for magnification of affect, the technique is applicable to any type of interpersonal analysis.

Many of the shortcomings associated with use of motion picture films and video recordings result from a lack of understanding or neglect of the conventions of filmmaking. Michaelis issues the warning that "the film can and does lie!"[41] The camera's narrow angle of vision, for instance, may influence the film record. The restricted field of vision excludes many items, which may or may not be desirable. Human vision subtends an angle of approximately 120° whereas the camera lens ranges from 37° for 16-mm film to 50° for 35-mm film and even less for long-focal or telephoto lens. While the telephoto lens has the advantage of bringing objects into close view, it also foreshortens the perspective and distorts the image. The convention of slow or rapid editing—the length of individual shots—may give the impression of excitement, disturbance, and rapid action if a succession of short shots are taken and an impression of tranquility if there are slow and infrequent changes of view. Conventions of camera position and motion are also potential sources of subjectivity in motion picture films. The vertical distance between the camera and the subject is important. For example, Michaelis cautions that "if the camera is above the subject, so that it looks down on him, he will appear dwarfed . . . if the camera looks up to a subject, then his size . . . will appear greatly exaggerated."[42] Movement of the camera while filming a subject, such as a tilt from head to toe, may suggest "looking the person over." Michaelis also indicates that lighting should be given careful consideration. Bright lighting produces a cheerful atmosphere, while low-key lighting gives the impression of gloominess or even danger. Several books and articles have been written about film and videotape techniques, and these resource materials address problems such as the ones already mentioned in addition to discussing other basic issues and procedures in the scientific use of video records.[43]

In spite of the problems created by the subtle conventions in filmmaking and by the other more practical consideration of cost, the increasing popularity of film and video techniques for the study of children is evidence that the disadvantages of these methods are overshadowed by their advantages. As a data collection medium, films and videotapes aid in observation, description, classification, and in the formulation and testing of hypotheses. Indeed, they have been used with considerable success not only in the natural habitat but also in therapeutic and classroom settings.[44]

## VIDEO STUDY OF BEHAVIOR AND DEVELOPMENT

Biographical film recordings of an individual child's development over an extended period of time have been undertaken in a few cases.[45] Langmuir studied a male child between the ages of two and seven years and filmed his development over this period of time at both nursery school and at home.[46] Using film techniques, Behrens traced the growth and development of a boy from the age of six weeks through five years.[47] Another biographical study of a female child was filmed by Fries.[48] She recorded the life of a girl, Mary, from birth to fifteen years of age, and discovered that disturbed family interaction led to psychopathology in the child. In a biographical film study of Anna, Fries examined the emotional problems of a child reared in a neurotic environment.[49] Allen recorded cinematographically the development of a boy who had been isolated from other children for sixteen years as a result of epileptic seizures.[50] More recently, Massie investigated the early natural history of childhood psychosis and utilized family-made home movies of the infancies of ten children who were later diagnosed as psychotic.[51] Frame-by-frame analysis provided data regarding the youngsters' constitutional qualities, neuromuscular functioning, early psychotic signs, and mother-child interaction.

Less extensive motion picture recordings are more commonplace than biographical film records. A number of these more restricted films that deal with normal behavior and development and pathological conditions of children have been reviewed elsewhere.[52] High speed cinematography which produces the slow motion effect has been particularly advantageous in the analysis of certain pathological conditions where rapid movements cannot be followed by the unaided eye.

The individual who had the greatest impact on scientific cinematography involving children was the late Arnold Gesell of the Yale University Child Development Clinic. He designed a one-way vision dome for observation that was constructed of steel ribs and specially painted wire-mesh screening. Outside the hemispheric structure, a cinematographer films infant subjects during developmental examinations. Cinema records are then studied and quantified by the method of cinemanalysis. This technique involves the careful analysis of individual frames or chronophotographs depicting seventeen parts of the infant's body during intervals of twenty consecutive seconds of behavior. A chronophotograph, in Gesell's words, is "one of a series of photographs of a moving object taken for the purpose of recording and exhibiting successive phases of motion."[53] Cinemanalysis is made possible by five features of the technique:

1. The film being propelled at a known speed minutely records time values and sequences.

2. Simultaneously and also minutely, the film records space relationships and configurations.

3. The film records these spatial and temporal data in a series of discrete, instantaneous registrations.

4. These registrations can be serially reinstated at normal, retarded, and accelerated rates.

5. Any single registration can be individually studied, in terms of time and space, as a delineation of a single phase of a behavior pattern or a behavior event.[54]

Using cinemanalysis, Gesell compiled and published his first major monograph, *An Atlas of Infant Behavior,* which contained over 3,000 photographs taken from motion picture films.[55] These pictures and thousands of others taken in subsequent research have provided developmental norms for children. Gesell and his associates have produced a normative series of films that deal with the growth of posture, prehension, locomotion, and adaptive behavior at monthly intervals through the first fifty-six weeks of life.

A recent investigation by Kessen and his associates that was designed to develop a measure of movement in the human newborn used motion picture photography as its technique.[56] The techniques employed in the investigation illustrate some of the procedures involved in scientific cinematography, especially the complex steps necessary in analyzing the data. The subjects in the study were fifteen normal infants in their first few days of life. An infant was placed supine on a mattress. Overhead, a 16-mm camera equipped with a wide-angle 10-mm lens photographed the child at sixteen frames per second. Meanwhile, an operations recorder permitted the recording of other data. Six frames from each thirty-second filmstrip were selected and marked for analysis. Then, through use of a filmanalyzer, permanent copies of these film frames were made. The film drive was stopped each time a marked frame was projected, and the significant details of the infant's image were traced. Dots representing each of seven body parts (visible ear, right palm, left palm, right knee, left knee, right ankle, left ankle) were used for sketching, and only these seven dots on the tracing paper were used to arrive at the movement measure. Next, a summary sheet showing all of the reference points from the selected film frames was drawn and then color coded to indicate the specific frames. The "index of displacement" was the linear distance measured for the different parts of the body, from ear-mark (frame 1) to ear-mark (frame 81), and so on. Findings of the study indicated that there were stable individual differences for this movement measure over the five days of the lying-in period.

Nordquist used a video recorder and other equipment to study nursery-school children's verbal behavior in a free-play setting.[57] The subjects were six children, three of whom had moderate to severe speech deficits and three of whom did not have speech problems. The investigation was conducted in a classroom which included an observation area with one-way mirrors. In order to control for extraneous noise, each subject was wired for sound with a wireless microphone that was secured to a harness at chest level. The microphone transmitted radio signals to an FM receiver that was connected to a mixer in the observation booth. The mixer had three channels so both peer-peer and teacher-child verbalizations could be simultaneously recorded. Every ten seconds, an audio tape recorder fed time-interval signals into the mixer and then into the video recorder at the microphone-in jack. The camera operator, who was stationed in the observation booth, wore a headset which permitted him to monitor the transmission and to adjust the FM receiver for clear reception. One speech impaired and one normal child was observed each day until five fifteen-minute observation periods had been recorded for each child. Responses for speech impaired children were coded as either fluent or disfluent; responses for the normal children were scored for use of the pronouns *we* and *I*. Only one occurrence per interval was recorded if the behavior took place. Satisfactory inter-observer reliability was obtained in the interval sampling. Nordquist reported that this system eliminated many of the problems previously experienced by researchers in child development and that use of the video recorder and related devices was especially appropriate for the observational study of verbal and nonverbal behavior in children.

## OTHER TYPES OF MECHANICAL EQUIPMENT

### EVENT RECORDERS

The event recorder has been used as an electromechanical recording device in child development research.[58] An event recorder registers the occurrence of a particular type of incident or event. Some event recorders are also capable of recording the duration of the selected events. Hutt and Hutt provide a general description of this widely used apparatus:

> In the kymograph type, the drum revolves at a constant and known speed while a metal arm, connected at one end via an electric circuit, or mechanically, to the displacing agent, makes a mark on the drum with the other. A mobile and some-what primitive model may be constructed by using a roll of paper whose central axis is made to rotate at a constant speed; a slit or window in the enclosing box permits marks registering the occurrence of an event, as the paper passes the slit.[59]

The Esterline-Angus Event Recorder has been employed frequently in studies with children. When event keys are depressed, they activate the corresponding pens on the recorder, and a mark is made on the paper that is driven by a mechanism. An Esterline recorder was used by Hendry and Kessen in an investigation designed to examine the tension or drive-reducing properties of oral behavior in infants.[60] Observations were made at different intervals after feeding since feeding is assumed to be associated with drive. Nineteen healthy, full-term newborns were observed during the lying-in period at a hospital for evidence of two kinds of oral behavior, hand-mouth contacting and mouthing. The observer manually depressed one silent telegraph key to record the hand-mouth contacts and depressed another key during mouthing. The following measures were obtained from the records: total duration of hand-mouth contacting; average length of hand-mouth contacting; total duration of mouthing; and total duration of hand-mouth contacting accompanied by mouthing. Interobserver reliability ranged from .96 to .99. Although the authors offered no evaluative statement concerning the instrument, the procedure appeared to work very well for their study.

A number of electronically sophisticated portable event recorders are available. The SSR system is an event-recording system that encodes the incidence, duration, coincidence, and sequence of entries in real time onto magnetic tape for transcription by a computer.[61] The device has a light-weight and battery-powered keyboard of alphanumeric characters and special grammar characters that are used to record categorical observations of events, an audio tape recorder for recording the keyboard output, a Sony high-speed playback tape deck, a signal conditioner, a small computer, and software for transcription and timing. Recently improved,[62] this system has been used successfully to study spatial behavior of children.

The DCR-II Event Recorder is a portable, digital cassette unit for recording the occurrence of single or simultaneous events.[63] It has two interchangeable keyboards that each permit the recording of thirty-two events. The keys are of the silent, push-button variety, which insures quiet operation. An event switch can activate an audio recorder for a supplementary verbal record, if needed. Approximately 31,000 events can be collected on a single cassette, and play-back time is only twelve minutes. The occurrence, time, duration, simultaneous nature, and/or sequence of every event can be recorded with DCR-II. An audible signal warns the observer when the cassette tape is running out and should be replaced. Since the unit includes decoding circuitry, it can be processed by any computer equipped with an appropriate input/output interface. This system has been employed in investigations of mother-infant interaction.[64]

Another very popular portable event-recording system is Datamyte 900.[65] Shown in Figure 6.1, this hand-held, solid-state electronic event recorder measures ten-by-ten-by-two inches and weighs only four pounds. It has fourteen keys (ten numeric and four alpha) which allow considerable flexibility in the development of coding schemes. A built-in interval timer facilitates time sampling. Datamyte 900 also has an integrated circuit memory that accepts and stores from 16,000 to 32,000 characters. Data are recorded in computer format and are ready for immediate transmission via a connecting cable. Transmitted data are printed, recorded on cassette or paper tape, or stored in the computer. Most users of the system write their own computer program so it is consistent with the objectives of their research.

A number of studies have used the Datamyte recorder,[66] and one such investigation will be discussed very briefly. Sawin, Langlois, and Leitner, who examined ethnic differences in parent-infant interactions, employed the Datamyte 900 for data collection, short term storage, and data interface with the computer.[67] Objectives of the study were to establish frequencies and durations of behavior, patterns of interaction, and conditional probability estimates between behaviors of one member of the dyad and those of the other member. The behavioral categories included approximately sixty parent and sixty infant behaviors that were represented by four-digit code numbers.

> The first digit indicates the actor; the second digit indicates the general class of behaviors to which the specific observed behavior belongs (e.g., holding positions, feeding activities, visual activities, tactual stimulation); the third indicates the behavior to be recorded within the general class of behaviors (e.g., ventral hold, adjusts feeding, eye contact, touch/pat); the fourth digit indicates whether the

entry is the onset (1) of behaviors defined as continuous (e.g., smile), the termination of those behaviors (0), or the simple occurrence of behaviors defined as discrete events (e.g., touch, pat) (2).[68]

Mother-infant and father-infant interaction was recorded in naturalistic settings within seventy-two hours following the child's birth and at three-month intervals during the first year. The observer was present in the room during ten-minute feeding and playing sessions, and recorded the behavior with the Datamyte unit. After the observation session, the Datamyte was connected to a teletype computer terminal for transmission of the data to the computer for storage on magnetic tape. A computer program written especially for the project inspected the input for error and sorted the data by code. Corrections were edited into the record, and a permanent file was created for each parent-child dyad. Results were presented and discussed based upon preliminary analyses for only a part of the sample and only a portion of the data. Frequency analyses revealed that there were no differences among ethnic groups in the number of times mothers adjusted the position in which they held babies during feeding and playing. The conditional probability analyses indicated that black mothers were more likely to adjust their hold following an infant distress signal than were other mothers. The researchers concluded that time-based recording devices such as Datamyte are valuable tools for child development studies like theirs.

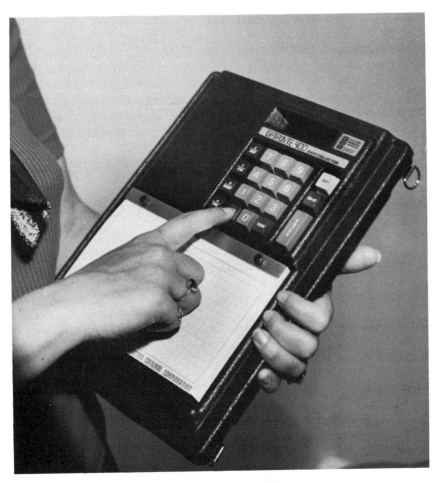

**Figure 6.1.** Datamyte 900

## BEHAVIOR COUNTERS AND AUDIBLE TIMERS

Mattos has reported the use of a compact five-channel manual counter that permits the simultaneous recording of multiple behavior categories for one subject or the recording of a single category for more than one subject.[69] This device, which is available commercially, is approximately five-by-two inches. Thus, it can be held and operated with one hand. Limitations of the instrument are the audible click signal that accompanies each operation and the fact that the reset knob resets all channels at the same time. After repeated use, there has been no evidence of operational malfunction.

Lindsley has described a wrist counter for recording behavior rates.[70] It allows two-digit recording, and is essentially a wrist-type golf-score counter that is also available commercially through sporting goods stores. Some difficulty has been reported with occasional jamming at the ten digit turns.

Traditionally, stopwatches have been used in observational studies in the systematic timing of intervals for occurrence or nonoccurrence of a behavior. However, visually monitoring a stopwatch to determine interval boundaries has the disadvantage of breaking eye contact with the subject. To remedy this problem, audible signal devices have been developed. Leifer and Leifer have described an auditory prompting device that produces a brief click which is audible only to the observer.[71] The click is generated at regular intervals from one to thirty seconds. A small, lightweight unit, the auditory prompter is battery powered and can be worn as a pendant or in a shirt pocket. The researchers report that the device has been reliable and easy to service.

Glynn and Tuck have developed a portable observation timer that emits differential tones for signalling observation and recording intervals.[72] Two audible signals occur, one at a ten-second interval and then another at the next five-second interval. Worthy has designed a similar instrument.[73] His miniature, portable timer and audible signal unit consists of two astable multivibrators and a transistor switch. A solid-state signalling device may be used instead of one of the astable-multivibrator circuits. Tone interval repeatability has been reported to be generally constant, but the instrument shows some loss in the reliability of the interval when used for very long periods of time. Other signal generators have been developed which are suitable for time sampling studies.[74] Readers who are interested in instrumentation aids for child study should consult such publications as *Behavior Research Methods & Instrumentation, Journal of Applied Behavior Analysis, Educational Technology,* and *Transactions of the Society of Instrument Technology.*

## ONE-WAY OBSERVATION DEVICES

No discussion of equipment used to instrument observational child study would be complete without a consideration of the one-way observation booth. One-way observation facilities have been used for many years in studies that require concealment of the observer and any apparatus that he or she may be using. In the words of Arnold Gessel, "one-way-vision adds to the intimacy, the piquancy, and the objectivity of observation."[75] Observation booths are usually small rooms with tables and chairs, desks, or stools for the observers. Their interiors are typically painted dark colors. Provision is made for air circulation and ventilation either through air conditioning and heating ducts or by electric fans. Although the latter may be less desirable because they can create noise that interferes with recording, some investigators[76] contend that the constant hum made by a fan has the advantage of muffling sounds that emanate from the booth into the subject room (e.g., writing, talking, shuffling feet, and apparatus noise).

Observation facilities are often equipped with windows covered by specially painted wire-mesh screening, referred to as Gesell screening, which allows sound to flow without obstruction from the subject room to the observation room. The surface of the Gesell screen that faces the subject room is painted with white enamel "to produce a diffuse dazzle which makes the screen appear opaque. Thus, the screen is transparent in one direction only."[77] In *The First Five Years of Life,* Gesell describes the procedure for processing the observation screen:

> Ordinary 16-mesh wire screen can be used. Thin, white enamel paint may be applied with painter's brush in the regular manner, if done with care so as not to clog the mesh. The paint should dry between the several coats. No. 30 wire cloth has definite advantages, particularly if casein paint instead of ordinary enamel is used. The casein paint should be thinned down with water to the consistency of thin cream and then applied with an air brush. At intervals, the air brush should be used to force air only through the screen in order to blow out any excess paint which may have clogged the mesh. This process is repeated four or five times. Casein paint dries rapidly and the successive coats may be applied in the course of one day.

> It is best to apply the paint before the screens are permanently mounted. If the screens are already in position, an absorbent barrier should be placed behind the screen to collect the transmitted paint spray.[78]

The primary shortcoming of this inexpensive means of achieving one-way vision is that almost absolute silence must be maintained by the observer and his or her recording apparatus; also, a substantial difference in illumination on both sides of the screen is necessary.[79] If lighting conditions are not completely favorable, two specially treated screens can be placed one behind the other approximately 1½ to 2 inches apart to produce decreased visibility from the subject room into the observation station. Observation rooms having windows with one-way mirrors rather than screens necessitate some type of electronic sound projection system so that subjects can be heard by the observer. With such a system, the sound level in the observation room can be amplified so that it is higher than that in the subject room. Many users of sound monitoring systems complain about distortion or the inability to distinguish which child is doing the talking, a problem which is minimized when painted wire screen is used.

The term *one-way mirror* refers to half-silvered or partial mirrors. Pinneau explains that partial mirrors differ from regular mirrors only in the thinner layer of silver deposited on the glass and in the type of protective coating applied to the silvered surface.[80] The phenomenon of one-way vision is dependent upon unequal illumination between the subject and observation room. Ideally, the lighting-level differential between the two rooms should be ten to one, as Horowitz elaborates:

> When the illumination level in an observation room is lowered to a level approximately one tenth or less of that in the subject area, the desired effect of an apparent one-way vision is obtained. Under these lighting conditions transparent glazing materials of all degrees of light transmission will appear to be mirrors when viewed from the bright subject side.[81]

Techniques for making one-way mirrors and alternative observation window screens and for constructing portable observation booths have been described in child development and psychological journals.[82] Horowitz has provided perhaps the best commentary on specifications, materials, and design considerations for observation room windows.[83]

Several features are important to consider in designing or modifying a one-way vision observation booth for use in observational study. It is essential that a properly engineered vision screen or one-way mirror be installed. If glass is used, an adequate sound monitoring system will be necessary. The observation station should be designed so that it can be kept as dark as possible and still make note-taking possible. Doors leading to the hallway should be positioned so that direct rays of light allowed into the room are minimized when the doors are open. The interior of the observation room should be painted black, dark brown, or midnight blue. Walls, ceilings, and floors should be painted with flat paint. If possible, the room should be carpeted in a dark material; this will help reduce noise. An acoustical tile ceiling is also recommended to keep noise to a minimum. Only furniture and equipment with dull or mat finishes should be used. Equipment painted with enamel may cause unwanted reflections. Stationary table-type desks are preferred over furniture that is movable and a possible source of noise. Desks should be situated as far from the observation window as possible. The observer who is situated too close to the window can be seen, particularly if he or she is wearing light clothing and bright jewelry. The observer station should be located on the window side of the subject room so that direct light from the windows does not strike the one-way screen. If this is impossible, venetian blinds or draperies should be installed on the windows of the subject room. Light fixtures inside the observation room should be placed so that their brightness cannot be seen through the screen. Finally, if the booth serves two subject rooms, it is usually necessary to install a black drapery partition to reduce incoming light and to increase observer visibility of the subject room.

## CHAPTER NOTES

1.  A. E. Scheflen, A. Kendon, and J. Schaeffer, "On the Choices of Audiovisual Media," in *Videotape Techniques in Psychiatric Training and Treatment*, ed. M. M. Berger (New York: Bruner/Mazel, 1970).
2.  Ibid.
3.  S. J. Hutt and C. Hutt, *Direct Observation and Measurement of Behavior* (Springfield, Ill.: Thomas, 1970).
    W. C. McGrew, *An Ethological Study of Children's Behavior* (New York: Academic Press, 1972).
    C. Z. Waxler and M. R. Yarrow, "An Observational Study of Maternal Modes," *Developmental Psychology* 11 (1975): 485-94.
4.  H. F. Wright, *Recording and Analyzing Child Behavior* (New York: Harper, 1967).
5.  M. L. Patterson, "Tape-recorded Cuing for Time Sampled Observations of Nonverbal Behavior," *Environmental Psychology and Nonverbal Behavior* 2 (1977): 26-29.
6.  R. M. Dreger, "Spontaneous Conversation and Story-telling of Children in a Naturalistic Setting," *Journal of Psychology* 40 (1955): 163-80.
7.  Ibid., p. 176.
8.  W. D. Loban, *The Language of Elementary School Children* (Champaign, Ill.: National Council of Teachers of English, 1963).
9.  G. F. Mahl, J. Dollard, and F. C. Redlich, "Facilities for the Sound Recording and Observation of Interviews," *Science* 120 (1954): 235-38.
10. Ibid.
11. R. E. Jones, J. B. Reid, and G. R. Patterson, "Naturalistic Observation in Clinical Assessment," in *Advances in Psychological Assessment*, vol. 3, ed. P. McReynolds (San Francisco: Jossey-Bass, 1975).
12. J. Herbert and J. Swayze, *Wireless Observation* (New York: Bureau of Publications, Teachers College, Columbia University, 1964).
    M. Hoshiko and G. Holloway, "Radio Telemetry for the Monitoring of Verbal Behavior," *Journal of Speech and Hearing Disorders* 33 (1968): 48-50.
    D. R. Miklich, "Radio Telemetry in Clinical Psychology and Related Areas," *American Psychologist* 30 (1975): 419-25.
    R. H. Moos, "Behavior Effects of Being Observed: Reactions to a Wireless Radio Transmitter," *Journal of Consulting and Clinical Psychology* 32 (1968): 383-88.
    K. Purcell and K. Brady, "Adaptation to the Invasion of Privacy, Monitoring Behavior with a Miniature Radio Transmitter," *Merrill-Palmer Quarterly* 12 (1966): 242-54.
    W. F. Soskin and V. P. John, "The Study of Spontaneous Talk," in *The Stream of Behavior*, ed. R. Barker (New York: Appleton, 1963).
13. D. R. Miklich, K. Purcell, and J. H. Weiss, "Practical Aspects of the Use of Radio Telemetry in the Behavioral Sciences," *Behavior Research Methods & Instrumentation* 6 (1974): 461.
14. Soskin and John, "Spontaneous Talk."
15. Ibid., pp. 230-231.
16. Ibid., p. 247.
17. Ibid., pp. 234-235.
18. Purcell and Brady, "Adaptation."
19. Ibid., p. 251.
20. Purcell and Brady, "Adaptation."
21. Soskin and John, "Spontaneous Talk."
22. Miklich, Purcell, and Weiss, "Practical Aspects."
    A. J. Wooten, "Talk in the Homes of Young Children," *Sociology: The Journal of the British Sociological Association* 8 (1974): 277-95.
23. Miklich, Purcell, and Weiss, "Practical Aspects."
24. Ibid.
25. Purcell and Brady, "Adaptation."
26. R. L. Schwitzgeben and R. M. Bird, "Sociotechnical Design Factors in Remote Instrumentation with Humans in Natural Environments," *Behavior Research Methods & Instrumentation* 2 (1970): 99-105.
27. Ibid.
28. M. H. Nichols and L. R. Rauch, *Radio Telemetry* (New York: Wiley, 1956).
    G. Swoboda, *Telecontrol: Methods and Applications of Telemetry and Remote Control* (New York: Van Nostrand, 1971).
29. A. R. Michaelis, *Research Films in Biology, Anthropology, Psychology, and Medicine* (New York: Academic Press, 1955).
30. Ibid., pp. 97-98.
31. Scheflen, Kendon, and Schaeffer, "Choices."
32. Ibid.
33. J. L. Efrein, *Videotape Production and Communication Techniques* (Blue Ridge Summit, Pa.: TAB Books, 1975).
34. Scheflen, Kendon, and Schaeffer, "Choices."
35. A. T. Dittmann, S. N. Stein, and D. Shakow, "Sound Motion Picture Facilities for Research in Communication," in *Methods of Research in Psychotherapy*, eds. L. A. Gottschalk and A. H. Auerbach (New York: Appleton, 1966).
36. Ibid., p. 27.
37. Ibid.
38. Dittmann, Stein, and Shakow, "Motion Picture," p. 29.
39. Michaelis, *Research Films.*
40. J. C. Peery, "Magnification of Affect Using Frame-by-frame Film Analysis," *Environmental Psychology and Nonverbal Behavior* 3 (1978): 58-61.
41. Michaelis, *Research Films*, p. 168.
42. Ibid., p. 177.

43. Dittmann, Stein, and Shakow, "Motion Picture."
    C. E. Engel and P. Hansell, "Use and Abuse of the Film in Recording the Behavior and Reactions of the Newborn Infant." *Cerebral Palsy Bulletin* 3 (1961): 472-80.
    R. La Bruzzo, "The What and How of Video Hardware and Tape," in *Videotape Techniques in Psychiatric Training and Treatment*, ed. M. M. Berger (New York: Bruner/Mazel, 1970).
    A. Nichtenhauser, *Films in Psychiatry, Psychology, and Mental Health* (New York: Health Education Council, 1953).
    W. H. Offenhauser, *16 mm Sound Motion Pictures* (New York: Interscience, 1949).
    Scheflen, Kendon, and Schaeffer, "Choices."
    E. R. Sorenson and D. C. Gajdusek, "Investigation of Non-receiving Phenomena: The Research Cinema Film," *Nature* 200 (1963): 112-14.
    R. Spottiswoode, *Film and Its Techniques* (Berkeley, Calif.: University of California Press, 1951).
    L. J. Stone, "Some Problems in Filming Children's Behavior: A Discussion Based on Experience in the Production of Studies of Normal Personality Development," *Child Development* 23 (1952): 227-33.
    J. Van Vlack, "Filming Psychotherapy from the Viewpoint of a Research Cinematographer," in *Methods of Research in Psychotherapy*, eds. L. A. Gottschalk and A. H. Auerbach (New York: Appleton, 1966).
44. M. M. Berger, ed., *Videotape Techniques in Psychiatric Training and Treatment* (New York: Bruner/Mazel, 1978).
    E. S. Cooper and J. D. Ingleby, "Direct Observation in the Infant-School Classroom," *Journal of Child Psychology and Psychiatry* 15 (1974): 263-74.
    E. A. Haggard, J. R. Hiken, and R. S. Isaacs, "Some Effects of Recording and Filming on the Psychotherapeutic Process," *Psychiatry* 28 (1965): 169-91.
    J. S. Kounin, W. V. Friesen, and A. E. Norton, "Managing Emotionally Disturbed Children in the Regular Classroom," *Journal of Educational Psychology* 57 (1966): 1-13.
    N. J. Maccoby et al., *Sound Film Recordings in Improving Classroom Communications: Experimental Studies in Non-verbal Communication* (Stanford, Calif.: Stanford University Institute for Communication Research, 1964).
    V. M. Nordquist, "A Method of Recording Verbal Behavior in Free-play Settings," *Journal of Applied Behavioral Analysis* 4 (1971): 327-31.
45. H. D. Behrens, producer, *A Study in Human Development. Parts I, II, III, IV* (State College, Pa.: Pennsylvania State University Psychological Cinema Register, 1946-48).
    M. E. Fries, producer, *A Character Neurosis with Depressive and Compulsive Trends in the Making: Life History of Mary from Birth to Fifteen Years* (New York: New York University Film Library, 1950).
    M. S. F. Langmuir, L. F. Stone, and J. Bucher, producers, *This Is Robert: A Study of Personality Growth in a Preschool Child* (State College, Pa.: Pennsylvania State University Psychological Cinema Register, 1942).
46. Langmuir, Stone, and Bucher, *This Is Robert.*
47. Behrens, *Human Development.*
48. Fries, *Character Neurosis.*
49. M. E. Fries, producer, *Anna N.—Life History from Birth to Fifteen Years: The Development of Emotional Problems in a Child Brought Up in a Neurotic Environment* (New York University Film Library, 1950).
50. D. T. Allen, producer, *The Development of Eugene, a 23-year-old-Boy Isolated by 16 Years of Epileptic Seizures* (Cincinnati: Children's Hospital, 1940).
51. H. N. Massie, "The Early Natural History of Childhood Psychosis," *Journal of the American Academy of Child Psychiatry* 17 (1978): 29-45.
52. L. F. Beck, "A Review of Sixteen-Millimeter Films in Psychology and Applied Sciences," *Psychological Bulletin* 35 (1938): 127-69.
    Michaelis, *Research Films.*
53. A. Gesell, "Cinemanalysis: A Method for Behavior Study," *Journal of Genetic Psychology* 47 (1935): 4.
54. Ibid.
55. A. Gesell, *An Atlas of Infant Behavior: A Systematic Delineation of the Forms and Early Growth of Human Behavior Patterns*, 2 vols. (New Haven: Yale University Press, 1934).
56. W. Kessen, L. S. Hendry, and A. M. Leutzendorff, "Measurement of Movement in the Human Newborn: A New Technique," *Child Development* 32 (1961): 95-105.
57. Nordquist, "Method of Recording."
58. L. S. Hendry and W. Kessen, "Oral Behavior of Newborn Infants As a Function of Age and Time Since Feeding," *Child Development* 35 (1964): 201-08.
    O. I. Lovaas et al., "Recording Apparatus and Procedure for Observation of Behaviors of Children in Free Play Settings," *Journal of Experimental Child Psychology* 2 (1965): 108-20.
    R. G. Wahler et al., "Mothers As Behavior Therapists for Their Own Children," *Behavior Research and Therapy* 3 (1965): 113-24.
59. Hutt and Hutt, *Direct Observation*, pp. 85-86.
60. Hendry and Kessen, "Oral Behavior."
61. G. R. Stephenson, D. P. Smith, and T. W. Roberts, "The SSR System: An Open Format Event Recording System with Computerized Transcription," *Behavior Research Methods and Instrumentation* 7 (1975): 497-515.
62. G. R. Stephenson and T. W. Roberts, "The SSR System: A General Encoding System with Computerized Transcription," *Behavior Research Methods and Instrumentation* 9 (1977): 434-41.
63. L. Celhoffer et al., "The DCR-II Event Recorder: A Portable High-speed Digital Cassette System with Direct Computer Access," *Behavior Research Methods and Instrumentation* 9 (1977): 442-46.
64. K. Minde et al., "Mother-Child Relationships in the Premature Nursery—An Observational Study," *Pediatrics* (1977).
65. L. Torgerson, "Datamyte 900," *Behavior Research Methods and Instrumentation* 9 (1977): 405-06.
66. R. D. Conger and D. McLeod, "Describing Behavior in Small Groups with the Datamyte Event Recorder," *Behavior Research Methods and Instrumentation* 9 (1977): 418-24.
    D. B. Sawin, J. H. Langlois, and E. F. Leitner, "What Do You Do After You Say Hello? Observing, Coding, and Analyzing Parent Infant Interactions," *Behavior Research Methods and Instrumentation* 9 (1977): 425-28.
    K. G. Scott and W. S. Masi, "Use of the Datamyte in Analyzing Duration of Infant Visual Behaviors," *Behavior Research Methods and Instrumentation* 9 (1977): 429-33.
    R. E. Sykes, "Techniques of Data Collection and Reduction in Systematic Field Observation," *Behavior Research Methods and Instrumentation* 9 (1977): 407-17.
67. Sawin, Langlois, and Leitner, "Say Hello."
68. Ibid., pp. 426-27.
69. R. L. Mattos, "A Manual Counter for Recording Multiple Behavior," *Journal of Applied Behavior Analysis* 1 (1968): 130.
70. O. R. Lindsley, "A Reliable Wrist Counter for Recording Behavior Rates," *Journal of Applied Behavior Analysis* 1 (1968): 77-78.
71. A. D. Leifer and L. J. Leifer, "An Auditory Prompting Device for Behavioral Observation," *Journal of Experimental Child Psychology* 11 (1971): 376-78.
72. E. L. Glynn and D. L. Tuck, "A Portable Observation Timer Emitting Differential Tones for Signalling Observation and Recording Intervals," *New Zealand Psychologist* 2 (1973): 40-42.
73. R. C. Worthy, "A Miniature Portable Timer and Audible Signal-generating Device," *Journal of Applied Behavior Analysis* 1 (1968): 159-60.
74. R. M. Foxx, and P. L. Martin, "A Useful Portable Timer," *Journal of Applied Behavior Analysis* 4 (1971): 60.
    J. H. Reynierse and J. W. Toevs, "An Ideal Signal Generator for Time-sampling Observation," *Behavior Research Methods and Instrumentation* 5 (1973): 57-58.
75. A. Gesell, *The First Five Years of Life: A Guide to the Study of the Pre-school Child* (New York: Harper, 1940), p. 357.
76. R. V. Burton, "An Inexpensive and Portable Means for One-way Observation," *Child Development* 42 (1971): 959-62.
    S. R. Pinneau, "A Technique for Making One-way Mirrors," *Child Development* 22 (1951): 235-41.

77. Gesell, *First Five Years,* p. 354.
78. Ibid., p. 356.
79. C. B. Hindley and F. Falkner, "A One-way Window," *British Journal of Psychology* 48 (1957): 105.
80. Pinneau, "One-way Mirrors," p. 235.
81. H. Horowitz, "Observation Room Windows," *American Psychologist* 24 (1969): 304.
82. M. O. Bergman, "A Mobile Laboratory for Research in Child Psychology" (Master's thesis, University of Minnesota, 1964).
    S. W. Bijou, "A Child Study Laboratory on Wheels," *Child Development* 29 (1958): 425-27.
    J. L. Gewirtz, "Plans for the Construction of a Portable One-way Observation Booth," *Child Development* 23 (1952): 307-14.
    Hindley and Falkner, "One-way Window."
    Horowitz, "Observation Room Windows."
    R. H. Passman, "The Smoked Plastic Screen: An Alternative to the One-way Mirror," *Journal of Experimental Child Psychology* 17 (1974): 374-76.
    Pinneau, "One-way Mirrors."
83. Horowitz, "Observation Room Windows."

# 7

# Structured Tests and Scales

As the first chapter emphasized, child study moved historically from philosophical treatises about children to scientific approaches to studying children. With these approaches came the need to quantify the variables under study through appropriate testing and measurment techniques and statistical tools.

Measurement is needed to describe and evaluate characteristics of children and to determine differences among them. Through such measurements, we are better able to guide and teach our children. *Measurement* may be defined as "finding out *how much* by a process of assigning numerals according to rules." The meanings of the words *test* and *measurement* overlap. However, they are not synonymous. A *test* is defined as "a standardized situation designed to elicit a sample of an individual's behavior." Either test or measurement is an appropriate term when that sample can be expressed as a numerical score.[1]

## TEST SELECTION

Tests and scales present the person tested with a set of constructive stimuli to which he or she responds. The person is then assigned a numeral or numerals to indicate his or her possession of the attributes that the test is supposed to measure. Actually, a sample of the person's behavior is measured. Some test developers provide tables of norms or scores earned by groups of representative subjects. Such tests are sometimes called standardized tests. The word *standardized* also is used to refer to clearly defined testing and scoring procedures. A test may have norms without standardized procedures, and vice versa a test with standardized procedures may not have established norms.

A few words of caution are in order regarding the use of tests. The amount of specialized training needed to administer and interpret test results varies with different instruments. Therefore, the purchaser of a test should evaluate his or her own qualifications when determining which tests to use. While studying children, sometimes an individual may administer, score, and interpret tests. At other times, a person may use the results of tests administered, scored, and/or interpreted by other professionals. In either case, the material in this book should serve as a guide to *types* of tests and their uses in studying children. Only a few examples of specific tests will be given. References that discuss additional tests and that present more detailed test descriptions are included.

Before selecting a test for use, an individual must know the precise objective of the testing. The tests or test chosen must meet that objective and must be valid, that is, measure what is supposed to be measured. An individual also should consider the reliability of the test, the ease in administering, scoring, and interpreting it, as well as the time and costs involved. Several sources of information are available. Test standards have been developed collaboratively by the American Psychological Association, the American Educational Research Association, and the National Council on Measurement in Education.[2] Buros's *Tests in Print*[3] presents a comprehensive bibliography of tests, and his *Mental Measurements Yearbooks*[4] list most of the published standardized tests in print at the time the yearbooks went to press. These tests are also described and reviewed in the yearbooks. Other source books are available which list and describe tests and measurements appropriate for children.[5] Some of these references deal with numerous unpublished tests. Before making a final test selection and ordering large quantities, an individual should order a specimen set of tests from the publisher for examination.

Tests vary in objectivity. If a test is truly objective, the final scores assigned by independent scorers will be the same. In Chapter 1, objective (or structured) tests and scales were divided into several classes: intelligence tests, aptitude tests, achievement tests, personality scales, and attitude and value scales. Some of these traits also can be measured in more subjective ways. Subjective measurement techniques are discussed in other chapters.

## MEASURES OF RELATIONSHIP

### CORRELATION

The relationship between two sets of scores or the changes in two variables is expressed mathematically as a correlation coefficient and graphically as a scatter diagram. (See Figures 7.1, 7.2, and 7.3.) In the graphs a point represents a person as the intersection of his or her two measurements. Correlations lie between the limits of +1.0 and –1.0, which represent a perfect direct (positive) relationship or inverse (negative) relationship, respectively. A positive relationship means that as the measures for one of the variables increase the measures for the other variable also increase. Likewise, as one decreases the other decreases. A negative (or inverse) relationship means that as the measures for one variable increase the measures for the other variable decrease. The correlation technique is used when there are scores or measures on two variables for each individual in a group and the researcher wishes to determine whether there is a relationship between these variables.

To determine the degree of correlation between the scores on two tests, we will examine hypothetical scores for eight children on a psychology test and on a child development test:

| Student | Psychology Score | Child Development Score |
|---------|------------------|-------------------------|
| A | 60 | 60 |
| B | 40 | 40 |
| C | 30 | 30 |
| D | 20 | 20 |
| E | 80 | 80 |
| F | 50 | 50 |
| G | 10 | 10 |
| H | 70 | 70 |

A quick examination of these data reveals that the scores for each individual on the two measures are identical and therefore a perfect correlation exists. To show this relationship graphically, the data are plotted on a scatter diagram as illustrated in Figure 7.1.

A hypothetical scatter diagram showing a perfect negative correlation is present in Figure 7.2. In this diagram, it is evident that preferences for dark colors are inversely related to preferences for light colors. It is a perfect negative correlation because when a straight line is drawn through the dots, the dots fall exactly on the line, indicating that the amount of increase in one variable is in proportion to the amount of decrease in the other variable.

An imperfect relationship between variables is illustrated in Figure 7.3. The dots tend to lie in a positive direction, indicating a positive correlation. By using a statistical formula, such as the Pearson product-moment correlation, the correlation coefficient can be computed from the two sets of scores. The coefficient is an estimation of the closeness of the points to the line, which is the same thing as the estimation of the closeness of the relationship of the measurements to a perfect relationship. Magnitude as well as direction is provided by the correlation coefficient. In the behavioral sciences perfect positive or negative correlations are seldom approached. A correlation of .20 is positive but low; .89 is high positive. A correlation of -.15 is low negative, whereas -.60 is moderate negative.

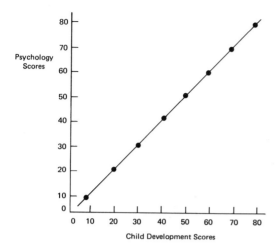

**Figure 7.1.** A Perfect Positive Correlation

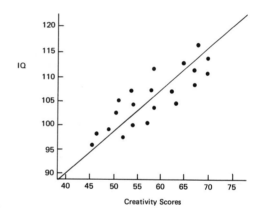

**Figure 7.3.** Scatter Diagram of I.Q. and Creatvitivy Scores

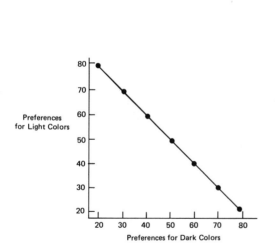

**Figure 7.2.** A Perfect Negative Correlation

Through statistical tables one can determine whether the correlation coefficient is sufficiently significant to reject the hypothesis of no significant relationship between the two sets of scores. The Pearson product-moment correlation involves the use of a scatter diagram unless a calculator or a computer program is used. The computation requires just one step in addition to those necessary for finding the means and standard deviations of two sets of data. The additional step, which can be taken simultaneously with the other steps, can be found in the computational procedures set forth in Garrett.[6]

The Spearman rank order correlation is particularly adaptable to small groups in which the number of paired scores is thirty or less. Since this correlation depends upon placing scores in order, from highest to lowest, it may be used when only rankings but not exact scores are available. Rank order correlation assumes that the measures are independent of each other.

# VALIDITY OF MEASUREMENT

To determine the validity of measurement, this question must be answered, Am I measuring what I think I am measuring? It is not possible to study validity without inquiring into the nature and meaning of one's variables. Validity is no great problem when measuring certain physical properties, such as the length and weight of an object. In this case, a direct and close relationship often exists between the nature of the object being measured and the measuring instrument.

On the other hand, in regard to a study on the relationship between children's creativity and their attitudes toward authority figures (e.g., parents or teachers), no rules or scales exist that allow the researcher to weigh accurately the degree of creativity possessed or the attitudes. In cases such as this, less direct means of measuring these nonphysical properties must be developed. These means are often so indirect that their validity may be questioned.

When choosing a test or other measuring device, the most important factor to consider is its validity— its ability to do what the user is trying to accomplish. Validity is concerned with what the test measures and with how well the test fulfills its function. It is not possible to answer the question Is this a valid test? Rather the researcher's concern should be how valid the test is for the decision that he or she wishes to make.

The American Psychological Association has defined three types of validity, each of which is involved in making a different kind of judgment.[7] The three types— content, predictive, and construct — are discussed in the sections which follow.

## CONTENT VALIDITY

Content validity is used to determine how an individual would perform at the present time in a given universe of situations of which the test constitutes a sample. The questions or situations included in the test must represent the content areas or behavioral patterns to be assessed. They must be appropriate for the individuals under study and for the circumstances in which they are being used. Content validity is determined by a logical process, that is, by examining the representativeness of the test content. Representativeness or sampling adequacy of the content of a measuring instrument is determined by analyzing the topics covered. The American Psychological Association has suggested that four factors determine content validity of a test: (1) item selection, (2) item description, (3) range and balance of items, and (4) manner of item presentation.[8]

If a nursery school teacher prepares a test to determine children's form perception (ability to distinguish between different shapes) and wishes to determine its validity, he or she should examine each item on the test for its relevancy to measure a child's perception. Ideally, if the test is to be high in content validity, it should contain a random sample of *all* items that could possibly be included in a test to measure form perception. Unfortunately, a random sample of items from a universe or population of test content is not possible. Thus, the content validity of a collection of test items must be based upon judgment. The teacher, often with the assistance of others, must judge the representativeness of each item as a measure of a child's perception of form.

## PREDICTIVE VALIDITY

Predictive validity is used to estimate an individual's success or future behavior from the results of a present measurement. This form of validity is useful in predicting the success of a job applicant in a particular position. Also, it is useful in selecting students for admission to college and professional schools. The method involves administering the test, waiting for the events the test is attempting to predict to occur, and then correlating the test scores with some measure of performance appropriate to the event. Academic achievement, performance in specialized training, and on-the-job performance are among the criteria for validating scores on a predictor (such as a scholastic aptitude test or a test battery).

The greatest difficulty of predictive validation concerns the criteria. In some cases obtaining possible criteria may be difficult, and in other cases the validity of criteria that have been obtained may be doubtful. For example, what criterion can be used to test the predictive validity of an artistic or musical aptitude test? What criterion can be used to validate a measure of teacher effectiveness?

The Hunter Science Aptitude Test is an example of an instrument that has been studied in relation to its predictive validity.[9] The test, which is designed for use with six- and seven-year-old children, assesses prior knowledge and the ability to learn new material. Items included in the test are designed to measure recall of scientific information, ability to assign meanings to observations, and capacity to use the scientific method.

Several determinations have been made of the *predictive validity* of the Hunter Science Aptitude Test. The principal predictive validity criterion was performance on seven science achievement tests. High positive correlations occurred between results on the Hunter aptitude test and science achievement test scores. The correlations between scores on the aptitude test and teachers' rankings on ability to learn science were also high.

## CONSTRUCT VALIDITY

A construct is a theoretical, imaginary mechanism or theory that accounts for behavior as it is observed. Construct validity focuses more on the property being measured than on the test itself. To know why a relationship exists between two measures, one must know the meaning of the constructs entering the relation. The theory behind the test must be validated. Actually, whenever hypotheses are tested, construct validity is involved.

Construct validity is valuable for scientific purposes rather than for immediate practical purposes. It is more complex than the other types of validity since it involves developing a theory about what a score means psychologically and what causes a person to get a certain score. Construct validity is important in measuring abilities, attitudes, personality characteristics, and complex behavior patterns.

One method used by Sarason and his colleagues to determine the validity of their Test Anxiety Scale for Children (TASC) was to correlate the TASC with teacher ratings of children's anxiety. The TASC was administered to over 2,200 second- through fifth-grade pupils, who were also rated by their teachers on a seventeen-item anxiety rating scale. The correlations between the TASC and the ratings were low. However, since the correlations were for the most part statistically significant, they yielded evidence of the validity of the TASC. The relations between the TASC and intelligence and achievement also were examined by Sarason and his colleagues. As predicted, the correlations were low and negative. The important relation between general anxiety and test anxiety also supported Sarason's expectations, adding further evidence to his confidence in the construct validity of the TASC.[10]

Another method that illustrates construct validity and construct validation is the technique of correlating test items with total scores. Since the total test score of any individual is assumed to be valid, an item is valid to the extent that it measures the same thing the total score does.

In order to study the construct validity of any measure, correlation of the measure with a large number of other measures is advisable. There are statistical tools available for doing this. One such tool, *factor analysis,* tells what measures assess the same thing and to what extent these measures assess what they assess. "In fact, factor analysis may almost be called the most important of construct validity tools."[11]

# RELIABILITY OF MEASUREMENT

Reliability of measurement indicates the consistency of independent but comparable measures of the same individual, group, or situation. There are three possible sources of variation affecting an individual's scores: variation arising from the measurement itself, changes within the individual over a period of time, and differences in the samples of tasks covered by the instrument. Several methods have been developed to control these variations and to obtain estimates of reliability.

## COMPARISONS OVER TIME (STABILITY)

Stability refers to the consistency of measures on repeated applications. If the measuring instrument is based upon observations, numerous repeated observations may be made. When an interview, questionnaire, or projective test is used, two administrations of the instrument are normally conducted. This method is often called the test-retest procedure. Two weeks to one month is usually considered a suitable interval between two administrations of many psychological tests. The common practice is to compromise between waiting long enough for the effects of the first testing to wear off but not long enough for a significant amount of real change to take place.[12] Stability is determined by calculating correlation coefficients from the scores on the two administrations of the same instrument.

## COMPARABILITY OF FORMS (EQUIVALENCE)

Equivalence involves arriving at consistent results from two parallel measurements that were used with the same individuals at approximately the same time. Parallel or equivalent forms are similar in content and difficulty. When the measuring device requires observations, two different observers might use the instrument to measure the same individuals at the same time. When individual subjects respond to tests or scales, two parallel forms of the test are applied with the same individuals at the same sitting or at two different times. The coefficient of equivalence is determined by correlating the scores or ratings resulting from the two forms. When two or more observers are used, the correlations are based on independent ratings given by the observers.

## INTERNAL CONSISTENCY (SPLIT-HALF METHOD)

Based upon a single administration of a test or other instrument, two scores can be obtained for each individual by dividing the test into equivalent halves. Usually this involves one score based on the odd-numbered items and another score based on the even-numbered items. The correlation between these scores is used to estimate the reliability that would result from a full-length test. Sometimes an analysis of variance method is used (Kuder-Richardson technique).

In general, the reliability of a test can be increased by adding items, provided that the additional items are similar in difficulty and discrimination to the original items. Practical limitations to this technique should be considered, however. For example, a lengthy test may tire and bore the subject, and as a result, distorted test scores may occur. Another factor that can boost reliability is clarity— clarity in the wording of items, in the directions for responding, and in scoring procedures. Reducing the possibility of getting correct answers by guessing and providing an inflexible scoring key (one that lists all acceptable answers) also make scoring more accurate and objective, thereby increasing reliability.

Validity and reliability are closely related in that a valid test must be reliable. Nevertheless, a test can be reliable without being valid. Reliability is concerned with the precision of measurement: to be reliable, a test must give accurate and consistent results, regardless of what it measures.

# NORMS AND PROFILES

Test scores must be interpreted and understood if they are to be of value. One aid in interpreting scores is the summarization of scores through the use of certain statistical methods. The use of norms and profiles also assist in interpretations of test scores.

## STANDARDIZED TEST DEFINED

Although the term *standardized test* was introduced at the beginning of the chapter, a formal definition is in order here. A standardized test is a measure that is usually prepared commercially by a uniform procedure; it is composed of a fixed set of questions to be administered by all investigators with the same set of directions and timing constraints; it has a carefully delineated and uniform scoring procedure. A standardized test is usually administered by the test developers to a reference group, or groups, in order to establish norms.[13]

## NORMS DEFINED

Test norms are based upon actual performance of people, not upon predetermined standards of performance. They are a measure of what *is,* the status quo, rather than what ought to be. A norm is an average score (mean or median) for a specified group of people that is known as the *reference group* or norm group. Norms are usually presented in the form of tables that show a relationship between the raw scores (usually the number of correct responses on a test) and some type of derived scores (scores that have been converted from raw scores to units of other scales). Derived scores indicate a child's relative standing in the normative sample and enable evaluation of his or her performance in reference to other children. In addition to their usefulness in making these inter-individual comparisons, derived scores also provide comparable measures that permit intraindividual (within-individual) comparisons. (See Table 7.1 for an example of a norm table from a test manual).

Raw scores may be transformed into many different types of derived scores such as *z* and *T*-scores, stanines, grade and age equivalents, mental age, and deviation IQ scores. One popular type of derived score that is frequently used by teachers and that is reported in standardized test manuals is the *percentile*. A percentile is defined as a point on the distribution below which a certain percent of the test scores fall. The percent of students' scores falling below an individual's obtained score is that individual's *percentile rank.*[14] For example, in Table 7.1 a score of 77 in total adjustment has a percentile rank of 60. Therefore, a child attaining a score of 77 would have a score higher than 60 students out of every 100 in a representative sample of children in grades one through three.

## PURPOSE OF NORMS

Norms serve as a means of comparing an individual's score, or the scores of students in a given school or school district, with the scores attained by others (the norm or reference group). Of course, norms must be updated continuously if they are to be representative of current groups. When current norms are not available, an investigator must be cautious in his or her interpretations. A person's score by itself is not as meaningful as it is when compared with other scores. For example, if a child takes a test consisting of 100 items and gets 75 correct answers, we know that he or she answered 75 percent of the items correctly. If other children in the child's same age group usually answer 95 percent correctly, the child's score would have a different meaning than if most of the children typically answered only 50 percent correctly.

## PROFILES

A profile is a form of plotting two or more scores for the same person or groups of people. For such a comparison, raw scores must be converted to the same type of derived score based upon the

## PERCENTILE NORMS—CALIFORNIA TEST OF PERSONALITY—1953 REVISION—PRIMARY SERIES

| Percentile: | 1 | 2 | 5 | 10 | 20 | 30 | 40 | 50 | 60 | 70 | 80 | 90 | 95 | 98 | 99 |
| --- | --- | --- | --- | --- | --- | --- | --- | --- | --- | --- | --- | --- | --- | --- | --- |
| | (0-1.4) | (1.5-2.4) | (2.5-7.4) | (7.5-14.9) | (15.0-24.9) | (25.0-34.9) | (35.0-44.9) | (45.0-54.9) | (55.0-64.9) | (65.0-74.9) | (75.0-84.9) | (85.0-92.4) | (92.5-97.4) | (97.5-98.4) | (98.5-100) |
| 1. Personal Adjustment    Score: | 1-14 | 15-19 | 20-22 | 23-25 | 26-28 | 29-31 | 32-34 | 35-36 | 37-38 | 39-40 | 41-42 | 43-44 | 45 | 46 | 47-48 |
| 2. Social Adjustment    Score: | 1-16 | 17-20 | 21-24 | 25-28 | 29-31 | 32-34 | 35-37 | 38-39 | 40-41 | 42-43 | 44 | 45 | 46 | 47 | 48 |
| Total Adjustment    Score: | 1-30 | 31-39 | 40-46 | 47-53 | 54-59 | 60-65 | 66-71 | 72-75 | 76-79 | 80-83 | 84-87 | 88-90 | 91-92 | 93-94 | 95-96 |
| Percentile: | 1 | 2 | 5 | 10 | 20 | 30 | 40 | 50 | 60 | 70 | 80 | 90 | 95 | 98 | 99 |

### SUB-SECTION SCORES AND PERCENTILES

**1. Personal Adjustment**

| Score: | 1 | 2 | 3 | 4 | 5 | 6 | 7 | 8 |
| --- | --- | --- | --- | --- | --- | --- | --- | --- |
| A. Self-reliance | 1 | | 10 | 20 | 40 | 60 | 80 | 95 |
| B. Sense of Personal Worth | 1 | 2 | 10 | 20 | 30 | 50 | 80 | 90 |
| C. Sense of Personal Freedom | 1 | | 10 | 20 | 40 | 50 | 70 | 90 |
| D. Feeling of Belonging | 1 | | 10 | 20 | 30 | 50 | 70 | 90 |
| E. Withdrawing Tendencies | 1 | 10 | 20 | 30 | 40 | 60 | 80 | 90 |
| F. Nervous Symptoms | 1 | 10 | 20 | 30 | 40 | 60 | 80 | 90 |
| Percentile: | 1 | 2 | 3 | 4 | 5 | 6 | 7 | 8 |

**2. Social Adjustment**

| Score: | 1 | 2 | 3 | 4 | 5 | 6 | 7 | 8 |
| --- | --- | --- | --- | --- | --- | --- | --- | --- |
| A. Social Standards | 1 | | 10 | 20 | 30 | 40 | 60 | 80 |
| B. Social Skills | 1 | 2 | 10 | 20 | 30 | 50 | 70 | 90 |
| C. Anti-social Tendencies | 1 | 5 | 10 | 20 | 30 | 50 | 70 | 90 |
| D. Family Relations | 1 | 2 | 10 | 20 | 30 | 50 | 80 | 90 |
| E. School Relations | 1 | | 10 | 20 | 30 | 40 | 60 | 80 |
| F. Community Relations | 1 | 2 | 10 | 20 | 30 | 40 | 60 | 90 |
| Percentile: | 1 | 2 | 3 | 4 | 5 | 6 | 7 | 8 |
| Score: | 1 | 2 | 3 | 4 | 5 | 6 | 7 | 8 |

Table 7.1. Percentile Norms for California Test of Personality (1953 Revision—Primary Series)

DIRECTIONS: To find the percentile value of Personal, Social, or Total Adjustment score, use the upper table, locate the score, and read the percentile above or below the heavy black lines. Thus a score of 77 in Total Adjustment has a percentile rank of 60. To find the percentile value of a component or sub-section score, use the lower table, locate the score above or below the black lines, and read the percentile opposite the appropriate component. Thus a score of 7 in the Self-reliance component has a percentile value of 80.

same norm or reference group. Figure 7.4 is a sample profile chart for one child, John Williams, on the California Test of Personality. This profile graphically illustrates the child's adjustment in percentile ranks for the total test and for the separate areas of Personal Adjustment and Social Adjustment. When the scores are significantly low, as in John Williams's case, the percentile ranks suggest areas of difficulty. These are comments concerning interpretation of the sample profile for John Williams:

> The profile of John Williams is rather unusual. Although he evaluated himself so as to earn scores of 9 or 11 in Sense of Personal Freedom and Feeling of Belonging, he is only at the 2nd percentile in Personal Adjustment when compared with his classmates. On the other hand, his scores in Social Adjustment, with the exception of School Relations, are fairly typical. His scores on Sense of Personal Freedom and Feeling of Belonging are in harmony with his Social Adjustment. However, he reveals a serious lack of Self-reliance; he has serious withdrawing tendencies and nervous symptoms.
>
> To understand this case properly, it is necessary to know that John Williams has an I.Q. of 127 on the California Test of Mental Maturity, Intermediate, 1951 Edition. He also recently took the California Achievement Test, Intermediate, Form AA and made the following grade placements: Reading Vocabulary, 9.9; Reading Comprehension, 12.8; Arithmetic Reasoning, 12.7; Arithmetic Fundamentals, 10.1; Mechanics of English, and Grammar, 10.8; and Spelling, 9.9.
>
> John feels so insecure and is so afraid he is going to fail in his work that he spends virtually his whole time studying. Although he was in the fifth month of the seventh grade when he took the California Achievement Test, his achievement averages about three years above norm.
>
> John is developing a seriously unbalanced personality. The moment an assignment is made he begins to work on it. He has little to do with his classmates because he is always so busy trying to keep from failing (he thinks). Obviously he has some very erroneous beliefs and some bad habit patterns.[15]

## INTELLIGENCE OR APTITUDE TESTS

### DEFINITION OF TERMS

In the selection and interpretation of an intelligence test, particular attention must be paid to the author's definition of *intelligence*. Theorists disagree on the structure of intelligence or aptitude, and a wide variety of tests are offered under the title "intelligence tests."

Generally, definitions of *intelligence* by psychologists fall into one or more of these categories: the capacity to (1) think abstractly, (2) learn, or (3) integrate new experiences and adapt to new situations.[16] Such definitions treat intelligence as an ability or capacity. However, some of the recent definitions tend to emphasize acquired behaviors (those gained through learning).

Some people use the terms *intelligence* and *aptitude* interchangeably. Others make subtle distinctions between them, using *intelligence* to refer to a general measure and *aptitude* to mean the measurement of specific factors. Another distinction is historically based. It is now recognized that intelligence is affected by environmental as well as by hereditary factors and is subject to some change. However, when intelligence tests were first developed, psychologists considered intelligence to be an innate characteristic. To avoid such an implication, many test developers prefer to call their tests aptitude tests.

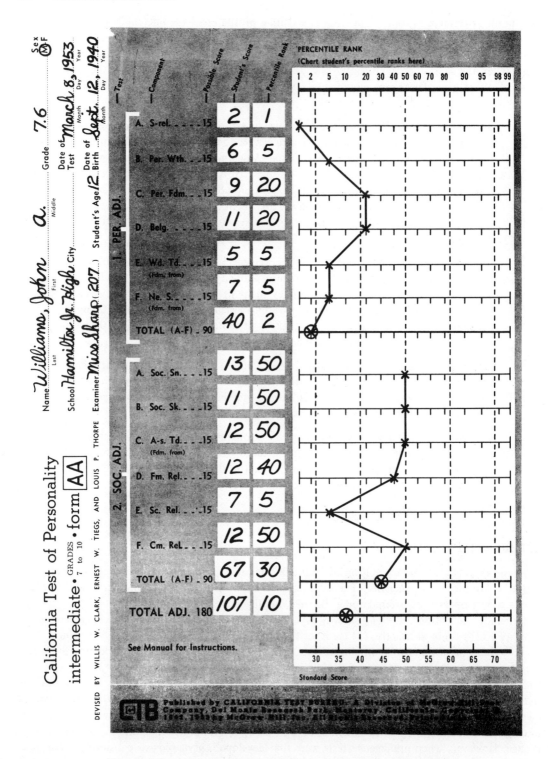

**Figure 7.4.** Sample Profile Chart for Child on California Test of Personality

Although theories of the structure of intelligence are far too numerous to describe here, most theorists recognize a general factor in addition to specific factors of intellect because positively correlated scores result when batteries of cognitive tests are given to samples of people. Also, because a general factor is the best predictor of academic performance, general intelligence tests continue to be widely used.

## JAMES McKEEN CATTELL

The term *mental test* was introduced by James McKeen Cattell in 1890 to refer to his precise measurements of muscular strength, speed of movement, pain sensitivity, weight discrimination, and reaction time. He used a combination of quantitative laboratory techniques that had been developed earlier by Sir Francis Galton, an English biologist, and by Wundt, who founded the first psychological laboratory in Leipzig, Germany, in 1879. Wundt established quantitative psychological laws similar to those in physics. These methods had obvious content validity but negligible validity for predicting behavior outside the laboratory. In addition, the behavior tested was elementary, being limited to clearly defined reactions and stimuli that could be controlled accurately.

## ALFRED BINET

A more practical form of mental testing, one that was geared to life performance, came to psychology from the field of medicine. Around 1890, Alfred Binet, a physician, tried a variety of tests to measure complex mental processes. He was concerned primarily with diagnosing pathological cases and mental defectives and with identifying slow learners in Paris schools. In collaboration with Simon, Binet developed the first individual intelligence test in 1905 (the Binet Scale), which was designed as a global measure of intelligence, producing a single score. Essentially, Binet viewed intelligence in terms of an individual's ability to deal effectively with his or her environment. Binet's original test was composed of thirty items that related to such abilities as following directions, defining words, and making judgments of appropriate behavior in everyday situations.

## THE STANFORD-BINET INTELLIGENCE SCALES

In 1916 Lewis Terman extended Binet's scale to include normal and superior children by producing the Stanford Revision of the Binet. This test has been central to psychological research and practice for many decades. From 1920 to 1940 the main function of the clinical psychologist was to "give Binets" in schools and other institutions.[17] The 1916 version was the first test to provide detailed administrative and scoring instructions and to recognize the need for a representative sample of subjects for test standardization.

In the 1960 Stanford-Binet Intelligence Scale (Third Revision),[18] items are grouped into twenty age levels. There is a separate test for each six-month level at the youngest age levels (ages two through five). For ages five through fourteen there is one set of subtests for each year. The instrument progresses to include three levels of superior adults.

This is a sampling of test items included in two of the young age levels:

### Age Two

Test items include sensory-motor skills, ability to follow directions, and identification of objects and parts of the body. Verbal and language skills are minimized.

1. Three-hole Form Board (placement of three geometric objects)

2. Delayed Response (identifying placement of hidden object after ten-second delay)

3. Identifying Parts of the Body (pointing out features on paper doll)

4. Block Building Tower (building four-block tower by imitating examiner's procedure)

5. Picture Vocabulary (naming common objects from pictures)

6. Word Combinations (spontaneous combination of two words)

**Age Six**

By age six the tests are heavily weighted with verbal skills and discriminations. Numerical concepts also begin to appear.

1. Vocabulary (defining six words on forty-five-word list)

2. Differences (telling difference between two objects)

3. Mutilated Pictures (pointing out missing parts of object in picture)

4. Number Concepts (counting number of blocks in a pile)

5. Opposite Analogies II (items of form "Summer is hot; winter is _____ .")

6. Maze Tracing (finding shortest path in simple maze)[19]

The Stanford-Binet is administered individually and requires a trained examiner because of the complexity of testing procedures. Typically, testing is begun with an individual child at the age level immediately below the child's chronological age. Testing is continued until every set of items is administered from the highest age level where all items are completed successfully (the *basal age*) through the lowest age where all items are failed (*ceiling* or *maximal* age).

Performance on the test is interpreted through the *mental age* (present level of intellectual development) and *IQ* (relative rate of child's intellectual development compared to agemates). The IQ computed is a *ratio IQ*, determined by taking the child's age in months, dividing it into the mental age in months, and moving the decimal two places to the right. Thus, a child with a chronological age (CA) of six and a mental age (MA) of six would have an IQ of 100.

The test is scored by comparing each response with an extensive list of correct response variations provided in the test manual. Scores are composed into an age scale by assigning a number of months credit to each answer.

Research with the Stanford-Binet has shown that performance reflects a general factor of verbal reasoning but that other abilities (e.g., memory, perceptual) also influence performance at some age levels. Studies on criterion validity of the instrument have resulted in positive correlations between scores on the test and a variety of measures of academic achievement (e.g., grades, years of education, teachers' ratings, and achievement test scores). Because of its technical quality and historical position, the Stanford-Binet serves as *the* standard for measuring intelligence—the standard against which all other purported measures of intelligence must be calibrated.[20] The popularity of the test is evidenced by reports of administration of the test to about 800,000 individuals each year from 1960 to 1972[21] and by a research list of 1,590 references from professional journals and books regarding the test.[22]

## THE WECHSLER SCALES

The first form of these scales was developed in 1939 by David Wechsler, a clinical psychologist at Bellevue Hospital in New York, with the purpose of measuring adult intelligence. In 1949 the Wechsler Intelligence Scale for Children (WISC) was first published, and it was revised in 1974 (WISC-R).[23] WISC-R covers ages five to sixteen. A test for children ages four to six-and-one-half was published in 1967—the Wechsler Preschool and Primary Scale of Intelligence (WPPSI).[24]

The Wechsler and Stanford-Binet tests correlate so highly at most age levels that the choice of which test to administer is only a matter of the test user's personal preference.[25] Both tests are individually administered, although the Wechsler scales are somewhat easier to administer and are now often used more frequently than the Binet scales. The performance items on the Wechsler scales are also useful for children with language problems—the deaf and "disadvantaged" children who have difficulty with more verbal tests. These performance tests require manipulation of objects rather than oral or written responses.

The Wechsler scales consist of five or six subtests that produce a Verbal score and five more subtests that generate a Performance score. These two scores combined give the Full Scale score. The subtests at each age level, which are listed in Table 7.2, are similar although not identical. Figure 7.5 provides an illustration from the Wechsler Preschool and Primary Scale (The Animal House Test), whereas Figure 7.6 illustrates the Object Assembly Test from the Wechsler Intelligence Scale for Children.

Unlike the Stanford-Binet which uses the *ratio IQ,* the Wechsler uses the standard form of IQ, that is known as a *deviation IQ.* The ratio IQ is based upon the assumption that a child's rate of mental development reflects his or her potentiality: that a five-year-old with a mental age of six is developing 25 percent faster than the average child and will continue to develop at that rate until adulthood. However, such a trend would not hold into adulthood. Therefore, when establishing a scale for adults, Wechsler introduced the deviation IQ. This IQ reports only the standing of the individual among others at his or her chronological age.

## INTELLIGENCE TESTS FOR INFANTS

All intelligence tests for infants are individual measures. Infant tests are difficult to standardize, administer, and score. They are less reliable than tests for older children, especially during the first six months. Infant scales primarily measure motor and sensory abilities, and reliability studies indicate that there is some consistency in the development of these attributes.[26]

**Table 7.2.** Subtests of the Wechsler Scales for Various Ages

| Preschool-Primary (WPPSI) | Children (WISC) | Adults (WAIS) |
|---|---|---|
|  | **Verbal** |  |
| Information | Information | Information |
| Comprehension | Comprehension | Comprehension |
| Arithmetic | Arithmetic | Arithmetic |
| Similarities | Similarities | Similarities |
| Vocabulary | Vocabulary | Vocabulary |
| (Sentences) | (Digit Span) | Digit Span |
|  | **Performance** |  |
| Block Design | Block Design | Block Design |
| Picture Completion | Picture Completion | Picture Completion |
|  | Picture Arrangement | Picture Arrangement |
|  | Object Assembly | Object Assembly |
|  |  | Digit Symbol |
| Animal House |  |  |
| Mazes | (Mazes) |  |
|  | Coding |  |
| Geometric Design |  |  |

Parantheses indicate tests used as alternates or supplements.

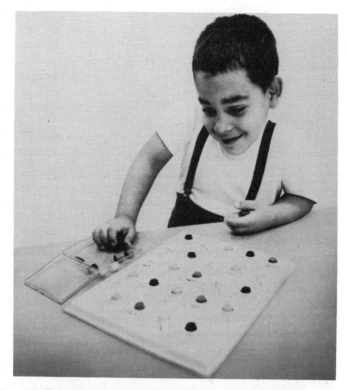

**Figure 7.5.** The Animal House Test of the Wechsler Preschool and Primary Scale

**Figure 7.6.** The Object Assembly Test of the Wechsler Intelligence Scale for Children

**Gesell Developmental Schedules.** One of the pioneers in infant testing was Arnold Gesell. His longitudinal studies of child development were mentioned in Chapter 1. On the basis of their observations of infants, Gesell and his colleagues prepared the Gesell Developmental Schedules.[27] These schedules are designed to measure these attributes:

**Motor behavior:**  standing, walking, holding balance, manipulating objects

**Adaptive behavior:**  solving problems in child's small world, obtaining objects, removing obstacles, solving puzzles, reacting to stimuli

**Language behavior:**  communicating, including use of gestures and primitive words

**Personal-social behavior:**  learning habits of personal care such as toilet training, dressing and feeding self. At later stages, managing self in social and play situations

Except for instruments with a Piagetian orientation, most current infant tests have a common ancestor in the Gesell Developmental Schedules.[28] During the first year of life most observations must be made about motor behavior.

**Bayley Scales of Infant Development.** This test by Nancy Bayley is designed for use with infants ages two through thirty months.[29] It provides two scores—mental and motor—plus thirty behavior ratings. A review of this test by Fred Damarin in *The Eighth Mental Measurements Yearbook* concludes that "fortunately for American baby-testers the BSID is a truly excellent instrument . . . the standardization of the mental and motor scales is as good as or better than that of any other individual test, whether for infants, children, or adults."[30] Damarin also emphasizes that the test grows out of the research traditions of Gesell and Bayley. The test demands a great deal of the examiner, who should be well trained not only in the mechanics of the instrument but also in the principles of normal development and its deviations. See Figure 7.7 for an illustration of objects used with the Bayley Scales.

**Figure 7.7.** Test Objects Employed with the Bayley Scales of Infant Development

**Cattell Infant Intelligence Scale.** This scale is considered a downward extension of the Stanford-Binet (ages three through thirty months).[31] It is based upon the foundation laid by Gesell and is similar to the Bayley Scales. A review of the Cattell Scale by Fred Damarin in *The Eighth Mental Measurements Yearbook* noted that "psychologists who want a reasonably well standardized Gesell-type instrument must apparently choose between the Cattell and the Bayley scales."[32]

**Piagetian-based Scales.** The scales of Gesell, Cattell, and Bayley are traditional scales that support a maturationally and genotypically controlled conception of development. By comparison, the Piaget-based scales are based upon the idea that qualitative changes in intelligence characterize growth.

Escalona and Corman designed the Einstein Scales of Sensorimotor Intelligence for infants between one month and two years of age.[33] The instrument consists of three scales totaling fifty-four items. The Prehension Scale covers the development of adaptive reflexes and early systematic behavior at the lowest age range. This behavior includes that which is spontaneous exploratory as well as that which is object-grasping, with these items being identical to those developed by Gesell. The Object Permanence Scale tests an infant's ability to follow objects to the limits of his or her visual field. The Space Scale elicits object manipulation in a three-dimensional perspective.[34]

The assessment procedure developed by Uzgiris and Hunt[35] is similar in coverage to the Einstein Scales but consists of six scales rather than three. Neither the Einstein Scales nor the Uzgiris-Hunt Scales have been widely reported in recent research literature but the increasing popularity of Piagetian theory suggests that their usage will increase.[36]

## PRESCHOOL INTELLIGENCE TESTS

After a child develops speech, he or she can be tested with more of the materials normally used in intelligence testing, although problems with test standardization and administration still remain. Test materials must consist primarily of pictures and performance tasks. The test examiner of preschool children must be skillful in holding their interest since many preschoolers are too active and distractible or too shy with strangers to give the cooperation needed for testing procedures.

**Minnesota Preschool Scale.** This is one of the most prominent tests for preschool children.[37] Many of the items are similar to those at the lower age levels of the Stanford-Binet, and scores for children over the age of three correlate highly with Binet scores obtained later.[38] Some of the test items from the Minnesota Preschool Scale are

1. Pointing to parts of the body on a doll

2. Telling what a picture is about

3. Naming colors

4. Digit span

5. Naming objects from memory

6. Vocabulary

7. Copying simple geometric designs

8. Block building

9. Doing a jigsaw puzzle

10. Indicating missing part in pictures[39]

Two other individual preschool scales worthy of consideration are the Merrill-Palmer Scale[40] and the Goodenough Draw-a-Man Scale.[41] Most of the major preschool techniques are at least fifteen years old and some over thirty years old.

### GROUP INTELLIGENCE TESTS

No tests dominate the group intelligence test field in the same way the Binet and Wechsler scales dominate the individual test field. Group tests correlate highly with individual tests at the teenage and adult levels. Both types of tests consist primarily of items of verbal comprehension, numerical computation, and reasoning factors.

Group testing is not considered feasible below the ages of five or six. At that level, only small groups of about a dozen children can be tested. Since the children cannot write their own responses, test instructions must be given orally and supported by illustrations.[42]

**Pintner-Cunningham Primary Test.** This test has been in use for over thirty years, and is one of the most widely used group tests for young children.[43] High correlations of about .80 have been computed between the Pintner-Cunningham and the Stanford-Binet. Sample items from the Pintner-Cunningham are shown in Figure 7.8.

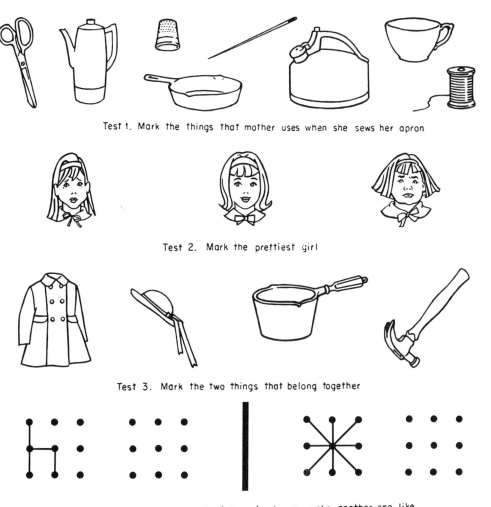

Test 1. Mark the things that mother uses when she sews her apron

Test 2. Mark the prettiest girl

Test 3. Mark the two things that belong together

Test 7. Look at how each picture is drawn; make another one like it in the dots

**Figure 7.8.** Sample Items from Form A of the Pintner-Cunningham Primary Test

**Lorge-Thorndike Intelligence Tests.** This is one of the best test batteries for use with children from kindergarten through twelfth grade.[44] Items through grade three are nonverbal, being comprised of pictures and designs. Administration time is about thirty minutes. The test is reliable and scores correlate highly with the Stanford-Binet and some achievement tests. Sample items from the Lorge-Thorndike Tests are given in Figure 7.9.

## SPECIAL APTITUDE OR ABILITY TESTS

It was indicated earlier in this chapter that some people make subtle distinctions between the terms *intelligence* and *aptitude,* using intelligence to refer to a general measure and aptitude for the measurement of specific factors or abilities. These specific factors will be considered in the sections that follow.

**Psychomotor Abilities.** Fleishman isolated eleven factors from many studies of psychomotor ability:

> *Speed:* speed of arm movement, wrist or finger speed, reaction time
>
> *Simple control:* steadiness, aiming
>
> *Coordination:* finger dexterity, manual dexterity, control precision, multi-limb coordination
>
> *Judgment:* response orientation, rate control[45]

Psychomotor abilities are measured with testing apparatus or machines or by pencil-and-paper measures. However, printed tests are not recommended for complex dexterity and coordination.

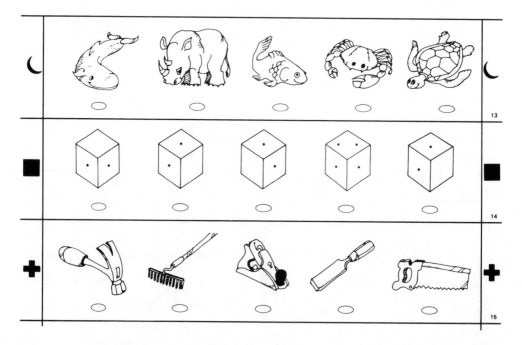

**Figure 7.9.** Sample Items from the Lorge-Thorndike Intelligence Tests, Kindergarten and First-grade Level

Among the oldest motor dexterity tests are the pegboards, which require the subject to place pegs into holes as fast as possible. There is no general psychomotor ability despite popular ideas about boys who are "good with their hands." Psychomotor abilities are often of value in predicting job performance but tend to be less relevant than intellectual abilities.[46]

**Artistic Aptitude.** Although there has been longstanding interest among psychologists in the nature of art and artistic ability, measurement and research on artistic ability lag far behind the study of other ability functions. Not only has there been less urgent need for identifying artistic ability than for intellectual and vocational measurement but also the nature of artistic ability is very complex.

A few tests have been designed to measure artistic ability in terms of artistic production or art judgment. Most of these tests are intended for high-school or college students and adults. Two art tests that can be used with small children are included in *The Eighth Mental Measurements Yearbook:* the Bryant-Schwan Design Test and the Taylor-Helmstadter Paired Comparison Scale of Aesthetic Judgment.

The Bryant-Schwan Design Test is a matching and identification test developed to measure art design knowledge in elementary-school children and mentally retarded children.[47] It can be used with children from kindergarten through grade twelve. Five items for each of five design elements (line, shape, color, value, and texture) make up each of the two parts of the test. One part of the test consists of matching items; the other part consists of identification items.

The Taylor-Helmstadter Paired Compairson Scale of Aesthetic Judgment is designed for use with preschool children through adults.[48] Thirty-eight pairs of color slides depicting paintings, sculptures, and common household items comprise the instrument. One slide of each pair was judged by art experts as higher than the other on an eleven-point successive category scale of aesthetic quality. The subject chooses the one in each pair that he or she likes best. The score is computed by totaling the number of slides chosen that corresponds to the preference of the art experts.[49]

## CREATIVITY AND ITS MEASUREMENT

The creative process has been defined as "a process of change, of development, of evolution in the organization of subjective life."[50] It is the imaginative re-combination of known elements into something new.

Research evidence indicates that creative thinking represents not a single ability but instead a number of abilities and personal characteristics. Intellectual factors appear to include sensitivity to problems, originality (production of ideas off the beaten track), fluency (production of a large number of ideas), and flexibility (variety of approaches to a problem). Motivational characteristics also are important in creativity. Highly creative people usually exhibit great dedication to their work, intellectual persistence, pleasure in manipulating ideas, a need for recognition and achievement, a need for variety, a need for independence, and a strong desire to improve upon currently accepted techniques and organization. High energy, accompanied by vast output through self-discipline, is usually found. Creative people also tend to differ from noncreative individuals in several personality characteristics. The former tend to be more concerned with autonomy, more stable, lower in sociability, more dominant and self-assertive, more self-accepting, more resourceful and adventurous, and more complex as persons.[51]

General confusion about the capacity of children for creative thinking has existed. However, the beginnings of creative thinking may be found at infancy in the child's manipulative, exploratory, and experimental activities; use of facial expressions; and efforts to discover the meanings of the facial expressions and gestures of others.[52]

### MEASURING CREATIVITY

The process of acquiring existing knowledge is different from the process of producing new knowledge and ideas. Since current intelligence tests do not involve the ability to create new ideas or things on one's own, tests should be extended beyond the I.Q. measurement.[53] Both Getzels and Torrance have reported that if an I.Q. test is used to select highly creative talent, about 70 percent of the persons who have the highest 20 percent of the scores on creativity test batteries will be missed.[54] In other words, more people with high creativity scores are missed than are identified by using current I.Q. tests to locate creative talent.

**Torrance Tests of Creative Thinking**. The tests most widely used by researchers on creative thinking have been a set of tests designed by Torrance.[55] Figural and verbal tests have been developed. The verbal tests (forms A and B) are appropriate for group testing from fourth grade through graduate school and for individual testing from kindergarten through third grade. The figural tests (forms A and B) may be used from kindergarten through graduate school. The word *test* is not used on the booklets or in the printed instructions in order to encourage a game-like, thinking, or problem-solving atmosphere and to avoid the threatening situation often associated with testing.

The verbal tests are structured around seven activities:

1. *Asking Questions.* A picture is shown to the child (or older subject) who is instructed to ask questions to find out what is happening in the picture.

2. *Guessing Causes.* The child is instructed to give (or list) as many *possible* causes as he can of the action shown in the picture.

3. *Guessing Consequences.* The child is instructed to give as many possibilities as he can of what might happen as a result of what is taking place in the picture.

4. *Product Improvement.* A small stuffed toy elephant is shown the child who is asked to think of the "cleverest, most interesting and unusual ways you can think of for changing this toy elephant so that children will have more fun playing with it. Do not worry about how much the change would cost. Think only about what would make it more fun to play with as a toy."

5. *Unusual Uses of Cardboard Boxes.* The child is instructed to give as many interesting and unusual uses he can think of for empty cardboard boxes.

6. *Unusual Questions.* Instructions are to think of questions about cardboard boxes that might arouse interest and curosity in others concerning boxes.

7. *Just Suppose.* An improbable situation is given "that will probably never happen." The subject is asked to use his imagination to think out all of the other exciting things that would happen IF this improbable situation were to come true.[56]

The Torrance Tests of Creative Thinking are scored for *fluency* (total number of relevant responses); *flexibility* (number of different categories into which responses fall); *originality* (rarity of occurrence of a response, given by less than 2 percent of the subjects); and *elaboration* (extent to which an idea is spelled out or elaborated). A summary score for creativity is also computed. Systematic norms are not available for the Torrance Tests. However, scores on the figural form do not appear to increase at all with age, and the verbal scores change very little after grade six.[57]

**Barron-Welsh Art Scale**. This instrument is designed for use with subjects of age six and above.[58] The test consists of eighty-six abstract line drawings and designs that range from simple geometric forms to complex asymmetrical figures and patterns. The individual indicates like or dislike of each drawing by circling *L* or *D*.

Research studies with this scale have shown that creative individuals demonstrate a marked preference for complex asymmetrical designs. This finding appears to indicate the creative individual's preference for complexity of experience. Several authorities believe that this test is exceedingly promising as a forecaster of creativity.

**Adjective Check List.** This test is designed by Harrison Gough for use from grade nine through the adult level.[59] It is comprised of 300 adjectives, and the individual is asked to check those that describe him or her. While not originally designed to measure creativity, this test is reported to differentiate highly creative people from those less creative. Creative individuals tend to check such descriptive adjectives as independent, inventive, enthusiastic, versatile, impulsive, excitable, self-demanding, worrying, thorough, sensitive, restless, preoccupied, and moody. Less creative or non-creative individuals see themselves as sincere, responsible, tolerant, clear thinking, logical, dependable, life-of-party, polite, popular, cheerful, obedient, sociable, fashionable, practical, and organized.

## DETERRENTS TO CREATIVITY

Creative imagination during early childhood seems to peak at about four years and drops about the time the child first enters school. There are indications that this drop is a cultural phenomenon. An extremely peer-oriented culture which emphasizes conformity to norms in behavior constitutes a block to creativity. A success-oriented culture that regards errors as fatal, that considers divergency as equal to abnormality or delinquency, and that emphasizes security and conventional career choices does not foster creativity. An educational system which emphasizes acquisition of knowledge and memorization of facts, a closely prescribed curriculum, over-reliance upon textbooks, trust in authority, and the lecture method of teaching is also a deterrent to creativity. It has been suggested that there is a need for selecting and developing leaders in the field of school administration who are interested in progress and are ready to take and permit new steps ahead.[60]

## CREATIVITY-INTELLIGENCE DISTINCTION

For many years Wallach and Kogan have studied the modes of thinking in young children, and have specifically dealt with the question, Is there an aspect of cognitive functioning which can be appropriately labeled "creativity" that stands apart from the traditional concept of general intelligence? Their examination of research reports in the professional literature has brought them to the conclusion that the various creativity measures utilized are almost as strongly, equally strongly, or even more strongly related to general intelligence than they are related to each other.

Preparatory to beginning their research, Wallach and Kogan noted that the majority of introspective accounts of highly creative artists and scientists share a concern with associative freedom and uniqueness. Introspections about times of creative insight reflected a kind of task-centered, permissive, or playful set on the part of the creative artists and scientists. Such a permissive, playful attitude would imply freedom from time pressure. By contrast, the creative studies reviewed by Wallach and Kogan usually referred to their creativity procedures as "tests," administered them to large groups of students in a classroom, and generally imposed relatively brief time limits.

Wallach and Kogan's conclusions that creativity represents a mode of cognitive functioning which matters a great deal in the life of the child and that his or her joint status on creativity *and* intelligence should be considered can be illustrated by one of their studies.[61] This study was conducted with 151 children (70 boys and 81 girls) who comprised the entire fifth-grade population of a suburban public school system in a middle-class region. A game-like, nonevaluational atmosphere was established for administration of the procedures. The experimenters were introduced as visitors interested in children's games. They spent two initial weeks with each class to gain rapport and also worked with individual children.

Creativity was measured by computing a uniqueness and productivity score for each of five procedures. These procedures were similar to those used in other attempts to measure creativity, such as thinking of uses for objects and possible meanings of visual patterns and forms. To assess general intelligence of the children, ten indicators were used, including verbal and performance subtests from the Wechsler Intelligence Scale for Children.

Results from the sample as a whole, and separately for the 70 boys and 81 girls, showed the ten creativity measures to be highly intercorrelated and the ten intelligence measures to be highly inter-correlated. However, the correlation *between* the creativity and the intelligence measures was extremely low. Therefore, Wallach and Kogan concluded their measure of creativity to be independent of the traditional concept of general intelligence.

The researchers then proceeded to determine the pyschological significance of their findings. They divided the creativity and intelligence scores to yield four groups of children that represented the four possible combinations of creativity and intelligence levels. The four groups were then compared to determine psychological differences among them. The experimenters used the observational technique to rate the children along specifically defined behavioral dimensions. Clinical accounts of various children in the sample reinforced the conclusions of the quantitative study. This is a summary of the "psychological nature" of the children in the four cognitive groupings:

> *High creativity-high intelligence:* These children can exercise both control and freedom within themselves and both adult-like and child-like kinds of behavior.

> *High creativity-low intelligence:* These children are in angry conflict with themselves and their school environment and have feelings of unworthiness and inadequacy. However, they can blossom forth cognitively in a stress-free context.

> *Low creativity-high intelligence:* These children are described as "addicted" to school achievement. They must continually strive for academic excellence in order to avoid the possibility of pain from academic failure.

> *Low creativity-low intelligence:* These children are basically bewildered and engage in defensive maneuvers ranging from adaptations like intensive social activity to regressions such as passivity or psychosomatic symptoms.[62]

## ACHIEVEMENT TESTS

Traditionally, aptitude testing has been based upon hereditary talents—innate differences among people—and achievement testing has been based upon what individuals had learned through experience. Actually, much overlap exists between aptitude and achievement tests, with the primary distinction relating to purpose. Aptitude tests are used as predictors of an individual's performance in some area, whereas achievement tests are used to evaluate an individual's accomplishments or the adequacy of his or her education and experience.[63]

### PURPOSES OF ACHIEVEMENT TESTS

Achievement tests are used primarily for student placement, to determine the development of individual children for guidance purposes, and to measure the effectiveness of teachers and different teaching methods.

### TYPES OF ACHIEVEMENT TESTS

Achievement tests may be classified as specially constructed or as standardized. *Specially constructed tests* are those that are usually developed by teachers to determine students' mastery of subject matter taught in the classroom or read in textbooks. *Standardized tests* are published group tests whose contents are deemed common to most educational systems at specific grade levels. Tables of norms (or average scores) are provided for comparative purposes. Also, these tests usually have been submitted to reliability and validity studies.

Standardized achievement tests can be classified into general and special tests. Usually general achievement tests consist of batteries of tests that measure achievement of children in primary school subjects such as reading comprehension, arithmetic, grammar, and social studies. Special achievement tests cover individual subjects such as history achievement and science achievement.

Examples of two achievement test batteries are the Stanford Achievement Tests (grades one through nine) and the Iowa Tests of Educational Development (grades nine through twelve).

# PERSONALITY SCALES

## PERSONALITY DEFINED

Many years ago Allport defined *personality* as "the dynamic organization within the individual of those psychophysical systems that determine his unique adjustments to his environment."[64] The measurement of personality is considered to be the most complex problem in psychological measurement because human personality is probably the most complex phenomenon in existence. For measurement purposes, personality can be viewed as the organization of the traits of the individual.[65]

**Traits.** A *trait* has been defined as "some relatively permanent and broad reaction tendency."[66] One way of describing personality is to assign scores to people on a group of traits. A person can then be compared with others in respect to the quantity of certain traits possessed. The individual's personality also can be described by expressing these trait scores on a graph or chart called a psychogram, or psychograph personality profile.

Developing methods for measuring and classifying traits is a complex matter. A special branch of psychology called psychometry has been formed to deal with such problems. One question facing psychologists is how to determine the number of traits that is sufficient to describe personality. Researchers have counted about 18,000 trait words in the English language. Recognizing the need to avoid personal preferences and prejudices in the selection of traits for study, researchers employ a statistical method called factor analysis to determine the traits that go together. In this manner, traits are arranged into a small number of groups or clusters which are thought to be adequate to describe personality. Personality scales are often developed through such an approach.

**Personality Types.** Types are simply organizations of traits. As shown in Eysenck's conception of types (Figure 7.10), specific responses or behavior of people, when repeated habitually, become habitual responses.[67] For example, an observation of Mary may show that she continues with a task until she masters it (specific response). Over a period of time, the observer may note that Mary is not easily distracted from a task and sticks with it instead of abandoning it for other activities (habitual response). In many situations, Mary may appear to be persistent in doing things that she has set as goals. Such a pattern is integrated into a trait of persistence. If Mary also tends to be high on the other traits enumerated in Figure 7.10—rigidity, subjectivity, shyness, and irritability—the researcher would have some justification for placing her into the personality type that Eysenck calls *introversion*. In this respect, traits with significant positive correlations among them define a type.

These trait and type approaches are not without their critics. In fact, they have been the topic of a great deal of controversy in psychology, although attempts to classify personality in this manner may be traced far back in human history.

The scientific study of personality is based upon the idea that individuals differ in various characteristics. Just as various species of animals may be categorized according to specific characteristics in biology, people also may be classified into personality patterns. Any observer can classify together those attributes that seem to be similar and can designate people with these attributes under a

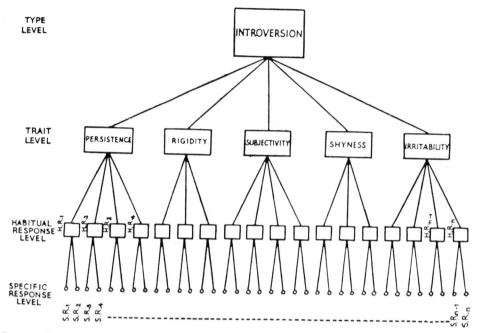

**Figure 7.10.** Eysenck's Conception of Types. In this diagram introversion is represented as a "type" which is identified by determining the common components in a series of related traits: persistence, rigidity, etc.

common label or type. However, one of the difficulties in applying type theories to personality rests with the assumption that people must be classified into distinct pigeonholes, although actually most of the population fails to fit the proposed types (Figure 7.11), tending instead to possess characteristics along a continuum (Figure 7.11). In Figure 7.11, the extrovert and introvert types are shown to represent the extremes of the distribution and the ambivert type to represent the middle range since the behavior of most people fluctuates between the extremes of extroversion and introversion.

Trait and type names are also confusing. The same name is often defined differently on different tests. Therefore, it is important to take special note of the meanings of the traits or types intended by the test developer in order to determine what that particular test measures.

## PERSONALITY MEASUREMENT

There are numerous approaches to the measurement of personality. In this chapter we are concerned only with the structured tests and scales. Most of the personality tests and scales used today are of the structured paper-and-pencil type in which the subject is presented with a series of questions dealing with typical behavior patterns. The subject is usually scored according to the number of questions he or she answers in a direction purported to display the trait or traits being measured. Some tests measure only one trait dimension such as security-insecurity, while other tests measure numerous traits.

Most personality instruments are designed for use with subjects from grade nine through adult levels. However, we will discuss only examples of tests designed specifically for younger children or those which extend from the young child to the adult years.

Most of the self-report instruments used with small children are semiprojective, with the child responding to pictures instead of completely verbal choices. A large proportion of the personality measures for young children are projective. This method will be discussed in Chapter 9.

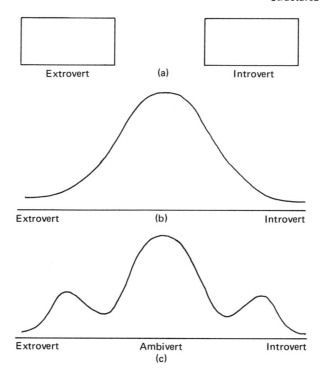

**Figure 7.11.** Curves Representing Extroversion-Introversion Personality Types

**California Test of Personality.** This instrument provides primary (kindergarten through third grade), elementary (fourth through eighth grade), secondary (ninth through twelfth grade), and adult forms.[68] The tests are in questionnaire form requiring yes or no answers. Reviews in the *Mental Measurements Yearbooks* point to the conclusion that the California Test of Personality is one of the most carefully prepared questionnaires of its type.

Questions are classified into two groups, one dealing with personal adjustment and the other with social adjustment. A table of norms and a sample profile for this test were presented earlier. Scores are computed for these personality traits as measured on the test:

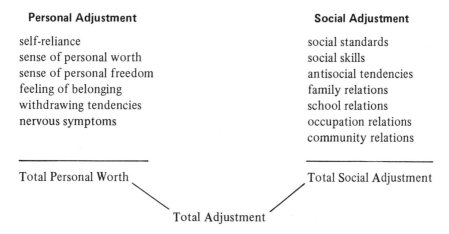

| **Personal Adjustment** | **Social Adjustment** |
| --- | --- |
| self-reliance | social standards |
| sense of personal worth | social skills |
| sense of personal freedom | antisocial tendencies |
| feeling of belonging | family relations |
| withdrawing tendencies | school relations |
| nervous symptoms | occupation relations |
| | community relations |
| Total Personal Worth | Total Social Adjustment |

Total Adjustment

**Children's Personality Questionnaire (1975 Edition).** This instrument was designed for group administration to children from eight through twelve years of age.[69] The test booklet title is "What You Do and What You Think." Young children may be helped with words on the test that are unfamiliar to them. The test is a downward extension of the IPAT High School Personality Questionnaire (HSPQ) and the Sixteen Personality Factor Questionnaire (16PF). The Early School Personality Questionnaire is a further downward extension to ages six through eight. All of these tests were developed by Raymond B. Cattell, who believes that the same dimensions of personality run the gamut from early childhood through adulthood.

Reviewers of the Children's Personality Questionnaire generally conclude that the booklet format is practical for use by children, that the questions are clearly stated, and that the items are easily scored. However, they suggest that the instrument should not be used for counseling with individual children until further research presents additional data on its reliability and validity. The Children's Personality Questionnaire covers these fourteen traits:

reserved versus warm-hearted
dull versus bright
affected by feelings versus emotionally stable
undemonstrative versus excitable
obedient versus assertive
sober versus enthusiastic
disregards rules versus conscientious
shy versus venturesome
tough-minded versus tender-minded
vigorous versus circumspect individualism
forthright versus shrewd
self-assured versus apprehensive
uncontrolled versus controlled
relaxed versus tense

**Early School Personality Questionnaire.** As indicated previously, this instrument is a downward extension of the Children's Personality Questionnaire to ages 6 through 8.[70]

**Institute of Child Study Security Test.** This test consists of a primary form for children in grades one through three and an elementary form for grades four through eight.[71] The primary form is entitled "The Story of Tommy," and the elementary form, "The Story of Jimmy."

The elementary form is reviewed in *The Fifth Mental Measurements Yearbook*, with the recommendation that the test merits consideration, at least for children ten to eleven years old. In this form the child reads "The Story of Jimmy" and is interrupted fifteen times to rank five statements that are designed to measure the child's independent security, deputy agent (equivalent to the use of various defense mechanisms), and insecurity. Although the test is in a structured paper-and-pencil format (and classified as "nonprojective" in the *Mental Measurements Yearbook*), it is based upon the child's projection of his or her security-insecurity into the story. The fact that the stories on both the primary and elementary forms are about boys makes its use with girls questionable.

**Eysenck Personality Questionnaire.** This instrument is a revision of the Eysenck Personality Inventory and Junior Personality Inventory.[72] The questionnaire is available for two levels: junior (ages seven through fifteen) and adult (ages sixteen and over). It results in four scores: psychoticism (P), extroversion (E), neuroticism (N), and lie (L). (Note again the illustration of Eysenck's introversion (the opposite of extroversion) in Figure 7.10.) Only one-half page of text in the manual deals with the junior level of the questionnaire. Data are presented on reliability and norms are given for different English age groups but no validity data are provided. In *The Eighth Mental Measurements Yearbook* the statement is made that the junior EPQ can be used only for research.[73]

**STS Junior Inventory**. The STS Junior Inventory is designed for use with children in grades four through eight.[74] The STS Youth Inventory is available for grades seven through twelve. Children are presented with problems in the forms in which they normally express them, such as "I want . . . " or "I need . . . . " Three response boxes of different sizes are presented for each item. The child checks the big box to indicate a "big problem," the middle-sized box for a "middle-sized problem," and the little box for a "little problem." A circle is checked to indicate no problem.

A reviewer of the STS Junior Inventory stated that it could serve teachers and counselors as a very useful evaluational tool and as a stimulus for discussions with students. Children's replies to specific items should also provide teachers and counselors with useful information about individual students. Analysis of group responses may provide a basis for evaluation of a school's success in achieving nonacademic objectives. Although the reviewer considered the inventory to be a "valuable supplement to general evaluational techniques in the area of personality at the elementary school level," he did question the refinements of scoring and profile analysis suggested by the authors, or the treatment of the inventory as a multiscored measuring instrument, at the time of his review (1957).[75]

**Embedded Figures Test**. This test was designed by Herman Witkin for persons age ten and over.[76] A Children's Embedded Figures Test for ages five through twelve is a revision of the Goodenough-Eagle modification of the Embedded Figures Test. It is available for research use only.[77]

The Embedded Figures Test consists of twenty-four complex colored figures, each of which contains one of eight simple figures. A card with a complex figure is shown to the subject for fifteen seconds and he or she is asked to describe it. Then a card containing a simple figure embedded within the complex figure is shown for ten seconds; the subject's task is to locate the simple figure and to trace it with a blunt stylus. The score received is the total time taken to locate the figures within the designs. The test is a measure of field dependence: a high score indicates field dependence, and a low score, field independence.

As Harrison Gough comments in his review in *The Sixth Mental Measurements Yearbook,* "one of the most attractive features of this test is its firm anchoring in a systematic context of theory and empirical evidence." The theory behind the test is based upon Witkin's concepts of psychological differentiation and "body as perceived."[78] An understanding of the manner in which the individual becomes aware of self and of his or her world is basic to any adequate understanding of human behavior. When exposed to the world for the first time, the newborn's perceptual field is blurred and confused and the ability to differentiate or organize the world into definable objects and people is lacking. For a period of time the infant is unaware of any separation between self and the other persons and objects in his or her environment. As the infant grows older, perceptual development enables him or her to mark off and to react to objects and people as separate entities. With this increasing ability, the child begins to make the distinction between self and not-self. The clearness of people's demarcation of their bodies from their surroundings or environment is believed to have important behavioral implications.

This ability of people to experience themselves as separate entities from their environment has been investigated by Witkin in his studies of field dependence, which use different techniques to measure this trait. In some studies, individuals were subjected to a tilted or otherwise distorted visual surrounding and were given the task of adjusting their bodies to an upright position. An individual's ability to straighten his or her body regardless of the position of the surrounding field indicates that the individual experiences his or her body as an entity separate from the field. Women have been found to be more dependent than men on the field or surroundings in their perception. Witkin's

Embedded Figures Test is also one of his techniques for measuring field dependence since, with this instrument, the subject must separate the small figure from its complex surrounding.

**ETS Locus of Control Scale.** This scale was developed by Virginia Shipman for use with children 5½ to 7½ years of age.[79] It is administered individually to determine whether a child perceives the things that happen to him or her to be due to his or her own behavior (internal control) or to outside forces (external control). Cartoon drawings of children are presented to the child, and the child is asked to pick an explanation for the character's success or failure from a pair of forced-choice responses.

**Brown IDS Self-Concept Referents Test.** This inventory is designed for use with preschool and kindergarten children.[80] Norms and validity studies were provided through the ETS Head Start Longitudinal Study. The test measures the self-concept of young children. At the beginning of the test session, a fast-developing, full-length picture is taken of the child. The child verifies the image in the picture as himself or herself, and then, while looking at the picture, responds to twenty-one bipolar questions that are phrased in an either-or format.

## ATTITUDE, VALUE, AND INTEREST SCALES

Attitudes, values, and interests are formulated as properties of an individual personality. They are classified as *dynamic traits* because of their focus on why and how a person is moved to do what he or she does. They deal with the "generalized dynamic dispositions of personality which direct and determine the type of response which an individual will make to the varied situations confronting him in his daily life."[81] Numerous experiments demonstrate a clear relationship between attitudes and values and conduct.

### DEFINITION OF TERMS

Some working definitions are in order to enable discussion of the measurement of attitudes, values, and interests. The terms are used interchangeably in some writings while others treat them as distinct concepts. Yarrow summarizes the distinctions often made between attitudes and values.[82] The concept of *attitude* is most frequently expressed in terms of a "state of readiness for motive arousal" or a "readiness to act" in a given consistent manner toward a specified class of stimuli. Although the concept of *value* has been discussed less often in psychology, there is general consistency from psychological, psychoanalytic, and sociological orientations to attach the dimensions of acceptability or unacceptability, good or bad, should or should not to an individual's or society's value frames of reference. For example, psychoanalytic theorists refer to values as internalized parents. In this sense, values represent conscience. Value is concerned with feeling whereas an attitude is a value expression. Teachers may have a value of acceptance of children. The attitudes reflected in their behavior may be described as being accepting, permissive, and warm.

*Interests* are less generalized than attitudes and values. They change rapidly as the mode of satisfying needs changes. For example, a person may score high on aesthetic value but the interests that he or she pursues in satisfying this aesthetic drive may change from reading books on art and design to visiting art galleries and museums to producing works of art.

### MEASUREMENT OF CHILDREN'S ATTITUDES AND VALUES

An understanding of the development of children's attitudes and values is an important part of child study for it leads toward an understanding of children's orientations toward their physical and social environments and toward themselves. The *self* has been defined as "the meaning life has for an individual in relation to his or her values." Attitudes and values initially tend to be adopted ready-made from our culture. They are passed on from parents and teachers to the child through the socialization process. As the child develops, his or her values are subject to refinement. Values represent to the individual what is worth seeking in living—what he or she stands for.

Children's sensitivity in perceiving and adopting attitudes and values at a very early age have been illustrated in studies of children's awareness of group morals and social prejudices. A case in point is Goodman's study of kindergarten children's awareness of racial differences and their preferences associated with these differences.[83]

The study of attitudes and values is difficult with young children. Attitudes and values are abstract concepts that are usually expressed verbally. Therefore, language skills, understanding of the concepts being studied, and communication ability are important in attitude and value research. The young child is oriented to his or her immediate experiences in the environment and to dealing with concrete concepts rather than abstract ones. Instruments for the study of attitudes, values, and interests of small children are very limited. A few examples follow.

**Interest Inventory for Elementary Grades.** This instrument was developed to measure the general interest patterns of boys and girls in grades four through six.[84] It contains 250 items that seek reactions to such things as movies, radio, games and toys, hobbies, things to own, school subjects, people, occupations, and activities. The child responds *like, indifferent,* or *dislike* to each of the 250 items. A review of this instrument recommends its usefulness as a checklist for item-by-item study but not as a scored measuring instrument.[85]

**What I Like to Do: An Inventory of Children's Interests.** This inventory is designed for use with children in grades four through seven.[86] Like most other inventories of this type, What I Like to Do lacks validity, and its norms are questionable. The perusal by teachers of item responses rather than scores is suggested. On the inventory, children indicate what they would like to do, would not like to do, or neither like nor dislike to do for 294 items that deal with art, music, social studies, active play, quiet play, manual arts, home arts, and science.

**IT Scale for Children.** This is a self-report semiprojective inventory for children five to six years of age.[87] It measures *sex-role preferences* of young children. "It," a figure drawing of indeterminate sex, is shown, and the child selects toys that "It" would like to play with from among thirty-six pictures of toys (each of which is stereotyped masculine or feminine one).

## CHAPTER NOTES

1. L. E. Tyler and W. B. Walsh, *Tests and Measurements,* 3rd ed. (Englewood Cliffs, N.J.: Prentice-Hall, 1979).
2. American Psychological Association, *Standards for Educational and Psychological Tests and Manuals* (Washington, D. C.: American Psychological Association, 1974).
3. O. K. Buros, ed., *Tests in Print: II* (Highland Park, N.J.: Gryphon, 1974).
4. O. K. Buros, ed., *The Eighth Mental Measurements Yearbook* (Highland Park, N.J.: Gryphon, 1978).
5. B. A. Goldman and J. L. Saunders, *Directory of Unpublished Experimental Mental Measures,* vol. 1 (New York: Behavioral Publications, 1974).
   B. A. Goldman and J. C. Busch, *Directory of Unpublished Experimental Mental Measures,* vol. 2 (New York: Human Sciences Press, 1978).
   W. L. Goodwin and L. A. Driscoll, *Handbook for Measurement and Evaluation in Early Childhood Education* (San Francisco: Jossey-Bass, 1980).
   R. Hoepfner, C. Stern, and S. G. Nummedal, eds., *CSE-ECRC Preschool/Kindergarten Test Evaluations* (Palo Alto, Calif.: Consulting Psychologists Press, 1971).
   R. Hoepfner et al., eds., *CSE Elementary School Test Evaluations* (Palo Alto, Calif.: Consulting Psychologists Press, 1971).
   O. G. Johnson and J. W. Bommarito, eds., *Tests and Measurements in Child Development: A Handbook* (San Francisco: Jossey-Bass, 1971).
   O. G. Johnson, *Tests and Measurements in Child Development: Handbook II,* vols. 1-2 (San Francisco: Jossey-Bass, 1976).
   D. K. Walker, *Socioemotional Measures for Preschool and Kindergarten Children* (San Francisco: Jossey-Bass, 1973).
   R. H. Woody, *Encyclopedia of Clinical Assessment,* 2 vols. (San Francisco: Jossey-Bass, 1980).
6. H. E. Garrett, *Statistics in Psychology and Education,* 6th ed. (New York: McKay, 1966).
7. American Psychological Association, *Standards for Educational and Psychological Tests and Manuals* (Washington, D. C.: American Psychological Association, 1966).
8. American Psychological Association, "Technical Recommendations for Psychological Tests and Diagnostic Techniques," *Psychological Bulletin* 51 (1954): 201-38, supplement.
9. Johnson and Bommarito, *Tests and Measurements.*
10. S. B. Sarason, *Anxiety in Elementary School Children: A Report of Research* (New York: Wiley, 1960).
11. F. N. Kerlinger, *Foundations of Behavioral Research* (New York: Holt, Rinehart and Winston, 1964).
12. C. Selltiz et al., *Research Methods in Social Relations* (New York: Holt, Rinehart and Winston, 1966).
13. W. A. Mehrens and I. J. Lehmann, *Measurement and Evaluation in Education and Psychology* (New York: Holt, Rinehart and Winston, 1975).
14. Ibid.
15. L. P. Thorpe, W. W. Clark, and E. W. Tiegs, *California Test of Personality* (Monterey, Calif.: McGraw-Hill, 1953).

16. Mehrens and Lehmann, *Measurement and Evaluation.*
17. L. M. Terman and M. A. Merrill, *Stanford-Binet Intelligence Scale: Manual for the Third Revision, Form L-M* (Boston: Houghton-Mifflin, 1960).
18. L. J. Cronbach, *Essentials of Psychological Testing,* 3rd ed. (New York: Harper and Row, 1970), p. 202.
19. F. G. Brown, *Principles of Educational and Psychological Testing* (Hinsdale, Ill.: Dryden, 1970), p. 325.
20. Ibid., p. 325.
21. R. L. Thorndike, "Mr. Binet's Test 70 Years Later," *Educational Researcher* 4 (1975): 3-7.
22. Buros, *Eighth Mental Measurements Yearbook,* vol. I.
23. D. Wechsler, *Wechsler Intelligence Scale for Children* (New York: Psychological Corp., 1974).
    K. L. Hobby, *Wechsler Intelligence Scale for Children Profile Form* (Jacksonville, Ill.: Psychologists and Educators, 1974).
24. D. Wechsler, *Wechsler Preschool and Primary Scale of Intelligence* (New York: Psychological Corp., 1967).
25. J. C. Nunnally, *Introduction to Psychological Measurement* (New York: McGraw-Hill, 1970).
26. Ibid.
27. A. Gesell and C. S. Amatruda, *Gesell Developmental Schedules* (New York: Psychological Corp., 1949).
28. Buros, *Eighth Mental Measurements Yearbook,* vol. I.
29. N. Bayley, *Bayley Scales of Infant Development* (New York: Psychological Corp., 1969).
30. Buros, *Eighth Mental Measurements Yearbook,* vol. I.
31. P. Cattell, *Cattell Infant Intelligence Scale* (New York: Psychological Corp., 1960).
32. Buros, *Eighth Mental Measurements Yearbook,* p. 296.
33. H. H. Corman and S. K. Escalona, "Stages of Sensorimotor Development: A Replication Study," *Merrill-Palmer Quarterly* 15 (1969): 351-61.
34. P. McReynolds, *Advances in Psychological Assessment* (San Francisco: Jossey-Bass, 1975).
35. I. C. Uzgiris and J. McV. Hunt, *Toward Ordinal Scales of Psychological Development in Infancy* (Champaign, Ill.: University of Illinois Press, 1974).
36. McReynolds, *Psychological Assessment.*
37. F. Goodenough and M. J. Van Wagenen, *Minnesota Preschool Scale: Forms A and F,* rev. ed. (Minneapolis: Educational Test Bureau, 1940).
38. Nunnally, *Psychological Measurement.*
39. Ibid.
40. R. Stutzman, *Guide for Administering the Merrill-Palmer Scale of Mental Tests* (New York: Harcourt, 1931).
41. F. L. Goodenough, *Measurement of Intelligence by Drawings* (Chicago: World Book Co., 1926).
42. Nunnally, *Psychological Measurement.*
43. R. Pintner, B. V. Cunningham, and W. N. Durost, *Pintner Cunningham Primary Test* (New York: Harcourt Brace Jovanovich, 1966).
44. I. Lorge and R. L. Thorndike, *The Lorge-Thorndike Intelligence Tests* (Boston: Houghton Mifflin, 1957).
45. E. A. Fleishman, "The Description and Prediction of Perceptual-Motor Skill Learning," in *Training, Research and Education,* ed. R. Glaser (Pittsburgh: University of Pittsburgh Press, 1962), pp. 137-76.
46. Cronbach, *Essentials.*
47. A. S. Bryant and L. B. Schwan, "Art and the Mentally Retarded Child," *Studies in Art Education* 12 (1971): 50-63.
    A. S, Bryant and L. B. Schwan, *Bryant-Schwan Design Test* (Mankato, Minn.: Campus Publishers, 1973).
48. G. C. Helmstadter, *Taylor-Helmstadter Paired Comparison Scale of Aesthetic Judgment* (Tempe, Ariz., Arizona State University, 1973).
    A. P. Taylor and G. C. Helmstadter, "A Preliminary Pair Comparison Test for Measuring Aesthetic Judgment in Young Children" (Paper presented at the annual meeting of the American Educational Research Association, New York, 1971).
49. Johnson, *Tests and Measurements,* pp. 277-78.
50. B. Ghiselin, *The Creative Process* (Berkeley: Regents of the University of California, 1952).
51. N. H. Compton, "Creativity—A Way of Life," *Canadian Home Economics Journal* 17 (1967): 3-7.
52. E. P. Torrance, *Creativity* (Washington, D. C.: National Education Association, Research Pamphlet Series, April 1963).
53. Compton, "Creativity."
54. Torrance, *Creativity.*
55. E. P. Torrance, *Torrance Tests of Creative Thinking* (Princeton, N.J.: Personnel Press, 1966).
56. Ibid.
57. Cronbach, *Essentials.*
58. G. S. Welsh and F. Barron, *Barron-Welsh Art Scale* (Palo Alto, Calif.: Consulting Psychologists Press, 1963).
59. H. G. Gough and A. B. Heilbrun, *Manual for the Adjective Check List* (Palo Alto, Calif.: Consulting Psychologists Press, 1965).
60. Compton, "Creativity."
61. M. A. Wallach and N. Kogan, "A New Look at the Creativity-Intelligence Distinction," *Journal of Personality* 33 (1965): 348-69.
62. Ibid.
63. L. E. Tyler and W. B. Walsh, *Tests and Measurements.*
64. G. W. Allport, *Personality, A Psychological Interpretation* (New York: Holt, 1937).
65. F. N. Kerlinger, *Foundations of Behavioral Research,* 2nd ed. (New York: Holt, Rinehart & Winston, 1973).
66. R. B. Cattell, *The Scientific Analysis of Personality* (Chicago: Aldine, 1966), p. 28.
67. H. J. Eysenck, *The Structure of Human Personality* (New York: John Wiley, 1953).
68. L. P. Thorpe, W. W. Clark, and W. Tiegs, *California Test of Personality.*
69. R. B. Cattell and R. B. Porter, *Children's Personality Questionnaire* (Champaign, Ill.: Institute for Personality and Ability Testing, 1975).
70. R. W. Coan and R. B. Cattell, *Early School Personality Questionnaire* (Champaign, Ill.: Institute for Personality and Ability Testing, 1976).
71. M. F. Grapko, *Institute of Child Study Security Test* (Toronto: Guidance Center, 1968).
72. H. J. Eysenck and S. B. Eysenck, *Eysenck Personality Questionnaire* (San Diego: Educational and Industrial Testing Service, 1975-76).
73. Buros, *Eighth Mental Measurements Yearbook,* p. 814.
74. H. H. Remmers and R. H. Bauernfeind, *STS Junior Inventory* (Bensenville, Ill.: Scholastic Testing Service, 1972).
75. O. K. Buros, ed., *The Fifth Mental Measurements Yearbook* (Highland Park, N.J.: Gryphon, 1959).
76. H. A. Witkin et al., *Embedded Figures Test* (Palo Alto, Calif.: Consulting Psychologists Press, 1971).
77. S. Karp and N. Konstadt, *Children's Embedded Figures Test* (Palo Alto, Calif.: Consulting Psychologists Press, 1971).
78. H. Witkin, "Development of the Body Concept and Psychological Differentiation," in *Body Percept,* eds., S. Wapner and H. Werner, (New York: Random House, 1965).
79. V. Shipman, *ETS Locus of Control Scale* (Princeton, N.J.: Educational Testing Service, 1968).
80. B. R. Brown, *Brown IDS Self-Concept Referents Test* (Bethesda, Md.: ERIC Document Reproduction Service, 1966).
81. H. Cantril and G. W. Allport, "Recent Applications of the Study of Values," *Journal of Abnormal and Social Psychology* 28 (1933): 259-73.
82. M. R. Yarrow, "The Measurement of Children's Attitudes and Values," in *Handbook of Research in Child Development,* ed. P.H. Mussen (New York: Wiley, 1960), pp. 645-687.
83. M. E. Goodman, *Race Awareness in Young Children* (Cambridge, Mass.: Addison-Wesley, 1952).
84. M. Dreese and E. Mooney, *Interest Inventory for Elementary Grades* (Washington, D. C.: George Washington University Center for Psychological Service, 1941).
85. L. J. Cronbach, "Interest Inventory for Elementary Grades," in *Third Mental Measurements Yearbook,* ed. O. K. Buros (New Brunswick, N.J.: Rutgers University Press, 1949).
86. L. P. Thorpe, C. E. Meyers, and M. R. Sea, *What I Like To Do: An Inventory of Children's Interests* (Chicago: Science Research Associates, 1958).
87. D. G. Brown, *IT Scale for Children* (Missoula, Mont.: Psychological Tests Specialists, 1956).

# 8

# Self-report Methods: Interviews and Questionnaires

## THE INTERVIEW

A dictionary definition of *interview* is "a meeting of persons face to face, especially for the purpose of formal conference on some point." It is a conversation with a purpose. The man who was surprised to learn that he had been speaking prose all his life would likely be just as surprised to learn that he had been interviewing all his life.[1] The interview is a face-to-face method of verbal communication in which one person, the interviewer, asks another person, the respondent, questions designed to elicit information or opinions. Interviews may be placed on a continuum from a very informal discussion to a very structured research interview.

Among the major advantages of an interview is the possibility of obtaining information that very likely could not, or would not, be obtained by any other method. For example, a person might be willing to talk about certain family problems on which he or she would not wish to comment in writing. A person may be willing to spend more time giving information when he or she has direct personal contact than when asked to take time to complete a questionnaire. In some instances, the personal contact encourages cooperation from persons who might neglect to respond to a questionnaire.

An interview provides more flexibility in obtaining information than the self-administered questionnaire provides. It may yield more accurate information and greater depth of response than could be obtained through a questionnaire. This is particularly true in regard to children and respondents who are poorly educated or from a low socioeconomic area. These people might have difficulty reading or understanding the questions, or they may not be able to express themselves clearly. An interview can be adapted to the level of understanding of the interviewee. The interviewer can clarify by repeating or rephrasing questions, follow up leads in responses, or probe more deeply to obtain a clear picture of the interviewee's ideas. However, in so doing, the interviewer must be careful not to influence the respondent's answer.

An interview permits greater control regarding the sequence of questions than a questionnaire. Since questions are hidden from the respondent during an interview, later questions cannot affect earlier replies. Moreover, the respondent cannot consult with someone else about how to answer a question.

### FUNCTIONS OF THE INTERVIEW

The main function of an interview is to elicit facts about the individual being interviewed. Lawyers, doctors, psychologists, social caseworkers, counselors, teachers, employers, and researchers are all concerned with getting information from their clients, patients, students, employees, or research subjects through interviews.

A treatment or therapeutic interview is usually initiated by the respondent (or parent or teacher of a child) for the purpose of obtaining relief for a problem or a therapeutic change. Counseling and psychiatric interviews are of this type. The respondent gives facts or information to the interviewer (e.g., counselor, psychiatrist), and, in turn, the respondent should receive support and insight from the interviewer as a "treatment" or "therapy." Therapeutic interviewing is a highly specialized interpersonal transaction.

Job applicants and students seeking college admission are often subjected to interviews to determine their qualifications for specific jobs or programs. Interviews also are conducted by teachers or job supervisors for the purpose of evaluating or appraising performances of students or subordinates on the job.

The interview is one method of collecting data for research purposes. The questions for such an interview are usually highly structured to meet the objectives of the research project for description, explanation, or prediction. The respondent provides information for use by the researcher in carrying out his or her project objectives.

## QUESTIONNAIRES

The term *questionnaire* refers to any kind of instrument that has items or questions to which individuals respond directly. The questionnaire format is usually associated with self-administered instruments that are composed of items of a closed- or fixed-alternative type. Questionnaires are either handed to subjects or mailed to them. In either case, a minimum of explanation is given. The respondent can take as much time as necessary to think about his or her answers without feeling pressure to respond. Since the questionnaire is an impersonal instrument with standardized instructions and wording, it may include items relating to unusual or personal kinds of activities more freely than is possible in an interview. Moreover, there may be less desire on the part of a questionnaire respondent than an interviewee to try to impress the investigator. The questionnaire is less expensive and requires less skill to administer than the interview. Also, it can provide anonymity of respondents and can be administered to a large group simultaneously.

Among the limitations of questionnaires are the diversity of meaning that may be attributed to a question by various respondents, the amount of education that may be required of a person in order to understand the questions and procedures, the difficulty of securing valid personal or confidential information, and the uncertainty of whether an adequate number of responses will be received to represent the population. Obviously, self-administered questionnaires cannot be used with young children. For this reason, the interview will be the self-report method of emphasis in this chapter.

## VALIDITY OF SELF-REPORT

Self-administered questionnaires and interviews are often used simply for gathering facts. However, both are also time-honored assessment methods and should be used to test hypotheses and to study relations between variables. In this respect, they become measuring instruments subject to the same criteria of reliability and validity as other measuring instruments.

Walsh compared the accuracy of the interview and the questionnaire for collecting data that are, in principle, verifiable.[2] The sample consisted of 300 female and 240 male college students. One control group of students provided personal information by interview and another control group responded by questionnaire. Two experimental groups (one for each method) were given a social incentive to distort their self-reports. Two other experimental groups were given a social and financial incentive to distort their reports. The validity of the students' self-reports was determined by university records. Findings indicated that for seven of the eight questions for female subjects and for six of the eight questions for male subjects, one method of self-report did not elicit more accurate information than the other. Both interview and questionnaire methods yielded generally valid biographical information for items such as number of courses failed, quarter hours completed, and overall cumulative grade point average. However, for the females the interview yielded more accurate self-report information than the questionnaire for the question: How many quarters have you been on academic probation? For male subjects the questionnaire method yielded more accurate self-report for this question as well as for the question: What was your previous quarter grade point average?

## USE OF THE INTERVIEW AT DIFFERENT AGE LEVELS

Developmental factors must be taken into account when considering the use of the interview technique. Because of its dependence on language, motivation, and interpersonal relationships, the interview is not generally used with children under six years of age. However, a few researchers have attained positive results from interviewing preschool children. Radke compared direct interview reports of superior children just under four years of age with those of their parents on parental roles and control techniques. The degree of correspondence was high.[3] Ammons combined a verbal interview with doll play to study racial awareness in children two through five years of age. There was a high percentage of refusals to respond among two-year-olds but above this age the interview appeared applicable.[4] Based upon his review of the research evidence, Yarrow suggests that the direct interview can be used effectively with four-year-olds. Below this age, special adaptations of the conventional interviews can be used, such as picture choice and doll play.[5] These special adaptations will be discussed later in this chapter.

In psychiatry, the structured interview is extensively used with adult patients for clinical and research purposes. In child psychiatry, instruments that ask questions about children have been developed for use with parents, teachers, and other adults. One study attempted to determine the reliability of children as reporters.[6] The study was conducted in an attempt to develop an interview for collecting data directly from children in a mental health clinic. The researchers interviewed fifty children, ranging in age from six to sixteen years, and their mothers using a structured interview similar to the usual psychiatric examination of a child. An 80 percent average agreement was found between the children's and mothers' answers on all questions. Also girls were found to be more reliable informants than boys. The researchers concluded that children are reliable reporters and that the use of a structured interview with children is worthy of further study.

Two other researchers studied the reliability and validity of the psychiatric assessment of a child through the interview technique.[7] In the study, the psychiatric assessment or diagnosis concerned *whether* the child had any psychiatric disorder and *what* was the nature of the disorder. Psychiatric disorder was defined as abnormalities of emotions, behavior, or relationships that were developmentally inappropriate and of sufficient duration and severity to cause persistent suffering or handicap to the child and/or distress or disturbance of the family or community. Test-retest reliability and interrater reliability were sufficiently high. Validity was determined by comparing findings of half-hour interviews that were conducted with children aged nine and ten years from a "normal" population and with children regarded as having significant psychiatric disorder on the basis of information from parents and teachers. These short psychiatric interviews with the children were found to be sufficiently senstive diagnostic instruments to give rise to reliable and valid judgments on whether a child exhibits any psychiatric disorder, although depression proved to be more difficult than anxiety to rate reliably. Also, it still might be questioned whether a psychiatric interview with a child can add anything to the diagnostic process that cannot be better obtained from a parent's or teacher's accounts of the child. The researchers believe their findings provide a very tentative answer that a child's emotional responsiveness and interpersonal relationships can be better evaluated by a psychiatric interview with the child.

## INTERPERSONAL RELATIONS AND INTERVIEW SETTING

In an interview there is always interactions between people. The interviewer and the person being interviewed are talking to and affecting each other. Any interview has both formal and informal elements. The most common error made by the untrained interviewer is to observe only the formalities and to lose sight of the personal interactions—the informalities.[8]

The primary advantage of using the interview over the more impersonal personality inventory or attitude questionnaire is the assistance that the personal relationship provides in the communication process. Therefore, in planning for use of the interview, it is important to set the stage to facilitate the communication process. Yarrow offers some good suggestions for interviews with children.[9]

The key to successful communication in interviews with children is to build rapport by establishing a common ground with the child. The child will not communicate if he or she is hampered by fear, suspicion, or hostility. Nonverbal communication plays a part in establishing an atmosphere before the formal verbal part of the interview begins. If the building, the interview room, and the interviewer's appearance resemble a schoollike situation, the child gets a different message than from a setting with a homelike atmosphere. The child should be allowed sufficient time to become familiar with the physical setting prior to the interview. A quiet room that suggests privacy should facilitate the interview process best. The seating arrangement also should foster rapport and communication. A different expectation is created when a desk separates the interviewer from the child than when they are seated side by side. However, children sometimes feel more comfortable in a strange situation if they are seated at a table with paper and crayons. Play materials may put small children at ease.

The interviewer should explain the nature of the interview and roles to be played within it to the child. The relationship between the interviewer and child in a therapeutic interview is different from that in a research interview. The research interview often consists of only one meeting with the child, whereas therapeutic and counseling interviews often extend over months or years. In the treatment or therapeutic interview, the child receives support or insights into his or her problems from the interviewer. In a research interview, the purpose of the information supplied by the child is to meet the research objectives of the interviewer. It is important to explain purposes to a child in language that he or she understands: "We want to hear the different ideas that six-year-old-girls have about this."

The sex of the interviewer is believed to influence rapport and responses, particularly during middle childhood and adolescence. The social code for boys in the latency period requires overt rejection of girls and women. Some studies show that women analysts work with success with boys in this period in child therapy, whereas others report that ten-year-old boys did not respond as well to a female as to a male therapist. Therefore, Yarrow suggests that boys' difficulty in relating to a woman in an interview situation is not universal and undoubtedly is modified by the specific experiences of the child.

Interviews that probe feelings, attitudes, and other personal orientations require deeper relationships and sensitivity than those focusing primarily on the collection of factual information.

## INTERVIEWING TECHNIQUES—METHODOLOGY

Interviewing is an art that consists largely of creating a situation in which the respondents will be cooperative and honest. We have already described the importance of the physical setting and rapport between interviewer and respondent. Special skills in social relations are needed to convey a genuine liking and acceptance of the child and at the same time to maintain a sense of neutrality and objectivity.[10] Successful interviewing therefore requires two contradictory attitudes:

1. Empathy, in which the interviewer feels the same emotion as the child.

2. Detached and scientific objectivity that enables him to recognize the emotion and not be swamped by it.[11]

Once the setting and the rapport for the interview have been established, the interviewer's tasks are to ask the questions properly to obtain accurate responses and to record the responses carefully. A detailed discussion of interviewer training is beyond the scope of this book.

## INTERVIEW APPROACHES

Interviews vary with respect to the degree of their standardization, the directiveness of the interviewer, and the structure of the questions used in the interview.[12] In a *standardized interview* the questions are fixed, having been formulated prior to the interview. The sequence and manner of presentation to respondents are also fixed. Carefully prepared interview schedules are normally used. In an *unstandardized or free interview* suggested topics may be outlined which are geared by the interviewer to the language of the respondent at appropriate times during the interview. This form of interview is desirable for use with children. Ordinarily no interview schedules are used.

The amount of direction or degree of control exercised by the interviewer can also vary. A very *directive interview* is comparable to a questionnaire in that the interviewer keeps complete control of content areas and directs responses to keep them within the prescribed structure. The *nondirective interview* is better suited to children. In this type of interview, the interviewer may simply open up an area of discussion and follow the child's lead in the direction of the topic.

The questions asked in an interview vary in degree of structure. Possible variations range from a highly *structured question* in which both the stimulus and the response frameworks are structured to the *unstructured question* in which both stimulus and response are ambiguous. This is Yarrow's schematized example of structured and unstructured questions based on a doll-play interview with four- and five-year-old children in regard to mother-child relationships.[13]

### Possible Variations in Structure of Interview Questions

| Stimulus Framework | Response Framework |
| --- | --- |
| **Structured** | **Open** |
| Example: "This little boy is busy playing and his mother stops him and says it's time to go to bed." | "What does he say?" |
| **Structured** | **Structured** |
| Example: "If this little boy is busy playing and his mother stops him and says it's time to go to bed." | "Does he get mad or does he say, All right mother?" |
| **Open** | **Open** |
| Example: "This little boy is playing and his mother comes in." | "Let's make up a story about what she says to him and what he says to her." |
| **Open** | **Structured** |
| Example: "This little boy is busy playing and his mother comes in." | "Does the boy ask his mother to play with him or does he just go on playing as if his mother was not there?"[14] |

Highly structured questions are most suitable for very specific topics such as a child's feelings about mealtime, but less structure is desirable in probing broader topics such as a child's relationship to his or her mother. However, at the youngest age levels, children need some structure within which to focus their limited language.

Piaget expresses the problem facing the interviewer of children:

> It is so hard not to talk too much when questioning a child, especially for a ped-
> agogue! It is so hard not to be suggestive! And above all, it is so hard to find the
> middle course between systematisation due to preconceived ideas and incoherence
> due to the absence of any directing hypothesis! The good experimenter must, in
> fact, unite two often incompatible qualities; he must know how to observe, that is
> to say, to let the child talk freely, without ever checking or sidetracking his ut-
> terance, and at the same time he must constantly be alert for something defin-
> itive; at every moment he must have some working hypothesis, some theory,
> true or false, which he is seeking to check. When students begin, they either suggest
> to the child all they hope to find, or they suggest nothing at all, because they are
> not on the look-out for anything, in which case, to be sure, they will never find
> anything.[15]

## CONSTRUCTION OF INTERVIEW SCHEDULES

**Pretesting.** A good deal of study and practice is required to produce a good interview schedule. Even with adults, multiple meanings and ambiguity of words present problems. No matter how astute the researcher or interviewer may be in wording the questions, he or she should try out the questions and procedures on a small scale before conducting an actual interview. Such *pretesting* helps to eliminate unclear or anxiety-arousing questions and to determine whether the questions elicit the kind of responses desired for the objectives of the interview. Pretesting should be conducted on a population similar to that to be used in the full-scale interview. To develop a schedule for inter-viewing preschool children, considerable pretesting comparable to the type used by Piaget may be necessary.[16] Piagetian pretesting methods begin with a detailed recording of the spontaneous conver-sation of children in situations arranged to elicit verbal comments on the subject being studied. Questions for an interview schedule are then formulated on the basis of the children's own vocab-ulary. Next, the interview schedule developed by this procedure is subjected to pretesting to de-termine such factors as the children's comprehension of the questions and the quality of rapport established with the children.

**Interview Questions.** Yarrow suggests three considerations in the formulation of interview questions for children:

1. The question should be readily understood by the child.

2. The meaning or interpretation of the question should not vary significantly from one child to another.

3. The form of the question should not "lead" the child to a given response.[17]

Ammons's study of racial awareness in children provided some suggestions for interview questions. Questions that called for *yes* or *no* answers or a choice between concrete alternatives like *white* or *colored* usually resulted in responses. The highest rate of refusals to answer was to open-ended questions. Children also responded more easily to questions about their *actions* than to questions about what they would *say*.[18]

It is also important when interviewing children, as well as adults, to make the respondent feel comfortable in expressing ideas on behavior that may be socially undesirable. For example, questions may be worded to suggest that other children may have similar feelings: "Some girls like to let other children play with their toys. Other girls don't like to do this. How do you feel about it?"

The order in which questions are presented influences rapport as well as accuracy of response. The opening questions are important in establishing rapport and should be ones the child can answer easily and without embarrassment. More difficult questions should not be introduced until rapport is established.

In developing interview schedules for children, special consideration should be given to limiting the total time of the interview to fit the child's attention span. The spacing of questions to provide variety will help reduce boredom and fatigue, however the number of topics introduced in a single interview should be limited.

This imaginary interview was prepared by Rich to illustrate good interview technique:

> Twelve-year-old Frank has been referred to the school psychologist because he is working below his capacity. They are already well into the interview and the child has relaxed and is talking quite freely. The relationships at home appear good, and Frank spends his spare time in the usual pursuits of his age and culture.
>
> *Psychologist:* Let me see now, you have a younger brother, David, haven't you? Isn't he in grade three?
>
> *Frank:* Yes, he wants to be a chemist.
>
> There is a note of scorn in this remark, and the psychologist picks it up.
>
> *Psychologist:* It sounds as if you don't think he'll make it.
>
> *Frank:* You've got to be pretty good to be a chemist, and he is only average.
>
> This sounds like sibling rivalry and could be highly relevant, so the psychologist casts around to see what will come up.
>
> *Psychologist:* Do you have any other brothers and sisters?
>
> He knows the answer to this question, but he wants to see what Frank will do with it.
>
> *Frank:* Yes, there's Annette—she's married—and then there's Geoffrey.
>
> Again there was a slight change in his expression as he mentioned his older brother, and it is necessary to find out why.
>
> *Psychologist:* What does Geoffrey do?
>
> *Frank:* He's a chemist.
>
> *Psychologist:* Oh. Is that where David got the idea from?
>
> *Frank:* Yes.
>
> *Psychologist:* What do you want to do when you leave school?
>
> *Frank:* Oh, I guess I'll work in a shop or something.
>
> The pattern is now beginning to fall into place. The highly successful older brother is being held up at home as a model that the younger boy should emulate, and Frank feels so far inferior to him that he is giving up in despair. Further questioning is needed to confirm this impression and to find out whether the source of the comparison is Father or Mother or Geoffrey.
>
> *Psychologist:* What does your dad want you to be?
>
> *Frank:* Oh, I don't know.
>
> *Psychologist:* And your mother, does she have any ideas?

*Frank:* Oh, she doesn't mind.

He answered the first question in a very offhand manner and the second with some relief. It was evident that he was evading the first and covering up. It had already been established that the relationship between Frank and his father was good, so it would appear that there was friction only in this one area.

*Psychologist:* Does your father put a lot of store by education, or does he think other things are just as important?

This is a simple multiple-choice question that does not imply that Father ought to think one way or the other, so Frank is free to answer.

*Frank:* I guess he sets a lot of store by education.

*Psychologist:* What do you feel about it?

*Frank:* Oh, yes, they're always telling you in the papers about school dropouts not being able to get work and all that.

By now it is evident that Frank would like to do better in school, and the psychologist risks summing up what the boy has been hinting at, but not quite saying.

*Psychologist:* When you've got an older brother who's done well, it's pretty tough to come along afterwards, isn't it?

*Frank:* (who has been sitting very still and tense during the previous few remarks, suddenly relaxes and grins) It sure is.

The feeling he puts into these few words and the sudden relaxation of his body both confirm the tentative diagnosis of the situation.[19]

## RECORDING RESPONSES AND ANALYZING INTERVIEW RESULTS

Responses should be recorded accurately at the time they are made either through tape recording or detailed notes made by the interviewer. There are differences of opinion regarding the use of a tape recorder. It is often more inhibiting to the interviewer than to the child, especially if the tape is to be played to the interviewer's colleagues at a later time. With either recording or note taking, a simple statement like "I am writing down (or recording) some of your ideas so I won't forget them" should be made to the child. Ethical and confidential aspects of these procedures will be discussed in Chapter 12—"Ethical Guidelines for Child Study."

In addition to a verbatim record of the interview, attention should be given to the child's behavior before and after the interview. Sometimes when a child believes the interview is over he will talk about things he refused to discuss earlier. The interviewer should also record descriptions of the child's physical appearance, posture, gestures, movements, and changes in expression (his nonverbal communication). Spontaneous actions of children often take the place of spontaneous remarks made by adults, and special notes should be made of these actions.

Before data are collected through an interview, consideration should be given to the method of analysis because the manner in which responses are recorded affects analyzation. If simple yes or no or approve-disapprove answers are required by the questions, these responses are recorded in their simple categories and can be analyzed quantitatively in terms of the frequencies with which the responses occur. Data can be pooled easily for different children and norms established. However, qualitative data acquired through responses to open-ended questions require the setting up of special categories and coding prior to quantitative statistical analysis.

Many factors can influence the accuracy of interview data, such as the personality and skills of the interviewer, the interview setting, and numerous factors that relate to the respondent like motivation, memory, language skills, and emotions. Therefore, the interview should be regarded as only one part of the study of a child. In assessing the results of an interview for an individual child, consistent patterns should be looked for as well as contradictions in the child's responses and behavior. Are the child's behavior and actions during the interview consistent with his or her verbal responses? Does the child keep returning to the same topics? Does the child evade or refuse to answer some questions?

Used in conjunction with the observational approach to child study, the interview is valuable because it permits the exploration of children's wishes, attitudes, fears, and other subjective phenomena not available through direct observation. The interview's ultimate value, however, is dependent upon the interviewer's knowledge of theories of child development and his or her ability to apply them in relating to children.

## SPECIAL ADAPTATIONS OF INTERVIEW TECHNIQUES

A number of adaptations to conventional interview techniques have been made to meet the needs, motivations, interests, and language limitations of children. These adaptations vary from the use of visual aids to the combination of the interview with direct observations in natural settings to combinations with various projective techniques such as story and sentence completion and doll play. Since projective techniques will be discussed in Chapter 9, they will not be covered in detail here.

### VISUAL AIDS IN INTERVIEWING

Visual aids in the form of photographs, line drawings, dolls, and other items are sometimes introduced in an interview as a substitute for verbal statements; the respondent is asked to react to the visual aid. The most common use of this approach has been in studies of racial awareness or attitudes of young children. Horowitz developed several approaches with pictures and photographs for these studies.[20] White and brown dolls have been used in similar work by Clark and Clark[21] and by Goodman.[22] Visual aids also have been valuable in introducing topics about which people are reluctant to discuss when questioned directly.

One researcher conducted a study to determine the relative effectiveness of a strictly verbal interview in comparison to one using photographs. He found that respondents showed much greater interest and gave more information in the interviews using photographs.[23]

Dolls are often used effectively with young children in conjunction with the verbal interview. As Yarrow points out, the distinction between "projective" doll play and the doll-play interview is not a sharp one.[24] Doll play has been extensively used in clinical therapy with children. David Levy is credited with being the first to use the technique in his research on sibling rivalry. The experimenter creates a series of problem situations by manipulating the dolls, states each problem verbally, and probes the child's reactions to the situations.[25] Ammons's use of doll play with verbal interviews was mentioned earlier in this chapter. Radke and Trager combined a variation of the doll-play interview with a multiple-choice technique in studying social role perceptions of five- to eight-year old children.[26] They used a series of plywood formboards with cutout figures of white and black adults. The children dressed the forms in "dress-up," "work," and "shabby" clothes and were asked what a man would be doing if he were wearing those clothes, which he liked best, and why. They were also asked to tell stories about the forms. A similar interview was conducted with cutouts of two kinds of houses, a "good" house and a "poor" house.

The primary advantage of visual aids in interviewing is in maintaining the interest of the child, thereby increasing his or her willingness to respond.

## THE LIFE-SPACE INTERVIEW

The life-space interview, developed by Fritz Redl through his research and therapy with disturbed delinquent children, is a variation of the standard interview. The life-space interview is structured around the child's direct life experience in connection with the issues that become the focus of the interview. The child is interviewed immediately after the occurrence of an incident. Usually the interviewer is someone who is part of the child's "natural habitat or life space." The two major categories of goals and tasks established for life-space interviewing are (1) clinical exploitation of life events and (2) emotional first aid on the spot. Essentially, the life-space interview is "making use of a momentary life experience in order to draw out of it something that might be of use for long-range therapeutic goals."[27]

## INTERVIEW INSTRUMENTS FOR USE WITH CHILDREN

*Socioemotional Measures for Preschool and Kindergarten Children* is "a comprehensive guide to all socioemotional measures available for use with children aged three to six."[28] As its author points out, most of the self-report measures used with children are semiprojective, with the children being asked to respond to pictures or drawings. Interviews combine self-report measures with observational and rating techniques. These are some of the interview instruments that are described in the book:

*Ammons Doll-Play Interview.* Situational, semistructured doll-play interview. Measures interracial feelings and attitudes.

*Clark Doll Test–Revised.* Situational, structured doll-play interview. Measures racial attitudes, racial cognition, and sense of racial identification.

*Child Nurturance-Control Scale.* Situational, structured doll-play interview. Measures a child's identification with his or her parents.

*Hartup Imitation Schedule.* Situational, structured doll-play interview. Measures a child's preference for the like-sex parent.

*Structured Doll-Play Interview (Dreger and Haupt).* Situational, structured doll-play interview; teacher questionnaire. Measures a child's evaluations of his or her competence.

*Stevenson and Stewart Racial Awareness Battery.* Situational, structured doll-play interview; incomplete stories. Measures a child's ability to discriminate among races.

*Morland Picture Interview.* Situational, partially structured picture interview. Measures four aspects of social awareness: racial acceptance, racial preference, racial self-identification, and racial cognition ability.

*Social Episodes Test (Radke, Yarrow, and Trager).* Situational, partially structured, semiprojective picture interview. Measures racial and ethnic attitudes.

*Self-Concept Interview (Fitzgibbon and Nimnicht).* Situational, partially structured picture interview. Measures self-concept with regard to school and to peers.

*Social Perception Interview (Estvan).* Situational, semiprojective picture interview. Measures children's social perceptions: rural and urban differences, upper-class and lower-class differences, and child-adult age differences.

*Sechrest's Structured Interview Schedule.* Situational, structured interview. Measures a child's attitudes toward his or her classroom teacher through the use of structured and open-ended questions.

# SOCIOMETRIC TECHNIQUES

## SOCIOMETRY DEFINED

The importance of social relations and social adjustment to the normal development of personality and to the learning process has long been recognized by educators and psychologists. This recognition resulted in the need for an objective approach to improved social relations in the school classroom. Sociometry has provided this approach. The term *sociometry* is a Latin derivative meaning "social or companion measurement." This type of measurement was originated by J. L. Moreno and designated by him as a sociometric test,[29] although it is not a test in the sense in which that term is usually understood. Moreno used the term to distinguish it from other methods that he developed in the general area of sociometry.

Sociometric studies ordinarily use questionnaires and interviews, although observational data and other kinds of records may be used for a sociometric analysis. In sociometry, an individual is usually asked to specify which other members of the group he or she would like to have as a companion in some activity (e.g., play with, study with). The individual is sometimes allowed to name as many people as he or she wishes, but more frequently is limited to naming a specific number. Occasionally the individual is asked also to name the people that he or she would least like or would not like to have as companions.

Gronlund's *Sociometry in the Classroom* offers many suggestions for use of the sociometric technique with children.[30] Some of these suggestions are summarized in this chapter.

## CRITERIA FOR USING THE SOCIOMETRIC TECHNIQUE

Since the sociometric test is an informal instrument usually designed by the person administering it, skill and understanding of the approach are important to the teacher or others using it. The more informal and less structured the measuring instrument, the more knowledge required in its use.

From the time Moreno developed the technique, he emphasized the importance of basing socio-metric choices on criteria reflecting an actual situation or activity in which the group members have an opportunity for participation. Because the situation is so important, sociometric tests are classified as *situational tests* rather than as rating scales. They are the most commonly used situational tests with younger children. Asking children questions such as "Whom do you like best?" or "Who are your best friends?" is not using the sociometric technique, for the situational criterion of choice is lacking. Asking children to choose others they would like to have as play companions, to study with, or to sit beside in school would meet the situational criterion.

The group of children to be tested should have sufficient opportunity to become acquainted with each other before the sociometric test is administered. This does not imply that each child must know every other child because research has indicated that the number of choices received on a sociometric test is not influenced by the number of group members known.

Group members should be assured of the confidentiality of their choices, especially if their choices differ widely from their actual associations.

After the situational criteria have been selected, the number of choices to be permitted for each criterion must be determined. This decision should be influenced by the age of the children and the stability of the results. With nursery school and kindergarten children, studies have indicated that there is little discrimination beyond the first choice. During the early elementary school years, three choices for each criterion are appropriate. Five choices can be made without difficulty from the third grade on. Research studies show that five choices provide the most stable sociometric results except for small children.

## TEST PROCEDURES

Individual interviews are needed in testing children below the fourth grade level but group testing is usually used above that level. The classroom teacher most often administers the test except in some research projects or in a school-wide testing program.

Figure 8.1 is an example of a sociometric instrument used at the later elementary school level. Note that the word *test* is not used in the instructions and that children are told what uses will be made of their choices.

---

Name _____   Date _____

During the next few weeks we will be changing our seats around, working in small groups and playing some group games. Now that we all know each other by name, you can help me arrange groups that work and play best together. You can do this by writing the names of the child you would like *to have sit near you, to have work with you,* and *to have play with you.* You may choose anyone in this room you wish, including those pupils who are absent. Your choices will not be seen by anyone else. Give first name and initial of last name.

Make your choices carefully so the groups will be the way you really want them. I will try to arrange the groups so that each pupil gets at least two of his choices. Sometimes it is hard to give everyone his first few choices so be sure to make five choices for each question.

*Remember!*

1. Your choices must be from pupils in this room, including those who are absent.
2. You should give the first name and the initial of the last name.
3. You should make all five choices for each question.
4. You may choose a pupil for more than one group if you wish.
5. Your choices will *not be seen* by anyone else.

I would choose to *sit near* these children:

1. _____   3. _____
2. _____   4. _____
                5. _____

I would choose to *work with* these children:

1. _____   3. _____
2. _____   4. _____
                5. _____

I would choose to *play with* these children:

1. _____   3. _____
2. _____   4. _____
                5. _____

---

**Figure 8.1.** Sociometric Form Used at Later Elementary School Level

## MODIFICATIONS FOR USE WITH YOUNG CHILDREN

A picture modification of Moreno's original sociometric technique was first made by Biehler to permit the use of the technique with young children.[31] Examples of picture sociometric techniques in which the child selects with whom he most wants to do something from a large board of pictures are presented in this section. These measures are also described in Walker's *Socioemotional Measures for Preschool and Kindergarten Children.*[32]

**McCandless-Marshall Sociometric Status Test.**[33] A board with pictures of each child in the preschool or kindergarten is presented to each child individually, and he or she names all children in the photos. Then the child points to or names the three children with whom he or she likes to play best in three different situations named by the tester (outside play, inside play, and listening to stories). Additional choices given by the child are also recorded and scored. This test is adapted from Biehler's technique.

**Dunnington Sociometric Status Test.**[34] In this sociometric interview the child is asked to select both the three children with whom he or she likes to play best and the three with whom he or she likes to play least. The child is then asked to respond yes or no to his or her desire to play with the remaining children.

**Minnesota Sociometric Status Test.**[35] This test combines the methods used by McCandless-Marshall and Dunnington. Each child is asked to point out on a picture board, in order of preference, four children whom he or she especially likes and four he or she does not like very much. The tester then determines if the child likes the remaining children.

## TEACHER JUDGMENT VERSUS SOCIOMETRIC STUDY

Observational techniques are of value in studying the interaction of groups of children. However, the internal structure of the group, measured by the sociometric test, and the external structure of the group, which provides the clues for teachers' judgments, are often quite different. Teachers are frequently surprised to discover that students they think are leaders are only moderately accepted by the group through sociometric measurement and that small groups of children who seem so close on the playground do not choose each other on the sociometric test. Gronlund states that the need for an objective measure of interpersonal relations in the social sphere is roughly equivalent to the need for an intelligence test in the academic area—that teachers' ability to judge the intelligence of their pupils is approximately equivalent to their ability to judge the sociometric status of their pupils.[36]

## USES AND LIMITATIONS OF THE SOCIOMETRIC TECHNIQUE

The sociometric technique may be used for these purposes and others: to improve the social adjustment of individual children, to organize or arrange children in groups, to improve the social structure of a group, and for action research.

The sociometric technique indicates the present social status of individuals and groups but does not indicate why they became that way nor what should be done to change the situation. However, the use of sociometric choices to identify interpersonal conflicts and to rearrange social groups may have therapeutic value for individual students and may improve the working effectiveness of various groups.

## ANALYZING, PRESENTING, AND INTERPRETING RESULTS

**The Sociogram.** Sociometry yields very simple scores—basically ones and zeros. Yet it can involve analysis at a high level of sophistication mathematically. These mathematical methods will not be

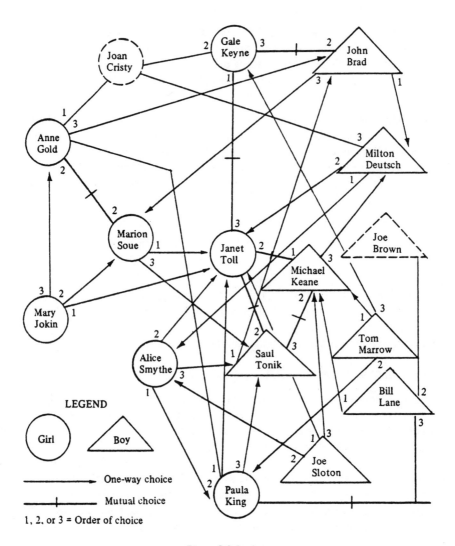

**Figure 8.2** Sociogram

discussed here. However, the type of analysis shown in Figure 8.2 in the form of a sociogram is frequently used, especially for practical purposes. The data plotted in this sociogram may be manipulated to describe several properties of group structure or to define an individual member's social relationships with other members of the group. Whenever a conceptual arrow from one person to another person can be drawn—with the arrow indicating interacts with, dominates, leads, likes, is friendly with, is like me, and so forth—sociometric methods have potential usefulness for observation and measurement of variables.

**Sociometric Terms.** The number of choices the individual receives in a sociometric test is called his or her *sociometric status, social status,* or *group status.* Other terms used in sociometric analysis are

>   *Star:* the individual who receives more choices than would be expected by chance

>   *Isolate:* individual who receives no choices

*Neglectee:* individual who is neglected by a majority of the group members (receives fewer choices than would be expected by chance)

*Rejectee:* individual who receives negative choices when respondents are asked to indicate those whom they would least prefer (negative choices are seldom used, however)

*Mutual choice:* two individuals choose each other on the same sociometric criterion (reciprocated choice or a pair)

*Sociometric clique:* a number of individuals choose each other on the same criterion and give relatively few choices of individuals outside the closely knit group

*Sociometric cleavage:* lack of sociometric choices between two or more subgroups (example: between sexes at the elementary school level when boys seldom choose girls and girls seldom choose boys)[37]

**Typical Patterns.** Sociometric results vary from one group to another, but certain phenomena occur with sufficient frequency to be considered typical sociometric patterns. One such pattern is the tendency for a larger percentage of children to appear in the low sociometric status than in the high status categories at all age levels, between both sexes, and over different sociometric criteria. Sociometric results at various grade levels indicate that between 11 and 22 percent of the pupils were neglected or ignored by their classmates.[38] Such results point to the need for assistance in improving social relations. Another pattern is the sex cleavage or preference of children for members of their own sex. An increase in mutual choices tends to occur during junior and senior high school.

**Caution in Interpretation.** The results of a sociometric test indicate current status of *desired* association, not *actual* relations among group members. Too often, a high sociometric status is interpreted to mean leadership ability and good personal adjustment, and receiving no sociometric choices is commonly equated with maladjustment. Receiving many choices could just as reasonably be interpreted to mean high conformity to a group, and rejection could be associated with independence and creativity. Supplementary evidence would be needed to verify such interpretations. Sociometric choices provide no evidence for *why* individuals are either chosen or rejected by their peers.

**Stability of Sociometric Results.** Sociometric status scores have a relatively high degree of stability at various age levels. High and low sociometric scores show more stability than average scores. Since individuals tend to maintain the same level of sociometric status on numerous criteria, a general social acceptability factor appears to be operating in the choice process.

## CHAPTER NOTES

1. J. Rich, *Interviewing Children and Adolescents* (New York: St. Martin's Press, 1968).
2. W. B. Walsh, "Validity of Self-report: Another Look," *Journal of Counseling Psychology* 15 (1968): 180-86.
3. M. J. Radke, "The Relation of Parental Authority to Children's Behavior and Attitudes," in *Institute of Child Welfare Monographs* 22 (Minneapolis: University of Minnesota Press, 1946).
4. R. B. Ammons, "Reactions in a Projective Doll-Play Interview of White Males Two to Six Years of Age to Differences in Skin Color and Facial Features," *Journal of Genetic Psychology* 76 (1950): 323-41.
5. L. J. Yarrow, "Interviewing Children," in *Handbook of Research Methods in Child Development,* ed. P. H. Mussen (New York: Wiley, 1960).
6. B. Herjanic et al., "Are Children Reliable Reporters?" *Journal of Abnormal Child Psychology* 3 (1975): 41-48.
7. M. Rutter and P. Graham, "The Reliability and Validity of the Psychiatric Assessment of the Child: I. Interview with the Child," *British Journal of Psychiatry* 114 (1968): 563-79.
8. Rich, *Interviewing.*
9. Yarrow, "Interviewing Children."
10. Ibid.
11. Rich, *Interviewing.*
12. Yarrow, "Interviewing Children."
13. B. Winstell, "The Use of a Controlled Play Situation in Determining Certain Effects of Maternal Attitudes on Children," *Child Development* 22 (1951): 299-311.
14. Yarrow, "Interviewing Children," p. 576.
15. J. Piaget, *The Child's Conception of the World* (Highlands, N.J.: Humanities Press, 1951).
16. J. Piaget, *The Language and Thought of the Child* (Highlands, N.J., Humanities Press, 1951).
17. Yarrow, "Interviewing Children."

18. Ammons, "Reactions."
19. J. Rich, *Interviewing*, pp. 92-95.
20. E. L. Horowitz and R. E. Horowitz, "Development of Social Attitudes in Children," *Sociometry* 1 (1938): 301-38.
    R. E. Horowitz, "Racial Aspects of Self-identification in Nursery School Children," *Journal of Psychology* 7 (1939): 91-99.
21. K. B. Clark and M. P. Clark, "Emotional Factors in Racial Identification and Preference in Negro Children," *Journal of Negro Education* 19 (1950): 341-50.
22. M. E. Goodman, *Race Awareness in Young Children* (Reading, Mass.: Addison-Wesley, 1952).
23. J. Collier, Jr., "Photography in Anthropology: A Report on Two Experiments," *American Anthropologist* 59 (1957): 843-59.
24. Yarrow, "Interviewing Children."
25. D. M. Levy, "Use of Play Technique As Experimental Procedure," *American Journal of Orthopsychiatry* 3 (1933): 266-77.
26. M. J. Radke and H. G. Trager, "Children's Perceptions of the Social Roles of Negroes and Whites," *Journal of Psychology* 29 (1950): 3-33.
27. F. Redl, "The Life Space Interview Workshop: Strategy and Techniques of the Life Space Interview," *American Journal of Orthopsychiatry* 29 (1959): 1-18.
28. D. K. Walker, *Socioemotional Measures for Preschool and Kindergarten Children* (San Francisco: Jossey-Bass, 1973).
29. J. L. Moreno, *Who Shall Survive?* (New York: Beacon House, 1953).
30. N. E. Gronlund, *Sociometry in the Classroom* (New York: Harper, 1959).
31. R. F. Biehler, "Companion Choice Behavior in the Kindergarten," *Child Development* 25 (1954): 45-50.
32. Walker, *Socioemotional Measures*.
33. B. R. McCandless and H. R. Marshall, "A Picture Sociometric Technique for Preschool Children and Its Relation to Teacher Judgments of Friendship," *Child Development* 28 (1957): 139-48.
34. M. J. Dunnington, "Investigation of Areas of Disagreement in Sociometric Measurement of Preschool Children," *Child Development* 28 (1957): 93-102.
35. S. Moore and R. Updegraff, "Sociometric Status of Preschool Children Related to Age, Sex, Nurturance-giving and Dependency," *Child Development* 35 (1964): 520-24.
36. Gronlund, *Sociometry*, p. 11.
37. Ibid.
38. Ibid.

# 9

# Projective Techniques

## HISTORICAL FOUNDATIONS

In Chapter 1 we defined a projective technique as one that provides a relatively ambiguous, unstructured stimulus which the individual is assumed to structure in terms of his or her own personality and functioning. For example, people's delight in unfolding their imaginations on unstructured stimuli like clouds can be traced back to the beginning of recorded history. It is evident in the oracles of the ancient Greeks.

The history of inkblots, one of the most popular projective stimuli, can be traced to Leonardo da Vinci in the fifteenth century, who said in his *Introduction for the Painter:*

> He is not well rounded who does not have the same love for all things that are included under art: as is the case for example when one does not like landscapes and decides to give it only brief and ordinary study. In this connection our Botticelli said that such study is idle, for when nothing more than a sponge full of various colors is thrown against the wall, it leaves a blot on the wall in which one can perceive a beautiful landscape. It is quite true that various experiences can be seen in such a blot, provided one wants to find them in it—human heads, various animals, bottles, cliffs, seas, clouds or forests and other things—and it is just as when a bell is ringing in which you can read words if you want to. But if such blots already give you ideas, then they teach you not to completely finish any specific part of them. For the painter who does that, paints very sad landscapes.[1]

In the early days of mental test development, inkblots were used to portray imagination. In 1895 Binet and Henri wrote about their use of them for this purpose:

> It is necessary to recognize the state of these different forms of imagination in the individual by means of several rapid tests . . . let there be a spot of ink with an irregular contour on a white paper; to some this will mean nothing, to others who have a lively visual imagination (Leonardo da Vinci for example) the small inkblot will appear full of figures, whose number and type can be noted, without, of course pushing the experiment to the kind of hypnosis which the English like to evoke with their crystalgazing.[2]

A number of other studies using inkblots as a test of imagination were conducted during the late nineteenth and early twentieth centuries. Dearborn at Harvard used them in experimental psychology in 1897. In the early 1900s several researchers studied children's development in relation to differences in their responses to inkblots. During this same period, pictures were used to evoke stories (the forerunner of the Thematic Apperception Test or TAT). The word-association projective technique has a distinguished clinical and experimental history, from Galton to Wundt's laboratory and to Jung's consultation room.[3] In this approach the stimulus is a word, usually presented verbally rather than visually, and the subject responds with the first word that comes to his or her mind.

These early uses of what later became projective techniques were limited in scope. The concept of personality was not part of the psychology of the times. A new era in the development of psychology and psychiatry began in the 1920s, and during that period, projective techniques came to the fore. As indicated in Chapter 1, this was the time of the establishment of the university child development programs and the evolvement of the child guidance clinics from the mental hygiene movement. The child guidance clinics adopted a clinical psychiatric approach, with heavy emphasis on psychoanalytic principles which were not generally accepted in academic circles in the 1920s.

Actually, projective techniques arose as a protest to the testing movement and to the entrenched approaches to the evaluation of personality which psychometrics developed. Psychometrics developed tests for the measurement of intelligence, aptitudes, interests, and achievement, however it remained for projective techniques to fill the gap in such areas as motivation, emotion, and aspects of personality reflecting psychopathology.[4]

The concept of *projection* in personality theory is credited to Freud who used it as early as 1896. He later elaborated his ideas to define projection as a tendency to ascribe one's own drives, feelings, and emotions to other people or to the outside world, in such a manner as to defend oneself against awareness that these are part of oneself. In this sense, projection is a defensive element.[5]

As we have indicated, early experiments with inkblots dealt primarily with imagination. Rorschach broadened the scope to include the determinants of responses, modes of perception, and their relationship to personality and psychopathology. The Rorschach inkblot test was the first major clinical and research instrument to be classified later as a projective technique.[6] David Levy, appointed chief of staff of the Institute for Child Guidance in New York City in 1927, brought the Rorschach test to America in 1925.

In 1935 Murray developed the Thematic Apperception Test (TAT). He and his coworkers set out to construct both a theory of personality as well as techniques for its assessment. The term *projection tests* was first introduced in Murray's *Explorations in Personality,* which was published in 1938.[7]

During that same year, Frank first used the term *projective methods,* and in the following year—1939—he published the first theoretical paper, which was expanded later into the monograph *Projective Methods.* In this monograph Frank defines *projective technique* as "a method of studying the personality by confronting the subject with a situation to which he will respond according to what the situation means to him and how he feels when so responding."[8]

## CURRENT TRENDS

Projective techniques have been used with increasing frequency in child development research in recent years. They are especially appropriate for use with children because of their relatively nonverbal nature. A limiting factor with children is the relatively meager, matter of fact responses they give to unstructured stimuli.[9]

Clinical psychologists have a higher regard for the techniques than many measurement specialists. The validity of the techniques is not well established psychometrically, even for the Rorschach and TAT.[10] However, many of their research disadvantages do not apply in clinical use.

Varble cites several studies which indicate that projective techniques are declining in importance. In a comparison of university clinical psychology programs in diagnostic training practices between 1965 and 1970, the trend was shifting away from projective to objective approaches. Also, while psychological research in general was increasing tremendously during that period, the use of projective techniques remained stable or declined.[11]

Projective techniques provide a broad, integrative approach to the study of the individual by indicating the quality of his or her adjustment, his or her contact with reality, and his or her way of attacking problems and organizing experiences. Of course they also reveal the individual's originality, creativeness, rigidity, and other similar factors. A good background in the psychology of personality and clinical psychology is required before one is well qualified to use projective techniques.

We will give examples of projective techniques classified according to five types of response, as proposed by Lindzey: association, construction, completion, choice or ordering, and expressive.

## ASSOCIATION TECHNIQUES

In association techniques, the subject is presented with the stimulus and is asked to respond with the first word, image, or percept that comes to his or her mind. The two most commonly used forms of association are word association and inkblots.

### Word Association

The word association technique is one of the oldest procedures used in personality study. It may well be considered the forerunner of projective techniques. With this method, clues to personality of the subject are obtained in three typical ways: (1) by analyzing stimulus words on which the subject "blocks"; (2) by analyzing associations or actual responses to stimulus words on which the subject shows some emotional disturbance, blocking, etc.; and (3) by analyzing usualness or unusualness of the subject's responses as compared to the norm for his or her culture or group. In the word association method, emotionally charged words are ordinarily included with neutral words, and subjects are asked to respond with the first word that comes to mind. The words they express presumably indicate their feelings and attitudes, especially toward other persons.

#### Kent-Rosanoff Free Association Test

The word association technique is more often used with adults than with children. However, the Kent-Rosanoff Free Association Test was designed for use with individuals four years of age and older.[12] The child responds to one hundred stimulus cards by giving the first word that comes to his or her mind. The examiner reads the words to the child one at a time and records the child's responses, reaction time, and any related observed behavior. This is an old instrument, having been developed in 1910. Over the years norms have been collected from preschool children through adults. All studies with the test have shown marked differences between children's and adults' responses.

### Inkblots

#### Rorschach

Another example of an association technique is the Rorschach.[13] With this instrument, the individual is asked by highly trained persons to respond to ten inkblots of varying shapes and colors. The subject is shown each card in a series, one at a time, and is asked to tell what he or she sees in it or what it may be. After the subject has responded to each of the ten cards, a period of inquiry follows in which the psychologist administering the test probes for information to clarify what the subject saw and what aspect of the blot determined his or her perception. Every response to the inkblots is determined both by the qualities of the blot and the individual response of the subject. Perceptual responses play an important part. See Figure 9.1 for a sample of a Rorschach inkblot.

Scoring systems provide for the analysis of both structure and content of responses. In scoring responses to each card, each response is considered separately and scored on four primary dimensions as shown in Table 9.1. The researcher is concerned with the way the subject uses movement, color, shading, and form in determining a response. These are called the *determinants* of the response. Once the responses are scored and tabulated, they are interpreted according to Rorschach's hypotheses concerning the meaning of movement and color. These hypotheses have been well validated clinically, and students of Rorschach's method find from their actual study of patients that they hold up in practice. The tendency to project movement into the blots reflects intrapsychic activity and fantasy-thinking. The tendency to utilize color in determining responses reflects responsiveness to emotionally toned stimulus material. The need to take interrelationships of various factors into account makes Rorschach's interpretation very complex. Its primary use is as a clinical diagnostic tool.

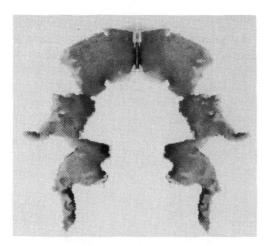

**Figure 9.1.** Rorschach Inkblot

**Table 9.1.** Four Primary Dimension on Which Each Response to a Rorschach Card is Scored

| Location | | Determinant | | Content | | Popularity | |
|---|---|---|---|---|---|---|---|
| W | Whole Response (all or nearly all of blot used) | F | Form | A | Animal figure | P | Popular |
| | | M | Human movement | Ad | Animal with detail | O | Original |
| D | Large usual detail | FM | Animal movement | H | Human figure | | |
| d | Small usual detail | m | Abstract movement | Hd | Human with detail | | |
| Dd | Unusual detail | C | Color, pure | | | | |
| S | White space | FC | Form-color | | | | |
| | | CF | Color-form | | | | |
| | | Fc; cF; c | Shading with texture or surface | | | | |

Volumes of studies have been conducted using the Rorschach technique. The 1972 edition of *The Mental Measurements Yearbook* cites 4,204 references, most of them dealing with adult subjects. Numerous reports of individual case studies also document its use as a tool in clinical diagnosis of children.[14]

Uses of the Rorschach with children, emphasizing diagnostic problems, scoring techniques, and case studies that compare the Rorschach and other projective techniques in clinical work with young children, is provided by Francis-Williams.[15] The first extensive use of the Rorschach in research with children was in a study reported in 1946 of 123 middle-class children ages three to eight.[16] The Gesell Normative Study included typical Rorschach responses for children from ages two through eight.[17] A longitudinal study of developmental changes in Rorschach responses of 1,000 people from ages two to seventy has also been conducted.[18]

Louise Ames and Richard Walker of the Gesell Institute of Child Development rescored the 650 Rorschach records and added nearly 900 supplementary records at different socioeconomic levels. Longitudinal follow-ups were made on 300 children. Two of their studies provide good illustrations of the use of the Rorschach in helping to understand children: (1) contrasting Rorschach records of children of normal and distrubed emotional functioning, and (2) comparing early Rorschachs of children who later became good and poor readers. The following are a few findings from these studies as described in *Child Rorschach Responses–Developmental Trends from Two to Ten Years* by Ames and her associates.[19]

**Rorschach and Emotional Disturbance.** Ames and Walker drew records from their clinical service files of fifty boys of average intelligence or higher, aged six to twelve, who had been diagnosed as emotionally disturbed independent of their Rorschach responses. Each of these subjects was matched individually for age, intelligence, and socioeconomic status with a subject from their normal research sample. An item analysis of sixteen Rorschach response characteristics, determined previously to be "danger signals" or indicators of disturbed functioning in children, was done to determine which response characteristics were contributing most to differentiating the emotionally disturbed boys from the "normal" boys. The number of these danger-signal responses for the disturbed boys was 5.0 compared to 1.6 for the normal boys, a clearly significant difference. The majority of disturbed boys had scores of 4 or more whereas hardly any of the normal boys had scores that high. Table 9.2 summarizes the type of responses which significantly differentiated the disturbed from the normal boys. Eleven danger-signal responses significantly differentiated the two groups.

To summarize Table 9.2, disturbed boys had a significantly higher percentage of various types of responses to the Rorschach than normal boys: They manipulated the cards more often (turned them around, placed them upside down, etc.), and position alone determined responses more often. The disturbed boys' responses to form or shape within the cards showed a lower quality and accuracy of form perception. F% exceeded F+%, where F%= total responses in which the child responded only to the shape of the blot divided by R (the total number of scorable responses) and F+ represents quality and accuracy of form perception. F+ is scored from established norms of usual responses and statistically determined lists. It indictes agreement with other people's responses. In responding to a whole blot (W responses), the disturbed boys showed greater contamination and confabulation. Contamination indicates odd combination responses such as "That's a furniture house" or "a cow barber pipe." Confabulations are overgeneralizations from a detail to a whole, where the response is also F– (low in accuracy of form perception as described in our definition of F+ above). For example, in one sample record of a four-year-old girl, the child responded to the red color in one card as "splatters of paint." She then interpreted "center hands" as a "church steeple" but generalized from this into "church" for the whole blot. The disturbed boys also evidenced static perseveration (repetition of the same response on more than three cards) which did not occur with the normal boys.

The disturbed boys also differed from the normal boys in the *content* of their responses to the inkblots. As shown in Table 9.2, they had a higher percentage of no H or Hd or Hd:H>2.1. A response is scored for H if a human figure is seen, and Hd for a human figure with detail. Hd: H>2.1 indicates *more* than 2.1 Hd responses to every H response. (The expected ratio for adults is usually given as 2:1.) Considering human responses as indicating an interest in people, this result indicates lower interest among the disturbed boys. The contents of their responses were also more bizarre,

**Table 9.2.** Percentage Occurrence of "Danger Signals" in Disturbed and Normal Subjects

| Type of Rorschach Response | Disturbed | Normal Control |
|---|---|---|
| Excessive card manipulation | 24 | 0 |
| F% exceeds F+% | 38 | 8 |
| No H or Hd or HD:H>2:1 | 40 | 14 |
| Elimination or sex responses | 14 | 2 |
| Static perseveration | 30 | 0 |
| Bizarre content, F-originals | 46 | 8 |
| Troubled content (hostile, anxious) | 56 | 16 |
| Personal reference | 16 | 2 |
| Contamination | 32 | 2 |
| Confabulation | 38 | 10 |
| Positional | 16 | 4 |

contained more personal references, expressed more hostility or anxiousness, and were more highly related to elimination and sex.

**Rorschach and Reading.** Ames and Walker also examined the Rorschachs of fifty-four kindergarten children whose reading ability was evaluated at the end of fifth grade. Correlations were computed among the kindergarten I.Q. scores, reading-prognosis scores, and fifth-grade reading scores from the reading sections of the Stanford Achievement Test. Kindergarten Rorschach scores were compared for children falling in each of the four quartiles of fifth-grade reading ability. Several Rorschach scores differed significantly for these groupings. The children who scored as better readers at the end of the fifth grade had Rorschach responses during kindergarten with lower W%, higher D%, lower F%, higher FM, and more responses than poorer readers. These Rorschach variables associated with reading ability tended to fall more into the cognitive than the emotional sphere. The differences in W%, D%, F%, and in total responses all relate to clarity, detailing, and accuracy of perceptions. The better readers differed from the poorer ones in variables that change most during the normal development of the child. The better readers showed more mature responses. Greater use of movement (M), as in FM responses, with lower F% (form) responses, presumably reflects greater emotional maturity, more differentiated experiences, and greater openness to stimulation.

Ames and Walker conclude that their findings do not suggest the use of the Rorschach specifically for predicting fifth-grade reading scores. Rather, they point to the usefulness of the Rorschach in assessing important individual characteristics that correlate with behaviors basic to school success. All of these characteristics should be viewed within a developmental child study framework.

### Holtzman Inkblot Technique (HIT)

Several attempts have been made to objectify the inkblot technique. The Holtzman Inkblot Technique was first published in 1961 and its use has increased steadily since that time.[20] However, the Rorschach continues to be the most widely used projective technique for the assessment of personality and differential diagnosis.[21]

Five years is considered the lower age limit for this test since children under five usually cannot finish the test. The HIT consists of two parallel sets of forty-five inkblots (forms A and B). Unlike the Rorschach, only one response is made for each inkblot, and a simple standardized inquiry follows to determine location and reasons for responses. Only one of the normative samples used by Holtzman and his associates in developing the test includes kindergarten children or younger.

## CONSTRUCTION TECHNIQUES

Construction projective techniques emphasize the product created or constructed by the subject. In this technique the subject is required to produce something like a picture or a story. This technique is relatively demanding of the subject, although the stimulus may be simple. Usually a standardized stimulus is used.

### Thematic Apperception Test (TAT)

The TAT (Thematic Apperception Test), or parts or variants of it, has been used to a great extent in research studies.[22] TAT is comprised of a set of vague pictures of relatively low structure to which the subject responds by telling a story about what is happening in each picture, what led up to this scene, and what the outcome will be. In so doing, the individual expresses a variety of feelings and needs.

The TAT, like most projective instruments, was developed for clinical use. As indicated previously, it was introduced in 1935 by Henry Murray and his associates at the Harvard Psychological Clinic. It also has a research history, particularly through the work of McClelland, Atkinson, and associates on achievement and related motives. The areas of hostility and aggression also have been explored through TAT responses. The assumption is that TAT pictures arouse motives in much the same manner as cues in real life situations and that these motives are based on the subject's past experiences.

The TAT consists of thirty black-and-white pictures and one blank card. (A TAT card is shown in Figure 10.3 in the next chapter.) From these pictures, four sets are selected for use with four groups: boys of fourteen and younger, girls of fourteen and younger, boys older than fourteen, and girls older than fourteen. Two examples of the content of the pictures are: A little girl is climbing a winding flight of stairs (for girls only), and a little boy is sitting on the doorstep of a log cabin (for boys only).

The child invents a story for each picture by telling what is happening, what led up to it, and what the outcome will be. From these stories, the child's motivations, attitudes, and habits are inferred. The average length of the stories of children who are five to seven years old is twenty-nine to thirty words.[23] Few studies have been conducted with young children although adolescents have been studied frequently.

### Children's Apperception Test (CAT)

The basic procedure and means of interpretation of the CAT are based upon the Thematic Apperception Test (TAT).[24] However, animals instead of people are used in the pictures, with the assumption that young children respond more easily to animals. Instructions are less formal than those for the TAT. The test was designed by L. and S. Bellak for use with children ages three through ten.[25]

The themes portrayed in the CAT pictures relate primarily to problems of human family-centered action as suggested by psychoanalytic theory. Examples of the pictures are an adult dog sitting in a bathroom holding a smaller dog and a crib holding two baby bears in a darkened room with a large bed in the background. For each picture the child tells a story about what is happening, what led up to the scene, and what the outcome will be. A checklist is provided with the test to assist in interpretation. This analysis sheet is designed for checking ten variables for each story: main theme, main hero (heroine), attitudes to parental figures, family roles and identifications, figures or objects or external circumstances introduced, objects or figures omitted, nature of anxieties, significant conflicts, punishment for crime, and outcome.

A reviewer of the CAT has stated:

> At its present stage of development the CAT is a very promising tool for the experimental student of children's attitudes and personality development and for the clinician who is ready to use the results of this test, like those of the TAT or interview material, to build up a clinically shrewd and (hopefully) consistent concept of a personality; it is not ready for those who wish quantitative or even qualitative guideposts to normative status or to differential diagnosis.[26]

### Blacky Pictures

The Blacky Pictures is a modified TAT for ages five and over.[27] It consists of twelve cartoons showing various scenes in the life of a dog named Blacky. Dogs, rather than humans, are used to facilitate personal expression in situations that might provoke inhibitory resistance. Each card is presented with a brief identification and the subject is requested to tell a story in TAT style.

Analysis is in terms of psychoanalytic variables of psychosexual development. Eleven psychosexual variables are assessed from responses to the cartoons: oral eroticism, oral sadism, sadism, oedipal intensity, masturbation guilt, castration anxiety or penis envy, positive identification, sibling rivalry, guilt feelings, and positive ego ideal or love object. For example, oral eroticism is assessed by the picture of Blacky nursing, and sibling rivalry, by Blacky watching Mama and Papa pet Tippy. .

A lengthy review of Blacky Pictures in *The Sixth Mental Measurements Yearbook* concludes:

> When used with children, especially boys, having mental ages of about five to ten years, the *Blacky Pictures* often provide adequate material for interpretations concerning problem areas, attitudes toward siblings and parents, characteristic defensive reactions, self-perceptions, and the like. Yet it is the reviewer's impression that, with children of both sexes, aged from about eight to about twelve years, Bellak's CAT is likely to have a higher interpretative yield than the Blacky. With subjects beyond early adolescence, the reviewer, in most cases, would consider the TAT, rather than the Blacky, to be the instrument of choice . . .[28]

### Rock-A-Bye Baby: A Group Projective Test for Children

This test was designed for use with children five to ten years of age.[29] It is a constructive projective technique combined with an interview. It assesses personality adjustment through feelings about sibling rivalry.

A thirty-five-minute filmed puppet show (entitled "Rock-A-Bye-Baby") is shown to groups of nine to sixteen children. Then the group suggests endings for the story, and each child is interviewed individually about his or her reactions.[30]

### Projective Drawings

In projective drawings, the subject projects his or her psychomotor activities on paper, with his or her conscious and unconscious perception of self and significant people in his or her environment determining the content of the drawing.[31] Figure drawing tests are simple to administer but complex to interpret.

Many of the figure-drawing projective tests grew out of the work of Florence Goodenough who developed the Draw-a-Man Test for appraising children's intelligence. This test was based primarily on the number of details and the complexity put into the drawing of a man. Although the test seems to tap chiefly visual motor coordination, it also is highly correlated with social adjustment. The same drawing can be used as a projective test, with different instructions.[32]

Drawing tests are also a suitable means of communication for a child who does not speak the same language as the examiner.

### Machover Draw-a-Person Test

This test, also called *Machover Figure Drawing Test,* is used with individuals ages two and over.[33] Instructions are to draw a person and then to draw a person of the opposite sex than the first. This task is followed by asking the subject to tell a story about the figures.

Both the content and structure of the drawings are analyzed and interpreted, such as parts of the body and clothing included and emphasized, size of the male and female figures, placement on the page, type of line, shading, and erasures. The overall tone and mood created through the facial expression and posture drawn are emphasized in the interpretation. As Machover explained:

> The process of drawing the human figure is for the subject, whether he realizes it or not, a problem not only in graphic skill, but one of projecting himself in all of the body meanings and attitudes that have come to be represented in his body image. Consequently, the drawing analyst should feel free to extract from the graphic product what the subject has put into it. He should feel free to interpret directly aspects which, with striking literalness, often reflect real life problems and behavior of the individual who is drawing. The figure is, in a way, an introduction

to the individual who is drawing. Thus, when a subject erases his arms and changes the position of them several times, it may be literally interpreted that the subject does not know what to do with his arms in his behavior. If the fist is clenched, he may literally be expressing his belligerence. If the eye of the figure has a pensive, furtive, or bewildered gaze, it may often be characteristic of the individual who is projecting.[34]

The Machover Draw-a-Person Test has gained a large following and is believed to be second only to the Rorschach in popularity. One reviewer cautions, however, that the examiner should be well versed on body symbolism, interpretation of expressive movements, and graphomotor functioning.[35]

Several other human figure drawing tests are available for use with children. Among them are the *Draw-a-Person Test*[36] by William Urban for children five years and older and the *Human Figure Drawing Test*[37] by Elizabeth Koppitz for children five to twelve years.

**Human-Figure Drawings as a Projection of Social Attitudes**. Badri and Dennis used human figure drawings to test the research hypothesis "that children who, when asked to draw a man, draw chiefly men in modern dress show thereby a preference for modern dress and for the complex of social changes of which it is a part . . . . On the other hand, children who for the most part draw men having the traditional appearance of men in their group are either (a) unacquainted with modern dress or (b) hold negative attitudes toward it."[38] The drawings for this study were obtained from four boys' schools in two major cities in Sudan as well as from a boys' school in each of two villages. A traditional aspect of the dress of a Sudanese man is his chief article of apparel: the *galabia,* a long loose garment that extends from the shoulders to the ankle. It is easily drawn, distinguishable from drawings of modern dress.

Results of this study showed that modern dress was seldom drawn in the two villages but that this finding was not due to lack of acquaintance with it. The teachers of the boys were men in modern dress, and the drawing test was administered by a psychologist in modern dress. The authors concluded that most of the village boys and some of the urban boys had not yet developed a preference for modern clothing although it was familiar to them. Also, the authors predicted that before these villages in Sudan adopt the technological changes associated with modernization, the drawings will begin to show a preference for modern dress.

### Bender-Gestalt Test for Young Children

This instrument was developed by Elizabeth Koppitz in 1964.[39] The original Bender-Gestalt test was developed by Lauretta Bender in 1938 to assess visual-motor performance. The Koppitz version assesses developmental level, intelligence functioning, brain damage, mental retardation, and emotional disturbances in young children.

A child is given nine geometric figures, one at a time, and asked to copy them. His or her drawings are scored using Koppitz's Developmental Bender Scoring System.

In the normative sample, most children at nine years of age could copy all nine figures with few errors. Studies indicate limited use for children below age five. Bender scores compare favorably with school readiness and achievement tests, which indicates its usefulness as a screening instrument for kindergarten children.[40]

### Lowenfeld Mosaic Test

This test is used for subjects ages two and over.[41] It consists of 456 mosaic pieces of different geometric shapes, colors, and thicknesses. First, the subject is shown a sample of each shape and of each color and told that each of the five shapes comes in six colors. The subject is then asked to make anything that he or she wishes on the tray provided, and upon completion of the pattern, the subject is asked to tell what it represents.

Lowenfeld's classification of mosaic productions, on which analysis is based, falls into three main groups:

1. *Representational:* designs representing an external object or set of objects. Designs are analyzed for projected movement, use of color, and skill.

2. *Conceptual:* designs representing an idea or concept of three types: abstract, emotional or mental, general.

3. *Abstract patterns or nonrepresentational designs*[42]

No normative data are available except for the mosaic characteristics of children that have been analyzed according to the above classification and then applied to the mosaics of mental retardates, the normal personality, neurosis, "mental disorders," and subjects with different cultural backgrounds. It was Lowenfeld's interest in cultural differences that prompted her to develop this instrument. In the late 1920s she was a child psychiatrist and founder of the Institute of Child Psychology in London. She observed that European communities had their own distinct folk costume patterns and designs and that different arrangements of form and color in dress embroidery provided reliable clues to an individual's village or community of origin.

## COMPLETION TECHNIQUES

The sentence completion method is the best known completion technique, but other measures such as story completion and argument completion are available also. The projective aspect of these completion techniques is that the subject is supplied with an incomplete stimulus which he or she is required to complete as personally desired.

### Sentence Completion

One of the simplest methods is that in which the beginning of a sentence is provided and the individual writes an ending. Responses can be analyzed for such items as content, moods, motives, feelings, expectations, and attitudes. Since the nature of the response is apparent, an individual may easily control his or her responses and not reveal inner feelings.

### Rosenzweig Picture-Frustration Study

The Rosenzweig Picture-Frustration Study consists of two anonymous figures in cartoon form reacting to mildly frustrating situations.[43] The respondent is asked to write in the blank caption box what the frustrated person would say. The assumption is that the respondent identifies with the frustrated character and projects his or her own reaction tendencies in replies.

Forms are available for adults and children. The Children's Form is intended for use with children ages four through thirteen. Instructions are as follows:

> We are going to play a game. Here are some pictures of people doing and saying different things. Look at the pictures carefully one at a time. One person is always shown talking. Read what the person is saying. Write in the empty space what you think the boy or girl would answer. The answer you give should be the first thing you think of. Do not make jokes. Work as fast as you can.[44]

These are two of the twenty-four situations included in the instrument:

> A women is telling a boy that she does not know how to fix his trucks.

> A girl on a swing is telling another girl that she is planning to keep the swing all afternoon.[45]

## Story Completion

### Structured Doll-Play Test

This preschool test is designed to measure the tendency to express behavior and feelings of guilt.[46] Using a dollhouse, the examiner asks the child to complete six stories about a same-sex doll. The child's story completions are scored into nineteen categories including delay, confession, tattling, denial, physical punishment, isolation, and crying.

## CHOICE OR ORDERING TECHNIQUES

Choice or ordering techniques provide multiple-choice responses to projective stimuli and, in this sense, are modified projective techniques. A multiple-choice Rorschach test is available.[47] Also, the *Szondi Test* consists of six sets of photographs from which the subject selects the two liked most and the two disliked most.[48] The pictures are of mental patients representing eight diagnostic categories. The assumption behind the test is that the photographs have meanings that correspond to need-systems characteristic of all persons. Interpretation is a complex process and the test is questionable to many psychologists.

## EXPRESSIVE TECHNIQUES

An expressive technique is similar to a constructive technique except that the end product is not as important in the expressive technique. Rather, the emphasis is placed upon the *manner* (the process) in which the subject forms a product out of raw material. Doll play is an expressive technique especially well suited for use with children because it is easy and natural for children to project themselves into the dolls. The child reveals attitudes toward family members as well as fears, aggressions, and conflicts. The examiner observes what the child chooses to play with, what the child says and does, and the child's emotional expressions.

### The World Test

This test for children ages four and over consists of 160 or 300 wooden toys that children use on the floor or table. Standardized instructions and recording procedures by Charlotte Buhler are included.[49] Scoring is accomplished by sorting or classifying various aspects of the completed productions under the heading of *signs*. The number of "elements" used are first recorded (i.e., kinds of toys such as men, animals, and trees). Then the presence of these signs is judged and recorded:

A-Signs (aggressions)

CDR-Signs (distortions, including closed-in-areas, disarrangements, and rigid arrangements)

S-Signs (symbolic arrangements in which important qualitative material is revealed)

A child's play with the World Test is similar to play with dolls except that the projection in the World Test permits the child to express his or her feelings toward people in general—toward the whole world. The question has been raised whether feelings regarding the whole world are primarily an outgrowth of family relationship experiences and the extent to which other life experiences contribute to them.

# CHAPTER NOTES

1.  J. Zubin, L. Eron, and F. Schumer, *An Experimental Approach to Projective Techniques* (New York: Wiley, 1965), p. 167.
2.  Ibid., p. 169.
3.  A. I. Rabin, ed., *Projective Techniques in Personality Assessment* (New York: Springer, 1968).
4.  Zubin et al., *Experimental Approach.*
5.  Ibid., p. 4.
6.  Rabin, *Projective Techniques.*
7.  H. A. Murray et al., *Explorations in Personality* (New York: Oxford University Press, 1938).
8.  L. K. Frank, *Projective Methods* (Springfield, Ill.: Thomas, 1948), p. 46.
9.  D. P. Ausubel and E. V. Sullivan, *Theory and Problems of Child Development,* 2nd ed. (New York: Grune and Stratton, 1970).
10. J. C. Stanley and K. D. Hopkins, *Educational and Psychological Measurement and Evaluation* (Englewood Cliffs, N.J.: Prentice-Hall, 1972).
11. D. L. Varble, "Current Status of the Thematic Apperception Test," in *Advances in Psychological Assessment,* ed. P. McReynolds (San Francisco: Jossey-Bass, 1975).
12. G. H. Kent and A. J. Rosanoff, *Kent-Rosanoff Free Association Test* (Chicago: Stoelting Co., 1910).
13. H. Rorschach, *Psychodiagnostics—A Diagnostic Test Based On Perception* (Bern: Huber, 1932). English translation by P. Lemhau and B. Kronenberg (New York: Grune and Stratton, 1942).
14  D. K. Walker, *Socioemotional Measures for Preschool and Kindergarten Children* (San Francisco: Jossey-Bass, 1973).
15. J. Francis-Williams, *Rorschach with Children: A Comparative Study of the Contribution Made By the Rorschach and Other Projective Techniques to Clinical Diagnosis in Work with Children* (London: Pergamon, 1968).
16. M. E. Ford, *The Application of the Rorschach Test to Young Children* (Minneapolis: University of Minnesota Press, 1946).
17. L. B. Ames et al., *Child Rorschach Responses: Developmental Trends from Two to Ten Years* (New York: P. B. Hoeber, 1952).
18. L. B. Ames, "Changes in Rorschach Responses Throughout the Human Life Span," *Genetic Psychology Monographs* 74 (1966): 89-125.
19. L. B. Ames et al., *Child Rorschach Responses* (New York: Bruner/Mazel, 1974).
20. W. H. Holtzman, *Holtzman Inkblot Technique* (New York: Psychological Corp., 1966).
    W. H. Holtzman, "The Holtzman Inkblot Technique," in *Introduction to Modern Projective Techniques,* ed. A. I. Rabin (New York: Springer, 1968), pp. 136-70.
21. W. H. Holtzman, "New Developments in Holtzman Inkblot," in *Advances in Psychological Assessment,* ed. P. McReynolds (San Francisco: Jossey-Bass, 1975).
22. H. A. Murray, *Thematic Apperception Test* (Boston: Harvard University Press, 1943).
23. Walker, *Socioemotional Measures.*
24. M. S. Hurvich, *Children's Apperception Test* (Larchmont, N.Y.: C.P.S., Inc., 1974).
25. L. Bellak and S. Bellak, "An Introductory Note on the Children's Apperception Test (CAT)," *Journal of Projective Techniques* 14 (1950): 173-80.
26. O. K. Buros, ed., *Fourth Mental Measurements Yearbook* (Highland Park, N.J.: Gryphon Press, 1953).
27. G. S. Blum, *The Blacky Pictures: Manual of Instructions* (New York: Psychological Corp., 1950).
    G. S. Blum, "The Blacky Pictures with Children," in *Projective Techniques with Children,* eds. A. I. Rabin and M. R. Haworth (New York: Grune and Stratton, 1960).
28. B. R. Sappenfield, in *Sixth Mental Measurements Yearbook,* ed. O. K. Buros (Highland Park, N.J.: Gryphon Press, 1965), p. 205.
29. M. R. Haworth and A. G. Woltmann, *Rock-A-Bye, Baby: A Group Projective Test for Children* (University Park, Penn.: Pennsylvania State University, 1959).
30. M. R. Haworth, "Films As a Group Technique," in *Projective Techniques with Children,* eds. A. I. Rabin and M. R. Haworth (New York: Grune and Stratton, 1960).
31. E. F. Hammer, "Projective Drawings," in *Projective Techniques in Personality Assessment,* ed. A. I. Rabin (New York: Springer, 1968).
32. J. O. Palmer, *The Psychological Assessment of Children* (New York: Wiley, 1970).
33. K. Machover, *Personality Projection in the Drawing of the Human Figure: A Method of Personality Investigation* (Springfield, Ill.: Thomas, 1949).
34. Ibid., p. 35.
35. P. M. Kitay, in *Sixth Mental Measurements Yearbook,* ed. O. K. Buros (Highland Park, N.J.: Gryphon, 1965).
36. W. Urban, *Draw-A-Person Test* (Los Angeles: Western Psychological Services, 1963).
37. E. Koppitz, *Human Figure Drawing Test* (New York: Grune and Stratton, 1968).
38. M. B. Badri and W. Dennis, "Human-Figure Drawings in Relation to Modernization in Sudan," *Journal of Psychology* 58 (1964): 421-25.
    W. Dennis, *Group Values Through Children's Drawings* (New York: John Wiley, 1966).
39. E. M. Koppitz, *The Bender-Gestalt Test for Young Children* (New York: Grune and Stratton, 1964).
40. Ibid.
41. M. Lowenfeld, *Lowenfeld Mosaic Test* (London: Badger Tests Co., Ltd., 1958).
42. Rabin, *Projective Techniques.*
43. E. E. Fleming and S. Rosenzweig, *Rosenzweig P-F Study: Form for Children,* manual, 1977.
44. S. Rosenzweig, E. Fleming, and L. Rosenzweig, "The Children's Form of the Rosenzweig Picture-Frustration Study," *Journal of Psychology* 26 (1948): 141-91.
45. Ibid., p. 142.
46. D. B. Lynn, *Structured Doll-Play Test* (Burlingame, Calif.: Test Developments, 1960).
47. J. B. Stone, *Structured Objective Rorschach Test (SORT)* (Los Angeles: California Test Bureau, 1958).
48. S. Deri, *Introduction to the Szondi Test* (New York: Grune and Stratton, 1949).
49. C. Buhler, "The World Test: A Projective Technique," *Journal of Child Psychiatry* 2 (1951): 4-23.

# 10

# Studying the Child's Family

The family exerts the single greatest influence on the behavior and development of a child. This is closely related to the parents' important position among the child's interpersonal relationships and to the extent of parental contact with the youngster especially during his or her early, formative years. Since the home has such a strong impact on the child, we must carefully investigate as many dimensions of family life as possible in order to arrive at an adequate understanding of the child's current functioning.

Family variables have been conceptualized in a number of ways. One taxonomy classifies aspects of family life that are closely related to child behavior and development. This schema, proposed by Hoffman and Lippitt,[1] will be adapted for our purposes and will be used as a general framework for discussion of techniques suitable for studying the child's family. The classification includes: (a) parental background and current family status, (b) personal characterisitics of parents, (c) parental perceptions of their roles and relationships in the home, (d) child-oriented parental attitudes, (e) parental behavior patterns, and (f) child's perceptions of parents and family relationships. Under these six headings, we will describe several methods of measuring the particular family life variable. It will become apparent that family dimensions may be examined in many of the same ways that we study individual children.

Family assessment techniques may be categorized broadly as either indirect or direct methods. Indirect approaches include methods like questionnaires, checklists, rating scales, tests—both objective and projective—and interviews. All of these approaches employ the "orientation of the respondent to filter the raw facts of his experience."[2] Traditionally, family study has been accomplished largely with the use of these measures. In addition to serving as an economical method for the collection of family data, an indirect technique can provide a focused means of investigating the individual's introspection about his or her behavior and feelings.[3] These are some of the assumptions that underlie the use of indirect methods in family measurement:

1. People conceptualize their lives in terms of the language used by the investigators so that their understanding of the questions is similar to that of the investigator.

2. People can accurately recall events and feelings of many years past with minimal forgetting.

3. People will report unpleasant events without selective forgetting, defensive distortion, and justification of actions by inaccurate elaboration.

4. People will report past events unaffected by social desirability or other response sets.[4]

In spite of the fact that high and consistent correlations are not always obtained between indirect reports and actual behavior, indirect approaches to studying the child's family continue to be used with at least moderate success.

Direct methods of family measurement involve observational techniques that are "aimed directly at the overt behavior of the subjects, avoiding reliance on secondhand reports."[5] Observational techniques were treated in detail in earlier chapters and will be considered here only as they relate to family assessment. As in the study of the individual child, a variety of methods should be used in combination if accurate appraisal of the family is desired. The discussion that follows describes significant family life variables and a few indirect and direct assessment techniques that are available for their investigation.

## PARENTAL BACKGROUND AND CURRENT FAMILY STATUS

This category of familial information includes family history data such as the social, cultural, and economic background of the parents; their place of birth; their ages, race, nationality, and religious background; their premarital and marital history; their educational history; their employment history, including present occupational income; and their health history and current physical condition. Other variables regarding family status include composition of the household, age and sex of siblings, physical characteristics of the home and neighborhood, and economic status. A good deal of this information can be obtained from existing school or agency files, but interviews with the family members and sometimes direct observation are required to insure complete and accurate data. Although used primaily for intake reception and evaluation of counselees, sections of the Individual and Family Developmental Review (IFDR) lend themselves well to studying these aspects of the child's family.[6] This series of history forms to be completed by parents provides a systematic framework for collecting and organizing family, personal, and child developmental history.

Present socioeconomic standing of the family is important in understanding a child's home background. Social class can be defined in several ways.[7] Some researchers have described a family's social class exclusively in terms of the occupation of head of household; others have used a combination of occupation, dwelling area, house type, and source of income as the basis for classification; and still others have rated socioeconomic status using occupation, education, and neighborhood as indices. Since the home and neighborhood are frequently used to determine social and economic class, observation of the child's environments may be undertaken as described in Chapter 3. These observations may be enhanced by structured scales that are available to assess the home.[8]

Two instruments, one developed by Gough[9] and the other by Sewell,[10] also provide the observer with a convenient means of quantifying variables that reflect social class. White and Hopkins have constructed another measure of socioeconomic status that can be completed by the child.[11] This multiple-choice questionnaire, which takes about fifteen minutes to fill out, asks the youngster to specify the educational attainment of his or her parents (e.g., high school, college) and to indicate the presence or absence of certain material possessions (e.g., telephone, fireplace, dishwasher) and experiences (e.g., travel). Items regarding parental educational attainment are scored 2 (yes), 1 (no), or 0 (I don't know), and those dealing with home characteristics and experiences are scored 1 (present) or 0 (absent). This self-report can be used by children as young as seven or eight. Despite the availability of these methods, information concerning socioeconomic position is usually obtained from existing files or through interviews with the child or other family members.

## PERSONAL CHARACTERISTICS OF PARENTS

Included as personal characteristics of parents are personality traits, values, philosophy of life, and other individual qualities not specifically oriented toward parental functions. These personal traits can be conveniently measured by either objective or projective tests and scales.

### OBJECTIVE TECHNIQUES

Objective, or nonprojective techniques as they are sometimes called, require the subject to respond to a series of structured questions that have a small number of possible answers. Responses to the limited-choice or forced-choice items are then scored and interpreted using the test's norms or classification schemes. Some of these instruments do not require that an examiner be present. These are a few of the personality and value measures which tap the personal characteristics of the child's parents:

Adjective Check List

Bell Adjustment Inventory

California Psychological Inventory

California Test of Personality

Comrey Personality Scales

Edwards Personal Preference Record

Emotional Profile Index

Gordon Personal Profile

Guilford-Zimmerman Temperament Survey

Internal-External Locus of Control Scale

Minnesota Multiphasic Personality Inventory

Mooney Problem Checklist

Myers-Briggs Type Indicator

Omnibus Personality Inventory

Rokeach Values Survey

Self-Disclosure Questionnaire

Sixteen Personality Factor Questionnaire

Study of Values

Survey of Interpersonal Values

Survey of Personal Values

Taylor Manifest Anxiety Scale

Taylor-Johnson Temperament Analysis

Of the preceding measures, three will be described briefly.

**Minnesota Multiphasic Personality Inventory.** The Minnesota Multiphasic Personality Inventory (MMPI)[12] is the most widely used nonprojective personality inventory. Originally developed in a psychiatric hospital, the MMPI consists of 550 items to which the subject responds in three possible ways: *true, false,* or *cannot say.* The latter response, which is indicated by leaving a blank when an answer sheet is used, is selected when the subject is undecided about the truth of a statement. An individual form is available with statements written on cards which the subject places in one of the three categories. A group form is also available. In the group version, the respondent reads the items printed in a test booklet and records his or her responses on an answer sheet. Items on the MMPI cover a wide range of personality-related areas such as health, family, religious beliefs, interests, attitudes, and neurotic and psychotic behavior manifestations. Five sample items of the instrument are shown in Table 10.1 to give some idea of the diversity of MMPI statements.

Responses to the MMPI are scored according to ten clinical scales and additional validity keys. The clinical scales and their abbreviations include:

| | |
|---|---|
| Hypochondriasis (Hs) | Paranoia (Pa) |
| Depression (D) | Psychasthenia (Pt) |
| Hysteria (Hy) | Schizophrenia (Sc) |
| Psychopathic deviate (Pd) | Hypomania (Ma) |
| Masculinity-femininity (Mf) | Social introversion (Si) |

Raw scores are converted to $T$-scores which have a mean of 50 and a standard deviation ($SD$) of 10. A score that falls 2 $SD$s or more above the mean (70 or more) is considered pathological. Scores are plotted on a profile chart like the one shown in Figure 10.1. It is the pattern of scores rather than individual scale scores which are of special importance in diagnosis. For this reason, only persons with appropriate training and experience should attempt to make these complex clinical interpretations.

**Calfornia Psychological Inventory.** Another objective personality instrument that is held in high regard is the California Psychological Inventory (CPI).[13] Although the CPI draws almost half of its items from the MMPI, it is not symptom-oriented like the MMPI. Rather, it was developed for use with normal or nonpsychiatrically disturbed populations. The self-administering paper-and-pencil inventory consists of 480 true-false items which deal with personality traits that are important for social living. Some sample items from the CPI are presented in Table 10.2.

The subject designates on a separate answer sheet whether a statement is true or false for him or her. Completion of the CPI requires about one hour. After the raw scores have been calculated, they are transferred to a profile sheet and converted to $T$-scores. Then, they are interpreted by someone who is familiar with the instrument. The CPI is scored for eighteen scales that are divided into four groups to facilitate profile interpretation.

| **Class I Scales** | **Class II Scales** |
|---|---|
| Dominance (Do) | Responsibility (Re) |
| Capacity for Status (Cs) | Socialization (So) |
| Sociability (Sy) | Self-Control (Sc) |
| Social Presence (Sp) | Tolerance (To) |
| Self Acceptance (Sa) | Good Impression (Gi) |
| Sense of Well-Being (Wb) | Community (Cm) |

| **Class III Scales** | **Class IV Scales** |
|---|---|
| Achievement via Conformance (Ac) | Psychological Mindedness (Py) |
| Achievement via Independence (Ai) | Flexibility (Fx) |
| Intellectual Efficiency (Ie) | Femininity (Fe) |

Class I scales assess poise, ascendency, self-assurance, and interpersonal adequacy; class II scales measure socialization, maturity, responsibility, and intrapersonal structuring of values; class III scales examine achievement and intellectual efficiency; and class IV scales investigate personal orientation and attitudes toward life. The CPI is an extremely valuable means of describing the characteristics of nondeviant, socially functioning individuals.

**Table 10.1.** Items from the Minnesota Multiphasic Personality Inventory

| Alternatives | | | Item | |
|---|---|---|---|---|
| True False | ? | | 1. | I like mechanics magazines. |
| True False | ? | | 2. | I have a good appetite. |
| True False | ? | | 3. | I wake up fresh and rested most mornings. |
| True False | ? | | 4. | I think I would like the work of a librarian. |
| True False | ? | | 5. | I am easily awakened by noise. |

# The Minnesota Multiphasic Personality Inventory

## Starke R. Hathaway and J. Charnley McKinley

Scorer's Initials_____

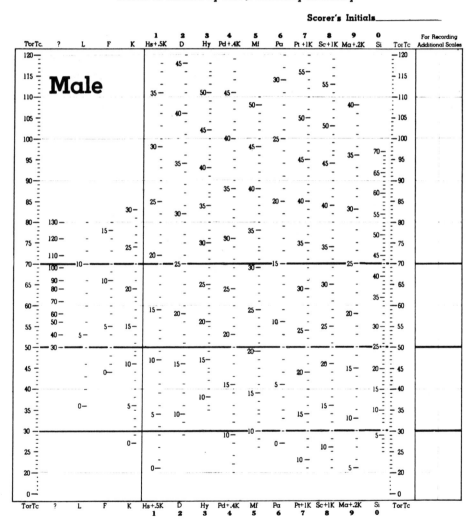

**Figure 10.1.** MMPI Profile Form. Validity scales ?, L, F, and K are shown in the upper left-hand side, and the ten clinical scales, numbered 1 to 0, are to the right. A similar form is used for females.

**Table 10.2.** Items from the California Pyschological Inventory

| Alternatives | | Item |
|---|---|---|
| True | False | I enjoy social gatherings just to be with people. |
| True | False | I gossip a little at times. |
| True | False | I like poetry. |
| True | False | People often expect too much of me. |
| True | False | My home life was always happy. |
| True | False | Only a fool would ever vote to increase his own taxes. |
| True | False | I love to go to dances. |
| True | False | Sometimes I feel that I am about to go to pieces. |

**Study of Values.** Among the objective measures of personal values, the Allport-Vernon-Lindzey Study of Values is perhaps the best known.[14] First published in 1931 and subsequently revised, this self-administered forced-choice instrument is designed to measure the relative prominence of six types of values: theoretical, economic, aesthetic, social, political, and religious. The *theoretical* person is one who is characterized by an interest in the discovery of truth. His or her behavior is governed by an empirical, rational, and intellectual orientation. The *economic* person is concerned with useful and practical values and holds attitudes that are in keeping with the stereotype of the average American businessman or woman. The *aesthetic* person is interested in form and harmony and places highest value on beauty rather than truth or utility. The *social* person is altruistic and philanthropic. The *political* person is dominated by a strong need for power and renown. Finally, the *religious* person is concerned with the unity of all experience and is preoccupied with a strong need to arrive at a transcendental understanding of the world as a whole.

The first part of the scale is made up of thirty items, and each value is paired twice, using different statements, with every other value. The second part consists of fifteen items, and each value is compared with all combinations of three other values. The format in which the items are cast is presented in Figure 10.2. Total raw scores for each value can be plotted to form an individual's profile.

**Part I**

8. When witnessing a gorgeous ceremony (ecclesiastical or academic, induction into office, etc.) are you more impressed: (a) by the color and pageantry of the occasion itself, (b) by the influence and strength of the group?

**Part II**

10. Which of the following would you prefer to do during part of your next summer vacation (if your ability and other conditions would permit)
   a. write and publish an original biological essay or article
   b. stay in some secluded part of the country where you can appreciate fine scenery
   c. enter a local tennis or other athletic tournament
   d. get experience in some new line of business

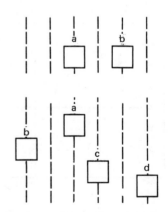

**Figure 10.2.** Items from A Study of Values

## PROJECTIVE TECHNIQUES

These subjective techniques involve unstructured situations or vague and ambiguous stimuli that permit self-expression in any way the subject chooses. Consequently, such techniques allow or encourage the subject to reveal certain covert, latent, or unconscious aspects of his or her personality.

There are numerous projective personality measures that are appropriate for use with adults. Among them are the Rosenzweig Picture-Frustration Study (adult form), the Holtzman Inkblot Technique, the Rorschach, the Rotter Incomplete Sentences Blank, the Szondi Test, and the Thematic Apperception Test. The Thematic Apperception Test will be discussed as an example of a projective method.

**Thematic Apperception Test.** The Thematic Apperception Test (TAT) is second only to the Rorschach projective method in use. Devised by Murray,[15] the TAT presents the subject with somewhat more structured stimuli than the Rorschach. The TAT uses ambiguous drawings, photographs, and paintings, in contrast to the amorphous blots of the Rorschach. As was indicated in the previous chapter, most of the TAT cards depict scenes that have personal and interpersonal relevance about which the subject is asked to tell a story (see Figure 10.3). Certain guide questions are used by the examiner to insure complete stories. There are no correct or incorrect answers to the TAT cards. A five-minute limit is usually imposed for each story which is recorded verbatim by the examiner.

The examiner first distinguishes the character with whom the subject has identified (i.e., the "hero"). The content of the story is then analyzed in terms of Murray's need-press system. *Needs* are the internal determinants of behavior which are classified as viscerogenic (e.g., *n* Food, *n* Water, *n* Air) and as psychogenic (e.g., *n* Aggression, *n* Nurturance, *n* Abasement, *n* Achievement). *Press* refers to attributes of an environmental object or person that facilitates or impedes a person's progress toward a goal (e.g., physical danger, family insupport, rejection by loved ones).

**Figure 10.3.** Card 12F of the Thematic Apperception Test

Murray's instructions for test administration and interpretation are not always followed. Instead, other more highly standardized administration and scoring procedures that have been developed for adaptations of the original TAT may be used. Among the newer quantitative scoring systems are those that allow in-depth analyses of three particular psychogenic needs: achievement, affiliation, and power.[16]

## PARENTAL PERCEPTIONS OF THEIR ROLES AND RELATIONSHIPS IN THE HOME

Family measurement has customarily been accomplished by assessing each individual family member through the use of personality inventories such as those already mentioned. However, another fruitful approach to family study involves the use of interpersonal measures that appraise relationships in the home rather than just the subject's own personal characteristics. This concept of assessment taps interpsychic as well as intrapsychic responses and provides a measure of a parent's feelings about his or her marriage partner, the marriage, the family as a whole, his or her role in the family system, and his or her perception of interaction patterns in the home. It includes such variables as decision-making processes, power relations, division of labor, degree of consensus, communication patterns, sex roles, and affective relationships. These interpersonal factors can be examined with indirect approaches such as objective and projective instruments and interviews as well as with direct methods such as behavioral observation.

### OBJECTIVE TECHNIQUES

One of the most immediate routes to understanding the properties of marriage and family life is the paper-and-pencil inventory. With this technique, the child's parents are asked to fill out instruments that describe their marriage and family relations. Examples of assessment devices in this category are listed here, and three of them will be subsequently described.

Autonomy for Women Attitude Inventory

Caring Relationship Inventory

Communication Between Husband and Wife

Conjugal Life Questionnaire

Day at Home

Decision Power Index

Dyadic Adjustment Scale

Familism Scale

Family Adjective Rating Scale

Family Adjustment Test

Family Attitude Measure

Family Concept Q-Sort

Family Environment Scale

Family Functioning Index

Family Integration Scale

Family Interaction Schedule

Family Interest Scale

Family Life Questionnaire

Family Problems Index

Family Relations Inventory

Family Relations Scale

Family Relations Test

Family Solidarity Scales

Family Unit Inventory

Feminine Role Attitudes

Fundamental Interpersonal Relations Orientation

Index of Marital Integration

Interpersonal Checklist

Interpersonal Communication Inventory

Interpersonal Method

Interpersonal Relationship Scale

Interpersonal Style Inventory

Inventory of Female Values

Locke Marital Adjustment Scale

Love Attitudes Inventory

Love Attraction Inventory

Marital Adjustment Scale

Marital Communication Inventory

Marital Conventionalization Scale

Marital Happiness Index

Marital Happiness Scale

Marital Power and Task Participation Measures

Marital Problems Checklist

Marital Roles Inventory

Marital Roles Questionnaire

Marital Satisfaction Indexes

Marriage Adjustment Inventory

Marriage Scale

Otto Family Strength Survey

Parenting Stress Index

Primary Communication Inventory

Relationship Quality Index

Role Segregation Index

Role Tension Index

Semantic Differential

Sexual Interest Test

Short Marital Adjustment Test

Similarity of Self-Perception Index

Success in Marriage Instrument

Traditional-Developmental Family Role Concepts Scale

Traditional Family Ideology Scale

Value Consensus Index

Yale Marital Interaction Battery

**Marital Roles Inventory.** The Marital Roles Inventory (MRI), developed by Hurvitz,[17] is one objective tool that examines marital adjustment within the framework of role theory. As its author explains, the rationale underlying the scale is that the family is an organization of interacting roles:

> Within the family, the roles of husband-and-father and wife-and-mother are units of conduct which stand out as regularities by their recurrence and form patterns of mutually oriented conduct. These roles, constituted into a role-set, have two aspects: each spouse's performance of the roles in his role-set, and each spouse's expectation of how the other spouse will perform the roles in his role set.[18]

The two general characteristics of roles—performances and expectations—are the basis for the MRI. Since complementary and reciprocal relationship of role performances and expectations make up the social structure of the family, an important aspect of adjustment in marriage results from the compatibility between the role performances and role expectations. This is what the scale measures.

The husband is given a form that lists in random order the "functions or roles of the American husband and father." He is asked to read the eleven statements and to decide which one he carries out as his most important function or role in his family; he assigns a number 1 to this role. Then he decides which role is his next most important one in his family situation and so on until he has ranked each statement with a different number from 1 to 11. On the reverse side of the form are listed functions or roles of the American wife and mother. The husband is instructed to rank his spouse's roles in the order of importance in which he wants or prefers her to perform them. Sample items are provided in Table 10.3. The wife is asked to fill out a parallel form on which she ranks her roles or functions in order of importance and also from 1 to 11 her husband's roles as she wants or prefers him to perform them.

After the response process has been completed, one spouse's ranking of the roles in his or her own role-set can be compared with the rank order of the same roles as the other spouse prefers them to be performed. The difference between these rankings is referred to as the Index of Marital Strain (IMS).

Thus, the husband's IMS is a measure of the difference between his and his wife's ranking of the husband's roles, and the wife's IMS is the difference between her and her husband's ranking of the wife's roles. Similarities in the assignment of rank orders by both spouses indicate good adjustment, whereas discrepancies between role performances and role expectations indicate marital mal-adjustment. In addition to the Index of Marital Strain, three additional scores are obtained with the Marital Role Inventory: Index of Deviation of Role Performances (IDRP), Index of Deviation of Role Expectations (IDRE), and Corrected Index of Marital Strain (C-IMS).

**Dyadic Adjustment Scale.** Another objective measure of marital relations is the Dyadic Adjust-ment Scale.[19] This scale is based upon the notion that marriage adjustment (and other dyadic rela-tionships such as unmarried cohabiting couples) is a constantly changing process with a qualitative dimension that can be measured at any time on a continuum from well-adjusted to maladjusted. The inventory is comprised of four factors related to dyadic adjustment: dyadic satisfaction, dyadic co-hesion, dyadic consensus, and affectional expression. The adjustment instrument yields a subscale score for each of the factors as well as a total adjustment score. The thirty-two-item Dyadic Adjust-ment Scale, which features a changing-alternatives format, asks for an indication of the approximate extent of agreement or disagreement between the respondent and his or her partner on each item. Selected items are presented in Table 10.4.

**Table 10.3.** Items from the Marital Roles Inventory

### American Husband and Father

_____ I do my jobs around the house.
_____ I am a companion to my wife.
_____ I help the children grow by being their friend, teacher, and guide.
_____ I earn the living and support the family.
_____ I do my wife's work around the house if my help is needed.

### American Wife and Mother

_____ She helps earn the living when her husband needs her help or when the family needs more money.
_____ She practices the family religion or philosophy.
_____ She cares for the children's everyday needs.
_____ She is a companion to her husband.
_____ She is the homemaker.

**Table 10.4.** Items from the Dyadic Adjustment Scale

|  | Always agree | Almost always agree | Occa-sionally disagree | Fre-quently disagree | Almost always disagree | Always disagree |
|---|---|---|---|---|---|---|
| 1. Handling family finances | 5 | 4 | 3 | 2 | 1 | 0 |
| 2. Matters of recreation | 5 | 4 | 3 | 2 | 1 | 0 |
| 3. Religious matters | 5 | 4 | 3 | 2 | 1 | 0 |
| 4. Demonstrations of affection | 5 | 4 | 3 | 2 | 1 | 0 |
| 5. Friends | 5 | 4 | 3 | 2 | 1 | 0 |
| 6. Sex relations | 5 | 4 | 3 | 2 | 1 | 0 |
| 7. Conventionality (correct or proper behavior) | 5 | 4 | 3 | 2 | 1 | 0 |
| 8. Philosophy of life | 5 | 4 | 3 | 2 | 1 | 0 |
| 9. Ways of dealing with parents or in-laws | 5 | 4 | 3 | 2 | 1 | 0 |
| 10. Aims, goals, and things believed important | 5 | 4 | 3 | 2 | 1 | 0 |

**Marital Communication Inventory.** A vital facet of family relationships is communication. Because of its correlation with success in marriage, marital communication and its measurement have received considerable attention in the research literature. One instrument designed to measure the process of marital communication is the Marital Communication Inventory.[20] Drawing from previous research and from marriage and family counseling, Bienvenu developed a forty-eight item scale that is designed to assess patterns, characteristics, and styles in communication rather than content of dialogue. It explores the couple's abilities to listen and understand each other and to express themselves. The inventory also examines the manner in which each spouse says things, as some of the items in Table 10.5 illustrate. The subject responds to each item by checking one of four possible answers: *usually, sometimes, seldom,* and *never.* Items are scored on a three-point scale, with 0 signifying an unfavorable response, and 3, the most favorable response.

**Interviews.** The interview is another popular method that has been used to obtain information from parents about their marriage and home life.[21] Interview techniques that examine child-rearing and other aspects of parent-child relations will be treated in some detail later in this chapter under "Parental Behavior Patterns."

## PROJECTIVE TECHNIQUES

Projective measures may be used as another means of studying the marital relationship. Some of these tests also yield insight into other areas of family life, including parent-child relations. Such methods are exemplified, among other things, by sentence- and story-completion instruments, projective picture techniques, and family drawings. Examples of this type of assessment are

Adult-Child Interaction Test

Adult Family Scene

Family Distance Doll Placement Technique

Family Drawings

Family Interaction Apperception Test

Family Interaction Report

Family Relations Indicator

Family Rorschach

Family Story Technique

Family TAT

Female Role Attitudes Test

Kell-Hoeflin Incomplete Sentence Blank: Youth-Parent Relations

Marital Projection Series

Marital Satisfaction Sentence Completions

Marriage Adjustment Sentence Completion Survey

Sentence Completion Test

Three examples of these measures will be discussed.

**Family Relations Indicator.** The Family Relations Indicator is a projective technique for assessing family relationships that can be used with parents as well as children.[22] It consists of forty pictures,

**Table 10.5.** Items from the Marital Communication Inventory

- Does your spouse have a tendency to say things which would be better left unsaid?
- Do you find your spouse's tone of voice irritating?
- Does your spouse complain that you don't understand him (her)?
- Does your spouse insult you when he (she) gets angry with you?
- Do you fail to express disagreement with him (her) because you're afraid he'll (she'll) get angry?
- Does it upset you a great deal when your spouse gets angry at you?
- Do you hesitate to discuss certain things with your spouse because you're afraid he (she) might hurt your feelings?

sixteen of which show a boy as the principal character and sixteen, a girl. The two parallel series of pictures portray the same family situations with the only difference being the sex of the child in the picture. The other eight pictures are appropriate for use with any family, irrespective of its composition. Parents of families with children of both sexes are shown all forty pictures.

The pictures are black-and-white pencil drawings with relatively sharp outlines (see Figure 10.4). They have minimum detail and are structured as little as possible. Furnishings in the interior scenes are socially ambiguous; likewise, clothing worn by characters is not indicative of any particular social class. Children depicted in the family scenes appear to be between eight and eleven years of age, and the parental figures are portrayed as being an appropriate age for parenting the children. There is a minimum of emotional expression shown by the characters. Ambiguity is achieved through the arrangement of the human figures rather than by blurring or shading their outlines. Howells and Lickorish emphasize the need to establish rapport with the subject before introduction of the picture cards. Their rationale for this recommendation is that a person who is placed in a secure and friendly situation will usually ascribe to the figures in the pictures the feelings, attitudes, and actions that are actually representative of his or her own immediate experience. For this reason, the authors suggest that the measure not be administered during the first interview.

When the picture cards are introduced during the second interview, the examiner tells the subject that the pictures show typical family situations. The examiner then asks the mother or father to look at each picture and to tell what the people are saying or doing. Simple statements rather than a story are encouraged. By using this procedure, it is assumed that the responses will be more factual than imaginative. The scenes are replicated with slight variations which have a cumulative effect upon the information volunteered. In addition, the replications provide an internal verification of what is said by the parent. Replies are recorded verbatim, and the use of a tape recorder is suggested. The responses are then scored by selecting from the protocol those words and phrases that describe relationships within the home.

Since limited evidence regarding the scale's validity exists at this time, its authors advise that the Family Relations Indicator be used only in conjunction with other parent-child measures in order to insure a complete description of family dynamics.

**Marital Satisfaction Sentence Completions.** Another widely used projective technique that is appropriate for the measurement of marriage and family relations is the sentence completion method. Pioneered by Payne[23] and Tendler,[24] sentence completion procedures have been constructed to suit the special needs of the particular population being studied.[25] The subject is presented with a series of incomplete sentences and is asked to provide endings for them. The stimulus stems used by Inselberg are listed here to show how the sentence completion technique can be used to study marital happiness:

In-laws are . . .
Our income  . . .
Sex relations are . . .

I wish . . .
My husband (wife) and I. . .
I regret . . .
The future . . .
The happiest time . . .
Getting married at the age that I did . . .
Getting tied down after marriage . . .
Making decisions in our home . . .
What annoys me . . .
If only . . . [26]

Each of these introductory stems is designed to elicit responses that reveal an individual's attitudes and feelings about his or her marriage. For example, *In-laws are* presumably illustrates feelings about in-laws or aspects of relationships with the spouse's parents. Other stems, such as *Our income,* would elicit a narrower range of responses because of the use of *our* which insures greater specificity of content. As indicated by the examples, some statements employ the first person, and others, the third person.

**Sentence Completion Test.** Of the several other instruments of this type, Forer's Sentence Completion Test[27] has been the most useful in the assessment of marriage and family relations. Two 100-item forms are available, one for each sex. Several items deal with attitudes toward important interpersonal figures in the individual's life, ranging from members of the immediate family to less closely related persons. For example, these sentence stems are included in section A of the test: *His (her) father always . . . , Most men . . . , Mothers . . . ,* and *Most women act as though . . . .* Section D is an analysis of the characteristic ways in which the respondent reacts or thinks of reacting to various interpersonal relationships, including marriage. Some typical stems from this part of the test are *A person who falls in love . . . , Love is . . . , Most marriages . . . , After a year of marriage, he (she) . . . ,* and *When I think of marriage . . . .*

Content analysis and qualitative interpretations are usually made from sentence completion responses, although some attempts at quantification have been made. Because of the difficulties inherent in most standard objective scoring systems, subjective inferences drawn from the responses are generally the rule.

**Figure 10.4.** Specimen Card from the Family Relations Indicator

## DIRECT METHODS

The child's parents may also be studied using direct methods, that is, observational techniques. Although observations of the family have been undertaken which examine typical behavior in natural settings, a recent trend in observational family study has been to use artificial situational tests whose aim is "to provide a standard milieu for revealing and comparing family interaction."[28] Against this backdrop, family interaction is pictured and observed. Usually, simulations of three types of "tasks" have been used to stimulate sequences of interaction for analysis: decision-making,[29] conflict resolution,[30] and problem-solving.[31] Although these techniques represent ambitious efforts in the area of family assessment, they have demonstrated methodological difficulties specific to the study of families in addition to those inherent in all observational approaches.[32] Direct observation techniques for family study will receive greater attention in the section "Parental Behavior Patterns."

## CHILD-ORIENTED PARENTAL ATTITUDES

Child-oriented parental attitudes include conceptions of the parent and child roles, attitudes toward parenthood, child-rearing goals, attitudes about disciplinary techniques, and acceptance or rejection of children. Many measures of this nature are available, and some of them are

Ackerly Parental Attitude Scale

Anders' Child Rearing Survey

Attitude Toward Children's Freedom Scale

Attitude Toward Self-Reliance

Attitudes Toward Parental Control of Children

Child Rearing Practices Report

Child Responsibility and Independence Indexes

Family Attitude Measure

Family Problems Scale

Intra-Family Attitude Scales

Inventory of Family Life and Attitudes

Mark Attitude Survey

Maryland Parent Attitude Survey

Maternal Attitude Questionnaire

Maternal Attitude Scale

Maternal Attitudes Scale

Minnesota Scale of Parent Opinion

Mother-Child Relationship Evaluation

Nebraska Parent Attitude Scale

Parent Attitude Research Instrument

Parental Concern Test

Parental Control Attitude Scale

Parental Developmental Timetable

Parental Opinion Inventory

Parent As a Teacher Inventory

Parent Attitude Inventory

Parent Attitude Survey

Parent Questionnaire

Perinatal Rigidity Scale

Stanford Parent Questionnaire

University of Southern California Parent Attitude Survey

**Parent Attitude Research Instrument.** Although there are a number of widely used child and family attitude instruments, the best known and most popular measure of this kind is the Parent Attitude Research Instrument (PARI) developed by Schaefer and Bell.[33] This questionnaire consists of twenty-three five-item scales:

| | |
|---|---|
| Encouraging Verbalization | Rejection of the Homemaking Role |
| Fostering Dependence | Equalitarianism |
| Seclusion of the Mother | Approval of Activity |
| Breaking the Will | Avoidance of Communication |
| Martyrdom | Inconsiderateness of the Husband |
| Fear of Harming Baby | Suppression of Sexuality |
| Marital Conflict | Ascendance of the Mother |
| Strictness | Intrusiveness |
| Irritability | Comradeship and Sharing |
| Excluding Outside Influences | Acceleration of Development |
| Deification | Dependency of the Mother |
| Suppression of Aggression | |

The PARI format involves the use of third-person statements about child-rearing and family life such as *Children who are troublemakers have most likely been spanked too much, Sometimes it's necessary for a wife to tell off her husband in order to get her rights,* and *A good mother should shelter her child from life's little difficulties.* Four response alternatives are possible, including strongly agree, mildly agree, mildly disagree, or strongly disagree. The score for each subscale is obtained by summing the rating.

The instrument, which should be administered personally or in closely supervised group situations, was initially designed for use with mothers only, but a slightly different form has since been developed for fathers.[34] The father's version of the PARI is composed of thirty scales, each measured by eight items. Scales included in this form but not in the mother's are Harsh Punishment, Deception, Inconsiderateness of Wife, Autonomy of Child, and Suppression of Affection. A critical research review on the PARI has been published by Becker and Krug.[35]

**Parent Attitude Survey.** Another frequently used parent attitude instrument is that constructed by Shoben.[36] Referred to as the University of Southern California Parent Attitude Survey because it was developed at that institution, this paper-and-pencil scale consists of eighty-five items that measure three categories of parental attitudes plus an additional miscellaneous category which defies classification. The *Dominating* subscale includes items reflecting a tendency for the parent to put the child in a subordinate role. The second subscale, called the *Possessive* variable, consists of items referring to an inclination on the part of the parent to "baby" the child and to overemphasize the parent-child affectional bond. The *Ignoring* subscale is composed of items that relate to a tendency for the parent to disregard the child as an individual member of the family and to disclaim responsibility for the youngster's behavior. Each item is answered by one of four weighted response categories: strongly agree, mildly agree, mildly disagree, and strongly disagree. These are examples of items for the three parent attitudinal themes:

### Possessive

21. Children should be forbidden to play with youngsters whom their parents do not approve of.

40. A child should feel a deep sense of obligation always to act in accord with the wishes of his parents.

51. Parents are not entitled to the love of their children unless they earn it.

### Dominating

23. Severe discipline is essential in the training of children.

36. It is wicked for children to disobey their parents.

45. Strict discipline weakens a child's personality.

### Ignoring

22. A good way to discipline a child is to tell him his parents won't love him any more if he is bad.

25. Parents cannot help it if their children are naughty.

56. Children should not interrupt adult conversation.[37]

Technical data regarding the University of Southern California Parent Attitude Survey are available in Shoben's monograph which describes the development of the scale.

## PARENTAL BEHAVIOR PATTERNS

Two methods of studying parental behavior patterns will be highlighted in this section: the interview and the observation of parent-child interaction.

### INTERVIEW

Interviewing techniques have long been used as a vehicle for obtaining information about parental behavior.[38] A conversational encounter between two or more persons which encompasses verbal and nonverbal interactions,[39] the interview can provide descriptions of parent-child relations as well as detailed accounts of the child's current behavior and past development.

> Usually, the differentiation of role between interviewer and respondent is pronounced. The interviewer not only initiates the conversation; he presents each topic by means of specific questions, and he decides when the conversation on a topic has satisfied the research objectives (or the specific criteria which represent them) and another topic shall be introduced. The respondent in the research interview is led to restrict his discussion to the specific questions posed by the interviewer.[40]

**Sears Interview Schedule.** A widely cited interview study concerning the examination of patterns of child rearing was conducted by Sears, Maccoby, and Levin over twenty years ago.[41] The original interview schedule, because of its comprehensive nature, has been adapted for use in a number of studies and in clinical practice. Using a type of interview described as "somewhere between the flexible, unstandardized, 'depth' interview which is characteristic of clinical interviewing, and the completely structured interview,"[42] Sears and his associates investigated the child-rearing practices of 379 mothers with five-year-old children.

The interview schedule includes open-ended questions with a series of suggested probes that the interviewer is free to use or omit depending on the comprehensiveness of the respondent's answer to the original question. This is an example of a question and its probes (9a and 9b):

> 9. There has been a lot of talk about whether it is better to have a regular feeding schedule for a baby, or to feed him whenever he is hungry. How do you feel about this?
> 9a. How did you handle this with X?
> 9b. (If schedule) How closely did you stick to that schedule?[43]

These questions were designed to provide information that could be used to rate the mother's treatment of her youngster on a scale that ranged from extreme rigid scheduling to complete self-demand. If the mother answered the initial question fully, the interviewer did not ask the probe questions. However, if she gave a vague answer which did not provide a basis for an accurate rating, further probing was pursued. Standard probes were included in the interview schedule to insure that the interviewer obtained the child-rearing data that were necessary.

A number of questions in the interview schedule deal with neatness, orderliness, and care of the household.

> 21. Now we want to change the subject: the question of being neat and orderly and keeping things clean. What do you expect of X as far as neatness is concerned?
> 21a. How do you go about getting him to do this?
>
> 22. How important do you think it is for him to be careful about marking on the walls and jumping on the furniture and things like that?
> 22a. What do you do about it if he does these things?
> 22b. And how about teaching children to respect the things that belong to other members of the family? What have you done about this with X?[44]

Other questions explore maternal stimulation of cognitive development and expectations for the child's achievement.

> 34. Before X started kindergarten, did you teach him anything like reading words or writing the alphabet, or drawing, or telling time—things like that?
> 34a. Anything else you taught him?
> 34b. How did you happen to teach him these things?
>
> 35. How important is it to you for X to do well in school?
> 35a. How far would you like him to go in school?[45]

The matter of parental sanctions in child rearing is examined in this series of questions and probes.

> We have been talking about how you handle X in many different kinds of situations: table manners, neatness, and so on. Now we'd like to know something about how you go about correcting X and getting him to behave the way you want him to, regardless of the particular kind of behavior that is involved.

45. Do you have any system of rewarding him for good behavior?

    45a. Do you have any ways that he can earn money?

    45b. Can he earn points or gold stars or anything like that?

46. Some parents praise their children quite a bit when they are good, and others think that you ought to take good behavior for granted and that there's no point in praising a child for it. How do you feel about this?

47. In training X, do you ever say: "Your daddy and mother do it this way?" Do you say that? Under what circumstances?

    47a. Who else do you hold up as an example—his older brother (sister)? grandparents? other relatives? playmates?

    47b. Is there anyone you mention as an example of what not to do? For instance—you're acting just like so-and-so—you wouldn't want to be like him, would you?[46]

To overcome stereotyping in answers, a number of devices are incorporated into the wording of the interview schedule, including these:

1. (*Face saving*) "Do you ever find time to play with Johnny just for your own pleasure?" (instead of "Do you ever play . . . .")

2. (*Assuming the existence of negatively valued behavior*) "In what ways do you get on each other's nerves?" (instead of "Do you ever get on each other's nerves?")

3. (*Making a wide range of answers appear socially acceptable*) "Some people feel it's very important for a child to learn not to fight with other children, and other people feel there are times when a child has to learn to fight. How do you feel about this?"

4. (*Pitting two stereotypes—values—against each other*) "Do you keep track of exactly where Johnny is and what he is doing most of the time, or can you let him watch out for himself quite a bit?" (Here the value of being a careful mother, who protects her child from danger, is pitted against the value of training a child to be independent.)[47]

The lengthy standardized interview was recorded on a portable Audograph machine, and verbatim typed transcripts were prepared later. Interview protocols were then coded for 188 scales by two independent raters. Some of the rating scales for the mothers' questions already mentioned are listed here, along with their respective point values as they appear in the *Patterns of Childrearing*, Appendix B.

II   36  Scheduling of feeding. . . . . . . . . . .3=vague attempts
                                          6=rigid schedule

II   61  Standards for neatness and
               orderliness . . . . . . . . . . . . . . . .1=low standards
                                        9=high standards

II   62  Restrictions relating to care
               of house and furniture . . . . . . . .1=few restrictions
                                        2=many restrictions

II   63   Pressures for neatness and
orderliness . . . . . . . . . . . . . . . . . .1=no pressure
9=high pressure

III   16   Amount of teaching before
child starts school . . . . . . . . . . .1=no teaching
5=considerable teaching

III   17   Child's demand for
teaching. . . . . . . . . . . . . . . . . . .1=none
5=considerable

III   18   How important that child do
well in school? . . . . . . . . . . . . .1=unimportant
9=very important

III   19   How far is child expected
to go in school?. . . . . . . . . . . . .1=grade school
9=graduate school[48]

The Sears procedure was successful in identifying customary child-training practices in a New England sample, in surveying the effects of certain rearing practices on the personality development of children, and in revealing what kinds of mothers use different methods of child rearing. Moreover, the study demonstrated that interviews with parents can provide a variety of data regarding a child's family life and that the interview method is vital to effective child assessment.

**Hereford Interview Schedule.** A brief and versatile interview procedure for parents has been developed by Hereford.[49] Less comprehensive than the Sears procedure, this interview schedule includes some fairly general questions in seven areas of parental attitudes and behavior: difficulties in raising children, what parents like about parenthood, parental worries, amount of freedom for children, methods of punishment, family troubles, and ideal child/parent. The scope of the questions is indicated in Table 10.6. Like the Sears schedule, the Hereford Schedule includes probe questions which assist the interviewer by suggesting ramifications to the major question so that more complete information may be elicited from the interviewee.

Interview data are tabulated according to a content code. Depending on the complexity of the question, the number of response codes for each item varies from 2 to 24. A code of 0 is assessed if the parent gives insufficient information or if a response is not covered by the code. For the lead

**Table 10.6.** Questions from the Hereford Interview Schedule

---

1. All parents have some difficulties in raising children. In general, what has been the hardest thing about child-rearing for you?
   a. What have you done to help this situation?
   b. How has this worked out?
   c. [If nothing on causation.] What do you think caused this situation to develop?
   d. How common are situations like this with other parents and children you know?
   e. Have you ever sought outside help in this matter? [Talked it over with a friend, physician, guidance center, teacher, etc.]
   f. How did this work out?
4. Sometimes it's hard to know just where to draw the line with children. How much freedom do you allow your children? [Strict? Lenient? Flexible?]
   a. Can you give some examples? [Activities, responsibility for school, allowance, choice of playmates, etc.]
   b. How do other families in the neighborhood handle situations like this?
   c. Are there some children you would prefer he or she didn't play with? [If so, why?]
   d. How does he or she feel about this?

---

in the interview regarding difficulties in raising children, there are twenty-four possible responses that are covered by codes (see Table 10.7).

Although the interview questions and probes were selected on the basis of their relevance for the hypotheses of Hereford's research, they nevertheless encompass a broad domain of parental attitudes and practices and examine many areas of family life that are important in understanding individual children.

**Evaluation of Parental Interviews.** In spite of the fact that much of the data on parent-child relations has been generated by means of the interview, not all child and family specialists are willing to accept information deriving from it at face value. In a very critical review, Yarrow has questioned the validity of the interview technique for several reasons: (a) in a brief period of time, usually only minutes, the interviewer extracts information on many complicated behaviors; (b) responses by parents may be influenced by their needs and defenses, child-rearing values, as well as social-class identification and the mores attached to it; (c) parents are sometimes requested to make difficult discriminations and syntheses, many of which require recall of past feelings and behaviors; and (d) parents are asked to rate themselves, and their frames of reference vary considerably.[50] To these potential pitfalls of the interview technique in parent-child studies, Wenar has added other possible sources of bias.[51] Parents have a good deal of personal involvement and investment in their youngsters and consciously or unconsciously view their offspring as representing them and as reflecting the adequacy of their socialization practices. Parents may go so far as to distort or omit facts that reflect negatively on their competence as childrearers. In response to previous research on the problems of retrospective data,[52] Wenar points out that it is the nature of the information and not necessarily the passage of time that affects recall, although just what its influence will be is difficult to determine. For example, the parents of a child who is having a serious behavior problem

Table 10.7. Interview Code for Question 1 of the Hereford Interview Schedule

| Code | | Question 1. Difficulties in raising children |
|------|------|------|
| 00 | No information, or not covered by code | |
| 01 | Discipline—minding, obeying, making child do something, etc. | |
| 02 | Sibling rivalry, problems between children | |
| 03 | | Interpersonal—getting along with others |
| 04 | | Responsibility |
| 05 | Normal adjustment or | Passivity—shy, won't fight back |
| 06 | developmental problems | Aggressiveness—rowdy, noisy |
| 07 | | Dawdling |
| 08 | | Other |
| 09 | | Thumbsucking |
| 10 | | Wetting or soiling |
| 11 | | Eating problems |
| 12 | Specific symptoms | Nailbiting |
| 13 | | Withdrawal, extreme shyness |
| 14 | | Extreme destructiveness or aggression |
| 15 | | Phobias or fears |
| 16 | | Other |
| 17 | Physical health or illness, safety | |
| 18 | Financial | |
| 19 | | Inadequacy |
| 20 | | Indecision |
| 21 | Problem within parents | Inconsistency between parents |
| 23 | | Lack of patience |
| 23 | | Other |
| 24 | States that he has no problem | |

for the first time may remember details of the youngster's earlier satisfactory behavior because discontinuity may have increased accuracy through contrast. Perhaps if the child had experienced behavioral disturbance for some time, the continuity of present and past behavior or the relative homogeneity of events might have decreased memory. Or, perhaps an element of "social desirability" colors the responses of parents.[53]

Not all researchers take a dim view of parental interviews. In fact, a few validity studies have revealed that the interview is a feasible procedure.[54] Moreover, the credibility of interview data is increased when efforts are made to reduce some of the possible areas of distortion by such means as structuring the interview carefully,[55] focusing on relatively recent events and examining questions about feelings separately from more factual ones,[56] confining questions to those encompassing only recent events,[57] and informing interviewees that data will be cross-checked with different sources (i.e., others in the child's environment will also be asked questions).[58]

Most of the disadvantages of parental interviews also plague paper-and-pencil self-report measures of parent-child relations since both involve accounts of what goes on or has gone on in the home. But the interview justifies its continued use in family study because it can sample a wide range of feelings and behaviors, data which may be unattainable through observation. In addition, the interview is helpful in generating and testing hypotheses about the child's behavior and environments, and it also provides insight into the parents' *interpretation* of certain events. Finally, Lytton provides an encouraging summary note and prospectus for the future use of interviews in parent-child studies when he writes:

> With the modifications introduced recently which mean that the information input is more strictly controlled, the interview has shown reasonable agreement with other data and will have a useful role to play, particularly in obtaining data that are inaccessible to direct observation and for information about internal cues. Above all, verbal reports by parents will inspire greater confidence in their veracity and validity if they are supplemented by, and checked against, observational measures.[59]

## DIRECT OBSERVATION

Perhaps because of dissatisfaction with the frequent lack of correspondence between parental reports and actual behavior or possibly because of the desire to get closer to primary data, child development and family researchers have turned more and more to direct observation of parent and child interacting in some situation.[60] Perusal of recent issues of developmental and clinical journals reveals that the number of parent-child observation studies is increasing monthly.

Parent-child observational studies share many common features, but at the same time, they differ methodologically in several ways. Among these variations are amount of control exercised over stimuli and behavior, method of recording data, conceptualization of variables, range and type of behavior sampled, and reliability and validity of data.[61]

Some parent-child observation approaches involve completely unstructured situations in the home,[62] whereas others use highly structured tasks in a standardized laboratory setting.[63] Between these two extremes is the arrangement in which external circumstances are standardized, while the child's behavior is allowed to vary as in "free-play" parent-child interaction studies.[64] Minimum control of stimuli is found in the unstructured, natural setting of a family's home.[65]

There are a number of ways to approach the recording of parent-child observation data. Recording procedures may be viewed as comprising a continuum from global to specific.[66] Global recording provides the least amount of information on actual behavior and involves the most abstraction. Conversely, specific recording gives the most information about behavior with a minimum of abstraction. Methods that require ratings *after* observation are representative of the global type.[67] In these, behavior is noted informally or not at all during the course of observation, and ratings on global characteristics of the parents and children are subsequently made. Some global behaviors or summary variables, as they are sometimes called, include affection, rejection, anxiety, and stimulation.

Parent and child behavior may also be recorded in narrative-style summaries that are prepared following home visits.[68] Unlike the recording techniques just mentioned that use postcategorization of variables and which provide the least information on behavior observed as well as the greatest amount of abstraction, the narrative-style summary involves slightly less abstraction. Another possible way to record parent-child data is the selected narrative record written at the time of observation.[69] Here, only certain aspects of the parent-child interaction are recorded on-the-spot. Yet another narrative recording technique which lends itself to parent-child study is the specimen record.[70] As described in Chapter 3, specimen recording is a sequential, narrative account of *all* of the behavior observed. Because of its comprehensiveness, this recording scheme gives the greatest amount of information and abstracts the least.

The use of precoded behavior categories is the most popular method of recording parent-child interaction today. This approach employs predetermined classes of carefully defined behaviors, the occurrences of which are noted with code symbols or are indicated as "present" or "absent" at specified and usually brief intervals of time.[71] A recent journal article written by Roberts and Forehand provides an excellent description of available direct observation technologies for measuring parent-child interactions and should be consulted for an extended discussion of the topic.[72]

The range and type of parent-child behaviors sampled vary according to the observer's objectives and preferences. For instance, naturalistic observations in the home may enable the observer to obtain uncommon socialization data,[73] thereby extending the range of behavior open to investigation. However, home observations may also restrict this range since some significant behavior will not always occur during the times arranged for observation.[74] Moreover, the type of parent-child behavior examined seems to be influenced by the child's age. Lytton has pointed out that unstructured naturalistic methods are most often used with infants because their mobility is limited, making them captive subjects.[75] Consequently, the infant's behavior, usually simple reactions, is easily brought into focus for careful scrutiny. But this is not necessarily the case for older children. There are relatively few studies investigating the naturally occurring behavior of noninfant subjects in domestic settings because of the problems involved in observing the wider ranging activities of older subjects.[76] Typically, home observations involving these children have taken the form of structured tasks in which parent-child interaction is observed.[77] Significantly more parent-child studies that include older preschool children have been carried out in the laboratory, using either free play or structured tasks. Despite the restrictions the laboratory situation places on the possible range of responses, the variety of actual behaviors examined in the lab is a tribute to the ingenuity of observers as Hughes and Haynes have demonstrated in a recent review article.[78] The increasing use of instrumental aids in these studies appears to have contributed to an overall improvement in the quality of the parent-child observation record in recent years.[79]

An important methodological concern in parent-child interaction investigations involves two related issues: reliability and validity. Most recent studies have achieved adequate intercoder reliability. However, findings of intersession consistency across behaviors have been less consistent, with some investigations demonstrating this type of reliability[80] and other not.[81] Some studies of parent-child interaction do not even report reliability data, leaving their findings open to question.[82] Factors that affect the reliability of observational studies were discussed in Chapter 4, and these apply equally to parent-child investigations.

Another way in which parent-child interaction studies vary is in the validity of their data. Although most interactional studies of this nature have face or content validity, results regarding predictive and concurrent validity are rare, and findings concerning criterion-related validity are mixed. The latter type of validity refers to the extent to which the data are representative of normal interactions between parents and their children. With a few exceptions,[83] investigations have found that some parent-child observations demonstrate criterion-related validity.[84]

Closely related to the issue of validity is the matter of observer interference. The potential bias introduced by the parent's knowledge that he or she is being observed has continued to receive attention in the research literature. A number of studies have discovered reactive effects,[85] while a few others have shown that there are no significant effects.[86] White has attempted to explain these inconsistencies in terms of several factors that include the setting, length of observation, constraints placed on the parent and child by the conditions of the observation, the research paradigm employed, and the dependent variables examined.[87] These factors must be examined carefully before inconsistent findings regarding observer interference can be completely understood.[88] Even then, obtaining experimental evidence on parents' reactions to observations may still be difficult because this requires the collection of baseline data unknown to the observation subjects, something that is both practically and ethically difficult to do.[89]

In the following sections, three observational approaches to the study of parents and their children are described.

**Fels Behavior Rating Scales.** One of the first systematic observational investigations of parent-child relations were conducted by Baldwin, Kalhorn, and Breese[90] using the Fels Behavior Rating Scales.[91] This assessment procedure involves both direct observation and inferences made by an observer who visits the home for a total of approximately four hours. After the home visit, the observer writes a narrative case summary and also evaluates the parent's behavior in terms of the thirty variables on the Fels instrument. Of these, twenty-five are grouped into eight clusters, and five are listed separately.

1. *Warmth*—acceptance of child, direction of criticism, affection, rapport, child centeredness, intensity of contact

2. *Adjustment*—adjustment of home, discord, effectiveness of policy, disciplinary friction

3. *Indulgence*—babying, protectiveness, solicitousness

4. *Democracy*—democracy of policy, justification of policy

5. *Intellectuality*—readiness of explanation, accelerational attempt, understanding

6. *Restrictiveness*—restrictiveness of regulations, coerciveness of suggestions

7. *Clarity*—clarity of policy, readiness of enforcement

8. *Interference*—quantity of suggestion, readiness of criticism, severity of punishment

9. *Activeness*

10. *Coordination*

11. *Sociability*

12. *Duration of contact*

13. *Emotionality*

The observer is assured of obtaining a relatively complete record of parent-child relationships inasmuch as he or she prepares not only a narrative summary but also completes the more objective, quantitative ratings. Originally, the scales were developed to help social workers structure their reports of parental behavior and its relationship to the child as well as to assure complete coverage of all significant areas of parent-child relations. Eventually, the determination was made that such a technique for home data collection, with its use of a standardized vocabulary and a prescribed list of parent-child behavior variables, would serve as a valuable adjunct to the case summary and would contribute toward greater comparability among clinical reports. As an observational aid, the battery of Fels Parent Behavior Scales helps the observer present an integrated description of the family situation.

Ratings on the home environment of a child are made separately even if the observation subjects are siblings. There is a separate rating sheet for each of the thirty variables. The rating form for "readiness of enforcement" is illustrated in Figure 10.5. As you can see, a form may be used for more than one child. This particular rating sheet summarized the parent-child behavior of ten different youngsters. Ratings are made by placing an X on the vertical line at or near the cue that describes the parent's behavior toward the child on the dimension in question. In addition, the observer provides two supplementary ratings. The first, Tolerance, is indicated by horizontal dashes, and signifies the observer's region of uncertainty. It demonstrates within what limits he or she would consider a rating by an independent observer to be in close agreement with his or her own. The second supplementary

FELS PARENT BEHAVIOR RATING SCALE NO. 3.12     Readiness of Enforcement
                                                        (Vigilant—Lax)

Serial Sheet No.

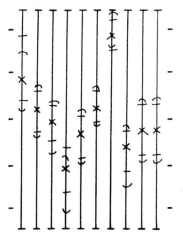

Rate the parent's tendency to enforce the standards of conduct set up for the child. Does the parent follow up to see that the child conforms, or sustains a penalty? Or are lapses in compliance disregarded?

This variable applies only to situations where there is an opportunity for the parent to enforce an accepted standard which has been, or is being, or is about to be violated by the child. Disregard the methods of enforcement and the severity of penalties. Disregard effectiveness of enforcement, and clarity to the child of standards involved. Do not confuse with the non-regulational type of parental domination covered by the "suggestion" scales.

Eternally vigilant. Goes out of way to discover and discipline misconduct. Often pounces before lapse occurs.

Seldom lets child "get away with anything." Enforces rules strictly whenever violations come to attention, but seldom deliberately hunts for misbehavior.

Moderately firm. Strict about important requirements and prohibitions; but rather lax with minor violations, especially when they are not an issue at the moment.

Reluctant to enforce standards. Tends to overlook violations unless they are flagrant, cumulative, or threaten serious consequences.

Extremely lax. Disregards obvious misbehavior. Enforces regulations only when pressed by the strongest motives or the severest circumstances.

| 71 | 59 | 53 | 34 | 48 | 59 | 90 | 43 | 50 | 50 | Score | Rater: J̈ | Date of Rating: 10/13/47 |
| 27 | 17 | 14 | 18 | 17 | 13 | 13 | 16 | 21 | 21 | Tolerance | Scored by: RG | Date: 10/19/47 |
| 24 | 21 | 22 | 34 | 23 | 17 | 14 | 26 | 26 | 27 | Range | Checked by: MN | Date: 10/23/47 |
| 1 | 2 | 3 | 4 | 5 | 6 | 7 | 8 | 9 | 10 | Number | Tabulated by: | Date: |

Rater's Remarks: (continue on back of sheet)

Figure 10.5 Sample Rating Form from the Fels Behavior Rating Scale

rating, Range, is denoted by horizontal parentheses, and designates the range of variability in the parent's behavior that was actually observed or what the observer believes would occur in other situations. At the bottom of the form is room for notation of remarks by the observer. Baldwin and his associates suggest that this space be used for

1. Mention of anything unusual about the conditions of observation

2. Exceptions taken to definitions or cues

3. Peculiarities of the observer of the mother or child subject relative to that variable

4. Any other qualifying remarks or mention of difficulties in using that particular scale[92]

Ratings should be completed in sequence, each one done before going on to the next.

The bottom of the scale line is 9.5, and the top, 99.5. Scoring is accomplished by measuring the distance from the bottom of the vertical line to the X with a millimeter rule. This results in a two-digit number, anywhere from 10 to 99. After the raw score has been noted in the box at the bottom of the rating sheet, it is transformed into a standard score, called a sigma index. This derived score is actually nothing more than a $T$-score distribution with a mean of 50 and a standard deviation of 10 (sigma index $= \dfrac{X\text{-}M}{\sigma} \cdot 10 + 50$). To facilitate the transcription, a tabulation sheet is provided. The observer may then interpret the scores further by transferring them to the profile sheet shown in Figure 10.6. Dots are placed at the appropriate points on the horizontal lines that correspond to the particular variables, revealing intraindividual variation. A dot at the midpoint signifies a sigma index of 50 (i.e., the mean), and dots to the left and right indicate scores below and above the average rating, respectively. Thus, a score of 30 is $-2$ standard deviations from the mean; a score of 60, $+1$ standard deviation from the mean, and so forth. Additional technical information and recommendations for interpretation of the Fels Behavior Rating Scales are available in the 1949 Baldwin et al. monograph.[93]

**Bishop Category System.** Another pioneering effort in the field of direct observation studies of parent-child interaction using precoded categories was conducted by Bishop.[94] In this investigation, Bishop observed the stimulus properties of maternal behavior in a standardized play situation outside the home. She explains the objectives of her category system:

> The categories chosen as most useful for characterizing the mother's behavior toward her child were selected partly on theoretical grounds and partly on empirical grounds. From a theoretical standpoint it was desired to have categories which would reflect accurately the direct amounts and kinds of influence the mother's behavior had on the child, i.e., the stimulus properties of her behavior. From an empirical standpoint it was necessary to select categories that were already definable, easily recognized in the rapid flux of social interaction, and comprehensive enough *in toto* to permit the categorization of all possible behavior incidents that appeared during the play session.[95]

Some of the categories are given in Table 10.8. Uppercase $M$ stands for mother, and $C$ for child. Symbols are used to record the mother's behaviors irrespective of the child's reaction. For instance, the category $dM$ indicates that the mother demanded that her child do something. It is marked $d$ no matter what the response of the child was. Similarly, if the mother stopped a particular child behavior, this action is recorded $i$ whether or not the youngster was receptive to the interference. Of the thirty-two behavior categories used, eleven were finally analyzed for Bishop's recording system: lack

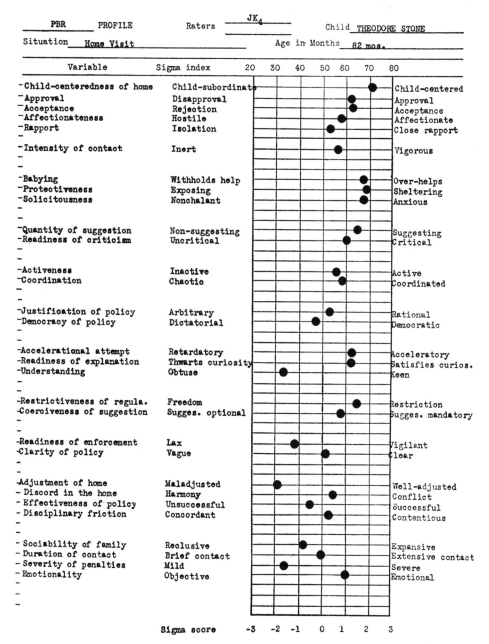

**Figure 10.6.** Profile Sheet from the Fels Behavior Rating Scale

of contact, structurizing, structurizing a change in activity, teaching, interactive play, helping, directing, interfering, criticizing, cooperation, and noncooperation. The mother's behavior was recorded behind a one-way screen at five-second intervals during two thirty-minute observation sessions.

Bishop's study of mothers and their three- to five-year-old children revealed some of the relationships that exist between mother and child behavior in the context of stimulus-response learning theory. More importantly, however, it presented an innovative method for the direct measurement

**Table 10.8** Behavior Categories from Bishop's Study of Mother-Child Interaction

**M=mother**

*a* M is carrying on independent activity at the adult level—any act divorced from the experimental set-up or C, such as reading magazines, looking out the window, busying self with contents of pocketbook.

*o* M is a silent onlooker. M sits in adult chair, which together with the large table and its magazines are slightly apart from the toys with which C is playing; although she watches C, she is not in contact with him as explained under category *c*.

*c* M is in contact with C either physically, conversationally, or on a play level. "Physically" means sitting or being near C as he plays, even though she says nothing. "Conversationally" means purely social talk with C; M is apparently not trying to shape or influence C's actions. Example: "This is a nice water tank— we'll have to see if daddy can build one for you like it."

*s* M structurizes. She uses indirect means to stimulate or influence the child. M attempts to encourage C to think or decide for himself, usually with the aid of a few cues. M may be also trying to inspire C's imagination and creativeness. Essentially, by this form of stimulation C is oriented toward several possible courses of action, any one of which he may choose, or he is given the option of accepting one offered suggestion or not. The quality of the guidance is to C apparently unobtrusive and unimposing. With regard to the play situation, the purpose is to further and enrich play content. With reference to teaching, the aim is to have C reach his own conclusions. In respect to discipline, the basic idea is to obviate the necessity for arbitrary demands. Examples: M: "I imagine these animals would like a nice boat ride in the water." C: "But what can I use for a boat? —these little boats aren't large enough." M: "Do you see something in this room out of which you could make a boat?" C: "Oh yes, I could make one out of the wood."

*S* M introduces by suggestion the possibility of play activity other than the one C is engaged in, in terms of the play units offered in the experimental room. Example: "Did you see those pretty blocks over there—and the dolls—they look as though they might need a house to live in."

*t* M teaches. She gives information to C for the purpose of increasing C's knowledge. Example: "This is a duck and that is a swan—swans have longer, thinner necks than do ducks." If the information is given to clarify and stimulate play possibilities, it should be marked *s*. Example: "Turtles make houses in the sand—do you suppose this turtle needs a house?" If teaching is done by structurizing, it should be marked *s*. Example: "How do swans differ from ducks?"

*p* M plays interactively on C's level; she plays as though she were another child. Example: "I'll be the garage man and I'll fix your car."

*ps* M plays by herself while in contact with C for the purpose of interesting C in that particular play activity.

*h* M gives C physical help. Example: M pounds nail for C.

**C=child**

*oh* M offers help to C before giving it; in other words, she asks C's permission. Example: "Would you like me to help you carry those blocks over there?"

*d* M specifically directs C's actions by command or statement. She gives unequivocal impetus to a certain action; she offers C only one course of action. She tells C what to do, with the exception that C will do that. Example: "Put that block on top of the other ones . . . then make a door right there."

*i* M interferes with an activity on C's part with the intent of stopping it completely. This is interpreted as a stimulus which causes a break in C's action pattern and which may conceivably be felt by C as thwarting or interrupting his course of action. Explicit directing is implied in this category. Example: 'No, don't put that sand in the water . . . did you hear what mother said!"

*r* M restricts C's activity. She modifies his behavior by reducing intensity, speed, manner of executing, etc. Example: "Don't splash the water so high."

*si* M interferes by structurizing. She indicates the undesirability of certain action and/or the consequences of the act if carried out. She suggests that is would be wiser to refrain from continuing the particular behavior and may give the reason for her judgment. The final decision is relegated to C. Example: "You know other boys and girls will want to play with those toys (floating celluloid animals) and if you mash them together like that they will be spoiled."

*we* M cautions C against possible injury. Example: "You are going to hurt your thumb if you don't hold it back out of the way of the hammer."

*wi* M interferes with (stops) C's activity because it is involving a threat to his welfare. Example: "Don't drink that water—the cup is not clean."

*w* M worries over C's welfare. Example: "Oh dear, now you've gotten your suit wet and there's quite a draft in this room."

*m* M praises or encourages C. Example: "That's a very fine boat you've made."

*n* M blames, criticizes, scolds, or punishes C. Example: "You know better than to be so careless."

*−q* M refuses to answer C's question by being silent or evasive. Example: "I don't know—Mother is busy reading."

*+* M cooperates with a verbal request by C. The plus sign may appear in connection with an appropriate behavior category (for example, +*h*, or +*p*, indicating that the mother has agreed to help or play with the child in response to his request for such activity); or it may stand alone if none of the given categories apply.

*−* M ignores or refuses to comply with a verbal request by C. The minus sign is used alone or with an appropriate category in the same manner described for the plus sign.

**Table 10.9.** Behavior Categories in the Behavior Coding System

| First Order | | Second Order | |
|---|---|---|---|
| **Verbal** | | | |
| CM | Command | TA | Talk |
| CN | Command Negative | | |
| CR | Cry | | |
| HU | Humiliate | | |
| LA | Laugh | | |
| NE | Negativism | | |
| WH | Whine | | |
| YE | Yell | | |
| **Nonverbal** | | | |
| DS | Destructiveness | AT | Attention |
| HR | High Rate | NO | Normative |
| IG | Ignore | NR | No Response |
| PN | Physical Negative | RC | Receive |
| | | TH | Touch |
| **Either Verbal or Nonverbal** | | | |
| AP | Approval | SS | Self-stimulation |
| CO | Compliance | | |
| DI | Disapproval | | |
| DP | Dependency | | |
| NC | Noncompliance | | |
| PL | Play | | |
| TE | Tease | | |
| WK | Work | | |

of mother-child relationships under experimental conditions, and served as the basis for development of subsequent category systems designed for the study of parent-child interaction.

**Behavioral Coding System.** Patterson et al. have developed the Behavioral Coding System (BCS), a psychometrically sophisticated system that records parent-child interactive sequences in natural settings.[96] Using a time-sampling procedure, the observer records the behavioral interactions among family members using BCS categories as shown in Table 10.9. The designation of first order and second order behaviors helps the observer decide which behavior should be coded if more than one behavior is exhibited by the subject during a single time sample. When a choice must be made among multiple behaviors, first order ones are always coded. Division of the categories into verbal, nonverbal, or either verbal or nonverbal facilitates cataloging of the different codes.

An observer witnessing this interaction between a mother and her seven-year-old daughter would enter the BCS codes shown:

| | | |
|---|---|---|
| MOTHER: | Please clear off the table. | CM |
| KAREN: | (Walks into den and begins to play with her kitten.) | NC,PL |
| MOTHER: | (Ignores her daughter's noncompliance.) | IG |
| KAREN: | (Continues to play with kitten.) | PL |
| MOTHER: | Come in here *now* and help me clear off the table. | CN |
| KAREN: | I'm tired and don't want to. | NE |
| MOTHER: | (Ignores her daughter's noncompliance.) | IG |
| MOTHER: | You have to help more around the house now that I am working (yells from kitchen). | YE |

| KAREN: | All right. I will. | CO |
|---|---|---|
| MOTHER: | You're a good girl. | AP |

The BCS coding manual, which includes complete definitions of the various behavior categories, is available from Microfiche Publications.[97] A series of investigations have demonstrated the reliability and validity of the Behavioral Coding System.[98]

## CHILD'S PERCEPTIONS OF PARENTS AND FAMILY RELATIONSHIPS

Oftentimes, study of the child's family is achieved by obtaining the youngster's responses to structured questions regarding his or her family life. This approach to the assessment of interpersonal family experiences represents a phenomenological point of view. According to the phenomenological school of thought, it is not enough to know only the objective stimulating conditions that surround a child since a considerable portion of behavior is influenced by stimuli *as experienced.* To put it another way, the child's behavior is also influenced by his or her phenomenological perception of persons and situations.[99]

### OBJECTIVE TECHNIQUES

These are some available objective measures of the child's perception of his family:

Adolescent-Parent Adjustment Measure

Adolescent Perception of Conjugal Power Index

Adult Role Perception Index

Bristol Social Adjustment Guides

Bronfenbrenner Parent Behavior Questionnaire

Childhood Experiences Rating Scale

Child-Parent Dissidence Scale

Child-Parent Relations Index

Child-Parent Relationship Scale

Child's Report of Parental Behavior Inventory

Children's Dependence Scale

Composite Measure of Family Relations

Conflicts with Mother Checklist

Cornell Socialization Inventory

Day at Home

Emancipation from Parents Scale

Family Adjective Rating Scale

Family Adjustment Index

Family Adjustment Test

Family Image Scales

Family Interaction Schedule

Family Inventory

Family Life Questionnaire

Family Participation Scale

Family-Peer Group Orientation Questionnaire

Family Relations Inventory

Family Relations Test

Hawkes-Lewis Family Control Scales

Heston Personal Adjustment Inventory

Index of Reliance

Interpersonal Relations Scale

Intra-Family Attitude Scale

Intra-Family Relationships Questionnaire

Inventory of Child's Report of Parental Behavior

Maternal Interest and Control Index

Nye Family Relationship Scale

Parent Behavior Form

Parental Aggression Training Scale

Parental Authority Love Statements

Parental Contact Scale

Parental Expressivity Scale

Parental Nurture and Control Scales

Parental Punitiveness Scale

Parental Role Patterns

Parent-Behavior Question Schedule

Parent-Child Identification Measures

Parent-Child Interaction Scales

Parent-Child Relations Questionnaire

Parent-Child Relationship Indexes

Parent Evaluation Scale

Perceived Parent Attitude Rating Scale

Perception of Parent Role Performance Questionnaire

Perceptions of Family Questionnaire

Power Inventory

Relationship with Father Scale

Satisfaction with Family Role Performance Indexes

Semantic Differential

Source of Emotional Support Measure

SRA Junior Inventory

SRA Youth Inventory

Three frequently used scales that assess family variables *as perceived by children* are the Child's Report of Parental Behavior Inventory, the Bronfenbrenner Parent Behavior Questionnaire, and the Family Relations Test.

**Child's Report of Parental Behavior Inventory.** The Child's Report of Parental Behavior Inventory, which is designed for use by children ten to eighteen years old, is a 260-item questionnaire that measures a child's perception of his or her parents on twenty-six concepts.[100] The selection of these concepts or scales was based upon a conceptual model derived from factor analyses of parent ratings by psychologists. Each of the twenty-six scales is made up of ten items that describe specific, observable parental behavior. The scales are

| | |
|---|---|
| Extreme Autonomy | Intellectual Stimulation |
| Lax Discipline | Child-Centeredness |
| Moderate Autonomy | Possessiveness |
| Encouraging Sociability | Protectiveness |
| Positive Evaluation | Intrusiveness |
| Sharing Activities, Plans, and Interest | Suppression of Aggression |
| Expression of Affection | Strictness |
| Encourages Independence | Punishment |
| Emotional Support | Control Through Guilt |
| Equalitarianism | Parental Direction |
| Negative Evaluation | Nagging |
| Irritability | Neglect |
| Rejection | Ignoring |

The child is asked to indicate the answer—*like* or *not like*—that most closely describes the way the parents act toward him or her. Sample items for seven of the twenty-six concepts measured by the instrument are shown in Table 10.10. Separate parallel forms are provided for reports of the mother's and the father's behavior.

**Bronfenbrenner Parent Behavior Questionnaire.** The Bronfenbrenner Parent Questionnaire likewise assesses children's perceptions of parental behavior.[101] One form is filled out in regard to the mothering person, and another form with identical items is filled out in regard to the fathering person. The instrument, which is designed primarily for children nine to twelve years of age, consists of forty-five items grouped into fifteen scales:

Nurturance

Affective Reward

Instrumental Companionship

Affiliative Companionship

Prescriptive

Social Isolation

Expressive Rejection

Physical Punishment

Deprivation of Privileges

Protectiveness

Power

Achievement Demands

Affective Punishment

Principled Discipline

Indulgence

Three statements comprise each scale. Samples of the items that make up some of the scales are shown in Table 10.11.

The child is requested to indicate the degree to which the statements are descriptive of his or her parents. For the first twenty-five items, the child selects responses from the following options: *in every case, in most cases, sometimes, seldom,* or *never*. In the last twenty items, the child's five choices are *almost every day, about once a week, about once a month, only once or twice a year,* or *never*. The scoring on each item ranges from 1 (for a response of *in every case* or *almost every day*) to 5 (for a response of *never*), on each item. Therefore, a high score would indicate absence or denial of a parental behavior, and a low score, affirmation of the behavior. Three items, separated from each other on the questionnaire, comprise each of the fifteen scales. As a result, the range of scores for each scale is 3 to 15.

Siegelman factor-analyzed the Bronfenbrenner Parental Behavior Questionnaire and identified three major components: loving, punishing, and demanding. The results of the factor analysis and other technical information about the instrument are available in his article.[102]

**Family Relations Test.** The Family Relations Test (FRT) is a complex forced-choice measure designed to assess the quality and intensity of relationships in the home.[103] According to its authors, the purpose of this technique is to

> indicate objectively, reliably, and rapidly the direction and intensity of the child's feelings toward various members of his family, and, of no less importance, his esti- mate of their reciprocal regard for him.[104]

**Table 10.10.** Items from the Child's Report of Parental Behavior Inventory and the Concepts They Are Designed to Measure

| Concepts | Sample Items |
|---|---|
| Extreme autonomy | Allows me to go out as often as I please. Lets me go any place I please without asking. |
| Lax discipline | Lets me get away without doing work she's (he's) told me to do. Excuses my bad conduct. |
| Moderate autonomy | Allows me to pick my own friends. Gives me the choice of what to do whenever possible. |
| Encouraging sociability | Helps me give parties for my friends. Enjoys it when I bring friends to my home. |
| Positive evaluation | Often praises me. Often speaks of the good things I do. |
| Sharing | Enjoys talking things over with me. Enjoys working with me in the house or yard. |
| Expression of affection | Almost always speaks to me with a warm and friendly voice. Smiles at me very often. |

**Table 10.11.** Items from the Bronfenbrenner Parent Behavior Questionnaire

| Concepts | Sample Items |
| --- | --- |
| Nurturance. . . . . . . . . . . . . . . . . . . . . | I can talk with him (her) about everything. |
| | Comforts me and helps me when I have troubles. |
| Affective reward . . . . . . . . . . . . . . . . | Is very affectionate with me. |
| | Praises me when I have done something good. |
| Instrumental companionship . . . . . . . . . | Teaches me things which I want to learn. |
| | Helps me with hobbies or handiwork. |
| Affiliative companionship . . . . . . . . . . . | Goes on pleasant walks and outings with me. |
| | Is happy when with me. |
| Prescriptive . . . . . . . . . . . . . . . . . . . | Expects me to help around the house. |
| | Wants me to run errands. |
| Social isolation . . . . . . . . . . . . . . . . . | Punishes me by sending me out of the room. |
| | As punishment she (he) sends me to bed early. |
| Physical punishment . . . . . . . . . . . . . . | Threatens to spank me. |
| | Spanks me. |

Since the FRT involves direct questions to the subject, with possible replies printed on cards, it cannot be termed a projective device in the strictest sense. However, the FRT may be considered a marginally projective technique since the child chooses the family member to whom the statements apply. The materials include ambiguously drawn cardboard figures that are attached to boxes with slotted tops. The child indicates which member of the family is represented by each figure. All family members are represented including the youngster participating in the test. An additional figure, called Nobody, is placed apart from the others. Next, the child is presented cards on which are statements that describe attitudes, feelings, and relationships within the family. Included are statements such as *"This person in the family does not love me enough"* and *"This is the person in the family whom father spoils too much."* The child reads a card or the examiner reads the card aloud if the child cannot read. Then the child puts the card into the box attached to the figure representing the family member to whom the statement best applies. (See Figure 10.7.) If the statement fits two family

**Figure 10.7.** Examiner Administering the Family Relations Test to an Eight-Year-Old

members equally, both figures receive a card. Since there is only one card with each statement, the examiner uses a slip of paper to jot down the statement number for the second family member in such cases. If the statement does not apply to anyone in the home, the card is posted in the box attached to the figure called Nobody.

The level of the Family Relations Test that is appropriate for children eight years or younger consists of forty-seven statements. An adult form is also available. In the children's version, the statements are broken down into positive feelings coming from the child, negative feelings coming from the child, positive feelings going toward the child, negative feelings going toward the child, and dependence. Scoring is accomplished by recording and counting the number of incoming and outgoing positive and negative statements attributed to the various family members. The patterns of scores are of considerable interest in understanding family dynamics.

## PROJECTIVE TECHNIQUES

Projective techniques have been used with some success in studying family life through the eyes of the child. Several projective measures are available for use with children.

Adult-Child Interaction Test

Blacky Pictures

Child's Perception of Parental Behavior

Children's Apperception Test

Doll Play

Family Distance Doll Placement Technique

Family Drawings

Family Interaction Apperception Test

Family Pictures Test

Family Relations Indicator

Family Rorschach

House-Tree-Person Projective Technique

Incomplete Story Test

Kell-Hoeflin Incomplete Sentence Blank: Youth-Parent Relations

Kinetic Family Drawings

Parental Attributes Technique

Parent and Child Role Conception Pictures

Parent-Child Conflict Stories

Parent-Child Relations Picture Series

Projective Film Technique for Studying Adolescent-Parent Relationships

Punishment Situation Index

Radke Projective Pictures

Rock-A-Bye-Baby

Rosenzweig Picture-Frustration Study

Sentence Completion Test of Children's Views of Parents

Sentence Completion Wish Test

Stein Family Attitudes Sentence Completion Test

Story Completion Test

Symond's Picture Story Test

Test of Family Attitudes

Two Houses Technique

The Test of Family Attitudes and Kinetic Family Drawings are described in this section.

**Test of Family Attitudes.** The Test of Family Attitudes, developed by Jackson, is a projective technique which examines the child's attitudes toward his or her parents and siblings and which also probes ideas concerning the family's attitudes toward the child.[105] The test consists of seven pictures drawn in black and white with slightly blurred outlines that represent common situations between children six to twelve years old and adults. (The seventh picture was added after publication of Jackson's original study.) One of these pictures is reproduced in Figure 10.8. These are descriptions of all the pictures and the aspects of family life that they are designed to examine:

*Picture 0:* Female figure bending over a cradle (child's dependence on the mother).

*Picture 1:* Man and woman sitting on chairs side by side with their backs turned to a child who is sitting on the floor; outside a closed door, a man standing (child's exclusion from intimacy between the parents with the consequent threat to its security).

*Pictures 2 and 2A:* Man and woman are sitting side by side; the woman is holding an infant; a small boy (2) or girl (2A) is standing some way off, looking at them (jealousy of a sibling).

*Picture 3:* Child is sitting on a stool looking down; he is alone and the door is closed (transgression and the ensuing loneliness and guilt).

*Picture 4:* A rather small woman is holding up a young child and a large man is facing them with his right arm up and fist clenched (fear of aggression from parents).

*Picture 5:* A child is crawling and stretching out toward a vaguely defined object; a male figure is standing behind with his arms raised (longing for the forbidden and the threat of punishment).

*Picture 6:* Man and woman are facing each other and gesturing; child is sitting on a chair observing them at a short distance (child's reaction to clash between parents).

The child is asked to tell a story about each picture using simple language. The examiner says, "It need not be a very good story, but it must be your own, and not something you've read in a book."[106] There is no time limit, but if the child's story becomes too diffuse, the examiner may urge the child to stick to the main subject. Prompting, in the form of standard lead questions, is also allowed if necessary. The entire test takes a little less than one hour. Scoring consists of summarizing the family attitudes and relationships disclosed by the the child.

**Kinetic Family Drawings.** Projective drawing techniques have been used for several years to study the child's family. Although the origin of the draw-a-family procedure has remained undetermined, it has nevertheless gained widespread acceptance as an integral part of most batteries of tests to study children. Hammer has commented that "this technique is most popular in its use with children, where

**Figure 10.8.** Specimen Card from the Test of Family Attitudes

a determination of the essential relationship to one's parents and siblings is of prime importance."[107] Whereas most drawing procedures ask children simply to draw a person, a family, or house, tree, and person[108] and usually result in static productions, one expressive technique called Kinetic Family Drawings[109] uses action instructions. That is, the child is asked to produce drawings in which the figures are doing something. The authors of this projective measure, Burns and Kaufman, included the instruction to add movement to the drawings in the belief that it would "help mobilize a child's feelings not only as related to self-concept but also in the area of interpersonal relations."[110]

In an individual session, the child is given a plain white sheet of paper and a pencil and receives these instructions from the examiner:

> Draw a picture of everyone in your family, including you, *doing* something. Try to draw whole people, not cartoons or stick people. Remember, make everyone *doing* something—some kind of action.[111]

After giving the directions, the examiner leaves the room, although he or she returns periodically to check the child's progress. No time limit is imposed; the procedure is terminated when the child indicates that he or she has finished the drawing. The examiner then asks the subject to explain the drawing. No method of questioning for the examiner is specified in the manual.

The Kinetic Family Drawings measure is analyzed according to four categories: characteristics of K-F-D figures, K-F-D actions, K-F-D styles, and symbols. Scoring is facilitated by using an analysis sheet which contains

### Characteristics of K-F-D Figures

1. Arm extensions

2. Elevated figures

3. Erasures

4. Figures on the back of the page

5. Hanging

6. Omission of body parts

7. Omission of figures

8. Picasso eye

9. Rotated figures

### K-F-D Actions

1. Actions of individual figures

2. Actions between individual figures

### K-F-D Styles

1. Compartmentalization

2. Edging

3. Encapsulation

4. Folded compartmentalization

5. Lining on the bottom

6. Lining on the top

7. Underlining individual figures

In addition, Burns and Kaufman recommend the use of a grid sheet to analyze the drawings. The grid, which is made of transparent paper marked off in millimeters, is of value in obtaining important K-F-D data, as they explain:

> By superimposing the grid over a K-F-D, a number of measurements may be made. The grid may be of help in obtaining the measurements of the Self and other K-F-D figures. The distance of the Self from the other figures is also at times very important. The location of the Self and the other figures on the grid may also be of interest.[112]

Other scoring methods for the K-F-D are also available.[113]

## OTHER APPROACHES TO STUDYING THE CHILD'S FAMILY

Although we have attempted to survey a number of approaches to studying the child's family, we have not done justice to any one area because of space limitations. Other excellent sources are available, however, which provide more in-depth treatment of family assessment techniques, and these[114] are included in the Chapter Notes along with a number of other sources[115] in which family measures are described.

## CHAPTER NOTES

1.  L. W. Hoffman and R. Lippitt, "The Measurement of Family Life Variables," in *Handbook of Research Methods in Child Development,* ed. P. H. Mussen (New York: Wiley, 1960).
2.  G. Levinger, "Supplementary Methods in Family Research," in *Research in Family Interaction,* eds. W. D. Winter and A. J. Ferreira (Palo Alto, Calif.: Science and Behavior Books, 1969), p. 18.
3.  Ibid.
4.  A. F. Fontana, "Familial Etiology of Schizophrenia: Is a Scientific Methodology Possible," *Psychological Bulletin* 66 (1966): 214-27.
5.  Levinger, "Supplementary Methods."
6.  I. W. Charny, *Individual and Family Developmental Review Manual* (Los Angeles: Western Psychological Services, 1969).
7.  R. T. Centers, *The Psychology of Social Classes* (Princeton, N. J.: Princeton University Press, 1949).
    A. B. Hollinghead and F. C. Redlich, *Social Class and Mental Illness: A Community Study* (New York: Wiley, 1958).
    W. H. Sewell and A. O. Haller, "Social Status and the Personality Adjustment of the Child," *Sociometry* 19 (1956): 114-25.

W. L. Warner and P. S. Lunt, *The Social Life in a Modern Community* (New Haven: Yale University Press, 1941).

W. L. Warner, M. Mecker, and K. Eells, *Social Class in America* (Chicago: Science Research Associates, 1949).

8. E. O. Laumann and J. S. House, "Living Room Styles and Social Attributes: The Patterning of Material Artifacts in a Modern Urban Community," *Sociological and Social Research* 54 (1970): 321-42.

9. H. G. Gough, "A Short Social Status Inventory," *Journal of Educational Psychology* 40 (1949): 52-56.

10. W. H. Sewell, "A Short Form of the Farm Family Socio-economic Status Scale," *Rural Sociology* 81 (1943): 161-70.

11. K. D. Hopkins, *Colorado State Assessment* (Boulder, Colo.: Laboratory of Educational Research, University of Colorado, 1972).

12. S. R. Hathaway and J. C. McKinley, *Minnesota Multiphasic Personality Inventory (Revised Manual)* (New York: Psychological Corporation, 1948).

13. H. G. Gough, *California Psychological Inventory* (Palo Alto, Calif.: Consulting Psychologists Press, 1956).

14. G. W. Allport, P. E. Vernon, and G. Lindzey, *Study of Values* (Boston: Houghton-Mifflin, 1960).

15. H. A. Murray, *Thematic Apperception Test* (Cambridge, Mass.: Harvard University Press, 1943).

16. J. W. Atkinson, ed., *Motives in Fantasy, Action, and Society* (Princeton, N.J.: Van Nostrand, 1958).

D. C. McClelland et al., *The Achievement Motive* (New York: Appleton, 1953).

D. G. Winter, *The Power Motive* (New York: Free Press, 1973).

17. N. Hurvitz, *Marital Roles Inventory Manual* (Beverly Hills, Calif.: Western Psychological Services, 1961).

18. Ibid., pp. 377-78.

19. G. B. Spanier, "Measuring Dyadic Adjustment: New Scales for Assessing the Quality of Marriage and Similar Dyads," *Journal of Marriage and the Family* 38 (1976): 15-28.

20. M. J. Bienvenu, "Measurement of Marital Communication," *Family Coordinator* 19 (1970): 26-31.

21. H. B. Biller, "Father Dominance and Sex-Role Development in Kindergarten-age Boys," *Developmental Psychology* 1 (1969): 87-94.

G. W. Brown and M. Rutter, "The Measurement of Family Activities and Relationships," *Human Relations* 19 (1966): 241-64.

E. Chance, "Measuring the Potential Interplay of Forces Within the Family During Treatment," *Child Development* 26 (1955): 241-65.

L. D. Eron, L. O. Walder, and M. M. Lefkowitz, *Learning of Aggression in Children* (Boston: Little, Brown, and Company, 1971).

J. R. Eshleman, "Mental Health and Marital Integration in Young Marriages," *Journal of Marriage and the Family* 27 (1965): 255-62.

S. L. Fink, J. K. Skipper, Jr., and P. N. Hallenbeck, "Marital Satisfaction Scale," *Journal of Marriage and the Family* 30 (1968): 64-73.

J. L. Hawkins, "Associations Between Companionship, Hostility, and Marital Satisfaction," *Journal of Marriage and the Family* 30 (1968): 647-50.

R. S. Ort, "A Study of Role Conflicts As Related to Happiness in Marriage," *Journal of Abnormal and Social Psychology* 45 (1950): 691-99.

C. F. Wells and E. L. Rabiner, "The Conjoint Family Diagnostic Interview and the Family Index of Tension," *Family Process* 12 (1973): 127-44.

22. J. G. Howells and J. R. Lickorish, *The Family Relations Indicator* (Edinburg, England: Oliver and Boyd, 1967).

23. A. F. Payne, *Sentence Completions* (New York: Guidance Clinic, 1928).

24. A. D. Tendler, "A Preliminary Report on a Test for Emotional Insight," *Journal of Applied Psychology* 14 (1930): 122-36.

25. P. Goldberg, "A Review of Sentence Completion Methods in Personality Assessment," *Journal of Projective Techniques and Personality Assessment* 29 (1965): 12-45.

26. R. M. Inselberg, "Social and Psychological Factors Associated with High School Marriages," *Journal of Home Economics* 53 (1961): 770.

27. B. R. A. Forer, "A Structured Sentence Completion Test," *Journal of Projective Techniques* 14 (1950): 15-30.

28. Levinger, "Family Research," p. 19.

29. R. D. Carter and E. J. Thomas, "Modification of Problematic Marital Communication Using Corrective Feedback and Instruction," *Behavior Therapy* 4 (1973): 100-09.

A. J. Ferreira and W. D. Winter, "On the Nature of Marital Relationships: Measurable Differences in Spontaneous Agreement," *Family Process* 13 (1974): 355-69.

D. W. Goodrich and D. S. Boomer, "Experimental Assessment of Modes of Conflict Resolution," *Family Process* 2 (1963): 15-24.

T. Jacob and J. Davis, "Family Interaction As a Function of Experimental Task," *Family Process* 12 (1973): 415-27.

W. F. Kenkel and D. K. Hoffman, "Real and Conceived Roles in Family Decision Making," *Marriage and Family Living* 18 (1956): 311-16.

30. E. A. Blechman, "The Family Contract Game," *The Family Coordinator* 23 (1974): 269-81.

D. Kieren and I. Tallman, "Spousal Adaptability: An Assessment of Marital Competence," *Journal of Marriage and the Family* 34 (1972): 247-56.

F. L. Strodtbeck, "Husband-Wife Interaction Over Revealed Differences," *American Sociological Review* 16 (1951): 468-73.

31. M. Deutsch and R. M. Krauss, "Studies of Interpersonal Bargaining," *Journal of Conflict Resolution* 6 (1962): 52-76.

M. A. Straus and I. Tallman, "SIMFAM: A Technique for Observational Measurement and Experimental Study of Families," in *Family Problem Solving,* ed. J. Aldous (Hinsdale, Ill.: Dryden, 1971).

R. Usandivaras et al., "The Marbles Test," *Archives of General Psychiatry* 17 (1967): 111-18.

C. Wild et al., "Measuring Disordered Styles of Thinking: Using the Object Sorting Test on Parents of Schizophrenic Patients," *Archives of General Psychiatry* 13 (1965): 471-76.

32. L. Y. Rabkin, "The Patient's Family: Research Methods," in *Research in Family Interaction,* eds. W. D. Winter and A. J. Ferreira (Palo Alto, Calif.: Science and Behavior Books, 1969).

33. E. S. Schaefer and R. W. Bell, "Development of a Parental Attitude Instrument," *Child Development* 29 (1958a): 339-61.

34. E. S. Schaefer and R. W. Bell, "An Adaptation of the Parental Attitude Research Instrument" (Unpublished ms., National Institute of Health, 1958b).

35. W. C. Becker and R. S. Krug, "The Parent Attitude Research Instrument–A Research Review," *Child Development* 36 (1965): 329-65.

36. J. R. Shoben, Jr., "The Assessment of Parental Attitudes in Relation to Child Adjustment," *Genetic Psychology Monographs* 39 (1949): 101-48.

37. Ibid., pp. 140-41.

38. D. Baumrind, "Child Care Practices Anteceding Three Patterns of Preschool Behavior," *Genetic Psychology Monographs* 75 (1967): 43-88.

L. D. Eron et al., "Comparison of Data Obtained from Mothers and Fathers on Child-rearing Practices and Their Relation to Child Aggression," *Child Development* 32 (1961): 457-72.

I. Hart, "Maternal Child-rearing Practices and Authoritarian Ideology," *Journal of Abnormal and Social Psychology* 55 (1957): 232-37.

C. F. Hereford, *Changing Parental Attitudes Through Group Discussion* (Austin: University of Texas Press, 1963).

M. L. Hoffman, "An Interview Method for Obtaining Descriptions of Parent-Child Interaction," *Merrill-Palmer Quarterly* 4 (1957): 76-83.

R. Lapouse and M. A. Monk, "Behavior Deviations in a Representative Sample of Children: Variation by Sex, Age, Race, Social Class, and Family Size," *American Journal of Orthopsychiatry* 34 (1964): 436-46.

D. R. Miller and G. E. Swanson, *The Changing American Parent* (New York: Wiley, 1958).

V. Nowlis, "The Search for Significant Concepts in the Study of Parent-Child Relationships," *American Journal of Orthopsychiatry* 22 (1952): 286-99.

R. R. Sears, E. E. Maccoby, and H. Levin, *Patterns of Child Rearing* (Evanston, Ill.: Row, Peterson, 1957).

R. R. Sears et al., "Some Child-rearing Antecedents of Aggression and Dependency in Young Children," *Genetic Psychology Monographs* 47 (1953): 135-236.

J. R. Wittenborn, "A Study of Adoptive Children," *Psychological Monographs* 70 (1956): 93-115.

J. W. M. Whiting, I. L. Child, and W. W. Lambert, *Field Guide for Study of Socialization* (New York: Wiley, 1966).

M. R. Yarrow, J. D. Campbell, and R. V. Burton, *Child Rearing: An Inquiry into Research and Methods* (San Francisco: Jossey-Bass, 1968).

39. B. Pope, *The Mental Health Interview* (New York: Pergamon, 1979).

40. C. F. Cannell and R. L. Kahn, "Interviewing," in *Handbook of Social Psychology,* eds. G. Lindzey and E. Aronson (Reading, Mass.: Addison-Wesley, 1968).

41. Sears, Maccoby, and Levin, *Patterns.*

42. Ibid., p. 19.

43. Ibid., p. 492.

44. Ibid., p. 494.

45. Ibid., p. 495.

46. Ibid., pp. 497-98.

47. Ibid., p. 21.
48. Ibid., pp. 503-10.
49. Hereford, *Changing Parental Attitudes.*
50. M. R. Yarrow, "Problems of Methods in Parent-Child Research," *Child Development* 34 (1963): 215-21.
51. C. Wenar, "The Reliability of Mothers' Histories," *Child Development* 32 (1961): 491-500.
52. E. A. Haggard, A Brekstad, and A. Skard, "On the Reliability of the Anamnestic Interview," *Journal of Abnormal and Social Psychology* 61 (1960): 311-18.
   J. W. Macfarlane, "Studies in Child Guidance, I, Methodology of Data Collection," *Monographs of the Society for Research in Child Development* 3 (1938), no. 6.
   M. K. Pyles, H. R. Stolz, and J. Macfarlane, "The Accuracy of Mothers' Reports on Birth and Developmental Data," *Child Development* 6 (1935): 165-76.
   L. C. Robbins, "The Accuracy of Parental Recall of Aspects of Child Development and of Child-rearing Practices," *Journal of Abnormal and Social Psychology* 66 (1963): 261-70.
   M. R. Yarrow, J. D. Campbell, and R. V. Burton, *Child Rearing.*
53. H. Lytton, "Observation Studies of Parent-Child Interaction: A Methodological Review," *Child Development* 42 (1971): 651-84.
   Wenar, "Reliability."
54. J. W. B. Douglas, A. Lawson, and J. E. Cooper, "Family Interaction and the Activities of Young Children," *Journal of Child Psychology and Psychiatry* 9 (1968): 157-71.
   M. L. Kohn and E. E. Carroll, "Social Class and the Allocation of Parental Responsibilities," *Sociometry* 23 (1960): 372-92.
   H. J. Smith, "A Comparison of Interview and Observation Methods of Maternal Behavior," *Journal of Abnormal and Social Psychology* 57 (1958): 278-82.
55. H. F. Antonovsky, "A Contribution to Research in the Area of the Mother-Child Relationship," *Child Development* 30 (1959): 37-51.
56. M. Rutter and G. W. Brown, "The Reliability and Validity of Measures of Family Life and Relationships in Families Containing a Psychiatric Patient," *Social Psychiatry* 1 (1966): 38-53.
57. Douglas, Lawson, and Cooper, "Family Interaction."
   Hoffman, "Interview Method."
58. Kohn and Carroll, "Social Class."
   J. O. Palmer, *The Psychological Assessment of Children* (New York: Wiley, 1970).
59. Lytton, "Observation Studies," p. 667.
60. S. Santostefano, "Miniature Situations and Methodological Problems in Parent-Child Interaction Research," *Merrill-Palmer Quarterly* 14 (1968): 285-312.
61. Lytton, "Observation Studies."
62. A. L. Baldwin, J. Kalhorn, and F. H. Breese, "The Appraisal of Parent Behavior," *Psychological Monographs* 63 (1949): (4, whole no. 299).
63. R. D. Hess and V. C. Shipman, "Cognitive Elements in Maternal Behavior," in *Minnesota Symposia on Child Psychology,* vol. 1, ed. J. P. Hill (Minneapolis: University of Minnesota Press, 1967).
64. B. M. Bishop, "A Measurement of Mother-Child Interaction," *Journal of Abnormal and Social Psychology* 41 (1946): 37-49.
   B. M. Bishop, "Mother-Child Interaction and the Social Behavior of Children," *Psychological Monographs* 65 (1951): (11, whole no. 328).
65. R. G. Barker and H. F. Wright, *Midwest and Its Children: The Psychological Ecology of an American Town* (Evanston, Ill.: Row, Peterson, 1955).
66. Lytton, "Observation Studies."
67. B. M. Caldwell and L. Hersher, "Mother-Infant Interaction During the First Year," *Merrill-Palmer Quarterly* 10 (1964): 119-28.
   E. Powers and H. Witmer, *An Experiment in the Prevention of Delinquency: The Cambridge-Somerville Youth Study* (New York: Columbia University Press, 1951).
68. Baldwin, Kalhorn, and Breese, "Appraisal."
69. D. Baumrind, "Child Care Practices Anteceding Three Patterns of Preschool Behavior," *Genetic Psychology Monographs* 75 (1967): 43-88.
   Hess and Shipman, "Cognitive Elements."
70. Barker and Wright, *Midwest.*
71. Bishop, "Social Behavior of Children."
   R. R. Jones, J. B. Reid, and G. R. Patterson, "Naturalistic Observation in Clinical Assessment," in *Advances in Psychological Assessment,* vol. 3, ed. P. McReynolds (San Francisco: Jossey-Bass, 1975).
   H. Lytton, "Three Approaches to the Study of Parent-Child Interaction: Ethological, Interview, and Experimental," *Journal of Child Psychology and Psychiatry* 14 (1973): 1-17.
   G. R. Patterson et al., *Manual for Coding Family Interactions,* 1969 revision (Available as Document #01234 from ASIS National Auxiliary Publications Service, New York).
   C. E. Moustakas, I. E. Sigel, and M. D. Schalock, "An Objective Method for the Measurement and Analysis of Child-Adult Interaction," *Child Development* 27 (1956): 109-34.
   M. W. Roberts and R. Forehand, "The Assessment of Maladaptive Parent-Child Interaction by Direct Observation: An Analysis of Methods," *Journal of Abnormal Child Psychology* 6 (1978): 257-70.
   P. Steinglass, "The Home Observation Assessment Method (HOAM): Real-Time Naturalistic Observation of Families in Their Homes," *Family Process* 18 (1979): 337-54.
72. Roberts and Forehand, "An Analysis of Methods."
73. J. Newson and E. Newson, *Four Years Old in an Urban Community* (London: Allen and Unwin, 1968).
74. D. Baumrind, "Naturalistic Observation in the Study of Parent-Child Interaction" (Paper presented at the annual meeting of the American Psychological Association, San Francisco, September, 1968).
75. Lytton, "Observation Studies."
76. G. R. Patterson, J. A. Cobb, and R. S. Ray, "A Social Engineering Technology for Retraining Aggressive Boys," in *Georgia Symposium in Experimental Clinical Psychology,* vol. 2, eds. H. Adams and L. Unikel (New York: Pergamon, 1970).
   Santostefano, "Miniature Situations."
77. E. Bing, "Effect of Child-Rearing Practices on Development of Differential Cognitive Abilities," *Child Development* 34 (1963): 631-48.
   B. C. Rosen and R. D'Andrade, "The Psychosocial Origins of Achievement Motivation," *Sociometry* 22 (1959): 185-217.
78. H. M. Hughes and S. N. Haynes, "Structured Laboratory Observation in the Behavioral Assessment of Parent-Child Interactions: A Methodological Critique," *Behavior Therapy* 9 (1978): 428-47.
79. J. S. Hatfield, C. R. Fergusin, and R. Allport, "Mother-Child Interaction and the Socialization Process," *Child Development* 38 (1967): 365-414.
   Hess and Shipman, "Cognitive Elements."
   S. M. Johnson and R. A. Brown, "Producing Behavior Change in Parents of Disturbed Children," *Journal of Child Psychology and Psychiatry* 10 (1969): 107-21.
   G. R. Patterson et al., "Reprogramming the Social Environment," *Journal of Child Psychology and Psychiatry* 8 (1967): 181-95.
   D. B. Sawin, J. H. Langlois, and E. F. Leitner, "What Do You Do After You Say Hello? Observing, Coding, and Analyzing Parent Infant Interactions," *Behavior Research Methods and Instrumentation* 9 (1977): 425-28.
   R. G. Wahler, "Setting Generality: Some Specific and General Effects of Child Behavior Therapy," *Journal of Applied Behavioral Analysis* 2 (1969): 239-46.
   H. C. Wimberger and K. L. Kogan, "A Direct Approach to Altering Mother-Child Interaction in Disturbed Children," *Archives of General Psychiatry* 30 (1974): 636-39.
80. Bishop, "Social Behavior of Children."
   S. M. Eyberg and S. M. Johnson, "Multiple Assessment of Behavior Modification with Families: Effects of Contingency Contracting and Order of Treated Problems," *Journal of Consulting and Clinical Psychology* 42 (1974): 594-606.

M. E. Scarboro and E. Forehand, "Effects of Two Types of Response-Contingent Time-out on Compliance and Oppositional Behavior of Children," *Journal of Experimental Child Psychology* 19 (1975): 252-64.

R. G. Wahler et al., "Mothers as Behavior Therapists for Their Own Children," *Behavior Research and Therapy* 3 (1965): 113-24.

81.  Hatfield, Fergusin, and Allport, "Socialization Process."

E. W. Herbert et al., "Adverse Effects of Differential Parental Attention," *Journal of Applied Behavioral Analysis* 6 (1973): 15-20.

Johnson and Brown, "Producing Behavior Change."

82.  S. W. Bijou, "Experimental Studies of Child Behavior, Normal and Deviant," in *Research in Behavior Modification*, eds. L. Krasner and L. Ullman (New York: Holt, 1965).

E. J. Mash, L. Terdal, and K. Anderson, "The Response-Class Matrix: A Procedure for Recording Parent-Child Interactions," *Journal of Consulting and Clinical Psychology* 40 (1973): 163-64.

83.  Eyberg and Johnson, "Multiple Assessment."

Moustakas et al., "Objective Method."

J. F. O'Rourke, "Field and Laboratory: The Decision-making Behavior of Family Groups in Two Experimental Conditions," *Sociometry* 26 (1963): 422-35.

84.  Baumrind, "Child Care Practices."

Johnson and Brown, "Producing Behavior Change."

Mash, Terdal, and Anderson, "Response-Class Matrix."

F. R. Schulman, D. J. Shoemaker, and I. Moelis, "Laboratory Measurements of Parental Behavior," *Journal of Consulting Psychology* 26 (1962): 109-14.

85.  C. G. Baum, R. Forehand, and L. E. Zegiob, "A Review of Observer Reactivity in Adult-Child Interactions," *Journal of Behavioral Assessment* 1 (1979): 167-78.

A. Harris, "Observer Effect on Family Interaction" (Ph.D. diss., University of Oregon, 1969).

G. R. Patterson and J. B. Reid, "Reciprocity and Coercion: Two Facets of Social Systems" (Unpublished ms., Oregon Research Institute, University of Oregon, 1969).

L. E. Zegiob and R. Forehand, "Parent-Child Interactions: Observer Effects and Social Class Differences," *Behavior Therapy* 9 (1978): 118-23.

86.  Barker and Wright, *Midwest*.

Schulman, Shoemaker and Moelis, "Laboratory Measurements."

87.  G. D. White, "Effects of Observer Presence on Mother and Child Behavior" (Ph.D. dissertation, University of Oregon, 1972).

88.  S. M. Johnson and O. D. Bolstad, "Methodological Issues in Naturalistic Observation: Some Problems and Solutions for Field Research," in *Methodology, Concepts, and Practice*, eds. L. Hamerlynk, L. C. Handy, and E. J. Mash (Champaign, Ill.: Research Press, 1973).

89.  Lytton, "Three Approaches."

90.  Baldwin, Kalhorn, and Breese, "Appraisal."

91.  H. Champney, "The Measure of Parent Behavior," *Child Development* 12 (1941): 131-66.

92.  Baldwin, Kalhorn, and Breese, "Appraisal."

93.  Ibid.

94.  Bishop, "Measurement."

95.  Ibid., p. 39.

96.  Patterson et al., *Manual for Coding*.

97.  Ibid.

98.  Jones, Reid, and Patterson, "Naturalistic Observation."

99.  P. C. Goldin, "A Review of Children's Reports of Parent Behavior," *Psychological Bulletin* 71 (1969): 222-36.

100. E. S. Schaefer, "Children's Reports of Parental Behavior: An Inventory," *Child Development* 36 (1965): 412-24.

101. M. Siegelman, "Evaluation of Bronfenbrenner's Questionnaire for Children Concerning Parental Behavior," *Child Development* 36 (1965): 163-74.

102. Ibid.

103. E. Bene and J. Anthony, *Manual for the Children's Version of the Family Relations Test* (Windsor, England: National Foundation for Educational Research Publishing Co., 1978).

104. Ibid., p. 15.

105. L. Jackson, "Emotional Attitudes Towards the Family of Normal, Neurotic, and Delinquent Children," *British Journal of Psychology* 41 (1950): 35-51.

106. Ibid., p. 36.

107. E. F. Hammer, "Recent Variations of the Projective Drawing Techniques," in *The Clinical Application of Projective Drawings*, ed. E. F. Hammer (Springfield, Ill.: Thomas, 1971), p. 291.

108. J. N. Buck and I. Jolles, *H-T-P: House-Tree-Person Projective Technique* (Beverly Hills, Calif.: Western Psychological Services, 1946).

J. H. DiLeo, *Young Children and Their Drawings* (New York: Bruner/Mazel, 1970).

W. C. Hulse, "The Emotionally Disturbed Child Draws His Family," *Quarterly Journal of Child Behavior* 3 (1951): 152-74.

K. Machover, *Personality Projection in the Drawing of the Human Figure* (Springfield, Ill.: Thomas, 1949).

M. Reznikoff and H. R. Reznikoff, "The Family Drawing Test: A Comparative Study of Children's Drawings," *Journal of Clinical Psychology* 12 (1956): 167-69.

C. R. Shearn and K. R. Russell, "Use of the Family Drawing as a Technique for Studying Parent-Child Interaction," *Journal of Projective Techniques and Personality Assessment* 33 (1969): 35-44.

109. R. C. Burns and S. H. Kaufman, *Actions, Styles and Symbols in Kinetic Family Drawings (K-F-D): An Interpretive Manual* (New York: Bruner/Mazel, 1972).

R. C. Burns and S. H. Kaufman, *Kinetic Family Drawings (K-F-D)* (New York: Bruner/Mazel, 1970).

110. Burns and Kaufman, *Interpretive Manual*, p. 2.

111. Burns and Kaufman, *Kinetic*, pp. 19-20.

112. Burns and Kaufman, *Interpretive Manual*, p. 286.

113. R. P. O'Brien and W. F. Patton, "Development of an Objective Scoring Method for the Kinetic Family Drawings," *Journal of Personality Assessment* 38 (1974): 156-64.

D. V. Myers, "Toward an Objective Evaluation Procedure of the Kinetic Family Drawings (KFD)," *Journal of Personality Assessment* 42 (1978): 358-65.

114. A. M. Bodin, "Conjoint Family Assessment," in *Advances in Psychological Assessment*, vol. 1, ed. P. McReynolds (Palo Alto, Calif.: Science and Behavior Books, 1968).

R. D. Conger, "The Assessment of Dysfunctional Family Systems," in *Advances in Clinical Child Psychology*, eds. B. B. Lahey and A. Kazdin (New York: Plenum, 1981).

R. E. Cromwell, D. H. L. Olson, and D. G. Fournier, "Diagnosis and Evaluation in Marital and Family Counseling," in *Treating Relationships*, ed. D. H. L. Olson (Lake Mills, Iowa: Graphic Publishing, 1976).

E. E. Filsinger and R. A. Lewis, eds., *Assessing Marriage* (Beverly Hills, Calif.: Sage, 1981).

L. Fisher, "Dimensions of Family Assessment: A Critical Review," *Journal of Marriage and Family Counseling* 4 (1976): 367-82.

J. L. Framo, "Systematic Research on Family Dynamics," in *Intensive Family Therapy*, eds. I. Boszormenyi-Nagy and J. L. Framo (New York: Harper, 1969).

Goldin, "Children's Reports."

G. Handel, "Psychological Study of Whole Families," *Psychological Bulletin* 63 (1965): 19-41.

Hoffman and Lippitt, "Measurement."

Hughes and Haynes, "Methodological Critique."

L. E. Humphreys and M. R. Ciminero, "Parent Reports of Child Behavior: A Review," *Journal of Clinical Child Psychology* 8 (1979): 56-63.

J. R. Lickorish, "The Psychometric Assessment of the Family," in *Theory and Practice of Family Psychiatry,* ed. J. G. Howells (New York: Bruner/Mazel, 1971).

Lytton, "Observation Studies."

C. E. Phillips, "Some Useful Tests for Marriage Counseling," *Family Coordinator* 22 (1973): 43-53.

Roberts and Forehand, "An Analysis of Methods."

B. Semeonoff, *Projective Techniques* (New York: Wiley, 1976).

D. K. Snyder, "Advances in Marital Assessment: Behavioral, Communications, and Psychometric Approaches," in *Advances in Personality Assessment,* eds. C. D. Spielberger and J. N. Butcher (Hillsdale, N.J.: Erlbaum, 1982).

M. A. Straus, "Measuring Families," in *Handbook of Marriage and the Family,* ed. H. T. Christensen (Chicago: Rand McNally, 1964).

L. K. White and D. B. Brinkerhoff, "Measurement Problems in Family Research," *International Journal of Sociology of the Family* 7 (1977): 171-79.

W. D. Winter and A. J. Ferreira, eds., *Research in Family Interaction* (Palo Alto, Calif.: Science and Behavior Books, 1969).

115.  C. A. Beere, *Women and Women's Issues: A Handbook of Tests and Measures* (San Francisco: Jossey-Bass, 1979).

C. N. Bonjean, R. J. Hill, and S. D. McLemore, *Sociological Measurement: An Inventory of Scales and Indices* (San Francisco: Chandler, 1967).

O. K. Buros, ed., *Mental Measurements Yearbooks,* vols. 1-8 (Highland Park, N.J.: Gryphon, 1938-1978).

K. T. Chun, S. Cobb, and J. French, *Measures for Psychological Assessment* (Ann Arbor, Mich.: Institute for Social Research, University of Michigan, 1975).

A. L. Comrey, T. E. Backer, and E. M. Glaser, *A Sourcebook for Mental Health Measures* (Los Angeles: Human Interaction Research Institute, 1973).

R. E. Cromwell and D. G. Fournier, *Diagnosing Relationships: A Measurement Handbook for Marital and Family Therapists* (San Francisco: Jossey-Bass, in press).

R. E. Cromwell and G. W. Peterson, "A Framework for Multimethod Multisystem Assessment," in *Marital Observation and Behavioral Assessment: Recent Developments and Techniques,* eds. E. Filsinger and R. Lewis (Beverly Hills, Calif.: Sage, 1981).

O. G. Johnson, *Tests and Measurements in Child Development: Handbook II,* 2 vols. (San Francisco: Jossey-Bass, 1976).

O. G. Johnson and J. W. Bommarito, *Tests and Measurements in Child Development: A Handbook* (San Francisco: Jossey-Bass, 1971).

D. G. Lake, M. B. Miles, and R. B. Earle, Jr., eds., *Measuring Human Behavior* (New York: Teachers College Press, 1973).

P. Rosen, ed., *Test Collection Bulletin* (Princeton, N.J.: Educational Testing Service).

M. A. Straus and B. W. Brown, *Family Measurement Techniques* (Minneapolis: University of Minnesota Press, 1978).

D. K. Walker, *Socioemotional Measures for Preschool and Kindergarten Children* (San Francisco: Jossey-Bass, 1973).

# 11

# The Case Study

The case study is a process that brings together data collected by a variety of child study techniques in such a manner as to permit systematic review and analysis. Strang describes the method further:

> The case study is a synthesis and interpretation of information about a person and his relationship to his environment, collected by means of many technics. If the individual has been parceled out to specialists, the case study attempts to put him together again. At its best, it is a personality picture that becomes clearer and more lifelike as each new item is added. By preserving details that would otherwise be lost or distorted by lapse of time, a case study makes possible a comparison of conflicting evidence or a reinforcement and clarification of initial impressions. Trends, too, are revealed. To accomplish these ends requires psychological insight and critical thinking based on the best available data viewed as a whole.[1]

The case study has been characterized by Allport as being a completely synthetic method of studying individuals which embraces all assembled facts.[2] The manner in which it is employed determines its ultimate utility. "Unskillfully used, it becomes a meaningless chronology, or a confusion of fact and fiction, of guess-work and misinterpretation. Properly used it is the most revealing method of all."[3]

Although its origins are found in medicine and psychiatry, the case study has not been limited to pathology and its treatment. In fact, there are two basic types of case studies, the methodologies of which were developed relatively independently of each other.[4] One is the case study of genetic orientation that is used in medicine, psychiatry, and clinical psychology, and the other involves the nonmedical use of case material. The latter approach is represented by human development and education, as well as by business and law. At approximately the same time Freud was revolutionizing psychiatry with the development of his psychoanalytic theory based on the case method, Gesell and Piaget, representing child development, were using observation and the case method to study individual children. Because of its value, the case study has become a mainstay in both the medical sciences and child development.

Use of the word *case* may not be as appropriate in some fields as it is in the medical sciences. *Case* has traditionally referred to a person who is suffering from a physical or emotional illness, but all "cases" in child development and education are not pathological. Similarly, the term *case history* in medicine and psychiatry has meant the history of the patient's present illness and other past illnesses (i.e., medical history), whereas in nonmedical areas, *case history*, or the somewhat parallel term *life history*, has typically been used to designate data that are not necessarily medical. As more and more clinically oriented personnel have entered the fields of psychology, child guidance, social work, and education, the case history has evolved into a combination of the medical and nonmedical type histories. Cottingham describes the case history in this manner:

> The case history stresses the collection of a comprehensive series of developmental facts concerning the past and current life of the individual pupil as they relate to a particular problem. The purpose is to obtain a chronological view of the essential phases of the pupil's life. These data are obtained from the child's own account,

from relatives, from official records, as well as teachers and other guidance person-nel.[5]

In Traxler's words, the case history "presents the story of an individual in as complete and objective form as possible."[6] It includes information pertaining to family history, developmental history, sociological history, and educational and vocational history.[7] An integral part of the case study, the case history is a longitudinal survey which does not highlight problem areas, nor does it synthesize and interpret data. This is done within the framework of the larger case study. The case study goes beyond the raw data provided by the case history. Case history material and other additional data that may be obtained are incorporated into the case study to the extent that they contribute to answers that are being posed. The case history is strongly advocated for a number of reasons, including these:

1. It furnishes leads which contribute toward understanding the behavior of a child.

2. It facilitates evaluation of long-term trends in development.

3. It enriches interpretation when integrated with test results and other data.

4. It aids in prediction by indicating more or less what can be expected of a child, barring any radical or significant influences which may alter patterns of behavior.

5. It helps uncover multiple causes of behavior and constellations of contributing factors.

6. It permits all data to be viewed discriminately, thereby assisting in a more scientific methodology.[8]

If a school district maintains a complete cumulative record system, it has an ongoing and up-to-date, though perhaps incomplete, case history for every child enrolled. An example of a cumulative record form is provided in Figures 11.1 and 11.2.

The case method of investigation may be conducted at various levels of sophistication. It may deal with typical or atypical behavior and development. In its most elementary form, the case method is used as a learning tool by students and teacher trainees to further their understanding of child development and behavior. The students' observations are usually restricted to the classroom, since additional information on the child is normally limited. At the next level, case studies are conducted by classroom teachers who are interested in planning effective educational programs to meet the needs of individual students. A teacher may also ask other school personnel to provide additional data on a particular child. The teacher's professional training may or may not allow him or her to develop a truly in-depth case study. Nevertheless, a preliminary study conducted by a teacher may serve as an initial step in the referral process. A third level is represented by the type of case study that school counselors undertake when they are consulted by teachers who, in their instructional capacity, cannot answer important questions about a student. The child may have an academic deficit in a certain subject matter area, or the child may have emotional problems. Although the counselor will probably have test scores and personal and family information on the child, he or she may choose to expand upon these data with interviews involving not only the child but also the parents and others who have contact with the child. Moreover, the counselor may decide to test the child or to refer the child for psychological testing. Therefore, the case study may be helpful to the counselor in planning programs of developmental guidance and counseling or in arranging remedial measures for a child who is experiencing difficulties. At the most sophisticated level, a clinical case study may be developed by a school psychologist, clinical psychologist, or psychiatrist. The case is usually a child who is exhibiting maladaptive behavior that interferes with his or her personal, social, and scholastic

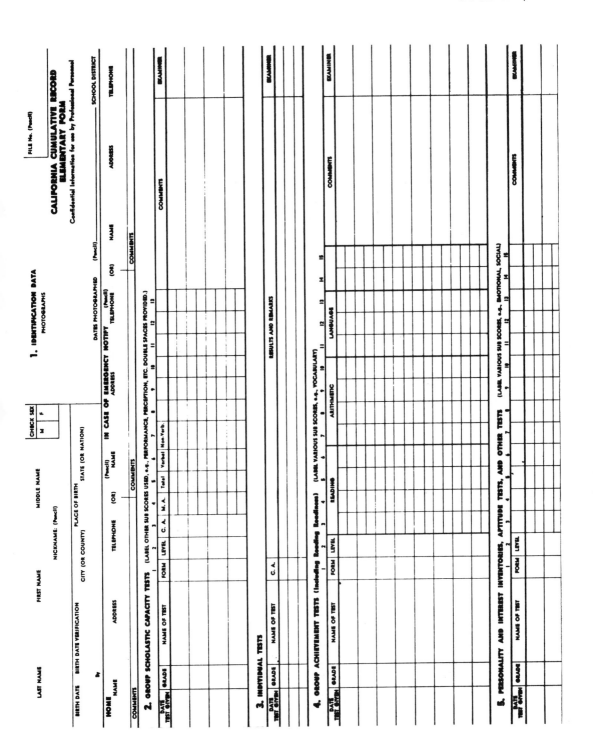

**Figure 11.1.** Inside Half of an Elementary School Cumulative Folder

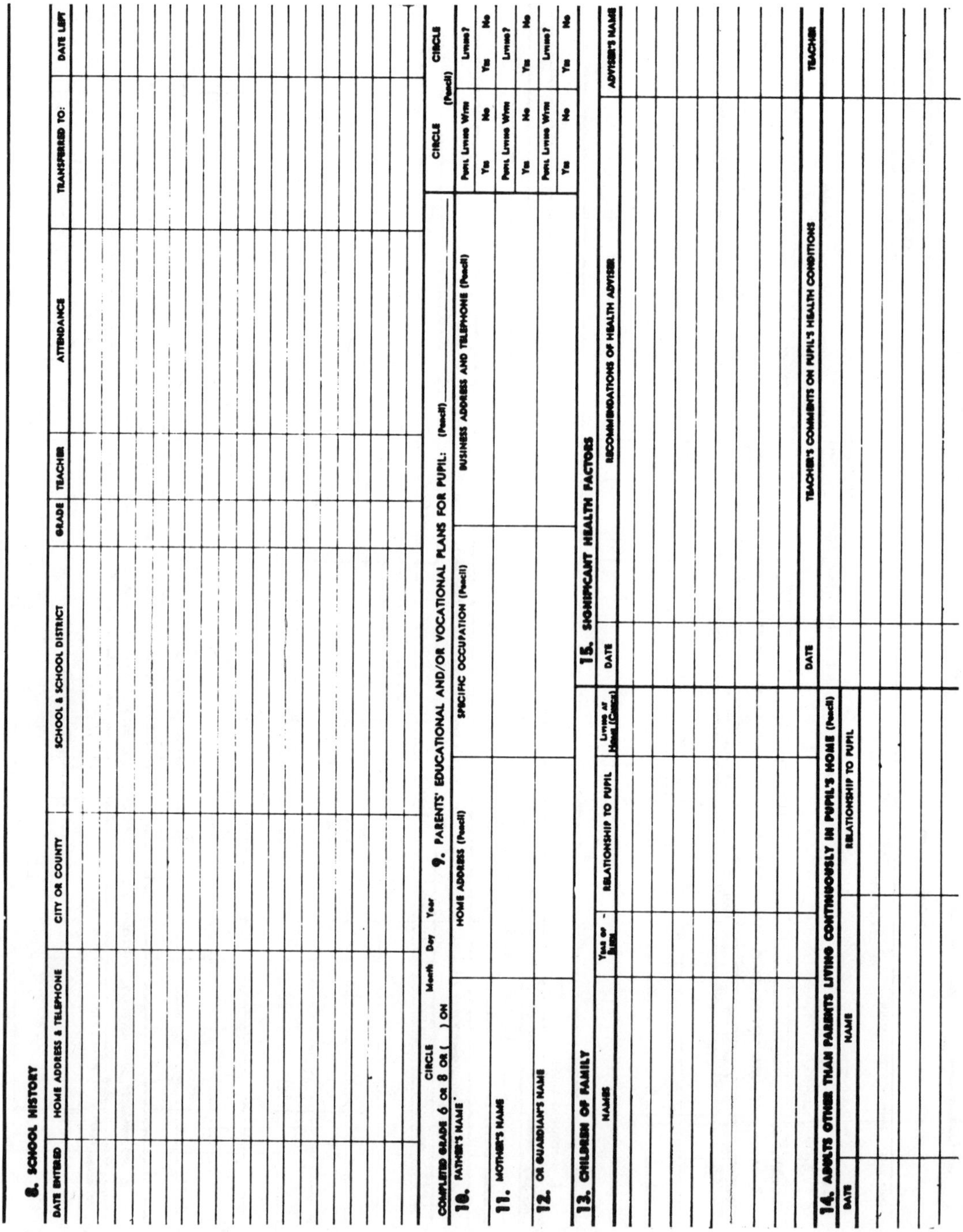

**8. SCHOOL HISTORY**

| DATE ENTERED | HOME ADDRESS & TELEPHONE | CITY OR COUNTY | SCHOOL & SCHOOL DISTRICT | GRADE | TEACHER | ATTENDANCE | TRANSFERRED TO: | DATE LEFT |
|---|---|---|---|---|---|---|---|---|
| | | | | | | | | |

COMPLETED GRADE 6 OR 8 OR ( ) ON Month Day Year (CIRCLE)

**9.** PARENTS' EDUCATIONAL AND/OR VOCATIONAL PLANS FOR PUPIL: (Pencil)

| | HOME ADDRESS (Pencil) | SPECIFIC OCCUPATION (Pencil) | BUSINESS ADDRESS AND TELEPHONE (Pencil) | CIRCLE (Pencil) | CIRCLE |
|---|---|---|---|---|---|
| **10.** FATHER'S NAME | | | | Pupil Living With: Yes No | Living? Yes No |
| **11.** MOTHER'S NAME | | | | Pupil Living With: Yes No | Living? Yes No |
| **12.** OR GUARDIAN'S NAME | | | | Pupil Living With: Yes No | Living? Yes No |

**13. CHILDREN OF FAMILY**

| NAMES | Year of Birth | RELATIONSHIP TO PUPIL | Living at Home (Check) |
|---|---|---|---|
| | | | |

**14. ADULTS OTHER THAN PARENTS LIVING CONTINUOUSLY IN PUPIL'S HOME (Pencil)**

| DATE | NAME | RELATIONSHIP TO PUPIL |
|---|---|---|
| | | |

**15. SIGNIFICANT HEALTH FACTORS**

| DATE | RECOMMENDATIONS OF HEALTH ADVISER | ADVISER'S NAME |
|---|---|---|
| | | |

| DATE | TEACHER'S COMMENTS ON PUPIL'S HEALTH CONDITIONS | TEACHER |
|---|---|---|
| | | |

**Figure 11.2.** Outside Half of an Elementary School Cumulative Folder

functioning. This highly clinical approach to the case study involves a diagnostic formulation regarding the type of disorder and its possible causes, a proposed treatment plan, and a statement of prognosis. The treatment and its results are usually recorded as part of the case study if the person who initiates the study also provides the treatment. When the case has been referred to another person for treatment, reporting of the treatment and its results is not always possible. However, clinical case studies are of much greater value if they are concluded with a report concerning the nature of the treatment and any progress made with the child.

Thus, the case study can be used to provide information that leads to a plan which will insure maximum development of a normal child, or it can be used to diagnose a problem for a child who is experiencing difficulty and to recommend a plan of treatment or remediation for that child.

## STEPS IN THE CASE STUDY

Preparation of a case study parallels the steps in the scientific method. With the scientific method, a problem is selected and carefully defined, a body of objective data is amassed, hypotheses are made and tested, additional information is gathered, hypotheses are retested and restated as valid conclusions, and strategies are planned to solve the problem in light of validated conclusions. The *first step* in the initiation of a case study is to determine precisely what its purpose is. The specific problem could be Why is Mary aggressive toward her classmates? or Why is Fred not achieving at a level compatible with his ability? A preliminary statement must always be made regarding the specific reason(s) for studying a child.

The *second step* is to collect and organize the data. Since most schools have an adequate cumulative record system, a good part of the case history work has usually been done already. School records supply at least some social and medical history data, family information, and other data such as test scores, grades, extracurricular activities, and anecdotes on the child. However, an effort should be made to verify this information. All of the facts needed for a comprehensive case history will not be available in the child's file. It is therefore necessary to interview the child's teachers and parents as well as the child. Information collected in the interviews may then be supplemented by additional tests, self-reports written by the child, samples of the youngster's school work, and records from the courts, police, truant officers, and social welfare agencies. Another rich source of information is observational material on the child that is collected in the school, on the playground, at home, and in social settings. Various observational techniques (anecdotal records, running records, time sampling, etc.) were described in Chapter 3. There is no better way to study a youngster's behavior than to witness it firsthand in a multitude of situations.

The data should then be organized in some meaningful way to facilitate analysis. A six-area framework for analysis with subheadings has been suggested by Prescott to highlight the dynamics in a child's development:

### A Framework for Analysis

1. Physical Factors and Processes
   a. Growth rate and physical-maturity level.
   b. Characteristic rates of energy output, of fatiguing, of recovery from fatigue, and characteristic rhythms of activity and rest.
   c. State of health, health history, and health habits.
   d. Physical limitations and handicaps, how they are managed by the individual, and how the individual thinks and feels about them.
   e. How the individual uses his body, including game skills.
   f. Attractiveness of face, physique, and grooming in terms of their impact on adults, peers, and self.

2. Love Relationships and Related Processes
   a. Relationships of the individual with each parent and sibling and how these relationships are expressed.
   b. Relationship between the parents, between each parent and each sibling, and between the various siblings, and how these relationships are expressed.
   c. Relationship between each of the above individuals and any other adults living in the home and how these relationships are expressed.
   d. Relationships of the individual with pets and how these relationships are expressed.
   e. How difficulties in relationships within the family are managed by the individual and by others in the family.
   f. Relationship of the individual to any person outside the family who sincerely values him personally and who becomes a source of security to him, such as teacher, neighbor, relative, scoutmaster, priest or pastor, psychiatrist, nurse, etc.

3. Cultural Background and Socialization Processes
   a. Subcultures carried by the family and the characteristics of these cultures: masculine-feminine, rural-urban, regional, ethnic, social-class, caste.
   b. Processes by which the child is internalizing these cultural factors.
   c. The functioning of the individual in the school as a social institution.
   d. The functioning of the individual in other community institutions and social processes: church, play and recreation; earning, saving, and spending money; scouts; 4-H clubs; museums, etc.
   e. Progress in the individual's internalization of the wider American culture through school-mediated, family-guided, and community-available experiences.
   f. The individual's concepts of and feelings about the American society, his sense of how its present institutions and processes have evolved gradually through the roles played by individuals and groups in the past and his sense of his own responsibility for playing roles that will maintain and develop it further.
   g. Inconsistencies which may exist between the cultures the individual is internalizing at home, or in his neighborhood, and the expectancies that are pressed upon him at school, in his church, in business or industry, or by the government.
   h. Special pressures felt by the child if his family is geographically or social-class mobile or if he elects to become mobile himself.
   i. Special pressures felt by the child if his family belongs to an ethnic group in a minority in his community or to a caste-discriminated racial group.

4. Peer-group Status and Processes
   a. Characteristic activities of the individual's peer group, roles available in these activities, knowledge and skills required for these roles, customs and codes of behavior of the peer group, and personality characteristics esteemed by the peer group.
   b. Roles sought and won by the individual in his peer group, and the status accorded him through this role playing.
   c. Failures of the indivdual to win desired roles in the peer group and the causes of these failures in terms of lack of knowledge or skills, failure to

follow peer-group customs or codes, lack of the necessary personal characteristics or the possession of unacceptable personality characteristics, or inappropriate behavior.

   d. How the individual manages himself when he fails to win peer-group roles or when he fails to play accorded roles successfully.

   e. The effects of physical, affectional, and cultural factors upon the individual's peer-group status and role playing.

5. Self-developmental Factors and Processes
   a. The individual's *conception of himself and feelings about himself,* as influenced by physical processes and factors, love relationships and related processes, cultural background, socialization processes and social experiences, peer-group status and processes.
   b. How the individual's many-sided *conception of himself influences his perception* of situations, or the meaning that each successive experience has for him.
   c. The individual's unique accumulation of experiences and the *meanings,* including both knowledge and skills, which he has *distilled out of these experiences,* meanings which *constitute his conceptions of the universe, of society, and of events.*
   d. How the individual's many-sided *conception of the universe, of society, and of events influences his perception* of persons and situations and his perception of their meanings for him.
   e. The *conceptions* and feelings the individual has *of the relationships* that exist *between himself* (as he conceives himself) *and the universe, society, other individuals and events* (as he conceives them). These conceptions of relationship between self and universe, self and society, and self and others are the bases of the individual's attitudes, codes of conduct, philosophy of life, and values.
   f. The individual's potential and operating capacities and aptitudes for learning and doing, as evaluated objectively through tests and subjectively by persons who have interacted functionally with him through time.
   g. The mental processes which the individual habitually uses to work out the meanings for himself, for others, and for society of various experiences and situations, including symbolizing, abstracting and generalizing, reasoning, and imagining.
   h. The long-term purposes and the immediate goals which the individual reveals through his behavior; and the patterns of action which he permits himself to use as he works toward these goals and purposes.
   i. The conceptions which the individual's parents, siblings, teachers and peers have of him as a person and the expectancies as to his behavior and competencies which result from these conceptions.

6. Self-adjustive Factors and Processes
   a. The quality of the individual's feelings about his own physical adequacy. Whether he feels: abundantly adequate, physically sufficient to meet situations, physically limited as to what he can undertake, physically handicapped in what he must undertake, physically inferior to others, or physically ill.

b. The quality of the individual's feelings about his love relationships: is completely secure in his sense of being loved, intermittently feels loved and unloved, is uncertain and confused about whether he is loved, feels unloved and therefore essentially alone, feels actively rejected by those whom he wants to love him.

c. The quality of the individual's feelings about being socially significant: constantly feels socially important, intermittently feels socially important, feels himself to be without social importance, feels in conflict with the expectancies and demands of social processes, feels actively excluded from social roles, feels antisocial.

d. The quality of the individual's feelings about his status among his peers and about the roles accorded him in peer-group activities: feels that he is a high-prestige person privileged to play leadership roles, feels that he belongs and effectively plays roles in the group, feels anxious about his belonging because he only intermittently wins roles, feels isolated and without significance to the peer-group, feels in conflict with peers about his roles and status, feels actively rejected by peers who refuse him roles.

e. The quality of the individual's feelings about his adequacy as a total person, as a self: feels he can face successfully whatever comes, feels reasonably adequate to meet life, feels that he may fail to achieve some goals but will succeed in others, feels that success or failure depends upon luck, feels he is more likely to fail than to succeed in any task, feels he is sure to fail at everything.

f. The individual's way of acting when he is experiencing any of the feelings listed above, or particular combinations of them.

g. The adjustment patterns used by the individual when some of the unpleasant feelings listed above are experienced repeatedly or at a high level of intensity: rationalization, withdrawal, projection, compensation, fantasy, creative activity, sublimation or others.

h. Whether the individual is facing continuing adjustment problems that are limiting or damaging his conception of self, distorting his conceptions of the universe and of society, warping his felt relationship with persons, group, or society.

i. Whether the situations giving rise to continuing adjustment problems are being altered for the better or worse by known factors, and whether the effects of these continuing problems are being neutralized by known factors.

j. Whether the individual's continuing adjustment problems are of such severity that therapeutic assistance is necessary.[9]

Another possible way to organize case material is to list recurring patterns. Recurring patterns are behaviors, events, or situations that occur several times. Yet another means of organizing the case record is presented later in this chapter under "Form of the Case Study."

The *third step* in preparing a case study is to formulate multiple tentative hypotheses. After considerable objective data have been gathered, the case investigator should list tentative hypotheses about events or relationships. According to Perkins, these hypotheses can be of three types: "(1) hypotheses suggested by the particular circumstances under which the behavior occurred, (2) hypotheses suggested by other case record information on the person, and (3) hypotheses suggested by scientific concepts and principles of human development and learning."[10] The data usually point to several plausible explanations for the child's recurring patterns of behavior, and these are stated formally. In the case study of a child who consistently failed to complete his artwork, the teacher offered twenty hypotheses as tentative explanations for the pupil's behavior. These are ten of the teacher's hypotheses:

1. Scotty is in competition with another student in the class. (Hence he does not want his work to appear in comparison.)

2. Scotty is ambivalent in his attitude toward art.

3. Scotty believes that art is sissyish and feminine.

4. Other children laugh and make fun of Scotty's pictures.

5. Scotty expresses an interest in sports and games. (This he views as incompatible with an interest in art.)

6. Scotty is asserting that he is independent of adult authority. (He showed this by not finishing the picture that the teacher liked.)

7. Scotty has a warm, friendly, permissive relationship with the teacher. (He feared that his completed picture might not fulfill her expectations.)

8. Scotty has a short attention span.

9. Scotty has a preference for realism rather than for things imaginary.

10. Scotty gains emotional support by depending on others.[11]

The *fourth step* is to test the hypotheses against available facts in the case record to determine whether the data support or refute the hypotheses. In analyzing Scotty's failure to complete his art projects, the teacher found evidence which confirmed hypotheses 6, 7, 9, and 10. Prescott has recommended that the case record be examined carefully and a plus mark placed by each hypothesis that is supported by the data and a minus mark by each hypothesis that is weakened by the facts presented. To show how the hypotheses were evaluated for a case involving a pupil who persistently avoided working at reading tasks, the tabulation for seven of the twenty-four hypotheses listed in that case is presented:

| Hypotheses | Plus score | Minus score |
|---|---|---|
| 1. Chester is just stubborn and won't work unless he is forced to. | 0 | 2 |
| 2. Chester's mother has kept after him about reading until he hates it. | 7 | 0 |
| 3. Chester's earlier teachers have let him get away with not working on reading for so long that he thinks he can still get away with it now. | 0 | 2 |
| 4. Chester has failed at reading for so long that he is thoroughly discouraged and avoids trying so that he will not feel like a failure again. | 13 | 0 |
| 5. Chester has no real reason to want to read, since no one ever reads in his home. | 0 | 10 |
| 6. Chester is not bright enough to read better at present. | 3 | 0 |

7. Chester is not liked by the other children; he avoids trying
   to read because he doesn't want them to see him fail . . . . . . .   11      $0^{12}$

From the foregoing, it can be seen that hypotheses 2, 4, and 7 were supported by many facts, such as those garnered from anecdotes, home visits, test scores, and cumulative records, and that hypothesis 5 was clearly refuted. Hypotheses 1, 3, and 6 probably required additional data before a definite judgment could be made.

The *fifth step* is to gather additional information. The case study outline or framework for analysis adopted for organizing the data usually helps the case writer spot significant gaps in his or her knowledge about the child. The data collection procedures mentioned in step 2 are used to obtain new facts about the youngster to correct this imbalance of information. Frequently, the case investigator finds that insufficient data exist to test some of the hypotheses formulated in step 4, so further information must be sought. The additional data permit reevaluation of existing hypotheses and testing of new ones.

The *sixth step* is to synthesize and summarize the data and to draw conclusions or make diagnoses. For purposes of analysis, the child has been segmented in previous steps. But in this stage of the case study, the youngster is put back together again and viewed as a whole. Final analysis and conclusions may take the form of (a) validated hypotheses or explanations of the child's behavior in the particular situation chosen for study; (b) a series of general statements regarding the child's present status (e.g., physical health, interpersonal relationships, and psychological adjustment); (c) a listing of the child's assets and liabilities; (d) a recurring pattern summation; (e) a developmental tasks interpretive survey; (f) a self-structure interpretive summary; or (g) a combination of these. In the case of Bob, which is presented at the end of this chapter, we will see how objective raw data can be summarized and interpreted using options *d, e,* and *f.*

The *seventh step* is to apply what has been learned about the child and to make recommendations based upon the increased knowledge. At this point, the case writer indicates changes in conditions or new experiences that will maximize the youngster's development and adjustment. The case investigator may make concrete and specific recommendations for accenting optimal development such as suggesting supportive and helping actions that are designed to facilitate developmental task achievement, to enhance the child's self-image, to improve the youngster's school performance, and to promote the child's personal-social adjustment. In the case of Chester mentioned in step 4, the teacher eventually uncovered a number of reasons why the student avoided reading activities. Based upon her findings, she noted several constructive ideas about how to help the child at school. Some of there were

1. Continue to give Chester personal warmth, acceptance and support whenever it is appropriate.
2. Continue to give Chester concrete help in getting started on specific limited tasks, especially in reading.
3. Continue to give Chester responsibilities and roles in the day-to-day life of the classroom.
4. Give Chester more direct praise whenever he completes a task or does something reasonably well.
5. Have patience with Chester's slowness and deliberateness.
6. Utilize Chester's interest in music, art, and science as bases for activities to give him success and ways of working off emotional tensions.[13]

Another case, reported by Ringness, involved a seven-year-old boy who exhibited withdrawal and self-conscious behavior. After some study at school, the child was referred to a local child-study clinic. There, the professional staff discovered that the youngster's main problem was a deep-seated feeling of inferiority due to neglect by his mother and lack of acceptance by his father. The team of workers offered these recommendations to the school:

1. Teachers should not force Jerry to talk in class but let him move at his own speed into group participation.

2. Teachers should provide individual remedial instruction for Jerry in academic and physical education classes.

3. Teachers should not call attention to Jerry's behavior through their comments, nor should the child be subjected to strong pressures to achieve.

4. Teachers should provide Jerry with friendly support and reinforcement.

5. Teachers should manipulate Jerry's assignments at first so that work was on his level and he would be helped to know success; his strong points should be taken advantage of, rather than attention be given to his weak points.[14]

In cases like Jerry's, recommendations usually include remedial treatment such as tutoring, counseling, and sometimes even special-education placement. Recommendations should be congruent with diagnoses. Following the recommendations, a prognosis is usually made which predicts the future development of the child or the outcome of treatment.

The *eighth step* is to follow up the case to determine progress. A case described by Traxler illustrates the follow-up procedure very well.[15] Fred's reading test scores were low and indicated a deficiency in this area. Consequently, a remedial reading program was recommended to stimulate interest in reading, to inspire habits of independent reading, to increase rate of reading, to improve vocabulary and comprehension, and to overcome the student's tendency to reverse certain letters. Fred then met with the remedial teacher for one class period a week for eight months. To evaluate the results of the special work, the case investigator examined Fred's latest reading test scores and course grades and reviewed reports by teachers and observations by the remedial reading instructor. The test scores indicated improvement in most areas, and year-end academic reports by Fred's teachers did not cite any marked deficiencies in reading. The remedial teacher noted that Fred had evidenced slow but consistent growth in reading ability and that he had achieved almost grade-level reading skills. Interviews with the child revealed that he anticipated doing a fair amount of informal reading during summer vacation. In the interest of continuing follow-up of the case, the remedial reading teacher planned to meet with Fred at the beginning of fall semester in order to study his progress and possibly to test him again. Further remedial instruction would probably be unnecessary if no significant loss in reading skill was found and if the student had reached the point where he could guide himself in his reading activities. This follow-up process serves as a check on the final analysis or diagnosis and may lead to changes in the plan of action for the child. Follow-up also aids in understanding subsequent cases that may be similar in nature.

To summarize, the general steps in executing a case study are

1. Explain the purpose of the study.

2. Collect and organize the data.

3. Formulate multiple tentative hypotheses.

4. Test the hypotheses.

5. Gather additional information.

6. Synthesize and summarize the data; draw conclusions.

7. Make recommendations and a prognosis.

8. Follow up the case.

## FORM OF THE CASE STUDY

There is no standardized form for the case study because the outline used will vary with the nature of the case. However, a number of different formats have appeared in the case study literature.[16] The one included in this section is similar to those that are described in the literature and those that are being used in some schools, clinics, and agencies. The outline is quite comprehensive but it may be adapted to a wide variety of cases. More than anything else, the outline is intended to call attention to the different types of information that might be helpful in a case. The guide questions overlap somewhat with Prescott's six-area framework for analysis presented in the previous section, and when considered together, the questions and framework should insure more than adequate coverage of details for most case studies of children.

**SUGGESTED OUTLINE**

I. **Identifying Information**

What is the child's full name, address, telephone number, age in years and months, place of birth, sex, school, grade (class and teacher's name), race, nationality, and religion? The name of the person making the study and the date of the report should also be included at the beginning of the write-up.

II. **Sources of Information**

What are your sources of information about the child (e.g., cumulative records; personal observations; interviews with child, parents, relatives, neighbors, friends, teachers, principal, school psychologist, juvenile officer, police, social welfare agencies, clinics, hospitals, psychological reports)? All notations should be dated to indicate when the information was reported or provided.

III. **Reason for Study**

What is the purpose of the case study? A statement should be made regarding the situation that has led to the study, or if a problem is involved, it should be stated as clearly as possible. Problems may be classified into four general areas: educational (intellectual deficiency, learning disability, poor performance, attendance, etc.); physical (health, physical handicaps, etc.); social-emotional (personality disorders, conduct problems, delinquency, relationships with peers and adults); and family (socioeconomic status and finances, relationships in the home, parental absence, abuse, etc.). If the child has been referred to you, the name of the person who made the referral and his or her reason for the referral should be included.

IV. **Data**

A.    Family History

1. Members of the Immediate Family and Close Relatives

The names of all persons in the immediate family should be recorded as well as those of persons who are closely related to the study child but not living in the home. The age, race, nationality, and religious background of each person should be noted. The social, cultural, and economic background of the parenting persons should be given. If a family member or close relative is deceased, the age at death and cause of death should be included. Special care should be taken to describe the marital status of the parents. Are both natural parents in the home? If so, how long have they been married? Where has the family lived in past years? If the home is not intact, notation should be made regarding the atypical nature of the family structure (one natural parent only, one natural parent and one stepparent or nonmarried partner, adoptive or foster parents, relatives, etc.). Divorces, separations, and remarriages in the immediate family should be indicated, and the age of the study child at the time of such occurrences should be given.

2. Health and Physical Characteristics

   The physical characteristics of all family members should be described. In addition, any physical and mental handicaps should be designated. Serious injuries and illnesses should be noted.

3. Education

   Educational attainment and area of training of parents, siblings, and relatives who are close to the child should be provided along with the family's attitudes toward education, particularly their aspirations for the study child.

4. Socioeconomic Status

   Socioeconomic status of the family should be carefully studied and reported. What is the employment history and present job status of the parenting persons? Specifically, what are their occupations and incomes? What is the level of job satisfaction, and how are their relations with fellow workers? Is the family on welfare? Does the family own or rent their home? Are accommodations adequate for the size of the family? Describe housing and living conditions (community and neighborhood; nearby recreational facilities; home; yard; material possessions in the home; automobile ownership; debts; quality of food and clothing; availability of books, magazines, and other cultural resources; recreation; etc.). What is the child's perception of his or her environments?

5. Socioemotional Climate in the Home

   What is the family organization (e.g., patriarchal, matriarchal, egalitarial)? Who is the disciplinarian in the home? What are the sources of family tension (parent compatibility, parent-child and child-child relations, finances, religion, alcoholism, gambling, delinquency, drugs, etc.)? How is the family thought of in the neighborhood and community? What are the parents' attitudes toward their community? Does the family have many friends, and who are they? What are the family's recreational activities, and how does the study child participate? Does the family currently belong to a church or synagogue, and if so, how often do they attend? What seem to be the major interests of the family members (intellectual, social, athletic, etc.)? What is the overall atmosphere in the home and what are the important family attitudes and values (loving, harmonious, cooperative, unhappy, competitive, dysfunctional, religious, permissive, suppressive, organized, chaotic, community-minded, liberal, conservative, etc.)? How does the study child fit into the family's psychosocial system? What are the family's strengths and weaknesses?

B. Child's Developmental History

   1. Health and Physical Development

      What was the mother's general health and attitude during pregnancy? What was the length of pregnancy and labor, and were there any complications during pregnancy? Where was the child born? What were the infant's length and weight at birth? What was the infant's condition at birth (birth injuries; malformations, etc.)? What illnesses and injuries have occurred since birth, and when? What is the child's surgical history? Notation should be made of the height and duration of temperature during illnesses, and injuries should be mentioned that may have neurological implications. Regarding the rate of development, when was the child weaned? When did the child first crawl, sit, stand, walk, talk, achieve bladder and bowel control, cut teeth, etc? Preferably, a complete developmental record of growth in height and weight should be obtained. The child's sleep habits, diet, and exercise history also should be indicated as well as any unusual behavior problems related to the child's development. Describe any nervous habits of the child such as thumb sucking, tics, masturbation, etc. How would you describe the child's build, strength, and other physical capacities relative to other children his or her age? What is the child's current health status? Include a report of a recent medical examination of the child that provides information concerning vision, hearing, speech, coordination, dental health, nutritional status, height-weight ratio, immunizations, etc. If medical records are unavailable, a physical examination is necessary. The name of the child's present physician should be indicated in case there is a need to check on any medical information.

2. Educational Development

What was the child's age at school entrance, and what other schools has he or she attended? Describe the environment of the child's present school. What is the child's level of performance in classwork (reading, mathematics, writing, spelling, science, etc.)? Provide teacher reports, course grades, achievement test scores, and results of other standardized tests (intelligence, aptitude, personality, interest inventories, etc.). When test data are listed, the complete name of the measure should be given along with the form and level used and the date on which the test was administered. Derived scores (percentile, grade equivalent, deviation I.Q., etc.) rather than raw scores should be noted for the total scale as well as subtests. Any test behavior or situation that may have invalidated the measure or made it unreliable should be indicated. Most of this information is available in the cumulative folder. What is the child's history of promotion, retention, and acceleration? What is his or her past record of conduct? What are his or her study habits? What is the child's attitude toward school? Does the child have any special abilities or difficulties in school? What courses does the child like or dislike? Does he or she have any special interests? Has he or she thought about any tentative educational or vocational plans? Is the child a member of any school-sponsored organizations? How does the child relate to teachers and classmates? Is school attendance regular? If not, what are the reasons for absences?

3. Personal-Social Development

What are the child's relations in the home with parents and siblings? What is the nature of the child's interpersonal relations in the neighborhood and community? Who are his or her playmates, and what are their races, ages, sexes, and socioeconomic status? Who are his or her closest friends? What people influence the child? Is the child a member of the Scouts or the "Y"? Is he or she affiliated with a gang? What is the child's attitude toward self, family, peers and authority figures? Describe the child's personality. Does he or she have any special personal problems? Has he or she ever been referred for treatment? What are the child's likes and dislikes? What is his or her general mood state?

What are his or her modes of psychological defense? What are the child's hobbies and leisure-time activities?

V.  **Tentative Multiple Hypotheses**
    Plausible explanations for the child's behavior

VI.  **Evaluation of Hypotheses**
    Tests of the hypotheses in light of the data collected

VII.  **Additional Data**
    More interviews, observations, questionnaire and sociometric techniques, standardized tests, teacher reports, school and community records, etc.

VIII.  **Synthesis and Summary of Data/Conclusions**
    Final analysis and summary of case record

IX.  **Recommendations and Prognosis**
    Recommendations (numbered in order of priority) should be made for maximizing the development of a child, or in the case of problems, a plan for treatment and remediation should be suggested. A recommendation may be made for further professional attention and referral. A prognosis should be attempted if at all possible.

X.  **Follow-up**
    This is the procedure used to determine the child's progress or to learn the results of treatment and the accuracy of the final analysis or diagnosis. It may be necessary to obtain still additional data and modify the ameliorative plan.

## CRITERIA FOR CASE MATERIAL

After the data have been collected and organized but before the case study is written in its final form, it is helpful to stop and consider the adequacy and range of the materials at hand. Rothney suggests that the case writer evaluate the case on the basis of these twenty questions:

1.  Are there any serious omissions in the data?

2.  Was more than one method employed in the collection of the data?

3.  Has more than one school of thought been considered in the interpretation of the data?

4.  Are the sources of all data specified?

5.  Have independent judgments been made by use of tests, judges, and those who provided behavior descriptions?

6.  Have reference points for statistics been given?

7.  Has consideration been given to the possibility of deception by the subject?

8.  Is the cultural situation given in enough detail?

9.  Is a description of the family situation presented?

10.  Is the developmental story told as far as it is relevant?

11.  Has adequate attention been given to current trends of behavior?

12.  Are future plans given enough consideration?

13.  Are data presented as evidence when predictions are made?

14.  Has due care been exercised in the interpretation of the motivation of the subject?

15. Are concrete illustrations of general categories presented?

16. Have censorial terms been avoided?

17. Is the writing good?

18. Has maximum brevity been sought?

19. Does the opening paragraph set the tone for the study?

20. Do you feel that you really know the person when you have finished reading the case study?[17]

## ILLUSTRATION OF CASE STUDY PROCEDURES

To demonstrate the use of some of the case study procedures discussed in this chapter, material will be presented from a case reported in Brandt's *Studying Behavior in Natural Settings.*[18] This case illustrates what can be learned about the processes of development and the forces which influence that development by careful study of a youngster over a period of time. The subject is Bob, a fairly well-adjusted child with the usual problems of preadolescence. The case investigator was Bob's Latin teacher, who also served as a part-time counselor in Bob's school.

Most of the case study was completed during Bob's ninth-grade year. It includes anecdotal descriptions of Bob's behavior in different situations, records of conferences with parents and teachers, and some of Bob's own writings (notes, autobiography, etc.). Because of space limitations, only excerpts from the original data that represent typical examples of the teacher's record are presented.

### SAMPLE OF ORIGINAL DATA

#### December 10

When I entered the classroom, Bob was standing talking to a group of students: among them were Jane Myers and Mike Finkler. When he saw me he rushed over and saluted me, saying: "Again I say, *Morituri te Salutamus!*"

I pretended to choke him, and he said, "Hey, that's my good neck!"

He didn't settle down to work as usual, but was rather talkative—working with David Jones more loudly than usual, correcting David's Latin. Twice I asked him to put all four legs of his chair on the floor. He was swinging far back on two legs of his chair.

I passed out the corrected Latin tests—again he tied with Margaret Kopak—101 points out of a possible 104. He busied himself discussing the test with his neighbors.

After class was dismissed, I heard him yell loudly, "Give me that!"

He was angrily going after Mike Finkler—his face was very flushed and whatever Mike had he quickly relinquished.

Out in the hall, as I was locking the door, Bob insisted on reading to me a verse from Jane Myer's wallet.

#### December 12

As I was locking the door after class, Bob came from his locker with a small brown paper bag which he handed to me saying, "Don't open this now, and don't thank me for it in class."

I must have looked puzzled, because he laughed and added, "It isn't a joke. Don't be afraid of it: but don't open it here."

I opened it in the counselor's office and found a Christmas corsage of ribbon and ornaments. I pinned it on my jacket, and at lunch time, as I was returning to the A building, I passed Bob with a large group of boys. He said loudly, "Where did you get your corsage?"

"I found it! Pretty, isn't it?"

He grinned and said, "So you did. So you did."

### December 13

The class was busily working on translations, when I was startled to see Bob precariously perched on the edge of his chair, again with only two of its legs on the floor. Rather sharply I said, "Bob!" and with indignation in her voice Jane Myers said, "He didn't do anything!"

It was so unlike her that I had to laugh, and said, "So now you're Bob's guardian angel?"

Bob proceeded to draw a picture of an angel with horns. It looked surprisingly like Jane who wears her hair in bangs which curl two ways.

### December 14

As I hurried to class, Mr. Brown came across the hall to meet Jane and me at our classroom door. He said, "I hear that you have a guardian angel in your Latin class."

"Where did you hear this?"

"At radio club last night, the boys were teasing Bob. He seemed to enjoy it."

Jane had gone on into the room, and was looking at me with a strange expression.

I asked, "Did I start something?" "You certainly did! Do I have to sit there?"

"Of course not!"

So Jane pulled her chair to another table, and Bob looked peeved.

### December 17

Jane started to pull her chair to another table, and I asked, "Do you mean you are still peeved, even over a weekend?"

"Well, if certain people would stop making remarks."

To which both David and Bob said, "We promise! We won't say another word."

(From Mrs. Falkner: Bob gave Robert Falkner a big fuzzy animal for Christmas. He and Max Hammer had manufactured a "Time Bomb" for Mrs. Falkner. It was ticking when they left it at her home. It was an ingenious device that they must have spent hours putting together.)[19]

The foregoing represents only a little over 3 percent of the total record. The only changes made by the author were the names of persons and other identifying information.

## RECURRING PATTERN SUMMATION

Recurring pattern summation was one of the procedures mentioned earlier under "Steps in the Case Study." This process involves examining the record and then listing the behaviors that are repeated. In Bob's case, the teacher looked for all of the recurring patterns in the youngster's behavior and in the behavior of others toward him. She organized the behaviors under five headings and indicated the date each pattern was reported in the record (see Figure 11.3). The case investigator withheld any judgments about the child until she had collected and organized the information. Coding reliability is high if case writers have been trained to make behavioral statements and not interpretive statements. In fact, over 90 percent agreement on the recurring behaviors is common between persons who have independently formulated recurring pattern lists from a given record.

After the list of behaviors has been made, interpretation is appropriate. Two conceptual schemes were used in the case of Bob to interpret the recurring behaviors. The first involved an itemization of

---

*A. Relationship with Teachers*

1. Uses first name or other informal phrases such as "Buddy, Buddy" to address Latin teacher. 9—10, 10—5, 10—10, 10—22, 10—24, 11—26, 11—29, 12—5, 1—2, 1—15, 1—15, 1—28, 1—29, 1—29, 2—1, 2—1, 2—14, 3—8

2. Teases or jokes with teachers.
   (a) With Latin teacher. 10—30, 11—2, 11—30, 12—22, 1—21, 1—21, 1—24, 1—25, 1—28, 1—30, 1—31, 2—1, 2—6, 2—11, 2—14, 2—20, 3—1, 3—19, 3—26, 3—26, 4—22, 5—3, 5—3
   (b) With other teachers. 12—17, 1—25, 1—30, 1—30, 4—1, 4—1

3. Gives a present to a teacher.
   (a) Latin teacher. 9—18, 12—12, 1—21, 3—26
   (b) Sick algebra teacher. 5—1

4. Makes telephone call to teacher at her home.
   (a) Latin teacher. 2—12, 2—20, 3—13, 3—19, 3—26, 5—13
   (b) Sick algebra teacher. 5—1

5. Talks to Latin teacher about Jane, a classmate. 2—6, 2—7, 3—1, 3—11, 4—22

6. Asks Latin teacher if she had noticed something which he had done or if she wants to see something he has to show her. 10—8, 2—11, 2—13, 2—15, 2—20, 4—22, 5—14

7. Tells Latin teacher about his out-of-school activities. 2—11, 2—20, 3—1, 3—13, 3—19, 3—25, 4—10

8. Did not answer Latin teacher's question about how science fair was going. 4—6, 4—6, 4—11

9. Bob is restricted by the Latin teacher from doing something he wants or has already started to do. 12—10, 12—13, 2—20, 2—20, 3—13, 3—19 (latter two incidents are group restrictions)

10. Latin teacher takes Bob some place he wants to go. 2—1, 3—1, 3—19 (twice at Bob's request)

11. Stops by counselor's office. 1—14, 1—15, 3—7, 3—21

12. Corrects Latin teacher. 2—11, 3—26

13. Writes or gives note to teachers. 11—28, 11—29, 1—30, 1—30, 1—31, 2—11, 4—1

14. Approaches Latin teacher outside class to talk casually with her. 11—26, 1—28, 2—11, 5—17

*B. Relationship with Peers*

15. Seen with groups of boys after school or between school classes (in only one instance were girls included in the groups). 10—2, 10—30, 11—13, 11—26, 12—10, 12—12, 1—30, 3—1, 3—19, 3—26, 5—6

16. Teases Jane. 12—10, 12—17, 1—21, 1—28, 2—6

17. Asks Jane to go with him to special event. 2—7, 4—22

18. Classmates defend Bob's behavior in discussion with teacher. 11—28, 11—28, 12—13

19. Bob is nominated by classmates for seatmate or special role. 11—27 (5 nominations), 1—14 (2nd in class)

20. Peers comment to teacher about Bob.
    (a) Favorably: 11—28, 12—13
    (b) Neutrally: 10—5, 11—28

21. Bob is teased by others about Jane. 12—14, 2—12

22. Bob kids classmates. 11—28, 1—21, 4—29

---

**Figure 11.3.** Recurring Pattern Summation

C.  *School and Community Activities and Roles*

23.  Assumes teaching or special report-making roles in class. 9—11, 12—7, 1—15, 3—21, 4—4, 4—29
24.  Participates in extracurricular activities.
  (a) Picture taking and other photography activities: 9—25, 10—8, 1—18, 2—14, 2—20, 3—4, 3—7, 3—8, 3—21, 5—16
  (b) Radio club: 10—30, 12—14
  (c) Talent show and special events: 1—15, 2—1, 4—6, 4—10, 5—10
  (d) Attended sports events and social parties: 2—11, 2—15
  (e) Attended concerts and shows: 2—27, 3—25
  (f) Student council: 2—28
  (g) Piano playing: 5—13
25.  Sits on chair with legs off the floor. 12—10, 12—13
26.  Uses Latin phrases in writing or talking. 10—10, 12—5, 12—10, 1—25, 1—29, 2—11, 2—12, 2—14
27.  Refers to Roman characters or writings. 9—11, 9—17, 1—28, 1—29, 1—31, 2—11
28.  Adults comment about Bob to teacher:
  (a) Favorably: 3—4, 3—29, 5—17
  (b) Unfavorably: 10—17, 1—18
  (c) Neutrally: 9—11
29.  Receives A in semester grades (five in academic subjects, one C in physical education). 1—25
30.  Receives less than top citizenship grade in eight instances and top citizenship ratings in five instances. 1—25
31.  Receives top or near-top grade on Latin class tests. 9—27, 10—11, 10—29, 12—10, 2—1
32.  Is permitted to leave class for extracurricular projects. 10—8, 3—8, 5—16
33.  Goes on school trips. 1—10, 4—10

D.  *Family Relationships*

34.  Mother or father comes to school, generally to attend school events Bob is in. 11—7, 11—26, 2—1, 3—1, 3—4, 4—25
35.  Mother supports, condones, defends, or praises Bob's behavior. 11—26, 2—11, 4—5 letter, 5—13, 5—13, 5—23
36.  Mother comments to the effect that Bob is not unusual. 3—4, 3—4
37.  Bob spontaneously mentions his father. 10—22, 11—13, 3—4, 4—6,
38.  Mother arranges for him to attend concerts or shows. 3—25, 4—22
39.  Bob teases members of his family. 2—1, 3—1, 5—13

E.  *Physical and Personality Make-up*

40.  Classmates mention Bob's small size. 1—24, 5—16
41.  Bob's voice cracks. 3—21, 5—6
42.  Absent from school for physical reasons. 10—15, 4—5, 5—10, 5—19 thru 5—23
43.  Mentions need for more sleep. 10—24, 4—12
44.  Fidgets. 3—11, 3—13
45.  Makes derogatory comments about his intellect or his academic performance, especially when he turns in tests. 9—11, 10—25, 11—15, 2—1, 3—8, 4—11, 5—17, 5—27
46.  Blushes and face turns pink. 11—1, 11—28, 12—10, 4—4
47.  Writes poems. 1—25, 2—3, 2—13
48.  Remains nontalkative in a social situation. 10—5, 11—29, 3—7, 5—23
49.  Carries notebooks, cigar box, or books with him. 3—7, 3—13, 3—21, 4—22
50.  People laugh at Bob's antics.
  (a) Peers: 11—2, 1—28, 1—30, 2—6, 2—11, 3—19
  (b) Adults: 11—29, 1—28, 2—1, 2—6, 3—19, 5—23

**Figure 11.3.** — Continued

the developmental tasks the youngster seemed to be working on, and the second involved the generation of a hypothesized model of Bob's self-structure as revealed in the case material. For both types of interpretation, additional information was used in conjunction with the recurring pattern data.

## DEVELOPMENTAL TASK INTERPRETIVE SUMMARY

Developmental tasks are tasks that all individuals within a given society face as they progress toward maturity. Successful achievement of the tasks at the time they are encountered leads to personal happiness and approval by society. It also provides a good foundation for the accomplishment of subsequent tasks. Failure with a task leads to unhappiness, societal disapproval, and difficulty with later tasks.

The various developmental tasks that Bob seemed to be attempting during the ninth grade are summarized. here along with supporting evidence from the recurring pattern list (RPs) and other available data.

1. *Establishing and maintaining close personal contact with adults outside the family.* Adolescence is a time when normally developing youngsters pattern themselves after adult model composites taken from many sources. Bob may not have shown much evidence yet of actually modeling teacher behavior, but he certainly related closely to the Latin teacher and shared his thoughts and concerns with her regarding out-of-school as well as in-school life. He seemed to be genuinely interested in this teacher as an adult friend, and to a lesser extent in other teachers.

   Evidence included: RPs 1–7, 11–14

2. *Obtaining and retaining adult recognition and affection, while at the same time testing the limits of their acceptance.* Adult support and understanding were highly important to Bob, as they are to most adolescents, especially as he tested the limits of his relationships.

   Evidence included: RPs 1–4, 6, 7, 11–14

3. *Meeting school expectations for mature behavior.* Bob's teasing, prankish behavior seemed to decrease as the year went on. Most of the preadolescent types of behaviors were not seen after February.

   Evidence included: RPs 1, 2, 9, 20, 21, 23, 25, 28, 30, 44

4. *Finding appropriate outlets for his mental interests and capacities.* Bob's brightness and general alertness led him to pursue a variety of activities, both in class and out. Even with a heavy extracurricular life, he did not lose interest in school work.

   Evidence included: RPs 7, 10, 14, 17, 19, 21, 23, 24, 26, 27, 32, 43 and autobiography, reading about Mars, and other specific behaviors in the record.

5. *Extending his facility with language.* Improving writing and speaking patterns, articulating ideas, and expressing thoughts are life-long tasks for many people. Bob was clearly striving to use his Latin class learnings in other situations, as well as to experiment with language in other ways.

   Evidence included: RPs 23, 26, 47 and several verbal expressions used in particular incidents.

6. *Finding appropriate roles to assume in society, that is, in school and community.* Those who do not find accepted roles in which they can succeed within the institutions society establishes are likely to fill the ranks of the maladjusted, delinquent, and downtrodden. In spite of some teacher rejection of Bob for his antics, considerable teacher acceptance of him did exist, especially by the Latin teacher. Even more important, he filled numerous extracurricular roles successfully in addition to performing well in school work.

   Evidence included: RPs 19, 23, 24, 26–32

7. *Maintaining good peer belongingness with other boys.* Bob was seen frequently with other boys and seemed to be well accepted by them in spite of his superior mental ability and certain physical limitations. These qualities are often drawbacks to peer acceptance. His humorous antics at school and overt modesty about his academic abilities may have been the qualities for which he was especially appreciated by other boys.

Evidence included: RPs 15, 16, 18, 19, 20, 22, 45, 50

8. *Relating to the opposite sex.* While many ninth-grade boys have been "going with" girls for some time and others do not yet even know what to say in their company, Bob seemed to have become interested in Jane by the middle of the year and to have begun making what were probably his first overtures to a girl. His efforts appeared to be unsuccessful, as she rejected his invitation to a concert and complained about his attentions to her; yet she seemed to enjoy being teased by him.

Evidence included: RPs 5, 16, 17, 21

9. *Adjusting to a changing body and the heavy energy demands imposed on adolescents by a variety of agencies, each with expectations* (that is, home, school, church, Boy Scouts, Little League, etc.). Bob's then small stature and health status may not have been sufficient to meet all his obligations easily. A cracking voice suggests that he may have been starting his adolescent growth spurt, which in turn was likely to have increased the demands to be made on what may have been limited physical resources.

Evidence included: RPs 40–44[20]

These are but a few interpretations possible from the data. Certainly, additional generalizations could have been made. For example, more could have been said regarding other forces that either helped or hindered Bob in the accomplishment of his developmental tasks. Among other things, the influence of family relationships on the youngster's development and adjustment could have been examined in greater detail. An advantage of this procedure is that a second interpreter can inspect the same data and decide whether or not the generalizations reached have been sound.

Readers who are interested in a listing and description of developmental tasks for the different maturity levels (infancy, early childhood, middle childhood, etc.) are referred to Havighurst's *Developmental Tasks and Education.*[21]

## SELF-STRUCTURE INTERPRETIVE SUMMARY

In the self-structure interpretive summary, recurring patterns and other data in the record are examined and grouped. As shown in Figure 11.4, the case writer divided each section of the Level I list of recurring behaviors with arrows; items representing Bob's behavior were listed on one side, and the reactions of other persons were enumerated on the other side. The case investigator then constructed "self-other" hypotheses which were consistent with the groupings of information. She did this by asking herself how Bob probably felt in order to do these things. The hypotheses were examined again to see if the hypothetical statements were consistent with the underlying behavior and whether they adequately covered this behavior in the case record. Like the developmental task interpretive summary, the self-structure summary and interpretation procedures can be replicated by others.

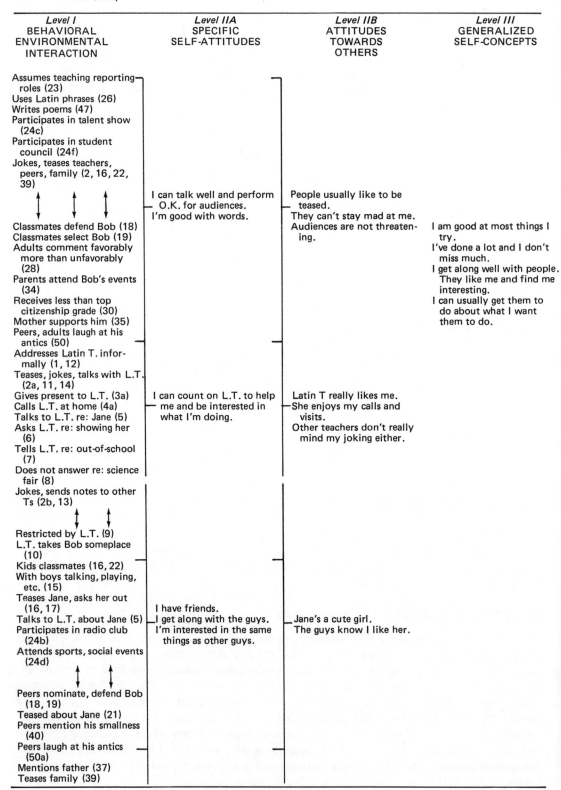

| Level I<br>BEHAVIORAL<br>ENVIRONMENTAL<br>INTERACTION | Level IIA<br>SPECIFIC<br>SELF-ATTITUDES | Level IIB<br>ATTITUDES<br>TOWARDS<br>OTHERS | Level III<br>GENERALIZED<br>SELF-CONCEPTS |
|---|---|---|---|
| Assumes teaching reporting roles (23)<br>Uses Latin phrases (26)<br>Writes poems (47)<br>Participates in talent show (24c)<br>Participates in student council (24f)<br>Jokes, teases teachers, peers, family (2, 16, 22, 39) | | | |
| Classmates defend Bob (18)<br>Classmates select Bob (19)<br>Adults comment favorably more than unfavorably (28)<br>Parents attend Bob's events (34)<br>Receives less than top citizenship grade (30)<br>Mother supports him (35)<br>Peers, adults laugh at his antics (50) | I can talk well and perform O.K. for audiences.<br>I'm good with words. | People usually like to be teased.<br>They can't stay mad at me.<br>Audiences are not threatening. | I am good at most things I try.<br>I've done a lot and I don't miss much.<br>I get along well with people. They like me and find me interesting.<br>I can usually get them to do about what I want them to do. |
| Addresses Latin T. informally (1, 12)<br>Teases, jokes, talks with L.T. (2a, 11, 14)<br>Gives present to L.T. (3a)<br>Calls L.T. at home (4a)<br>Talks to L.T. re: Jane (5)<br>Asks L.T. re: showing her (6)<br>Tells L.T. re: out-of-school (7)<br>Does not answer re: science fair (8)<br>Jokes, sends notes to other Ts (2b, 13) | I can count on L.T. to help me and be interested in what I'm doing. | Latin T really likes me.<br>She enjoys my calls and visits.<br>Other teachers don't really mind my joking either. | |
| Restricted by L.T. (9)<br>L.T. takes Bob someplace (10)<br>Kids classmates (16, 22)<br>With boys talking, playing, etc. (15)<br>Teases Jane, asks her out (16, 17)<br>Talks to L.T. about Jane (5)<br>Participates in radio club (24b)<br>Attends sports, social events (24d) | I have friends.<br>I get along with the guys.<br>I'm interested in the same things as other guys. | Jane's a cute girl.<br>The guys know I like her. | |
| Peers nominate, defend Bob (18, 19)<br>Teased about Jane (21)<br>Peers mention his smallness (40)<br>Peers laugh at his antics (50a)<br>Mentions father (37)<br>Teases family (39) | | | |

**Figure 11.4.** Hypothesized Model of Bob's Self-Structure

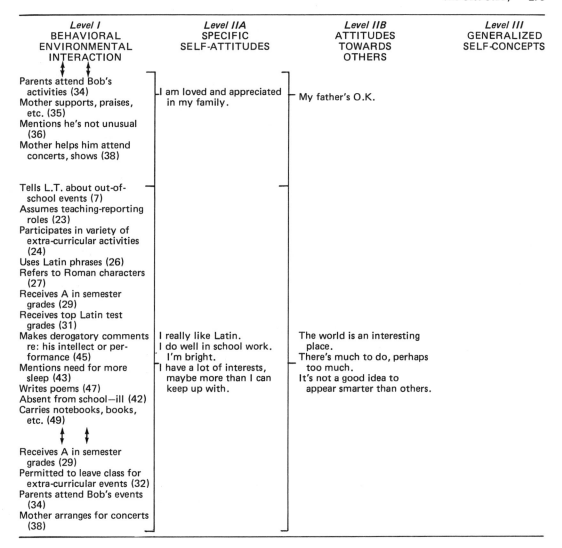

| *Level I*<br>BEHAVIORAL<br>ENVIRONMENTAL<br>INTERACTION | *Level IIA*<br>SPECIFIC<br>SELF-ATTITUDES | *Level IIB*<br>ATTITUDES<br>TOWARDS<br>OTHERS | *Level III*<br>GENERALIZED<br>SELF-CONCEPTS |
|---|---|---|---|
| Parents attend Bob's activities (34)<br>Mother supports, praises, etc. (35)<br>Mentions he's not unusual (36)<br>Mother helps him attend concerts, shows (38) | I am loved and appreciated in my family. | My father's O.K. | |
| Tells L.T. about out-of-school events (7)<br>Assumes teaching-reporting roles (23)<br>Participates in variety of extra-curricular activities (24)<br>Uses Latin phrases (26)<br>Refers to Roman characters (27)<br>Receives A in semester grades (29)<br>Receives top Latin test grades (31)<br>Makes derogatory comments re: his intellect or performance (45)<br>Mentions need for more sleep (43)<br>Writes poems (47)<br>Absent from school—ill (42)<br>Carries notebooks, books, etc. (49) | I really like Latin.<br>I do well in school work.<br>I'm bright.<br>I have a lot of interests, maybe more than I can keep up with. | The world is an interesting place.<br>There's much to do, perhaps too much.<br>It's not a good idea to appear smarter than others. | |
| Receives A in semester grades (29)<br>Permitted to leave class for extra-curricular events (32)<br>Parents attend Bob's events (34)<br>Mother arranges for concerts (38) | | | |

**Figure 11.4.** — Continued

## WHAT THE CASE OF BOB REPRESENTS

The case of Bob demonstrates the scientific value of the case study in understanding an individual child. When objective facts are recorded and when systematic and at least moderately rigorous procedures are used to interpret the data, the results are heartening.

# ADVANTAGES AND DISADVANTAGES OF THE CASE STUDY

A good case study is a very valuable appraisal technique. It organizes information into patterns[22] and leads to an understanding of the child in all his or her uniqueness.[23] Because of its comprehensiveness, the case study discourages the interpretation of facts in isolation, offers a safeguard against analysis based upon incomplete information or unsubstantiated impressions, and provides an opportunity for the cross-validation of data.[24] It also aids in the prediction of future behavior.[25] Since a variety of persons are called upon to provide information about the child, the case method brings together a number of individuals who are interested in the child's welfare.[26] The case study procedure also benefits its writer. Through writing case studies, teachers and counselors become better acquainted with different approaches to child study and may develop into more sensitive observers of human behavior and more effective teachers and counselors.[27] The case method helps professionals become aware of the complexities of child behavior and development and of the needs and problems of children.[28] Hence, case studies assist in the understanding of not only the study child but also of children in general. The case study, as interpreted by a teacher or counselor, may even help the child understand some of the factors that are affecting his or her performance and happiness.[29] Finally, the case study reduces errors in analysis or diagnosis, and insures informed decisions regarding the selection of instructional strategies, remedial measures, and treatment techniques that will help the child achieve, adjust, realize his or her potentialities, and grow toward maturity.[30]

There are some drawbacks to the case study as well. The most prominent one is that the method requires a great deal of effort and time for the collection and analysis of extensive data.[31] Consequently, the case study may delay aid to the child.[32] The wealth of data collected by the case method may encourage overinterpretation and obscuration of minor but important facts.[33] Frequently, shortcuts to save time are at the expense of accuracy and thoroughness.[34] The reliability of case materials cannot be calculated by statistical techniques, and validity is difficult to establish.[35]

It is accurate to say that the case study method represents the culmination of approaches to child study. It involves the use of a variety of appraisal techniques, and as such, insures the inclusion of a great deal of information about the child from different perspectives. It provides the most complete and valid picture of the child that is possible. Every child in certain respects is like other children, like some other children, and like no other child.[36] That is, each child shares certain universal characteristics with all other children, shares group characteristics with a few other children, and possesses characteristics that are not duplicated by those of any other child. The case study is especially well-suited for the examination of these universal, group-related, and unique characteristics. It is particularly appropriate for the latter, as Allport explains:

> Each single life is lawful, for it reveals its own orderly and necessary process of growth. . . . Most studies of personality are comparative. . . . and these tools are valuable. The danger is that they may lead to a dismemberment of personality in such a way that each fragment is related to corresponding fragments in other people, and not to the personal system within which they are embedded. . . . Psychology is truly itself only when it can deal with individuality.[37]

The preceding is essentially a statement of rationale for the *ideographic* approach to the study of child development. In contrast to this method which is aimed at understanding a particular child, the *nomothetic* approach necessitates the statistical study of groups of children in order to determine group trends. It allows generalizations about selected groups of children and statements about differences among various groups and subgroups (age, race, social class, etc.). The nomothetic point of view is unconcerned about the individual children who comprise these groups. Obviously, the case investigation represents an ideographic method inasmuch as it involves study of a single child; but it also includes data that are nomothetically based such as nomothetically derived norms and generalizations (psychological tests standardized on large samples, tables of developmental norms based upon groups of children, etc.). However, the group is considered only as it provides a background for describing an individual child. The case study probably represents the best of both worlds, as Murray so aptly states:

> By the observation of many parts one finally arrrives at a synthetic conception of the whole, and then, having grasped the latter, one can reinterpret and understand the former.[38]

# CHAPTER NOTES

1. R. Strang, *Counseling Technics in College and Secondary School* (New York: Harper, 1949), p. 207.
2. G. W. Allport, *Personality, a Psychological Interpretation* (New York: Holt, 1937).
3. Ibid., p. 390.
4. H. Bolgar, "The Case Study Method," in *Handbook of Clinical Psychology*, ed. B. B. Wolman (New York: McGraw-Hill, 1965).
5. H. F. Cottingham, *Guidance in Elementary Schools* (Bloomington, Ill.: McKnight and McKnight, 1956), p. 84.
6. A. E. Traxler, *Case-study Procedures in Guidance* (New York: Educational Records Bureau, 1937), p. 3.
7. J. M. Hadley, *Clinical and Counseling Psychology* (New York: Knopf, 1958).
8. Ibid., pp. 309-13.
9. D. A. Prescott, *The Child in the Educative Process* (New York: McGraw-Hill, 1957), pp. 205-208.
10. H. V. Perkins, *Human Development* (Belmont, Calif.: Wadsworth, 1975), p. 22.
11. Ibid., 23.
12. Prescott, *Child,* p. 142.
13. Ibid., p. 148.
14. T. A. Ringness, *Mental Health in the Schools* (New York: Random House, 1968), pp. 314-15.
15. A. E. Traxler, *Techniques of Guidance* (New York: Harper, 1957), pp. 271-76.
16. W. Barbe, "Preparation of Case Study Reports," *Education* 79 (1959): 570-74.
    G. M. Blair, R. S. Jones, and R. H. Simpson, *Educational Psychology* (New York: Macmillan, 1968).
    C. Buhler, F. Smitter, and S. Richardson, *Childhood Problems and the Teacher* (New York, Holt, 1952).
    Cottingham, *Guidance.*
    H. B. English and V. Raimey, *Studying the Individual School Child* (New York: Holt, 1941).
    R. L. Gibson and R. E. Higgins, *Techniques of Guidance: An Approach to Pupil Analysis* (Chicago, Ill.: Science Research Associates, 1966).
    M. E. Hahn and M. S. MacLean, *General Clinical Counseling* (New York: McGraw-Hill, 1950).
    G. E. Hill and E. B. Luckey, *Guidance for Children in Elementary Schools* (New York: Appleton, 1969).
    A. J. Jones, *Principles of Guidance* (New York: McGraw-Hill, 1951).
    D. A. Leton and L. G. Schmidt, "Case Studies and the Case Conference," in *School Psychological Services in Theory and Practice: A Handbook,* ed. J. F. Magary (Englewood Cliffs, N.J.: Prentice-Hall, 1967).
    C. V. Millard and J. W. M. Rothney, *The Elementary School Child: A Book of Cases* (New York: Dryden, 1957).
    Prescott, *Child.*
    N. C. Ralston and G. P. Thomas, *The Child: Case Studies for Analysis* (Scranton, Pa.: Intext Educational Publishers, 1972).
    H. N. Rivlin, *Educating for Adjustment: The Classroom Applications of Mental Hygiene* (New York: Appleton, 1936).
    J. W. M. Rothney, *Methods of Studying the Individual Child: The Psychological Case Study* (Waltham, Mass.: Blaisdell, 1968).
    J. E. Simmons, *Psychiatric Examination of Children* (Philadelphia: Lea and Febinger, 1969).
    Strang, *Counseling Technics.*
    Traxler, *Case-study Procedures.*
    R. DeV. Willey, *Guidance in Elementary Education* (New York: Harper, 1969).
    K. Young, *Personality and Problems of Adjustment* (New York: Crofts, 1946).
17. Rothney, *Methods of Studying,* pp. 86-89.
18. R. M. Brandt, *Studying Behavior in Natural Settings* (New York: Holt, 1972), pp. 221-34.
19. Ibid.
20. Ibid.
21. R. J. Havighurst, *Developmental Tasks and Education* (New York: McKay, 1972).
22. Gibson and Higgins, *Techniques of Guidance.*
23. G. W. Allport, *Pattern and Growth in Personality* (New York: Holt, 1961).
24. Gibson and Higgins, *Techniques of Guidance.*
    Hadley, *Psychology.*
25. B. Shertzer and S. C. Stone, *Fundamentals of Guidance* (Boston: Houghton Mifflin, 1966).
26. Gibson and Higgins, *Techniques of Guidance.*
    Traxler, *Case-study Procedures.*
27. Gibson and Higgins, *Techniques of Guidance.*
    Strang, *Counseling Technics.*
    Traxler, *Case-study Procedures.*
28. Gibson and Higgins, *Techniques of Guidance.*
    Strang, *Counseling Technics.*
29. H. J. Peters, B. Shertzer, and W. Van Hoose, *Guidance in Elementary Schools* (Chicago: Rand McNally, 1965).
    Strang, *Counseling Technics.*
30. Shertzer and Stone, *Fundamentals.*
    Strang, *Counseling Technics.*
31. Barbe, "Preparation."
    Gibson and Higgins, *Techniques of Guidance.*
    Strang, *Counseling Technics.*
32. Gibson and Higgins, *Techniques of Guidance.*
    Shertzer and Stone, *Fundamentals.*
33. Gibson and Higgins, *Techniques of Guidance.*
34. Ibid.
35. Shertzer and Stone, *Fundamentals.*
    Strang, *Counseling Technics.*
36. C. Kluckhohn and H. A. Murray, "Personality Formation: The Determinants," in *Personality in Nature, Society, and Culture,* eds. C. Kluckhohn and H. A. Murray (New York: Knopf, 1961).
37. Allport, *Personality,* pp. 572-573.
38. H. A. Murray, *Explorations in Personality* (New York: Oxford University Press, 1938), p. 605.

# 12

# Ethical Guidelines for Child Study

It is the vision of all children, as the assets of the race, to be conserved at any cost —as the torch bearers to the civilization of the future, as the links in the chain of human endeavor. With this vision before mankind, the child has in our own day entered into his rights . . . His life has become an autonomous world set within that of maternity.[1]

A great deal of attention has been devoted to the sociopolitical rights of various groups of people who have historically been denied many rights and privileges—blacks, women, consumers, and—more recently—children.

The rights of children have been directly implicated in numerous social issues such as adoption policies, foster home placement, child labor, child abuse, desegregation, intelligence testing, and compulsory schooling.[2] Coverage of children's rights in this book will be limited to those involved in procedures used to study children.

Attitudes toward children's rights fall within two different frameworks, one dealing with their rights to be nurtured and one dealing with their rights to self-determination. The issues involved are complex and the opinions diverse. Children are persons, not objects, but they do not have the experience and judgment of adults. Therefore, the right of self-determination must be related to the developmental level of the child and the type of determination or judgment required of him or her. Children's rights also depend upon cultural values and norms.

## ETHICAL CODES OF PROFESSIONAL ASSOCIATIONS

Thirty-nine associations have been identified with codes of ethics that can be classified according to whether or not they contain materials explicitly dealing with the protection of human subjects in research. Twenty-one gave some recognition of problems in this area either through codes of ethics, letters, or documents.[3]

### AMERICAN PSYCHOLOGICAL ASSOCIATION

The Division of Developmental Psychology of the American Psychological Association published ethical standards for research with children in a 1968 newsletter. These standards are reproduced here.

#### Ethical Standards for Developmental Psychologists

Children as research subjects present problems for the investigator different from those of adult subjects. Our culture is marked by a tenderness of concern for the young. The young are viewed as more vulnerable to distress (even though evidence may suggest that they are actually more resilient in recovery from stress). Because the young have less knowledge and less experience, they also may be less able to evaluate what participation in research means. And, consent of the parent for the study of his child is the prerequisite to obtaining consent from the child. These characteristics outline the major difference between research with children and research with adults.

1. No matter how young the subject, he has rights that supersede the rights of the investigator of his behavior. In the conduct of his research the investigator measures each operation he proposes against this principle and is prepared to justify his decision.

2. The investigator uses no research operations that may harm the child either physically or psychologically. Psychological harm, to be sure, is difficult to define; nevertheless, its definition remains a responsibility of the investigator.

3. The informed consent of parents or of those legally designated to act *in loco parentis* is obtained, preferably in writing. Informed consent requires that the parent be given accurate information on the profession and institutional affiliation of the investigator, and on the purpose and operations of the research, albeit in layman's terms. The consent of parents is not solicited by any claims of benefit to the child. Not only is the right of parents to refuse consent respected, but parents must be given the opportunity to refuse.

4. The investigator does not coerce a child into participation in a study. The child has the right to refuse and he, too, should be given the opportunity to refuse.

5. When the investigator is in doubt about possible harmful effects of his efforts or when he decides that the nature of his research requires deception, he submits his plan to an *ad hoc* group of his colleagues for review. It is the group's responsibility to suggest other feasible means of obtaining the information. Every psychologist has a responsibility to maintain not only his own ethical standards but also those of his colleagues.

6. The child's identity is concealed in written and verbal reports of the results, as well as in informal discussions with students and colleagues.

7. The investigator does not assume the role of diagnostician or counselor in reporting his observations to parents or those *in loco parentis.* He does not report test scores or information given by a child in confidence, although he recognizes a duty to report general findings to parents and others.

8. The investigator respects the ethical standards of those who act *in loco parentis* (e.g., teachers, superintendents of institutions).

9. The same ethical standards apply to children who are control subjects, and to their parents, as to those who are experimental subjects. When the experimental treatment is believed to benefit the child, the investigator considers an alternative treatment for the control group instead of no treatment.

10. Payment in money, gifts, or services for the child's participation does not annul any of the above principles.

11. Teachers of developmental psychology present the ethical standards of conducting research on human beings to both their undergraduate and graduate students. Like the university committees on the use of human subjects, professors share responsibility for the study of children on their campuses.

12. Editors of psychological journals reporting investigations of children have certain responsibilities to authors of studies they review; they provide space for the investigator to justify his procedures where necessary and to report

the precautions he has taken. When the procedures seem questionable, editors ask for more information.

13. The Division and its members have a continuing responsibility to question, amend, and revise the standards.[4]

## AMERICAN PERSONNEL AND GUIDANCE ASSOCIATION

This association has established ethical standards for the six major areas of professional activity which encompass the work of its members: counseling, testing, research and publication, consulting and private practice, personnel administration, and preparation for personnel work. Here is a summary of the ethical guidelines for counseling, testing, and research and publication:

### Counseling

1. The member's *primary* obligation is to respect the integrity and promote the welfare of the counselee or client with whom he is working.

2. The counseling relationship and information resulting therefrom must be kept confidential. . . .

3. Records of the counseling relationship including interview notes, test data, correspondence, tape recordings, and other documents are to be considered professional information for use in counseling, research, and teaching of counselors but always with full protection of the identity of the client and with precaution so that no harm will come to him.

### Testing

1. Generally, test results constitute only one of a variety of pertinent data for personnel and guidance decisions. Adequate orientation or information should be provided the examinee so that the results of testing may be placed in proper perspective with other relevant factors.

2. Different tests demand different levels of competence for administration, scoring, and interpretation. It is therefore the responsibility of the member to recognize the limits of his competence and to perform only those functions which fall within his preparation and competence.

3. In selecting tests for use in a given situation or with a particular client the member must consider not only general but also specific validity, reliability, and appropriateness of the test(s).

4. Any prior information, coaching, or reproduction of test materials tends to invalidate test results. Therefore, test security is one of the professional obligations of the member.

5. The member has the responsibility to inform the examinee as to the purpose of testing.

6. The criteria of examinee's welfare and/or explicit prior understanding with him should determine who the recipients of the test results may be.

**Research and Publication**

1. In the performance of any research on human subjects the member must avoid causing any injurious effects or after-effects of the experiment upon his subjects.

2. The member may withhold information or provide misinformation to subjects only when it is essential to the investigation and where he assumes responsibility for corrective action following the investigation.

3. In reporting research results or in making original data available, due care must be taken to disguise the identity of the subject, in the absence of specific permission from such subject to do otherwise.

4. The member has the obligation to honor commitments made to subjects of research in return for their cooperation.[5]

## AMERICAN MEDICAL ASSOCIATION

Within the American Medical Association's Ethical Guidelines is a specification that minors be used in nontherapeutic research only when the nature of the investigation is such that mentally competent adults are not suitable subjects.[6]

## SOCIETY FOR RESEARCH IN CHILD DEVELOPMENT

In its "Ethical Standards for Research with Children" this organization lists twenty-one principles. Among them are these:

1. The child must be free to participate or not (a freedom which is to be based on informed consent on the part of the child, its parents or guardians, and those persons whose interaction with the child is a focus of inquiry).

2. The investigator must honor all commitments and not harm the child either physically or psychologically.

3. Full disclosure is the ideal. When a particular methodology requires deception, a committee must give prior approval, and corrective action must be taken afterward.

4. All information must be kept confidential.

5. Special safeguards must be taken when consulting institutional records.

6. If the investigator learns of circumstances which may seriously affect the child's well-being, he is obliged to discuss these with experts so "that the parents may arrange the necessary assistance for their child."[7]

# LEGISLATION

## THE BUCKLEY AMENDMENT

Many of the ethical guidelines developed by the professional associations were translated into law when the Buckley Amendment became effective in November, 1974. This amendment, entitled Protection of the Rights and Privacy of Parents and Students, was introduced by Senator James

Buckley as an amendment to the 1974 elementary and secondary education bill (General Education Provisions Act).

The Buckley Amendment requires institutions, under the penalty of losing federal funds, to provide parents and students aged eighteen or enrolled in college access to all official files, records, and data containing information directly related to the students. This material specifically includes, but is not necessarily limited to, identifying data, academic work completed, level of achievement (grades, standardized achievement test scores), attendance data, scores on standardized intelligence, aptitude, and psychological tests, interest inventory results, health data, family background information, teacher or counselor ratings and observations, and verified reports of serious or recurrent behavior patterns.

This amendment also gives parents and eligible students the right for a hearing to challenge any portion of the records that may appear "inaccurate, misleading, or otherwise inappropriate." Confidentiality of the records is assured by prohibiting schools from releasing them to third parties without a parent's or student's written consent.

The U. S. Office of Education and professional organizations have set up guidelines for use in complying with this law. Critics of the Buckley Amendment object to its lack of clarity in areas such as letters of recommendation, "official" files, and research. The curbs on data-gathering activities and the protection of "personally identifiable" data such as social security numbers could hamper evaluation and make longitudinal research studies virtually impossible.[8] A federal attorney commented that "research will be much more cumbersome administratively and that the opportunity for naturalistic experimentation will be eliminated."[9] The amount and kinds of data maintained by schools also may be curtailed.

The Buckley Amendment was presented and passed because of thousands of letters sent to national organizations by parents who expressed concern with their children's records being given to third parties by schools.[10] In proposing his amendment, Senator Buckley cited examples of abuses in the preparation and handling of student records. An article from *Parade Magazine* entitled "How Secret School Records Can Hurt Your Child"[11] was printed at the end of his remarks and proposed amendment in the *Congressional Record*. Among the problems and abuses cited were these:

> Results of surveys of school systems throughout the country showed that CIA and FBI agents and juvenile court and health department officials had access to the entire records in more than half the school systems, local police in 33 percent and parents in less than 10 percent.

> Children may become permanent victims of their teachers' prejudices and misconceptions. Examples from the Parade Magazine article by Diane Divoky include:

> A school principal reads on the telephone from a child's record to a community project secretary that the child is a bed wetter and that his mother is an alcoholic with a different boy friend in the house every night.

> A parent is told by a guidance counselor, asked to write a college recommendation for her son, that his "psychological" file labeled him a "possible schizophrenic" back in elementary school.

> In a sneak glance at her junior high school son's record a mother sees a note "exhibitionist tendencies" written by his second-grade teacher. After locating the teacher, who no longer taught in the school system, she learned that the comment was based on a single incident when the child hurriedly returned from the lavatory unzipped.[12]

These examples point up the serious consequences of a nonscientific approach to observing and recording data on children. On the other hand, many professional researchers are suffering from the results of these abuses. It has been suggested that it may be in order to press for the passage of legislation to protect the rights of ethical researchers.[13]

## NATIONAL RESEARCH ACT OF 1974

The National Research Act of 1974 mandated the establishment of the National Commission for the Protection of Human Subjects of Biomedical and Behavioral Research to make recommendations to the secretary of Health, Education and Welfare concerning guidelines for the protection of human research subjects. It also stipulates that any institution applying for funds from HEW must have established an Institutional Review Board "to review all biomedical and behavioral research involving human subjects conducted at or sponsored by" the institution. Such reviews are to consider

1. whether the research subjects are at risk

2. whether the risks are outweighed by any benefit to the subject or by the importance of knowledge gained

3. that the right and welfare of the subjects will be adequately protected

4. that legally effective informed consent will be obtained

5. that the research will be reviewed at timely intervals

The National Commission for the Protection of Human Subjects of Biomedical and Behavioral Research submitted a report in 1977 entitled "Report and Recommendations—Research Involving Children."[14]

## INFORMED CONSENT

The principle of informed consent has been one of the ethical guidelines for psychological research for many years, although it has not always been put into practice. *Legally effective informed consent* is defined as "the knowing consent of the individual (or his legally authorized representative) who is in a position to exercise free choice and who is not subjected to any element of force or deceit. Each subject should be given an explanation of the procedures to be followed, a description of any risks to be expected, a description of any benefits, an offer to answer any questions, and an instruction that he or she is free to discontinue participation at any time. With very limited exceptions, legally effective informed consent must be documented by a written form signed by the research subject."[15]

Levine lists eleven elements of information needed to meet the requirements of informed consent:

1. Statement of overall purpose

2. Defining the role of the subject

3. Informing the prospective subject why he or she has been selected

4. A fair explanation of the procedures, including the setting, the time involved, with whom the subject will interact

5. Description of discomforts and risk

6. Description of benefits

7. Disclosure of alternatives

8. Offer to answer questions

9. Offer of consultation

10. Noncoercive disclaimer

11. Consent to incomplete disclosure[16]

## INFORMED CONSENT FOR CHILDREN AS RESEARCH SUBJECTS

In considering children's rights as research subjects, the application of informed consent becomes an important issue involving the question of their capacity for self-determination. Proposed HEW guidelines specify that no child of "sufficient understanding should participate in a nonbeneficial research activity without his or her consent (or assent)."[17] The assessment of "sufficient understanding" becomes the issue here. Such an assessment must be based upon our current knowledge of the child's cognitive development. The requirement of consent by parents or legal guardians prior to research participation of children is intended to protect the rights of those whose capacity is not sufficiently developed for "informed consent." However, parental consent is sufficient only for infants and very small children. For older children, both parental consent and the consent of the child are required.

The establishment of a specific chronological age for "sufficient understanding for informed consent" is unsatisfactory because children's rates of development differ. However, the Buckley Amendment provides parents of children and students aged eighteen or enrolled in college access to student's official records, and the British Medical Research Council specifies age twelve as the age criterion for "sufficient understanding." The Department of Health, Education and Welfare (HEW) tentatively proposed that the "age of discretion" for children be set at seven years.[18]

Lucy Ferguson sets forth some special considerations which apply to four developmental groups: (a) infants and preverbal toddlers; (b) preschool and beginning-school-age children, generally those below the age of seven; (c) preadolescent children; and (d) adolescents.[19] A summary of these considerations follows.

**Infants and Toddlers**. The infant and very young child cannot be expected to make informed judgments about participation in research. Therefore, informed parental consent is sufficient for the child's participation in research activities that are nontherapeutic and nonharmful to the child. The general requirements for the informed consent of research subjects apply to the parents of these children.

**Preschool and Primary-age Children**. In Piagetian terms, children at these ages are in the preoperational stage of cognitive development. They understand more than they can express. They can understand explanations stated in concrete terms, in relation to the immediate situation and to their recent personal experiences. Within these limitations, the researcher should explain the research (e.g., "We want to find out more about how children play or what they think about things"). It also is often helpful to tell a child that the investigator needs his or her help in this work or game. Such contacts and explanations to the child should follow prior parental consent.

**The Preadolescent (School-age) Child**. Around the age of seven, children are capable to some degree of understanding a problem from another person's perspective and of understanding the consequences of their actions for others. Considerable capacity for self-determination is present in the school-age child. Therefore, his or her informed consent should be obtained directly, including the signing of appropriate consent forms, following prior parental consent.

**The Adolescent**. For purposes of research participation, the adolescent should be treated as an adult. Adolescents who are still minors legally must also have the consent of their parents, but these adolescents should be treated as colleagues of the investigator in the pursuit of knowledge.

## PARENTAL CONSENT FOR PSYCHOLOGICAL EVALUATIONS

There appears to be a lack of uniformity concerning whether psychologists in school settings should obtain permission from parents prior to the administration of psychological evaluations of their children. However, the Education for All Handicapped Children Act of 1975 settled the parental consent question for school-based services for handicapped children in schools that receive funds under the act (Pub. L. 94-142).[20] Although the statute specifies "notice" rather than consent, it authorizes the Office of Education (Department of Health, Education and Welfare) to write regulations for clarification of the law. Their rules state that "parental consent must be obtained before an evaluation is conducted."

# CONFIDENTIALITY

Maintaining confidentiality and anonymity is an ethical obligation of researchers, counselors, and others having access to personal information about human beings. However, various threats to the individual's right to privacy do occur. In some instances, information is obtained about people without their knowledge. In other instances, information may be obtained with the informed consent of the subject and passed on to third parties by the investigator at a later time. Requests for confidential information may come from many sources, such as from the research participant's friends and relatives, employers, teachers, data banks, and law enforcement officers.

## CONFIDENTIALITY AND THE COUNSELOR-CLIENT RELATIONSHIP

Clients are generally assured that communications with a professional counselor will not be revealed to others without the clients' informed consent. Of course, it also has been common practice to exclude the clients themselves from access to much of this information.[21] The information is generally shared only with other professionals who are directly involved with the clients.

The question recently has been raised as to whether counselors are covered by the Buckley Amendment. As indicated previously, official files specifically include scores on standardized intelligence, aptitude, and psychological tests; interest inventory results; health data; teacher or counselor ratings and observations; and verified reports of serious or recurrent behavior patterns. (All of this material is to be accessible to parents and to students aged eighteen or enrolled in college.)

Another section of the amendment, however, specifically excludes certain materials from the definition of *educational records:*

> Records relating to an eligible student which are (i) created or maintained by a physician, psychiatrist or other recognized professional or paraprofessional capacity, or assisting in that capacity; (ii) created, maintained or used only in connection with the provision of treatment of the student, and (iii) not disclosed to anyone other than individuals providing the treatment.[22]

These records need not be made available to parents or students.

Needless to say, confusion reigns with respect to the definition of *educational records* in the amendment. The definition of the type of material considered part of a student's educational record appears to hinge not so much on the nature of the materials as on the primary purposes or uses of the materials and accessibility to them.[23] Materials obtained and maintained solely for the purpose of providing professional diagnostic or counseling service to students appear to be excluded, as well as records accessible only to those professionals and support personnel who are directly involved in the treatment of the student. These materials need not be made available to parents or students. However, other psychoeducational data that subsequently become part of a student's cumulative records are considered educational records subject to accessibility to parents or students.

## CONFIDENTIALITY, INFORMED CONSENT, AND MEDICAL RECORDS

Ronald Shlensky, M.D., J.D., provides a good discussion of approaches in Illinois to the problem of confidentiality of medical records.[24] He points out that patients are often asked to relinquish their privacy regarding their medical records to third parties. However, those controlling medical records have a statutory and civil duty to protect privacy and cannot give access to the records without the patient's consent. He raises the question whether one consents to allowing access to his or her medical records when one does not possess knowledge of the content of those records. Is such consent *informed* or is it *submission?*

The state of Illinois is acting to resolve this dilemma in regard to mental health records. A person may see his or her own mental health record, and for all practical purposes, health records in general. The person must be twelve years old; up to age eighteen, the parents also may have access. If a patient disputes information in the record, he or she may enter a written statement in the record and request it to be modified. Consent must be in writing and specific as to who receives the information, the nature of the information, and the consequences of refusal to consent. Blanket consents and redisclosures are prohibited.[25]

## SUBPOENA OF CONFIDENTIAL RECORDS

No promise made by a researcher to maintain confidentiality of data can legally withstand a subpoena from a court of law (unless the researcher is willing to refuse and accept the consequences), although the Privacy Commission has recommended to Congress that government collected or sponsored research data be protected by statute so that data for research could not be used against a research subject. Some states have enacted statutes that protect certain types of research data in limited areas, but none of the statutes applies to *all* of social research.[26] Both research data and consent forms can be subpoenaed. Therefore, consent forms sometimes protect the researcher at the expense of the research participant. In studies such as those dealing with prostitution, alcohol and drug abuse, gambling, and criminal behavior, a subpoena could be fateful for the research participant.[27]

Some researchers take extra precautions to safeguard the confidentiality of research data, as this incident illustrates:

> We were doing a longitudinal study of student behavior and, hence, had to keep the student's identity signs associated with each piece of data, even where it involved legally touchy matters, like drug usage, participation in illegal demonstrations, etc. Knowing that we could be asked by the courts to supply this information, we used a code number for each individual and deposited the key in another country.
>
> This procedure was expensive and tedious (and probably leaves the researcher open to contempt proceedings), but we felt it necessary if we were to safeguard our subjects and retain their confidence.[28]

## SOCIAL RESPONSIBILITY VERSUS ETHICAL PROCEDURES

A dilemma with serious implications for the issues of privacy and confidentiality involves discovery during the progress of research of personal problems of the subject that the investigator believes need the attention of others. In such cases with children, the question is often raised as to whether parents, teachers, or others should be notified.[29] Guidelines of the Society for Research in Child Development state:

When, in the course of research, information comes to the investigator's attention that may seriously affect the child's well-being, the investigator has a responsibility to discuss the information with those expert in the field in order that the parents may arrange the necessary assistance for their child.[30]

## EQUIPMENT AND TECHNOLOGY

Advances in scientific technology have made it possible to observe and record data on the characteristics and behavior of individuals to the extent that the public is expressing increasing concern over threats to personal freedom. Concealable tape recorders, small photographic and TV cameras, extension telephones, one-way vision screens, drugs such as LSD, and computerized information in data banks are examples of widely used techniques.

Data banks are especially threatening to the maintenance of confidentiality. A data bank is defined as "any collection of coded information about individuals that is kept in a form so that the information is easily retrievable, often by automatic means."[31] Because access to data is so much easier when data are computerized than when they are retained in manual records and because the researcher and others collecting data lose control of their data, ethical concerns arise. If data in the data bank identify individuals, the data could be used to the disadvantage of these individuals; people with access to the data may not be adequately trained to interpret the data; and the data may be used later for purposes for which the subjects did not consent. Before contributing data to data banks, investigators must assure themselves that safeguards exist to protect confidentiality and the anonymity of the subjects.

In addition to research data, many other types of information are stored in data banks, such as employee records, medical records, and credit information. Departments or agencies of the federal government as well as many private agencies maintain files on billions of people. In a 1974 report of a four-year study on the extent and nature of personal data collections in federal agencies, a Senate Subcommittee on Constitutional Rights commented that 54 agencies had reported 858 data banks containing more than 1.25 billion records on individuals.[32]

The use of automated data systems is the wave of the future in health care. In about half of the states, psychiatric information in data banks has been directly matched to names or social security numbers. However, a better trend is emerging in some states where community health centers are refraining from placing identifiable personal confidential information in computer data banks. Some are using code numbers assigned at the treatment facility and are decoding the information only at the mental health facility where the person is served.[33]

## CHILDREN'S SCHOOL RECORDS

Concern regarding the kinds and numbers of records collected on school children and how these records are disseminated has arisen with the increased use of data storage and retrieval systems. Russell Sage Foundation guidelines suggest that information be classified into three categories based upon its importance to the school and its trustworthiness:

> *Category A.* Official administrative records necessary for the operation of the school, which normally are valid. These records include parents' names, pupils' grades, and attendance records. This information would be maintained indefinitely and a student or his parents should have access to it.
>
> *Category B.* Verified information of clear importance but not absolutely essential to the school. Included in this category are IQ or aptitude test data, systematically gathered teacher or counselor observations, verified family background data, and

other information which can be of use and in which trust can be placed. These data should be eliminated from files at various transition points in a child's life (e.g., when he moves from elementary to junior high school) and should be destroyed when the child leaves school. Parents should have access to Category B data and also the child should have access with his or her parents' permission.

*Category C.* Data which are potentially useful but which are not verified or are not definitely needed beyond the immediate present (e.g., legal or clinical findings, including some personality test scores, and unverified or unsystematic teacher or counselor reports). Information in this category should be reviewed at least once a year and destroyed if its usefulness is ended. If verified and useful, it may be transferred to Category B. Category C information should be released only under judicial order.[34]

## TESTING

Testing has come under public scrutiny and criticism because of its widespread use and its influence in making decisions regarding people's lives. Among the criticisms are these:

1. Tests represent an invasion of privacy.

2. Tests create anxiety and interfere with learning.

3. Tests permanently categorize students.

4. Tests penalize bright and creative students.

5. Tests discriminate against minority groups.

6. Tests measure only limited and superficial aspects of behavior.

In Chapters 7 through 9 we described testing procedures and gave numerous examples of tests, questionnaires, and other related techniques used for assessing many characteristics of children. In Chapter 1 we defined *child study* as "the process of collecting, organizing, synthesizing, and interpreting pertinent information of many kinds about individual children." We also have emphasized the importance of specialized training in child development and in the processes of scientific observation, measurement, and data analyses and interpretation. Many of the criticisms against testing relate to the manner in which the tests are administered and the way in which the results are interpreted and communicated to others. In Chapter 1 we provided ten principles of analyses to guide in the appraisal process. These principles emphasized rigid adherence to ethical standards, the need for training in the use of analytical tools, the uniqueness of individuals, and the fact that analytical techniques provide only samplings. In its code of ethics the American Psychological Association includes four principles concerning testing: test security, provisions for confidentiality, test interpretation, and test publication.

Attacks on psychological testing reached a new height in 1965, climaxing in Congressional investigations accompanied by executive directives banning or restricting the use of psychological instruments. Testimony ran to thousands of typescript pages.[35] These are several headlines that appeared in the *Washington Post* newspaper that year: "Pupils Given 'Offensive' Personality Test," "Psyching Out—You Can't Flunk This Test But It Tattles on Your Id," "Personality X-Rays or Peeping Toms," and "Shriver Defends Personality Tests for Peace Corps." The well-known cartoonist Herblock contributed the cartoon shown in Figure 12.1 to the *Washington Post*.

As we have already indicated, steps are being taken to protect the privacy of test subjects, to give parents and students access to scores, and to require their consent prior to communicating results to third parties. Limitations to such protection as court subpoenas and misuse of computerized data banks also have been emphasized.

The *American Psychologist* published numerous articles between 1965 and 1967 concerning the issue of psychological testing. One such article by Anne Anastasi is apropros to our insistence on the use of child development theory and research to aid in test interpretation.[36] The main assertion of her article is that psychological testing has become dissociated from the mainstream of contemporary psychology. She points out that psychologists specializing in psychometrics have been devoting more and more of their efforts to refining the techniques of test construction, while losing sight of the behavior they set out to measure. Outdated interpretations of test performance may, therefore, become insulated from the impact of subsequent behavior research. Anastasi contends that this isolation of psychometrics from other relevant areas of psychology is one of the conditions which incites public hostility toward testing.

**Figure 12.1.** "You've Been Deciding Who's All Right and Who Isn't?"— from *The Herblock Gallery* (Simon and Schuster, 1968).

## NATURALISTIC STUDY

Studying behavior in natural settings presents ethical problems when individuals are observed through the use of one-way vision screens or other equipment without their knowledge or consent or through the participant observation technique if the participant observer has not been identified as an observer. In an attempt to overcome subjects' self-conscious control or concealment of real feelings when the presence of an observer is known, some researchers mingle secretly with subjects, become participants with them (as patients, drug addicts, etc.), and establish relationships with them in order to elicit information. There is little need for ethical concern when the participant observer clearly identifies himself or herself and his or her purposes upon joining a group.[37] Children are routinely subjected to observation through one-way vision screens, in many instances without their knowledge.

Disguised and undisguised participation studies range along a continuum, so there is no absolute cutoff where they definitely become unethical. There is also no general agreement among social scientists about whether disguised participant observation is justified. However, Diener and Crandall suggest several safeguards to minimize detrimental effects if a researcher decides to proceed with a disguised observation study:

1. Deceive as little as possible. Do not deceive subjects when it serves little purpose, and remember that it is better to let others draw incorrect conclusions or simply be ignorant of your scientific study than to actively lie.

2. Enter private spheres with the maximum informed consent consonant with the research goals. When a private sphere has been observed without participants' knowledge, obtain their informed consent post hoc whenever possible.

3. Plan procedures that absolutely guarantee subject anonymity, especially in published reports. One safeguard, especially where sensitive information is reported, is to let the subjects read a draft of the report and point out any passages they feel were given in confidence or any statements that might jeopardize their anonymity.

4. Review the potential influences of the observers on the group and rework the study if any negative consequences are foreseen.

5. Fully inform research assistants about the research before it begins and give them free choice whether to participate.

6. Consider whether the study could cause indignant outrage against social science, thus hampering other research endeavors. If so, consider canceling the study or using a different methodology.[38]

## EXPERIMENTAL STUDY

We have discussed the professional ethics of child study primarily with respect to general ethical guidelines of informed consent to participate in such study, anonymity of subjects, and confidentiality of data. The actual design of the research studies and the validity and reliability of the instruments used is seldom mentioned in these ethical guidelines. The issues of adequate experimental design, analysis procedures, and interpretation of results are often considered to be different from ethical issues.[39] Yet, as Rutstein explains

. . . When a study is in itself scientifically invalid, all other ethical considerations become irrelevant. There is no point in obtaining "informed consent" to perform a useless study. A worthless study cannot possibly benefit anyone, least of all the experimental subject himself. Any risk to the patient, however small, cannot be justified. In essence, the scientific validity of a study on human beings is in itself an ethical principle.[40]

### LONGITUDINAL RESEARCH DESIGN

The major feature distinguishing longitudinal from most other types of research is the continuation of the relationship between the experimenter and subject over an extended period of time, even for many years. Maintaining confidentiality becomes more difficult when subjects must be contacted over a period of years. A coded system (with identities of subjects secured in a locked file with access limited to authorized personnel only) is most commonly used to protect confidentiality. Since losing subjects is a serious problem in longitudinal study, the experimenter too often pressures subjects to remain involved in the study.

## CONTROLLED EXPERIMENTS

The purpose of controlled experiments is to test hypotheses about the effects of certain treatments or experiences on specific characteristics of individuals or objects. In human experiments the treatment or experience would be given to a group of subjects (the experimental group), and a control group of subjects—who are not given the treatment or experience being studied—would be used for comparison. Ethical questions arise when a treatment or experience believed to be useful is withheld from subjects who are in need of the benefits of the treatment. For example, a longitudinal study comparing the effects of an inadequate diet on the cognitive development of children who receive supplemental diets (experimental group) and children who are "naturally" poorly nourished (control group) would raise ethical questions especially since the deleterious effects of malnutrition on cognitive development have already been established. The most acceptable solution in both biomedical and psychological research is to use the best known treatment on the control group for comparison with the effects of the experimental treatment.[41]

# DECEPTION

*Informed consent* implies that a subject has been told about the procedures to be followed in a study in which he or she has been asked to agree to participate. Yet, *concealment* (withholding information from the subject) and *deception* (misinforming the subject) are frequently practiced by behavioral scientists. Deception is difficult to defend unless it is absolutely essential to the validity of the research findings for the subject to be unaware of what is being investigated.

Hoch specifies several kinds of manipulation of human subjects that occur in research. These are illustrated in Figure 12.2. Diener and Crandall suggest two fictitious behavioral experiments as examples similar to those actually staged by psychologists. These two examples were designed to confirm a theory about how adults react to and protect small children. They are good examples of the use of deception in research.

> Sunbathers soak up the warm Florida sunshine while children build sand castles and collect shells up and down the beach. The water is warm and calm; swimmers float lazily about as a group of teen-agers splash by. Suddenly the beach erupts into pandemonium, as the cry "Shark!" sounds out. Swimmers rush madly for shore; parents scramble to grab confused children who are playing in the shallow water. Everyone who is safely on the beach stares toward the azure water, trembling, trying to spot the shark or perhaps a victim of his jaws.

> Across the continent in San Francisco, a forlorn child about to cry wanders in the downtown area, looking up into the faces of adults as she goes. The urchin apparently is unaccompanied by an adult; her blond hair is ragged and dirty, her sundress torn and threadbare. Two blocks away another little girl wanders about, also apparently lost, but this child is dressed in expensive clothes. Her hair is curled as if styled at a beauty shop. An elderly gentleman stops, smiles, and gently inquires if she needs help.[42]

# DEBRIEFING

In dealing with college students and adults, investigators typically handle the ethical problems of studies involving deception by a *debriefing* procedure (carefully explaining the reason for the deception after the study is over). In research with young children, however, debriefing is not an adequate solution, for a full explanation of procedures to them is seldom desirable.[43] However, results of a research study on the effects of deception and debriefing on fifth-grade children's attitudes concluded that children generally viewed participation favorably and that debriefing, in contrast to encouraging children's skepticism, influenced children to view the value of experimentation more positively.[44] Generally positive evaluations of experiments involving deception and debriefing also were made in a study of college students' reactions.[45]

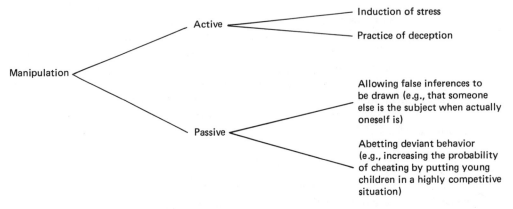

**Figure 12.2.** Several Kinds of Manipulation of Human Subjects that Occur in Research

## BEHAVIOR MODIFICATION

Behavioral technology, sometimes called behavior modification, behavior therapy, applied behavior analysis, contingency management, or conditioning therapy, is spreading rapidly through schools, clinics, mental hospitals, missions, homes, vocational and industrial settings, and social planning. There is a lack of consensus regarding definitions as well as for the best name for the field. However, it has been suggested that enough elements are common in the variety of interpretations to warrant a single generic label: behavior modification.[46]

Behavior modification involves measuring the occurrence of the behavior to be changed and of the desired behavior. It is based on a model of human behavior that assumes that human behavior follows natural laws and that behavior is an adaptation of people to their circumstances. Behavior modification holds that behavior can be changed or modified through the application of learning principles. Behavior modification study generally involves observation in the setting where the problem behavior occurs.[47]

In our discussion of "Theoretical Approaches to Child Study" in Chapter 1, we included behavioristic approaches and pointed out that the behavioristic concept of operant conditioning has been incorporated into the applied system of interventions called behavior modification.

Behavior modification is fraught with ethical questions, for many view such control over people as a machinelike process suppressing individual freedom. Critics have expressed concern over some of the technical terms used, such as *shaping, reinforcement,* and *control,* and over the use of punishment or unpleasant stimuli or denial of privileges. Proponents argue that all types of psychological interventions attempt to control people's behavior. Less formally, people's behavior is also controlled or influenced by education, advertising, and political campaigns.[48] As Bandura puts it, "the basic moral question is not whether man's behavior will be controlled, but rather by whom, by what means, and for what ends."[49]

Both the courts and Congress have been actively involved in issues dealing with behavior modification. The Senate Subcommittee on Constitutional Rights of the Committee of the Judiciary published a report of over 600 pages based upon a three-year investigation of behavior modification. This report documents the extent of federal support for behavior modification research, criticizes the government's involvement in such projects, and calls for "continuing legislative oversight . . . to ensure that constitutional rights and privacy are well protected" when behavior modification is used.[50]

The National Commission for the Protection of Human Subjects was also charged with investigating the implications for the protection of subjects of "research advances such as behavior modification."

The American Psychological Association established a Commission on Behavior Modification that identified issues of importance in considering psychological interventions:

Identification of the client

Definition of the problem and selection of goals

Selection of the intervention method

Accountability

Evaluation of the quality of the psychologist and the intervention

Record keeping and confidentiality

Protection of client's rights

Assessment of the place of research in therapeutic settings[51]

Each of these issues is discussed in some detail by Stolz and associates in *Ethical Issues in Behavior Modification.*[52]

## RISKS VERSUS BENEFITS

The literature on ethical guidelines for use in studying humans is replete with concerns for the need to protect subjects participating in investigations from physical and psychological harm. Little consideration is given to the benefits accruing from such participation, although federal regulations do specify that the risk to subjects should be weighed against the benefits from proposed research.[53]

One's attitudes toward considering risks versus benefits in considering approaches to scientific study depend not only upon one's view of science, but also upon one's general ethical philosophy. Schlenker and Forsyth have examined and contrasted three philosophical positions on the nature of ethics within the context of psychological research: teleology, deontology, and skepticism.[54]

*Teleology* considers the balancing of the potential benefits of research (e.g., advancement of science, beneficial technological applications, advantages to subjects) against the potential costs (e.g., harm to subjects, detrimental technological applications). The American Psychological Association's *Ethical Principles in the Conduct of Research with Human Participants* maintains a teleological position: "The general ethical question always is whether there is a negative effect upon the dignity and welfare of the participants that the importance of the research does not warrant."[55]

The *deontology* ethical position involves adherence to rigid, universal rules that hold irrespective of the situation or consequences. *Skepticism* involves denying the ability to apply universal rules and asserts the individuality of moral codes. Theologian Paul Ramsey is close to the deontology position in asserting that the ethical justification for child research must rest with the rigid application of the patient-benefiting principle: proxy consent (by parents) is acceptable only when the child stands to benefit from the experimental procedure.[56]

We have enumerated many guidelines for protecting the rights and well-being of children and other humans participating in various types of studies. In child study we are concerned with the needs and rights of individual children and also with the need to improve the opportunities for the development of all children through scientific studies. As Frankel concludes in an article regarding ethical issues in the use of children as experimental subjects:

> The current emphasis on human rights in this country has unquestionably swung the pendulum toward more stringent safeguards for protecting the subjects of clinical research. Yet, in our efforts to promote the interests of the child-subject, we must be constantly mindful of the many benefits that the child-subjects and other children like them stand to gain from the well-designed clinical experiment.[57]

A final word should be said about the ethics of data collection. It bears repeating that all information obtained about children and their families must be kept confidential. Student observers, teachers, and other professionals must conceal the identity of the children they are studying. Anonymity is easily accomplished by assigning a code number to the subject, so that the data are identifiable only by that number. Or, the study child may be given a fictitious name. The principle of confidentiality applies to both written reports and informal discussions. If the use of names or identifiable responses is unavoidable, the data should be safeguarded in a locked file cabinet and destroyed when no longer needed. It is a special privilege to study children firsthand—one that requires a professional attitude and strict adherence to ethical guidelines.

For further consideration of ethics in child study, the reader is referred to recent handbook chapters by Rheingold[58] and Cooke.[59]

## CHAPTER NOTES

1. Simeral, *Reform Movements on Behalf of Children in England in the Early Nineteenth Century, and the Agents of Those Reforms* (Ph.D. Dissertation, Columbia University, 1916).
2. N. D. Feshbach and S. Feshbach, "Toward an Historical, Social and Developmental Perspective on Children's Rights," *Journal of Social Issues* 34 (1978): 1-7.
3. R. T. Bower and P. deGasparis, *Ethics in Social Research–Protecting the Interests of Human Subjects* (New York: Praeger, 1978).
4. American Psychological Association Division of Developmental Psychology, "Ethical Standards for Developmental Psychologists," *Newsletter* (1968): 1-3.
5. American Personnel and Guidance Association, *Ethical Standards* (Washington, D.C.: APGA, 1974).
6. J. Katz, *Experimentation with Human Beings* (New York: Russell Sage, 1972).
7. Bower and deGasparis, *Ethics in Social Research*, p. 74.
8. S. Trotter, "Buckley Amendment Sparks Controversy, Gives Students Access to School Files," *APA Monitor* 5 (1974).
9. C. R. Davis, "The Buckley Regulations: Rights and Restraints," *Educational Researcher* 4 (1975): 11-13.
10. Ibid.
11. D. Divoky, "How Secret School Records Can Hurt Your Child," *Parade Magazine* (March 31, 1974).
12. J. Buckley, in the *Congressional Record* 120 (May 9, 1974).
13. Davis, "Buckley Regulations."
14. National Commission for the Protection of Human Subjects in Biomedical and Behavioral Research, *Report and Recommendations: Research Involving Children*, DHEW publication no. (05) 77-0004 (Washington, D.C.: U.S. Government Printing Office, 1977).
15. K. Bond, "Confidentiality and the Protection of Human Subjects in Social Science Research: A Report on Recent Developments," *The American Sociologist* 13 (1978): 150.
16. R. J. Levine, *The Nature and Definition of Informed Consent in Various Research Settings* (Washington, D.C.: National Commission for the Protection of Human Subjects, December, 1975).
17. National Commission for the Protection of Human Subjects, *Children and the Mentally Disabled As Research Subjects*, staff report (Washington, D.C.: National Commission, October, 1975).
18. A. C. Rosen, G. A. Rekers, and P. M. Bentler, "Ethical Issues in the Treatment of Children," *Journal of Social Issues* 34 (1978): 122-36.
19. L. R. Ferguson, "The Competence and Freedom of Children to Make Choices Regarding Participation in Research: A Statement," *Journal of Social Issues* 34 (1978): 114-21.
20. W. B. Pryzwansky and D. N. Bersoff, "Parental Consent for Psychological Evaluations: Legal, Ethical, and Practical Considerations," *Journal of School Psychology* 16 (1978): 274-281.
21. J. M. McGuire and T. D. Borowy, "Confidentiality and the Buckley-Pell Amendment: Ethical and Legal Considerations for Counselors," *Personnel and Guidance Journal* 56 (1978): 554-57.
22. "Privacy Rights of Parents and Students: Final Rule on Educational Records," *Federal Register* (1976), p. 24671.
23. McGuire and Borowy, "Confidentiality."
24. R. Shlensky, "Informed Consent and Confidentiality: Proposed New Approaches in Illinois," *American Journal of Psychiatry* 134 (1977): 1416-18.
25. Ibid.
26. Bond, "Report on Recent Developments."
27. Ibid.
28. American Psychological Association, *Ethical Principles in the Conduct of Research with Human Participants* (Washington, D.C.: American Psychological Association, 1973), p. 93.
29. P. Keith-Spiegel, "Children's Rights As Participants in Research," in *Children's Rights in the Mental Health Professions*, ed. G. P. Koocher (New York: Wiley, 1976).
30. Society for Research in Child Development, *Ethical Standards for Research with Children*, Newsletter, Winter 1973, 3-5.
31. American Psychological Association, *Ethical Principles in the Conduct of Research with Human Participants* (Washington, D.C.: American Psychological Association, 1973), p. 93.

32. V. R. Kelley and H. B. Weston, "Computers, Costs, and Civil Liberties," *Social Work* 20 (1975): 15-19.
33. Ibid.
34. D. Goslin, *Guidelines for the Collection, Maintenance and Dissemination of Pupil Records* (New York: Russell Sage Foundation, 1970).
35. M. Amrine, "The 1965 Congressional Inquiry into Testing: A Commentary," *American Psychologist* 20 (1965): 859-70.
36. A. Anastasi, "Psychology, Psychologists, and Psychological Testing," *American Psychologist* 22 (1967): 297-306.
37. R. M. Brandt, *Studying Behavior in Natural Settings* (New York: Holt, Rinehart and Winston, 1972).
38. E. Diener and R. Crandall, *Ethics in Social and Behavioral Research* (Chicago: University of Chicago Press, 1978).
39. Keith-Spiegel, "Children's Rights."
40. D. D. Rutstein, "The Ethical Design of Human Experiments," *Daedalus* 98 (1969): 524.
41. Keith-Spiegel, "Children's Rights."
42. Diener and Crandall, *Ethics,* p. 72.
43. M. B. Smith, "Conflicting Values Affecting Behavioral Research with Children," *American Psychologist* 22 (1967): 377-82.
44. C. S. Weissbrod and T. Mangan, "Children's Attitudes About Experimental Participation: The Effect of Deception and Debriefing," *Journal of Social Psychology* 106 (1978): 69-72.
45. E. P. Gerdes, "College Students' Reactions to Social Psychological Experiments Involving Deception," *Journal of Social Psychology* 107 (1979): 99-110.
46. S. B. Stolz et al., *Ethical Issues in Behavior Modification,* report of the American Psychological Association Commission (San Francisco: Jossey-Bass, 1978).
47. Ibid.
48. Ibid.
49. A. Bandura, "The Ethics and Social Purposes of Behavior Modification," in *Annual Review of Behavior Therapy, Theory, and Practice: 1975,* vol. 3, eds. C. M. Franks and G. T. Wilson (New York: Bruner/Mazel, 1975), p. 85.
50. U.S. Congress, Senate Committee on the Judiciary, Subcommittee on Constitutional Rights, *Individual Rights and the Federal Role in Behavior Modification,* 93rd Cong., 2d sess. (Washington, D.C.: U.S. Government Printing Office, 1974).
51. Stolz et al., *Ethical Issues.*
52. Ibid.
53. Code of Federal Regulations, *Protection of Human Subjects* (45CFR46, 1977).
54. B. R. Schlenker and D. R. Forsyth, "On the Ethics of Psychological Research," *Journal of Experimental Social Psychology* 13 (1977): 369-96.
55. American Psychological Association, *Ethical Principles,* p. 11.
56. P. Ramsey, *The Patient As Person* (New Haven: Yale University Press, 1970).
57. M. S. Frankel, "Social, Legal, and Political Responses to Ethical Issues in the Use of Children As Experimental Subjects," *Journal of Social Issues* 34 (1978): 112.
58. H. L. Rheingold, "Ethics as an Integral Part of Research in Child Development," in *Strategies and Techniques of Child Study,* ed. R. Vasta (New York: Academic Press, 1982).
59. R. A. Cooke, "The Ethics and Regulation of Research Involving Children," in *Handbook of Developmental Psychology,* ed. B. B. Wolman (Englewood Cliffs, N.J.: Prentice-Hall, 1982).

# Credits

FIGURE CREDITS

**Chapter 1.** *Figure 1.1.* From N. H. Compton and O. A. Hall, *Foundations of Home Economics Research, A Human Ecology Approach.* Burgess Publishing Company, Minneapolis, 1972. *Figure 1.2.* From *Techniques of Guidance: An Approach to Pupil Analysis* by Robert L. Gibson and Robert E. Higgins. Copyright 1966, Science Research Associates, Inc. Reprinted by permission of the publisher.

**Chapter 2.** *Figure 2.1.* From H. Levin and I. Silverman, "Hesitation Phenomena in Children's Speech," in *Language and Speech* 8 (1965): 74. Reprinted by permission of Kingston Press Services, Ltd. *Figure 2.2.* Reprinted from "Criteria for Use in Describing Facial Expressions of Children" by N. G. Blurton Jones in *Human Biology,* Volume 43, Number 3 (1971) by permission of the Wayne State University Press. Copyright 1971 by Wayne State University.

**Chapter 3.** *Figures 3.3 and 3.4.* From M. A. Kiley, *Personal and Interpersonal Appraisal Techniques,* 1975. Courtesy of Charles C. Thomas, Publisher, Springfield, Illinois. *Figure 3.5.* From Allen et al., "Effects of Social Reinforcement on Isolate Behavior of a Nursery School Child," *Child Development* 35 (1964), p. 513. Reprinted by permission of The Society for Research in Child Development, Inc. Copyright 1964 by the Society for Research in Child Development, Inc. *Figure 3.6.* From: Mattos, R. L., "Some relevant dimensions of interval recording," *Academic Therapy* 6:3. Reprinted by permission of the publisher. *Figure 3.7.* From A. E. Boehm and R. A. Weinberg, *The Classroom Observer.* Teachers College Press, 1977. Reprinted by permission of the publisher. Copyright 1977 Teachers College, Columbia University. *Figure 3.8.* Selected items from "The Child's Room Checklist," 1975. Reprinted by permission of Harriet L. Rheingold. *Figure 3.9.* "Living Room Checklist" reprinted by permission of Edward O. Laumann. *Figure 3.10.* From Jane A. Stallings, *Learning to Look.* Wadsworth Publishing Company, Belmont, California, 1977. Reprinted by permission of the publisher and author. *Figure 3.11.* Reprinted from *Children's Play and Playgrounds* (Allyn and Bacon) by Joe Frost and Barry Klein. By permission of Joe Frost (copyright holder).

**Chapter 5.** *Figure 5.1.* From David G. Ryans, *Characteristics of Teachers: Their Description, Comparison, and Appraisal* (Washington, D.C.: American Council on Education, 1960), p. 86; used by permission. *Figure 5.2.* Reproduced from the Haggerty-Olson-Wickman Behavior Rating Schedules by permission. Copyright 1930 by Harcourt Brace Jovanovich, Inc. All rights reserved. *Figure 5.3.* Selected items from Walker Problem Behavior Identification Checklist. Copyright 1970 by Western Psychological Services. Reprinted by permission. *Figure 5.4.* The Trait Information checklist by American Guidance Service, Inc., 1966. Reprinted by permission of American Guidance Service, Inc. *Figure 5.5.* From R. W. Tyler, "A Test of Skill in Using the Microscope," *Educational Research Bulletin* 9 (1930) pp. 493–496. Reproduced by permission of the Ohio State University, College of Education. *Figure 5.6.* From E. G. Boyer et al., *Measures of Maturation: An Anthology of Early Childhood Observation Instruments* (Philadelphia: Humanizing Learning Program, Research for Better Schools and Communications Materials Center, 1973). Reproduced by permission of Communications Materials Center, Wyncote, Pa. 19095. *Figure 5.7.* From R. F. Bales, *Interaction Process Analysis.* The University of Chicago Press, 1950. Reprinted by permission of the University of Chicago Press and the author. Copyright 1950 Addison-Wesley Press, Inc. *Figure 5.8.* From J. N. Webb, "Taxonomy of Cognitive Behavior," *Journal of Research and Development in Education* 4 (1970), p. 31. Reproduced by permission of the College of Education, University of Georgia.

**Chapter 6.** *Figure 6.1.* Courtesy of Electro General Corporation, Minnetonka, Minnesota.

**Chapter 7.** *Figure 7.4.* From the *California Test of Personality Manual* by L. P. Thorpe, Willis W. Clark, and Ernest W. Tiegs. Reproduced by permission of the publisher, CTB/McGraw-Hill, Del Monte Research Park, Monterey, CA 93940. Copyright 1953 by McGraw-Hill, Inc. All Rights Reserved. Printed in the U.S.A. *Figures 7.5, 7.6 and 7.7.* Courtesy of The Psychological Corporation, 757 Third Ave., New York, N.Y. 10017. *Figure 7.8.* Reproduced from Form A of the Pintner-Cunningham Primary Test by permission. Copyright 1938, 1964, 1965 by Harcourt Brace Jovanovich, Inc. All rights reserved. *Figure 7.9.* Reproduced from Cognitive Abilities Test, Form 3, Level 1, Copyright 1978, Houghton Mifflin Company, with permission from The Riverside Publishing Company. *Figure 7.10 and 7.11.* From H. J. Eysenck, *The Structure of Human Personality.* Methuen, Inc., 1970. Reproduced by permission of Methuen, Inc.

**Chapter 8.** *Figure 8.1.* Reproduced with permission from N. E. Gronlund, *Sociometry in the Classroom.* New York: Harper and Row Publishers, Inc., 1959, p. 50. *Figure 8.2.* Source: Helen Hall Jennings, *Sociometry in Group Reactions: A Work Guide for Teachers* (Washington, D.C.: American Council on Education, 1948), p. 22. Used by permission.

**Chapter 9.** *Figure 9.1.* Reproduced from H. Rorschach, *Psychodiagnostics—A Diagnostic Test Based on Perception.* Bern: Hans Huber Publishers, 1932. English translation by P. Lemhau and B. Kronenberg. New York: Grune and Stratton (distr.), 1942. Blot VII. By permission of Hans Huber Publishers.

**Chapter 10.** *Figure 10.1.* Reproduced from the Minnesota Multiphasic Personality Inventory, copyright 1948, by The Psychological Corporation. All rights reserved. *Figure 10.2.* From G. W. Allport, P. E. Vernon, and G. Lindzey, *A Study of Values* (Boston: Houghton-Mifflin, 1960). Reprinted by permission of The Riverside Publishing Company. *Figure 10.3.* From Henry A. Murray, Thematic Apperception Test (Cambridge, Mass.: Harvard University Press, 1943). Copyright 1943 by the President and Fellows of Harvard College; Copyright 1971 by Henry A. Murray. Reprinted by permission. *Figure 10.4.* From J. G. Howells and J. R. Lickorish, The Family Relations Indicator (Edinburg, England: Oliver and Boyd, 1967). Reprinted by permission of the authors and the publisher. *Figures 10.5 and 10.6.* Reproduced from A. L. Baldwin, J. Kalhorn, and F. H. Breese, "The Appraisal of Parent Behavior," *Psychological Monographs* 63 (1949): 4, Whole No. 299. *Figure 10.7.* Photograph of Family Relations Test materials by permission of NFER Publishing Company Ltd., Windsor, England. Full rights reserved. Photo by Marie Coventry. *Figure 10.8.* Reproduced from the Test of Family Attitudes by L. Jackson. By permission of the publishers, Methuen & Co., Ltd.

**Chapter 11.** *Figures 11.1 and 11.2.* Reproduced by permission of Pisani Carlisle Graphics, San Francisco, California. *Figures 11.3 and 11.4.* From Richard M. Brandt, *Studying Behavior in Natural Settings* (New York: Holt, Rinehart and Winston, 1972). Reprinted by permission of the author.

**Chapter 12.** *Figure 12.2.* Hoch, E. L., "The Privacy Issue and a Professional Response at the Departmental Level." *Journal of Educational Measurement,* Spring 1967, p. 17. Copyright 1967, National Council on Measurement in Education, Washington, D.C. Reprinted by permission of the National Council on Measurement in Education.

**TABLE CREDITS**

**Chapter 2.** *Table 2.1.* From J. R. Davitz, *The Communication of Emotional Meaning,* p. 63. McGraw-Hill Book Company, New York, 1964. By permission of McGraw-Hill. *Table 2.2.* From W. C. McGrew, *An Ethological Study of Children's Behavior,* p. 25. Academic Press, Inc., New York, 1972. By permission of the author and the publisher. *Table 2.3.* Adapted from N. G. B. Jones, "Criteria for Use in Describing Facial Expressions of Children," *Human Biology* 43 (1971): 365–413. By permission of the Wayne State University Press.

**Chapter 3.** *Table 3.1.* Reprinted from *Ecological Psychology* by Roger G. Barker, with the permission of the publishers, Stanford University Press. Copyright 1968 by the Board of Trustees of the Leland Stanford Junior University. *Table 3.2.* From R. Barker (Ed.), *Stream of Behavior.* 1963. Irvington Publishers, Inc. Reprinted by permission of the publishers. *Table 3.3.* From Bettye M. Caldwell and Robert H. Bradley, "Home Observation for Measurement of the Environment." Unpublished manuscript, Little Rock, Arkansas, College of Education, 1979. By permission of Bettye M. Caldwell. *Tables 3.4 and 3.5.* From *Environmental Psychology: Man and His Physical Setting* edited by Harold M. Proshansky, William H. Ittelson, and Leanne G. Rivilin. Copyright 1970 by Holt, Rinehart and Winston, Inc. Reprinted by permission of Holt, Rinehart and Winston. *Table 3.6.* Reprinted with permission from *Journal of Behavior Therapy and Experimental Psychology,* Volume 1, R. G. Wahler and W. H. Cormier, "The Ecological Interview: A First Step in Out-patient Child Behavior Therapy," Copyright 1970, Pergamon Press, Ltd.

**Chapter 5.** *Tables 5.1 and 5.2.* From Bettye M. Caldwell and Alice Sterling Honig, "APPROACH—A Procedure for Patterning Responses of Adults and Children." Unpublished manuscript. By permission of the authors.

**Chapter 7.** *Table 7.1.* From the *California Test of Personality Manual* by L. P. Thorpe, Willis W. Clark, and Ernest W. Tiegs. Reproduced by permission of the publisher, CTB/McGraw-Hill, Del Monte Research Park, Monterey, CA 93940. Copyright 1953 by McGraw-Hill, Inc. All Rights Reserved. Printed in the U.S.A. *Table 7.2.* Table 7.1 (p. 208) in *Essentials of Psychological Testing,* 3rd edition by Lee J. Cronbach. Copyright 1960, 1970 by Lee J. Cronbach. Reprinted by permission of Harper & Row, Publishers, Inc.

**Chapter 9.** *Table 9.2.* Adapted from *Child Rorschach Responses* by L. B. Ames, M. A. Metraux, J. L. Rodell, and R. N. Walker, (New York: Brunner/Mazel, 1974).

**Chapter 10.** *Table 10.1.* Reproduced by permission from the Minnesota Multiphasic Personality Inventory. Copyright 1948, by The Psychological Corporation. All rights reserved. *Table 10.2.* Reproduced by special permission from the California Psychological Inventory, by Harrison G. Gough, Ph.D., copyright 1957, published by Consulting Psychologists Press, Inc. *Table 10.3.* From Nathan Hurvitz, Marital Roles Inventory. Western Psychological Services, Beverly Hills, California, 1961. By permission of the author. *Table 10.4.* From Spanier, Graham B., "Measuring Dyadic Adjustment: New Scales for Assessing the Quality of Marriage and Similar Dyads," *Journal of Marriage and the Family,* February 1976. Part of scale on page 27. Copyrighted 1976 by the National Council on Family Relations. Reprinted by permission. *Table 10.5.* From Bienvenu, Millard J., Sr., "Measurement of Marital Communication," *The Family Coordinator,* January 1970. Part of Table 1 on page 28. Copyrighted 1970 by the National Council on Family Relations. Reprinted by permission. *Tables 10.6 and 10.7.* From C, F. Hereford, *Changing Parental Attitudes Through Group Discussion.* University of Texas Press, Austin, 1963. By permission of the publisher. *Table 10.8.* From B. M. Bishop, "A Measurement of Mother-Child Interaction," *Journal of Abnormal and Social Psychology* 41 (1946): 40-41. *Table 10.9.* Adapted from Paul McReynolds' *Advances in Psychological Assessment III.* San Francisco: Jossey-Bass, 1975. With permission of author and publisher. *Table 10.10.* With permission of the author. Schaefer, E. S., "Children's Reports of Parental Behavior: An Inventory," *Child Development,* 1965, *36,* 413-423. *Table 10.11.* Reprinted with permission from M. Siegelman, "Evaluation of Brofenbrenner's Questionnaire for Children Concerning Parental Behavior," *Child Development* 36 (1965): 165. Copyright The Society for Research in Child Development, Inc.

## EXCERPT CREDITS

**Chapter 1.** *Pages 5-6:* Excerpt from *Child Development* by E. B. Hurlock. Copyright 1978 by the McGraw-Hill Book Company, Inc. Used with the permission of McGraw-Hill Book Company. *Page 9:* Excerpt from *Piaget's Theory of Intellectual Development* by H. Ginsburg and S. Opper. Copyright 1969. Reprinted by permission of Prentice-Hall, Inc.

**Chapter 3.** *Pages 76-78:* Excerpts from *Studying Behavior in Natural Settings* by Richard M. Brandt. Holt, Rinehart and Winston, New York, 1972. Reprinted by permission of the author. *Pages 53-54:* Excerpts from J. A. Randall, "The Anecdotal Behavior Journal," *Progressive Education* 13 (1936): 22. Reprinted by permission of the John Dewey Society. *Page 61:* Excerpts from *The Nature and Use of Anecdotal Records* by A. E. Traxler. Harper, New York, 1949. Reprinted by permission of the Educational Records Bureau. *Page 75:* Excerpt from *The Child in the Educative Process* by D. A. Prescott. Copyright 1957 by the McGraw-Hill Book Company, Inc. Used with the permission of the McGraw-Hill Book Company. *Page 81:* Excerpt from Roger G. Barker, "On the Nature of the Environment," *Journal of Social Issues,* Volume 19, Number 4 (1963): 26-27. Reprinted by permission of the author and the Society for the Psychological Study of Social Issues. *Pages 59-60:* Excerpts reprinted by permission of the publisher from Kenneth D. Wann, Miriam Selchen Dorn, and Elizabeth Ann Liddle, *Fostering Intellectual Development in Young Children.* (New York: Teachers College Press, Copyright 1962 by Teachers College, Columbia University.) *Pages 64-66:* Excerpt from *Recording and Analyzing Child Behavior* by Herbert F. Wright. Harper & Row, New York, 1967. Reprinted by permission of the author.

**Chapter 5.** *Page 135-137:* Excerpt from Herbert, J. and Attridge, C., "A Guide for Developers and Users of Observation Systems and Manuals." *American Educational Research Journal* 12, 1975, pp. 4-18. Copyright 1975, American Educational Research Association, Washington, D.C. *Pages 128-130:* Excerpt from "APPROACH: A Procedure for Patterning Responses of Adults and Children—Coding Manual" by Bettye M. Caldwell and Alice S. Honig (unpublished manuscript, University of Arkansas at Little Rock). Reprinted by permission of the authors.

**Chapter 7.** *Pages 164-165:* Excerpt from the *California Test of Personality Manual* by L. P. Thorpe, W. W. Clarke, and E. W. Tiegs. Reproduced by permission of the publisher, CTB/McGraw-Hill, Del Monte Research Park, Monterey, CA 93940. Copyright 1953 by McGraw-Hill, Inc. All Rights Reserved. Printed in the USA. *Pages 167-168:* Excerpt from *Principles of Educational and Psychological Testing* by Frederick G. Brown. Copyright 1970 by The Dryden Press, Inc. Reprinted by permission of Holt, Rinehart and Winston.

**Chapter 8.** *Page 192:* Excerpt from J. Piaget, *The Child's Conception of the World.* Humanities Press, Atlantic Highlands, New Jersey. Reprinted by permission of Humanities Press, Inc. *Pages 193-194:* Excerpt from J. Rich, *Interviewing Children and Adolescents.* St. Martin's Press, Inc., Macmillan and Co., Ltd., New York, 1968. Reprinted by permission of St. Martin's Press, Inc.

**Chapter 9.** *Pages 210-211:* Excerpt from K. Machover, *Personality Projection in the Drawing of the Human Figure: A Method of Personality Investigation* (1949). Courtesy of Charles C. Thomas, Publisher, Springfield, Illinois. *Page 209:* Excerpt reprinted from *The Fourth Mental Measurements Yearbook* by Oscar Krisen Buros by permission of University of Nebraska Press. Copyright 1953 by Oscar Krisen Buros. *Page 210:* Excerpt reprinted from *The Sixth Mental Measurements Yearbook,* Oscar Krisen Buros, editor, by permission of University of Nebraska Press. Copyright 1965 by Oscar Krisen Buros.

**Chapter 10.** *Pages 227-228:* Excerpt from R. M. Inselberg, "Social and Psychological Factors Associated with High School Marriages," *Journal of Home Economics,* Volume 53 (1961). Reprinted by permission of the American Home Economics Association. *Page 231:* Excerpt from Edward J. Shoben, Jr., "The Assessment of Parental Attitudes in Relation to Child Adjustment," *Genetic Pyschology Monographs,* Volume 39 (1949). Reprinted by permission of the Journal Press, Provincetown, Massachusetts. *Pages 232-234:* Excerpted from *Patterns of Child Rearing,* by Robert R. Sears, Eleanor E. Maccoby, and Harry Levin, with the permission of the publishers, Stanford University Press. Copyright 1957 by the Board of Trustees of the Leland Stanford Junior University.

**Chapter 11.** *Pages 272-279:* Excerpts from *Studying Behavior in Natural Settings* by Richard M. Brandt. Holt, Rinehart and Winston, New York, 1972. Reprinted by permission of the author. *Pages 261-264:* Excerpt from *The Child in the Educative Process* by D. A. Prescott. Copyright 1957 by McGraw-Hill Book Company, Inc. Used with the permission of McGraw-Hill Book Company.

**Chapter 12.** *Pages 284-285:* Excerpt adapted from *Ethical Standards* (Washington D.C.: American Personnel and Guidance Association 1974). By permission of the American Personnel and Guidance Association. *Pages 282-284:* Excerpt from Statement of Division of Developmental Psychology of the American Psychological Association, Newsletter, 1968, pp. 1-3. Copyright 1968 by the American Psychological Association, and reproduced by permission of the Division on Developmental Psychology. *Pages 293-294, 295, 296:* Excerpts reprinted from *Ethics in Social and Behavioral Research* by E. Diener and R. Crandall by permission of The University of Chicago Press. Copyright 1978 by the University of Chicago.

# Index of Subjects

# Index of Names